Holy Fab

Volume I

The Old Testament Undistorted by Faith

Robert M. Price

Tellectual Press
tellectual.com

Tellectual Press
tellectual.com
Valley, WA

Print ISBN: 978-1-942897-14-9

Tellectual Press is an imprint of Tellectual LLC.

Cover design by Edwin A. Suominen, based on an engraving by Gustav Doré ("St. John at Patmos") and an image from Robert M. Price's Wikipedia page. Done with The GIMP free image processing software.

In some Scripture quotations, paragraph breaks have been inserted for clarity of dialogue, lyrical formatting has been added, and, using the convention for author interpretation of quoted material, words substituted as indicated by brackets.

Table of Contents

"Robert M. Price's *Holy Fable* is a remarkable hybrid, combining the genre of Biblical Introduction (for both Testaments) and comprehensive commentary. The book aims–and succeeds–in conveying highly specialized material in plain and even humorous speech. It is like listening to the Bible Geek podcasts he is famous for. It is straightforward enough that no one should get lost in the weeds but even serious scholars should be able to discover new and surprising insights here. Price has learned much–and has much to teach–from biblical scholars from the great Higher Critics of the Nineteenth Century, Baur, Strauss, Wellhausen, et. al., all the way to today's controversial "Minimalists" like Lemche, Davies, and Thompson. Believers and skeptics alike will probably find things in *Holy Fable* to annoy as well as delight them!"

    —**Robert Eisenman**, author of
    James the Brother of Jesus and *The New Testament Code*

"Every serious biblical scholar should read this book. None will agree with everything in it, some will dismiss the lot, but most will recognise the questions that Price raises. These are questions that biblical scholars prefer to avoid. Price does not treat the Bible as a sacred text to be pondered and treasured by the community that produced and preserved it, but rather engages with those who treat the Bible as a deposit of literal historical truth, the position of many Bible users today. These people should ponder his questions.

"Price has an easy-to-read and fast-moving style which is a breath of fresh air. But do not be deceived: This is not a lightweight book. It is an accessible feast of well-digested learning."

    —**Margaret Barker**, author of
    Temple Theology, *The Great Angel*, *The Older Testament*, and *The Mother of the Lord*

"Robert Price has succeeded brilliantly in what seems to me an almost impossible project: producing a commentary on the entire Protestant Bible. Not only has he amassed mountains of information from all the most important primary and secondary sources, he has made everything wonderfully clear and delightful to read . . . . Again and again, Price reveals features that have been invisible to the eyes of those of us who have been reading the Bible since childhood, but still have difficulty seeing how it really looks without the distorting optics retained from our believing years. *Holy Fable* would serve as a great textbook for courses on the Christian Bible taught at secular colleges and universities."

    —**Frank R. Zindler**, author of *The Jesus The Jews Never Knew*

"*Magna est veritas et prævalebit.* 'Mighty is truth and it will prevail.' What is presumed to be holy can turn out to be a fable, yet even some fables and fairy tales can convey profound truths. We need not understand them literally or historically to benefit morally and intellectually from them, only critically. Robert M. Price's *Holy Fable* is a search for truth, and as such it serves what is most sacred, and manages to do so with impressive wit and deft insight. Price is that rare soul able to combine the supposed opposites of critical scholarship and genuine spiritual sensibility."

    —**Samuel Zinner**, author of
    Textual and Comparative Explorations in 1 and 2 Enoch and *Christianity and Islam*

Introduction

The Old Testament of History versus the Scripture of Faith

Many of us who consider ourselves biblical critics were introduced to the study of the Bible as a function of Christian piety. We read the book for spiritual and moral guidance and were not disappointed. The trouble came from having been taught to read the text through the lenses of a particular theology.

The founders of our denominations, whether Lutheran, Baptist, Pentecostalist, Presbyterian, etc., had shaped their beliefs according to a selection of biblical passages that seemed to them of central importance. The churches they founded understandably passed these interpretations down through the generations as *the* meaning of scripture. Paramount among these interpretations was the doctrine that the Bible is inspired by God and thus infallible and without error. We gladly embraced this view.

But then, excited at the prospect of deep and detailed biblical study, we found that too many passages appeared not to comport with this belief about scripture. We found various contradictions between scriptural authors, between "historical" narratives, and between the Bible and other ancient historical and archaeological records.

Sure, there were books full of elaborate and clever rationalizations of all these "apparent contradictions," but after a while they became just too much. We had to conclude that such apologetics were little more than stonewalling and spin. They had all been offered as instruments to protect our faith in the Bible and, perhaps more importantly, the Christian beliefs based upon its supposed authority. Yet they can have the opposite effect. You look at, e.g., Gleason Archer's *Encyclopedia of Biblical Contradictions* and you think, "*Encyclopedia?*" If there are *that* many problems, maybe it's time to go back to the drawing board.

Some people come to this point and turn away from the Bible disillusioned. It comes to seem like the charlatan behind the curtain in *The Wizard of Oz*. But others of us drew a different conclusion. We knew we had arrived at a crossroads, but not quite the same one. Our love for the Bible had not come into question. We were still enormously curious about plumbing its depths, ferreting out its tantalizing secrets. It was simply that we came to realize that the faith assumptions that originally motivated our interest in Bible study turned out to hamper any real understanding of it!

We had to choose between faith and understanding, between a deductive and an inductive approach, between studying the text as a means to some theological end and studying it for its own sake. In each case we chose the latter. What else could we do? We knew too much to retreat into the Toyland of dogma, reading scripture with blinders on. Too late for that. And to reject the Bible as bunk would have been another version of the same thinking: Is the Bible to be considered a *true* or a *false* magic book? To be embraced if you believe it to be true, rejected like a counterfeit bill if you decide it is false? No, we decided the books of the Bible were of new and enormous interest, precisely the same way the Iliad and the Odyssey are of interest to Classicists, which is sort of what we became.

The irony is that, as I see it, the true partisans and best friends of the Bible turn out to be those who have sacrificed faith for the sake of understanding. To believe the Bible is to serve it ill, to try to suppress what it is saying because we would prefer that it said something else.

Holy Fable: The Old Testament Undistorted by Faith, is the first of a two-volume set of books (the second volume covering the New Testament, naturally) that attempt to introduce readers to the "Bible of history," not "the scripture of faith." The goal is not to attack the Bible, though I will not hesitate to debunk common Christian readings of the text which seek to make the text conform to dogma. This is to invoke the truism that often one must *un*learn what one has first learned insofar as one has learned misconceptions.

We have to clear the decks. We might never arrive at some definitive "final truth" about the Bible, but we will still have made great progress now that we can dispel misconceptions substituting for understanding. Isn't that what theologians say about God? If there is a deity, infinite and absolute, it seems unlikely that human minds could ever really understand him (or it). But we will be ahead of the game if we can at least set aside foolish, childish, and unworthy notions of the deity.

The Bible, too, is plenty mysterious (though by no means infinite and absolute). Everyone, even fundamentalists, understands this, as witness the common default to "Well, I guess we'll find the answer to that one when we get to heaven." I don't expect any such "Advanced Bible Seminar" (or much of anything else) after death, but there are very many answers to Bible puzzles that turn out to be readily available right now if we care to look closely at the text without the lenses of the inspiration dogma.

And that, ultimately, is the greatest vindication of our choice of the critical method over the dogmatic: Which approach can make more sense of the text? Again and again, the critical method offers explanations where the credulous method offers rationalizations. You will see that in the pages of *Holy Fable*.

––––––

The Bible, as everyone knows, is a library of very different writings (the "books" of the Bible) representing very different genres. We find myths, "history" (of an ancient sort), poetry, song lyrics, aphorisms, epistles, apocalypses, prophetic oracles, royal propaganda, object lessons and cautionary tales. This diversity calls not only for a variety of interpretive methods, but also a variety of formats of presentation. In a few cases, I believe the close attention required to understand important complexities in the text make it needful to provide extensive quotations of it. In others, summaries and citations will be enough (though I encourage you to have a copy of the Bible at hand to consult).

A related issue is that of comprehensive versus selective scrutiny of particular biblical books. *Holy Fable* does not pretend to be a commentary on every bit of the Bible. While many of the individual episodes of Genesis, Exodus, Leviticus, Numbers, Joshua, Judges, Samuel, and Kings invite individual consideration, we need not linger in such detail, e.g., in the Old Testament Prophets. Here I will focus on passages important to our purposes. For instance, I will choose passages traditionally read as messianic prophecies and those understood as predictions of Jesus Christ (not quite the same thing), showing how they originally meant something altogether different. I will also indicate where and why books like Isaiah must be divided into writings by several different authors. And I will attempt to show how the main business of the Prophets was, as some say, "forth-telling, not foretelling."

Likewise, space forbids me expounding every one of the one hundred fifty Psalms, but I will set forth the sub-genre categories of the Psalms and their intended use, focusing on representative samples. I do not want to miss the forest for the trees, but I think the best way to appreciate the forest is to examine representative types of trees in close detail. I intend *Holy Fable* as more of a book to be read straight through than a reference work like *The Jerome Biblical Commentary* (an excellent resource!), which is designed for the reader to dip into here and there.

Karl Barth once said that, despite (or even because of) his extensive theological education, he discovered a whole new world when he opened the Bible. *Holy Fable* is an invitation and a guidebook to that new world. You will find that the Bible is not the same book you once believed and obeyed, nor the one you rejected as a tool of oppression.

————

Finally, let me address a point of concern given the hypersensitivity, as I view it, of our culture. Some lament the very use of the term "Old Testament" because of its roots in Christian theological conceptuality. Mustn't it denote the inferiority of the Jewish scriptures as merely preparatory to the superior Christian New Testament? Is not continued scholarly use of the term "Old Testament" the same as continuing to use the old "B.C./A.D" framework, the latter presupposing a Christian understanding of history? I agree that it is inconsiderate to expect Jews to refer to dates "before Christ" and "in the year of our Lord (Jesus)." I go with the revised, ecumenically neutral nomenclature *B.C.E.* ("Before the Common Era") and *C.E.* ("Common Era," denoting the time when Judaism shares the stage with Christianity).

But when it comes to naming the pre-Christian books "the Old Testament," I see things differently. Some urge us to speak of the Tanakh (the Jewish designation, a kind of acronym based on the first letters of the Hebrew names for the three chief sections of scripture: Torah (Law, Pentateuch), Nebiim (Prophets), and Ketubim (Writings). Or maybe we should just refer to the Hebrew (or Jewish) Scriptures. Yet I reject that. It seems to me that these designations imply reference to these writings as canonical Jewish scripture, denoting a Jewish theological understanding of their contents, just as "Old Testament" carries Christian theological baggage. It is misleading to refer to "the Torah" when you are discussing the component sources J, E, D, and P (more about them later).

So then, is it proper to retain Christian terminology? While it may not be ideal, there is an integrity to it, since the Higher Criticism of the Bible began with Benedict Spinoza (who was kicked out of the synagogue for his "heretical" views on scripture) and various radical Protestant scholars. These men sat loose to any theological orthodoxy and refused to allow it to control their results. Many of them were soon (and still are) considered apostates from the traditional faith. And they referred to "the Old Testament," the term they had inherited.

I stand in their tradition, and I employ their terminology, "Old Testament" along with others like "form criticism" and "redaction criticism." In this case, I am afraid we are best advised to use one term in two different senses: "Old Testament" may refer either to the pre-Christian writings from Genesis through Malachi as understood by Christian theology *or* to these same books as understood via historical and literary criticism. I view it all as analogous to the legitimate equivocality of the term "Indians." We may use the word to denote people from the Asian subcontinent or the Apaches, Sioux, Iroquois, Mayans, etc. Many prefer to call these pre-Columbian Americans "Native Americans," but in point of fact they are not. They are not aboriginal Americans but are descended from Siberian ancestors. None of these labels is without ambiguity. So I'm sticking with "Old Testament" just as I do "American Indians."

Something else you might want to know is that the Bible texts were not originally divided into chapters and verses. The ancient Hebrew text did not have any vowels! And neither biblical Hebrew nor Greek featured spaces between words! These conventions invited occasional ambiguity: Does it mean this or that? Is it supposed to be read as "God is now here" or "God is nowhere"? It turns out to be much less of a problem than you might think. But I mention these matters, especially chapter and verse divisions, because otherwise you might find it confusing when I say, for example, that the Six Day Creation story concludes at Genesis 2:4b, and the very different Garden of Eden creation story begins in Genesis 2:4b. Those who inserted the chapter and verse divisions (to make it easier to look up passages) just failed to notice what now seem the natural divisions of the text.

Finally, let me address a common concern about the texts of the Bible. Obviously they are very, very old. They were for the longest time passed down by hand copying. They were translated into several languages. Do not these factors afford considerable space for suspecting extensive rewriting or unintentional distortion?

I am all for skepticism, for raising every question we can raise. But popular skeptical talk about the Bible often suffers from understandable ignorance. For instance, the objection that "It's been translated so many times, who knows what it originally said?" seems to presuppose that the texts were serially translated, the new version replacing the old. As if someone translated the Hebrew into Greek, the Greek into the Latin, the Latin into English, etc., without retaining copies of each previous version. But that isn't the way it happened.

We still have plenty of copies of the Masoretic Hebrew Text, the Dead Sea Scrolls copies of scripture, the Greek Septuagint, the Old Latin, the Old Syriac, the Syriac Peshitta, the Latin Vulgate, etc. We can compare the various translations, and our modern versions are based on the earliest extant manuscripts in the original languages. The ancient translations, though, are quite helpful because they were made from earlier Hebrew and Greek manuscripts than those available to us and thus provide vital clues on the way still earlier manuscripts read.

The Greek Septuagint Old Testament had God dividing the human race into nations "according to the number of the sons of God," implying an early Israelite polytheism with the High God making sure each lesser deity had his own people to rule. But the Masoretic Hebrew had "according to the number of the sons of Israel," whatever that might mean. It looks like an editorial attempt to strip the polytheism out of scripture. Was it? Yes, as the discovery of the Dead Seas Scrolls proved. A thousand years older than the Masoretic Text, the Dead Sea Scroll of Genesis agreed with the Greek Septuagint, confirming suspicions that the Greek translators were using an earlier Hebrew version. So the existence of several ancient translations actually makes it clearer what the original text was like rather than obscuring it.

What I just said also confirms that scribes were not above altering the text in order to adjust scripture to developing theological norms.[1] But even here there is less of a problem than one might imagine. Since we possess thousands of biblical manuscripts spanning many centuries of scribal hand-copying, we can compare them and weed out many errors and distortions. For instance, it has become clear that at least three particularly juicy passages are subsequent additions: the last eight verses of Mark's gospel with the crazy business about handling poisonous snakes and chug-a-lugging strychnine, the story of the woman taken in adultery in John 8, and the Trinity proof text of 1 John 5.

But problems do remain. For one thing, it is not possible in very many cases to determine the original reading since the manuscript evidence is divided pretty much evenly. Did Luke have Jesus pray from the cross, "Father, forgive them, for they know not what they do"? I think he did because it fits so well with Luke's understanding elsewhere in his gospel and the Book of Acts, but about as many manuscripts lack it as have it, and some scribe may have inadvertently skipped it. Or one may have found the notion offensive that Jesus could have asked God's pardon for "those Christ-killing Jews" and cut the sentence. Who really knows? There are many such puzzles.

Another difficulty is that while we do have many centuries worth of manuscripts to check, we are out of luck when it comes to the earliest (and thus most crucial) period of copying. We have no copies of the Pauline Epistles before about 300 C.E. Yikes![2] But there are certain irregularities in the earliest extant manuscripts similar to those accompanying interpolations and edits that we can trace in our later manuscripts: abrupt charges of subject, changes in style, contradictions to the context, vocabulary uncharacteristic for the author, etc. These imply that, though we lack the manuscript evidence to prove it (or to *disprove* it), passages where these aberrations occur were not in the original and are no more authentic than the ending of Mark.

Most scholars get pretty nervous about suggestions of this kind because, once we admit the likelihood that the texts have already been corrupted before we have manuscripts to check, then it becomes more difficult to pontificate about what 'The Bible says" on this or that subject. So, where the natural implication would seem to be skepticism ("We can't be sure if most of Romans 1, where we find the only clear condemnation of homosexuality, was originally part of the epistle."),[3] these scholars flip over into pious fideism ("Since we can't prove the passage wasn't original, we're entitled to go on assuming it was."). But this is just letting our theological preferences control (and supersede) the text again.

If we step back even further, we can see how the common skeptical jibe about scribal tampering the text is off-base. And yet the situation may be worse, not better. You see, the real issue is not so much whether people have screwed up the texts once they were definitively written and circulated (something John of Patmos warned scribes about in Revelation 22:18-19). Rather, the problem is the evolving character of the texts before they were "finalized."

Were stories told and retold for decades or centuries before someone included them in Genesis or Matthew? Have new prophetic oracles, or whole chapters or even books of them, been added to the original oracles of Isaiah or Jeremiah? Is it possible that the Pauline Epistles we are reading are composites of texts written by rival Paulinists and juxtaposed by later scribes, rather than single missives written by a single apostle?

It is the pre-history rather than the post-history of the biblical text that presents the challenge of an all-engulfing void which scholars may never successfully plumb. As I say, this condition induces panic in scholars who would like to retain some version of "scriptural authority." But for historians, such irresolvable uncertainly is nothing new. In fact, it is the name of the game. Historians know that the coin of their realm is speculation, that all hypotheses and reconstructions of the past (including the history of texts) must remain forever provisional and tentative, always open to revision in light of new evidence or more illuminating paradigms. Again, we see an unbridgeable chasm between the theological use of the Bible as scripture and the scholarly scrutiny of the same book as a historical artifact—or artifiction. We must not suppress the truth in self-righteousness.

—Robert M. Price

July 16, 2014

Notes

1. Bart D. Ehrman, *The Orthodox Corruption of Scripture: The Effect of Early Christological Controversies on the Text of the New Testament* (New York: Oxford University Press. 1993).

2. Brent Nongbri, "Reconsidering the Place of Papyrus Bodmer XIVXV (P75) in the Textual Criticism of the New Testament." Journal of Biblical Literature vol. 135, no. 2 (2016), pp. 405-37, shows that this papyrus, containing the Pauline epistles, is contemporaneous with Codex Vaticanus, fourth century.

3. J.C. O'Neill, *Paul's Letter to the Romans* (Baltimore: Penguin Books, 1975), pp. 52-54. The quotation marks here denote my summing up a position, not a passage quoted from O'Neill's book.

I
Genesis

Patchwork Pentateuch

Source Criticism

"Pentateuch" is a Greek word meaning "five books," referring to Genesis ("The Beginning"), Exodus ("The Way Out"), Leviticus ("Concerning the Levites"), Numbers ("The Census"), and Deuteronomy ("The Second Law"). Collectively they are traditionally called the "Five Books of Moses." In Hebrew they are called the Torah, which means "the Law" (or "Instruction").[1] This last is a case of synecdoche, using a part to stand for the whole thing, since the body of laws (613 of them), dominates the Pentateuch, though there is a great deal of narrative as well.

Why did anyone ever imagine, as the ancient scribes and rabbis did, that Moses was the author of the Pentateuch? If there ever was a historical Moses, which is highly doubtful,[2] he did not and could not have been our author. This ought to be obvious from the fact that the text several times refers to events long after the time of Moses,[3] who is already regarded as an ancient figure even in the Pentateuch (Deut. 34:10).

For instance, we are told that Abraham and Lot went their separate ways, back at the time of the Canaanites and the Perizzites (Gen. 13:7). Uh, wait a minute: The Canaanites were exterminated under Joshua, Moses' successor. And yet Moses wrote this? He recorded *his own death* as a past event (Deut. 34:7)? How could Moses have listed the kings of Edom "before any king reigned over the Israelites" (Gen. 36:31)? The first Israelite kings came centuries after the ostensible time of Moses.

The same ancient scribes also nominated Joshua as the author of the book bearing his name, David as the author of the Psalms, etc. It is surely a gratuitous inference, even a wild one, that the major character in a book is the same as its author. That would be erasing the line between biography and autobiography. My guess is that the ancients tagged the books with the names simply to denote the major subject of each. The "Books of Moses" would first have denoted "the Books *about* Moses." Most of them were.

Why the transition? Well, the narrative does say all the laws were given to Moses by his divine Patron. When he did not write them himself, he would have dictated them to someone else, as Paul is said to have done, pontificating as his secretaries struggled to keep up.

In fact, as Julius Wellhausen[4] demonstrated beyond reasonable doubt, the Pentateuch is a compilation (at the earliest, in the fifth century B.C.E. or later, i.e., about a thousand years after the supposed lifetime of Moses) of four earlier narrative and legal sources, collections of legends and laws. It is fairly simple to tell the sources apart even in English translation, once you know what to look for.

The earliest of these, as well as the most stylistically beautiful, is the **J** source, so called, partly, because it consistently uses the divine name Yahweh, which used to be transliterated as "Jehovah." Most English Bibles have substituted for it the more generic terms "LORD" or "GOD" (printed in all capitals). This is because of an ancient Jewish tradition of safeguarding the sacred name from casual and profane use ("But all I said was, 'That piece of halibut was good enough for Jehovah.'").[5]

The goal was to secure obedience to the third commandment, "Thou shalt not take the name of [Yahweh] thy God in vain" (Exod. 20:7, KJV). What this probably meant was that you must not invoke the divine name when making a contract or guarantee ("As Yahweh lives, I will have the job done by June 23 and under budget.") and then defaulting, or when pledging to testify truthfully in court ("As Yahweh lives, I did not steal your yak."), and then lying. But no one could say for sure *what* the commandment might refer to.

So better safe than sorry: Best not to use the name at all! Not even in the public reading of scripture. When the reader came to the divine name, which of course peppers the text, he would read "Adonai" ("the Lord," also a divine name, as with the Syrian-Greek deity Adonis, but a lesser one). If Adonai preceded the name Yahweh as a title, "the Lord Yahweh," then Adonai gets translated as "Lord," and Yahweh gets hidden, this time, behind "GOD." We won't be doing any of that here.

We also call this source "J" because it seems to be a collection of material from the southern Hebrew kingdom, Judah. The J source gives us raw mythology (God often appears as a character on stage) as well as unretouched, entertaining portraits of biblical characters, not yet "sanitized" as holy saints. J is anachronistic, paying little attention to when various laws actually began to be observed in Israel, sometimes describing the ancients as if they followed the customs of the writer's own day, as when Noah is shown already observing the distinction between "clean" (kosher) and "unclean" (nonkosher) animals in Genesis 7:2.[6]

J's story begins with the creation (the Garden of Eden story, Gen. 2:4b-chapter 3) and continues on through Moses. J may have compiled his epic, at the earliest, in Rehoboam's reign (just after Solomon), but may even be as late as Post-Exilic times. We can imagine that J (whoever he was) was much like the Brothers Grimm who collected fairy tales from elderly nurses and grandmothers, compiling the old, oral tales before they died out and were forgotten. Likewise, J would have traveled throughout Judah, visiting every local shrine, oracle, and sacred grove he could find, taking notes as the attendant priest would tell him the story behind the place, what made it so holy, as today when tourists are told that Glastonbury, England, is the burial site of Joseph of Arimathea, King Arthur, and Queen Guinevere.

The second Pentateuchal source is a collection of similar materials, the **E** source, so called because it calls the deity **E**lohim ("God" or "gods") up until the burning bush story (Exod. 3:15), when it introduces the name Yahweh. E was a collection of stories from the Northern Hebrew kingdom, Israel, also called **E**phraim (after the leading Northern tribe). E is more subtle in its depiction of God, having him speak from offstage in dreams and visions. It also tries to clean up the faults of the characters, as we can see by comparing the J and E versions of the same story.

The scope of E's narrative is narrower than J's. E lacks a creation account and begins with Abraham and extends through Moses. E seems to be later than J, and some scholars think it was compiled in the ninth century, the dawn of the prophets, since it calls Abraham a prophet (Gen. 20:7), as if it were synonymous with "holy man." But again, it may be much later.

The third source is **D**, the basis of the Book of **D**euteronomy, consisting of sermons and sets of laws fictively ascribed to Moses, from chapter 4 through 34. Gerhard von Rad thought D incorporated sermonic material from the old Shiloh shrine in the North,[7] but others suggested the book was put together by prophets and priests (perhaps including the priest Hilkiah and the prophetess Huldah) associated with the "discovery" of the book (2 Kings 22:8-16) in Jeremiah's day, in the seventh-century B.C.E.

Moshe Weinfeld[8] makes a strong case that D was actually the work of Temple scribes, a kind of rival or alternative to the Priestly Code (see just below). Someone later added a historical preface (Deuteronomy 1-3), a summary of the Moses and Exodus sections of J and E, which someone had already combined.

Like D, the fourth source is mainly a vast law code, or set of them, called **P**, or the Priestly Code, traditionally thought to have been compiled by the exiled Jewish priests while in Babylon in the sixth century B.C.E. but may be later. It contains the sketchiest summary of Israelite history, beginning with the Six Day Creation (Gen. 1:1-2:4a), pausing to dwell on Noah's Flood, and going on through Moses. The Creation, Flood, and Moses stories are told at some length.

But by far most of P is legal material. We do not know to what extent these were actual laws that had governed Israel and Judah, or if they may have been an ideal blueprint like Plato's *Republic* or Thomas More's *Utopia*. It is tempting to think the laws of P (and the whole Torah) were like the myriad regulations set down in the much later Talmud, a kind of "Fantasy Football" game devised by a clique of scholars who had no authority to enforce them. Had most Jews ever even heard of them?

This source-critical way of slicing the Pentateuchal pie into four slices, J, E, D, and P, is vastly illuminating. It makes so much sense of the text, solving many of the old conundrums of the Bible, that it's permanently reshuffled the deck as far as biblical scholars are concerned. Once I entered a major New York City synagogue with my friend and mentor, the Jewish theologian Michael S. Kogan. Pointing at the five prominently displayed Torah scrolls behind the pulpit, I quipped, "Hmmm. I see J, E, D, and P, but what's the fifth one?" I was kidding (but not really).

Mosaic Tiles

Form Criticism

Hermann Gunkel delineated five major types of stories or legends in Genesis, though we will find many of them throughout the rest of the Bible, too. By far most of them are attempts to answer various questions in a pre-scientific, yet ingenious and inventive, way. You might first be inclined to disdain their "answers" as monuments of superstition and credulity, but that would be a mistake.

It is one thing for modern educated people to feel they must believe these old stories as factual when science proves otherwise. It is quite another for ancient people living before the dawn of scientific technology to venture clever but inevitably mistaken explanations. My guess is that many secular folks in our day take a dim view of biblical tales of a six-day creation, a universal flood, etc., blaming these stories for the oppressive use of them by religious leaders who ought to know better. But that's not fair. Who, after all, scorns and ridicules the Greek or the Norse myths? No one, because no one catechizes us to believe these literally. They haven't left a bad taste in our mouths. Nor should the myths of Genesis.

If we could somehow visit the past and explain to the authors of Genesis the true origins of the earth and its life-forms, of languages, and of ethnicities, I suspect they would rejoice to learn the truth of the matter, just as Professor Jacob Barnhardt is delighted when the alien Klaatu clears up scientific mysteries for him in *The Day the Earth Stood Still*.

Etiological stories[9] are narrative attempts to explain how remarkable things got to be the way they are. Why is there death? Why do we wear clothes? Why must we work for a living? Why do people hate snakes? What is the rainbow? Why do spiders spin webs?[10]

Etymological stories[11] explain, by means of puns, the supposed origins of names no one understood anymore or that had unsavory pagan origins and needed a more wholesome Hebrew explanation.

Ethnological stories[12] depict the relations of nations, tribes, and groups in the narrator's day, symbolizing each group as a fictive ancestor who has the stereotyped traits of the group,[13] sort of like Uncle Sam, John Bull, and the Russian bear in political cartoons. Why do the Israelites and the Edomites always fight, despite being neighbors and even kin? Because Esau and Jacob got off to a bad start, and now it's in the blood.

Geological stories[14] are folktales told to explain the origin of remarkable features of the landscape, whether oases, springs, wind-eroded rock formations, man-made cairns, glacial megaliths, etc.

Ceremonial (or *cult*) **stories**[15] supply a rationale for performing some ritual that was either so archaic that no one remembered why it was first done, or else was pagan in origin and thus required a new "orthodox" rationale.

To these five we might add another, suggested by anthropologist Bronislaw Malinowski: **Legitimization stories.**[16] In order to reinforce a society's laws and customs, a story tells that at the dawn of creation God or the gods decreed that it be this way. Who are we to change it now? Of course, the story is told after human beings have created the custom, not before.

Many biblical stories fall into more than one of these categories, doing double or triple duty to answer many questions. Probably the stories grew in the telling, as each telling prompted new questions from the audience: "Oh! I'll bet that's *also* why . . . ."

The Stories

The Six Day Creation
Gen. 1:1-2:4a

Though placed at the head of the Bible, this is not the earliest biblical version of the creation. It comes from the Priestly source and represents a sophisticated rationalizing of earlier creation myths. This may seem surprising in view of how fundamentalists have waved this story like a battle flag in their crusade against evolutionary science. That is quite ironic since the Priestly creation account is itself an example, not of mythology, but of early science.[17] This becomes evident when we compare the story, on the one hand, with earlier and overtly mythic creation accounts, and, on the other, with contemporary natural philosophy (pre-technological scientific speculation).

As we will shortly see, the immediately adjacent Garden of Eden story is decidedly mythic in character. The Six-Day Creation is not dependent on the Eden tale, but it does preserve and reinterpret elements of yet a third version of creation attested pretty widely elsewhere in the Bible as well as in the myths of neighboring cultures (and possibly borrowed from them).[18] This myth depicts creation as a by-product of an epic battle between a young warrior god and one or more sea dragons at the dawn of time.

At first there is no world to speak of, only the home of the gods in heaven and the waters of Chaos in which great monsters sport. The dragons have risen up to threaten the gods, who, however, are aged and not up to their challenge. A young and virile deity, usually the storm god, steps forth with an offer: If the others will acknowledge him as their king, he will take on the monsters.

They readily agree, and the battle commences. Though initially defeated, even devoured, he bursts forth from the monster's gullet and dismembers it, creating our earth from the dragon's remains. Henceforth he reigns over the pantheon, either as co-regent with his father or as his successor.

There is more to be said about this widespread myth later, but for the moment, suffice it to note how the Priestly writer has sought to "demythologize" it. The sea dragons seem to have originated as personifications of seas or rivers. The name of the nine-headed dragon slain by Hercules, the Hydra, simply means "water" in Greek, while Lotan (= the biblical Leviathan,[19] mentioned in Pss. 74:13-14; 89:9-10; 104:25-26; Job 3:8; 26:13; 41:1-34; Isa. 27:1; 51:9), the seven-headed dragon slain by Baal in Canaanite myth, embodies the Syrian Litani River.[20]

These combat myths seem to have started out as chants reciting the primordial victory of the god over the threatening flood, in hopes that he would deliver his people from it once again.[21] Later, the creation by combat story was repurposed as part of the annual re-investiture of the king, who was supposed to be God's vicar on earth. (Again, more of this later on.)

During the Babylonian Exile (from about 586 to about 435 B.C.E.), the Jewish priests and scribes who had been deported to the metropolis of Babylon were concerned lest traditional Jewish lore be lost as Jews began to learn Babylonian ways. Much of the Old Testament may have been written (or compiled from various oral and written sources—and/or, ironically, borrowed from surrounding cultures) at this time. The combat myth was alive and well in Babylon. In their version it was the storm god Marduk who whelmed the dragons Apsu and Tiamat, using their carcasses to create the earth.

It is obvious that the Priestly creation account drew from this story. The Priestly writer has demythologized the dragon Tiamat, speaking instead of the *tehom*, or ocean depths from which God causes the earth to emerge, as well as in the description of the earth's initial chaotic state as "without form and void" (*tohu* and *bohu*). *Tohu* is an abstraction of Tiamat, while *bohu* is another form of "Behemoth," [22] another primordial monster mentioned in Job 40:15-24. The sea monsters do show up in Genesis 1, but further along, where they have become mere sea beasts created along with other marine animals in verse 21.

Many scholars think we can detect Babylonian influence also in the division of the creation process into seven days, six of work and one of rest. The division may reflect an organizing feature of an ancient Babylonian creation epic called the *Enuma Elish* (the opening words, "When on high . . .").[23] There the gods take turns contributing this and that portion of the world, and this happens in seven stages.

While no individual deities are differentiated in Genesis 1, there are broad hints that polytheism at least lurks in the background.[24] The Hebrew word translated "God" is actually grammatically plural, which might denote fullness of power for a single deity but seems to imply a pantheon when we read "And God said, 'Let us make man in *our* own image, and in *our* own likeness.' So Elohim created them in his own image and likeness: male and female he created them." That is best explained, I think, as meaning the Elohim consisted of gods *and goddesses*, who were the template for the two sexes among their human replicas.

Modern readers balk at the idea of several gods in the Bible, as well as the notion of God having a physical body of some sort,[25] even if made out of superior materials. But all the ancients believed in anthropomorphic deities, and the Bible often describes God as sitting in state on a throne. In the Eden story, God takes daily evening strolls with the man and the woman in the shade of the Garden.

We might find the narrative less embarrassing if we took "the image of God" in man as denoting "rational intelligence" or some such, but this seems to be reading modern notions back into an ancient text. I have had fundamentalist students and acquaintances who truly believed God possesses a body. In the eighth century, the liberal, philosophical faction of Muslims, the Mu'tazilites,[26] could not believe Allah exists in bodily form in heaven and posited a purely transcendent God-concept. They were met with outraged accusations of heresy from Islamic traditionalists.[27] My point is that belief in a God or gods with physical form was apparently universal until the late Middle Ages when Jews, Christians, and Muslims alike began to question the notion.

So the Priestly author of Genesis 1 has edited out the combat myth, demythologizing Tiamat and Behemoth. But then we might ask him, why not go the whole way and demythologize God? Well, not every God concept is mythological. Some, like Anselm's or Spinoza's, are philosophical. Roman Catholic thinker Blaise Pascal summed up the same point with his famous maxim, "The God of Abraham, Isaac, and Jacob is not the God of the philosophers." And in fact the Priestly writer was at least headed in that direction: His creator deity is no primeval "crocodile hunter" but calls creation into being by his mere command.

A few centuries later, the Jewish Middle Platonist philosopher Philo of Alexandria had no trouble interpreting the "Let there be's" of Genesis One in terms of the creative *logos* (Greek for "word" or "reason, logic") of Heraclitus and the later Stoics. And that's practically already catching up to the eighteenth-century Pantheist Spinoza.

Let's return to the seven-days schema for a moment. Whether or not it was borrowed from the *Enuma Elish*, the division of the creation process into days of a week was motivated by a concern to reinforce Sabbath-keeping by Jews who were tempted to drop the custom as they adopted the cosmopolitan ways of their (pagan) neighbors. The same thing happened with Jews in the Roman Empire, and of course in modern Europe and America. Assimilation is probably more of a threat to Judaism than is persecution.

There are other reasons given for Sabbath observance elsewhere in scripture, but the Priestly account urges readers to follow the example set by God himself: After laboring six days, thou shalt kick back on the seventh, as the Creator himself did. That's bringing in the big guns.[28]

As Wellhausen[29] showed, the Priestly writer had much in common with the roughly contemporary pre-Socratic natural philosophers, who advanced various theories of world origins. All sought to explain how the amazing diversity of our world had emerged from one common element. Thales suggested all things are made from water, Anaximenes posited air, Heraclitus fire, Anaximander "the Indeterminate Boundless." And so on.

Many of these theories pictured some process, perhaps centrifugal, that produced different forms or combinations of elements. We can see something very much like this going on in the Six-Day Creation, where each day witnesses the emergence of specific classes and species, stage by stage: light and darkness (the former further coalescing into sun, moon, and miniature stars), oceans and dry land, sea life, vermin ("creeping things" including insects, lizards, snakes, salamanders, mice and rats, all lumped together in the ancient Hebrew taxonomy), birds, mammals, humans. And, just as in some Asian Indian cosmogonies,[30] Genesis 1 starts the whole thing off with the disturbance of the primordial waters with "a mighty wind" stirring the face of the deep. This causes the turbulent churning of the primal ocean which then casts up the various land-forms and life-forms.

Already we are glimpsing genuine natural philosophy beginning to supplant raw mythology, since the story has God set in motion a process *operating under its own steam*. Just as Thales reasoned that, even if it does rain because Zeus wills it, there must be some *way* that he does it, some *process*, and we are on our way to the water cycle.

Speaking of the scientific thinking of the ancients, we must draw a vital distinction between *mythology* and *speculation*. When Genesis 1 describes the universe with a flat earth floating upon a universal ocean, protected from a cosmic ocean above it by means of a solid dome (a *"firmament,"* Hebrew *raqiya*, "a dome beaten out of metal plates") with windows in it to let in the rain and with stars set in it like ceiling lights—we are dealing not with myth but with scientific speculation. A mythic cosmology (world-schema) would be, for example, one where the earth hatches out of an egg or rests on the back of a giant turtle. But just about all the ancients in the biblical environment thought (not "believed in") the flat, domed earth with oceans above and below. And they weren't stupid to think so, either.

Take a look around you: Doesn't the earth appear to be basically flat, albeit bumpy here and there? You can't see very far, but you can chalk that up to plain old distance, right? And doesn't the sky seem to come down to meet the ground in every direction? A world-dome begins to make a lot of sense. You dig wells and find water deep in the ground, which implies that the earth is built over water. And where does the rain come from? The sky, which means there must be a huge amount of water up in the cosmic attic, too! Nobody had invented telescopes yet, so I submit that what I have just described was the best thinking of the day.

The Priestly writer was therefore a natural philosopher, and this fact has three important implications for modern attitudes about the Bible.

First, literalists, "creationists," like to champion the Six-Day Creation story as true fact and wind up repudiating science (except when it comes to TV broadcasting technology) or fabricating elaborate pseudo-science. This is tragically ironic, since, as I've suggested, the Priestly writer would surely have ditched his theory (and that's all it ever was; he never said, "God told me this.") in a split second had somebody presented him the facts at our disposal.

Second, theological liberals like to assure us that the Genesis writer wasn't really trying to set forth an accurate account of world origins. No, he was just using the assumptions of his day to communicate a religious message, namely that, contrary to the belief of Gnostic ascetics (or some such), the world is *good*, that God wants us to enjoy the good things of life.

The story is indeed wholesomely world-affirming, but it is just preposterous to say the writer was not doing his best to describe what he thought must have happened.[31] The liberal approach is just a step removed from the fundamentalist approach. The fundamentalist wants to say the Bible was not wrong at all, but the liberal says the Bible wasn't *really* wrong, since it wasn't really *trying to say* the part of it that it got wrong.

Third, the Bible-hater blames the Bible for being an ancient book, not a modern one. Of course, he would never do this if the fundamentalist wasn't making ridiculously inflated claims for the Bible. Once we drop the absurd pretense that the Bible is a miraculously inspired, infallible, and inerrant revelation from God, the Bible is no longer an old battle axe wrested from the hands of a threatening barbarian. It ceases to be a weapon and becomes a fascinating artifact, like *Beowulf*, the *Nibelungenlied*, and the *Iliad*.

One last note: Bible-haters like to condemn this story because of the business about God commanding his[32] humans to "fill the earth and subdue it" (Gen. 1:28). They read it as if it said "Thou shalt strip-mine the planet, pollute it, and exhaust its resources." Of course this is ludicrous. The point is that humans are stewards of the earth. And "it is appointed to stewards to be faithful" (1 Cor. 4:2). The reference is to farming, clearing land for building homes, etc.

The Garden of Eden

Gen. 2:4b-3:24

This is an entirely different creation story, and unlike the Priestly Six-Day Creation story, this one is pure myth. No science here, not even early science. The Garden of Eden story is one of J's. The story is built from *etiological* tales: why snakes crawl, why we and snakes hate each other, why childbirth is painful, why we wear clothes, why we work for a living, why there is sex and death. There are also *etymological* notes explaining the names of Adam and Eve. If the Priestly account is implicitly polytheistic, the Garden of Eden story is explicitly so. The order of events, where there is any overlap between the P and J stories, is significantly different, and the harmonizations offered to reconcile them are *ad hoc* contrivances that would never look good to anyone not looking to get out of a tight spot.

Significantly, J does not have God intend for humans to "be fruitful and multiply and fill the earth" as the Priestly writer did. Nor does Yahweh want his fledgling humans to bear his image and likeness. In fact, as in the *Enuma Elish*, Yahweh and his fellow deities create man as a servant, a slave. Yahweh and his colleagues require a groundskeeper to keep up the Garden of Eden, a Paradise or oasis for the gods' use. The fruit trees are first and foremost the food of the gods, even the Tree of Life, from which the gods eat to renew their immortality.

This sounds outrageously strange when we read the story through the lenses of Christian theology, but it all makes perfect sense when viewed against the background of ancient mythology. The Greek gods ate ambrosia and were nourished on the smoke of sacrifices (as God is in Genesis 8:21), as were the Vedic gods. Yahweh allows the man to eat from most of the trees, just as the Torah provides for the poor, ordering farmers to leave the edges of their grain fields unharvested for the indigent to glean (Deut. 23:25; cf., Deut.25:4, "You shall not muzzle the ox as it treads out the corn."). Only one type of fruit is off limits. It is, of course, that of the Tree of the Knowledge of Good and Evil.

Though a natural inference, it is probably incorrect to assume that the fruit somehow provides him who eats it with moral judgment or conscience. If this were the case, how could one be blamed for committing the "sin" of deciding to disobey his creator by eating the fruit? "It was wrong? What's a 'wrong'?"

No, "good and evil" is more likely a figure of speech: a *hendiadys*, in this case the indication of the whole range of things, "from A to Z."[33] Yahweh does not want the man to become too smart. It is just like Pierre Boule's novel, *The Planet of the Apes* (the loose inspiration for all those movies): People train chimps and gorillas to act as domestic servants. They are docile and obedient—until somebody gets the bright idea of enabling them to *speak*. It takes only a simple operation on the vocal apparatus. The power of speech fuels a rapid rush to full intelligence, and the newly self-confident apes rebel. That is pretty much what happens in the Garden of Eden myth. The trigger is eating the forbidden fruit.

But there is a specific aspect of the godlike knowledge which dominates the story as the focus shifts slightly.

Apparently Yahweh needs but a single employee to do the job. The notion of a whole human race never crosses his mind, unlike the Priestly account, where God (Elohim) makes several human males and females at the same time and directs them to get busy breeding and populating the new-made earth. Fundamentalists have never solved the problem of the whole human race stemming from so tiny a gene pool as a single pair would afford. Ditto the problem of where Cain gets his wife in Genesis 4. We might not have this issue to deal with if we recognized that Genesis 1 has God create numerous unrelated men and women simultaneously, but fundamentalists do not have that option, since it would mean admitting that P and J are telling very different stories. Too bad.

One day, Yahweh realizes there is not enough work to keep the man busy, and the poor thing is lonely. Taking pity upon him, Yahweh resolves to arrange companionship for him. To this end he experiments by creating one creature after another out of the ground from which he had molded the man. But every creature that appears (like the Golden Calf spontaneously appearing, without previous design, from the furnace in Exodus 32:24) proves unsuitable to the task.

The man (who is not yet given a name, despite many Bible versions translating the common noun *adam*, "man," as a proper name, which it does later become) is more choosy than his counterpart Tarzan, for whom the company of chimps and elephants seemed sufficient. As soon as one fails the test, Yahweh tries another, raising each one up from the dirt. This is the occasion as well as the reason for Yahweh creating animals at all, according to J.

But once they are there, he (presumably) creates a mate for each so they can produce various species. Here, by the way, is one of the major differences between J's Garden of Eden creation myth and P's Six-Day creation: In the Priestly version, whole classes of animals are created before humanity appears on the scene, none after, whereas in the former, the animals are an afterthought, created after the man, as failed attempts to provide him a fitting pet or pal.

This series of experiments having failed, Yahweh goes back to the drawing board. This time he "clones" the man, breaking off one of his ribs while he keeps the man under anesthesia and fashioning it into a second human, a female. Not that he wants them to have sex, mind you, just companionship, not even scintillating conversation, since at this point they are still basically just trained apes, a point the text underlines by describing them as "naked and not ashamed," i.e., like an animal or a little child. He pointedly does *not* tell them to "be fruitful and multiply." As an aside, anticipating what is soon going to happen, the J writer tells us that this "birth" of the woman (*ish-sha*) from the man (*ish*) occasions the sex drive: The two sundered halves seek reunion.[34]

This may sound contrived: Didn't Yahweh *know* what was likely to happen? And why didn't he simply make another *man*? Why not Adam and Steve? But remember, in the fashion of all etiological "shaggy dog" stories, the story is a piece of "reverse engineering," working backward from the phenomenon it is trying to explain. If we were dealing with the work of an author freely spinning out a story in whatever direction he preferred, like a modern novelist, the story would not read this way. The etiological story-teller has certain dots he is obliged to connect the best he can.

The ancient Gnostics probably had it right, in my opinion, when they suggested that the Tree of Knowledge stands, at least in the latter portion of the story, for *carnal* knowledge, and that Yahweh (and his fellow gods whom he addresses in tones of panic at the end of Genesis 3) means to prevent the couple from learning about procreation. The "knowledge" refers to sex, as "knowledge" and "to know" do ten other times in the Old Testament. Yahweh tells them they will die as soon as they eat the fruit because it is poison. But, as the serpent tells them, it actually is not. Instead, it will impart divine wisdom. They eat and gain wisdom, especially the ability to reproduce.

Please note that throughout the narrative it is Yahweh who deceives the man and the woman, while the serpent tells them the truth. Yahweh warns them that tasting the knowledge fruit will kill them on the spot: "In the day that you eat of it you shall die." They don't. The serpent tells them the fruit is "good for food," i.e., not poison after all, and that it will open their eyes and make them like God or gods. Events corroborate the serpent's claims: The narrator[35] tells us that "their eyes were opened," while Yahweh himself admits (to the other gods), "they have become like one of us." All this is quite clear if one reads the text closely, but it remains invisible to Christian readers because, saturated with later Christian theology, they simply cannot imagine that the Bible would depict God as a liar.

Yahweh fears that if humans possess both godlike knowledge–especially including the power of reproduction–and personal immortality, they will outnumber and overpower Yahweh and his divine compatriots. It has become too late to prevent their breeding like rabbits, but at least he can bar them from the Tree of Life. Up till this point, they had been allowed to eat from it so that Yahweh would never have to replace them with new caretakers. But it seems they had not availed themselves of the opportunity.

Since, via sex, mankind as a species can thus continue in perpetuity, Yahweh now forbids individual immortality, so the man and the woman are exiled from the source of eternal life, which Yahweh himself eats. J's Garden of Eden tale is just like the *Atrahasis Epic*, where the gods flood the world because they are sick of the incessant noise made by the teeming multitudes of pesky humans.

The whole Eden scene finds its parallel (if not perhaps its origin?) in the *Gilgamesh Epic*. The demigod Gilgamesh (whom the ancient Hebrews numbered among the semi-divine champions called the *Nephilim* in Gen. 6:1-4)[36] has spurned the advances of the goddess Aruru, who plans revenge against him. From the ground she fashions, Adam-style, the Tarzan-like Enkidu, a wild man possessing strength nearly equal to Gilgamesh's.

Enkidu lives in the forest among the animals, raiding hunters' traps for food. The hunters prevail on King Gilgamesh to find and defeat this pest. Meanwhile, Aruru sends one of her priestesses to socialize Enkidu by initiating him into sexuality. They go at it for several days straight. Afterward, Enkidu visits his favorite watering hole. When he arrives, his old furry pals bolt in fear. Enkidu is flabbergasted! The priestess explains that he is no longer one of them, and they can tell: "Behold, Enkidu! You are become wise–like unto a god!" The two titans do meet in battle, but each comes to admire the other's might and prowess, and they become friends. Again, sexuality = knowledge = godlikeness.

The Garden of Eden story has nothing to do with Original Sin. Nor is the serpent supposed to be an incarnation or puppet of Satan. As we will see, on the rare occasions when Satan does appear in the Old Testament he is an agent, not an enemy, of God.

It was much later theological speculation that connected Satan with the Edenic serpent.[37] The latter is probably to be identified with the old Hebrew serpent deity Nehushtan (also called Leviathan)[38] of whom we shall have more to say later on. For now it is enough to note that in the Eden story he is strikingly parallel to the Greek Titan Prometheus, cousin to Zeus. Though Zeus had created humanity, it was their "uncle" Prometheus who had more concern for the shivering primitives huddled in their caves.

Twice he gets in serious trouble with Zeus by intervening on the mortals' behalf. When Zeus is trying to determine what portions of the butchered sacrifice he is to receive (as a burnt offering) and which parts the worshippers may keep for their sacrificial feasts, Prometheus pulls the old switcheroo, tricking Zeus into claiming the disgusting detritus for himself and assigning the tasty meat to the mortals.

As if this were not enough to rouse Zeus's ire, Prometheus outwits him again, this time, in the matter of fire, forbidden to mortals. Prometheus sneaks into the Olympian temple and steals a bit of the eternal flame, concealing it in a papyrus cone. He descends to earth and demonstrates to the humans how to make and use fire. Zeus sees the unaccustomed bright sparks down below and swears vengeance upon his cousin. Henceforth, Prometheus is to pass eternity crucified to a boulder on Mount Aetna, where he must be tortured every day by a vulture tearing at his liver. (Don't worry: Eventually Hercules rescues him.)

The similarities are striking. The serpent is "the wisest of creatures," while the very name "Prometheus" means "forethought." Neither is the creator of humanity,[39] but both show more concern for humans than their creator does. Both conspire to poach food that properly belongs to the gods and give it to mortals. Both bring knowledge (for which fire is an obvious symbol) to mankind.[40] Both are punished for aiding mortals against the orders of the creator. Both are representatives of pantheons whose cults have been suppressed by more recent ones.

Prometheus was one of the Titans, the immortals whose king was Cronus until Zeus overthrew him. The serpent god Nehushtan/Leviathan had been part of the Hebrew pantheon with his own chapel in the Jerusalem Temple until King Hezekiah ejected most of these gods in a clean sweep of zeal for Yahweh (2 Kings 18:4).

And right here we find a clue as to how on earth the biblical writer could possibly depict Yahweh as what the author of the Nag Hammadi scripture *The Testimony of Truth* (one of several alternative versions of the Eden story) called "a malicious grudger," jealously guarding his divine prerogatives. My guess is that both the Eden and Prometheus stories are the work of secret partisans of their respective "heretical" gods. Once their worship had been overthrown and banned, these out-of-favor priests had no choice but to give lip service to the official deity, whether Zeus or Yahweh, but they could still get their licks in!

So each told a story in which his god, though he could no longer be depicted in his rightful glory, showed himself the self-sacrificing benefactor of mankind, as against the oppressive injustice of the gods who (i.e., whose priests) had overthrown him. History went on, and later generations who gathered up the old stories were oblivious of old, long-dead theological controversies. If it was a story about Yahweh (or in Greece, Zeus), into scripture it went, make of it what one will.

The etiological functions of the Eden myth come into play following the eating of the knowledge fruit. This event precipitated several developments that set the course of the future, "explaining" how things wound up as they did. For instance, it seemed puzzling that humans wear clothing when animals don't (or didn't until our day when Chihuahuas started wearing sweaters). Of course, had the Bible writers lived in a colder clime, there would have been no mystery!

At any rate, we are first told that the man and the woman paraded around naked, unaware of anything amiss. But after a taste of the knowledge fruit, they suddenly "knew that they were naked" and hastened to make loincloths (and a bra?) out of fig leaves. One supposes they knew how to do this automatically from that knowledge juice (brain fluid?), like Neo and Trinity uploading new skills direct from the computer in *The Matrix*.

When Yahweh shows up for his evening constitutional, he finds he has been stood up. "Hey! Where *is* everybody?" An omniscient deity has to ask? Remember, we are not dealing with Thomas Aquinas or St. Anselm here. This is J, not Paul Tillich or Karl Barth, after all. From the bushes come the quavering accents of the humans: "We were ashamed, for we were naked." "Oh, that's . . . *Wait* a second! Who *told* you you were naked? You must have sampled that fruit I told you not to eat, *didn't* you?"

I am guessing the problem was that Yahweh surmised what must have happened, discretely left tacit in the narrative, or would soon happen: The nakedness was unremarkable before, but once their eyes were opened, nudity provoked sexual arousal. And that is why public nakedness is forever after forbidden. This is obviously why Muslim women cover themselves in *burkhas*. Men know their sexual urges too well and shroud their females from head to toe lest the mere sight of their charms incite other men to molest them.[41] So "Papa, why do we wear clothes?" *That's* why.

Why do women have to endure labor pains? Why would the Creator inflict such abuse? It must have been a punishment for something the first woman did, namely, getting pregnant. Yahweh did not want his wards to reproduce, but, with the serpent's assistance, they had outwitted him. Yahweh had proven unable to prevent it, so now he would make them pay dearly for the privilege. The punishment was made to fit the "crime."[42]

Yahweh tells the woman to be careful what she wishes for: Along with sex come children, and with children comes a home, complete with domestic slavery and domination by her blustering husband, like Ralph Kramden, "the king of the castle." You wanted it, lady? You got it! A woman might see this coming and decide to skip marriage, though her father would try his best to nudge her out of the nest. Even married, she might think, like Scarlett O'Hara, to lock her husband out of the bedroom (1 Cor. 7:5), but Yahweh says that's not going to work either. Her libido, now that it's been awakened, will make her give in sooner or later.

This story legitimatized male domination over women. The purpose is to prevent women demanding equal treatment. They had their chance: Describing the woman as a "helper" or "helpmeet" for the man in no way implied inferiority, as if she were to walk around in a French maid outfit, feather duster in hand. The word *ezer* does mean "help," but all the rest of the times it is used in the Hebrew Bible it refers to God (and once to King David). No, the subordination is a subsequent development, after the first couple partook of the Tree of Knowledge. "You don't like the arrangement, girlie? Better take it up with God! It was his idea, not mine!" Obviously, the reverse was the case: Male chauvinism was imposed by males, then, via ventriloquism, attributed to God, as is the case with all legitimization myths.

Is it more likely that this story was the work of a man or of a woman? If it weren't already obvious, recall how the Eden story has the first woman born from the first man!

And the snake? As already suggested, there is an earlier myth, another creation myth, in fact, behind this one. Originally, the enmity between Yahweh and the serpent was the primordial battle in which Yahweh, "a man of war" (Exod. 15:3), "crushed the heads of the dragons on the waters" (Psalm 74:13). Jehovah's victory over his foe somehow reflects the purge of Nehushtan/Leviathan's worship from the Jerusalem Temple.

By the time J makes use of the myth, there is not much left of it: The ophidian deity has sunk to the level of being "Mr. Snake," the progenitor of all future snakes.[43] And it is as the representative of the whole subsequent species that he is punished. Because he conspired, like some mischievous Disney character, with the humans to get around Yahweh's commands, all future snakes will have to wallow in the dust and mud.[44] How would they have locomoted otherwise? The ancient Hebrews were probably thinking of the *Seraphim*, winged serpents whose name means "fiery ones" (denoting poisonous snakes in Numbers 21:6). They are shown with wings, hovering about the throne of Adonai in the Temple, in Isaiah 6. The serpent of Eden was apparently pictured as one of these—until Yahweh clipped his wings.

Needless to say, it is only from the human point of view that crawling along the ground seems repugnant. Snakes are quite pleased to navigate on their bellies across the earth. But the story does at least preserve someone's sharp-eyed observation: Some snakes do have tiny vestigial legs embedded in their underside, which means their reptile forbears were pretty much long lizards whose little Dachshund legs provided such negligible advantage that the species lost them over the generations and didn't even notice.

We like to call a treacherous rogue "a snake in the grass" (unless, of course, the Ophidian Anti-Defamation League gets wind of it). The Eden story attempts to account for this, too. Why do humans and snakes get along so poorly? Rattlesnakes bite us when they get the chance, and we waste no time beating their brains out with a garden hoe. As Rodney King once mused, "Why can't we all just get along?" Because Yahweh wanted to prevent further ruinous collaborations between us and snakes, he turned us against each other. Divide and conquer, that's the ticket. (We'd still have to ask what's up with the snakes and the mongooses.)

All right, the man and the woman didn't die as soon as they ate the forbidden fruit, for the simple reason that it turned out not to be poisonous after all. But at the end of the story, Jehovah does condemn them to eventual death, denying them access to the Tree of Immortality. And that's why we die. After all we do, after all we become, once we are in sight of maturity and prosperity—we die! "Vanity of vanities! All is vanity!" (Eccl. 1:2). How can this be the natural plan? Something seems wrong. And the Eden story says it is, and this is how it happened.

Not just condemned, the man and the woman are exiled, too. No more leisurely picking grapes off the vine! From now on, man, cast out of Paradise, will be forced to wring crops out of the stubborn, rocky ground. He is sentenced to hard labor, and that, boys and girls, is why we have to work for a living. Nothing here about the dignity of labor. So much of ancient work was necessary but meaningless. How futile, but better than starving to death, because the Eden story holds out absolutely no glimmer of hope for any life after death. God's in his heaven, and man's in his grave. It is a dreary, pessimistic worldview perfectly summed up in the bumper sticker: "Life's a bitch and then you die" (cf. Gen. 47:9; Psalm 90:7-10; Eccl. 2:13-17; Matt. 7:34).

Genesis 3:20-21 looks like a clumsy interruption of the narrative, which seems to progress naturally from the end of verse 19 straight to verse 22. Besides, the word *adam*, a common noun up to this point, here suddenly becomes a proper name, anticipating the man naming his wife. This is an etymological note, explaining her name as if a pun on the similar-looking Hebrew word for "life."

The problem here is the naive assumption of the story-teller that the first human being already spoke Hebrew. It is just like pulp science fiction stories where American astronauts land on a distant planet and find the bug-eyed aliens all speaking English! Of course! Doesn't everyone? Our story-teller has the man think it appropriate to name his wife "Livia" (so to speak) because, he says, "she is the mother of all living." But this is a retrospective comment, as when anthropologists call the fossil female "Lucy" the mother of all humans today. Such a remark assumes there are plenty of people around in the speaker's day. But at that moment, Eve was *it*.

As with the serpent, Eve is a vestige of earlier mythology. The name ("Eve," "Heba," "Hebe") belonged to an important Near-Eastern goddess.[45] In Greece, she was married to Hercules. In Asia Minor she was another version of the mother goddess Cybele, consort of the dying and rising god Attis. And the title "Mother of All Living" was the title of the equivalent goddess Aruru,[46] whom we have already met in connection with Gilgamesh and Enkidu. Two things become clear. First, the Bible is the tip of a larger, submerged iceberg of ancient mythology. Second, the one-time goddess Eve has been ignominiously demoted to the role of a primordial Lucy Ricardo, precisely like her Greek sister Pandora ("all gifts," a divine Creatrix).[47] Don't eat that fruit! Don't open that box!

The Cain Cycle

Gen. 4:1-17

Cain is known today as the first murderer and, even more famously, for apparently pulling his wife out of thin air. Fundamentalists have never been able to answer the old stumper, "Where did Cain get his wife?" But the blinders they wear prevent them from seeing the answer, or, rather, that, as so often, they are asking the wrong question. The key thing is to realize that some editor or compiler has done his best to stitch together the disparate fragments of legends and stories available to him. These bits and pieces seem to be remnants of what must have been an extensive body of Cain material. But the J compiler has come onto the scene too late; most of the Cain lore had already been forgotten, so he had no connected narrative to pass on to us.

This is one of several hints that J may have been historically later than the great Higher Critics of the nineteenth century estimated. The fragments that had survived till his day owed their preservation to the use that had been made of them in the meantime (probably the reasons for creating them in the first place).

The birth of Cain (Gen. 4:1) is an *etymological* tale: The name "Cain" is punningly derived from *qanah*, "to get." "I have gotten a man [child] with the help of [Yahweh]." What is this supposed to mean? It sounded just as odd to some of the ancient scribes who thought they sniffed the mythic theme of gods begetting demigods upon mortal women— and they were probably right!

I believe that the various other biblical tales of angels appearing to supposedly barren women, announcing they will have a son after all, are probably censored versions of such demigod nativities. The notion was abhorrent to later, monotheistic Jews, as the Cain birth story came from earlier, polytheistic times. They couldn't believe the text originally read this way, so they surmised that the original was "I have gotten a man with the aid of *Satan*"![48] Uh, that's an im*prove*ment?

That they "fell back" to something like this implies they felt they simply couldn't evade the present text's implication of a supernatural conception. And, being monotheists, they had a limited number of paternity suspects. If not Yahweh, then who? And the whole idea seemed more appropriate to the devil than to God. Thus Cain must have been Rosemary's Baby.

He is certainly viewed this way in the New Testament. In 1 John 3:12, Cain is said to have been born "of the evil one." Second Corinthians 11:2-3 speaks of Eve having been seduced by the devil, and this is obviously a component of the Cain nativity. It was an attempt to explain Cain's evil behavior. What do you expect? He was half devil! (Just one horn?)[49] But none of this is hinted in Genesis 4:1, which celebrates the first birth from a woman (unlike that of Eve from Adam in Genesis 2:21-22). In fact, the more seriously one takes the likelihood of Yahweh's begetting Cain, the more likely it seems that Cain was first supposed to be a demigod hero, not some murderer. The evil Cain only appears in some, though by no means all, of the subsequent verses.

Another surviving tradition derives the name Cain from "cornstalk." One legend says baby Cain hopped up and fetched a cornstalk for mommy.[50] This innocuous nonsense would seem to be a secondary version, again, attempting to supplant an earlier, "pagan" characterization of Cain as some sort of embodiment of the Corn Spirit.

Note that he is described here in Genesis as a tiller of the soil, an agriculturalist, in contrast to his brother, a shepherd.[51] Still another version explains "Cain" as denoting "metal worker,"[52] reflecting the fact that Cain appears also as the character Tubal-Cain[53]

(Gen. 4:22), the eponymous ancestor of the tribe of Tubal (Ezek. 38:2; 39:1), or the Tibarenes, bronze-workers near the Black Sea.[54]

The anecdote of the offerings of Cain and Abel (Gen. 4:2-7) seems to be an *ethnological* myth, contrasting shepherds like the ancient Israelite nomads with settled farmers such as the Canaanites whom the invading Israelites supplanted.[55] It is tempting to think that, this time, "Cain" stands for the *Can*aanites. Notice that nothing is said of any hypocrisy or insincerity on Cain's part (an accusation leveled at hypocritical worshippers, e.g., in Isaiah 1:10-20).

Yahweh notices Cain sulking and tells him, "Sin is waiting by the door; it hungers for you, but you must master it" (Gen. 4:7, my paraphrase). Doesn't this mean Cain was guilty of something after all, some moral turpitude that disqualified his sacrifice in the eyes of God? Not at all; we must keep in mind that "sin" was primarily ritual in nature, a ceremonial infraction, as when God incinerates the careless priests Nadab and Abihu for getting the incense formula wrong (Lev. 10:1-3).

The moralization of the concept of sin was a later development as seen, e.g., in Isaiah, who lambasted the congregation for presuming to appear for worship while the rest of the week they were exploiting their workers, etc. They were no doubt baffled, as no one had ever told them moral behavior was a prerequisite for pleasing the deity. Thus the "sin" of which Yahweh warns Cain must be a repetition of his mistake in offering God the greenery.

God is not said to reject Cain's worship because it is not heartfelt. The Almighty is depicted in a manner reminiscent of one of the judges on the Food Network show *Iron Chef America*: He just prefers Chef Abel's dish over Chef Cain's. Maybe Yahweh's like me: He just doesn't like vegetables.

The lack of any moral or spiritual criticism of Cain implies the story means to reject one type of worship, one whole class of worshippers, one religious group. Who would have told such a story? In Jeremiah 35, 1 Chronicles 2:55, and 2 Kings 10:15-17 we read of a group of ascetics called the Rechabites, roughly analogous to the Amish in our day, a self-segregated clan of pious nonconformists who rejected town and farm life (perhaps because of the pagan fertility magic often associated with it) and idealized a (possibly imaginary) past of Wahabi-like desert severity and simplicity.[56]

Such a past is represented in the tales of Moses leading the Israelites around from oasis to oasis in the Sinai Desert. To them, Cain would have represented the complacent religion of townsmen and farmers, while Abel symbolized the Rechabite option.

Though the redactional juxtaposition of the "two offerings" tale with the episode of Cain murdering Abel invites one to infer a connection between the two episodes, originally there was none. We take for granted that Cain was disgruntled at Yahweh's rebuff and, jealous of Abel, attacked and killed him. But there is no mention of such motivation. And we don't need it. The murder is preliminary to Cain founding the city called Enoch (Gen. 4:17), and this is a pattern we find elsewhere, as in the myth of the founding of Rome by Romulus–who killed his brother Remus first.[57] It looks like the murder of Abel is a parallel myth or a variant version of it (if there's a difference).

These myths were probably recounted at the breaking of ground for a new city, accompanied by a human sacrifice (on the rationale that in this manner they could satisfy the angel of death so he would not return too soon for his due tribute).[58] We see a case of this in 1 Kings 16:34, when Hiel of Bethel offers up his first-born son Abiram to consecrate the foundation of Jericho.

Joshua 6:26 preserves from an older context the ancient law governing such situations: "At the cost of his first-born shall he lay its foundation, and at the cost of his youngest son shall he set up its gates." The fact that Cain names the city after his (apparently) first-born Enoch may denote that in another version of the tradition, it was his son, not his brother, whom Cain sacrificed at the foundation of his city.

When Yahweh confronts Cain (4:9-16) about the fratricide, he does not execute him, which might surprise us, but rather exiles him. God's sentence is virtually a repetition of his order of exile of Adam from Eden. Apparently, Adam and Eve had settled in near proximity to Eden, but Cain is denied even that. He is doomed to tread the earth forever like the Wandering Jew of Christian legend.[59] It says he went on to "dwell in the land of Nod" (4:16), but "Nod" means "wandering," so it's just a poetic way of saying he hit the road.

And, though Yahweh does not kill Cain on the spot, Cain feels his life is not worth a plugged shekel anyway, as he is sure to be killed by the first person he encounters. (And who might *that* be, as Cain is at this point one of a total of three members of the human race? We will address that puzzle in a moment.)

This episode is another *ethnological* myth, this time using Cain to represent the bloodthirsty marauders, the *Ken*ites (the names are even more similar in the original Hebrew), who are later counted among the allies of David. The point is to account for the characteristic tribal tattoo that tipped off outsiders not to mess with the Kenites lest one provoke a disproportionate vendetta: You kill one Kenite, the Kenites will kill *seven* of yours, so take care![60]

If this anecdote was really about a "historical Cain," we are faced with the absurdity of Cain's universal infamy. *Anyone* who spots him will try to kill him? Were there wanted posters? Police alerts? Had he done the perp walk on televised news? No, the notion of public notoriety fits an infamous *gang, group, or tribe*, not an individual. "*Uh*-oh! That guy's a Kenite! You better get out of his way, Stan!"

By this time you might be asking where Cain came up with his wife (4:17), *a* wife, *any* wife? Was she a hitherto-unmentioned sister? Yikes! Actually, it's worse than *that*. Cain married his *mother*, Eve. As Nicolas Wyatt[61] shows, the present version of the Cain story seems to be a much-demythologized version of an even older myth of a type widespread in the ancient world, one reflecting the *hieros gamos* (sacred marriage) rite of the king and his (favorite) queen. The king played the role of the First Man (like Adam, Enosh, Yama, etc.), the son of the King of the gods and his queen. When time came to produce some more humans, the First Man mated with his divine Mother. In playing out this scenario, sometimes the earthly king might actually marry the Queen Mother if she had outlived the old king.

Now what has all this weirdness to do with Cain? Cain must have been, according to some of the ancient Hebrews, the first man. His mother Eve, remember, was originally a mother goddess, apparently identified with Astarte, a major object of worship by "idolaters" (polytheists) throughout the Old Testament.

Remember, too, what Eve said in greeting Cain's birth: "I have gotten a man with the help of [Yahweh]." Wyatt shows that the Hebrew might better be rendered as "I have gotten a husband, Yahweh," and that he was the father of Cain, the first man, a demigod hero.[62] Then it becomes no coincidence that Cain is expelled from the "ground" even as Adam was, since, in this version, Cain, so to speak, *was* Adam. Anyway, when Cain decided to produce some offspring, he mated with his mother, Eve/Astarte. This is not what the present Cain story wants us to understand; just the opposite. But this earlier, suppressed but still discernable version offers the solution to the problem that was created when the story was sanitized to its present form.

And, again, who was Cain afraid of? Did he think Adam and Eve were gunning for him? And why did he build a city if there was nobody else around to sell real estate to? Plainly, these little story notes presuppose that Cain lived considerably later in human history as part of an amply populated world. There must have been a whole cycle of Cain stories told for entertainment around the campfire. The story-tellers scarcely bothered to work out a consistent chronology. Who cared?

Some tales featured Cain at the dawn of humanity, others placed him in later times. Herodotus the historian supposed there had once been a real historical Hercules and set about trying, from the various references to kings and kingdoms in the Hercules myths, to figure out when the mighty hero had lived.[63] He gave up in frustration. Or, to appeal to a perfect modern parallel, the title character in the TV series *Xena, Warrior Princess* jumps from one historical period to another in every episode. In one we see her on the walls of Troy. In another she meets Julius Caesar. Next she chances to meet Mary and Joseph on their way to Bethlehem. Then she meets the titan Goliath, then Galen the physician. How old *was* this woman? Of course, history is being used as fodder for fantasy adventure. She's active in "the ancient world," anywhere and everywhere there's a good story to be told. And so with Cain.

Interestingly, J also includes a variant version of Cain killing Abel. Cain appears in Genesis 4:22 as Tubal-Cain (see above). Abel appears as Jabal,[64] who, like Abel, is said to be a nomadic shepherd. Tubal-Cain does not himself strike down Jabal, but he supplies the metal weaponry his father Lamech uses to kill his brother. "I have killed a man for wounding me, a *young man* for striking me."

This item culminates a series of subtle clues as to a hidden agenda item in J's primeval "history," namely a running contrast between that which is created directly "from the ground" (a recurring refrain: Gen. 2:7, 9, 19) and that which is born of parents like itself. There seems to have been a psychological struggle in the mind of primitive man, likely stemming from the first (and repeated) discovery that sex led to childbirth. After all, not every act of intercourse results in pregnancy, so the link is not self-evident. The remote ancients, it seems, somehow understood "Mother Earth" in a literal fashion, even if it would seem to make more sense to posit an unseen *Father* impregnating human females.[65]

An echo of this belief survives in the tales told to children even today that mommy and daddy found them under a cabbage leaf, etc. As the sexual nature of procreation became evident, people (like maturing children learning "the facts of life") naturally found themselves compelled to understand themselves as the children of two human parents, beings like themselves. Alas, it is difficult to say goodbye to a cherished belief, even if only subconsciously.

The ripples of this disturbance in the depth-psychological pond became manifest in myths like those underlying the Oedipus Cycle[66] and the Garden of Eden.[67] We find an opposition between being born from the earth and being born of fellow creatures ("born from one" versus "born from two"). Humans embrace their fellow-human parentage, but this seems a betrayal (however necessary) of their debt to Mother Nature. They pay for this betrayal (much like that of a man whose mother resents his wife "stealing" him from her)[68] by discovering problems that result from embracing human parentage.

As long as Jehovah creates plants, the man, and the animal species "from the ground," all goes smoothly. The trouble begins when he tries creating a woman from a fellow human, Eve from Adam. She instigates their downfall, whereupon the couple is driven from the garden. "Cursed is *the ground* because of you." Hitherto, their clothing was made of leaves (from trees grown from the ground), but henceforth animals (with like parents) are slain to provide clothing. (In parallel fashion, Cain is "driven forth from the ground" he used to farm.) Now Yahweh rejects the offering of produce in favor of slaughtered animals.

Cain, celebrated as the first human-born human, goes on to murder the second human-born human, implying that the new arrangement doesn't work out too well. Eve already knew that, because childbirth was so painful, the price she had to pay for sexual procreation. Thus the "progress" of advancing to "the facts of life," the forbidden knowledge, exacts a very heavy price. Is this exclusively a quaint concern on the part of ignorant ancients? Not really. We find it both mirrored and magnified in our own concerns over humanity's alienation from and consequent exploitation of Mother Earth's resources.

The Pre-Flood Patriarchs

Gen. 4:18-5:32

Biblical genealogies are notoriously tedious. Modern readers have no interest in them and wonder why on earth the Bible bothers to include them. But of course they are there for a good reason. These lists of generations served as credentials for priests, kings, etc. Priests had to be descended from Aaron or Zadok, kings from David, etc. As with the genealogies of Jesus in the Gospels of Matthew and Luke, they may be fabrications, which may not be as bad as it sounds. After all, do modern tracers of family trees always possess complete data? Sometimes they have to connect the dots as best they can even if it's part guesswork. Muslim traditionists used to document the validity of *hadith*, ostensibly the word-of-mouth tales of what the Prophet Muhammad did and said, in the same way, by citing long chains of attestation: "I got it from A, who got it from B, who got it from C," and so all the way back to the Prophet. Of course, all of them were fabrications.[69]

But the genealogies of the descendants of Adam are an exception to the general rule of tedium. The life-spans of these ancient personages beggar credibility. Old Methusaleh beat them all, retiring from this mortal coil at the ripe old age of 969 years. No, not your typical genealogy, not even for the Bible.

And just as Matthew and Luke present us with two different, contradictory genealogies of Jesus, the Pentateuchal sources J and P offer two somewhat different versions of the descendants of Adam. In the J version (Gen. 4:18-26), Cain is Adam's son, whose line it traces from Cain to Lamech, doubling back to tell us Adam also fathered Seth, who fathered Enosh. But the P version (Gen. 5) makes Cain ("Kenan") the son of Enosh and includes Seth in the same line: Adam, Seth, Enosh, Kenan/Cain. And for some reason, Enoch and Mahujael (= Methusaleh) are reversed. The oddity that the Priestly writer lists Cain (Kenan) as Enosh's son makes sense if we recognize that P has already harmonized two lists. In one of them Cain (Kenan) was still the first son of the first man, but the first man was not Adam but Enosh! And thereby hangs a tale.

Enosh must have been the original Israelite mythical "first man," since his name means "man." "Adam," on the other hand, must originally have been the mythic ancestor of the Edomites (= "Adamites"). Keep in mind that Semitic languages are based on clusters of two or three consonants with no written vowels, the result being that the pronunciation comes to vary, as with the Arabic Muhammad/Mohammed and Omar/Umar. Thus "Adam" and "Edom" come out to the same name. The Edomites were related to the Israelites as Spaniards are to Portuguese. Some of the Israelites simply shared the same first man character with their Edomite cousins, just as they shared the god El with other Canaanite neighbors. But other Israelites came up with their own first mythical progenitor, Enosh.

The Edomites, like many ancient peoples, simply equated their own tribe with the human race *per se*; thus their (imaginary) tribal ancestor was *ipso facto* the father of the human race.[70] The Israelites regarded the Edomites as elder brothers (as implied in the Jacob-Esau stories later in Genesis), so the ultimate progenitor of the Edomites was automatically the father of Israel, too: Adam. The Priestly writer has, as I say, harmonized an Adam version with an Enosh version, each having Cain/Kenan for his son. It looks like one of the lists P used skipped Cain's line altogether, as well as Abel who produced no descendants, going directly from Adam to Seth, etc., and ascribing the rest of the pre-Flood patriarchs to Seth instead of Cain. Many later Jews took Seth to be a quasi-messianic character,[71] a necessary replacement for Abel, supplied in order to take up the destiny and mission of his murdered brother.

It is worth noting in this connection that later Sethian Gnostics made a great deal of the implied Seth vs. Cain contrast, regarding their own membership (possessors of a superior, esoteric enlightenment) as "the kingless race" of Seth's descendants, as opposed to the common run of ignorant mankind. The Mandaean Gnostics (still going today) revered Abel, Seth, and Enosh as angelic saviors in the heavens.

All this may be merely subsequent embellishments of scripture, but it is tempting to suspect that some of this lore preserves very ancient beliefs about these mythic figures. After all, these names occurring in the genealogies of Genesis must denote characters famous in Hebrew legend or no one would have bothered including them. More, possibly much more, must have been "known" about them than Genesis 4-5 tell us.

This is true especially with regard to Enoch, to whom several long works are ascribed, one of them actually quoted in Jude verses 14-15, namely, 1 Enoch (or Ethiopic Enoch, since the only extant copy is an Ethiopic (Ge'ez) translation, though it was composed in Hebrew or Aramaic). This one was an Enochic Pentateuch of sorts, an anthology of five originally independent Enoch books: *The Book of the Watchers*, the *Similitudes of Enoch*, the *Astronomical Book*, the *Dream Visions* or *Animal Apocalypse*, and the *Epistle of Enoch*.

The Pseudepigraphical book Testaments of the Twelve Patriarchs mentions other Enoch literature from the same period, i.e., first century B.C.E. to first century C.E. Second Enoch (or Slavonic Enoch or the Secrets of Enoch) appears to be slightly later, while 3 Enoch is a Medieval Hebrew text, a collection of mystical revelations. Enoch is said in Genesis 5:22 to have "walked with God." God "took him" (Gen. 5:24). Early on, scribes interpreted this to mean that Enoch was so righteous that God rewarded him with immortality through a bodily ascension to heaven. That was a boon granted to a very few in Old Testament legend, since most people were not believed to die, then go to heaven, but only to die and linger as ghosts in the dreary netherworld of Sheol, as in Job 7:9; 17:16; Pss. 6:5; 49:14; 55:15; Eccles. 9:14; Isa. 14:11; 38:18.

Jewish scribes had plenty of speculations about the set-up of the universe, the sections of the heavens (skies) devoted to good or bad souls, fallen angels, stars, raindrops, snowflakes, etc. They also thought they knew what God had planned for the future, and they could not resist the opportunity to couch these opinions as heavenly secrets revealed to the ascended Enoch. Of course, for us to be reading them, one must posit that Enoch returned to earth briefly to report on what he had seen, then returned to heavenly glory. Some Gnostic texts have the risen Jesus do the same thing.

The ancient scribes were substituting all this for an earlier understanding of Enoch from the old days of Hebrew-Canaanite polytheism. Originally it seems that Enoch was the personification of the sun.[72] He "walked with God" across the sky every day, from his appearance at dawn to his retirement at dusk. Enoch's ascent to heaven was, of course, the sun's daily rising to its zenith at noon. Hence his life-span of 365 "years," an obvious reference to the length of a year in the solar calendar.

Someone still understood this much in later centuries, because one of the major topics in 1 Enoch is the solar versus lunar calendar debate, a headache for the rabbis because rival calendars resulted in some factions celebrating the holy days on the "wrong" days and thus not at all. Not only so, but, as the sun (or sun god), Enoch must originally have been the Flood hero who built the ark to survive the deluge. The symbolism is natural: The sun triumphs over the flood waters by drying them up. But wasn't Noah the Flood hero? Yes indeed, but "Noah" appears to be a garbled version of the name "Enoch." The "ch" in one is really the same as the "h" in the other, as we can see in one of the adjectival forms of Noah, e.g., "the Noachian Flood" or "the Noachian covenant."[73]

The fantastic life-spans of the pre-Deluge patriarchs, as well as their names, have been derived from the Babylonian list of antediluvian kings[74] who together reigned for a total of 86,400 *sosses* (5 year periods used in Assyrian reckoning), which comes out to 432,000 years. The Priestly author, writing during the Babylonian Exile and having access to the vast libraries of Babylonia and Assyria, thought a *soss* must be the same as a sabbath (i.e., a week). On this erroneous assumption he must have posited a total period of 86,400 *weeks*, or 1,646 years, for the combined, overlapping life-spans of the Hebrew antediluvians. [75]

The names of the mythical kings roughly correspond etymologically to those of the biblical patriarchs, so the Priestly writer thought he had found a record of the life-spans of Lamech, Enoch, Methusaleh and the rest. The life-span assigned to each patriarch was symbolic. Enoch represents the sun and the solar calendar of 365 days, while Lamech's age of 777 recalls his vow to avenge, not *seven*fold but *seventy-seven*fold (4:24). What did the other numbers denote? We might be able to figure it out if we possessed any of the "facts" about these men that once formed part of Hebrew legend but have not survived.

The Sons of God and Daughters of Men
Gen. 6:1-2, 4

This *ethnological* myth explains the origin of the Nephilim/Anakim, a tall people (Num. 13:32; Deut. 3:11; 1 Sam. 17; 2 Sam. 21:15-22) believed to be descended from epic heroes and demigods like Goliath, Nimrod (whom ancient sources equate with Orion the Hunter),[76] and Gilgamesh. How else to explain their remarkable height (over six feet, per 1 Sam. 17:4),[77] quite tall by ancient standards? A demigod is of course, the offspring of a god and a mortal. The "sons of God" mentioned here and elsewhere in the Old Testament (Job 1:6; 2:1; Psalm 82:1; 89:5-7) are a vestige of Hebrew polytheism. There were apparently some seventy of these gods, one to rule each nation.

Deuteronomy 32:8 preserves part of an already ancient poem recounting how God decided there would be enough nations of humanity for each of his sons to receive one to rule, and the Hebrews counted seventy nations. These sons of God are the other deities to whom God speaks in both the J and the P creation stories. Originally no shame attached to this kind of divine-human hybridization, any more than in Greek mythology. "So tall? Here's why." Sort of like today's "ancient astronaut" theories.[78] And at first it had nothing at all to do with the Flood.[79]

Needless to say, later Jewish scribes could not brook this polytheistic "heresy" and so reinterpreted the sons of God as *angels*. But the idea of angels impregnating human females was no less distasteful theologically. Short of omitting the story, something the scribes and compilers were generally unwilling to do, the only option was to portray such miscegenation as perversion and blasphemy.[80] Such a reinterpreted story had its uses, too.

As we have seen, the Eden story seems not to have been intended as a depiction of a "Fall of Man" into immorality. But the story of the sons of God and daughters of men *was* understood as the origin of evil. As biblical and Pseudepigraphical sources (books like The Testaments of the Twelve Patriarchs, 1 Enoch, and the Book of Jubilees) tell it, these angels (also called the Watchers) were seduced by the wiles of women or taught the immoral arts of Delilah-like enticement to women and the arts of metallurgy, weapons, and warfare to men.

Genesis 6:1-4 implies more than this, though: The pollution of the human genome (as we should call it) by demonic infection. As such, the story has been inserted into its present location in order to provide narrative motivation for the Flood. How did the human race suddenly become reprobate enough to deserve being drowned like rats?

The Great Flood

Gen. 6-9

Any Bible reader who has paid close attention to the Flood story in Genesis 6-9 must have paused to scratch his head in puzzlement over a couple of whopping contradictions (not to mention the prolix repetitiveness). How long did the Deluge last? How many of each kind of animal did Farmer Noah bring on board? Here's a great example of how the critical approach can answer questions, unravel problems that remain insoluble as long as one approaches the Bible on the assumption that it records actual events and records them infallibly.

Once we recognize that Genesis 6-9 is a composite of two earlier Flood stories (those of J and P), things quickly fall into place. It turns out that the unknown editor of the Pentateuch stitched them together. Why not simply choose one and omit the other? Because each story had its own audience. If the compiler wanted to provide an ecumenical Jewish scripture acceptable to all factions, he could not afford to alienate anyone by leaving out a favorite version of a cherished story.

When the Revised Standard Version debuted in 1946, there were public book burnings of this Bible because the translators had changed things many Christian believers didn't want changed. Certain passages not adequately attested in the earliest manuscripts were removed from the translated text and relegated to the footnotes in smaller print. The Pentateuchal compiler must have known what would happen if he flipped a coin and decided to include either the J version or the Priestly version.

But why not just place them side by side as he did with the J and P Creation stories? That wasn't an option for one reason. Each Flood story ends with God promising never to inundate the earth again. If one Flood story followed another, we would read at the end of one version the assurance of no more floods–immediately followed by "another" flood! Yikes! This must be why the editor decided it would be best to weave them into one fabric, albeit one far from seamless.

The J version can be distinguished in Genesis 6:5-8; 7:1-5, 7-10, 12, 16b-17, 22-23; 8:2b-3a, 6-12, 13b, 20-22; 9:18-19. According to the J writer, the Flood is caused by rain, and the waters increase for 40 days, taking another three weeks to dry up, a total of 61 days. Noah observes kosher laws, taking aboard a single pair of unclean (non-kosher) animal species, seven pairs of kosher species.

By contrast, P's version (Gen. 6:9-22; 7:6, 11, 13-16a, 18-21, 24; 8:1-2a, 3-5, 13a, 14-19; 9:1-17, 28-29) has the waters deepen for 150 days and recede gradually, the whole flood lasting one year, 11 days. The Priestly author knew kosher laws would have originated much later, in Moses' time, so P has Noah, a vegetarian, bring only a single pair of animals. And the Flood results from the gushing up of the subterranean sources of the *Tehom*, the world ocean, mentioned in the Priestly creation account, not in the J account.

Yet these are far from the only versions of the Flood. The two biblical versions descend from previous Sumerian and Babylonian Flood epics. Utnapishtim, warned by his divine patron Ea of the plans of the gods to destroy all life with a deluge, follows the deity's instructions and builds a cube-shaped vessel, the dimensions of which are stipulated in the text just as in Genesis. He loads representative animals for breeding stock, plus his family and his hired laborers.

When the water recedes, his ark is found to rest on a particular named mountain peak. Utnapishtim releases a couple of birds to perform reconnaissance, then disembarks. An animal sacrifice attracts the gods who, pleased with the sacrificial aroma, repent of their genocidal hatred and promise not to flood the world again. As a token of their promise, the goddess Aruru drapes her lapis lazuli necklace across the clearing sky. Utnapishtim is granted immortality as a reward for his courage.

Though everything else is startlingly parallel, no gift of eternal life is reported of Noah— or is it? Remember, originally the Flood hero was Enoch, who was taken up by God and given divine immortality. So the parallel is complete after all.

Irving Finkel[81] offers a translation of the earliest known version of the Babylonian Flood story. The chief difference from previously known versions lies in the mandated shape of the ark: It is circular, the dividing walls of the animal pens radiating outward like spokes from the hub of a wheel, like slices of a pie.

The Flood hero constructed several tiers (representing the several heavens) on the ark, culminating in a roof (a copy of the firmament, or sky dome) though which the hero climbs to pray to his god. The symbolism of the round ark, a coracle, seems to confirm Geoffrey Tolle's theory[82] that the ark was not just a round boat but a floating microcosm, an artificial Mountain of God[83] built to allow the Flood hero to reach the floodgates in the heavens and close them, thereby shutting off the rains. Thus the original ark was a *micro-cosmic* world intended to allow the hero to affect the *macro*cosmic world through his actions.

The Noah stories are *geological* legends attempting to account for one of the attested floods in the Fertile Crescent, e.g., the flood of 3200 B.C.E.[84] The ancients could not imagine that such an event simply *happened*. That would imply God was not in providential control. So he must have sent the Flood, something he'd never have done without sufficient reason. So the human race must have deserved it.

The stories also have an *etiological* purpose, providing the origin of the rainbow.[85] But instead of Aruru's necklace, the J version understands the rainbow as Jehovah's war bow. He has made peace with his former targets. It is the bow Jehovah uses to shoot his arrows, the lightning bolts (Psalm 18:14). Now he has "hung up his gloves."

There is also a *ceremonial* function to the stories: They explain the origin of meat-eating, the blood taboo, and capital punishment.

Noah's Curse
Gen. 5:28-29; 9:20-27

This peculiar tale is one of J's. In addition to its plainly unedifying character, the story raises questions that have puzzled readers for millennia. For one thing, how can Noah be the first tiller of the soil? That Noah had not learned his trade from any predecessors agrees with the fact that he appears to have gotten stinking drunk, despite the earlier notice (6:9; 7:1) that he was the only righteous man! We have to suppose that Noah had not known what would happen if he guzzled that "grape juice."

But Cain was already a farmer (Gen. 4:2), wasn't he? Does this mean that the Noah story is independent of the Cain tales? Come to think of it, the same problem pops up back in 4:20-21, where Jabal is said to have invented herding *as still practiced in the writer's day*, while Jubal[86] invented music *as still practiced*, neither leaving room for the cultural rupture of the Flood. These traditions are independent and do not quite fit together. That must mean that the J source was not a continuous narrative but, like the Pentateuch itself, already a patchwork quilt of disparate traditional stories. Whoever told the stories of Jabal and Jubal (obvious folklore names, like Tweedledum and Tweedledee) never heard of a Flood myth.

In fact, we have two different Noahs! Or he was a very different character in different legend cycles. You can see this from the fact that in J Noah is the son of Lamech (Gen. 5:28-29), while in P Lamech's sons are Jubal, Jabal, and Tubal-Cain (4:19-22).[87] The Priestly writer introduces Noah, with no note about his parentage, at the beginning of his Flood story (6:13). In the J version we run into a Noah who has nothing to do with the Flood at all.[88] We know this because of the etymological legend begun in 6:28-29, originally followed immediately by the story of Noah's curse.

Remember, Genesis contains numerous name-origin stories rather like modern "shaggy dog" groaners. A name (whether of a person or of a place) receives a punning "definition." "They named him So-and-So, for they said . . ." (see Gen. 5:29; 4:1; 10:25; 11:9; 16:11; 19:20, 22; 25:25-26, etc.). Either people did not know the actual definition, had forgotten it, or did not like the original meaning because of some pagan or polytheistic connotation.

The pun always focuses on the most important thing about the character. The foreknowledge attributed to the one who assigns the name is really the hindsight of someone living long afterward. So what great feat is baby Noah named to commemorate and anticipate? Building the ark? No. *Inventing wine.*[89] "Noah" looks kind of like the Hebrew word for "rest." The connection? "Out of the ground which [Yahweh] has cursed this one shall bring us relief from our work and from the toil of our hands" (Gen. 6:29). After a hard day's work, *it's Miller time!* A man saves the human race from total destruction—and he's remembered as that little ol' winemaker Noah? Of course, the solution to this problem is that originally the Flood hero was not Noah at all, but *Enoch*.[90] As I already pointed out, it was easy to confuse the two names. And this would fit well, since in cognate Middle Eastern Flood epics, it is the immortal Enoch-analog who built the ark, e.g., the Babylonian Xisuthros and the Sumerian Utnapishtim.[91]

So we may detach the story of Noah's Curse from the Flood story completely. In its own right, what is Genesis 9:20-27 about? I believe that it was originally a version of the Greek myth of the brother Titans Cronus, Coieus, Crius, Hyperion, and Iapetus ganging up on their father Uranus to castrate and dethrone him.[92] In this Hebrew version, Uranus' place is occupied by Noah. The conspiring brothers are, this time, Shem, Ham, Japheth, and Canaan, though as we now read it, Canaan has been demoted to Ham's son and does not appear in the initial team-up against Noah. He shows up only to receive a blistering curse from the hung-over Noah. Why, if he wasn't involved?

This perennial problem is solved as soon as we realize that Canaan must have been the fourth brother, presumably the one who did the deed. It is not merely the "three/five against one" opposition that parallels the Greek version. Two of the names clinch it. "Japheth" is simply an alternate spelling of "Iapetus," while the ancients identified the Greek Cronus with the Carthaginian Baal Hammon, i.e., "Ham."

What exactly did the brothers do? Ancient rabbis recognized that the answer to that had been excised from the text as being just too distasteful. The scene as it now reads is ridiculous. All right, Ham stumbles upon the undignified sight of his father lying in a drunken stupor, naked. For some unstated reason he enlists his similarly prudish brothers to walk backwards toward the supine Noah, so they will not be scarred by the sight, and to drape a blanket over the snoring patriarch. "When Noah awoke and saw what they had done to him," he leveled his curse. For *that*? That they caught sight of him naked?

That cannot have been too uncommon in the time of the ancient readers or hearers. Something is missing all right. It might have been incest, because the Hebrew idiom "to uncover the nakedness of one's father" (Lev. 18:7) was a judicious way of saying "having sex with one's mother" (cf., 1 Cor. 5:1). Thus maybe the point is that Noah's son knew his father would be unconscious for a while and took the opportunity to sneak off and, *ahem*, rape his mother.

But if that had been the outrage, it is hard to understand why Noah would not have killed the offender on the spot. In a similarly disgusting vein, some have suggested that Noah's son *sodomized* his oblivious father. But, again, one might have expected a more severe reaction from Noah, along the lines of Marcellus's revenge on the depraved cop Zed in *Pulp Fiction* in a scenario similar to that envisioned here.

It looks like they castrated Noah. This would complete the parallel to the Greek myth as well as explaining why the help of all the brothers was required. They were needed to restrain their father. And the motive: to topple Noah from his position as the patriarch of the family and clan. In ancient thinking, virility was a prerequisite for rulers, as they were, as we might say, the father of their country.

What did Noah's curse intend? Here the story has been subsequently historicized and repurposed for political commentary. It is thus an *ethnological* and *legitimization* legend, justifying (long after the fact) Israelite (Shem) intermarriage with Philistines (who worshipped the Titan Iapetus) as in Judges 14:1-2 and their common enslavement of Canaanites (Ham/Canaan) as in Joshua chapter 9.[93]

The story of Noah's Curse has become infamous because of the Civil War era use of it to justify slavery in the South. Antebellum Presbyterians (e.g., Robert Dabney) and others believed Ham or Canaan to stand for black Africans, so that abolitionist efforts to free slaves would be contravening the will of God. But Africans are no more in view here than Eskimos. It actually wasn't dreamed up by pro-slavery Protestants: Some ancient rabbis also took the passage to justify the enslavement of Africans.[94] They were mistaken, too. But we cannot completely exonerate the story since it did mean to legitimatize enslaving an ethnic group, just not an African one.

We are used to thinking of Noah as standing pretty much at the beginning of history, Adam all over again, the new progenitor of the human race. This is natural, given his inclusion in the Flood story (in which he did not originally belong), as well as his position in the Table of Nations to follow. But the Noah's Curse story need not imply this. For him to dictate (not just predict) the future of whole nations (fictively) descended from him does not necessitate his placement so very far back. We read the same kind of stories with later, historical-era patriarchs predetermining their descendants' histories, e.g., Isaac (25:23; 27:27-29, 39-40) and Jacob (Gen. 49).

The Table of Nations
Gen. 10

The source for this genealogy of the nations known to ancient Israel is not clear, though my vote is for P, given that source's love for genealogies, statistics, and the like. The function of it, obviously, is *ethnological*, outlining a kind of ethnic taxonomy, positing the relations of ancient tribes and nations, inferring blood-relations from proximity, military alliances, and trade relations.

It is cut from the same cloth as the many episodes in which this and that group are linked by positing fictive common ancestors, as when Lot is made the progenitor of both the Ammonites and the Moabites, who thus are cousins of the Ishmaelites, Edomites, and Israelites, all fictively descended from Abraham, Lot's uncle. An even more obvious case is the supposed common ancestry of the twelve tribes of Israel, as if each tribe had an eponymous ancestor, all of them sons of the Patriarch Jacob (Israel). These pseudo-genealogies were no more than symbolic ways to seal treaties, alliances, and trade pacts between ancient tribes and groups. It made them officially (albeit fictive) "blood brothers."[95]

As often, the Priestly writer sprinkles a few fascinating bits of legendary lore amid his otherwise dry content. We learn a bit about the epic hero Nimrod the Hunter (identified with the Greek Titan Orion).[96] He is said to have founded a number of major cities including Babylon (Babel), Erech (the Uruk of the Gilgamesh Epic), Accad (Akkad), and Nineveh (modern Mosul). Of course, no single individual founded all these cities, nor were they established in the same period. Nimrod is said to have been the first "mighty man," or epic hero. There must have been much more told about him, presumably including some of the material associated with Nimrod's Greek alter ego, Orion.

How on earth, you may ask, did the name Nimrod become synonymous with "idiot" in modern American slang? When the public was more biblically literate, a "Nimrod" denoted an avid hunter. In an old Loony Tunes cartoon, Bugs Bunny scoffs at the efforts of his inept adversary Elmer Fudd, dressed up in his hunter's accoutrements, to bag the laughing lagomorph: "The poor little Nimrod!" It wasn't that Elmer was being called an idiot; he was being called a pathetic excuse for a hunter. But time passed, and a new generation arose that knew not Nimrod but did know Bugs Bunny, and it came to pass that they thought that "Nimrod" meant "idiot."

The Tower of Babel

Gen. 11:1-9

This J story clearly displays sedimentary layers, showing that the tale grew in the telling as it furnished opportunities to deal with new questions. First, it is *etiological*, explaining why there are many languages, not a bad question, since all peoples have the same vocal apparatus and talk about pretty much the same things. Naturally, the ancients, at least on the popular level, had no idea of the gradual dissemination and evolution of languages. But for anyone today to defend this story as historically true is precisely parallel to creationists claiming all species were created in six days and that the sedimentary layers of the Grand Canyon were laid down in forty days by Noah's Flood.

Second, as an *ethnological* story, it tries to account for the related phenomenon of the division of the human race into various nations. Why didn't they stick together? Because they couldn't communicate anymore. This raises the question of whether, as on a first reading, no two individuals, following Jehovah's little prank, found themselves speaking the same language. But this would mean that every single family unit would have been as unable to communicate with each other as they were unable to make themselves understood to their next-door neighbors. Did each *individual* depart and raise a whole new branch? If so, with whom? It's Cain's wife all over again!

Notice that this explanation of the origin of nations contradicts that of the Table of Nations, in which all nations stem from the gradual dispersion of Noah's sons. It also contradicts the myth in Deuteronomy 32 whereby God decided how many nations to create after taking a nose-count of his sons, the lesser gods, making sure each one would have a people to worship him.

Why does Yahweh confuse human language? The story depicts the same nervous, insecure deity we saw in J's Eden story. Here, too, he tells his fellow deities that trouble is brewing because the fledgling humans have turned out to be more resourceful than he had planned and now seem poised to poach on the prerogatives of the gods. Something must be done to nip it in the bud.[97]

As Yahweh earlier exiled the first couple from Eden, now he magically multiplies the languages. The result: "I shall be a foreigner to the speaker and the speaker a foreigner to me" (1 Cor. 14:11). The simple fact of working together to construct a tower is enough to show Yahweh how capable these primates are. The specific project is not said to threaten him. But we have to wonder if the story began as a variant of the Greek myth in which the Titans pile one mountain on top of another as a siege tower to invade Olympus.[98] Zeus knocks it down.

In fact, subsequent, post-biblical retellings of the story often borrow the Titan Nimrod from Genesis 10 and depict him as the King of Babylon who orders the erection of the tower as an act of hubris to reach heaven.[99] Perhaps one sees here some influence from Isaiah 14:13-14, "You said in your heart, 'I will ascend to heaven: above the stars of God I will set my throne on high; I will sit on the mount of assembly in the far north; I will ascend above the heights of the clouds, I will make myself like the Most High.'"

Third, there is the *etymological* dimension. It explains "Babel" (which actually means "Gate of God") as if the name were based on the Hebrew word *balal*, "confusion." The pun works even better in English translation, where "Babel" reminds us of "babble." Babel is actually the same name as "Babylon," and that is where the story is set,[100] in the plains of Shinar. The Babylonians had drifted in from the East, just as the story says, where they had worshipped atop mountains and hilltops (the Bible calls such shrines "high places"). But Shinar was flat. To get the same effect, they decided to build artificial hills, stepped pyramids called *ziggurats* with altars on top. The "gate of God" referred to these altars, portals to contact the gods.

This story might be classified also as a *geological* legend, though it does not attempt to account for a natural rock formation. It seems intended to explain the origin of a ruined ziggurat seen by Jewish exiles in Babylon. Perhaps it was old and neglected, some of its building stones moved elsewhere for new construction, but, beholding the jagged outline against the sky, some inferred that the tower's construction had been aborted, and the story supplied a colorful explanation.

The Patriarchal History

Abraham has always loomed large over the history of Middle-Eastern and Western religion. He is the sole link between Judaism, Christianity, and Islam. And that is quite appropriate, given the ancient function of the Genesis patriarchs as fictive/mythic links between hitherto feuding tribes and clans. If any of them forged political bonds, military alliances, or trade covenants, they would henceforth consider themselves blood brothers and seal the deal by positing a previously unknown ancestor from the remote past, someone from whom they could claim common ancestry.[101]

The most famous example would be Jacob (Israel), ostensibly the father of twelve sons, each of whose descendants begets a whole tribe. They remained united (in some measure) as "children of Israel." What actually must have happened is that twelve originally disparate Canaanite groups decided, for mutual benefit, to form an "amphictyony," or twelve-tribe league (a common arrangement all over the ancient Mediterranean) centered on rotating custodianship of a central shrine dedicated to a "federal god" whom all tribes would worship in addition to their own ancestral totems.[102]

In fact, the names of several of the Israelite tribes reflect either their religious allegiances or geographical locations: Gad was the god of good fortune all over the region, while Asher is named for the goddess Asherah, Yahweh's queen. Zebulun is named for the god Zebul. Issachar means "migrant laborer," while "Ephraim," not at first a personal name at all, denotes "those who live on Mount Ephrath." "Benjamin" signals "sons of the right hand," i.e., the south (as in "Yemen" today). And so on. Once they decided to federate, they chose as a common ancestor the mythic figure Israel/Jacob (probably already a fusion of two heroes, joined for similar ecumenical purposes, uniting Jacobites and Israelites).

Somewhere along the line, the tribe named for Isaac and venerating his god ("the Fear of Isaac," in Gen. 31:42) had similarly joined with the Jacob group (worshipping "the Strong One of Jacob," in Gen. 49:24) as well as the Abrahamic group (worshipping "the God of Abraham," in Gen. 31:42, 53), with the result that, according no doubt to tribal seniority, the three patriarchs became, purely on the political-geological drawing board, father, son, and grandson.[103] Nor was this the end.

When the Ammonites and Moabites allied with Israel, they all agreed that Abraham and Lot (Lot being already the symbolic progenitor of the other two) were uncle and nephew. When relations (rocky though they often were) with the Edomites were achieved, the national ancestor and stereotype Esau was added to the family tree. When covenants were forged with the Arab amphictyony, Ishmael became the first son of Abraham. And so on and so on. And this is what I mean about Abraham's central symbolic role today. He is a helpful though tenuous link between Arabs (Muslims), Jews, and Christians in an unstable region. If not for the ancient fiction that they are all related Peoples of the Book with an Abrahamic heritage in common, who knows how much worse the violence might be?

Had Abraham been an historical figure? There is no particular reason to think so. Conservative scholars, striving to secure a historical basis for every bit of the Bible they could, used to point out features of the Abraham stories that reflected social conditions of the second millennium B.C.E. when Abraham was supposed to have lived. Such arguments are equivocal and unconvincing. And, as Hermann Gunkel[104] observed, who can believe the Israelite nation preserved not one shard of memory of their whole 430 year sojourn in Egypt but did manage to preserve specific verbal exchanges between Abraham, his wives, slaves, and foes from centuries before that? No, it has to be fiction.

And they were fictions of a particular kind. Many of them, on one level, are ceremonial etiologies, official stories circulated to legitimatize certain Israelite religious or dietary practices, especially new ones requiring the clout of Abraham. One of these is the story of Abraham nearly sacrificing Isaac at Yahweh's behest, then being told to forget it and to sacrifice a sheep instead (Gen. 22:13). It must reflect the transition from the early law of firstborn sacrifice (Exod. 22:29-30) to the substitution of an animal for one's son (Exod. 13:12-13). Well, if it was good enough for Abraham . . .

But the Abraham stories had an earlier meaning still. At first Abraham was the moon personified. He was the "father of a multitude" not of Israelites, but of the stars, smiling protectors of the shepherding nomads who blessed the moon but execrated the blistering sun. Isaac was the sun. "Isaac" means "he laughs" and reflects the image of the smiling or laughing ("beaming") of the sun: "he who sits in the heavens laughs" (Psalm 2:4). When

Abraham sought to destroy his son, but was prevented, the first meaning was to depict the cycle by which the moon seeks to supplant the sun, ruling the night sky, only to be cast down daily as the sun rises. (Isaiah 14 refers to the identical myth, this time told of Venus, the upstart morning star, brightest object in the sky until the obliterating return of the sun.)

Many other Patriarchal characters and stories preserve ancient astronomy, as Ignaz Goldziher (*Mythology among the Hebrews*) showed, under the influence of Max Müller's once dominant solar mythology paradigm. He is still correct, as far as I am concerned.

Abraham's Itinerary

The Oaks of Moreh

Gen. 12:6-7

This J story is ceremonial in nature, providing a new, "orthodox" origin of the altar at Moreh, giving a Yahwist pedigree to what was originally some sort of Baal shrine. These stories are pedigrees for the "sacred groves"[105] denounced later on by the prophets in the wake of the Deuteronomic reform, when they tried to centralize all worship at Jerusalem (Deut. 12:2; 1 Kings 14:23; 2 Kings 16:4; Judith 3:8).

Why were groves of trees considered sacred in the first place? They were pretty much oases scattered over a largely barren landscape, and one had to wonder why these little zones of fertility existed in the midst of desolation. The answer: They were made fertile by the divine power of some local deity or sprite. These entities were believed to dwell in one of the trees or in the spring.[106] The Garden of Eden is just such an oasis or pleasure garden for Yahweh and his fellows.[107]

People would visit these groves to consult the spirit, in other words, to have their fortune told by the priest or shaman who attended the place. We have these little notes about Abraham stopping at these places because J made a point of visiting any of them he came across, interviewing the priests: "Why is this place holy?" And he would be told, "Why, don't you know, my son? Father Abraham stopped here to seek God's guidance, and to this day many follow his example. And thanks for the donation."

These sacred groves, sometimes connected with hilltop shrines ("high places"), originally dedicated to various gods, must have been re-christened as holy to Yahweh as Israelite worship became restricted to that deity. Later still, they were destroyed as worship was centralized in the Jerusalem temple, where the official priesthood could keep an eye on things.[108] These "George Washington slept here" notes about Abraham come from the period when sacred groves flourished.

Between Bethel and Ai

Gen. 12:8

Another *ceremonial* story collected by J, like the preceding, claims an Abrahamic/Yahwist pedigree for an older pagan altar. Of added interest, this tale is but one of many foundation stories (Gen. 28:10-22; 32:1-2, 22-32; 35:1-15) for Bethel, a major temple city (1 Kings 12:28-30).

The Sacred Tamarisk

Gen. 21:33

Here, considered out of order, is another of J's *ceremonial* stories. It gives a Hebrew pedigree to a previously pagan sacred grove.

Dishonest Abe

The story of one of the Israelite patriarchs sojourning in a foreign land who lies about his wife in order to save his skin circulated in various forms. J found two of them, while E collected a third. All three appear in Genesis, though separated by other material in order to mask the redundancy.

Once again, our compilers (J and the subsequent compiler of the whole Pentateuch) dared not leave anyone's favorite version on the cutting room floor. Comparing the three versions lays bare the dynamics of oral tradition: We can see how only the basic plot logic is preserved, all other details being negotiable. It is exactly like one of the genres of oral tradition that survives to our own day: jokes. How many times have you heard two or more versions of a joke with the names and circumstances changed, yet still recognizable as the same basic joke? "Did you hear the one about the Patriarch? I forget, which one was it? Oh, I guess Abraham." The next guy who repeats it picks Isaac.

We find J's *first* version in Genesis 12:10-20, which looks like an alternative version of the Exodus story but drawn from an originally unconnected cycle of stories. Note the famine, the plagues, and the escape with great riches, shared with the Mosaic Exodus.

Here "Abram" (a variant version of "Abraham," both meaning "great father"), with his wife "Sarai," dwells among the Egyptians (*Mizraim*), so the king must be a Pharaoh. In the other two versions, the same root consonants have been read as denoting the *Muzrim*, Hagar's tribe of Philistines, who lived at Gerar, and accordingly the name Abimelech is given for the kings.

In J's *second* version (Gen. 26:1-14, 16-17) the generic Patriarch and his wife have become Isaac and Rebecca, while the Mizraim (Egyptians) become the Muzrim (Philistines).[109] In E's version (Gen. 20), as is his habit, he has cleaned up the story, so that Abraham is no longer simply lying to save his skin. His wife Sarah *is* his sister, sort of. Also E makes extra clear that the king has not touched Sarah, something left open by J.

Genesis 17:15 has God rename Sarai "Sarah," to no particular purpose except to harmonize two sets of traditions, one calling her Sarah, the other Sarai, though in fact the difference is negligible. It is as if God said, "Your name shall no longer be Carl, but Carlos."

To underscore the patchwork character of Genesis, it is worth noting that, in Genesis 12:11 and 20:2, Abe cooks up the lie about Sarah being his sister, not his wife, because she is so beautiful that the foreign king, as soon as he sees her, will no doubt exclaim, "Va-va-va-*voom!*" and recruit her for his harem, killing Abraham if he stands in the way. But according to Genesis 17:17 Sarah is already *ninety* years old! Unless Pharaoh and Abimelech had a taste for prunes, this is hard to picture. But of course this hilarity is the unintended consequence of the compiler of the Pentateuch suffering from "editorial fatigue."[110] He just couldn't keep all the details straight as he tried to find a place for every anecdote, loose ends and all.

God's Covenant with Abraham

The J version is found in Genesis 15:1-12, 17-21, verses 13-16 being a Deuteronomic interpolation, supplying a "coming attractions" prophecy of the Exodus from Egypt and the Conquest of the Canaanites (whom the Deuteronomist writer prefers, as here, to call "Amorites"). Why insert it here? In order to explain why Abraham's progeny did not immediately receive the land God has just promised them. There would be, ah, a little delay of four centuries!

We cannot help thinking of Luke 21:24, where the second advent of Christ, first promised to occur in the disciples' own generation (Mark 13:30; Matt. 24:34; Luke 21:32), gets pushed into the remote future while "the times of the Gentiles" put it on indefinite hold. Both are contrived attempts to make virtue of necessity.

But we can go deeper. The problem of the delay of the promise of inheriting the land is another side effect of patching together what were originally disparate, unrelated traditions. At first, the Patriarchal stories of Abraham, Isaac, and Jacob had nothing to do with Moses and the Exodus, which in turn had nothing to do with those of Joshua and the Conquest. As archaeology, linguistics, and comparative mythology have amply demonstrated, the ancient Israelites simply *were* Canaanites. If you look closely, several passages in Genesis come very close to admitting it.

All those stories stipulating kinship between Israel, the Edomites, Ammonites, Moabites, Ishmaelites, etc., certainly imply it. The Genesis stories of the Patriarchs know as little of the sojourn in Egypt and the Exodus from there[111] as the stories of Jabal, Jubal, and Tubal-Cain know of Noah's Flood. (And, as we have seen, the story of Abram and Sarai entering and exiting Egypt constitutes an autonomous "Exodus" within the Patriarchal tradition (though the redactional fusion of Patriarchal and Mosaic epics reinterprets the Abram version as a foreshadowing of the Moses version). And we will see, too, that the stories of the Wilderness Wanderings originally did not lead to the entrance into and the Conquest of Canaan. Instead, they presuppose a chosen Bedouin lifestyle on the part of Israel and Moses.[112]

What is unique about the J story of the Covenant is that it preserves information on the ancient ritual of "cutting a covenant." The underlying assumption is that the parties entering into a contract agreed that they would deserve the same treatment the sacrificial animals got if either failed to live up to the agreed-upon terms.[113] The slaughtered animals were intended to invoke God (or a god) to witness the contract and to keep an eye on the parties, who would fear his wrath if they broke it, as in Genesis 31:44, 48, though no sacrifice is recorded there. The present story is likely ceremonial in origin, laying out the pattern for a covenant sacrifice, though one between two mortals before God.

The Priestly version of God's Covenant with Abraham occurs in Genesis 17:9-14. It is very clearly *ceremonial*: It ordains circumcision, already an ancient practice, but adopted here as an infant initiation rite. Note the use of *Elohim* (God) and *El Shaddai* (God Almighty), the Priestly writer's favorite names for God, as well as the use of P's preferred formula, "I will make my covenant between me and you" (as in 17:2, 9:9, 11, 15). J makes Moses and Zipporah institute infant circumcision as a substitute for bridegroom circumcision in Exod. 4:24-26.

Laughing Boy

The name "Isaac" seems to mean "May he laugh," i.e., "May God rejoice in him" or "May God smile upon him." It was already a name commonly applied, but in several *etymological* stories it gets redefined in specific application to Abraham's son. One of P's versions (Gen. 17:15-17) explains Isaac's name as commemorating Abraham's hilarity upon hearing God's promise that, at this late date, he and his aged wife will have a baby.

The point is not to portray Abraham as a man weak in faith. After all, he believes that he is receiving messages from God in the first place! The point is to highlight the greatness of the miracle to come. Skepticism is often a component of miracle stories.[114] It sets the bar higher. It increases the odds against which God or the miracle-worker will prevail (as in Mark 2:7; 5:30-31, 39-40; 6:37, 49-50; 8:4, 10:48).

In J it is Sarah who laughs at God's promise (Gen. 18:9-15). P also has a story of Isaac's nativity (Gen. 21:6-7) in which Sarah predicts that all who hear of her improbable delivery will laugh with joy and amazement, the implicit assumption being that she decided to name Isaac for this happy circumstance. Genesis 21:9 seems to understand "Isaac" as reflecting his half-brother Ishmael laughing at him. But all of this represents a subsequent historicizing of Isaac who must originally have been the divine sun in the sky: "He who sits in the heavens laughs" (Psalm 2:4a).[115] One who laughs "beams."

Sodom and Gomorrah

Gen. 18-19

We owe this *geological* tale (Gen. 18:1-8, 16-33; 19:1-16, 24-25, 27-29) to J. It is meant to explain the origin of the salt waste surrounding the Dead Sea. It may well preserve the historical memory of the destruction of Sodom by a volcanic cataclysm. We know Sodom existed, as it is mentioned in trade records surviving from the Ebla Empire. The whole region is seismically unstable and honeycombed with pockets of bitumen and flammable gas.

It would not be too difficult to imagine the friction of an earthquake igniting the gas and bitumen, causing the fiery pitch to erupt into the sky and rain back down on the doomed metropolis.[116] Obviously, the ancients, at least on a popular level, would have no idea of these factors. They sought an explanation for the disaster in a different realm. "Suppose ye that these Galilaeans were sinners above all the Galilaeans, because they suffered such things?" (Luke 13:2, KJV). But it wasn't that the citizens of Sodom were known (or even believed) to be sinners before their destruction. No, the logic ran, they *must* have been pretty big sinners for God to nuke them like this!

One of the most striking parts of the Sodom and Gomorrah story is the dialogue between Abraham and Yahweh. Abraham has heard the unpleasant rumors about Sodom, just as Yahweh has, and, as the two undercover angels embark on their fact-finding tour, Abraham begins to reflect: His nephew Lot may be in considerable danger!

So Abraham dares to negotiate with the Almighty. He reminds God of his responsibility as the judge of all the earth. Surely he will not paint with too broad a brush, lest in pulling up the weeds, he uproot the wheat, too–if there *is* any wheat! Yahweh, surprisingly, turns out to be something of a pushover. He agrees to relent and let the wicked majority off the hook so long as there are some fifty righteous found in Sodom. This is going pretty well, Abraham thinks, so he presses his luck. Every time God accedes to his low-balling estimates, Abraham realizes his estimates have been far too optimistic! There may not be as many as five lousy righteous in Sodom! But there is really no lower he can go.

Why is God such a soft touch? It is because he already knows the state of things in Sodom; he knows he's not going to have to change his plans. And indeed he is not. There will not prove even to be five. Lot's future sons-in-law think the old man's urgings to flee are a joke, so they refuse to leave, and the joke's on *them*. Mrs. Lot lingers and becomes a pillar of salt. We have been assured that, for their part, the men of Sodom, *without a single exception*, are guilty (19:4). So it's time to push the red button.

The bargaining with God initially reminds us of two other Old Testament passages. In the Book of Job, Job goes on at great length reproaching God for Job's undeserved suffering. Job finally acquiesces. Who is he, a mere mortal with a worm's eye view, to hold accountable the Creator of the universe with all its mysteries? In Exodus 32:11-14, Moses just manages to persuade God to refrain from wiping out the whole of Israel in a fit of fury at their idolatry.

Moses does prevail upon God to keep his word, to honor the promises he once made to the Israelite Patriarchs. But it isn't just that the Judge of all the earth decides to keep his word after all. Moses also points out what a public relations disaster this would be! So God relents. But in Genesis there is no uncertainty about the outcome. Yahweh is happy to grant any concession Abraham proposes, knowing it will make no difference to the outcome.

But this raises another question: If Yahweh already knows of the unforgiveable villainy of Sodom, why does he send his angels on their reconnaissance mission in the first place? It would make sense if he had simply assigned them to alert Lot and his family and to escort them to safety. But he does tell Abraham that he needs to check out the rumors. I think we are again dealing with a composite narrative. I think the dialogue between Abraham and Yahweh is a subsequent addition (like the promise that Sarah would become pregnant). In the original story, God really does need to investigate. He does not already know if he ought to destroy Sodom any more than he knew where Adam and Eve were when they stood him up in the Garden.

So what was the terrible sin supposed to be? Like Yahweh himself, we must not rush to judgment, but must investigate whether familiar rumors about Sodom are well-founded. We have always heard that Sodom and Gomorrah (the Twin Cities?) were blasted because they practiced homosexuality, sort of an ancient Fire Island. But this reading of the text is not merely false but absurd. The overarching issue is that of *hospitality*, a major virtue in the ancient world where there were few motels where a traveler might pass the night in peace and security. It was no mere question of etiquette. Look at the space devoted to the issue even centuries later in 1 Clement 10:7- 12:7; 35:5.

Genesis 18 takes considerable pains to display Abraham's perfect hospitality as host to three travelers whom he does not know from Adam. He is not acquainted with them, and the point is that he doesn't *have* to be. They are hungry, weary travelers, and that's all Abraham needs to know to enthusiastically embrace his duty to see to their needs.[117] In Genesis 19, we see an instant replay starring "righteous Lot" (2 Pet. 2:7).[118] The point is to provide a good example with which to contrast the barbarism of the men of Sodom. They are as hostile to helpless strangers as Abraham and Lot are friendly to them. *That* is the issue.[119]

It is possible that the city's xenophobia is expressed in a threat to gang-rape the visitors. We know that the victors in battle sometimes did "sodomize" the vanquished. But this did not mean the victors were gay. In fact, it denoted precisely the opposite: They meant to show "who was a man and who wasn't." Such violated prisoners of war were being exhibited as "girly men." Thus, even if homosexual acts are to be envisioned in Genesis 19, the story does not have anything to do with homosexual *orientation*. How *could* it when the text goes out of its way to emphasize that *every last man* in the city joined the mob demanding Lot turn his visitors over to them? They were *all* gay? And why would Lot offer his virgin daughters to a bunch of homosexuals who he knew could not possibly be tempted by them? It is ridiculous.

So why does anybody read the story as being about homosexuality? It all comes down to a single word. "Bring out the men who came to you that we may *know* them!" The Hebrew words translated "knowledge" and "to know" are used, depending upon context, to denote "carnal knowledge," sex, a measly *ten* times. Genesis 19:8 ("I have two daughters who have not known man") is one of them. Genesis 18:19 ("I have known him [Abraham] that he may charge his children and his household after him to keep the way of Yahweh by doing righteousness and justice.") isn't. Into which category should we place

Genesis 19:5 ("Where are the men who came to you tonight? Bring them out to us that we may know them")?

The context certainly seems to imply that the Sodom Welcome Wagon, suspicious of strangers, wanted to get a look at them–and lynch them. Later rabbis certainly understood it this way, as they supplied an example of the abuse typically inflicted upon foreign visitors, borrowing (or paralleling) the Greek myth of Procrustes' bed.

Procrustes was an evil innkeeper with but a single bed to offer his guests. There were holes in the footboard, and if a guest proved too tall, he would advise him simply to put his ankles through the holes. Old Procrustes would listen outside the door until he heard the snoring begin, at which point he would produce a hacksaw and get to work. Of course he would "roll" the ruined corpse and help himself to the money. That is, until the superhero Theseus, "the second Hercules," put a stop to it. The rabbis said this was the practice of the men of Sodom, too. [120] Nothing about homosexuality there. As far as the prophet Ezekiel was concerned, "Behold, this was the guilt of your sister Sodom: she and her daughters had pride, surfeit of food, and prosperous ease, but did not aid the poor and needy." (Ezek. 16:49, RSV; cf., Matt. 25:41-46). What, no gays?

Lot offers his daughters to distract the brutish louts at his door: Maybe he can use sex to make these Neanderthals forget their murderous plan. They don't fall for it. Lucky for Lot, he has been "entertaining angels unaware" (Heb. 13:2), and they rescue him with supernatural power.

This brings up another parallel with Greek mythology. On account of the notorious cannibalism practiced by the depraved Pelasgians, Zeus decides to flood out the whole human race.[121] Hermes, reminiscent of Abraham bargaining with God over the fate of any righteous minority that Sodom might contain, asks Zeus to reconsider his extreme plan. Why not assume disguises and embark on a fact-finding tour? Maybe they don't *all* deserve death.

So Zeus and Hermes adopt mortal guise and make random calls upon mortals to see what treatment they might receive. First they drop in on King Lycaon, who serves up the carcass of his own son as the main course at dinner. Second, they show up on the doorstep of a hovel in which an aged couple named Baucis and Philemon dwell. Like the destitute Widow of Zarephath (1 Kings 17:11-14), they offer their last victuals and dregs of wine to their incognito visitors.

They begin to surmise they are on Candid Camera when they notice that the wine is not running out no matter how much anybody swills. Zeus and Hermes reveal themselves and promise to reward their hosts by allowing them to serve at Zeus' altar and finally to turn into trees on either side of the temple (this myth pops up twice in the New Testament, in Acts 14:8-18 and Revelation 3:12). Third and finally, they visit the righteous Deucalion and Pyrrha and warn them to build an ark to escape the coming flood and repopulate the earth. Zeus has decided to turn on the spigot and leave it to the righteous to take refuge on the mountaintops.

We have to suspect that the closely similar story of the two angels visiting Lot, who deserves deliverance, and the men of Sodom, whose inhospitality dooms them, was originally part of the Hebrew Flood story. It must have broken loose and found a new home. Now both the J and P versions of the Flood merely say the human race had become irredeemably corrupt, with no details.

The Sodom and Gomorrah story has attracted to its hull several "barnacles" including the episode of *Lot's Wife* (Gen. 19:19:26). This is the classic *geological* legend, explaining the origin of a wind-eroded stalagmite of rock salt. Such stories are by no means uncommon.[122] A similar legend told among Bedouins explains the origin of a group of wind-eroded rock outcrops which, from a distance, suggest the appearance of a herd of gazelles frozen in mid-gallop. The story goes that Allah found the sight so beautiful that he changed them into stone so that all passing that way might admire them in perpetuity. The story of Mrs. Lot (should we call her "Lotta"?) pausing in her headlong flight from Sodom's conflagration and getting caught in the descent of molten rock salt also echoes the mytheme "Don't look back!" seen in Orpheus' failed attempt to raise Eurydice from Hades.[123]

Lot, sent packing by the angels who rescued him, gets the jitters and fears he will not reach the safety of the mountains before the radius of the Sodom explosion overtakes him and his daughters. He pleads with the increasingly irritated angels to create a protective bubble over a tiny settlement near Sodom. The angel okays it, figuring God can afford to spare a few sinners. Because they owe their survival to the small size of their village, the people rename it "Zoar," i.e., "Smallville" (Gen. 19:17-23). This aspect of the legend is obviously *etymological*, explaining the name. It is also geological, accounting for why Zoar was exempt from the general desolation.[124]

Before someone decided to wedge the Zoar anecdote into the aftermath of Sodom's destruction, the story of Lot originally continued without interruption into that of *Lot and his Daughters* (J, Gen. 19:30-38). No stopover in Zoar, just straight to the mountains, where the old man holes up with his daughters. We have to wonder again if these stories originally formed part of the Flood story. Why have these three sought refuge high up in the mountains if not to escape a *flood*? Remember, in the Greek myth of the Flood, the righteous sought refuge atop the mountains. Lot's two daughters appear to believe there are no more men left *on earth*, as if a world-destroying cataclysm had struck, not merely the fall of a city.[125]

This is why they arrive at the loathsome scheme of raping their father. ("If you were the last man on earth!") As if Lot would be capable of ejaculation while passed out drunk! And here is another clue that the Lot story originally belonged with the Flood myth: Lot's drunkenness followed by a revolting sexual crime perpetrated by his own children parallels the Noah's Curse story in significant respects (though, as we have seen, the latter may not have been an original part of the Flood story either).

In any case, the thrust of this tawdry tale is *ethnological*. It seeks to explain the origin of Israel's hostile kinfolk, the Ammonites and the Moabites, in the manner of an ethnic joke.[126] "Want to know why our black sheep cousins the worthless Ammonites and the no-good Moabites are so stupid? Look at how they were conceived! There's your answer! *Haw haw!*" Crucial to the joke is the *etymology:* It explains "Moab" as if based on *me-ab*, "from a father," and "Ammon" as from *ben-ammi*, "of my people," both puns suggesting incestuous origins.

The Sacrifice of Isaac
Gen. 22:1-19

This story, preserved in the E source, evidences several distinct sedimentary layers, still traceable. One might consider each reading an alternate interpretation and choose one of them as the "real" meaning, but all seem quite compelling, and it makes plenty of sense to see them as a series of reinterpretations and reapplications stemming from different eras when different beliefs prevailed and different issues had come to the fore.

The earliest stratum understands the story as an astronomical myth, a story depicting as a one-time sequence of events what the hearers understood to be a repeating cycle. Remember, another of these can be found in Isaiah 14, the myth of Helal, son of the dawn goddess Shahar, exalting himself against Elyon, the Most High. His gambit is unsuccessful and he is cast down.

That story is about what we now call the planet Venus, appearing at dawn as the brightest object in the sky–until the sun rises and renders it invisible.[127] The myth of Abraham making to slay his son Isaac is the same sort of astronomical symbolism. "Abraham" means "great father" or "father of a multitude,"[128] which amount to the same thing, as the ancients did not think of a "great father" as denoting "a great dad" who spends "quality time" with his kids, etc. They were thinking of how many children he had fathered. Abraham stood for the moon, father of the stars, tiny lights in the night sky beside him.

When God invites him to try and count the stars and tells him his progeny will be just as numerous one day (Gen 15:5), the original myth shines through. It was no mere analogy. The innumerable stars *were* Abraham's (the moon's) progeny. Isaac, on the other hand, was (as we have seen) the sun. The sun could be imagined as the moon's wayward child because the sun appears after the moon (though you could view it the other way around: a chicken-and-egg problem), and when it does, it supplants its "parent." The moon strikes back, managing to drive the sun from his perch for another night, but his victory does not last, and so it goes.[129] The myth depicts this never-ending cycle as a one-time narrative.[130]

Now Abraham has been historicized, demoted to a human, albeit legendary, character. He attempts to slay his son but is prevented at the last minute by an angel who hastily explains it was just a test of Abraham's faith in God who had commanded him to sacrifice Isaac. The heavenly visitor indicates a ram, caught by his horns in a nearby bush. Abraham should offer him as a sacrifice instead.

The point of the tale thus retold would seem to be *ceremonial*, attempting to facilitate a major ritual innovation. If it was really just about Abraham's willingness to obey a terrible command of his Lord, *why must he still offer a sacrifice?* That feature of the story clearly signals that the question is "What sort of sacrifice does God require?" The story legitimizes the changeover from eighth-day infant *sacrifice* (commanded in Exod. 22:29-30; Ezek. 20:25-27) to eighth-day infant circumcision and substitution of an *animal* sacrifice for an *infant* sacrifice. The Sacrifice of Isaac story would seem to have bridged the command found in Exod. 22:29-30 and the revised version in Exod. 13:11-13.

This "historicized" version has been shaped as a close parallel to a Greek myth. King Athamas has a son, Phrixus, who is set to become his successor. But he has another, Melicertes, with another woman, Ino. She schemes to make *him* the royal heir. Ino bribes an oracle to fabricate a prophecy commanding Athamas to sacrifice his son and heir Phrixus to Zeus. Like Abraham, Athamas is tearfully willing to do it. He has no more idea that the command is a hoax than Abraham has that it is a trial. And just as the angel appears in the nick of time to stay Abe's hand, Hercules appears at the last moment to stop Athamas, exclaiming, "My father Zeus loathes human sacrifices!" Suddenly a golden ram conveniently appears, and a much-relieved Phrixus, not willing to take any chances, hops aboard and rides it all the way to Colchis on the Black Sea, where Jason will one day seek its miracle-working pelt.[131]

I would suggest that the words, "and come again to you" at the end of verse 5, then verses 7-8, are later interpolations to make the story less offensive to later readers. We usually read these bits as notes of dark irony, but I suggest we take them at face value, as if Abraham went up Mount Moriah in full cognizance of what would happen. He was so sure of God's prior promise that Isaac would be his heir that he knew his mission could not end in his son's death, that God must have something up his sleeve. He really meant it when he assured his servants that he and Isaac would return together, alive, after offering sacrifice–which wouldn't be Isaac.

How this would transpire, he didn't yet know, but *some*thing would work out. It looks like the Writer to the Hebrews was reading the story in such way when he says Abraham (must have) figured God would raise his butchered son from death if that's what it took (Heb. 11:19).

Finally, it is important to mention that, in one of the rare cases of speculative textual criticism posited by the old rabbis, some said that older manuscripts had Abraham actually going through with the sacrifice! (Note that in Genesis 22:19 it only says that Abraham, not both of them, returns from the mountain!) In this version, the spilled blood of Isaac served as an atonement for the future sins of Israel.[132] And then one must wonder if there was a version in which Isaac was resurrected in the manner of Near Eastern dying and rising savior gods.[133]

Hagar and Ishmael

Gen. 16:1-4; 21:9-21

We find the J version in Genesis 16:1-4, the E version in Genesis 21:9-21. E's account appears to be a later version of the same story. It bears the editorial signature of the Elohist compiler, who likes to "clean up" his heroes. Like J's version, E has Abraham give in to Sarah's nagging to send his concubine (and Sarah's rival) packing. In J, though, Abe has no real qualms about kicking out Hagar and their son Ishmael, just to shut Sarah up. E must not portray Abraham as being so heartless; it takes a direct revelation from the Almighty to get him to accede to Sarah's badgering. "Don't worry–I've got it covered."

Perhaps the major goal of the story in both versions is *ethnological*, explaining how the federation of twelve Ishmaelite tribes (stereotyped here) are related to Israel. To make the tribes descendants of Ishmael was already a fictive device to seal the tribes' alliance, but to make Ishmael in turn the son of Abraham is a way of cementing a subsequent alliance between the Ishmaelites and the Israelites. Notice the terms on which this linkage is negotiated: Ishmael is destined for greatness, true, but he is only the bastard son of Abraham and his "Plan B" concubine ("Ishmael Fitz-Abraham"), while Isaac is the miraculously conceived child of promise. It is a way of defining precedence in the Ishmaelite-Israelite alliance.

A word should be said about Isaac's miraculous conception. As we now read this story and similar ones starring Samson (Judg. 13:2-25), Samuel (1 Sam. 1:1-20), the Shunammite woman (2 Kings 4:11-17), and John the Baptist (Luke 1:5-25), the point seems to be that God or his angel has simply announced to disappointed would-be mothers that God will reverse their supposed barrenness, so that the husband's seed will take root and blossom.

M.J. Field[134] sees here either a mythologization of, or a euphemistic reference to, a common shamanic service. Even today, Field notes, local or wandering shamans in Africa and Arabia come to the aid of "barren" women, enabling them to become pregnant by impregnating the women themselves. It was the husband's fault, not the wife's. She wasn't barren; he was sterile. But the shaman isn't. And he fathers the child, giving the credit to God. The neighbors probably know what really happened, but all go along with the official version to save face for the husband as he beamingly hands out the cigars. Field believes the biblical accounts imply such shamanic, angelic, prophetic interventions. His theory need not be taken as assuming these individual nativity stories have any basis in historical fact, only that they take for granted the practice in general.[135]

Well, it seems to me that these miraculous conception stories are only slightly rewritten versions of originals in which the barren women were directly impregnated by God himself in human form, just as Zeus sexually impregnated Europa and Apollo impregnated Coronis, semi-divine heroes being the result. We have seen how the story of the Sons of God fraternizing with mortal women (Gen. 6:1-4) must originally have been a non-pejorative tale about the gods begetting demigods. It was reinterpreted in the interest of emerging monotheism. Same here.

The other major concern of the story of Hagar and Ishmael is the origin and naming of local watering holes. J's version explains the common name "Ishmael" (originally denoting a prayer on a boy's behalf: "May God hear [his prayers]") as having a special application to the son of Hagar and Abraham: "God hears," ostensibly referring to his survival due to God's hearing the infant's thirsty crying. The well that refreshes the child and his mother was originally called *Beer-lahairoi*, a topographical reference. It meant "the Well of the Antelope's Jawbone," a well adjacent to a rising ridge of rocks reminiscent of a skeletal jawbone.[136] The name served as a marker to help travelers find it.

But someone thought this name too mundane. The present tale redefines it, chopping up the syllables differently as "the Well of One Who Sees [God] and Lives" to tell it.[137] Thus someone getting a drink there must have been surprised by a visitation of God, whom one is not supposed to be able to survive seeing (Exod. 33:20).

The Elohist version (Gen. 21:9-21) repeats the *ethnological* business of how the Ishmaelite tribes are related to Israel as well as the *etymological* explanation of "Ishmael" as "God hears." But it is also *geological*, explaining the origin of the spring at Beersheba.

Another *ethnological* story defines the relations between Rebecca's twins (from J: Gen. 25:1-6, 11b, 18, 21-26a). One twin, Esau, is destined to be the progenitor of the Edomites, the other, Jacob, the father of the Israelite tribes. Remember, such stories are after-the-fact attempts to explain why things in the story-teller's day have turned out as they have. What is their relation?

Israel acknowledged the seniority of Edom, even though Israel had come to dominate them. By rights, then, one should have expected Edom to have the hegemony, but they didn't. These wheels were (supposedly) set in motion when the neonate Esau emerged from the womb with his brother's tiny hand grabbing his heel! (In fact, "Jacob" can be taken to mean "He who grasps the heel," i.e., "the supplanter.")[138] We will see how the same state of affairs, as well as its eventual reversal, is explained later on in another Jacob and Esau tale.

By the way, why does the father of the Edomite race bear the name "Esau" rather than that of "Edom"? I'm guessing that, once Israel had appropriated Edom (Adam) as their mythical First Man, the Edomites shifted over to another Canaanite deity, Esau, who still bears the tell-tale marks of a sun god, his "hairiness" denoting the sun's rays and his name meaning "red." A single pantheon may feature a number of solar deities representing the sun at different points in its daily journey: dawn, noon, evening, sunset. Esau was the red sun as it set and loomed large. Now he became the mythical ancestor of the Edomites.

Jacob Cheats Esau

Gen. 25:27-34; 27:1-45

Here are two more of J's *ethnological* stories designed to justify the then-current political relations between Edomites and Israelites. Like the story of their twin birth, these explain the triumph of Israel (the younger, once less powerful, people) over the older and superior Edomites, as well as (in 27:40b) the eventual breaking free of the Edomites (2 Kings 8:20 ff), events reflected also in Psalm 2:1-3; 137:7). This is a later insertion updating the story:

"Oh yeah! Isaac predicted *that*, too!"[139] Note how Esau is presented as a stereotype for all Edomites: red, hairy, powerful, but stupid.

The episode in chapter 27 is redundant. It makes the same point as the one in 25:27-34. There must have been several independent versions aimed at accounting for the current state of affairs. Typically, J wanted to preserve as many of these stories, even if redundant or contradictory, as he could. But this latter story has other interesting features, too.

It is a polished literary work, what with the repeated attempts by the old, blind Isaac to expose what he shrewdly suspects is a trick being played on him by a nervous Jacob, put up to the scheme by his sneaky mother. If this is really Esau, how can he have returned from hunting so quickly? Does he smell like the open fields, as outdoorsman Esau must? And so on, until he finally gives in and confers upon Jacob the blessing of primogeniture which rightly belongs to Esau. (Of course, if the "mess of pottage" story was originally supposed to be an earlier episode in the same story, Esau would already have forfeited his birthright.)

Below the surface we can detect vestiges of earlier myths. First, we have another story of the perpetual rivalry between sun and moon. Esau is the sun, as noted above; Jacob is the moon. This is why he is described as a "smooth man" (Gen. 27:12) as opposed to his brother who is a "hairy man."[140] There are flaming solar rays but only a gentle lunar halo. Similarly, Elijah, "a hairy man" (2 Kings 1:8), is the sun, replaced by the bald Elisha (2 Kings 2:23), the moon. Physical descriptions of Bible characters are very rare. When they do occur, they are clues. Who gets the priority? Who gets to rule the heavens? Which one will succeed the old, declining sun, the *blind* Isaac?[141]

Second, there may be traces of another Hebrew version of the conspiracy of Cronus and his brothers to usurp their father's throne. It may be that the actantial roles (character functions) have remained the same but have been redistributed among different characters. Originally the conspirators were Cronus and his brothers; now they are Jacob and his mother. In both, they conspire against the father, whether Uranus or Isaac. And yet it is not old Isaac who stands to lose his position, as he is soon to die anyway. The one whose sovereignty is imperiled is Esau, the rightful successor to Isaac's leadership of the clan.

Jacob's Ladder

Gen. 28:10-22

I mentioned above that there were several foundation legends (*ceremonial* myths) for the temple at Bethel. Here are two more. They have been spliced together just like the J and P Flood stories. Why not simply use both and separate them by spacing them apart, as with the three stories of the lying Patriarch? Perhaps because there are so many Bethel origin stories, the compiler felt obliged to reduce the number, yet without leaving anything out. It is a great example (as is the Flood story) of how well the division of Pentateuchal sources works, leaving us with two complete and self-contained versions. We see the J version in Genesis 28:10, 13-16, 19 (in verse 13 we should translate "Yahweh stood *beside him*" where most translations render it "[Yahweh] stood *above it*").

The E version can be separated out as Genesis 28:11-12, 17-18, 20-22. Both versions are to be classified as *ceremonial*, giving a Patriarchal, Yahwist pedigree to the ancient shrine of Bethel–later the site of a major temple (1 Kings 12:25-33). Other stories with the same point include Genesis 32:1-2, 22-32 and 35:1-15. There is also the *etymological* aspect, explaining the name "Bethel" as meaning "house of God." It is virtually synonymous with "Babel," the "gate of God."

Jacob Wrestles with "God"

Gen. 32:22-32

This E story is an *etymological* legend, aimed at explaining the name "Israel" as "one who fights with God"–by having Jacob fight God! It also redefines the place-name "Peniel/ Penuel" as "Face of God," which originally denoted simply that it was a holy place, a shrine where one might come into the (invisible) presence of God and offer sacrifice or seek an oracle from the attending priest or shaman. Now it is said to get its name from a couple of specific incidents in the life of the Patriarch Jacob. Likewise, the story is to be categorized as *ceremonial*, providing a Patriarchal pedigree for the sacred "limping" dance[142] practiced there (see also 1 Kings 18:26), as well as the folk taboo on eating the muscle in the hollow of the thigh of any slaughtered animal. (That custom did not otherwise make it into the Torah of Moses.)

But the story is much more interesting than that. Like the story of Joseph, this story has been worked up into a real piece of literature, as witness its length, complexity, and polish. It follows on the excellent episode of Rebecca putting the reluctant Jacob up to the ploy of deceiving old Isaac about his identity, posing as Esau serving up his father's favorite dish, hoping to con him out of the deathbed blessing that rightfully belongs to Esau.

Not the least amusing touch is Isaac's disguise; he is more of a modern man, his brother more of a hirsute Neanderthal, so, to deceive his blind father's touch, Jacob straps some furry animal pelts around his forearms. (What, was Esau a full-fledged werewolf or something?) The trick works but is inevitably soon found out as Esau, returning from his hunt, brings his own bowl of stew to Isaac, and it's *déjà vu* all over again. "Uh, weren't you just here? *Burp!*"

In accord with ancient belief, the blessing Jacob had stolen through subterfuge was a real fate-turning conjuration. Just as a curse (a hex) would bring real misfortune upon its object, so would a blessing bring good fortune. In this case, the Patriarchal blessing should ensure a future of success for whomever received it.[143] So mechanical was it believed to be that it must benefit Jacob even though Isaac pronounced it on Esau, supposing it was he who stood before him, just as if he had handed a chest of gold to the wrong son. Too late now! It was far more than a mere gesture.

So when Isaac and Esau put the pieces of the puzzle together, Esau is furious at thus being defrauded. Rebekah, eavesdropping, goes and tells poor Jacob to take it on the lam, since a bloodthirsty Esau has sworn to have his hide. Of course, we know that's not going to work since, after all, Jacob does now possess the blessing! But Jacob is alarmed nonetheless; this is exactly what he was afraid of: "*Thanks*, Mom!"

I beg the reader's leave to skip ahead, passing by Jacob's adventures in the East after he has left town ahead of his brother's wrath. Suffice it to say that he takes up with his shifty uncle Laban and winds up marrying both his cousins, Leah and Rachel, before heading home again. We learn that Jacob has a pair of concubines, too. (A concubine was kind of an unofficial wife without a dowry, but her offspring were counted as legitimate heirs.)

Jacob has eleven sons (and eventually a twelfth) by them, plus a single daughter. With Leah Jacob produces Reuben, Simeon, Levi, Issachar, Judah, Zebulun, and Dinah. With his concubine Bilhah, he fathers Dan and Naphtali. With Leah's slave Zilpah he has Gad and Asher. Rachel bears Joseph and, much later, Benjamin. Why this careful tabulation? If these people are all sons of Jacob (and ultimately progenitors of the twelve tribes), what difference does it make who their various mothers were? The theory is that we are once again dealing with fictive genealogical links standing for alliances and federations of originally independent groups.[144]

There would have been one alliance of seven tribes who sealed their alliance by positing a common ancestress named Leah, originally a name attached to their object of worship, the setting sun.[145] In the same manner, there would have been three other, smaller alliances named for nature goddesses. "Rachel"[146] means "sheep," denoting fleecy rain clouds, of whom she was originally the divine personification. Bilhah[147] and Zilpah[148] appear to have been sun goddesses.

When all of these groups of groups eventually merged into one large group, they posited Jacob as "the father of us all." Later still, this twelve-tribe confederacy joined with another tribe named for their sun god Isaac, then with another devoted to the moon god Abraham. Other tribes along the way joined up, in looser or closer relations, e.g., Edomites, Ishmaelites, Moabites, Ammonites, patching themselves in as if cousins related to this or that legendary Patriarch.

Anyway, once Jacob, now fabulously wealthy and with hundreds of servants, retainers, and livestock, decides to take his chances back home, he learns that his estranged brother Esau is headed his way with a mighty host of his own. Jacob fears he cannot avoid a battle and plans to reduce his losses by dividing his entourage in two and sending them home by different routes. That way, if Esau attacks the one party, the other may escape. Sending them on their way, Jacob remains behind on the banks of the river Jabbok,[149] where in the wee hours he experiences an eerie encounter.

Suddenly "a man" jumps him, and they wrestle, neither gaining the advantage, till near sun-up. His assailant grows urgent: He must be away before the sun rises! So he short-circuits the fight by cheating: He manages to put Jacob out of commission by dislocating his thigh. Significantly, he neither robs nor kills him. So what was he trying to accomplish?

Jacob demands to know who it is who has attacked him and, implicitly, why. His erstwhile foe, still shrouded in shadow, refuses to answer but confers a new name on Jacob. "You will no longer be called Jacob, but Israel [= "He who strives with God"], for you have wrestled with God and prevailed." Off he goes, still incognito, but having implied he is the Angel of God who sometimes appears in human form (as in Gen. 16:7-14, Judg. 13:20-22). Limping from his injury, Jacob dubs the place "Peniel" ("Face of God") because he seems to have seen the very visage of God. This implies his antagonist had not managed to hide completely from the first rays of dawn after all. Jacob saw his face.

The next day, Jacob goes forth to meet the advancing host of his brother Esau, expecting a melee. He is in for a surprise, for his brother has long forgotten his thirst for vengeance. It is not hard to see why, because, even lacking the blessing of Isaac, he has grown as wealthy as Jacob anyway! He has learned that success is the best revenge. Jacob tells him that "Seeing your face is like seeing the face of God." And I believe that here I detect a double entendre.

We have heard one sandal drop in the enigmatic scene of the wrestling match, leaving the attacker's identity unresolved. This is the second sandal dropping. I believe we are to understand that now Jacob recognizes Esau, both men having visibly aged since last seeing each other, as the man who had attacked him in the darkness![150] He understood that Esau felt he must get his licks in, satisfying his grudge before reconciling with his brother. A wrestling match would be sufficient, and he hadn't even wanted Jacob to know it was he. Now Jacob acknowledges it with a wink, and they live happily ever after.

The Burials of Deborah and Rachel

Gen. 35:8, 19-20

This pair of *ceremonial* myths, both from the E source, are meant to account for the origins of sacred graves, where the shades of the two Israelite Matriarchs might be consulted through a medium. We see King Saul doing this in 1 Samuel 28, though not at a grave. This widespread practice is condemned with indignant mockery in Isaiah 8:19. Obviously, it would not be condemned if it was not happening. Still today, this sort of necromancy is common in the Near East[151] when people seek out the graves of local saints (*welis*), not to mention in modern America where a decent buck is to be made pretending to put the desperate in touch with their departed relatives.

The note about the resting place of Deborah, Rachel's nurse, is *etymological*. It explains the name of the shrine Allon-baccuth, "Oak of Weeping." But there is likely a bit more to it than the site being simply the place where this woman was once mourned. It seems likely that it was the site of repeated ritual mourning on behalf of Deborah, who must have been much more significant in Israelite belief than this brief mention would let on.

Possibly this was earlier supposed to be the grave of another Deborah, the leader ("judge") of Israel in an already ancient poem preserved in Judges chapter 5.[152] Alternatively, the place may have been a site where pubescent girls observed a ritual mourning for the impending loss of their virginity (Judg. 11:37-38). Again, it may have been a place for the annual ritual mourning for Tammuz (Ezek. 8:14) or Hadad-Rimmon (Zech. 12:11), who were dying-and-rising fertility gods.

Judah and Tamar

Gen. 38

This infamous story has absolutely nothing to do with masturbation, despite the (mis)use to which it has been put for centuries. The point rather is to reinforce the obligation of levirate ("brother") marriage (Deut. 25:9-10).

Suppose a man dies, leaving no heirs to carry on the family name or to keep property in the family. His brother, if he had one, must marry the widow. The firstborn son of such a union will be considered the legal heir of the biological father's late brother. In this story Judah's eldest son Er dies, a sinner struck down by God. Judah then calls on his second son, Onan, to do his duty by Er's young wife Tamar.

But Onan is not willing to beget a son that will not legally be his. It is due to his unwillingness to provide an heir for his dead brother that Onan "spills his seed upon the ground," which *could* mean he masturbated before going to meet Tamar with insufficient time to "reload." But it more likely denotes that in the midst of intercourse he pulled out, ejaculating outside of her.

Yahweh was neither pleased nor fooled, and he executed selfish Onan, too. Judah had a third son, a pretty young one, though post-pubescent. Judah apparently did not realize it was God who was killing his sons for cheating Tamar, thinking instead that she was cursed or something—like Sarah in the Book of Tobit, who was married seven times, only to have a jealous demon kill each one on the wedding night (Tobit 6:13-14). So Judah is afraid for the life of his third son, Shela. He puts off Tamar with the excuse that Shela is, ah, too young, and that she must wait some years to receive his attentions. Yeah, that's the ticket.

But Tamar can afford to wait only so long, so she decides to trick the only remaining male relative, old Judah himself, into impregnating her. She sets up shop as a roadside prostitute where she knows Judah will be passing. Sure enough, he stops by. We have to assume Tamar disrobes except for leaving her face veiled. Having left his Israelite Express card home, he promises to send her a young goat in payment, and she demands collateral: Judah's signet ring and other tokens.

Not long afterward, Judah sends a man to drop by with the goat, only to find the tent gone. Months later, Tamar is found to be pregnant with no known partner. She is condemned to death for harlotry, and Tamar offers to reveal the identity of the culprit. She produces Judah's possessions, whereupon he realizes what happened and why. He confesses the whole business, admits he was in the wrong for having cheated her, and they all live happily ever after.

Joseph the Hebrew Osiris

Gen. 37, 39-50

This one practically qualifies as a novella. In fact, centuries later, the biblical story of Joseph did inspire a Hellenistic Jewish novel, *Joseph and Asenath*, in which Joseph is revealed to be a quasi-supernatural figure. Surah 12 of the Qu'ran relates the story of Joseph, too. Muslims have traditionally had the same trouble with it that the Song of Solomon has occasioned for Jews and Christians: Why is there a romance included in scripture?

The Joseph story remains today a fascinating and effective story even as pure fiction, though there are other important elements to it. The narrative, like those of Daniel and Esther, offered an ideal for young Jews growing up in exile or Diaspora in foreign lands. It demonstrated that advancement was possible even under such adverse circumstances. Though they belonged to a subject minority people, young Jews could succeed even better than their non-Jewish neighbors by sticking to their Jewish identity and rejecting the ever-present temptation to take the easy way and assimilate to Gentile (pagan) culture.

In this way, they could also play the role God had assigned to Jews to be "a light to the nations" (Isa. 42:6), demonstrating the superior lifestyle available to those who live by the Torah. It worked, as many Gentiles, at least in the Roman Empire and perhaps earlier, were indeed attracted to Judaism and either converted outright or at least embraced Jewish "ethical monotheism," attending synagogues as "pious Gentiles" or "God-fearers" like the centurion Cornelius in Acts 10-11.

The descriptions of Joseph and Daniel depict them not only as high-rising court officials in pagan governments, but as skilled diviners and dream-interpreters: not exactly prophets in the classical sense, like Isaiah and Jeremiah, but something closer to shamans or magicians.[153] This role, too, may have been a function of their being exotic foreigners, as we see the trend continue for centuries in the reputation of Jewish occult specialists (exorcists, fortune-tellers, etc.) scattered through the Greco-Roman world,[154] as well as the attribution of magic texts to Moses and Solomon.

Source criticism reveals that the Genesis story of Joseph must be divided, as usual, between J and E. This explains certain inconsistencies. For instance, why was Reuben surprised when he returned secretly to rescue Joseph (37:22) only to find him gone (37:29-30)? According to the surrounding verses, *all* the brothers agreed to sell him to slavers. And were the slave-traders Ishmaelites (37:25-27, 28b) or Midianites (37:28a, 36)? (They're not two names for the same people.) J had it one way, E another.

The most neglected aspect of the Joseph story is also perhaps the most interesting, namely that the hero appears to be a Hebrew version of the pre-biblical Egyptian god Osiris. He was the god of the grain, brother to the sinister Set, god of the desert wastes. Set was jealous of his noble brother and plotted against him. During a banquet, Set had his henchmen carry in an elaborate sarcophagus, a very desirable item in the eyes of

Egyptians, given their obsession with burial rites and mummification. No one but Set knew who had sent it. He suggested that all present should lie down in it to try it on for size. Whoever was the best fit should have it for his own. The mighty Osiris was the winner, since Set had it designed to fit his brother's statuesque dimensions.

But before Osiris could sit up, Set's goons rushed forward, slammed the lid shut and hammered it closed. Like pallbearers in a race to the grave, they hoisted up the coffin, now occupied, and dashed out with it, finally setting it adrift on the Nile. Momentarily frozen with shock, Isis and her sister Nephthys, wives (and sisters!)[155] of Osiris, pursued Set's servants but were too late. Osiris, of course, suffocated in the drifting box. Isis set out to recover the casket, but by the time, long afterward, she found it, it had been enclosed in the trunk of a tree that had grown around it! But she lost it to Set again, who this time dismembered his brother's corpse and scattered the pieces all over the land (as in Judges 19:29).

Isis managed to recover all but the penis, for which she substituted a magical prosthesis. She resurrected the reassembled deity, who impregnated her with his heir and earthly reincarnation, Horus, the falcon-headed sun god, who grew up to avenge Osiris upon the wicked Set. Then Osiris descended to the Netherworld where he reigned henceforth as Judge of the dead, dispensing their fates as they appeared before him.

The original point of the myth was to set forth, as if a one-time event, the perennial, cyclical struggle between drought and harvest in Egypt. When the Nile floods and deposits alluvial soil, there will be an ample grain harvest. But this lasts only so long before the blistering sun scorches the land to desert. Back and forth it goes, just like the alternation between moon and sun in the myth of Abraham trying to sacrifice Isaac.

While the striking parallels to Jesus in the gospels are sometimes discussed and debated, it is less frequently noticed how closely this story corresponds to that of Joseph, and to such a degree that one may suggest Joseph's story is a rewritten version of Osiris'. That should occasion no surprise since Palestine had been part of the Egyptian Empire during the third millennium B.C.E. Influences would have been hard to avoid, as witness all the Egyptian names in the Old Testament, like Moses, Hophni, Merari, etc.

Young Joseph experiences dreams suggesting he will rule over his family, including his parents. The planetary imagery almost implies his godhood. (Osiris, too, will reign over all.) This seeming conceit on the part of the naïve youth does not win him any friends among his older brothers, especially since his father Jacob makes no attempt to hide his favoritism, Joseph being the only son (thus far) of his favorite wife, Rachel. (Here is the parallel to Set's murderous envy of his brother.)

When Joseph carries a message to them from his father while his brothers are at work in the pasture, they decide they have had about enough of this insufferable pest and drop him into a pit, from whence he is sold to travelling slavers, who of course extricate him. (This is the first of two echoes of Osiris' "burial," from which he will emerge.) Joseph had been sporting a luxurious garment his father had bestowed on him, either a robe striped with many colors or a robe with long sleeves depending on how you translate, either way a choice item.

The brothers strip the garment off Little Joe, tear it apart, and daub it in the blood of an animal they butcher. They return to old Jacob claiming they were unable to prevent Joseph getting ripped apart by a wild predator. (Set actually dismembers Osiris, while Joseph's brothers feign their sibling's dismemberment.) They pretend to commiserate with their stricken father. Really, though, what do they care? Maybe now he'll appreciate *them* for a change!

An Egyptian official named Potiphar purchases Joseph and makes him his estate's steward (something common enough in the ancient world). Joseph is only rising in his master's esteem through his excellent service–until one day when the lady of the house, in whose eyes Joseph has also been looking better and better, tries to seduce him. Joseph, being an honorable man, will have none of it. Hell hath no fury like a woman scorned, and she cries, "Rape!"

Joseph is sent to prison. (Here is the second "burial" of Joseph, recalling the second disposal of Osiris' body.) But there, too, Joseph proves his worth and rises to the position of assistant warden. While there, he uses his "wisdom," or psychic powers, to interpret the premonitory dreams of two inmates, both former staff of Pharaoh. Soon after, Pharaoh, too, has some strange and portentous dreams.

He learns of Joseph's oracular expertise and sends for him. The dreams are a warning from God that Egypt is soon to experience seven years of bountiful grain harvests, followed by another seven, this time, of bitter famine. Thus forewarned, Joseph tells Pharaoh, he ought to warehouse most of the wheat to dole out during the inevitable famine. With wise stewardship, he can save the world from starvation.

Pharaoh takes him seriously and readily decides Joseph is the man for the job. He will administer the stockpiling and the subsequent rationing. (Here is the contrast between feast and famine that is so central to the Osiris myth, and Joseph, as he who saves the world by means of grain, corresponds to the savior Osiris.) And so Joseph becomes the Grand Vizier of Egypt, second in command to Pharaoh (just as the risen Osiris is awarded the eternal throne of the Netherworld).

Later, Joseph is reunited with his fearful brothers and with his astonished father, a wonderful narrative sequence. But he is most surprised to learn of young Benjamin, the late-born son of Joseph's own mother Rachel. (Benjamin corresponds to Horus, a new Osiris, even as Benjamin was to Jacob a replacement for Joseph.)

This story seems to presuppose that Joseph would turn out to be a hero on a par with Abraham or Moses. Oddly enough, though, Joseph's main significance henceforth is merely that of one more (fictive) genealogical link. He has two sons, Ephraim and Manasseh, who are numbered among the tribes of Israel as distinct and separate entities. There is no "Tribe of Joseph," any more than there is a "Tribe of Rachel" or a "Tribe of Leah." It is as if Joseph is being used as a device for adding a thirteenth tribe as if, strictly for the purpose of keeping the magic number twelve intact, Ephraim and Manasseh are counted together.

There are clues that Joseph remained important in Israel in the north once that group of tribes seceded from Judah in the south, repudiating the Davidic dynasty. We will one day hear of a "Messiah ben Joseph" hailing from Galilee, a preliminary messiah whose battlefield death will open the way for a Judean Messiah ben-David to lead the Jews to victory over Rome. Whoever first told the Joseph story believed that Ephraim and Manasseh would lead the people of God. That would make more sense coming from the E source, but J has his own version, too.

How did the 1966 film, *The Bible: In the Beginning,* manage to squeeze the whole of scripture into three hours? Simple: It didn't try. The movie doesn't even get to the end of Genesis. Yet I have always thought the title was anything but misleading because my impression is that, when most people hear the words "the Bible," what comes to mind immediately is the Book of Genesis with its magnificent tales. And that's probably as it should be.

Notes

1. Hans-Joachim Schoeps, *Paul: The Theology of the Apostle in the Light of Jewish Religious History*. Trans. Harold Knight (Philadelphia: Fortress Press, 1961), p. 29.

2. D.M. Murdock, *Did Moses Exist? The Myth of the Israelite Lawgiver* (Seattle: Stellar House Publishing, 2014); Robert M. Price, *Moses and Minimalism: Form Criticism vs. Fiction in the Pentateuch* (Valley, WA: Tellectual Press, 2015).

3. Hermann Gunkel, *Genesis*. Trans. Mark E. Biddle. Mercer Library of Biblical Studies (Macon: Mercer University Press, 1997), p. viii.

4. Julius Wellhausen, *Prolegomena to the History of Ancient Israel*. Trans. Menzies and Black (New York: World Publishing Company/Meridian Books, 1957, orig. 1878). See also J. Estlin Carpenter, *The Composition of the Hexateuch: An Introduction with Select Lists of Words and Phrases* (London: Longmans, Green, 1902).

5. Graham Chapman, John Cleese, Terry Gilliam, Eric Idle, Terry Jones, Michael Palin, *Monty Python's Life of Brian (of Nazareth)* (New York: Ace Books, 1979), p. 20.

6. Gunkel, *Genesis*, p. 62.

7. Gerhard von Rad, *Studies in Deuteronomy*. Trans David Stalker. Studies in Biblical Theology No. 9 (Chicago: Henrt Regnery, 1953), Chapter One, "The Character of Deuteronomy and Its Sacral Traditions from the Point of View of Form-Criticism," pp. 11-24.

8. Moshe Weinfeld, *Deuteronomy and the Deuteronomic School* (Oxford at the University Press, 1972).

9. Hermann Gunkel, *The Legends of Genesis: The Biblical Saga and History*. Trans. W.H. Carruth (New York: Schocken Books, 1964; orig. 1901), p. 25. This book is a different translation of Gunkel's Introduction to his whole *Genesis* commentary, which was translated into English many years later. In the shorter work, etiological legends are made a separate category, while in the commentary all the types are discussed as sub-categories of etiology.

10. Robert Graves, *The Greek Myths*. Volume One (Baltimore: Penguin Books, 1960), p. 98.

11. Gunkel, *Genesis*, pp. xix-xx; Gunkel, *Legends*, pp. 27-30.

12. Gunkel, *Genesis*, pp. xviii-xix, 81; Gunkel, *Legends*. Watch out: In the Biddle translation of Gunkel's *Genesis*, when he gets to the "ethnological" category, he accidentally repeats "etymological" instead. So much for inerrancy.

13. Gunkel, *Genesis*, p. xvii.

14. Gunkel, *Genesis*, pp. xxi; Gunkel, *Legends*, p. 34.

15. Gunkel, *Genesis*, pp. xx-xxi; Gunkel, *Legends*, pp. 30-34.

16. Branislaw Malinowski, *Magic, Science and Religion and Other Essays* (Garden City: Doubleday Anchor Books, 1954), pp. 107-10.

17. Wellhausen, *Prolegomena*, pp. 297-99.

18. Hermann Gunkel, *Creation and Chaos in the Primeval Era and the Eschaton: A Religio-Historical Study of Genesis 1 and Revelation 12*. Trans. K. William Whitney, Jr. (Grand Rapids: Eerdmans, 2006; orig. 1895).

19. Ignaz Goldziher, *Mythology among the Hebrews and Its Development*. Trans. Russell Martineau (New York: Cooper Square Press, 1967; orig. 1877), pp. 184-86. Lot's name may denote he was understood to be a worshipper of Lotan/Leviathan, just as the harlot Rahab (Josh. 2:1) was likely a sacred prostitute ("priestitute"?) in the service of the dragon lord of the same name (Psalm 89:10), apparently the same as Leviathan.

20. Michael D. Goulder, *The Psalms of Asaph and the Pentateuch*. Studies in the Psalter, III. Journal for the Study of the Old Testament Supplement Series 233 (Sheffield: Sheffield Academic Press, 1996), pp. 68-69.

21. Another possible *Sitz-im-Leben* for the ritual rehearsal of the dragon-slaying myth is (unwittingly) suggested in Mircea Eliade, *The Sacred and the Profane: The Nature of Religion*. Trans. Willard Trask (New York: Harcourt, Brace & World, 1959), pp. 54-55: "Before the masons lay the first stone the astronomer shows them the spot where it is to be placed, and this spot is supposed to lie above the snake that supports the world. The master mason sharpens a stake and drives it into the ground, exactly at the indicated spot, in order to fix the snake's head. A foundation stone is then laid above the stake . . . . [T]he act of foundation repeats the cosmogonic [world-creating] act, for to drive the stake into the snake's head to 'fix' it is to imitate the primordial gesture of Soma or Indra, when the latter, as the *Rig Veda* expresses it, 'struck the Snake in his lair' (IV, 17, 9), when his lightning bolt 'cut off its head' (I, 52, 10)."

We have long understood the rehearsal of Yahweh's slaying of the dragon in Psalms 74 and 89, whereupon he established the earth and his throne, as renewing the Judean king's mandate of heaven in a yearly enthronement renewal ceremony. But what if, as Old Testament Minimalists contend, there *was* no such monarchy? What would the function of these Psalms have been? We can imagine them being chanted at the foundation of a new house, itself a microcosmic model of the universe. In so doing, one called the primordial time of creation into one's own day to make one's own efforts at construction effective.

22. Robert Graves and Raphael Patai, *Hebrew Myths: The Book of Genesis* (New York: Greenhouse House/Crown Publishers, 1983), p. 31; Gunkel, *Genesis*, p. 105.

23. Graves and Patai, *Hebrew Myths*, p. 25.

24. Gunkel, *Genesis*, p. 121.

25. Gunkel at p. 113.

26. Ignaz Goldziher, *An Introduction to Islamic Theology and Law*. Trans. Andras and Ruth Hamori. Modern Classics in Near Eastern Studies (Princeton: Princeton University Press, 1981; orig. 1910), pp. 92-94.

27. Think of Martin Luther's espousal, against Zwingli, of Consubstantiation on the grounds that, in the Words of Institution, "This is my body," "is" means "is," period.

28. Were the days of creation literal twenty-four hour days? Might they have been periods of indeterminate length, as some suggest, seeking to reconcile Genesis with geology? Nothing in the text would seem to suggest this. Clearly the age-day "hypothesis," though by no means inherently absurd, is an alien notion being shoe-horned into the text.

29. Wellhausen, *Prolegomena*, pp. 297-99.

30. Mircea Eliade, *Yoga: Immortality and Freedom*. Trans. Willard R. Trask. Bollingen Series LVI (Princeton: Princeton University Press, 1969), pp. 15-22.

31. Robert M. Price and Edwin A. Suominen, *Evolving out of Eden: Christian Responses to Evolution* (Valley, WA: Tellectual Press, 2013), pp. 108-109.

32. I refer to God as "he" because we are discussing a character in a book. If there is a real deity, it might transcend gender for all I know, but it is plain that the "God" character in both Testaments is just as much a male as Moses or Solomon.

33. Graves and Patai, *Hebrew Myths*, p. 81.

34. In fact the word usually translated "rib" can just as easily mean "side," and some ancient rabbis took the text to imply that the original *adam* was a hermaphrodite, as in Greek and Persian creation myths, and that what Yahweh did was to split it down the middle.

35. Gunkel, *Genesis*, p. 17.

36. The Qumran *Book of Giants* lists him as one of them.

37. Neil Forsyth, *The Old Enemy: Satan & the Combat Myth* (Princeton: Princeton University Press, 1987), pp. 107-23, 232.

38. Goldziher, *Mythology*, pp. 184-86.

39. In some versions of the Prometheus myth, he did create mankind.

40. Margaret Barker, *The Older Testament: The Survival of Themes from the Ancient Royal Cult in Sectarian Judaism and Early Christianity* (London: SPCK, 1987), demonstrates just how important this motif was in pre-Deuteronomic Hebrew religion. In fact, by setting forth the evidence for a multiform Israelite faith before its suppression by the Deuteronomic School, she does for Judaism exactly what Walter Bauer did for Christianity in his *Orthodoxy and Heresy in Earliest Christianity* (Trans. by a team from the Philadelphia Seminar on Christian Origins [Philadelphia: Fortress Press, 1971]).

41. I have always thought that feminists get it all turned around when they object to appeals to women not to dress "provocatively," as if the warning implied getting raped was their fault, when actually the point is not to underestimate the bestial lustfulness of men!

42. Gunkel, *Genesis*, p. 21.

43. Gunkel at p. 20.

44. If the Eden story establishes a doctrine of "the Fall of Man" and Original Sin for humans, shouldn't we also speak of a "Fall of Snake" and "Original Venom" or something? And why no redemption for sinful serpents? Unless we find it in Romans 8:19-22.

45. Graves and Patai, *Hebrew Myths*, pp. 15, 69.

46. Graves and Patai at pp. 79.

47. Graves and Patai, *Hebrew Myths*, p. 15; Graves, *Greek Myths*, p. 148. She was the same as Rhea.

48. Graves and Patai, *Hebrew Myths*, pp. 85; Forsyth, *Old Enemy*, pp. 236-37.

49. Actually, some in the Middle Ages thought Cain's "mark" was a unicorn horn! Sabine Baring-Gould, *Legends of Old Testament Characters from the Talmud and other Sources* (London and New York: Macmillan, 1871), p. 60.

50. Graves and Patai, *Hebrew Myths*, pp. 85, 88.

51. Compare the name of the cartoon character "Vegeta" in *Dragonball Z*.

52. Goldziher, *Mythology*, p. 113.

53. Graves and Patai, *Hebrew Myths* p. 124; Goldziher, *Mythology*, p. 113.

54. Graves and Patai, *Hebrew Myths* p. 51; Gunkel, *Genesis*, p. 51.

55. Archaeology makes clear that there *was* no Conquest. But this reading of the Cain and Abel story would still seem to reflect the ancient belief that there was.

56. Goldziher, *Introduction*, pp. 241-45.

57. Goldziher, *Mythology*, p. 113.

58. Samuel Ives Curtiss, *Primitive Semitic Religion Today: A Record of Researches, Discoveries and Studies in Syria, Palestine and the Sinaitic Peninsula* (New York: Fleming H. Revell Company, 1902), pp. 184, 187-90, 224-27.

59. Joseph Gaer, *The Legend of the Wandering Jew* (New York: Mentor Books/New American Library, 1961).

60. Gunkel, *Genesis*, p. 47; Graves and Patai, *Hebrew Myths*, pp. 95-96.

61. Nicolas Wyatt, "Cain's Wife," in Wyatt, *'There's such divinity doth hedge a King': Selected Essays of Nicolas Wyatt on Royal Ideology in Ugaritic and Old Testament Literature*. Society for Old Testament Study Monographs (Burlington, VT: Ashgate Publishing, 2005), pp. 27-30.

62. Though I guess the traditional translation, for our purposes, pretty much comes down to the same thing.

63. Paul Veyne, *Did the Greeks Believe in their Myths? An Essay on the Constitutive Imagination*. Trans. Paula Wissig (Chicago: University of Chicago Press, 1988), p. 32.

64. Goldziher, *Mythology*, pp. 111-12.

65. "In those days, when the world / Was young, and the sky bright-new still, men lived differently: / Offspring of oaks or rocks, clay-moulded, parentless." Juvenal, *The Sixteen Satires*. Trans. Peter Green. Penguin Classics (Baltimore: Penguin Books, 1974), p. 127.

66. Claude Levi-Srauss, "The Structural Study of Myth." In Levi-Strauss, *Structural Anthropology*. Trans. Claire Jacobson and Brooke Grundfest Schoepf (Garden City: Doubleday Anchor Books, 1967), pp. 202-28.

67. Edmund Leach, "Levi-Strauss in the Garden of Eden" in *Transactions of the New York Academy of Sciences* 23/4 [1961] 386-96. I find Leach's reading obscure, whereas Levi-Strauss's interpretation of Oedipus can be applied perfectly to the Eden myth.

68. Like Norman Bates's mother in *Psycho* and the ghostly mother in the *Twilight Zone* episode "Young Man's Fancy," written by Richard Matheson, May 11, 1962.

69. Joseph Schacht, "A Reevaluation of Islamic Traditions." In Ibn Warraq, ed./trans., *The Quest for the Historical Muhammad* (Amherst: Prometheus Books, 2000), p. 361.

70. Wyatt, "Cain's Wife," p. 26.

71. Graves and Patai, *Hebrew Myths*, p. 99.

72. Goldziher, *Mythology*, p. 127.

73. T.K. Cheyne, "Noah." In T.K. Cheyne and J. Sutherland Black, eds., *Encyclopaedia Biblica: A Critical Dictionary of the Literary, Political and Religious History, the Archaeology, Geography and Natural History of the Bible* (London: Adam and Charles Black, 1914), col. 3426.

74. Gunkel, *Genesis*, pp. 134-35.

75. S.R. Driver, *The Book of Genesis*. Westminster Commentaries (London: Methuen, 1911), p. 80.

76. Graves and Patai, *Hebrew Myths*, p. 128.

77. The Septuagint and the Dead Sea Scrolls biblical manuscripts agree that Goliath was 6 1/2, not 9 ½ feet tall, as against the corrupt Massoretic Text.

78. Zechariah Sitchin, *The Twelfth Planet* (New York: Avon Books, 1978), pp. 171-72, 198, 203, etc. Sitchen goes the whole way and makes the Nephilim actual space aliens enhancing the human stock with their DNA.

79. Gunkel, *Genesis*, p. 59.

80. Id.

81. Irving Finkel, *The Ark before Noah: Decoding the Story of the Flood* (New York: Doubleday, 2014).

82. Correspondence with Robert M. Price, August 22, 2014.

83. Eliade, *Sacred and the Profane*, p. 38; Richard J. Clifford, *The Cosmic Mountain in Canaan and the Old Testament*. Harvard Semitic Monographs Volume 4 (Cambridge: Harvard University Press, 1972).

84. Graves and Patai, *Hebrew Myths*, p. 116.

85. Goldziher, *Mythology*, pp. 169-70.

86. Jubal had been a music god, Graves and Patai, *Hebrew Myths*, p. 110.

87. Graves and Patai, *Hebrew Myths*, p. 110.

88. Goldziher, *Mythology*, p. 322.

89. Gunkel, *Genesis*, p. 55.

90. Graves and Patai, *Hebrew Myths*, p. 119.

91. On the other hand, the Greek Deucalion is both the ark builder and the discoverer of wine.

92. Graves and Patai, *Hebrew Myths*, pp. 14-15, 122.

93. Graves and Patai, *Hebrew Myths*, p. 122, accept this reading from Wellhausen, though Gunkel rejects it (*Genesis*, p. 82).

94. Goldziher, *Mythology*, p. 131; Graves and Patai, *Hebrew Myths*, pp. 114, 121, 122, citing *B. Sanhedrin* 72a-b, 108b; *B. Pesahim* 113b; *Tanhuma Buber Gen.* 49-50; *Tanhuma Noah* 13, 15; *Genesis Rabbah* 341. They believed God punished Ham by turning him black! (Cf., 1 Nephi 12:23; 2 Nephi 5:21-22, where the evil Lamanites are punished with black skin, too.)

95. Goldziher, *Mythology*, p. 286.

96. Graves and Patai, *Hebrew Myths*, p. 128.

97. Gunkel, *Genesis*, p. 98.

98. Graves and Patai, *Hebrew Myths*, p. 128.

99. Graves and Patai, *Hebrew Myths*, p. 126.

100. Graves and Patai, *Hebrew Myths*, p. 128; Gunkel, *Genesis*, p. 98.

101. Gunkel, *Genesis*, p. xiv.

102. The Israelite amphictyony may not have existed historically, but in any event this common arrangement seems presupposed by the legends for literary purposes.

103. Albrecht Alt, "The Gods of the Fathers." In Alt, *Essays on Old Testament History and Religion*. Trans. R.A. Wilson (Garden City: Doubleday Anchor Books, 1968), pp. 1-86.

104. Gunkel, *Genesis*, p. ix.

105. Graves and Patai, *Hebrew Myths*, p. 178; Curtiss, *Primitive Semitic Religion Today*, Chapter XI, "High Places and Sacred Shrines," pp. 133-43.

106. Gunkel, *Genesis*, p. 187.

107. Gunkel, *Genesis*, p. 7.

108. In Late Antiquity urban bishops followed the same plan when they co-opted outlying places of religious power by removing the relics of saints and martyrs from local shrines and mausoleums and transferring them to city churches under their supervision. Peter Brown, *The Cult of the Saints: Its Rise and Function in Latin Christianity* Haskell Lectures on the History of Religions, New Series, No. 2 (Chicago: University of Chicago Press, 1981), pp. 32-33, 42. Of course, this also explains the reluctance of the Vatican to recognize apparitions of the Virgin Mary in far-flung places of devotion.

109. Gunkel, *Legends*, p. 102.

110. Mark C. Goodacre, "Fatigue in the Synoptics." In *New Testament Studies* 44 (1998), pp. 45-58.

111. The similarity between Abram and Sarai's sojourn in and departure from Egypt in Genesis 12:10-20 and the Moses version in Exodus only reinforces the point: the redundancy implies they are alternative versions, just as the three Patriarchal stories themselves are. To make them episodes in the same sequential narrative (Genesis-Exodus) is a harmonization.

112. "It was a classic observation of Pentateuchal criticism that there were great blocks of tradition seamed together. The Exodus saga is joined to the saga of the patriarchs by the seaming in Exod. 3.13ff, where Yahweh is identified with the God of the patriarchs." Barker, *Older Testament*, p. 167.

113. Graves and Patai, *Hebrew Myths*, p. 154. Compare 1 Samuel 11:7.

114. Gerd Theissen, *The Miracle Stories of the Early Christian Tradition*. Trans. Francis McDonagh (Philadelphia: Fortress Press, 1983), p. 56.

115. Goldziher, *Mythology*, p. 96.

116. Gunkel, *Genesis*, p. 211.

117. Gunkel, *Genesis*, pp. 193, 198. Lot? *Righteous?* He was willing to toss his virgin daughters into the street to be gang-raped!? We are supposed to understand Lot to be willing to make any sacrifice rather than betray strangers whom he has offered shelter. Gunkel at p. 207.

118. Gunkel, *Genesis*, p. 207.

119. Derrick Sherwin Bailey, *Homosexuality and the Western Christian Tradition* (London: Longmans, Green, 1955), pp. 4-5.

120. Graves and Patai, *Hebrew Myths*, p. 168, citing *Sepher Hayashar* 62. (This was a twelfth-century C.E. attempt to supply the lost Book of Jasher mentioned in 2 Samuel 1:17-18.)

121. Graves and Patai, *Hebrew Myths*, p. 117.

122. Gunkel, *Genesis*, pp. 211-12.

123. Graves and Patai at p. 169.

124. Gunkel at p. 210.

125. Gunkel at p. 217.

126. Graves and Patai at p. 171.

127. Goldziher, *Mythology*, p. 117.

128. Graves and Patai, *Hebrew Myths*, offer the definition "Ram Is my Father," a theophoric name (p. 165), making "Abram" a variant of "Abiram."

129. Goldziher at pp. 92-93.

130. An episode of *Star Trek: The Next Generation*, "Masks," written by Joe Menosky, Season 7, episode 17, depicts the very same myth in striking fashion.

131. Graves and Patai at pp. 176-77.

132. Shalom Spiegel, *The Last Trial: On the Legends and Lore of the Command to Abraham to Offer Isaac as a Sacrifice: The Akedah.* Trans. Judah Goldin. A Jewish Lights Classic Reprint (Woodstock VT: Jewish Lights Publishing, 1993), pp. 38-44, 48-50.

133. Spiegel, *Last Trial*, p. 32-33.

134. M.J. Field, *Angels and Ministers of Grace: An Ethno-Psychiatrist's Contribution to Biblical Criticism* (New York: Hill and Wang, 1972), pp. 23, 34-35, 105-108.

135. René Girard, *Violence and the Sacred.* Trans. Patrick Gregory (Baltimore: John Hopkins University Press, 1979), p. 73; Robert M. Price, *Deconstructing Jesus* (Amherst: Prometheus Books, 2000), pp. 173-74.

136. Graves and Patai, *Hebrew Myths*, pp. 158-59.

137. Gunkel, *Genesis*, p. 188.

138. Graves and Patai, *Hebrew Myths*, p. 191.

139. Graves and Patai at pp. 16, 195, 200.

140. Goldziher, *Mythology*, pp. 127-28, 134-37, 139-40.

141. Gunkel at pp. 105-106.

142. Graves and Patai, *Hebrew Myths*, p. 229; Gunkel, *Legends*, p. 31.

143. Graves and Patai at p. 199.

144. Graves and Patai at p, 128.

145. Goldziher, *Mythology*, p. 162. Graves and Patai, *Hebrew Myths*, take "Leah" to mean "wild cow," a nomad's goddess or totem animal (p. 21).

146. Goldziher, *Mythology*, pp. 162-65; Graves and Patai, *Hebrew Myths*, p. 218.

147. Goldziher at pp. 171-73.

148. Goldziher at pp. 125-26.

149. Another version of the name "Jacob."

150. Graves and Patai, *Hebrew Myths*, p. 229; Jack Miles, "Jacob's Wrestling Match: Was it an Angel or Esau?" In Hershel Shanks, ed., *Abraham & Family: New Insights into the Patriarchal Narratives* (Washington DC: Biblical Archaeology Society, 2000), pp. 117-20.

151. Curtiss, *Primitive Semitic Religion Today*, pp. 75-95.

152. Gunkel, *Genesis*, p. 368.

153. Barker, *Older Testament*, pp. 94-97.

154. Dieter Georgi, *The Opponents of Paul in Second Corinthians*. Trans. Harold Attridge, Isabel and Thomas Best, Bernadette Brooten, Ron Cameron, Frank Fallon, Stephen Gero, Renate Rose, Herman Waetjen, and Michael Wiliams (Philadelphia: Fortress Press, 1986; orig. 1964), pp. 44-46. And see Juvenal's Sixth Satire: a "palsied Jewess/ Parking her haybox outside, comes round soliciting alms / In a breathy whisper. She knows, and can interpret, / The Laws of Jerusalem: a high-priestess-under-the-trees, / A faithful mediator of Heaven on earth. She too / Fills her palm, but more sparingly: Jews will sell you / Whatever dreams you like for a few small coppers." Juvenal, *The Sixteen Satires*. Trans. Peter Green. Penguin Classics (Baltimore: Penguin Books, 1974), pp. 147-48.

155. This reflects the practice of Egyptian Pharaohs wedding their sisters, though not impregnating them. A priest of this or that god, ostensibly temporarily incarnating him, would impregnate the queen. This pretense of sibling marriage was meant to maintain the fiction of a pure line of descent with no admixture of non-royal blood.

II

Exodus, Leviticus, Numbers, Deuteronomy

Moses, the Torah Made Flesh

Fleeing Phantoms

For a long time, Christians bragged how archaeological discoveries confirmed the biblical history in instance after instance. Only recently have we realized that this was an illusion created by people like William Foxwell Albright, a devout Presbyterian who set out to vindicate the accuracy of the Bible,[1] not exactly an objective approach. He would find some site and match it up with something in the Bible on the assumption that the Bible must be right ("Ruins of a city in the Dead Sea? Must be Sodom!").[2]

Since then, the situation has reversed itself in a dramatic way. Any would-be defender of the historical accuracy of the Old Testament is out on a creaking limb, sitting next to the defender of the Book of Mormon with its tales of Israelites in ancient America. It's a lost cause. It's time to get real. There was no historical exodus, no liberation of a group of Hebrew slaves from Egypt led by Moses, Charlton Heston, or anyone else. You can't even strip away the Technicolor of miracles and call what remains "history."

It is a simple matter of archaeological evidence. The trouble is, there *isn't* any. Pick any of the possible routes from Egypt, through the Sinai desert, and into Canaan proposed by scholars. Pick either of the suggested dates, 1200 B.C.E. or 1450 B.C.E. It's just not going to work because a mass migration of people and animals such as the Bible depicts must and will leave behind a great amount of detritus, and there is none.

We have infrared aerial photography capable of detecting ancient caravan routes though featureless deserts, and yet technology reveals no sign of the passage of the Bible characters. What could have happened, you ask? Uh, maybe God sent down an angelic clean-up crew like they do after tickertape parades through Manhattan, and they vacuumed up all the evidence? Just like Satan fabricated and planted all those dinosaur bones to dupe us into believing in evolution?

Most of the Old Testament "history" of Israel now appears to be nationalistic fiction, what G. Ernest Wright called "a theology of recital,"[3] implying an epic, not a history. It now appears that the ancient Hebrews were simply one more subgroup of Canaanites, as the cognate similarities between their religions and languages make clear. There is no archaeological evidence of either an exodus from Egypt or a conquest of Palestine. Knowing this, we are freed up to look for some alternate content and purpose to the stories, and there is indeed plenty of it.

For one thing, it may make the best sense to suggest, as Old Testament Minimalists do, that by far most of the narrative, pseudo-historical material in the Old Testament was assembled in order to provide a fabricated heritage for Jews moving "back" to Palestine (or Canaan, or the Holy Land or whatever you want to call it) from the Persian Empire.[4] It was the practice of the Persians to play a kind of shell game with their subject peoples, relocating them to hitherto-foreign lands and telling them they were doing them a big favor, "returning" them to their ancestral homelands, when in fact their ancestors had never dwelt there.[5] (There may be a hint of this in the Exodus 12:38 statement that a "mixed multitude" left Egypt in the exodus.)

The Book of Ezra plainly states that Ezra, an official of the Persian Empire, journeyed from Persia to Jerusalem "with the law of your God which is in your hand" (Ezra 7:14), a document which formed the basis for the subsequent reorganization of Judea and the building (rebuilding?) of the Temple. Part of this agenda was to "re"institute the celebration of the Passover, supposedly long "neglected" (1 Esdras 1:17-21).

More than likely, the Passover was an innovation, and the Exodus accounts which mention it were cooked up for the occasion to give the rite an ancient-seeming pedigree. As we will soon see, a great number of the anecdotes in Exodus, Leviticus, and Numbers serve in this manner to retroactively legitimatize later Jewish ritual practices.

Naturally this hardly means all this material was cooked up on the spot by some Persian writers staff. Many of the episodes may well go back much further as genuine folktales. We needn't imagine Judaism was completely the product of Ezra and some committee, but they *would* seem to have put it into its familiar, "official" form.

Basket Case

Very few of the stories featuring Moses can be considered biography, even as fictive biography. Moses figures in most of the tales as a kind of stand-in for God. It is he, for the most part, who reveals God's will and issues his commandments. He levels the Almighty's judgments and is the instrument of God's miracles. As Liberal Protestant theologian Albrecht Ritschl once said of Jesus, Moses "has the value of God for us" readers. By my count, there are really only seven stories in Exodus that center on Moses.

The first is the account of a paranoid Pharaoh fearing that one day the burgeoning Hebrew community, descended from Joseph's brothers and previously welcomed into Egypt as honored guests, may try to usurp power. Thus he deems it the wisest course to nip the next generation in the bud, ordering the Hebrew midwives to snuff out every male Hebrew baby.

The narrator names the midwives as Shiphrah and Puah, implying there are only two of them to serve a Hebrew community that is so numerous that Pharaoh fears their power! These women do not carry out his orders, and Pharaoh demands to know why. Thinking fast, these ladies "explain" that Hebrew women are so hardy and vigorous that they have no use for midwives, giving birth so quickly that midwives always arrive too late. Uh . . . and the Hebrews need midwives in the first place . . . *why*? It's as if a community of vegetarians employed a couple of kosher butchers. We are dealing with comedy here.

Similarly, in chapter 5, Pharaoh has sunk to the level of a melodrama villain, intent on tormenting the Hebrews by forcing them to find their own straw to make bricks, something he would never do if he wanted efficient work, as the frame story clearly supposes he does: He employs foremen, etc.

Pharaoh, depicted like a bumbling Nazi on the sitcom *Hogan's Heroes*, is stupid enough to fall for this but still orders that baby Hebrew boys must be exposed. Amram and Jochebed (named in Exodus 6:20) seem to have picked the wrong time to have a baby, but here he comes! His distraught parents entrust him to providence, packing the infant into a kind of picnic basket lined with blankets and set him adrift on the Nile, hoping for the best. His big sister, Miriam, runs along the river bank to keep an eye on him as long as she can. The basket comes to rest in the bulrushes at the edge of the water, where Pharaoh's daughter "happens" to spot it. She sends one of her handmaids to fetch it and is surprised to find a Hebrew boy aboard! (He is circumcised already, whereas Egyptians practiced circumcision as a puberty rite.)[6] She decides then and there to adopt the baby as her own.

Having followed these developments from her hiding place, Miriam pops up and says she happens to know a Hebrew woman who could probably be persuaded to serve as nursemaid to the boy. Approving, the princess sends Miriam off to recruit this woman–

who, of course, is the boy's mother. The irony here is rich. The boy was almost killed because Pharaoh wanted to prevent a possible Hebrew threat to his regime, but the scheme backfires royally. That very ploy results in bringing into his own palace the one who will overthrow Egypt! And Jochabed, willing to trust her newborn son to God's keeping, gets him back and is able to bring him up in the luxury of the royal palace. It is, all told, a masterpiece–of fiction.

The central device of exposing the infant and his providential rescue was already familiar from the myths of Oedipus, Romulus and Remus, Cyrus of Persia, Perseus, and the Assyrian Emperor Sargon. The Sargon version is especially close to Moses'. "I am Sargon, the mighty king, king of Agade [Akkad] . . . my mother, the high priestess, conceived me; in secret she bore me. She set me in a basket of rushes; with bitumen, she sealed my lid. She cast me into the river, which rose not over me . . ."[7]

The clincher (which makes this in part an etymological, or name-origin, myth) is the shaggy-dog story punch-line: Exodus 2:10 says, "She named him 'Moses,' for she said, 'I drew him out of the water.'" You see, "Moses" (Hebrew *Moshe*) is here imagined to be derived from the Hebrew *mashah*, "to draw forth from." That's why they borrowed this standard nativity myth, to account for the boy being named Moses, as if to commemorate the occasion and means of his rescue. (And why would his adoptive mother, an Egyptian, give him a Hebrew name?[8] Why would she let her nursemaid name him?) In fact, "Moses" is an Egyptian name, or half of one. It means "begotten" and forms part of various Pharaohs' names. "Tut*mose*" means "Thoth has begotten him." "Ra*mses*" means "Ra has begotten him." It would not be strange for an Egyptian prince to bear such a name, and such was Moses, by adoption. But later Hebrews felt uneasy that the great founder of their faith should not have borne a good Hebrew name, so they contrived a pun allowing them to pretend "Moses" was a Hebrew name after all. Pretty clever. But not historical.

Moses the Second Jacob

The remaining six "biographical" stories of Moses appear to have originated as rewrites of stories first told of the Patriarch Jacob. Consider these parallels between the biographies of Moses and Jacob.[9]

Moses vs. Jacob

Scene	Moses Version	Jacob Version
Flees eastward	Exod. 2:15	Gen. 27:41-28:5
Helps native woman at well	Exod. 2:16-17ff.	Gen. 29:1-12
Serves father-in-law as herdsman	Exod. 3:1	Gen. 29:18; 30:29, etc.
God appears, tells him to return west	Exod. 3:1-10ff.	Gen. 31:13
Returns with wife/wives & children	Exod. 4:20	Gen.31:17-21
God ambushes him	Exod. 4:24-26	Gen. 32:22-32

The second one is what Robert Alter[10] calls a "type scene" occurring throughout scripture. More of the same are to be found in Genesis 24 and John 4.

Which cycle of tales was original, and which is the copy? I suggest that the Jacob cycle came first, and this for two reasons. First, the Patriarchal traditions seem to remember the archaic period of "the gods of the Fathers" posited by Albrecht Alt,[11] when the God of Abraham, the Strong One of Jacob, and the Fear of Isaac were separate totems of separate clans, combined later, once the three clans joined together and their eponymous ancestors, in order of clan seniority, were fictively made father, son, and grandson. Jacob was the fictive ancestor of the southern, Judean tribes, while Abraham would have been the fictive ancestor of the Hebrew tribe of Raham, unattested in the Bible but mentioned in the Egyptian inscription of Sethos I about 1300 B.C.E. Thus "Abraham" might have been understood as meaning "Raham is my Father." This sub-tribe, merged into Judah, must have retained enough prestige to have their eponymous ancestor retained and even given top billing over Jacob.[12]

Second, form-critically, when we look at the specific *raison d'être* of each story in each cycle, it looks as if each of the Jacob tales, prior to its inclusion in a connected sequence, had a distinct purpose (etymological, ethnological, ceremonial. etc.), whereas most of the Moses stories in this sequence seem to function simply to move the narrative along to the exodus events, or to fill in the biography of Moses. With the exception of Exodus 4:24-26, they appear to have no form-critical prehistory, no function to account for their preservation and transmission. In short, the Jacob stories appear to be indigenous growths from various roots, not the result of copying from a prior source, while most of the Moses stories can be explained as copies since they do not serve other, prior, purposes.

The Plagues
Exod. 6-11

The grand narrative of the Plagues begins the story of the exodus proper, which continues through the crossing of the Sea of Reeds, then the giving of the Law. This sequence seems to have had nothing originally to do with either the Patriarchal legends or that of Joshua's conquest of Canaan. Not even the Wilderness Wanderings formed part of the original exodus motif. All these legend cycles have subsequently been sewn together.[13]

Not only that, but the story of the Plagues as we read it is itself a composite of three different versions. It was a tale told many times among groups of Jews who apparently traced their national origins no further back than as a slave population in Egypt.[14] Presumably, this was a story told by Diaspora Jews in Ptolemaic Egypt who wanted to minimize their "foreign" character by telling themselves that they had "really" *returned* to their original homeland. (In the same way, the story of Abraham setting out from his native Chaldea and making his way to Canaan seems to have been an attempt by Babylonian Jews, in the time of King Nabonidus, to claim a Mesopotamian origin and thus (fictive) kinship with their Babylonian neighbors.)[15]

Various versions of the Plagues story were making the rounds, and our collectors, J, E, and P, each chose the one most familiar to him. According to J (the Yahwhist) there were seven plagues:

1. Water turns to blood

2. Frog infestation

3. Flies

4. Cattle slain

5. Hailstorm

6. Locust devastation

7. Death of firstborn sons

Psalm 78 reflects this list (though that Psalmist need not have borrowed it from a written J document.). The Elohist has his own versions of 1, 5, 6, and 7, adding "thick darkness" (a dust storm?[16]). The Priestly writer repeats 1, 2, and 7, adding gnats and boils. The final, composite list has 10 in all, and Psalm 105 reflects this list.

Various of the plagues seem to reflect actual conditions in Egypt, especially connected with the annual flooding of the Nile in August. The water may turn red because of a concentration of red flagella ("whip-tails"), microbes washed down from the Mediterranean. This would poison the fish. As their finny little carcasses drifted downstream, the frogs, quite disturbed by this "dawn of the dead," would hop ashore, waiting their turn to die from the same microbe which they'd caught from the fish. Then they would lie about in stinking, rotting heaps, attracting flies and gnats, as well as diseases fatal to cattle and humans. A few months later the annual hailstorms, sandstorms, and locust devastations would have done their seasonal harm.

The story-tellers have thus retained some "local color" without realizing that these were fairly common and altogether natural events. They assumed these disasters were unique, miraculous occurrences. This means that the stories were told very far away from Egypt. It's as if someone did not know what had actually destroyed Hiroshima and Nagasaki and said it was Godzilla.[17]

The Priestly author has Aaron accompany Moses in these stories, elevating Aaron to the main miracle worker because, being a priest himself, the P writer wanted to magnify this symbolic figurehead of all priests.[18] The artificiality of this character, supposedly Moses' brother, is evident from the suspicious fact that he just pops up once Moses moves to Midian. Where was this guy during Moses' Nativity story? Floating down the Nile in a second basket?

Why does God repeatedly "harden Pharaoh's heart" so that he again and again reneges on his promises to let Moses' people leave Egypt? We don't have to guess. God explicitly tells Moses that he will just keep setting Pharaoh up to knock him down again (Exod. 4:21; 6:1; 7:3-5; 10:1-20). He doesn't want to make his deliverance of the children of Israel look too easy! He wants the bout to last the full number of rounds even if he must prop up his opponent.

Some have suggested that the story also implies God's triumph over the Egyptian pantheon, beating each god at his own specialty, since of course the Egyptians had a deity in charge of each of the natural phenomena that Yahweh uses to clobber Pharaoh. He learns the hard way that no help is to be expected from that direction!

Passover and the Feast of Unleavened Bread

Exod. 12-13

Passover (Exod. 13:11-15) was originally a shepherd's feast, the Feast of Firstlings, when you would sacrifice the firstborn lambs in gratitude to your god for a good bearing of sheep. Originally it had nothing to do with the exodus from Egypt (which never happened anyway), but was already celebrated as an ancient tradition even in the story *prior* to the "first" Passover (see 3:18). Ancient Bedouin herdsmen observed the feast in the desert as well. They offered it to the moon god, whose gentle illumination they preferred to the blistering glare of the daytime sun.

You would sacrifice to your god the firstborn lamb and eat it ritually, as if sharing the meal with the god, imagined to be invisibly present. You ate it raw and in haste, in order to be finished by the time the god departed, i.e., when the sun rose, blotting out the lesser orbs. Exodus 12:18 tells us the Passover feast had to be celebrated at the full moon (the middle day of the month by their lunar calendar), implying this was the original herders' god in whose honor the feast was first celebrated.[19] This must be why they had to eat it before sunrise (Exod. 12:9-11). As with all the sacred feasts, which were at first agricultural in nature, the Feast of Firstlings and of the First Fruits have been reinterpreted as memorials for great acts of God on Israel's behalf.

Whence the element of the blood being brushed on the doorposts and lintel of each house? This seems to reflect an ancient custom (still observed), whereby one sacrifices a lamb, etc., on the threshold of a new house in order to placate God or the jinn or the Grim Reaper so that death might skip the dwelling in the future. ("I gave at the office.") Every household, it is believed, must sooner or later lose a member to death, and this is a trick to get it out of the way with a token death to satisfy the Reaper.[20] But here the superstitious practice has been given a commemorative reinterpretation, a better, more pious reason for observing it. Even the prowling Grim Reaper against whom one sought exemption by the smearing of blood has been taken over into the biblical adaptation of the custom as "the Destroyer" (Exod. 12:23; cf., 1 Cor. 10:10; Rev. 9:11) who goes from house to house, slaying the unprotected firstborn.[21]

The unleavened bread (12:34, 39) was at first simply part of another agricultural feast: One ate bread without leaven so as to eat it in its purest possible form as a thank-offering to the god for his bounty. All three customs have been supplied with a Yahwist, theological-historical pedigree.

The Sea of Reeds

Exod. 13-14

The Hebrew text says the Israelites crossed the Sea of Reeds, not the Red Sea, which is a much larger body of water. (For some reason the translators of the Greek Septuagint mistranslated it as "Red Sea.") As its name would suggest, the Sea of Reeds (*Yam Suf*) was a marsh. What is supposed to have happened there?

Some have suggested that Mt. Sinai, a volcano, erupted just as the Israelites found themselves pursued by Egyptian troops and trapped, backs to the sea. The seismic activity caused a land bridge to rise from the sea bed, pushed up by subterrene gasses. It remained on the surface long enough for the Israelites to cross over but collapsed, the gasses already dissipating, beneath the heavier weight of the Egyptian host. Such events have been documented, e.g., near Naples, September 29, 1538, and near Martinique in 1902.

In both cases there was also a pillar of fire (i.e., a floating incandescent gas cloud) as in Exodus. But all this presupposes a real sea, not a marsh. (But then again, so does part of the Exodus account.) This approach was a product of the old Protestant Rationalism whose adherents rejected belief in divine interventions in the course of nature but still believed all the stories in scripture were historically accurate. They figured that the "real," scientific causes remained mysterious to the ancients who therefore described these striking events as miracles.

It had not yet occurred to the Rationalists that *nothing* had happened; the stories are myths and legends, pure and simple. They are based on traces of an earlier, less spectacular version according to which there was a straightforward military clash in which Israel was the upset winner. (This is all J material.)

> Now when Pharaoh had let the people go, God did not lead them by the way of the land of the Philistines, even though it was near; for God said, "The people might change their minds when they see war, and return to Egypt." Hence God led the people around by the way of the wilderness to the Red Sea; and the sons of Israel went up in martial array from the land of Egypt. (Exod. 13:17-18, NASB)

The Egyptians' chariot wheels got clogged up and slowed them down, not a surprising result of driving narrow hard rims on soft marshy ground. The Israelites would have crossed the reedy marsh at night and lain in wait, anticipating correctly that the heavy cavalry and chariots of Pharaoh's army would become mired in the mud. Horses threw their riders in panic, and the well-armed Israelites cut their discomfited foes to pieces.

Exodus 14:25-31 couples the clogged-up wheels with a story of the sea miraculously returning and leaving the Egyptians dead on the seashore. As in other Old Testament battles, the occasion got commemorated in mythic poetry suggesting that God alone won the victory (just as Evander Holyfield once claimed no credit for pounding Mike Tyson into submission, crediting the Holy Spirit with guiding his punches). This pious talk is later taken literally, as if Israel had been purely passive, watching from the sidelines. Had he decided to bring this version to the screen, Cecil B. DeMille could have saved a lot of money on the special effects.[22]

The Torah

Exod. 18-19

Moses is the figurehead of Hebrew law. His name appears on every Israelite law code except Ezekiel's, and that may be because some questioned the divine status of the latter.[23] Originally Moses may have been a sun god, a type of deity associated with giving laws. Notice the association of the law and the sun in Psalm 19, originally part of Akhenaten's *Hymn to the Sun*. Like the sun, Moses emerges from the tent (of meeting), glowing with light, to offer new laws (Exod. 34:29-35). Shamash the Babylonian sun god is depicted as giving Hammurabi's Code to him in the carving atop our stone copy of it. This story of the theophany atop Sinai must have been composed in Babylon, as the author depicts Moses' tables of the Law in terms that imply the writer thought of them as terra cotta tablets common in Babylon, easily broken, inscribed on both sides with the small lettering of cuneiform.[24]

But an earlier, simpler depiction of Moses as an inspired lawgiver had nothing to do with climbing a holy mountain or receiving stone tablets carved by the finger of an anthropomorphic deity. Exodus 19 shows us a recurring scene whereby, day after day, Moses sat beside the brook in the Wilderness of Kadesh (i.e., "the Holy Place"), patiently hearing cases (as ancient kings did–see 1 Kings 3:16-27), then rendering a verdict. These judgments would then be compiled as a set of legal precedents for use the next time a similar case came up. Here Moses is portrayed in the image of the oracular *kohenim*, or law-giving priests/seers (Hag. 2:11; Deut. 33:8, 10),[25] who would sit beneath the rustling palm trees (Judg. 4:4-5) or by the babbling brook and go into a trance, interpreting the sounds as the voice of God (Exod. 15:22-25; 18:13-16). The image of his receiving engraved stone tablets is a later, more spectacular version,[26] possibly suggested by the common sight of actual posted legal tablets in the Jewish quarters of Babylon (just as some champion the posting of the commandments in American courtrooms and classrooms today).

The Book of the Covenant

Exod. 20:20-23:33

The Sinai story combines older law codes. The first is *The Book of the Covenant* (Exod. 20:20-23:33). This is the earliest of the many "Mosaic" codes, often thought to have been composed about 740-640 B.C.E.[27] It commands the sacrifice of firstborn sons along with the firstborn of livestock (22:29-30). Elsewhere, e.g., Exodus 13:12-13, we find an amended version in which parents are allowed to substitute an animal for the offering of their sons.

But that doesn't change the fact that originally the Hebrew God had a taste for tender human flesh. The story of Abraham nearly sacrificing Isaac, then being prevented at the last moment (Gen. 22:1-14) seems to have been aimed at facilitating the transition from infant sacrifice to animal substitution. The prophet Ezekiel looks back on the old law with bemusement, imagining God later rationalizing his outrageous command: "I also gave them statutes that were not good and ordinances by which they could not live; and I pronounced them unclean because of their gifts, in that they caused all their firstborn to pass through the fire so that I might make them desolate, in order that they might know that I am [Yahweh]" (Ezek. 20:25-26, NASB). That seems kind of sadistic, but it must have been the best Ezekiel could come up with. He couldn't just deny God had ever commanded such a thing; it was too well known.

This code also gives instructions (Exod. 20:24-25) for the construction of local altars (the "high places") to mark any place where anyone had received a vision or a dream of God[28] (as Jacob does in Genesis 28:10-22). Subsequently all such altars were outlawed (Deut. 12) and shut down (2 Kings 23:5, 8, 13, 15, 19-20). Note that Moses is depicted as commanding the construction of local altars in Exodus but forbidding them in Deuteronomy. It is not that Moses changed his mind; rather scribes kept replacing old law codes with new ones, with different provisions, and all alike were fathered on Moses. It's easy to understand why: Are you going to junk the Law of Moses and substitute the Law of Phil or the Statutes of Bif?

Does "Mosaic" law address the topic of pre-marital sex? There is nothing about it in either of the two sets of Ten Commandments (see below). The Book of the Covenant comes the closest to treating the question.

> If a man seduces a virgin who is not engaged, and lies with her, he must pay a dowry for her to be his wife. If her father absolutely refuses to give her to him, he shall pay money equal to the dowry for virgins. (Exod. 22:16-17, NASB)

But this is not a matter of sexual morality at all. Instead, it is a case of property rights, those of the woman's father. The hypothetical case under discussion takes for granted that only a virgin is acceptable for marriage. Otherwise, she is "used goods."

Now suppose a young woman is swept off her feet by some burnoose-clad lothario with no honorable intentions. Well, her father is up the creek: Now he can't marry her off to anyone else, which means he is stuck with one more mouth to feed forever *and* he will not receive the bride-price a daughter's suitor would give for her. So what do they do? The answer is a shotgun wedding. The gigolo is going to have to marry her. Not exactly the ideal husband! But suppose the guy is *such* a stinker that dad cannot bring himself to hand over his daughter to him. The seducer is free to go his merry way to the next virgin, but not until he pays an amount equivalent to the bride-price. It's almost surprising he wasn't tasked with paying ongoing "father-in-law support"!

In any case, the value of female virginity in all this is purely economic, like that of a doll in mint condition, still in the box. Not much moral guidance here. The law itself certainly shows some practical wisdom; it's just that there is no *other* law that *does* deal with the ethical issue.

There are extreme fundamentalists who advocate the wholesale adoption of biblical law to govern modern America, but one may wonder whether they have ever actually bothered to *read* these laws. For example, the present code has quite a bit to say on the subject of slavery. One may sell one's daughter as a slave if one needs a few extra bucks

(Exod. 21:7). If you have a slave (in this case, an indentured servant, perhaps someone working off a debt) and you supply a wife for him, when his term is up and he is free to leave, he can't take his wife and children with him. They remain the property of ol' Massa. If the husband is reluctant to leave his family behind, he is welcome to accept permanent slavery to stay with them (21:3-6).

Suppose the slave angers his master (too slow in bringing him his Mint Julep?), and the master hauls off and slugs him. Guess what happens? "If a man strikes his male or female slave with a rod and he dies at his hand, he shall be punished. If, however, he survives a day or two, no vengeance shall be taken; for [the slave] is his property." (Exod. 21:20-21, NASB). Can someone who wants to make *this* the law of the land even be considered *sane*?

Anyone who thinks such commandments really are the revealed word of God might as well be a card-carrying member of the Taliban. Or how about *this* one? "Whoever curses his father or his mother shall be put to death" (21:15). "Tough love," huh? The only way to mitigate the horrific character of this stuff is to remind ourselves that these commandments are part and parcel of an ancient, alien culture. But that really does not help much. Even if you are willing to grant that these ancients lacked our more enlightened perspective, surely God did not lack it. Go ahead; chalk it up to "progressive revelation" if you want, but that's just a dodge. You mean God knew he would be expecting too much from these Neanderthals if he tried teaching them the basics of civilized morality? That is just absurd.

Remember, the Old Testament is all about God giving the Torah to his chosen people to make them "a light unto the nations" (Isa. 42:6), showing how superior to heathenism a nation's life can be if it lives as God's law directs. Granted, Hammurabi's Code is even more severe; this Book of the Covenant constitutes a real advance, but can we really imagine it is a transcript of the will of God? Good luck![29]

The provisions of this code (and those of Leviticus and Deuteronomy) are anachronistic, grossly ill-suited to the lifestyle of a bunch of desert nomads. They presuppose a settled, agricultural mode of life. To picture Moses giving this set of laws to a generation that wouldn't have known what to do with them, laws that would apply only to subsequent, settled generations, is fully as ridiculous as imaging the Hebrew prophets predicting events centuries, or even millennia in the future.[30] "Yeah, so what?"

It has long been known that this particular "Mosaic" law collection bears certain striking similarities to the much older Code of Hammurabi, but it now looks as if the Exodus version is directly based on the Hammurabi Code.[31] I recall once hearing porn-star-turned-televangelist Pastor Melissa Scott dismissing a similar theory of some Bible story being based on another ancient tale: "God's not a copycat." Presumably not, but that doesn't mean that ancient scribes weren't copycats. What it does is raise some doubt as to whether the whole thing came directly from God's mouth to the biblical writers' ears.

The Book of the Covenant mixes, from multiple older sources, two distinct types of commandments, the *casuistic* and the *apodictic*.[32] The former typically start, "If your neighbor's ox eats your Chihuahua . . ." Much of this is tort law. All mundane rules are placed under the aegis of divine authority as part of the larger code ascribed as a whole to God, but they are essentially secular and come from Hammurabi's Code or Near Eastern legal tradition generally. Apodictic laws, on the other hand, are brief, terse, and usually negative in form ("Thou shalt not . . ."). These seem to be oracular verdicts pronounced in a mantic state by the priests (the same word also means "soothsayers"), as in Haggai 2:11 or 1 Maccabees 4:46. In general, they match the apodictic laws in Hammurabi's Code, so some of them may have been adopted from there, but then the originals were probably the product of Babylonian oracles in the first place.

Ten Plus Ten Commandments
Exod. 20 // Exod. 34, Deut. 5:4-21

A second set of laws is two-fold. We have two very different lists of Ten Commandments, both said to be received by Moses atop Mt. Sinai. As with most sets of parallel passages, these represent rival, variant versions of the same tradition. Each offers what someone considered to be the "top ten" commandments. The rabbis used to kick around the hypothetical question: "Which commandment is the first of all?" (Mark 12:28). The most important, that is.

Which is the center of gravity? Jesus suggests not only the first but the runner-up as well. In the same way, earlier in Jewish history the scribes must have ranked what they regarded as the ten most important, and there were competing lists. But why *ten*? Some have suggested it was a mnemonic device. It would help to remember them if you could count them on your fingers:[33] "Hmmm . . . I've got a finger left. Which commandment am I forgetting? Oh yes! 'Thou shalt not put thine elbows on the table!'" Psalm 15 suggests a possible occasion and purpose for such checklists (ASV):

> Jehovah, who shall sojourn in thy tabernacle?
>   Who shall dwell in thy holy hill?
>
> He that [1] walketh uprightly, and [2] worketh righteousness,
>   And [3] speaketh truth in his heart;
> He that [4] slandereth not with his tongue,
>   [5] Nor doeth evil to his friend,
>   [6] Nor taketh up a reproach against his neighbor;
> In whose eyes [7] a reprobate is despised,[34]
>   But who honoreth them that fear Jehovah;
>   He that [8] sweareth to his own hurt, and changeth not;[35]
> He that [9] putteth not out his money to interest,
>   Nor taketh [10] reward [*a bribe*] against the innocent.
>
> He that doeth these things shall never be moved.

This poem (hymn lyrics) can be read very naturally as something analogous to the baptismal creed used in liturgical churches. Notice that, depending on how you divide them up, Psalm 15 may be counted as a set of ten commandments in its own right. These would be the requirements for any pilgrim looking to enter the Temple on Mt. Zion. The point would be to prompt self-reflection before entering into the presence of God,[36] much as in 1 Corinthians 11:27-30. "Am I worthy?" You wouldn't want to incur God's wrath in the very act of worshipping him, as they did in Isaiah's day (Isa. 1:10-23)!

Our compiler did not feel at liberty to leave either Decalogue out, since each had its following, and he wanted to include all the material his readers would complain about if it were excluded. The first set is more familiar to us, and it is the one which we call "the Ten Commandments," though the Bible reserves that phrase to the next one, over in chapter 34, verse 28. The one we know best (Exod. 20:1-17) is often called the *Moral Decalogue*. The commandments (in both lists) must have begun as single sentences, though they are now embedded in later scribal commentary.

I. (v. 3) *"You shall have no other gods beside/before me."* This commands *monolatry*, the worship of one god, but not necessarily the belief that there *is* only one god. That would come later: "I am [Yahweh]! Beside me there is no other god!" (Isa. 44:6). Israel owes allegiance only to the God who liberated them. Had, say, Thoth or Dagon led them out of Egypt, then Israel would owe *them* worship. But it *wasn't* them, it was Yahweh.

II. (v. 4) *"You shall not make yourself a graven image."* Don't carve one, apparently to worship, even if it is intended to depict Yahweh himself. But this is not explicit, which is why we have all these further qualifications. No loopholes!

III. (v. 7) *"You shall not take the name of [Yahweh] your God in vain."* To know what "taking his name in vain" is supposed to mean, we have to ask what it would mean to take it (invoke it) *not* in vain. I think the commandment means to prohibit *perjury* and *breach of contract*: On the witness stand you would be sworn in with the charge, "Give glory to Yahweh, God of Israel!" as in Joshua 7:19. You might answer, "As Yahweh lives, I did not steal Herschel's karaoke machine!" And if you were making a legally binding pledge, you would invoke God to keep an eye on you and punish you if you neglected to hold up your end of the deal: "As Yahweh lives, I swear I will have your hot tub finished by the Spring." Laban invokes God to solemnize an agreement between himself and Jacob in Genesis 31:49-50. Thus you would be taking unto yourself the name of Yahweh in vain, i.e., falsely, if you lied under oath or if you broke your contract.

By contrast, there was nothing forbidden about invoking God's name to curse someone who had abused you. Noah curses Canaan in this way in Genesis 9:24-26.[37] Imprecatory Psalms such as 17:13-14; 35:1-6; 58:6; 59:11; 79:12; 137:7-9 might be considered instances of leveling curses invoking Yahweh.

IV. (v. 8) *"Remember the Sabbath to keep it holy."* To this short-and-sweet mandate have been added verses 9-10. They are the contribution of the Deuteronomic redactor (the editor of the Book of Deuteronomy and the Deuteronomic History, i.e., Joshua-Judges-Samuel-Kings).This addition supplies the same reason for observing the Sabbath found in Deuteronomy 5:14, namely humane treatment for slaves and livestock.[38] But verse 11 is yet a later addition by the Priestly writer, repeating the reason for the Sabbath found in the Priestly creation story (Gen. 2:2-3): God took a day off after a week of work, and so should you. Everybody had to throw his two cents in.

The Sabbath is Saturday, though Christians have reapplied the name (and the commandment) to Sunday. "Sabbath" means "seventh." It is not unlikely that the choice of this day reflects the early worship in some Hebrew circles of the Titan Saturn (Amos 5:25-26),[39] the seventh planet according to ancient reckoning. Being mindful of the holiness, the special status, of the day entailed safeguarding it from profanation by secular concerns. This may seem superstitious, but it is simple common sense: As soon as you allow work on the Sabbath, its holiness will inevitably get lost in the shuffle, "choked out by the cares of the world" (Mark 4:19).

Early Jewish Christians must have observed the Sabbath and the Lord's Day (Sunday) alongside it. Some Gentile converts observed both with others celebrating only Sunday. But some of the Gentile believers were still attending synagogue as well as church in the time of John Chrysostom (349-407). It looks as if Christians met for church on Sundays but did not refrain from work for either practical or theological reasons. This changed when the Christian Emperor Constantine forbade work on Sunday for the sake of slaves and employees whose work schedules had prevented them from attending church. From then on, Sunday was the Christian day of rest.

V. (v. 12) *"Honor your father and your mother."* This may, some think, be a reworded version of an earlier prohibition of cursing or hitting one's parents.[40] The negative version is still found nearby in Exodus 21:15 ("Whoever strikes his father or his mother shall be put to death") and 21:17 ("Whoever curses his father or his mother shall be put to death").[41]

VI. (v. 13) *"You shall not murder."* The Hebrew word is not without some ambiguity, but the way it is used in most contexts implies pretty strongly that it refers to unjustified, victimizing killing, in short, murder. It is rather difficult, given the historical-cultural context, to imagine an *ahimsa* commandment, forbidding hunting, butchering, warfare, or self-defense.[42]

VII. (v. 14) *"You shall not commit adultery."* The definition of adultery is, naturally, a function of one's definition of marriage. From the look of things throughout the Old Testament, marriage seems not to have ruled out polygyny (a husband with more than one wife), though polyandry (a wife with more than one husband) was unheard of, as presupposed in Mark 12:18-23. Polygyny was more scarce, though it still existed, in New Testament times. And, as far as I can see, for a man to visit prostitutes did not constitute adultery, perhaps echoing the thinking of Plutarch:

> The Persian kings have their lawful wives sit with them at dinner and feast with them. But when the kings wish to be sportive and get drunk they send their wives away and call in music girls [i.e., dancing girls] and concubines. This procedure is correct, for it prevents wives from participating in debauchery and drunkenness. Hence if a private individual who is prone to incontinent indulgence transgresses with a courtesan or servant girl his wife ought not to be vexed or cross but rather to reflect that it is respect for her that makes him choose another outlet for his drunkenness and incontinence and wantonness.[43]

But if a married woman decides to turn tricks to make some extra cookie jar money, that *does* count as adultery (Gen. 28:34; Prov. 6:20-35; 7:1-27). And, obviously, sneaking off to have sex with another's spouse qualifies, too.

VIII. (v. 15) *"You shall not steal."* Originally this commandment probably referred to kidnapping, or shanghaiing as a means of recruiting slaves.[44] See Exodus 21:16 ("Whoever steals a man, whether he sells him or is found in possession of him, shall be put to death") and Deuteronomy 24:7 ("If a man is found stealing one of his brethren, the people of Israel, and if he treats him as a slave or sells him, then that thief shall die"). Obviously, this was the crime of Joseph's brethren in Genesis 37:27-28.

IX. (v. 16) *"You shall not bear false witness against your neighbor."* No slander, libel, gossip, incriminating perjury. There might be some overlap between this one and the command not to swear falsely by the divine name, but this one points in a slightly different direction. One focuses on the violation of God's name used in a guarantee; the other has to do with the actual damage done to another. Still, the redundancy is another sign of the eclectic character of this whole list.

X. (v. 17) *"You shall not covet anything that is your neighbor's."* The ensuing list is an attempt to close any loopholes. This might be viewed as an early example of the hair-splitting rabbinical casuistry that eventually led, e.g., to the delineation of thirty-nine different categories of "work" to be avoided on the Sabbath.

Deuteronomy 5:4-21 gives a slightly modified version of the Decalogue we have just discussed, but there is an almost completely different *Ritual Decalogue* in Exodus 34:14-26, and, again, this is the one the Bible actually calls "the Ten Commandments" (34:28). It is at first quite a challenge to disentangle the brief, apodictic mandates from an obscuring thicket of subsequent embellishment and commentary, but when you do, you can isolate these commandments.

I. (v. 14) *"You shall worship no other god."*

II. (v. 17) *"You shall make yourselves no molten gods."*

III. (v. 18) *"You shall keep the Feast of Unleavened Bread."*

IV. (v. 19) *"All that opens the womb is mine."*

V. (v. 21) *"You shall work six days, but on the seventh you shall rest."*

VII. (v. 22-23) *"You shall observe the Feast of Weeks, the First Fruits of Wheat Harvest, and the Feast of Ingathering at the turn of the year."*

VIII. (v. 25) *"Neither shall the sacrifice of the Feast of the Passover be left until the morning."*

IX. (v. 26) *"The first fruits of your ground you shall bring to the house of [Yahweh] your God."*

X. (v. 26) *"You shall not boil a young goat in its mother's milk."* What on earth? Ever been tempted to break this commandment? It sounds like a cooking tip from Alton Brown, but the discovery of the Ras Shamra texts revealed that what this commandment means to prohibit is the casting of a particular magic spell using milk.[45]

Note that this set overlaps with the Exodus 20 Decalogue at only three points: the first, second, and fifth. This is significant because we are told this set of commandments was just a second copy of the one in chapter 20, which it obviously is not. Our editor has tried to harmonize the two Decalogues, neither of which he dared omit. He could not just combine them, because each list was known as the "ten," not the "seventeen commandments"![46] He tries to get the reader to accept the Ritual Decalogue as a replacement copy of the Moral Decalogue, placing the two far enough apart that perhaps we will have forgotten the first set by the time we get to the second. But why would the first set need to be replaced? Wait and see!

The Golden Calf

Exod. 32:2-6, 24

These verses probably preserve what was originally a ceremonial story told in the northern kingdom of Israel to explain to pilgrims/tourists the origin of the golden bull images under which Yahweh was worshipped in the temples at Dan and Bethel. Note the striking similarity between Aaron's words in Exodus 32:4 and King Jeroboam's words in 1 Kings 12:28-29, "Behold your God(s), O Israel, who brought you up out of the land of Egypt!" As the original story would have read, Aaron must have told the people to dump their gold into the vat, and it *did* miraculously come out in the form of a calf. The idea was that only God could show us how he preferred to be depicted, since no mortal had ever seen him.

What is our (southern, Judaic) editor to make of *this* little story? He regards it as blasphemy to make an image of God, as per Exodus 20:4, so he could not very well simply include the story as it stands. So he made what was originally a miracle into a pathetic excuse for idolatry and immorality. It is this idolatry that makes Moses so mad that he smashes the tablets in disgust. *Voila!* The "first" set is smashed, so he needs another, which he is going to get in chapter 34.

Deuteronomy

This "second law" purports to be a long-winded lecture by Moses to the up-and-coming generation of Israelites who had to wait till their parents' generation died off before they could enter the Promised Land. God had had enough of their parents who had been such ingrates during the Wilderness Wanderings, and so he decided they should never arrive at their initial goal. He would start over with the new crop. But before Joshua led them into Canaan, Moses gave them, ostensibly, a refresher course in the Law. Maybe they would not make the same mistakes as their griping, faithless elders, whose stubbornness rivaled that of Pharaoh himself. But this is all fiction.

For one thing, as we shall see below, the whole motif of "murmuring" and rebellion is a secondary layer, a polemic designed to blacken the reputation of the Northern tribes, suggesting that God had negated his covenant because of their unbelief, choosing instead the Judeans in the South (replacing the failed Mosaic Covenant with the Davidic Covenant). For another, Deuteronomy presupposes the secondary conception of the Wilderness Wanderings as a generation-long diversion from the goal (Canaan) instead of, as originally understood, the natural, chosen existence of the Israelite nomads.

Yet again, there is the little matter of the Deuteronomic laws constituting a new and updated code quite different from the Book of the Covenant. The situation is precisely parallel to that of the Golden Calf story being used to harmonize the two different sets of Ten Commandments by pretending one was simply a copy of the other. In this case, the idea of Moses bringing the younger generation of Israel up to speed on the eve of the conquest of Canaan is intended to disguise the fact that Deuteronomy's laws represent a different code. Nor does it make any sense to view this "second law" as a revision or an update adjusting the Law to the new conditions the Israelites must face in Canaan, because, as we have seen, the Book of the Covenant's laws were never appropriate to nomadic desert life in the first place.

The first three chapters provide a historical prologue to the main body of the law code. It summarizes the Israel story up to this point. This is not a précis of our books of Exodus, Leviticus, and Numbers, but rather of only the narrative material from J and E. Nothing from the Priestly source. Furthermore, the summary is a kind of *Reader's Digest* version of a combined JE account of Moses. This implies J and E had already been woven together before Deuteronomy was written, and that, as Wellhausen believed, P had not been composed yet. Thus the order of the four Pentateuchal sources would be JEDP.

But another Moses, Moshe Weinfeld,[47] argued that Deuteronomy in several places seems to presuppose laws and concepts found in P and to develop them in new directions, implying that Deuteronomy is later than the Priestly Code. But relative theological differences do not necessarily coordinate with absolute dates. This is, I think, already implicit in Weinfeld's demonstration that the Priestly Code originated, obviously, with the priests, whereas Deuteronomy stems from the class of scribes,[48] hence Deuteronomy's relative disinterest in matters of ritual[49] as well as its ubiquitous humanism[50] and its inheritance from ancient Near Eastern Wisdom literature.[51]

The Priestly authors presumably did not fabricate their laws out of thin air when they sat down to write. Rather, they must have compiled and redacted long-standing traditional laws. So the Deuteronomists may have been reacting to these–and to the priestly approaches generally–before the Priestly material was compiled in our Priestly Code.[52]

Thus it is impossible to say which code was written first. "The problem at hand concerns two different ideologies arising from two different circles but not necessarily from two different historical periods. We would therefore regard the literary compositions of these schools as concurrent rather than successive documents."[53]

If Moses did not write (or speak) Deuteronomy, who did? Some of the more radical Old Testament critics thought that Deuteronomy (not counting the narrative prologue, obviously tacked on later) was a reform platform foisted on the young King Josiah of

Judah by a cabal including Huldah the prophetess, Hilkiah the priest, and their associates. In 2 Kings 22:8-13 (NASB),

> Hilkiah the high priest said to Shaphan the scribe, "I have found the book of the law in the house of [Yahweh]." And Hilkiah gave the book to Shaphan who read it.
>
> Shaphan the scribe came to the king and brought back word to the king and said, "Your servants have emptied out the money that was found in the house, and have delivered it into the hand of the workmen who have the oversight of the house of [Yahweh]." Moreover, Shaphan the scribe told the king saying, "Hilkiah the priest has given me a book." And Shaphan read it in the presence of the king.
>
> When the king heard the words of the book of the law, he tore his clothes. Then the king commanded Hilkiah the priest, Ahikam the son of Shaphan, Achbor the son of Micaiah, Shaphan the scribe, and Asaiah the king's servant saying, "Go, inquire of [Yahweh] for me and the people and all Judah concerning the words of this book that has been found, for great is the wrath of [Yahweh] that burns against us, because our fathers have not listened to the words of this book, to do according to all that is written concerning us."

The idea is that, just as the Emperor Constantine would later suppress all other forms of Christianity (e.g., Gnostics, Marcionites) in favor of his preferred version (nascent Catholicism/Orthodoxy), so did Hilkiah and his co-conspirators write up a manifesto/charter for Israelite religion as they wanted it to be. Not wanting to risk the king's possible indifference or even opposition, they sought to raise the stakes by claiming their Deuteronomic code was actually an ancient code[54] that appeared new and unfamiliar only because previous generations had callously disregarded, then forgotten, the code. Now it was time to get "back to the Bible," and quickly, since the wrath of God was looming.

This sort of pious fraud is by no means unparalleled in the history of religion. A notable modern example would be the Book of Mormon, undoubtedly the creation of Joseph Smith[55] but offered as a newly discovered scripture from ancient America.

Nowadays, it appears that even the theory of a Hilkiah-Huldah hoax is too naïve about biblical historicity. The theory still takes for granted that Hilkiah did bring a book to Huldah, then to Josiah. But why even give the story *that* much credit? Minimalists have shown that we have confused the "temporary, willing suspension of disbelief" of the reader of engaging fiction with a historian's credence.[56] Yet I think it premature to abandon the theory.

Something is going on here, the same thing we find in the *Book of Mormon* account of the Plates of Jared (Mosiah 8:5-19; 28:11-18; Ether 1-3).[57] In this story, the ancient Nephites learn of the discovery of an *already* ancient set of inscribed plates detailing an earlier cycle of salvation history. King Mosiah translates them by using a set of oracular lenses, the Urim and Thummim mentioned in the Bible. Some are skeptical, so it proves a test of the Nephites' faith: Will they welcome the new revelation?

Obviously, the story of the restored Plates of Jared parallels Joseph Smith's own claim to have unearthed the golden plates that constitute the *Book of Mormon* itself and to have translated them miraculously with the Urim and Thummim. King Mosiah corresponds, of course, to Joseph Smith, leader of the Latter-day Saints—and eventually literally crowned king of the sect! The controversy over the Jared scripture mirrors that surrounding the *Book of Mormon* in Smith's day. The whole story is a device to encourage Smith's contemporaries to drop their skepticism about his new scripture. It urges the nineteenth-century readers not to make the mistake the ancient Nephites almost made.

I think the 2 Kings 22 story of Hilkiah and Huldah is cut from the very same cloth: It smuggles into the text the actual situation of the scribes who fabricated the Deuteronomic law code long after the time of Josiah. We do not know their actual names, but we meet them in the guise of Hilkiah, Huldah, and the rest. They have placed themselves into 2 Kings to provide a fictive precedent for the acceptance of a new scripture in their own day. So the hoax theory is still good; it is just more extensive than we had thought. The implied date of the "discovery" (fabrication) of the Deuteronomic code is, then, not only much later than Moses' supposed time, but also much later than King Josiah's.

What Is Deuteronomy about?

The code of Deuteronomy has its own important distinctives, even its own distinctive literary style, but it is a revision and an expansion of the Book of the Covenant. The relationship between the two codes is analogous to that obtaining between Matthew and Mark, or between Luke and Mark. The new notes struck in Deuteronomy are numerous and significant. They reflect many of the recurring themes of the Israelite prophets, including humane benevolence toward the poor, servants, even animals.[58]

Deuteronomy is dead set against syncretism and polytheism. Its readers are urged to repudiate, e.g., the worship of the stars, an anachronism for the era of Moses. It was an import from Assyria, part of the tribute owed that empire, of whom Israel had become a vassal state. There is considerable railing against "Canaanite" and "Amorite" polytheism (Deut. 12:2-3).

Deuteronomy 20:16-18 has God direct Israel to displace (massacre) the Canaanite nations because of their polytheism, idol-worship, and fertility rites (sex magic). Defeating and subjugating them would not have been enough, since living side-by-side with the Ammonites, Edomites, Moabites, etc., would allow these peoples to remain a source of syncretism and corruption (Deut. 12:29-31). Israelites might be tempted to adopt their pagan ways (Deut. 12:29-30). And, as the Old Testament tells the story, it happened anyway! Hence all the thundering of the prophets against Israelites following heathen practices.

I have mentioned the recent observation that the Israelite people were simply one more group of Canaanites. They were about as distinct from the adjacent postage-stamp countries (Edom, Ammon, Moab, etc.) as each of them was from the next. Their fellow Canaanites also worshipped Baal, Asherah, Anath,[59] even Yahweh.[60] They described Yahweh and Baal in identical terms as a warrior and storm god.

So what are we to make of all the condemnation of "Canaanite" idolatry and polytheism? It is part of a drastic rewriting of history. What really happened was that at some point (retrospectively placed variously in the reigns of Hezekiah and Josiah), a group of scribes, prophets, and priests engineered a massive, systematic reform of traditional Hebrew religion, eliminating all deities but Yahweh, outlawing the former *Israelite* gods and goddesses, and then denying that Israel had *ever* worshipped them except insofar as their ancestors had mixed true, monotheistic Judaism[61] with "Canaanite" polytheism.[62] In fact, the heathen "Canaanites" whose reputation they blackened were their own Israelite forbears.[63]

The desire to eradicate polytheism and image-worship from Israel seems to have been the main reason for one of the most important stipulations of Deuteronomy: the centralization of worship (implicitly) in Jerusalem (Deut. 12:11). The countryside was sprinkled with local shrines and hilltop altars where Yahweh had to share worship and sacrifices with other deities including various Baals and Els, Anath, and Asherah. If you wanted to restrict worship to Yahweh alone, the only way to do it was to shut down all these outlying branches. You couldn't keep government supervisors on site all the time to control what went on there.

This seems to be a recurring pattern in the history of religions. Catholic bishops in Late Antiquity coveted the pious devotion offered at the many tombs of saints and martyrs dotting the countryside, so they eventually had the saints' relics removed and transferred to the urban churches where the bishops had their power base.[64] That very consideration, I believe, explains the historic reluctance of the Vatican to grant official recognition to the many outlying sites where Marian apparitions have occurred. The same concern appears also in the Acts of the Apostles, where the author schematizes the expansion of the Church in such a way as to make the Twelve Apostles in their Jerusalem "Vatican" the center from which all else radiates, and from which all developments must be granted approval. This is why Peter and John go to Samaria to authenticate the conversion of the Samaritans by Philip (Acts 8:14-17), why Paul must be brought to Jerusalem for apostolic approval (Acts 9:27-29), why Peter must defend his conversion of the Roman Cornelius before the Jerusalem elders (Acts 11).

Deuteronomy never quite has Moses name the legitimate center of Jewish worship as *Jerusalem*. Instead, Moses only speaks of "the place which Yahweh shall choose" (e.g., Deut. 17:8). Some scholars[65] have inferred from this fact that Deuteronomy contains traditions from the archaic period when Israelite tribes revered and served, serially, other central shines such as Shechem, Gilgal, and Shiloh (though none of them was exclusive like later Jerusalem). But my guess is that the intended reference of Deuteronomy was always to Jerusalem. It is left implicit for reasons of narrative plausibility, since a historical Moses could scarcely be pictured talking about centralizing Jewish worship in Jerusalem at a time when that city had no association with Israelite life or history. It was still in Jebusite hands.

I see a parallel to this "fill in the blank" caginess in the preaching of Mirza Ali Muhammad, or the Bab ("the Gate"), founder of the Bab'i Faith in Persia. On May 23, 1844, he began to proclaim the imminent advent of the Hidden Imam expected by all Shi'ite Muslims. He referred to him as "He Whom God Will Make Manifest" or "He Who Will Be Made Manifest."[66] As his ministry progressed, he admitted that he himself was the Hidden Imam, now revealed. The prediction of the Hidden Imam was not open-ended, and neither, I think, was Deuteronomy's "prediction" of God's choice of a central capital of Israelite worship.

Another key item on the Deuteronomic[67] agenda is the danger of any future monarch's abuse of power. Various provisions (Deut. 17:14-20) are made to rein in his prerogatives. Anyone can see that the whole discussion presupposes a previous unhappy record of royal excesses.[68] As we will see, there was an intense debate in Israel over the propriety of monarchy. Both sides are represented, for instance, in 1 Samuel, where, depending on what passage you read, monarchy is a regrettable borrowing from paganism, on the level with cult prostitution, or, on the other hand, an institution blessed by God.

One of the most important theological aspects of Deuteronomy is its emphasis on the *covenant* as the model for God's relationship to his people Israel. In short, it is a two-way street. The mutual loyalty of each party is conditional upon that of the other. If Israel does not keep up its end of the deal, they cannot expect Yahweh to keep up his. Deuteronomy 28 lists the provisions and conditions of the covenant. The chosen people are obliged to keep all the statutes of Deuteronomy. If they do so, they can count on rich harvests, battlefield victories, plenty of children, prolific herds, fair weather, and trade surpluses (Deut. 28:1-14). Neglect of the covenant and heedlessness of the commandments, on the other hand, will result in blight, drought, sterility and barrenness, military defeats, famine, plague, exile, poverty, insect devastation, and pretty much anything else one might dread (Deut. 28:15-68). There is quite a lot more cursing than blessing, much more stick than carrot. Of course, this is all seen in hindsight. These lists of blessings upon those who keep covenant with Yahweh and curses upon those who backslide form the basis of the so-called Deuteronomic theology or Deuteronomic philosophy of history upon which the long Deuteronomic History (Joshua-Judges-Samuel-Kings) is based.

As Weinfeld has shown with a Mount Sinai of evidence, Deuteronomy is largely based on the treaty-forms of the ninth through seventh centuries B.C.E., cross-pollinated with pronounced elements of ancient Near-Eastern law codes.[69] This fits with the scribal origin of Deuteronomy. The royal scribes would have had access to a library of such documents[70] and evidently borrowed freely from them, adding sermonic material here and there. Apologists have insisted that these formal similarities argue for a date for Deuteronomy more or less contemporary with the heyday of these treaties and codes from neighboring nations.[71] That argument rightly stresses form criticism as well as the principle of historical connection.[72] But the Achilles' Heel of the argument is the hybridization of the covenant treaty form with the law-code form. This indicates that the compilers of Deuteronomy were utilizing already ancient sources, not adhering to contemporary documentary protocols. This is no surprise: Deuteronomy is a pseudepigraph and a creative pastiche.

Give or Take a Teuch

Gerhard von Rad[73] thought Deuteronomy was the natural continuation of the books before it and that Joshua was the direct continuation of Deuteronomy. This means the whole Genesis, Exodus, Leviticus, Numbers, Deuteronomy, and Joshua collection originally formed one big *Hexateuch* before scribes decided Joshua would fit better as the beginning of the Deuteronomic History and detached it. At that point the Hexateuch became the Pentateuch.

By contrast, Martin Noth[74] believed that Deuteronomy was originally the beginning of the Deuteronomic History and was later detached from it and appended to an original *Tetrateuch* (Genesis, Exodus, Leviticus, and Numbers), making it into a Pentateuch. It is hard to decide which, if either, theory is correct. Both revolve around the fact that there are so many elements in common between Deuteronomy and Joshua. If these two belong together, which sequence does this linked material belong to, Genesis through Numbers or Judges through Kings? I tend to go with Noth, mainly because the joining of Deuteronomy to the Tetrateuch would provide a natural occasion for the Deuteronomic bits scattered here and there in Genesis through Numbers.

The Deuteronomic philosophy is basically a type of *theodicy*, a theory to explain the occurrence of evil and adversity despite one's faith in a righteous and watchful God. If he is not asleep at the switch, how can we explain disasters like the defeat of Israel by Assyria and of Judah by Babylon? It was customary for a defeated nation to infer that the gods of their enemies were stronger than their own gods, having trounced them and, so to speak, taken their human clients hostage. The defeated people would then switch to the gods of their masters, which only made sense: Why not go with a winner?

Well, that's certainly *one* way of explaining it! But then who wants to admit their god was not so mighty after all? To reduce cognitive dissonance, Israelite theologians came up with a very different way of looking at things. On one level, it is sour grapes, while on another it is actually quite profound. It suddenly occurred to them that Yahweh was all-powerful but had *disdained* to intervene on their behalf. They had naturally assumed that God was on their side–but what if *they* had not been on *his* side?

Israel must have failed God; he had not failed them. He couldn't have. And the Deuteronomic philosophy starts (and finishes) right there. There must have been a two-way covenant between Yahweh and Israel. By its terms, God was not automatically obliged to defend Israel. His commitment was conditional upon their keeping up their end of the deal by obeying his commands. So they must have forfeited his protection.[75]

On the one hand, this thinking brought religion to a new and higher level, elevating Yahweh above the status of Israel's genie or totem into a universal sovereign who prizes righteousness above partisan loyalty. On the other, it is a theodicy of blaming the victim. "You suffered setback and tragedy? You've no one but yourself to blame!" Is self-condemnation (without awareness of any real guilt) too high a price to pay to get God off the hook? So his reputation is not besmirched ("Why should the nations say, 'Where is their God?'", Psalm 79:10 NASB)? Not everybody was willing to take the blame for God, as we will see when we come to the Book of Job.

One must infer a connection between the elevation of Yahweh as something better than a national mascot (the traditional role of ancient deities) and Deuteronomy's internalization of religion: "Moreover the Lord [Yahweh] your God will circumcise your heart and the heart of your descendants, to love the Lord your God with all your heart and with all your soul, so that you may live" (Deut. 30:6, NASB). Here we approach the preaching of John the Baptist: "do not suppose that you can say to yourselves, 'We have Abraham for our father'; for I say to you that from these stones God is able to raise up children to Abraham" (Matt. 3:9, NASB). Or the teaching of Romans 2:28-29 (RSV): "He is not a real Jew who is one outwardly, nor is true circumcision something external and physical. He is a Jew who is one inwardly, and real circumcision is a matter of the heart, spiritual and not [merely] literal."

Finally, Deuteronomy promises that a prophet like Moses will one day appear, and it warns the people not to fail to heed his words (Deut. 18:9-22). They must take care equally that they not be led astray by anyone who claims to prophesy in the name of other gods (Deut. 13:1-5). But there might also be ostensible prophets for Yahweh who are actually charlatans. How can you tell the difference? If the prediction falls flat, he must have been a faker. But what if Karnack the Great says to get ready for imminent catastrophe and you wait to see the outcome before you take his warning seriously? Kind of a Catch-22, which implies this test was never actually intended to be used. Prophecy was a fabled thing of the past when Deuteronomy was written.

Who is intended as the prophet like Moses? Samaritans came to believe that Moses was predicting his immediate successor, Joshua, who is after all shown promulgating his own code of laws (Josh. 24:25) as well as repeating the Sea miracle, albeit on a smaller scale, leading the people to cross the Jordan dry-shod (Josh. 3:7-17). He appears almost to play Elisha to Moses' Elijah. But the prediction is usually taken to denote a Mosaic pedigree for the subsequent series of Israelite prophets, though that would seem a bit inconsistent with the eulogy of Moses that concludes Deuteronomy (34:10), which says that "There has not arisen *a prophet* since in Israel *like Moses*."

My guess is that the prediction is meant to pave the way for the writer/compiler of Deuteronomy[76] who is in a genuine sense a second Moses since he is posing as Moses and giving a "second law."

The Holiness Code

Lev. 17-26

The rest of the legal material in Exodus, Leviticus, and Numbers comes from the Priestly Code, traditionally supposed by scholars to have been compiled during the Babylonian

Exile of the sixth century. It incorporates an earlier[77] set of purity laws called the Holiness Code, found intact in Leviticus 17-26, and perhaps influenced by the code of the priest-seer Ezekiel in Babylon earlier in the same period. Most modern readers find this material pretty soporific. That is understandable, since it was never intended for them. Analogous to the Hindu *Yajur Veda*, the Priestly Code is a practical manual for priests (and Levites). It's not supposed to be a page-turner. But, even for laity like us, there are several points of interest.

It is easy to lose sight of the Levitical forest for the trees. So many of the regulations (e.g., kosher laws) appear so arbitrary, even bizarre, to non-Jews that we puzzle over them momentarily, then move on. Others, like the condemnation of homosexuality, seem clear enough but are so offensive to modern ears that we cannot take them seriously. But in fact there is an overarching method to the seeming madness. Anthropologist Mary Douglas[78] has, in my opinion, unlocked the mystery, laying out the logic whereby certain activities are forbidden and others allowed.

Basically, to "be holy" is to observe and to preserve the order of creation, not to compromise the categories God laid down or to violate them. This is why different kinds of trees are not to be planted together indiscriminately. This is why different types of animals, even if reproductively compatible, must not be hybridized. It explains why fields must not be sown with different kinds of seeds. And why one dare not wear clothing made of mixed fibers (Lev. 19:19).These things (and more) are stipulated as "abominations," literally "confusions" or "mixings" (better, "mix-ups").

No one ever thought it was "immoral" to do any of these things. Murder, theft, adultery, these acts were morally wrong. But the "abominations" were wrong in an entirely different sense. They were not offences against fellow human beings. They were *ceremonial* transgressions, transgressions against God by spurning the order of his creation. In fact, the original, proper meaning of "sin" as opposed to "wrong" was that, while the latter was a horizontal transgression against our fellows, the former was committed solely against God. "Against thee, thee only, have I sinned, and done that which is evil in thy sight" (Psalm 51:4a). Wrongs hurt mortals, but God cannot be hurt. Sins do not "wrong" him. But they are in effect blasphemies.[79]

The taxonomy of ancient Israel, upon which the kosher laws are based, set forth "true" types of each category of creatures based on habitat, means of locomotion, and physical traits. "True fish" were defined as creatures which lived in the water, possessed scales, and swam with fins. You could eat all the fish you wanted. But crustaceans were off the menu for, though they dwelt in the water, they lacked scales and fins. They did not swim. What's the problem with eating pork? It had nothing to do with trichinosis, which they knew nothing about. No, the issue was that pigs did not quite qualify as "true cattle." Real cattle were those creatures that had cloven hooves and chewed the cud (ruminants). Oops! Pigs had the right hooves, but they swallowed and digested only once. And so on.

It might occur to one to ask why God had created these "anomalous" life-forms in the first place. My guess is that originally the Jewish scribes thought someone *else* had created them. That's what the neighboring Zoroastrians of Persia (who had great influence on Judaism) thought. Whereas the good deity Ahura Mazda had created almost everything, the snakes, scorpions, worms, insects, etc. (the Bible's "creeping things") were the nasty inventions of the evil anti-god Ahriman. A hint of this idea surfaces in Luke 10:18-19 (RSV): "And he said to them, 'I saw Satan fall like lightning from heaven. Behold, I have given you authority to tread upon serpents and scorpions, and over all the power of the enemy; and nothing shall hurt you." Creeping things, then, are minions of the Evil One, hence his creations. This puzzle piece is missing because of later, stricter monotheism, which found the notion of a rival creator heretical.

How did the taxonomical issue bear on sexual acts? There were three axioms in play. First, some boundary lines can never be crossed. Second, some boundaries may be crossed but only by rites of passage (analogous to, say, puberty rites which mark and *effect* the transition between the categories of children and adults). Third, sex *within* a category is forbidden. Incest and homosexual acts are (ritually, ceremonially) unclean because the one occurs within the family circle and the other occurs within the same gender. Heterosexual acts constitute a crossover between genders, and marriage provides the bridge that legitimates it. But there is no ceremonial border-crossing between the categories of humans and animals, children and adults, or the dead and the living. Similarly, adultery is a transgression, an "unlicensed" crossing of the line between a married couple and a partner outside it.

Adultery was thus considered both an abomination (confusion) and an immoral act. An act might be wrong for both reasons. But not all ritual transgressions were moral transgressions. Nobody ever imagined it was *immoral* to eat a ham sandwich; that's not what was wrong about it. It was only *ceremonially* wrong.

I'm not even sure bestiality would have been considered immoral. Our first reaction to the whole idea is probably disgust, which seems to tilt in the direction of "uncleanness." Necrophilia[80] is so far out that I suspect that in that case we are not talking about immorality but rather *insanity*. So where on the spectrum do homosexual acts fall? That is not clear. It is quite clear that the Holiness Code deems male-male sex[81] a ritual transgression, and an intolerable one, given the death penalty attached to it (Lev. 20:13). So in ancient Israel the difference is moot.

But suppose one is a Pauline Christian who believes that the ceremonial aspects of the Torah are obsolete. Unless someone can show that the Old Testament somewhere condemned a ritually unclean act as *also* being immoral, I have to think the Reverend Troy Perry, founder of the Metropolitan Community Churches, was right in his retort to an anti-Gay fundamentalist.[82]

> She said, "Young man, do you know what the Book of Leviticus says?"
>
> I told her, "I sure do! It says that it's a sin for a woman to wear a red dress, for a man to wear a cotton shirt and woolen pants at the same time, for anyone to eat shrimp, oysters, or lobster–or your steak too rare."
>
> She said, "That's not what I mean!"
>
> I said, "I know that's not what you mean, Honey, but you forgot all these other dreadful sins, too, that are in the same book of the Bible."

This elaborate system of categories and distinctions does not sound to me like the traditional norms and worldview inherited by a culture from time immemorial, evolving and accumulating imperceptibly with no known author or founder. The whole thing strikes me as too redolent, again, of scribal and rabbinical hair-splitting.[83] I have to suspect that the Holiness Code originated much nearer in time to what would become Mishnaic Judaism, not just a remote precursor of it. This would make all the more sense given other indications that the Pentateuch stems from centuries later than we had long supposed.[84]

This similarity and continuity with rabbinical casuistry suggests a related point, namely that the laws of the Torah were never enforced or enforceable. They never actually regulated Israelite community life. Many of the laws did not pertain to civic affairs or criminal cases anyway. Very many pertained to cultic (ceremonial) matters only. Think of the role of Talmudic law in Judaism today: No one is forcing Orthodox and Hasidic Jews to keep these regulations. They are instead the rules of a particular game, the ground rules for a voluntary religious association. Any Jew may leave it, though, unless one lives in close proximity to a surrounding sea of non-Jews (as in contemporary America or in the Mediterranean Diaspora), leaving will involve painful familial dislocation. I am thinking that it was always thus.

I wonder if even the criminal laws, with their provisions for trial (by village elders?) and stoning by the mob, were not purely theoretical. Is the Torah like Plato's *Laws* and *Republic*? Like Thomas More's *Utopia*? Again, was it always more like the Talmud than Hammurabi's Code, in the sense that it never left the drawing board?[85]

Moses Stories Formally Classified

Most of the Moses episodes must be explained as having originated just like the myths of Genesis, to serve various explanatory purposes: to account (long after the fact) for certain rituals, dietary regulations, holy places, oases, etc. Often we will see, as we did in Genesis, that a single story, brief as it is, will serve more than one of these functions. This is a sure sign of the story having been augmented in the process of repeated oral transmission. The tales grew in the telling as new uses were found for them. Here are several of them, classified form-critically, not by their order of appearance. The order in which they are narrated is artificial anyway. Each one arose independently.[86]

George W. Coats[87] has shown how these tales originated as illustrations of Yahweh's watchful care for his people during their wilderness wanderings. The people report their needs, and God meets them. [88] There is no bitterness. As in Jeremiah 2:2-3 (cf. Hos. 2:14-20; 9:10), the time in the wilderness was a honeymoon period when God was only too happy to attend to his new bride's needs. But some time before J gathered the stories, someone had overlaid a new and alien motif, picturing Israel as bitterly griping, even repudiating both Yahweh and Moses.

Note how the people rue the fact that Moses ever dragged them out of Egypt where, in retrospect, things were actually pretty good![89] It is this gross ingratitude that prompts an exasperated Yahweh to wash his hands of them, leaving them to drop dead in the Sinai desert, never to set foot in the Promised Land. We can observe exactly the same view of things over in Psalm 78, which gleefully provides a rap sheet of the children of Israel–but not of the obedient and heroic Judeans! The target, in both Psalm 78 and the Wilderness Wanderings tales, is the northern kingdom of Israel. The J version of the murmuring episodes, then, implies God has abrogated the covenant he made with Moses and Israel in favor of a new covenant with the dynasty of David in Judah (2 Sam. 7:12-15; Psalm 89:19-38).

Ceremonial and Legal Precedents

Can You Guess my Name?
Exod. 3:1-15 // 6:2-8

These passages tell of the introduction of the divine name Yahweh to supersede the names El Shaddai and Elohim. Very likely what is really at stake here is a merger of two prior deities, subordinating both to a third one, the Kenite storm god Yahweh.[90] This would make a lot of sense given the business about Moses marrying into the family of Jethro, who is called "the priest of Midian" (Exod. 3:1). The Kenites were a Midianite tribe who eventually became part of Judah. Exodus implies that Jethro was a sheikh (a Kenite according to Jud, 1:15; 4:11) who had inherited priestly duties because Horeb, the mountain of God, was contained within his ancestral grazing domains. Moses is tending Jethro's flocks near Mt. Horeb when he beholds the mysteriously burning bush, then goes to investigate. This is the scene in which Yahweh appears to him and communicates the divine name.

It is plain in the narrative that Moses does not know this deity: "If I come to the people of Israel and say to them, 'The God of your fathers has sent me to you,' and they ask me, 'What is his name?' what shall I say to them?" (Exod. 3:13, RSV). When God replies that he is the God of the patriarchs, though they did not know to call him Yahweh, it looks like he is telling Moses that the deity of Jethro and his fellow Kenites is the same God worshipped by the Hebrews. In view of the new connection between the Hebrew Moses and the Kenites, God wishes to unify the worship of the two groups.

This is all fiction, but it has been designed to cement the merger of the deities of two allied groups. The unification is factual, just historically later. The maneuver is closely analogous to that by which various tribes, entering into political/military/trading relations together would "seal the deal" by declaring themselves to be "blood brothers" and positing that they shared a common ancestor in, e.g., Abraham.[91] In just the same way, during the Hasmonean struggle against the Seleucid Empire in the second century BCE, the forces of Judah Maccabee made common cause with the Spartans, who claimed to have discovered in old documents that the Jews and the Spartans were really kinsmen "separated at birth," both, you guessed it, descendants of Abraham (1 Macc.12:21).

It seems strange that God must reveal his preferred name to Moses twice, in Exodus 3:14-15 and Exodus 6:2-3. That is, until you remember that the Exodus narrative as we now read it is a patchwork, a scrap book, of sacred traditions, and that the compiler knew to expect a lot of pious outrage if anybody's favorite version got left on the cutting room floor.[92]

Similarly, how can God say he had not previously been known by the name Yahweh, when Genesis already had people invoking him by this name as far back as the days of Seth and Enosh (Gen. 4:26)? Simple: The J (Yahwist) writer just assumed that everyone had always known the God of the Bible by this name; to J, Yahweh was pretty much synonymous with God. By contrast, the Elohist and Priestly writers knew of the tradition that Yahweh had been introduced in historical times.[93]

Birth of Bureaucracy

Exod. 18:1-27 // Num. 11:11-12, 14, 16, 24-30

These two texts provide a holy pedigree for the institution of councils of elders, basically positing "apostolic succession" for later judges who would apply the laws of Moses in court. There were two versions, implying that more than one such local group got the same idea. This, ultimately, is where we get the Sanhedrin of New Testament times. But these passages had a different kind of importance for the New Testament writers. Both Pentateuchal passages were rewritten there.

The Exodus 18 version lies, barely concealed, behind Mark 3:19b-21, 31-35; 13-19a. In Exodus, Moses' father-in-law Jethro visits Moses in the Israelite camp following the victory over the Egyptians at the Sea, bringing with him Moses' wife and family. Moses, told of their arrival, welcomes them. Seeing how his son-in-law, busy every day hearing cases and mediating disputes, scarcely has a moment to stop and take a breath, Jethro warns him he is headed for "burnout" and advises him to appoint honest men to handle the lesser cases (presumably applying the statutes Moses has already established), while seeing to new and more serious cases himself. Moses sees the wisdom of this and chooses the first group of elders.

Early Christians reapplied the old story to Jesus. His family hears of his exhausting, hectic schedule of healing and teaching, and they fear for his sanity if it keeps up. So they go to him with the same advice: Appoint lieutenants to share the workload. Jesus happily receives them and heeds their advice by appointing twelve disciples to join him in his work. But the early church was rife with rival factions, some of whom preferred other leaders, e.g., Paul. Others looked to the Pillars (Gal. 2:9), the supposed relatives of Jesus, as his "dynasty."

The evangelist Mark (who opposed both the factions who looked to the Twelve and to the Pillars) did not care to use the story as he had heard it. So he cut the story in half, having Jesus appoint the twelve on his own initiative, no one else's. Then Mark has the family of Jesus enter the scene, thinking he has already lost his mind and bringing with them the Holy Straightjacket of Gilead for him to try on for size. And Jesus imperiously repudiates them, refusing even to give them audience. Ouch!

Mark saved some venom for the twelve, too, portraying them as hopeless buffoons at every opportunity.[94] In Mark 9:38-39 he has John, son of Zebedee, quite proud of himself, tell Jesus that he saw someone working their side of the street, casting out demons using Jesus' name as his exorcism formula, whereupon an exasperated Jesus asks him what on earth he could have been thinking! Surely Mark has in mind the sect of the twelve and their rivalry with Paul who was not one of their number. Mark has fabricated this one based on Numbers 11:24-30, where Eldad and Medad, two of the appointed elders, fail to join the rest at the appointed place where they are to receive the prophetic spirit, but they receive it anyway back at home. Joshua is alarmed at this, but Moses tells him to relax. The lone-wolf exorcist is Mark's version of Eldad and Medad.

The author of Acts used the same Numbers passage as the model for the descent of the Spirit upon the 120 at Pentecost (Acts 2:1-4). The parallel is even clearer once you realize that the "prophesying" the elders were doing (like that of the bands of prophets in 1 Samuel 10:5-6, 10-13; 19:20-24) would have been ecstatic possession-speech with no intelligible content, in other words, speaking in tongues.[95] Wellhausen refers to these ecstatic prophets as "bacchantes," "dervishes," and "flagellants."[96]

Origin of the Levites
Exod. 32:25-29

The privileged priesthood of the Levites was, we are to understand, a reward for their Yahweh-loyalty, demonstrated by their massacre of their fellow Israelites who had lapsed into Golden Calf idolatry (the violation of commands they had not yet received!). Jehu would do the same in 2 Kings 10:15-28, butchering the assembled priests of Baal. Ditto the prophet Elijah at Mt. Carmel in 1 Kings 18:40. Phineas proved his worthiness by skewering an Israelite who dared marry a Midianite woman (as Moses himself had done!), in return for which he and his posterity received God's promise of a perpetual priesthood (Num. 25:6-13). And of course, Judah Maccabee's father Mattathias, a priest, followed the example of Phineas, gutting a Jew who was about to offer pagan sacrifice (1 Macc. 2:23-28). Thus he sparked the Hasmonean liberation struggle against the Seleucids.

When Jews and Christians read these narratives they are caught up in the story and thus root for "the good guys." This is why they, and we, do not view such sectarian bloodshed the same way they and we do today's horrors of religious violence.

At any rate, the text implies that the sword-wielding Yahweh partisans had belonged to no particular tribal group. Rather, it was their bloody "purification" that elevated them to become a priestly caste called Levites. But there are other, conflicting clues as to Levite origins. In Judges 17:7-13 we learn of a man who was ethnically a member of the tribe of Judah yet occupied the position of a Levite, defined here as an oracle-monger. He becomes the private chaplain and fortune-teller for a family belonging to the tribe of Ephraim. This makes sense because the Hebrew word *kohen* ("priest") is cognate with the Arabic *kahin* ("soothsayer"), implying that the Jewish "priests" were originally oracles as well (or instead). At this stage, then, the Levites were a profession, not a tribe. And what set them apart was not religious violence (like the Mormon Danites of the nineteenth century) but rather their fortune-telling abilities.

But then why are the Levites elsewhere listed among the twelve tribes descended from Jacob?[97] It looks very much as if we are caught in the middle of multiple, mutually contradictory attempts to substitute a "sanitized" explanation for an original which had already passed beneath the dark cloud of heresy.

And the true explanation for the Levite caste is, I think, apparent in 2 Kings 23:8-9 and Ezekiel 48:11, where we read that those priests staffing the hilltop shrines throughout Judea suffered a significant demotion once King Josiah restricted worship to Yahweh alone and made the Jerusalem Temple the only legitimate place of worship.

> "But the Levites who went far from Me when Israel went astray, who went astray from Me after their idols, shall bear the punishment for their iniquity. Yet they shall be ministers in My sanctuary, having oversight at the gates of the house and ministering in the house; they shall slaughter the burnt offering and the sacrifice for the people, and they shall stand before them to minister to them. Because they ministered to them before their idols and became a stumbling block of iniquity to the house of Israel, therefore I have sworn against them," declares [the Lord Yahweh], "that they shall bear the punishment for their iniquity. And they shall not come near to Me to serve as a priest to Me, nor come near to any of My holy things, to the things that are most holy; but they will bear their shame and their abominations which they have committed. Yet I will appoint them to keep charge of the house, of all its service and of all that shall be done in it." (Ezek. 44:10-14, NASB)

These deposed priests were given duties as Temple door keepers, hymn writers, night watchmen, etc., as well as the administration of lesser offerings, e.g., of incense. There were too many of them to stay in the Temple all year round, so they were on a rotating schedule, living in the provinces most of the year and serving in the capital for a month each year, as John the Baptist's father Zachariah does in Luke 1:5, 8-10. These second-string priests and priestly flunkies were the Levites, hence the oft-occurring phrase "priests and Levites."

But it hadn't been solely a question of where they had worshipped. It was also a question of *whom*. King Josiah had also dumped out of the Temple the relics and idols of other Hebrew deities as well as imported ones. These included Asherah, the Queen of heaven, the stars ("hosts of heaven"), the images of the horses that pulled the sun god's chariot, and the serpent god Nehushtan or Leviathan. Both the Hebrew words *naas* and *levi* mean "serpent," and both these divine names bore the honorific suffix "-tan/than" (analogous to the Egyptian "-hotep"). The Levites, then, must have been "those skilled to awaken Leviathan" (Job 3:8),[98] the priests of the suppressed Nehushtan cult[99] who served his chapel in the Jerusalem Temple before Hezekiah put it out of commission (2 Kings 18:4).[100]

Numbers 21:4-9 and 2 Kings 18:4 seek to supply an orthodox Mosaic pedigree for the Nehushtan idol. Apparently, before the final step was taken, the ejection of the bronze effigy of the scaly god Nehushtan/Leviathan, there was an initial attempt to retain the beloved relic by redefining it. Perhaps it was *not* an artist's conception of the ophidian deity after all, but rather a caduceus, an apotropaic device to cure snake bite! Sure, that's it.

You want to know where it came from? Why, *Moses* had it made to turn back an infestation of poisonous "fiery" desert snakes. Look at this magic image, and, by a kind of imitative magic (like a Voodoo doll, only in reverse), the snake venom will be neutralized. Not any more, of course, but back in the old days it worked wonders. But apparently the original understanding was never completely stamped out, and people who *said* they were just coming to look at a museum exhibit were still praying to it on the sly. "Oh! Er, that's not incense! It's just, ah, *air freshener!* That's the ticket!" So out it went.

Cautionary Tales

Fire Extinguisher
Lev. 10:1-3

This little episode serves as a warning to priests not to be careless with mixing the incense formula, not to substitute or to skimp on required ingredients (Exod. 30:35; 37:29; Lev. 16:12). This would seem to be what "offering strange fire" (or "profane fire") means. It seems God had a pretty sensitive nose, and you wouldn't want to risk a divine sneezing fit! And presumably incense symbolizes the prayers of the people ascending before God as in Revelation 8:3-4.

Another possibility is that it is literal fire under discussion, and that the hapless priests' error was to have brought in some burning coals from outside the holy precinct instead of taking them from the altar as commanded in Leviticus 16:12.

Jockeying for Position
Num. 12:1-12

Better think twice before you decide to claim prophetic authority as a spokesman for Yahweh like Moses! (Aaron and Miriam represent such people here.) The danger envisioned here is that of the "dangerous supplement,"[101] claiming "merely" to add on to the revelations and laws of Moses while actually (even if not intentionally) undermining them. The simple fact of reopening (or keeping open) the channel of prophecy portends the abrogation of old revelation by new, as witness the "fulfillment" of the Old Testament by the New and of the New Testament by the Qu'ran. The new, simply by *being* new, implicitly supersedes and stultifies the old.

I see in this episode a parallel with Joseph Smith silencing those who stepped forth to add new revelations of their own to his as collected in the *Doctrine and Covenants*. No, that's enough prophecy, thank you! We are obviously looking at the diametrical opposite of Deuteronomy 18:15: Yahweh "your God will raise up for you a prophet like me from among you, from your brethren. Him you shall heed." Yahweh would raise up this prophet, Moses, "from among their brethren" and would put his words in the prophet's mouth. "And whoever will not give heed to my words which he shall speak in my name, I myself will require it of him," (vv. 18-19, both RSV). This "oracle" must have been the tendentious creation of those against whom Numbers 12-1-12 is aimed.

Was that Kindling Really Worth it?

Num. 15:32-36

How about a "scared straight" lesson about Sabbath violation? Did people ever really get *executed* for Sabbath-breaking? Once again, you have to wonder if these laws existed only on paper, in the minds of pious zealots who *wished* they had the ability to enforce their religious rules.

Two types of sanctions are brought to bear here. On the one hand, the rule is to be obeyed because God commanded it; hence it is no mere human convention like traffic laws. On the other, should you dare disobey it, the community (or its elders?) will bombard you with rocks. The situation might have been like that found today in Saudi Arabia, where pious mobs, possessing no official authority, take it upon themselves to enforce Shariah law, harassing, even stoning, young women who do not dress "modestly" enough in public.

Levitical Labor Dispute

Num.16:1ff

Korah and his allies are fictive ancestors of the Korah Guild, an order of Levitical singers in the Temple.[102] At some point they asked for a promotion to the status of sacrificing priests, which would have entitled them to a share of sacrificial meat, a prerogative reserved to the Aaronide priests. Their request was turned down summarily.

In order to prevent further attempts, the priests formulated this story in which Korah and his buddies make the same request of Moses and Aaron and wind up riding the dumbwaiter into the netherworld! You can read the Levitical singers' rejoinder[103] in Psalm 51:15-17: God doesn't *want* those bloody animal sacrifices! The sacrifices he prefers are purely spiritual, the offering of lamentation psalms—like Psalm 51 itself.

Numbers 17:1ff. is a very similar story calculated to secure the privileges of the Aaronide priesthood. No one else need seek ordination, just as the Vedic priesthood was reserved to the Brahmin caste alone. These stories, serving the interests of the priests, are what give us the old-fashioned polemical term "priestcraft," denoting fraudulent religious manipulation of the laity (especially by means of fear-mongering). Indeed, it is not hard to imagine the "miraculous" budding of Aaron's rod, authenticating the unique priestly status of his descendants, being a sleight-of-hand trick like that ascribed to Baal's priests in *Bel and the Dragon* (part of the Greek *Septuagint* version of Daniel).

Geological and Etymological Stories

Bittersweet Miracle

Exod. 15:22-25

Someone naturally inferred that, if a water spring was called Marah ("Bitterness"), the water must have been undrinkable. But in fact the water there was sweet! How come? Well, presumably the water had originally been bitter, *then* changed to sweet. And who might have done this favor for parched nomads? What better candidate than Moses? And so it must have been. Perhaps the story was borrowed from the exploit of Elisha at Jericho (2 Kings 2:19-22).

But all this is based on a false inference. The storyteller did not know that the name originally denoted a place of ritual lamentation and "bitter" mourning, just like the sacred grave of Deborah, Rebecca's nurse, which was called Allon-bacuth, "Oak of Weeping." Another such mourning site located beside a spring is mentioned in Psalm 139:1, "By the waters of Babylon, there we sat down and wept, when we remembered Zion."

We can bracket verse 24 as one more case of shoe-horning the murmuring motif into a simple story of need and provision.

Ol' Massah

Exod. 17:1-7

"Massah" means "proof," and "Meribah" means "contention." They must have marked a particular oasis as a place of legal arbitration. People would visit the oasis to ask a local oracle priest to settle their disputes. He would do just as Moses does in Exodus 15:22, going into a shamanistic state and allowing the babbling of the brook to stimulate his subconscious. The oracle would hear the sounds of the water as the words of God.

Again, we have to consider verses 2-4, 7 a later insertion, reinterpreting the story as one of Israel's stubborn unbelief in their God. Accordingly, "Massah" and "Meribah" were then taken to denote Israel putting *God* to the test and their contention against him (cf., Job 40:2: "Shall a faultfinder contend with the Almighty?")–as if anyone at the time would have actually named a place for a spiritual failure.

The original story is found in verses 1 and 5-6, a geological story explaining the origin of the oasis, replacing the original belief that local deities lived in the place, substituting for it the legend of a miracle of Moses. Ponds, springs, and groves were thought to be the habitations of various local deities, saints, and sprites. What else could account for such rare well-watered, shady spots in the middle of the desert? They were little Eden gardens of the gods. There are other Old Testament myths of the same kind, providing an "orthodox" pedigree for an originally pagan origin. For instance, God makes a spring gush up at Lehi for Samson's benefit (Judg. 15:18-19).

More Murmuring

Num. 20:1-13

The story of Massah and Meribah (this time without the redundant Massah) gets retold in order to make the theme of murmuring and rebellion central to the story. Another added element is Moses getting so sick of the Israelites' attitude that he flies off the handle and gets punished for it.

You see, Yahweh told Moses just to *speak* to the rock, commanding it to produce water, but Moses struck the rock with his staff (which is exactly what God told him to do in the other version!). Why on earth does God get so angry at what surely seems an insignificant infraction? You see, there were no stories of Moses entering the Promised Land, and this was because Moses was originally depicted as Israel's leader in a self-contained cycle of stories presupposing that the Israelites wandered the wilderness as nomads, not as people leaving one dwelling place and journeying to a new, settled home elsewhere.

The Conquest stories (equally fictive) starred a different hero, Joshua. When the compilers decided to join the Wilderness Wanderings cycle to the Conquest cycle, they harmonized them by making Joshua into Moses' assistant and successor. But it was too much to rewrite Moses into the Conquest stories, elbowing Joshua aside. So Moses' absence from the Promised Land had to be explained. Hmmm . . . maybe he committed some sin? But we're talking about Holy Moses here, so the redactor had to trump up a pretty minor infraction. Never mind that the story makes God look grossly unfair.

Feed me till I Want no More

Exod. 16:1-36 // Num. 11:4-9

These parallel passages preserve longer and shorter versions of the origin of manna, actually a naturally occurring flakey, sweet growth found in the desert, "traveler's bread." It is a kind of resin secreted by the bark of tamarisk trees pierced by plant lice.

Apologists for biblical accuracy[104] have long pointed to the existence of this stuff as proof of the truth of the Pentateuchal narratives. But they miss one crucial fact: The story-tellers to whom we owe these episodes were not aware of the commonplace, natural character of manna. They plainly regarded it as a miracle worked by God just for the occasion. As in the case of the Egyptian Plagues, the biblical narrators betray their distance from and ignorance of the natural phenomena they describe and distort. If this is what the manna really was, then the Bible was wrong, since it views manna as the bread of angels shared with man.

Etymological and Ethnological Stories in the Pentateuch

The names "Kibroth" in Numbers 11:31-35 and "Hormah" in Numbers 21:1-3 both represent inference (guesswork) from the place name to hypothetical events that might have led people to commemorate the places with the traditional names, which were no longer understood.

Ethnological stories include Exodus 17:8-16 (accounting for the age-old grudge against the no-good Amalekites), Numbers 20:14-21 (justifying the feud with the lousy Edomites), Numbers 21:1-3 (aimed at the rotten Canaanites), Numbers 21:21-35 (directed at the dirty Amorites, et. al.), and Numbers 22-25, 31 (blasting the highly annoying Midianites).

More than likely, no one even remembered the source of the traditional antipathies and so felt the need to justify them after the fact. No doubt the enemies of Israel circulated their own stories about the imagined crimes of Israel! Things don't change all that much.

————

By now, it ought to be clear that the Moses stories are something other than history. Not to say *less* than history; our goal is not merely to pick holes in these old tales. Rather, our observations have been aimed at demonstrating that these materials are something *else*: a mass of legal precedents and traditions, ceremonial legends, fanciful name origins, etc.

The Pentateuch is a treasure chest of fascinating relics whose value must be recognized. It is like the Ark of the Covenant, a golden chest in which precious ancient texts are stored. And it is equally crucial to understand that *value* is by no means the same thing as *authority*.

Notes

1. Burke Long, *Planting and Reaping Albright: Politics, Ideology, and Interpreting the Bible* (University Park: Penn State University Press, 2008); Thomas W. Davis, *Shifting Sands: The Rise and Fall of Biblical Archaeology* (New York: Oxford University Press, 2004).

2. Not unlike the procedure of Helena, the Emperor Constantine's mother, and her agents whom she dispatched to Jerusalem to "locate" the holy sites mentioned in the gospels. See Thomas L. Thompson, *The Mythic Past: Biblical Archaeology and the Myth of Israel* (New York: Basic Books, 1999), pp. 36-38, 104.

3. G. Ernest Wright, *God Who Acts: Biblical Theology as Recital.* Studies in Biblical Theology No. 8 (London: SCM Press, 1952), p. 38: "Biblical theology is first and foremost a theology of recital, in which Biblical man confesses his faith by reciting the formative events of his history as the redemptive handiwork of God." See also Gerhard von Rad, *Old Testament Theology Volume I: The Theology of Israel's Historical Traditions.* Trans. D.M.G. Stalker (New York: Harper & Row, 1962), pp. 72-73, 106-107. Wright and Von Rad wrestled with the extent to

which this *Heilsgeschichte* (holy history) reflected actual events, though neither dreamt of the real state of affairs now known to us.

4. Niels Peter Lemche, *The Israelites in History and Tradition*. Library of Ancient Israel (Louisville: Westminster John Knox Press, 1998), pp. 86-93.

5. Philip R. Davies, "In Search of 'Ancient Israel.'" Journal for the Study of the Old Testament, Supplement Series 148 (Sheffield: Sheffield Academic Press, 1992), pp. 78-79; Thompson, *Mythic Past*, pp. 192-95.

6. Exodus 4:24-26 seems to imply Moses had not, even as an adult, been circumcised, but that seems to be an alternative tradition.

7. Thompson, p. 13.

8. Sigmund Freud, *Moses and Monotheism*. Trans. Katherine Jones (New York: Vintage Books, 1939), Part I, "Moses an Egyptian," pp. 3-15, argued that Moses originally *was* an Egyptian, and that the redefinition of the name was an attempt to cover this up.

9. Robert Graves and Raphael Patai, *Hebrew Myths: The Book of Genesis* (New York: Greenwich House/Crown Publishers, 1983), p. 229.

10. Robert Alter, *The Art of Biblical Narrative* (New York: Basic Books, 1981), p. 48.

11. Albrecht Alt, "The God of the Fathers." In Alt, *Essays on Old Testament History and Religion*. Trans. R.A. Wilson (Garden City: Doubleday Anchor Books, 1968), pp. 1-86.

12. Giovanni Garbini, *History and Ideology in Ancient Israel*. Trans. John Bowden (New York: Crossroad, 1988), pp. 84, 126.

13. Von Rad, *Old Testament Theology*, pp. 4-5.

14. Garbini, *History and Ideology*, pp. 137-40.

15. Garbini at pp. 79-80.

16. Martin Noth, *Exodus: A Commentary*. Trans. John Bowden. Old Testament Library (Philadelphia: Fortress Press, 1962), p. 83.

17. James Barr, in *Fundamentalism* (Philadelphia: Westminster Press, 1978), pp. 241-42, notes the irony of attempts by K.A. Kitchen and others to vindicate the historical accuracy of the Plagues story as reflecting this yearly cycle of natural catastrophes. If this is indeed what Exodus is describing, then the Bible is actually *wrong*, because it clearly presents the Plagues as unprecedented miracles that would not have occurred without Moses' commands.

18. In the E source Aaron is said to be Miriam's brother and thus implicitly Moses' also, but he is not that important, mainly an eponymous ancestor figure for the Aaronide priesthood of a later time. Aaron probably did not originally appear in J at all, being interpolated later by way of harmonizing the narratives once combined. See W.E. Addis, "Aaron." In T.K. Cheyne and J. Sutherland Black, eds., *Encyclopaedia Biblica: A Dictionary of the Bible* (London: Adam and Charles Black, 1914), cols. 2-3, and Julius Wellhausen, *Prolegomena to the History of Ancient Israel*. Trans. Allan Menzies and J. Sutherland Black (1878; rpt. New York: Meridian Books/World Publishing, 1957), p. 354. His magnification into a second Moses mirrors the insertion of the priesthood as heroic miracle-workers in Chronicles, a priestly rewrite of Samuel and Kings.

19. Alfred Loisy, *The Religion of Israel*. Trans. Arthur Galton. Crown Theological Library (G.P. Putnam's Sons, 1910), p. 87. Or it might have been a peace-offering to roaming demons of the desert. See Noth, *Exodus*, p. 91. Walther Eichrodt, *Theology of the Old Testament*. Trans. J.A. Baker. Old Testament Library (Philadelphia: Westminster Press, 1961), vol. 1, p. 129.

20. Samuel Ives Curtiss, *Primitive Semitic Religion Today: A Record of Researches, Discoveries and Studies in Syria, Palestine and the Sinaitic Peninsula* (New York: Fleming H. Revell, 1902), pp. 188-89.

21. Helmer Ringgren, *Israelite Religion*. Trans. David E. Green (Philadelphia: Fortress Press, 1966), p. 187. Note that, while the rest of the narrative portrays Yahweh himself as passing through Egypt and Goshen, this verse escaped the editor's scrutiny, preserving the original identity of the Destroyer.

22. Alas, the Bible does not contain my favorite line from *The Ten Commandments*, when Pharaoh is suiting up for the battle. Warned of the odds against him, Yul Brynner says, gravely, "It is no shame to die in battle with a god."

23. Apparently, since Ezekiel's blueprint for the Temple had not been utilized, and various of his proposed ("revealed") provisions for the Temple service did not match those in the Pentateuch, some regarded the book as a false prophecy.

24. Garbini, *History and Ideology*, pp. 104-5.

25. Hamilton A.R. Gibb, *Mohammedanism: An Historical Survey* (New York: Mentor Books/New American Library, 1955), pp. 36-37; Von Rad, *Old Testament* Theology, pp. 244-45; Eichrodt, *Theology of the Old Testament*, p. 314.

26. The "Sinai pericope" is an insertion. "Kadesh traditions precede it, and Kadesh traditions follow it again. It is thus obvious that the Sinai tradition has been secondarily inserted into already extant traditions concerning the Wanderings in the Wilderness." Von Rad, *Old Testament Theology*, p. 187.

27. Wright, *God Who Acts*, p. 15.

28. Mircea Eliade, *The Sacred and the Profane: The Nature of Religion*. Trans. Willard R. Trask (New York: Harcourt, Brace & World, 1959), p. 26: "Every sacred space implies a hierophany, an irruption of the sacred that results in detaching a territory from the surrounding cosmic milieu and making it qualitatively different." Eichrodt, *Theology of the Old Testament*, p. 103: "It is possible, therefore, to observe from the first an effort to establish the character of the sacred localities as places not where Yahweh dwells, but where he manifests himself."

29. We can see a certain unease with some of these Old Testament provisions in Mark 10:5, where Jesus undermines the authority of the Mosaic allowance for divorce, saying, "For your hardness of heart he wrote you this commandment." In other words, they just weren't ready for the higher standards God preferred. (Cf. "I have many things to say to you, but you cannot bear them now," John 16:12). But this leaves us with the same problem as before: If you can dismiss any biblical command as an accommodation to ancient thick-headedness, you may as easily be justified in so relativizing (thus nullifying) them all. In that case, there is no guarantee that anything in the Bible really conveys God's will. The alternative? "Why do you not judge for yourselves what is right?" (Luke 12:57).

30. This is the approach of, e.g., Hal Lindsey with C.C. Carlson, *The Late Great Planet Earth* (New York: Bantam Books, 1973).

31. David P. Wright, *Inventing God's Law: How the Covenant Code of the Bible Used and Revised the Laws of Hammurabi* (New York: Oxford University Press, 2013).

32. Johann Jakob Stamm and Maurice Edward Andrew, *The Ten Commandments in Recent Research*. Studies in Biblical Theology Second Series No. 2 (London: SCM Press, 1967), pp. 31-33; Noth, *Exodus*, p. 262.

33. Sigmund Mowinckel, *The Psalms in Israel's Worship*. Trans. D.R. Ap-Thomas (New York: Abingdon Press, 1962), Vol. 1, p. 179.

34. The two parts of this one are "antithetical parallels," saying the same thing in positive as well as negative terms.

35. This probably means that things have changed since you made a promise so that keeping it will now put you at an unanticipated disadvantage, but you keep the promise anyway.

36. Mowinckel, *Psalms in Israel's Worship*, pp. 178-79.

37. He doesn't actually say, "Cursed by Yahweh be Canaan," true, but since this curse is juxtaposed with blessings on Shem and Japheth that do invoke the divine name, I think the same holds implicitly for the curse.

38. Moshe Weinfeld, *Deuteronomy and the Deuteronomic School* (Oxford at the Clarendon Press, 1972), p. 318, note 2.

39. Marten Stol, "Kaiwan." In Karel van der Toorm, Bob Becking, Pieter W. van der Horst (eds.), *Dictionary of Deities and Demons in the Bible (DDD)* (Leiden: E.J. Brill, 1995), cols. 899-900.

40. Stamm and Andrew, *Ten Commandments*, p. 19. Likewise, the Sabbath commandment may have first read, "You shall do no work on the Sabbath."

41. I can never read this one without thinking of an old *Saturday Night Live* skit in which Al Franken introduces his parents, intending to honor them, until old grudges surface and he blurts out "F–k *you*, dad!" The audience gasps, and the whole cringe-fest is hilarious. But fatal in ancient Israel.

42. Stamm and Andrew, *Ten Commandments*, pp. 98-99.

43. "Marriage Counsel" [or "Advice to the Bride and Groom"] par. 6. In Moses Hadas (ed. and trans.), *On Love, the Family, and the Good Life: Selected Essays of Plutarch* (New York: Mentor Books/New American Library, 1957), pp. 82-83.

44. Von Rad, *Old Testament Theology*, p. 191.

45. Von Rad at p. 27.

46. Mel Brooks notwithstanding.

47. Moshe Weinfeld, *Deuteronomy and the Deuteronomic School* (Oxford at the Clarendon Press, 1972).

48. Weinfeld, *Deuteronomy*, Part I, "The Typology of Deuteronomic Composition," Chapter III, "The Scribal Role in the Crystallization of Deuteronomy," pp. 158-78 (and p. 179).

49. Weinfeld, *Deuteronomy*, p. 213, etc.

50. Weinfeld, *Deuteronomy*, Part Three, "Deuteronomic Literature and Wisdom Literature," Chapter II, "Humanism," pp. 282-97.

51. Weinfeld, *Deuteronomy*, Part Three, "Deuteronomic Literature and Wisdom Literature," Chapter I, "Wisdom Substrata in Deuteronomy and Deuteronomic Literature," pp. 244-81.

52. I am capitalizing "Priestly" in reference to the Priestly Code, the P Source, but leaving it lower case when referring to the priests themselves.

53. Weinfeld, *Deuteronomy*, p. 180.

54. F.J. Foakes Jackson ("I and II Kings," in Arthur S. Peake, ed., *Peake's Commentary on the Bible* [London: T.C. & E.C. Jack, 1929], p. 312) sneered at the notion: "The suggestion that Hilkiah himself forged the book and pretended to discover it is unworthy of consideration." You have to suspect that Foakes Jackson mainly just found the word "forged" distasteful.

55. As recently demonstrated quite compellingly in Earl M. Wunderli, *An Imperfect Book: What the Book of Mormon Tells us about Itself* (Salt Lake City: Signature Books, 2013).

56. Apologists make the same mistake when they believe all will tacitly agree that Mary Magdalene went to the tomb to anoint the body of Jesus and found the sepulcher empty, and that only as of the resurrection appearances does the narrative become controversial.

57. Robert M. Price, "Joseph Smith in the Book of Mormon." In Price, *Latter-day Scripture: Studies in the Book of Mormon* (eBookit.com, 2013), pp. 42-43.

58. First Corinthians 9:9-10 (NASB) says, "For it is written in the Law of Moses, 'You shall not muzzle the ox while he is threshing.' God is not concerned about oxen, is He? Or is He speaking altogether for our sake? Yes, for our sake it was written, because the plowman ought to plow in hope, and the thresher to thresh in hope of sharing the crops." So little can the author imagine God sparing a thought for mere beasts that he can only take the Deuteronomic passage as an allegory about something else!

59. Raphael Patai, *The Hebrew Goddess* (New York: Discus/Avon Books, 1978), pp. 16-58.

60. Garbini, *History and Ideology*, Chapter 4, "The Origin and Development of Yahwism," pp. 52-65.

61. Isn't it anachronistic to use the name "Judaism" for the religion of this period? Yes, indeed: that's the whole point.

62. Davies, p. 85: "In Ezra-Nehemiah we encounter the 'people of the land' who are characterized as impure and of alien stock, with whom the true 'Israel' is not to mingle its 'holy seed.' It is these ... who become in Genesis-Kings transformed into the 'Canaanites', of whom very much the same is said. In each case we find antagonism towards the indigenous population, and separation from it, a separation based on the principles of ethnicity and religious adherence to the true ancestral cult." Obviously, the latter are a fictionalized version of the former.

63. But then what about the massacres recorded in Joshua? They never took place, as we will see when we come to that book.

64. Peter Brown, *The Cult of the Saints: Its Rise and Function in Latin Christianity*. Haskell Lectures on the History of Religion, new series, no. 2 (Chicago: University of Chicago Press, 1981), pp. 32-42, 123.

65. Gerhard von Rad, *Studies in Deuteronomy*. Trans. David Stalker. Studies in Biblical Theology No. 9 (Chicago: Henry Regnery Company, 1953), pp. 38-41.

66. See, for example, "A Tablet Addressed to 'Him Who Will Be Made Manifest'" in *Selections from the Writings of the Bab*. Trans. Habib Taherzadeh (Haifa: Baha'i World Centre, 1976), pp. 3-5.

67. Or "Deuteronomistic," if you prefer more syllables. Either form is acceptable.

68. A similar complaint must underlie the section of the Gilgamesh Epic in which Gilgamesh's subjects try to find tasks to keep their king busy to distract him from appropriating their women and exhausting their resources.

69. Weinfeld, *Deuteronomy*, Part I, Chapter II, "Treaty Form and Phraseology–Affinities with the Ancient Near Eastern Treaty Formulae," pp. 59-157.

70. Would they really have access to such sources? Well, *we do today*, millennia later.

71. Meredith G. Kline, *The Structure of Biblical Authority* (Grand Rapids: Eerdmans, 1975).

72. Van A. Harvey, *The Historian and the Believer: The Morality of Historical Knowledge and Christian Belief* (New York: Macmillan, 1966), pp. 14-15.

73. Gerhard von Rad, *The Problem of the Hexateuch and other Essays*. Trans. E.W. Trueman Dicken (London: SCM Press, 1984), Chapter 1, "The Form- Critical Problem of the Hexateuch," pp. 1-78. Heinrich Ewald first suggested the Hexateuch model in 1831, followed by Abraham Kuenen in 1886.

74. Martin Noth, *The Deuteronomistic History*. Trans. E.W. Nicholson. Journal for the Study of the Old Testament Supplement Series 15 (Sheffield: JSOT Press, 2nd ed., 1991), Chapter 3, "The Beginning of the History," pp. 27-33.

75. You see the same "blame the victim" theodicy in the case of Pentecostals who ask God to heal them but find themselves disappointed. God cannot have failed them, so it must be their fault: not enough faith.

76. I understand the analogous prediction of the Paraclete in John 16:12-15 in the same way: I take it to be a winking reference to the "Beloved Disciple" himself, the Fourth Evangelist. Indeed, that may be why that mysterious disciple is never named–it makes it more difficult to charge "forgery" if one cannot be sure who it is that the writer is impersonating!

77. But as we will see below, the whole matter of dating is now up for grabs. Traditionally, however, critics dated the Holiness and Priestly Codes to the time of the Exile. For the moment I am sticking with that.

78. Mary Douglas, "The Abominations of Leviticus." In Douglas, *Purity and Danger: An Analysis of Concepts of Pollution and Taboo*. Pelican Anthropology Library (London: Penguin Books, 1970), pp. 54-72

79. As we will see later, it was the prophets who first moralized and rationalized religion, redefining "holiness" as "moral righteousness" as opposed to majestic and unapproachable "Otherness." This resulted in reckoning immoral acts, and not just ritual transgressions, as sins against God. See Eichrodt, p. 278; Rudolf Otto, *The Idea of the Holy: An Inquiry into the Non-Rational Factor in the Idea of the Divine and its Relation to the Rational.* Trans. John W. Harvey (London: Oxford University Press, 1924), p. 144.

80. Necrophilia does not occur in biblical law, but it is a perfect instance of the category-transgression logic underlying the Holiness Code.

81. The Old Testament never even mentions female-female sex, much less condemning it. I do not believe Romans 1:26 ("Their women exchanged natural relations for unnatural") refers to Lesbianism, but rather to the Levitical prohibition of women having sex with animals (Lev. 20:16), in the same context.

82. Troy Perry with Charles L. Lucas, *The Lord Is my Shepherd and he Knows I'm Gay: The Autobiography of the Reverend Troy D. Perry* (New York: Bantam Books, 1973), pp. 137-38.

83. Cf., Mary Douglas, p. 69: "Everything would be quite straightforward were it not that the legal mind has seen fit to give rulings on some borderline cases."

84. Niels Peter Lemche, "The Old Testament–a Hellenistic Book?" *Scandinavian Journal of the Old Testament* (7/2), 1993, p. 191: "The time lapse between the composition of the major part of the Old Testament and the New Testament writings must . . . be considered minimal. The Old Testament was no creation of a distant and foreign *Israelite* world, but it came into being in a post-exilic Jewish society, presumably during the Hellenistic Age."

85. Wright, pp. 15-16, concludes this in the case of the Book of the Covenant. I would extend the notion to include the whole Torah.

86. Note that "//" means that the two references are parallel accounts, different versions of the same story.

87. George W. Coats, *Rebellion in the Wilderness: The Murmuring Motif in the Wilderness Traditions of the Old Testament* (New York: Abingdon Press, 1968).

88. Noth suggests that, in this early stage of the tradition, the Moses character had not yet been inserted as Israel's mediator with Yahweh. Martin Noth, *A History of Pentateuchal Traditions*, Trans. Bernhard W. Anderson (Englewood Cliffs: Prentice-Hall, 1972), pp. 166-67.

89. Remember the Irving Berlin song from the movie *White Christmas*, "Gee, I Wish I Was Back in the Army"?

90. Von Rad, *Old Testament Theology*, p. 9; Harry Emerson Fosdick, *A Guide to Understanding the Bible: The Development of Ideas within the Old and New Testaments* (New York: Harper Torchbooks / Harper & Brothers, 1956), pp. 2-3. The theory originated with L. Köhler, *Old Testament Theology*. Trans. A.S. Todd (London: 1957), pp. 45ff.

91. Hermann Gunkel, *The Legends of Genesis: The Biblical Saga and History*. Trans. W.H. Carruth (1901; rpt. New York: Schocken Books, 1964), pp. 25-27.

92. When the Revised Standard Version of the New Testament was introduced in 1946, many of the pious were outraged that certain favorite verses had been relegated to footnotes because of the advances of Textual Criticism in the centuries since the King James Version was published. These disputed verses ("The son of man came to seek and to save that which was lost;" "Father, forgive them, for they know not what they do;" the Longer Ending of Mark, the Woman Taken in Adultery, etc.) were absent from many or most ancient manuscripts. There were public burnings of copies of the RSV New Testament. History repeats itself.

93. But why did people begin to invoke Yahweh only in Enosh's time, not before? This is a vestige of the earlier Hebrew myth/belief that Enosh ("man") was the first man, before they borrowed Adam from the mythology of their kinsmen the Edomites. Naturally, they figured, the first man was told the name of his Creator.

94. Theodore J. Weeden, *Mark: Traditions in Conflict* (Philadelphia: Fortress Press, 1971).

95. Hermann Gunkel, *The Influence of the Holy Spirit: The Popular View of the Apostolic Age and the Teaching of the Apostle Paul.* Trans. Roy A. Harrisville and Philip A. Quanbeck II (Philadelphia: Fortress Press, 1979), pp. 28, 31, 53.

96. Wellhausen, pp. 267-268. Even the 120 on the Day of Pentecost are to be understood as "speaking with the tongues [i.e., languages] of angels" (1 Cor. 13:1), not foreign earthly languages. The ensuing confusion arises from the fact that each member of the crowd of international pilgrims heard the whole 120 as if *all* were speaking in

the same language as *each* (foreign) hearer. What the 120 were doing was the same as in Acts 10:46-48; 11:15-17; 19:6. See Richard I. Pervo, *Acts: A Commentary.* Hermeneia–A Critical and Historical Commentary on the Bible (Minneapolis: Fortress Press, 2009), pp. 64-65.

97. Comparing the various lists of Israelite tribes here and there in the Old Testament we see that the number and the particular names vary, much like the conflicting lists of disciples from gospel to gospel. See Garbini, Chapter 10, "The Twelve Tribes," pp. 121-26.

98. Cf., "Why sleepest thou, O [Yahweh]?" (Psalm 44:23) "Awake! Awake! Put on strength, O arm of [Yahweh]!" (Isa. 51:9). I am guessing that such urgings imply a mythic-ritual scenario like that of the Odinsleep depicted in Stan Lee and Jack Kirby, "To Kill a Thunder God," *Journey into Mystery* # 118, July 1965, and in the 2011 movie *Thor*.

99. Margaret Barker, *The Risen Lord: The Jesus of History as the Christ of Faith* (Valley Forge: Trinity Press International, 1997), p. 76; cf., Ignaz Goldziher, *Mythology Among the Hebrews and its Historical Development.* Trans. Russell Martineau (1877; rpt. New York: Cooper Square Publishers, 1967), pp. 183, 226.

100. I suspect that the Temple cleansings of Hezekiah and Josiah are two versions of the same event, especially as the Deuteronomic narrator says of both that "there was none like him among all the kings of Judah, nor among those who were before him" (2 Kings 18:5). "Before [Josiah] there was no king like him who turned to [Yahweh] with all his heart and with all his soul and with all his might, according to all the law of Moses; nor did any like him arise after him." (2 Kings 23:25, both NASB). That kind of narrows it down! If it could have been said of both, then they must have been the same man.

101. Jacques Derrida, *Of Grammatology.* Trans. Gayatri Chakravorty Spivak (Baltimore: Johns Hopkins University Press, 1976), p. 145.

102. They composed Psalms 42, 44, 45, 46, 47, 48, 49, 84, 85, 87, and 88.

103. This Psalm is anonymous, but the same issue seems to be under discussion.

104. Werner Keller, *The Bible as History.* Trans. William Neil (New York: Bantam Books, 1974), pp. 130-33.

III

Joshua, Judges, Samuel, Kings

A SHADY PAST

Our Bibles contain a series of books called Joshua, Judges, Samuel, and Kings, but originally all these were continuous segments of a single mega-narrative. Scholars call it the Deuteronomic[1] History. The Deuteronomist, however, did not simply create his epic from whole cloth. Rather, much like the New Testament evangelists (gospel writers), he compiled old materials into a larger narrative, editing and rewriting as he went.[2] We might compare his work to the *Histories* of Herodotus, as neither made much distinction between actual history and pious legends. On the other hand, in terms of basic purpose, the Deuteronomic Historian might be compared with the later Jewish historian Flavius Josephus (Joseph bar Matthias), author of *Antiquities of the Jews* and *Wars of the Jews*.

Just as Josephus wrote in the wake of the Jewish war with Rome, which culminated with the Roman destruction of the Jerusalem Temple in 70 C.E., the Deuteronomic Historian wrote after the defeat of Judah at the hands of the Babylonians in 586 B.C.E. (Or at least his narrative comes to a screeching halt at that point.) Josephus wanted to preserve the traditions of his people and to defend them from the blame for the war. He enumerated Roman provocations (including those by Pontius Pilate) as well as outrages committed by anti-Roman hotheads, blaming these "villains" for taking down the whole nation with them.

The Deuteronomic Historian, similarly, blamed the destruction of the Jewish state on its apostate kings whose repeated lapses into syncretistic idolatry led Yahweh, their only proper deity, to wash his hands of them. True, the people of Israel and Judah had asked for it: against the prophet Samuel's wise counsel they had insisted on placing power in the hands of a single ruler, replacing an earlier, decentralized system of autonomous tribes.

It seemed like a good idea at the time, since the lack of a powerful ruler had allowed for religious and political anarchy. But the abdication of the whole people's responsibility, handing it off to a monarch, proved only to make apostasy more efficient, a more direct and comprehensive drive over the cliff to ruin. As the Protestant Reformers would much later say, the religion (good or bad) of the prince automatically became that of the people, like it or not. With remarkable nuance, the Deuteronomic Historian preserved and portrayed this delicate balance of viewpoints by incorporating bits and pieces of pro- and anti-monarchial traditions, propaganda from both sides. Even his editorial asides point in both directions, as we will see.

The Deuteronomist, as we saw in the previous chapter, also incorporated a new set of laws, pretty much the same as our Book of Deuteronomy's legal sections.[3] It was filled with stern warnings that failure to keep these stipulations would forfeit Yahweh's promised benefits, notably his pledge of protection from foreign enemies. This covenant between God and his people provided an after-the-fact explanation of Israelite and Jewish disasters and defeats.

After all, one could not suspect *God* of welching on his promises,[4] so who's left to blame? Of course, like twentieth-century Jewish theologian Richard L. Rubenstein, in his book *After Auschwitz*,[5] one could just write off the whole idea of the Jewish covenant with God as a big mistake, never more than an imaginary illusion, but that would be to abandon any vestige of faith in divine Providence, and that would be even more depressing!

Our author, in pursuing his theological blame game, had to pound some square pegs into round holes, sending the historical splinters flying. He brackets individual episodes (received from tradition and national folklore) recounting heroic struggles of courageous Israelites against heathen oppressors, then adding arbitrary statements that God had sicced the bad guys on them in the first place in order to punish them for idolatry and apostasy, and that he had raised up the various freedom fighters only once the people had responded to the wake-up call.

None of this is apparent in the individual tales. And in what did this religious corruption consist anyway? The worship of various gods at local hilltop altars all over the countryside. But these practices were not perceived as wrong at the time. They were only rendered so retroactively from the perspective of much later monotheistic beliefs espoused by the Deuteronomic Historian(s).

In order to make the thread of his long story clear, the Deuteronomist punctuates his narrative with a series of "keynote" speeches put into the mouths of his major characters. Moses exhorts the people in Deuteronomy 1-4, Joshua in Joshua 1:10-18 and chapter 23, Samuel in 1 Samuel 12, and Solomon in 1 Kings 8:14-21. As Noth says, "at all the important points in the course of the story [the Deuteronomist] brings forward the leading personages with a speech, long or short, which looks forward and backward in an attempt to interpret the course of events, and draws the relevant practical conclusions about what people should do."[6]

The flip side of this belief in the covenantal blessings conditional upon Israel's faithful obedience is the notion that what good Israel receives it receives from the hand of God, not by token of their own might or ingenuity. "Otherwise, you may say in your heart, 'My power and the strength of my hand made me this wealth'" (Deut. 8:17, NASB). The Deuteronomic narrative provides several object lessons to this effect (though some of these make their point by virtue of redactional "spin"). The theme survives into the New Testament with even greater prominence, as in John 15:5; 2 Corinthians 3:4-5; 4:7-11; 12:8-10; Ephesians 2:8-9; Philippians 4:13.

The larger constellation of ideas in which this theology of "absolute dependence"[7] first appeared would seem to have been a kind of fanatical pacifism on display as late as the Dead Sea Scrolls manifesto, *The War of the Sons of Light and the Sons of Darkness*. It is an implicitly or explicitly apocalyptic disavowal of human military action in favor of miraculous divine intervention. Obviously, this is wishful thinking on the part of a group that knows itself hopelessly outmatched in any contemplated clash with powerful enemy forces. Modern examples are plentiful, e.g., the Boxer Rebellion in nineteenth-century China, some of the Melanesian Cargo Cults, and several Indian actions against the British colonial authorities.

Some of these movements were quietistic, leaving the whole matter in the hands of the gods. Others were ready to take an active role in the battle once divine aid should arrive to guarantee victory. Still others believed that, since the gods help those who help themselves, they should make the first move, lighting the fuse, after which they expected the gods or God to respond to their demonstration of faith and courage. But the common element was the confidence that victory was hopeless without divine intervention but certain with it, and the unshakeable faith that they would therefore prevail. In recent history, the usual belief was that the bullets of the foe would turn to water.[8] Of course, such hopes were and are doomed to tragic failure.

As Von Rad[9] shows, Deuteronomy has Moses exhort the readers to engage in fearless combat against heathen enemies. Von Rad thought he could show, mainly from the Conquest narratives of Judges, that the Deuteronomist, who wrote his history on the basis of the Book of Deuteronomy, had reworked authentic vestiges of archaic holy war rules, updating them. He thought that the holy war exhortations recorded in Deuteronomy were originally delivered as pep talks to the only armed forces left to King Josiah of Judah after the absorption of most of the country and its paid army by the Assyrians in 701.[10]

What remained must have been the untrained militia of Judean farmers, the same segment of the populace who had formed the original holy war legions in the far-off days of the Judges. Of course there had never been miraculous victories such as we read of in Joshua, and this is because the stories were not histories of what had happened in the past but rather predictions of what could and would happen in the future if only the people would heed the call, as the doomed, bare-chested Boxers did in modern times.

But the last-gasp effort of Josiah against his Assyrian overlords was a disastrous failure. And the Deuteronomic History was, Von Rad believed, composed in the aftermath of this defeat, even after the subsequent Babylonian conquest of 586 B.C.E., during the Babylonian Exile. Given this hindsight perspective, the Deuteronomist(s) had to reinterpret the holy war ideology in the manner I suggested above.[11] In exactly the same way, modern Muslims after the dissolution of the Ottoman Caliphate redefined *jihad* no longer as wars of evangelistic conquest waged against non-believers but rather as the interior struggle of the individual Muslim against his own personal sins.

It now appears that there had been no occasion for holy wars in pre-Deuteronomic times. It was all propaganda fiction. Who promoted this ideology before it was spiritualized by the Deuteronomic School? It must have come from a faction composed of (or heavily influenced by) the schools of "the sons of the prophets" (2 King 2:3-5, 7, 15; 4:1, 38; 5:22; 6:1; 9:1),[12] including the mysterious Rechabites (Jer. 35:1-10). These people maintained that Israel/Judah should abide by a holy war ideology which they had created and retrojected into holy antiquity.

This is why we have stories of Joshua's army losing a major battle because *one man* helped himself to a sharp-looking suit instead of turning it over to the well-stuffed coffers of the priests (Josh 7:1); of Saul forfeiting the mandate of heaven because he barbecued the sheep captured from the Amalekites (instead of saving them for the priests) and left King Agag alive, alone among the genocidally slaughtered population of Amalek (1 Sam. 15:8-9, 20, 32-33); of King David being clobbered by the Almighty (2 Sam. 24) for the sin of taking a military census (as Jesus assumes any secular ruler would be crazy *not* to do in Luke 14:31). Likewise, the Rechabites lived in a state of desert austerity as they imagined the ancient Israelites under Moses had.

These sectarians, like modern religious pacifists, advocated a policy of what we might call "political snake-handling." Isaiah, other prophets, and some of the Psalmists[13] demanded that the kings of Judah eschew reliance upon military alliances,[14] even weaponry, in the face of impending defeat, trusting only in Yahweh's mighty hand. "Some boast of chariots, and some of horses; but we boast of the name of [Yahweh] our God" (Psalm 20:7). It is doubtful whether any kings actually heeded such counsel, but if they did, and inevitably lost, one could always fall back on the handy excuse that the people lacked sufficient faith. If, however, one went into battle armed to the teeth but still lost, well, one should have heeded the prophets' advice!

The Book of Joshua

The Son of Nun

Again, biblical archaeology has completely eliminated the possibility that ancient Israelites journeyed from Egypt to Canaan and there conquered its inhabitants. This means that the Book of Joshua is altogether fictitious. Joshua himself appears to be a mythic character. He is called "son of Nun." This last, meaning "the fish," is not an attested proper name. It seems to denote that Joshua was the son of the Philistine fish-deity Dagon[15] or Oannes, who emerged from the waters to teach wisdom to men.[16]

We can still glimpse his god-like deeds (stopping the sun and moon in their orbits, stopping up the Jordan River, making a covenant of laws for his people, flattening the walls of Jericho), but he has been demoted to the status of a semi-historical (i.e., legendary) hero, as is standard in the evolution of myths.[17] The closer the Hebrews approached to monotheism, the greater the urgency to reinterpret old tales of gods and their exploits as edifying tales of heroes and prophets of Yahweh. Thus Joshua becomes Moses' (merely human) successor.

Some[18] have suggested that the Joshua character functions in the Deuteronomic History as a fictive anticipation (really a retrojection into antiquity) of King Josiah and his reform program. Joshua's extermination of "Canaanite" heathenism certainly symbolizes Josiah's celebrated reforms in any case. Garbini[19] points out that the depiction of Joshua in quasi-rabbinical terms (e.g., studying Torah night and day, Josh. 1:8) models Joshua upon the priestly version of Josiah on display in the Book of Chronicles more than the version of Josiah described in 2 Kings.

However, it seems quite likely that Josiah is himself a fictive retrojection of the second-century B.C.E. Hasmonean king John Hyrcanus,[20] and, in that case, so is Joshua!

Theology as History

Demythologizing the Book of Joshua requires perhaps less readjustment than does the critical approach to any other biblical writing. Christian readers[21] have always found in Joshua an allegory of the spiritual life as a series of struggles and triumphs for the one who depends upon God. The Canaanites, to whom no mercy can be shown, stand for the besetting sins in the Christian's life. The Christian must deal severely with them, i.e., with himself, with his own character (cf. Prov. 16:32).[22] This is in effect to apply the Deuteronomic theology to one's individual spiritual life. Admittedly, this is not exactly the point the Deuteronomist intended to make, but it is quite analogous.

Remember, the Israelites, like their cousins the Ammonites, Midianites, Amorites, and Edomites, were simply one more batch of Canaanites, as their cognate languages and myths attest.[23] The biblical portrayal of the Canaanites as dangerous foreigners tempting Israel to syncretism is a subsequent attempt to distance Israel from their own polytheistic, idolatrous past. The Deuteronomist must have intended the indigenous, idolatrous Canaanites of his narrative to symbolize the lingering vestiges (actually still-current "unreformed" tendencies, beliefs, and practices) against which the Deuteronomist Reformers sought to define their own new orthodoxy. What he really had in mind was not ancient blitzkriegs against pagan foreigners (which never took place) but rather the attempts in his own day to suppress the old, still-popular Israelite religion.

And shouldn't it come as something of a great relief not to have to take literally the statements in Joshua (e.g., 6:21) that God commanded his people to commit genocide, expressly mandating the merciless slaughter of whole peoples: men, women, children, and pets? When we say God did command such horrors and then try to justify it we make ourselves as morally demonic as the God we are defending. Thank God it didn't happen! In the manner of John Bunyan and *The Pilgrim's Progress*, we may now view the eradicated Canaanites as standing for so many besetting sins. Quite a gain!

We should have suspected all this anyway: Despite the blitzkrieg victories depicted throughout the book (e.g., 11:23), chapter 13 lists huge amounts of territory still unconquered, a very different impression than that left in the preceding chapters. Similarly, Judges 1 begins a wholly different account in which local Israelite groups only gradually win freedom from Canaanite overlords.

Additionally, certain later conquests appear to be back-dated in Joshua (and Judges). Judges 1:8 and Joshua 10 agree that Joshua captured Jerusalem, but according to 2 Samuel 5:6-9 it was first taken by David centuries later. Judges 1:18 has Joshua taking the Philistine cities of Gaza, Ashkelon, and Ekron, which however are still in Philistine hands in Samson's time. Joshua 11 has Israel defeat Jabin, King of Hazor, burning his city-state, but Judges 4 says Jabin was still around to subjugate Israel years after Joshua's death. All these inconsistencies show that the biblical Conquest led by Joshua is a complete fiction; nor does that story square with the ample archaeological evidence which yields no sign of a violent overthrow of the Canaanite states.

Harlot with the Heart of Gold

Josh. 2:1-24

Rahab the prostitute is an interesting character. Her name implies she is supposed to be no common whore but rather a so-called cult prostitute.[24] The sacred prostitutes (or hierodules) were priestesses of fertility gods with whom farmers would have sanctified sex as an act of imitative magic. Farmer Brown played the role of Baal (or whomever), while the woman stood in for the Earth Mother. As the man planted his seed in the woman, so would the sky god implant his semen, the rain, in the fertile fields, yielding a good harvest. That was the theory, anyway. Rahab would have been named for the divine sea dragon Rahab[25] (Psalm 89:9-10; Isa. 51:9) also called Leviathan, for whom the Levite priests were also named.

She harbors two spies sent by Joshua on a reconnaissance mission. Having heard of the supernatural victories of the Israelites, she can see the handwriting on the wall. The spies promise to spare her for her kindness to them once the city is taken. She is a "fifth columnist," a traitor. But loyalty to her own people is nothing to our author: The important thing is being on God's side. Rahab is in the same position as Jeremiah who advised his people to surrender to the Babylonian invaders because he knew they were being sent by God to punish Judah (Jer. 21).

Note that the prostitute is the heroine, and that God honors her lies to her countrymen just as he did the lie of the Hebrew midwives in Exodus 1:18-20.

On Jordan's Stormy Banks

Josh. 3-4

In order to show that he was with Joshua as he had been with Moses, God performs a miracle similar to the dividing of the Red (Reed) Sea. This time he divides the Jordan. How did he do it? The text seems to imply that, as often happened, a landslide upstream temporarily dammed up the river. Otherwise, what is the point of naming the point where the waters piled up (3:16) and saying it was a great distance away? The miracle is the providential *timing*. The implicit rationalism, providing a non-supernatural cause for the "miracle," may be a sign of the very late, Hellenistic-era origin of the story.[26]

Joshua tells them to appoint one man from each tribe to take a smooth riverbed stone to set up inland, at Gilgal, as a monument of this event. "Gilgal" means "circle," implying that the place was named for this cromlech, or circle of standing stones. Chapter 4, verses 1-7 and 21-24, tell us that this was the customary answer to children's curiosity when they would see the pile of stones for the first time. Thus it is originally both a *geological* story and an *etymological* one.

General Revelation

Josh. 5:13-15

To encourage Joshua, Yahweh sends his angelic war chief to appear to him. (Is this some sort of nod to the underlying myth of Joshua himself as a godlike warrior?) This is similar to the story in 2 Kings 6:15-17, where Elisha calms his fearful assistant on the eve of battle by asking God to "open his eyes" to behold the angelic horsemen and chariots of fire surrounding them: Yahweh's army. Here we glimpse the underlying mythic rationale for the faith-certitude of those embarking on a holy war.

Joshua Fit de Battle of Jericho

Josh. 6

This is the sequel to the Rahab story. In verses 17 and 21 all life in the city is sacrificed to Yahweh. So we are dealing here not only with genocide (although fictive), but with human sacrifice. The defeated are "offered" to God as a sacrifice, much, one might say, as a cat brings a slain bird or mouse to lay it before its owner.

The poem in verse 26 originally would have been part of a traditional ritual for the foundation of any new city. Such bloody rituals underlie myths such as Cain killing Abel before he founds the city of Enoch (Gen. 4:17) and Romulus slaying his brother Remus before breaking ground for the city of Rome.[27] Here it has been made a kind of epitaph for Jericho in particular, underlining its desolation.

Reading of the method by which the Israelites brought down the city wall, one cannot help but think of the modern strategy of surrounding terrorist compounds with troops and blaring heavy metal music at all hours. Biblical tactics?

Archaeology confirms the existence of Jericho, as well as its perimeter wall, but it was destroyed centuries before the ostensible time of Joshua.

One Expensive Suit!

Josh. 7

What was Achan's crime? No private individual was to take war booty (like the Nazi daggers my father brought back from World War II). It all had to go into the sacred treasury. Well, Achan saw a cloak he fancied and stashed it away. For this infraction God caused Israel to be defeated by Ai. The process which "discovered" Achan's supposedly unique sin is a classical piece of scapegoating, for we must suspect that *whomever* was finally fingered at random would have had his *own* stash of contraband.

Somewhat analogous to the story of Ananias and Sapphira in Acts 5:1-11 (and probably the basis for it),[28] the Achan episode must have been a cautionary tale. Though the story depicts the violation of the protocols of holy war,[29] that institution must have been long moribund by this point in the time of the Deuteronomist. The broader point, still relevant, would have been to reinforce the inviolability of the exclusive property of the priesthood.[30]

Why was Achan's *whole family* punished? And why by *stoning*? As in Exodus 14:12-13, God's holiness was a palpable and deadly force. It had attached itself to plunder rightly his, and from thence it had contaminated Achan by token of simple physical contact. Achan, in turn, had touched his family, rendering them all "holy," i.e., unavailable any longer for life in the profane world, which meant they were doomed to be sacrificed. Their executioners dared not touch them, lest the same thing happen to them, thus the stoning.

René Girard[31] explains how "physical contact with the anathema[tized] is avoided . . . To do violence to a violent person is to be contaminated by his violence . . . . It is best, therefore, to arrange matters so that nobody, except perhaps the culprit himself, is directly responsible for his death," lest reciprocal violence, i.e., escalating vendetta, erupt. This is also why the whole people (or a representative group of them) must stone Achan: That way, his death will not have been the result of any single executioner against whom retaliation might be plotted. All this has been mythologized into holiness or impurity as a palpable force. "Concepts such as impurity and contagion, because they translate human relations into material terms, provide a sort of camouflage."[32]

Whence the story? It began as a *geological* tale to account for a huge cairn of stones, enough to cover a whole family. It was situated at Achor, which means "trouble," hence something bad must have happened to the family: mass execution! So it is an *etymological* story, too.

Hands-on Astronomy

Josh. 10

This story, which assumes, as did all the ancients, that the sun orbits the earth, comes from the pre-biblical Book of Yashar/Jasher, or Book of the Just, i.e., of Hebrew heroes. (The same book is also quoted in 2 Samuel 1:18-27, the funeral dirge for Saul and Jonathan.)

Some have tried to minimize the miraculous character of the story, as if all Joshua had requested was a "stilling" of the fierce heat of the sun,[33] but this is ruled out by the parallel mention of the moon's halting in the sky (were they afraid of getting "moonburned"?), as well as the coordinates given for precisely where the tiny sun and moon stopped in their trajectories. The whole thing depends upon an ancient conception of astronomy and cannot survive it.[34]

Alternate Altar

Josh. 22

Three tribal groups (Reuben, Gad, Manasseh) lived beyond the Jordan, east of Palestine, what we call the Transjordan. They build their own altar, an act that nearly precipitates a war between them and the other tribes. Why? According to Deuteronomy 12:1-14, all worship was restricted to Jerusalem. But this was a much later development, presupposing that previously one might have constructed an altar pretty much anyplace a divine epiphany had occurred (like Marian apparitions today). Exodus 20:24-26 even provides instructions for building such altars.

But Joshua seems to read the Deuteronomic centralization back into the earlier period, insisting that worship be restricted to what was then the central shrine, namely the portable Tabernacle (wherever it happened to be at any given time). The Tabernacle itself was an imaginary analog to (or version of) Solomon's Temple, posited in order to root centralization more firmly in the period of the Exodus and Conquest. When it comes to pedigrees and precedents, the older the better.

The impending war is averted when the Transjordanian tribes explain that the structure was intended only as a nonfunctional reminder of the real thing![35] This story attempts to explain the embarrassing existence of an old, once-functioning Transjordanian Yahweh temple like those later built for Jewish colonies in Elephantine and Leontopolis, Egypt.[36] There shouldn't have *been* any, so the Deuteronomic Historian explains this one away. In Joshua's day, as is clear from 8:30-31, anyone could build his own altar anywhere.

A New Covenant

Josh. 8:30-35; 24:1-28, esp. vv. 1, 14-28

Here are two stories, or two versions of one story, in which Joshua leads the people in an affirmation of faithfulness to the covenant with God. In chapter 8, Joshua builds an altar on Mount Ebal as stipulated in the Book of the Covenant: out of uncut fieldstones, upon which he then carves the text of the laws. The priests stand at the foot of the mountain with the Ark of the Covenant to bless the people.

In chapter 24, Joshua challenges the people to get rid of their traditional gods and henceforth to serve only Yahweh. (What? Had God vanquished the Canaanites in favor of a pack of idolaters and polytheists such as Israel is now revealed to be?) The scene takes place at the shrine at Shechem. This time, instead of reading and copying older laws, as in chapter 8, Joshua is said to make a covenant of new laws for the people. He is depicted as another Moses or, perhaps better, a rival Moses.

Both stories must have been told (invented) by the priests in charge of the two named shrines.

The Book of Judges

The old title, Sefer Yashar, the "Book of the Just," i.e., of the heroes of Israel, would make an equally good title for the piece of the Deuteronomic History we call the Book of Judges. The protagonists of the book have virtually nothing in common, despite their being press-ganged into a literary agenda alien to their stories, except that they are one and all heroes of archaic Israel (or of the legends thereof). "Judges," a term used for rulers elsewhere in the ancient Near East, is purposely vague.

The Judges are not exactly kings: There is no real government in their era. They are charismatic, *ad hoc* leaders who emerge in times of crisis to marshal the troops and the tribes against their enemies. Some were like the prophetess Deborah, who literally judged her fellow Israelites, hearing cases and delivering oracular judgments. Others were military men whose victories proved after the fact that God must have anointed them. Still others, like Samson, hardly belong in the book at all, but this seems to have been the only catch-all where they could gain a foothold. If we think of Greek mythology, the Judges would be like Hercules, Agamemnon, and Teiresias.

The Deuteronomic Historian has made generous use of his theological shoe-horn to jam these old stories into his theological mold: They have been repurposed to serve as lessons of how Israel and Judah prospered when faithful to God (in terms of the Deuteronomic covenant which is plainly anachronistic for most of these stories, long post-dating them) and how they invited disaster when disobedient. That point is inescapably clear from his interpretive comments, but it is equally clear that the stories themselves do not fit that concept.

Instead of Israel as a whole losing a freedom won by Joshua, forfeiting it to pagans as the penalty for backsliding, most of the stories depict this or that tribal group gaining independence for the first time in valiant struggles against pagan kings. The Deuteronomist says God granted Israel victory once they repented for the sins that had led to their subjugation, but there is no note of repentance in the stories themselves; the editor does not even bother inserting it into the stories he has collected. We ought to be grateful for this superficial editing, though, since it enables us to recognize the original layer of meaning prior to his sketchy working over of it.

Judges also repeats the refrain, "There was no king is Israel in those days, and every man did what was right in his own eyes." The point seems to be to remind readers of the need for a righteous king like Josiah to implement the reforms of Deuteronomy in their own day (perhaps with the Hasmonean John Hyrcanus in mind). Elsewhere in the Deuteronomic History (e.g., 1 Samuel) we meet deep suspicions of monarchy, but I suspect those passages are really thinking of the pre-Exilic kings whose "sins" the Deuteronomist blamed for the Assyrian and Babylonian conquests.

Go Directly to Jael

Judg. 4-5

This fascinating sequence might be called the biblical counterpart of Marion Zimmer Bradley's Authurian novel, *The Mists of Avalon*. In it, the real movers and shakers are women, who steal the glory from the male heroes whom they manipulate from behind the scenes. Deborah is a tantalizing figure of whom we would love to know more. For one thing, her role as a "judge" is quite instructive: She hears cases sitting under the Palm of Deborah, passing into a mantic state to interpret the rustling of the overhead fronds as the word of Yahweh.

In our terms, she, like Moses at Kadesh in Exodus 18, would enter a dissociative state, allowing clear access to the subconscious and its wisdom. But she also commands great power as a kind of shamanic warlord like the Delaware Prophet (Michigan, 1762), the Shawnee prophet Tenskwatawa (Ohio Valley, 1805), and Smohalla the Dreamer (Pacific Northwest, 1860). Each of the military actions they inspired was carried out by a warrior (Pontiac, Tecumseh, and Chief Joseph respectively) playing the Barak role.[37]

It is tempting to take this story as evidence of a once-wider leadership role for women in Israel (in itself by no means impossible), but the story seems to belie such an inference by noting (4:9) the oddity that a woman should receive the credit for the victory. One first supposes that the woman in question must be Deborah, who organized the whole venture, but in the version we read, it is Jael who turns out to be the heroine of the prophecy.

We meet her later in the story, when Sisera, the general of the Canaanites of Hazor, fleeing from defeat, takes refuge in the tent of Jael and her husband, Heber the Kenite. She plays along with it, extending her protection, telling Sisera she will not tell anyone he is hiding there. And she keeps her word insofar as she does not *have* to turn him over to Israelite troops because she takes matters into her own hands. While the exhausted general snores away his troubles, Jael staples his head into the ground with a railroad spike! Her countrymen arrive, and she reveals the corpse: "Is *this* the guy you're looking for?"

Jael's husband's name, Heber, appears earlier in the Bible (Gen. 10:21) as the eponymous ancestor of the Hebrews, a wider group of which Israel was a subset. Obviously Heber the Kenite is not the same character, but the name has added interest here because he is a Kenite and a descendant of Moses' father-in-law Hobab.[38] The Kenites were important allies of David, and there is reason to believe Israel adopted the deity Yahweh from them. Note that Yahweh is said in 5:4 to have answered Israel's call, flying in from Mount Seir in Edom, which implies a broader Canaanite origin for this deity.[39] Thus "Heber the Kenite" is doubly redolent of archaic Israelite origins, for what that may be worth.

One of the most striking elements of the Jael tale is her assassination of a man to whom she had accorded safety and shelter. What a contrast to the typical treatment of hospitality in the Bible! Abraham hastens to provide a feast for travelling strangers as if he were a waiter in a posh restaurant (Gen. 18:1-8). Lot (Gen. 19:1-3) is so mortified at the thought of handing his guests over to the Sodom lynch-mob that he deems it a lesser offence to abandon his virgin daughters to the howling thugs (Gen. 19:8). Likewise the Ephraimite in Judges 19:23-24 (see below). Even given the fact that Sisera is a villain, it is still very surprising to see Jael blatantly violating the sacred protocols of hospitality and safe refuge. But my guess is that the narrator means to exonerate her by token of her having killed Sisera herself instead of betraying him to his pursuers.

Chapter 5 is a roughly parallel poetic version of the story of Deborah, Barak, and Jael. It is a traditional song of victory over the foe and goes on to execrate Israelite cowards who sat out the war effort. Though several of the specific allusions remain unclear to us after so many centuries, we cannot help noting the seeming mention of a "lost" Israelite tribe, that of Machir (5:14).**40**

Also note the apocalyptic imagery of the stars of heaven fighting invisibly alongside Israel (5:20). Angels are often symbolized by stars in biblical literature (Job 38:7; Jude 13; Rev. 1:20; 12:4; 1 Enoch 18:15-16), and if that is the intention here, we might have a parallel to Daniel, where an angel apologizes to the prophet for showing up late, having been occupied for three weeks in a fight with "the prince of Persia" (Dan. 10:13, 20), i.e., the angelic patron of that empire.

Gideon (Jerubbaal)
Judg. 6

As befits one of the great heroes, who give rise to whole cycles of legend, there are at least two different "calling" stories told of Gideon in Judges chapter 6. The first, Judges 6:11-24, is a *ceremonial* story, explaining the origin of the altar at the oracle Oak of Ophrah.**41** Gideon erected it to mark the occasion of God calling him.

The second, 6:25-32, is an *etymological* story, explaining how Gideon came to bear the name "Jerub-Baal" which seemed to smack of paganism. His parents would have named him at birth with a wish that the family's patron deity might favor and protect him in life, hence: "May Baal contend [on his behalf]." Hosea 2:16 may be taken to imply that Yahweh was sometimes called Baal ("Lord"), too.

So perhaps no foreign god is in view, but once people refrained from using the epithet "Baal" for Yahweh, as Hosea anticipates, pious Israelites took a second look at the name "Jerub-Baal" and thought it could use a convenient redefinition. This story makes the name a taunt to the pagan deity Baal. Gideon, under cover of night, vandalizes the local Baal altar.

Next morning, the irate neighbors gather at his family's house, demanding that Gideon answer for his hooliganism. But the lad's father challenges the Baalist lynch mob, replying that it is a poor deity who needs pathetic palookas like them to stick up for him! "He needs *you* to fight for him? *Let Baal contend* for himself!"

As if to assure the reader that the prophets are not acting out of self-seeking vainglory, the Bible often shows them initially reticent, like Moses (Exod. 4:10-14) and Jeremiah (Jer. 1:4-10). Likewise, here (6:36-40) Gideon seems to fear that maybe he is just hearing things, so he sets up a little experiment: He spreads out a fleece on the threshing floor, requesting that, if God really plans to give him victory over the Midianites, he cause the morrow's dew to soak the fleece but leave the surrounding floor dry. And so it happens. But he is still not convinced (and perhaps does not *want* to be!), so, just to be sure, he asks God to humor him by soaking the surrounding ground but leaving the fleece dry this time. God indulges him, making it official.**42**

In 7:2-7 we have the greatest single depiction of the Deuteronomic theology with its creed of entire reliance on God, not on the arm of flesh. Gideon recruits an enthusiastic legion of some 32,000 men, but God tells him to thin out the company by allowing those in danger of missing a favorite TV show to go home, then by seeing which of the remainder happen to lap up water like dogs (instead of cupping it in their hands)!

There are 300 of these left to him for his army, so that God may demonstrate that the victory comes from him alone. Never mind that the ensuing victory is won by means of a clever stratagem, deceiving the Midianites into believing the Israelite army outnumbers them. Strictly speaking, the real lesson would seem to be that brains are mightier than brawn.

Jephthah, A Devil's Bargain with God

Judg. 11; 12:1-6

Having been forced by circumstance, like David (1 Sam. chapter 27), into a life of highway robbery and brigandage, Jephthah is surprised to find himself courted by the elders of Gilead, who need a leader to fight off the Ammonites. He accepts their call but tries to fend off war by reasoning with the enemy: Why this territorial dispute? Why cannot they be content with the land their god Chemosh has assigned them, just as Israel is satisfied with the land Yahweh has apportioned them? This implies Israel was at that time not yet monotheistic but at most *monolatrous*, recognizing that other nations had gods of their own that they properly worshipped.

In 11:30-40, we have the Israelite version of Homer's story of Agamemnon who had to offer his daughter Iphigenia as a sacrifice before Athena would relent and allow the Achaean fleet to catch wind and embark for Troy for battle. Similarly, Jephthah had made a foolish bargain with God to sacrifice to him the first living thing he should lay eyes on once he returned from battle, should God grant him victory.

He returns home, victorious–and sees his daughter! She agrees to die but wins his permission to go with her girlfriends into the hills in a kind of Maenadic rite to lament that she will die a virgin. Was the biblical tale based on the *Iliad* version? Or were they spontaneous parallels? Or separate recountings of an original common legend?

This is no doubt a *ceremonial* myth told each year at a women's puberty rite, mourning the impending loss of virginity, not because they were about to die, but because they were about to enter the marriageable state.[43] As so often in the Bible, a piece of repeated ritual text has been turned into a story of a one-time event.

Finally there is the story (12:1-6) that gives us our expression "shibboleth," meaning a password. In the mopping-up operation after their victory over the Ephraimites, the Gileadites control a ford and will not let any pass who cannot pronounce the "sh" diphthong in the word *shibboleth*, knowing that the Ephraimites pronounced it as a simple "s."

Samson

Samson gets the lion's share of stories in the Book of Judges. He is very different from all the other judges and does not really fit in their ranks. He is no prophet, no seer, no military commander, just a rogue with superhuman strength. Samson is the Hebrew Hercules, perhaps actually two names for the same character.[44] Both were originally sun gods, as is clear from Samson's name ("the Sun"!),[45] his long hair (= the sun's rays),[46] etc. As with Joshua and others, Samson retained his place in scripture only by getting demoted from a god to a legendary hero.

This transposition of myth to heroic saga is a notable mechanism in ancient Indo-European traditions, wherever a certain cultic system has been supplanted in living religion and the superannuated former apparatus falls prey to literary manipulation.[47]

The tendency occurs in other cultural traditions as well, and Samson is the perfect example. The Hebrew cult (i.e., worship) of the sun eventually succumbed to Jewish monotheism, so the myths about him became transposed into legends of a demigod named Samson ("the sun"). There are two separate but partially parallel collections of Samson tales.

First Cycle

Miraculous Nativity

Judg. 13:2-5

Manoah of Zorah has no children; his unnamed wife is barren (like Sarah in Genesis 18:9-14, the Shunammite in 2 Kings 4:12-17, Hannah in 1 Samuel 1, and Elizabeth in Luke 1:5-23). A man appears, promising that she will after all conceive and commanding that the boy be raised with the strict discipline of the Nazirite vow *for his whole life*! The standard Nazirite vow was for a period of weeks, not a whole life. The point here is to try to explain Samson's long hair, unusual for Hebrew men, but quite natural for him as a sun god (the locks of hair symbolizing the sun's rays).

The Deuteronomist has, I suspect, like other biblical redactors and scribes, omitted a crucial element of the story, though we can still recognize it between the lines: The "man" or "angel of Yahweh" who appeared to the barren woman must originally have sexually impregnated her, as Zeus did with the mothers of Hercules, Perseus, etc. The result is, naturally, a powerful demigod. It seems that the old motif of the sons of God mating with the daughters of men (Gen. 6:1-4), begetting "men of renown," was originally not supposed to have been restricted to the antediluvian epoch but continued on through Hebrew history. Samson was of course one of these Nephilim.

The Lion and the Riddle

Judg. 14:1-19

The story's "local color" attests the Israelite-Philistine intermarriage that we saw legitimatized in the Curse of Noah story (Gen. 9:27).

We have two sun symbols here: First, Samson kills a lion, just as Hercules does. The mane (like Samson's own flowing hair) represents the rays of the sun.[48] Second, the wedding reception recalls Psalm 19:4b-5, "In [the skies] he has set a tent for the sun, which comes forth like a *bridegroom* leaving his chamber and like a *strong man* runs its course with joy."

Foxes in the Field

Judg. 14:20-15:8a

Samson gains vengeance on the tricky Philistines by catching 300 foxes (how long would this have taken, even for a man with superhuman strength? Tell me this is not folklore!), tying their tails together, and setting them on fire. Then he releases them into the Philistines' grain fields. The whole thing is symbolic of the sun withering the grain.

The Jawbone of an Ass

Judg. 15:8b-17

Pretending to come along quietly, Samson suddenly lays into his Philistine captors with the nearest weapon to hand, a sun-bleached donkey jawbone. With it he kills one thousand men! Did they line up to get brained one by one? Didn't the bone break? It is an *etymological* story told to supply a noble explanation for Ramath-lehi ("Hill of the Jawbone"), originally named for its topography, i.e., a declining rocky ridge. The story is based on a misunderstanding of the poem quoted ("With the jawbone of an ass, heaps upon heaps! With the jawbone of an ass I have slain a thousand men!") which originally meant, "At Ramath-lehi, heaps upon heaps! At Ramath-lehi I have slain a thousand men!"

This story is another version of the single recorded adventure of the similarly named Shamgar (Judg. 3:31). Like Samson, Shamgar was a demigod, son of the important goddess Anath. His accomplishment is to have dispatched six hundred Philistines with no more weapon than an ox-goad, a sharpened stick. Who knows whether the Samson or the Shamgar version was the original? Interestingly, several ancient copies place the Shamgar note as an adjunct to the Samson cycle, implying that someone understood that Samson and Shamgar were one and the same.

The Miraculous Spring
Judg. 15:18-19

Feeling pretty parched after killing a thousand foes, Samson petulantly calls out for God to provide a drink, lest thirst finish him off where the Philistines couldn't! God obligingly causes a spring to gush forth. It is an *etymological* story in that it redefines the old name, "En-hak-kore" ("Spring of the Partridge") as if it meant "the Spring of Him Who Calls."[49] This gave the place added dignity as a holy site by associating it with the superhero Samson. It is also a *geological* story, explaining the origin of the spring itself.

Verse 20 concludes the first cycle.

Second Cycle

The Ambush at the Gate
Judg. 16:1-3

Samson outwits a party of ambushers who wait for him at the city gates as he spends the night at a Philistine prostitute's apartment. He lifts the gates off their foundations and carries them to a hilltop. (Were the Philistines hanging on for dear life?) It may be some sort of zodiacal image, like the sun appearing in the aperture at Stonehenge, or perhaps a *geological* legend seeking to explain a pair of stalagmites jutting up from a hilltop.

Also, we may have the same image that underlies the famous Pillars of Hercules which marked the Western limit of the hero's travels.[50] Keep in mind that, like Samson, Hercules was at first a sun god. The Pillars would have denoted the end of the sun's heavenly circuit as it set daily in the West. Samson lifts and carries the gates at midnight, though one might have expected him to do it at dusk. In an earlier telling, perhaps, he did.

But Goldziher spotted something else underlying the story, an earlier myth of Samson "harrowing hell," descending to the Netherworld and bursting its confining gates to rescue someone held within, as Orpheus (very nearly) retrieved his beloved Eurydice and as Hercules liberated Theseus from Hades. (Of course, much later the same myth will be applied to Christ invading hell to "spring" the righteous souls of the Old Testament saints.)

These myths, too, are ultimately solar in nature, symbolizing the nightly descent of the sun into the Netherworld (some thought the sun sank into a well in Libya each night!) before returning in its glory at dawn. When Hercules returned from the Netherworld he had to smash his way through the infernal gates (Greek *pylos*), and eventually the story was retold with him engaging in an earthly battle at Pylos. The same thing appears to have happened in this Samson episode, where the impregnable gates of Sheol (cf. Matt. 16:18; Isa. 38:10; Jonah 2:6; Acts 2:24) have become the mundane gates of the city of Gaza ("Strong").[51]

Why, Why, Why, Delilah?

Judg. 16:4-31

Here is another instance of the theme of Samson and Philistine women. This is another version of the Lion and the Riddle. As there, we see Samson marrying a Philistine who betrays him to her countrymen by wheedling a secret out of him. She is a fictive character, named solely on the basis of her role in the story. "Delilah" means "Traitoress."[52] (In the real world nobody gives names like that to their children. "Bill, let me introduce my daughter, Bitchy.")

As before, Samson is temporarily outwitted but gains revenge, this time at the cost of his life. Note the threefold structure common to fairytales and jokes.

Samson's identity as the sun is absolutely clear from this story: He loses his strength when his hair is cut; in other words, when the rays of the sun are obscured, the sun is no longer shining in its strength. And he is *blind*![53] And his positioning himself between the pillars harks back to the hilltop gates of the previous tale.

Chaos without a King

Judg. 19-21

Here is one of the most revolting of all biblical stories. (That's not being overly critical, just honest.) These three chapters effectively paint a gruesome picture of the sort of careening chaos that finally led to Israel's adoption of monarchy. Some squeamish readers point to these episodes in order to show how vile a book the Bible is, but, as Jewish theologian Michael S. Kogan once pointed out, "niceness" is no criterion for truth.[54]

The travesties depicted in Judges 19-21 are offered as cautionary tales against a kind of optimistic anarchism. As the Deuteronomist shows quite clearly later in his story, having a king is also quite dangerous, but then even bad government is better than none. This is the germ of the profound biblical myth of the Principalities and Powers, the fallen angels who rule the world from behind the thrones of earthly rulers.[55]

We begin with a deceptively peaceful bit of domesticity in which a Levite[56] tries to patch up a quarrel with his estranged concubine.[57] He has journeyed, flowers and candy in hand, from their home in the hill country of Ephraim to her father's house in Bethlehem, where she has taken refuge. They are (presumably) reconciled, but the Levite seems happier to see his father-in-law than his concubine, as he spends the next several days eating, drinking, and just generally shooting the breeze with him. Finally he manages to tear himself away and leaves, heading home. The Levite, his concubine, and his manservant decide to stop the next night in the Benjaminite city of Gibeah.

The people there are suspicious, downright hostile, to outsiders, and so our trio starts to bed down in the open square. No room for them at the inn, you see. About this time a fellow Ephraimite, who happens to be staying in the town temporarily, chances upon them and warns them not to spend the night outside. He invites them to his quarters, and they go with him. The men are drinking and laughing it up until they hear fists pounding on the door. It is a mob of xenophobic Gibeonites demanding to see who he's hiding. At this point, we begin to detect definite signs of fiction: How has their host, as much a foreigner as the Levite, not incurred the wrath of the populace? And hadn't they already gotten enough of a glimpse of the visitors when they all earlier denied them shelter for the night?

One may experience a flash of *déjà vu* at the cry of the crowd: "Bring out the man who came into your house, that we may know him!" Isn't this virtually the same thing the ruffians of Sodom said to Lot in exactly the same situation (Gen. 19:5)? And doesn't the old Ephraimite sound just like Lot (Gen. 19:6) when he desperately tries to dissuade the mob from some unspecified atrocity? "No, my brethren! Do not act so wickedly, seeing this man has come into my house. Do not do this vile thing! Behold, here are my virgin daughter and his concubine. Let me bring them out now. Ravish them and do with them what seems good to you, but against this man do not do so vile a thing!" Uh, *what* vile thing, exactly? Does this mean "whatever vile thing you were planning to do to him" without specifying it? Or does it mean "as vile a thing as I'm suggesting you do to the women"? Did the mob intend to "ravish" the Levite?

There may be an answer in Judges 20:5, when the Levite subsequently explains to the elders of Israel what had happened in Gibeah: "The men of Gibeah rose up against me and beset the house round about me by night; they meant to kill me, and they ravished my concubine, and she is dead." This would seem to imply that the "vile thing" they had in mind for the Levite was *lynching*, not gang rape, especially since the fate of the concubine, gang rape, is specified as a different crime.

Otherwise, wouldn't we be reading, "They meant to ravish me but ravished my concubine instead"? This is important because of the extensive parallel with the Sodom story in Genesis chapters 18-19. It implies that the demand of the Sodom mob ("Where are the men who came to you tonight? Bring them out that we may know them!") was simply to *kill* the outsiders, not to engage in homosexual rape as is often supposed.[58]

The Levite unceremoniously shoves his concubine out the door into the waiting clutches of the Gibeonite degenerates who, uh, rape her all night long, rape her to death! But the narrator said just beforehand that they *rebuffed* the old man's offer to do just this! It becomes absolutely clear that we are reading fiction when we learn that the Levite, his servant, and their host somehow were willing and able to *sleep* through all this! ("Hey! Could you guys hold it down out there? We're trying to grab a few winks in here!") Next morning, as if nothing much had happened, the Levite opens the door, pokes the supine body of his beloved and says, "Get up! We've got a long trip ahead of us." Oops! She's a bloody corpse! Well, nothing for it but to sling the body over one of the mounts like a dead deer and head for home.

Once they get there, the Levite hacks the corpse to pieces like a kosher butcher and Fedexes the cuts of meat, one each, to the various Israelite tribes, informing them of the outrage. The tribal elders assemble a war council and resolve to take vengeance upon the men of Gibeah, demanding that the rest of the Benjaminites turn them over. But Benjamin refuses. So they, too, must be punished. The war goes forward until somebody realizes that things have gotten out of hand: They're about to totally destroy one of the tribes of Israel. So they put on the brakes.

Now they're in a pickle; they had already sworn that no one from the other tribes should give his daughter to marry a Benjaminite (hoping in that way to make the tribe die out?). But they had also slaughtered all the Benjaminite women! Someone points out that the town of Jabesh-Gilead had sat out the campaign, so why not kill off all their men and their wives and round up all *their* virgin daughters to marry the remaining Benjaminite men? Sure! *That's* the ticket! But it turns out there are *still* not enough virgins to go around. What to do next? Well, there's an annual religious festival up in Shiloh, where virgins participate in a ceremonial dance in the vineyards (the one mentioned in Judges 11:39-40?). Tell the Benjaminite men to go up there and grab the girls. They won't mind– much. Of course, this part of the story parallels that of the Rape of the Sabine Women.[59]

Judges 19-21 provide us with a breathless escalation from one horror to the next, even worse, one. And the Deuteronomist caps the whole disgusting business with the epitaph, "In those days there was no king in Israel; everyone did what was right in his own eyes." (Judg. 21:25, NASB). The Deuteronomist was, as we have seen, no fan of the Israelite and Jewish monarchies, but even their reigns saw nothing like this!

The Book of Samuel

Samuel is depicted as a "hinge" figure, the swivel joint between the judges and the kings.[60] Of the judges, he is perhaps most like Deborah (not to mention the later prophets Elijah and Elisha). He is a charismatic fortune-teller whose fame gave him considerable large-scale clout. He would ordinarily have been occupied as a kind of circuit-riding priest and oracle, often the same thing, as the Hebrew word for "priest," *kohen*, is cognate with the Arabic word *kahin*, "soothsayer." When young Saul has despaired of finding his father's stray oxen, he repairs to Samuel who is known to find lost objects for a small fee (1 Sam. 9:1-10). We also see Samuel presiding at local sacrifices (1 Sam. 9:12-13, 19, 25; 10:8). People sought out such figures to adjudicate disputes (as in Exodus 18:13; Luke 12:13) for two reasons.

On the one hand, they were believed to have direct access to God; on the other, as ascetics, they were obviously not "in it for the money" and so could be trusted to be impartial. They would not accept bribes, as they were propertyless ascetics. They could be pivotal in stirring the people to military action, as we saw with Deborah. Think also of the medieval Popes whipping up the Crusades. Samuel is pictured as active in the struggle against the Philistines and in the transition to the Israelite monarchy.

The Nativity of Samuel

1 Sam. 1:1-27

Note that verse 20 tries to explain Hannah naming her new son by reference to her prayer: "since she had asked [Yahweh] for him." This is actually an etymology for the name "Saul," which means "asked." "Samuel," on the other hand, means "Name of God." The Deuteronomic Historian obviously does not much care for Saul, as we will see. Can he have taken what was originally the nativity story of *Saul* and clumsily transferred it to his hero Samuel? (This would involve interpolating Hannah's vow, v. 11, and the subsequent business about taking her son to live as a Nazirite at Shiloh, vv. 21-23.)

But whomever the story was originally about, it seems to mask another "Nephilim" style rendezvous, marking either Samuel or Saul as another demigod hero.

Hannah's Song

1 Sam. 2:1-10

Originally this must have been a Royal Psalm like Psalms 2 and 110, celebrating any new king, who would, it was hoped, give justice to the oppressed. In the New Testament Luke uses Hannah's Song as a model for Elizabeth's (in some manuscripts) or Mary's Magnificat. It would fit the barren Elizabeth better than Mary.

The Corruption of Eli's Sons

1 Sam. 2:11-36

Clergy corruption is certainly nothing new, so why draw attention to the abuses by Eli's bad apple sons? The episode would seem to be aimed at legitimating the replacement of the older priesthood of Eli with the priestly line of Zadok in Solomon's day. The Zadokites controlled the priesthood for centuries until displaced by the Hasmoneans in the second century B.C.E.. At that time, the Zadokites retreated to the Qumran settlement in the Judean Desert.

But suppose the Deuteronomic History was itself the product of the Hasmonean period, as I suspect? If the Deuteronomist was himself a Hasmonean priest, would he have included an episode promoting the Zadokite lineage against that of Eli? Sure, why not? Noth[61] rightly says that the Deuteronomist "does not seem pedantic enough to reject traditional material just because it is not easily integrated into a set pattern." Morton Smith's insight should also be kept in mind both here and throughout.

> Thus what we have in the various Old Testaments is not the literature of a single party but the literature of a large number and long succession of parties which sometimes have come together by compromise in more or less enduring alliances, sometimes have been separated by quarrels, and finally, because of their separation, have preserved different collections of the literature–Pharisaic and Samaritan, Greek and Syriac. Evidence of their earlier differences appears in the contradictions between and within the various Old Testament books; evidence of their alliances appears in the common preservation of such contradictory material.[62]

First Revelation to Samuel

1 Sam. 3

The irony here is rich: God bypasses the priest Eli, speaking directly to Eli's young apprentice, Samuel. The latter, in his innocent humility, doesn't even consider the possibility that God Almighty would deign to speak to him, so he assumes it is Eli who has summoned him, and the sleepy Samuel asks him what he wants. The blinking priest tells him he must have dreamt it and that he should go back to bed. Only the third time this happens does the old priest begin to realize what is going on. So who hears God's voice, and who doesn't? (Of course, Samuel is sleeping at the foot of the Ark of the Covenant from which God speaks as he did to Moses,[63] so maybe the old man just wasn't in earshot.)

Philistine Raiders of the Lost Ark

1 Sam. 4-6

This sequence might be called the biblical version of the Trojan Horse. Readers may find themselves puzzled at Israel losing the battle with the Philistines and the latter's capture of the Ark of the Covenant, which, after all, denoted God's presence on the battlefield. How could the Israelites lose? Just wait for the other sandal to fall! Events will soon show that the Philistines have got much more than they bargained for! Yahweh has allowed his enemies to bring him behind the lines–where he will strike!

We see a replay of the plagues of Egypt (see 4:8; 6:6), only this time the enemies of Israel are afflicted with hemorrhoids and infested with mice! They try to solve the problem by using apotropaic devices. Just as Moses had cured snakebite in the wilderness by raising aloft a bronze effigy of a serpent, so now the Philistines fashion golden mice and, er, golden hemorrhoids. (Now what do you suppose *they* might have looked like?)

Meanwhile, they have displayed the stolen Ark in the temple of Dagon as a battle trophy. Then the darnedest things start to happen. Each morning the janitor finds the statue of Dagon more and more damaged, hands missing, fish tail broken off. It finally occurs to these geniuses that maybe the Hebrew God is harassing them, engaging in guerrilla warfare. To test their hypothesis, the Philistine bigwigs decide to load the Ark onto the back of a cart drawn by two cows that never before wore yokes, because it would insult Yahweh or any other god to use secondhand cattle (which is also why they are slaughtered after this one use).[64]

Like their sacred cousins in India, the cows are left to wander where they will, opening a window of indeterminacy through which the divine will may reveal itself.[65] If they head across the border to Israel, that will prove it was all the vengeful mischief of Yahweh who wants his Ark back. And, sure enough, that's just what Bessie and Elsie do. Case closed.

Death inside the Ark!

1 Sam. 6:19-21

The Ark comes to a halt in the town of Beth-Shemesh ("House of the Sun").[66] So it is home but still plenty dangerous! The corrupt Masoretic Text reads: "*Yahweh* was not *pleased with* the men of Beth-Shemesh *because* they saw [i.e., looked inside] the Ark of Yahweh, and *5,070* of them were struck down."[67] This is hopelessly absurd: Did they line up, shoving aside the bodies of their dead predecessors so they could get a look that they knew must be fatal? No one tells such a tale!

No wonder that we find in the Septuagint and the Dead Sea Scrolls manuscripts this earlier reading: "*The sons of Jeconiah* were not *pleased [along] with* the men of Beth-Shemesh *when* they *saw* the Ark of Yahweh [*arriving*], and *70* of them were struck down." There is no miracle here, only a report that one faction wanted to refuse reception of the Ark, probably fearing a Philistine trick, and the rest killed them for blasphemy.

Chapter 7 seems to be the original summing up of Samuel's story, though he will be brought onstage again for various stories about Saul and David later on. This chapter credits Samuel with ridding the country of the Philistines, something he certainly did not do according to the stories that follow.

Saul's Kingship Is Good

Various Versions

First we find material depicting Saul's kingship as good. It has been subjected to some editing, but the original version can be discerned in 9:1-10:7, 9-18 (up through "and addressed the Israelites"), verse 19 (beginning with "take your stand before [Yahweh] according to tribes and families") through verse 24. Here Saul is anointed king by divine choice. This is the grand moment to which the Book of Judges was leading: Now there *is* a king in Israel, so righteousness will prevail! (Or maybe not.)

Chapter 10 offers us the spectacle of Saul, newly anointed king by Samuel, joining a wandering band of ecstatic, tongues-speaking prophets whose contagious charisma at once envelops him, whereupon he, too, breaks into a mantic trance and "becomes another man" (10:6). The idea is that, just as Jesus imparts the Spirit to his disciples to equip them for their apostolic ministries (John 20:21-23), Saul must experience his own private Pentecost. All the Jewish kings were thought to receive the divine Spirit to give them the necessary wisdom and virtue to reign in an effective and godly manner. We see this in Isaiah 11:1-10 and 61:1-4, texts drawn from the enthronement (inauguration, coronation) liturgies.

Alongside this account the Deuteronomist has preserved another version of Saul's divine appointment as king (1 Sam. 10:20-27). In this one the king is chosen by lot and it turns out to be Saul, who is so humble that he hides once God's choice is known. This is to assure us that he is no power-hungry megalomaniac but must be prevailed upon to take up his assigned role. Even within this story we may detect a hint of still another, where Saul is chosen because he is the tallest man around (10:23).[68]

In chapter 11, there is yet another version. Saul proves his worth against the Ammonites. Both the Masoretic Text and the Septuagint are missing the beginning of this story, but the Dead Sea Scrolls text supplies it:[69]

> Nahash, king of the children of Ammon, sorely oppressed the children of Gad and the children of Reuben, and he gouged out all their right eyes and struck terror and dread in Israel. There was not left one among the children of Israel beyond the Jordan whose right eye was not put out by Nahash king of the children of Ammon; except that seven thousand men fled from the children of Ammon and entered Jabesh-Gilead.

Of course, as in the familiar text, Saul goes on to rescue them. Hearing of their desperate plight, he issues a rallying call to all the tribes. Reminiscent of the emergency alert of the Levite in Judges chapter 19,[70] Saul dissects an ox and sends the pieces to the tribal elders, calling them to abandon their impotent independence and to unite against a common enemy.[71] Once this decisive action leads to victory, the people realize the advantage of a strong central government, and who better to lead it than the hero who just brought them together?

There is no mention or need for lots, anointing, or measuring the height of candidates. According to this material, Saul is a great hero, as he is remembered in the early Book of Yashar (2 Sam. 1:19-27). That some in Israel never stopped revering Saul as a hero is evident from the fact that some folks continued to name their sons "Saul." Who ever named a daughter for Jezebel or Herodias?

Though the restored paragraph is not exactly spectacular, its discovery was quite significant in terms of confirming the validity of biblical criticism. For years scholars had believed something had been accidentally dropped from the text by scribes asleep at the switch. The problem was the abruptness of the beginning of the Masoretic and Septuagint version of the story.

Most of the Deuteronomic episodes of Israel's clashes with foreign enemies begin with the introduction of the enemy king as "Superfluus, king of the children of Slobbovia" (as in Judg. 3:8; 3:12; 4:2), but, without the missing piece, Nahash[72] was introduced without the expected epithet, "king of the Ammonites." Nor was it was clear how or why the men of Jabesh-Gilead had gotten into the fix from which Saul delivered them. Now it all finally makes sense, just as biblical critics had surmised.

What is 1 Samuel 10:17-19 doing here, rudely interrupting the account(s) of Saul's ascension to the throne? In the midst of all the lionizing, we suddenly find Samuel proclaiming what a terrible mistake Israel is making establishing a monarchy! By doing so, they are doing no less than repudiating their only true king, Yahweh himself. Obviously this passage is an attempt to "correct" all the pro-monarchial hoopla,[73] anticipating the following passages written from an anti-Saul, even anti-monarchial, viewpoint. The ancient redactors usually did not dare simply to excise earlier material of which they did not approve; the best they could do was to insert contradictory material pointing in the direction they favored.

Saul's Kingship Is Bad

Because David's Is Good

Saul's kingship was later deemed unsuccessful because he was unable to found a dynasty. According to later Deuteronomic and Priestly viewpoints, this fact alone was enough to prove that Saul must have displeased Yahweh. David, however, *did* manage to found a lasting dynasty. Many stories clustering about David feature Saul as a villain, fit only to be replaced by the heroic David. First Samuel 13:2-14 and 15:1-35 both offer late and contrived reasons for Yahweh rejecting Saul as king (in favor of David, who is anticipated in 13:14 and 15:28). The general impression we get from these traditions is of a striking parallel to the story of Camelot, in which Merlin first anoints Uther Pendragon as king but subsequently withdraws his imprimatur to endorse Arthur instead.

According to the first of these stories, Saul has dared to usurp priestly prerogatives, offering sacrifices himself instead of waiting to have Samuel the priest do it. Yet this would have been no offense at all in Saul's day or long afterward (see 2 Sam. 6:17-18; 24:25; 1 Kings 3:3-5; 8:62-64; 9:25; 1 Chron. 21:26).

In the second story, Saul's crime is simply that, instead of sacrificing the captured sheep of the butchered Amalekites as his patron Samuel had commanded him, he let his hungry soldiers roast and eat them. Plus he allowed the Amalekite king to live, contra Samuel's orders. And this was more odious in God's eyes than David's murder of Uriah and adultery with Bath-Sheba?

But were these various tales actually circulated as propaganda for the regimes of Saul and David? The problem is that there were not enough people in the area for either man to have ruled! No kingdom to be king of![74] The only way I can make sense of this material is to suggest that Saul and David were both fictive and mythic dynastic patriarchs invoked by rival factions who both cherished royal ambitions at some, much later, point. Their origin and function would be closely analogous to the fictive tribal patriarchs in Genesis: Their stories were really about the interrelations of the clans and tribes whose eponymous figureheads they were.

All Kingship Is Bad

A series of Deuteronomic interpolations (chapter 8; 10:18b-19a; 12:12-25) into traditional, pro-monarchic materials[75] seem to represent a priestly point of view on kingship: It was an error from the start, an accommodation to the idolatrous ways of the pagan nations surrounding Israel (8:20). Davies[76] notes that the Deuteronomist antipathy for "secular" kingship implies preference for priestly rulers.

Samuel's unheeded warning about the inevitable abuses of royal power (8:11-18) reads like a bitter satire of Deuteronomy's list of rules designed to curb such abuses (Deut. 17:14-20), which itself was based on the notorious abuses of Solomon. Those stories, in turn, must have been fictive cautionary tales like that of the equally mythic king Gilgamesh, who despoiled his subjects of their sons for his army, their wives and daughters for his harem.[77]

Samuel himself, a priest, not a king, yet ruler of Israel, reflects the position of the high priest in Judea after the Exile, when their Persian and Hellenistic imperial rulers denied them kings but allowed domestic self-rule to the high priests.

David and Goliath

1 Sam. 17

According to 1 Samuel 17:55-58, David and Saul meet here for the first time, on the eve of the battle with the Philistine champion Goliath.[78] David is a youth unaccustomed to either armor or battle. Yet according to chapter 16, Saul and David had already met, and David was already a skilled warrior by the time of chapter 17. The chapter 16 version must be the earlier of the Saul-David meeting, since it is the less spectacular compared with the David and Goliath version. If you already had the Goliath version, who would ever have made up the less spectacular one in chapter 16? But if that is what you started out with, you might welcome a new, more colorful version. They both survived in the tradition side by side.

And, according to 2 Samuel 21:19, it is not David but someone named Elhanan who kills Goliath! So we must conclude that the feat was only later ascribed to the more famous hero David. The David and Goliath story as we read it in 1 Samuel 17 must be a legend. As such it is another prime bit of Deuteronomic theology: God's power is shown in human weakness. (But again, isn't the point really that brains trump brawn?)

Interestingly, the much later Chronicler, who rewrote the Deuteronomic History, noticed this discrepancy and made Elhanan kill Goliath's *brother* (1 Chron. 20:5)! Subsequent Bible copyists liked the Chronicler's harmonization so well that they inserted it into the text of Samuel, which is why it appears that way in the late, corrupt text of the King James Version at 2 Samuel 21:19. Similarly, the Septuagint translators noticed the contradiction between the two versions of the first meeting of Saul and David, and they eliminated one of them!

Finally, note that Goliath's stature has literally grown in the telling. According to the Septuagint and the Dead Sea Scrolls texts, he is *six* and a half feet tall, not *nine* and a half feet tall as the corrupt Masoretic Text has it.

David versus Saul

1 Sam. 18-20, 24, 26

Initially, Saul is both impressed and delighted at David's victory, so he recruits him for his army, and indeed David proves to be almost a one-man army, dispatching the Philistines everywhere Saul deploys him. But David's success soon backfires, as he replaces Saul as the hero of the people. That makes Saul suspicious of him, wondering if David will ride popular acclaim all the way to the throne, just as Saul himself had done. David remains oblivious of all this, still pure in his devotion to his king, until one day Saul hurls a spear at him while David is playing the lyre for him! Rough crowd! Saul has now become fueled by an insane paranoia worthy of Herod the Great, who was in the habit of killing his wives and sons based on the flimsiest suspicions of disloyalty.

The narrator stresses the irrational character of Saul's murderous zeal by chalking it up to possession by "an evil spirit sent from [Yahweh]" (18:10). What? Did God *want* Saul to kill David? It is possible we are to infer that God is "hardening Saul's heart," as he did to Pharaoh, in order to direct events toward the ultimate replacement of Saul by David. But I think the real point is simply to highlight the arbitrary nature of Saul's act as inexplicable except as stemming from a supernatural source: It is "miraculous" hatred.

David is nimble enough to dodge Saul's spear—twice (18:11)! And still he continues in Saul's service, fighting for a king he knows seeks his death! Nor is Saul done with his attempts to skewer the slayer of Goliath, as he tries it yet again in 19:10. Something is wrong with the narrative here.

While the general direction remains clear, with Saul trying various expedients to have David killed, it looks like the repeated attempts to spear David are interpolations by someone who just wanted to "pile it on" but only succeeded in making the story absurdly implausible. Who can imagine David putting up with this? "Uh, sorry, Dave! I was aiming at that mosquito! Oops! Er, thought I had the little blighter *that* time!"

Saul offers to let David marry his daughter Merab if he will prove himself by still more fighting against the Philistines, hoping he won't have to make good on his promise. He figures David's luck has to run out pretty soon, and he will be killed in battle. But David prevails. Since Saul never intended to give Merab to David anyway, he gives her to another of his lieutenants, one Adriel the Meholathite, instead (18:17-19). This would have been no mere disappointment but a major public dishonor. So obviously undeserved a slap could only alienate the people from Saul, not from David.

But Saul tries the same stunt again (1 Sam. 18:18-29)![79] This time he promises his rival the hand of another daughter, Michal, requiring "only" a bride-price of one hundred Philistine foreskins.[80] Naturally, the Philistines aren't going to donate them freely! David is going to have to kill them first, and Saul, assigning him such a chore, hopes once again to maneuver him into fatal danger (the same shady tactic David himself will later use to get rid of his own champion, Uriah the Hittite, so he can have the man's wife, in 2 Samuel 11:14-15). Saul's plan fails, as a seemingly invulnerable David returns with double the number Saul had asked for.[81] So David marries into the family, but it's not going to last; David eventually shuts Michal out of the bedroom for henpecking him (2 Sam. 6:20-23) and later hands her off to Palti, son of Laish (1 Sam. 25:44).

Chapter 19, verses 8-10, preserve a shorter version of Saul's initial attempt to spear David at the impulse of an evil spirit from Yahweh after a successful campaign against the Philistines. It is immediately followed (19:11-17) by another attempt on his life by Saul. The connection to the preceding is artificial, in that we would have to imagine David dodging the spear, then heading home for the night as if everything were copacetic.

Lucky for him, his wife Michal learns of her father's evil intent and warns David to skip town fast. He escapes through the window as Saul's assassins approach the house. Michal hastily lugs a teraphim (a large image of a departed ancestor)[82] into the bed and draws a blanket over it. "He's sick and can't be disturbed. See for yourself." Saul sees through the ruse and demands to know why Michal conspired with David, whereupon she claims (lies) that he threatened to kill her if she didn't.

David makes for the dwelling of Samuel at Ramah. The two (perhaps suspecting that Saul will know to look for them there) retreat to Naioth. Word of this reaches Saul, who sends troops to arrest them there. The rest of the story bears a suspicious resemblance both to the earlier episode of Saul prophesying among the local dervishes at Gibeath-elohim ("the Hill of God") in 1 Samuel 10:5-12, and to that of King Ahaziah's sending of three successive groups of soldiers to apprehend Elijah near Ekron (2 Kings 1:9-15).

The former three are overcome with prophetic ecstasy, while two of the latter three squads are incinerated by fire from the sky. We have to suspect that these stories are related, recombining folk-traditional motifs in various ways. In particular, when Saul himself shows up at Naioth and succumbs to the Pentecostal glory, we recognize an alternate etiology of the enigmatic saying, "Is Saul, too, to be counted among the prophets?"[83]

Chapter 20 adds another, originally independent, story of Saul's enmity against David, as if we did not already know all about it. The next few chapters recount David's adventures while he is on the run from Saul, who is pursuing a fanatical vendetta against him. Chapters 24 and 26 are independent parallel accounts, both depicting a touching moment during Saul's pursuit of David.

In both versions, David finds himself in a position to assassinate Saul but refuses.[84] On the one hand, David dares not touch Yahweh's sacred king, even if he deserves it. Justice in such a case must be left to Yahweh. On the other, he still loves Saul. He has done nothing to merit Saul's hatred. Saul's rage against him seems so arbitrary to David that he is only mystified by it and does not think to blame Saul for it. Remember, the narrator attributed Saul's attempts on David's life to an evil spirit sent from Yahweh, the point being that Saul's hatred was unnatural and unmotivated. David appears to understand that Saul was, so to speak, criminally insane, dangerous but not really blameworthy.

In both versions, David calls out to Saul, telling him he could have killed him but didn't and explains why. Saul is cut to the quick and apologizes, swearing henceforth to eschew any and all attempts to kill David. He does this *both times*, which tells us that whoever told either story knew nothing of the other. We are not given to believe that, after his first promise to leave David alone, Saul had second thoughts. It is instead like Mark's two versions of the loaves and fish miracle (Mark 6:30-44; 8:1-10): The way that the first ends rules out the skepticism of the disciples in the second. We are in for more of the same when, right after Saul's second reconciliation with David, we find Saul in business as usual, persecuting[85] David (27:1)! This story is independent of both of the others.[86]

The Witch of Endor

1 Sam. 17

Here[87] is an honest-to-goodness ghost story in the Bible![88] Saul is coming up on a battle with the pesky Philistines, and he is plenty worried! He is desperate to know what will happen before it happens. There are means to do this: the ephod (a breastplate or an image of some sort), the oracular Urim and Thummim (apparently two flat, round stones, each black on one side, white on the other, something like fortune-telling dice), precognitive dreams, and prophets (see 1 Kings 22:5-6).

But Saul gets exasperated when every time he calls, it just keeps ringing.[89] So he decides to try the black market, resorting to Brand X techniques like necromancy (condemned in Isaiah 8:19).[90] Saul has painted himself into a corner; it was he who outlawed necromancers (spirit mediums)! This is interesting in its own right, as it portrays Saul as something of a Deuteronomic reformer cut from the same cloth as Hezekiah and Josiah (2 Kings 18:1-4 and 23:4-24, respectively, especially Josiah's ban on necromancers in 23:24).[91]

But it is common knowledge that the mediums are still active (like speakeasies during Prohibition). Saul has no trouble locating one and visits her in disguise. She senses it is a government sting operation and plays dumb, but Saul assures her he is sincere. So, at his request, she conjures up the shade of Samuel from Sheol, calling him "a god," which again fits the ancestor worship aspect of the teraphim.

Somehow, Samuel's appearance makes her realize who Saul really is. This would make a bit more sense if she said so *after* hearing a bit of their conversation, but that is probably the idea. Anyway, Saul explains his worries and asks the ghostly Samuel for some inside information. Samuel says, essentially, "Why are you wasting what little time you have left? You'll be with me in Sheol tomorrow—we can talk at leisure then!" This is appropriately chilling, worthy of Sheridan Lefanu or M.R. James.

One often hears the suggestion that it wasn't really Samuel who appeared but rather a sneaky demon impersonating him.[92] What the . . .? Absolutely nothing suggests this. Those who offer this contrived (mis)interpretation have taken the biblical prohibition of necromancy a bit *too* seriously. But the Bible doesn't say it isn't *possible* to get oracles from the dead, only that you're not *supposed* to do it. The Volstead Act said you weren't supposed to drink, not that booze didn't exist.

There is a striking formal parallel between this eerie episode and that in 2 Kings 1. I will discuss it later in the present chapter.

Chapters 27 and 29-30, astonishingly, depict David, sick of Saul's relentless harassment, becoming a turncoat against Israel! He crosses over to join the hated Philistines, serving as a bandit leader under the aegis of King Achish. It is no undercover scheme; David serves Achish as loyally as he once served Saul. On the eve of a major engagement with Israel, David is eager to enter the fray on the side of his new masters, but the other lords of the Philistines (kings of their five city-states) doubt his loyalty. So Achish asks him to sit this one out. Lucky thing as it turns out, because in his absence David's new home town, Ziklag, has been decimated by raiding Amalekites, his two wives taken hostage. When he and his men get home to this, they pursue the Amalekites and slay them, retrieving their property and people.

One important item, easily overlooked, is what David says about being forced out of Israel: "they have driven me out today so that I would have no attachment with the inheritance of [Yahweh], saying, 'Go, serve other gods.'" (1 Sam. 26:19, NASB). The implication is surely that David (or anyone else) has no business worshipping Yahweh outside of Israel.[93] When in Rome, do as the Romans do–and worship Jupiter and Mars. This is the flip side of the impatience of Elijah with the willingness of Israel to adopt Phoenician Baal worship alongside their traditional Yahweh worship. You don't see Elijah complaining about Phoenicians worshipping Phoenician gods in Phoenicia.

In Deuteronomy 32:8-9[94] we learn that when the king of gods, El Elyon, divided nascent humanity into enough nations that each of the sons of El might have one to rule, his son Yahweh chose Israel as his own. Rimmon, for instance, chose Syria, and this is why the Syrian general asked Elisha for two mule-loads of Israelite dirt to take home since otherwise he could not worship the God of Israel there (2 Kings 5:17). David's lament about having to forego his preferred Yahweh worship presupposes this *monolatry* (worshipping only one's national deity while by no means denying the reality of foreign gods).

Jephthah is depicted as sharing this assumption in Judges 11:24 (NASB) when he writes to the Ammonites, "Do you not possess what Chemosh your god gives you to possess? So whatever [Yahweh] our God has driven out before us, we will possess it." In 2 Kings 3:21-27 we are surprised to read that a timely human sacrifice to Chemosh successfully summoned the vengeful wrath of the Moabite god to vanquish the invading Israelites!

The Death of Saul

1 Sam. 31

Samuel's ghost knew what he was talking about: Saul perishes in battle against the Philistines the next day. But interestingly, Saul's uncircumcised foes do not kill him; he does the job himself, adding a further note of irony. Saul knows he's not getting out of this one alive. But he'd rather cheat the Philistines out of their fun. If you're going to die anyway, why not short-circuit the process and sidestep the torture and humiliation at the hands of your captors? So he asks his armor-bearer to run him through, but the lad is afraid to do it, perhaps showing the same caution David did when he refused to assassinate the king, leaving Saul's fate in the hands of God.

So then, it devolves upon Saul himself, who embraces the task, falling on his own sword. The Philistines find his body, decapitate it, and crucify the headless figure on a public wall. Learning of this, the people of Jabesh-Gilead, whom Saul had years before rescued from the Ammonites, show their gratitude in the only way left to them, by recapturing Saul's remains for a decent burial.

But wait! Next we hear a rather different version of the events (2 Sam. 1:1-16) when David, back in Ziklag, receives a visitor who claims not only to have witnessed the king's death but to have done the deed! To hear him tell it, it was he, an Amalekite, and not Saul's armor-caddy, whom Saul asked to dispatch him, and he did. To verify his report, the Amalekite produces Saul's bloody crown and armlet. If he expected some reward, he has another thing coming! Remember, David believed that no mortal had the right to lay violent hands on God's anointed king, which Saul still was. And so David has the Amalekite executed for his trouble.

In order to harmonize the two versions of Saul's death, some have suggested that the Amalekite was an opportunist who lied about having killed Saul, wrongly assuming that David would be grateful, given his troubles with Saul. But the narrator suggests no such thing. If the man made it all up, where did he get Saul's crown and armlet? Did the Philistines accidentally leave them behind? Not likely. Again, the Deuteronomic compiler found two different versions of the story and did not feel at liberty to eliminate either one, so he simply juxtaposed them. He was pursuing two aims simultaneously: telling a sequential story and preserving as much old material as he could. Contradictions and redundancies are the inevitable result.[95]

A poetic gem meets us in 2 Samuel 1:19-27. Besides its literary excellence, this text is further evidence of a persistent pro-Saul faction in Israel: The source of this poem is the fabled Book of Yashar ("Book of the Just"), a now-lost[96] collection of paeans to the heroes of Israel. As we have seen, another bit of verse from the same book celebrated Joshua's feat of making the sun and the moon stop dead in their tracks (Josh. 10:12-14).

The funeral lament (2 Sam. 1:26, ASV) for Saul and his son Jonathan reiterates the deep attachment between David and Jonathan:

I am distressed for thee, my brother Jonathan:
Very pleasant hast thou been unto me:
Thy love to me was wonderful,
Passing the love of women.

Some have taken this to denote a homosexual relationship between the two young warriors, like that between Achilles and Patroclus. That is not a contrived reading, but it must remain mere speculation in the absence of any clear confirmation in the text. It might mean "greater than romantic love per se" or "greater than romantic love for women." Who knows?

David Becomes King

2 Sam. 2-5

Next we read of the men of Judah anointing David as king to replace Saul. A war ensues with the rest of the Israelite tribes up north, still loyal to the house of the slain Saul. They fight on behalf of one of Saul's sons. The present Hebrew text calls him "Ish-Bosheth," which cannot have been his actual name because it means "Man of Shame." What sort of Baby Names book did Saul get *that* one out of?

It appears this term was a scribal substitution for an original "Ish-Baal" ("Man of Baal"), changed to suppress the fact that a king of Yahweh's people could have been dedicated as a worshipper of Baal. Keep in mind, at this time many did not draw a firm line between Yahweh and Baal. Their myths were certainly parallel. But later scribes understood the name as a positive reference to a false god and could not let it stand. Likewise, the extant text calls one of Ish-Baal's sons "Mephibosheth" ("Breaker of 'Shames,'" i.e., of idols), whose real name was Merib-Baal ("Baal's Champion").

The two kingdoms finally decide to put their differences aside, agreeing to have David reign over them. He then conquers the ancient city of Jebus (otherwise known as Salem and Jerusalem) and makes it his capital, presumably for the same reason Washington D.C. was chosen as the capital of the United States: It had been part neither of the North (Israel) nor of the South (Judah), so that neither region should feel slighted.

This all presents us with a major difficulty, as the archaeological evidence makes clear that Israel and Judah in fact were never united as a single kingdom.[97] One wonders if this stubborn fact lies behind the indications in the Deuteronomic narrative that the supposed unity of a united Israel was quite tenuous and did not last long.

According to the biblical narrative (as we will see below), the kingdom split for good upon the accession of Solomon's son Rehoboam to the throne, but already in David's reign there were two secessions of the Northern tribes, one under David's over-eager heir Absalom, the other under a usurper named Sheba.

Whence the idea that Israel and Judah had ever merged? My guess is that the fictive United Monarchy[98] was invented as a kind of land deed (like the medieval Donation of Constantine)[99] to legitimatize John Hyrcanus'[100] annexation of the Northern territories in the second century B.C.E. "Oh, we're just restoring the glory days of old!" It was impossible to pretend that the two groups of tribes had *always* been united. Too much history was predicated upon their parallel existence. Thus one had to posit an ancient unification that later dissolved.

But it gets worse: The very existence of King David is fully as dubious as that of King Arthur. It's not that such an epic hero couldn't have existed in reality. After all, there's Alexander the Great. The trouble is that no trace remains of David's palace or even of Jerusalem as a royal city.[101] So what was the purpose or the motive for the creation of David's epic? Here's a speculation: I wonder if the whole business was a fiction designed to enhance the credentials of Zerubbabel, the Jewish governor under the Persian Empire, who prided himself on his belonging to the house of David (Ezra 5:2; Hagg. 1:1; 2:21-23; 4:6-10).[102] I'm suggesting that he (and possibly other descendants of some nondescript man named David) fabricated an epic starring not the "David of history" (whoever he might have been) but the "David of faith," i.e., of propaganda, just as the Roman historian Livy made the mythic hero Aeneas, heroic refugee from Troy, the progenitor of the house of Iulus, from which Julius Caesar sprang.[103]

But there is reason to think there had never *been* any historical David. The name means "Beloved," a divine epithet.[104] It was applied to the David character as God's favorite, as if he had been named (by the author, not by his parents) in view of his narrative role, which he probably was.[105] David would seem to be another case of an ancient deity being reduced to a legendary hero.[106] But couldn't parents name their son "David" to mark their love for their infant? Sure. But there is no one else with the name David in the Bible, implying it was not considered an appropriate name for mortal man.[107]

Ark of Electricity

2 Sam. 6

Here is a notorious bit of classical "priestcraft," a "scare 'em straight" cautionary tale written *by* priests *for* priests, to teach them never to treat the Ark in a casual, secular manner. Those entrusted with the sacred object were no mere pit crew. Tending it was not like mechanics servicing Air Force One. It was more like scientists handling radioactive materials via padded sleeve-gloves through a radiation shield screen.

The divine aura of holiness is here described as a palpable current of force. Poor Uzzah sees that the ox cart upon which the sacred Ark rests is about to hit a pothole and spill its holy burden into the muddy ditch. The prospect horrifies him, as it ought to, and Uzzah acts instinctively to steady the Ark of the Covenant. The trouble is, he has not ritually decontaminated himself and thus touches the object with "hands defiled" (Mark 7:5). *Zap!* Man down!

Every reader at this point feels a sense of umbrage. It seems grossly unjust for God to punish a man whose intentions were so pure. But I think the priest who invented the story intended to highlight precisely this point! He sought to draw a clear line between moral righteousness, which poor Uzzah undoubtedly possessed, and ritual purity, which (inevitably, given the circumstances) he lacked. In the writer's mind, Uzzah was not exactly *punished*; it was simply as if he had stuck his finger into an electrical socket.

Of course we cannot say what the narrator thought Uzzah *should* have done! Which would have been worse: to let it go and demonstrate Yahweh's inability to protect his Ark from falling ignominiously into the mire? Or showing the very same thing by steadying the Ark, since then it would appear that Yahweh must be dependent on mere mortals like Uzzah to save face for him? "Let Yahweh contend for himself!"[108]

But there was another point to be communicated: Laymen and novice Levites must watch out and not touch the Ark! If they did, would they drop dead like the character in this story? Of course not. Nothing happened to the Philistines when they seized it on the battlefield. The goal was simply to safeguard the reverence due the Ark. If it is treated as untouchable and unapproachable, the dramatic mystique of the thing is preserved. If people saw the Levites getting out the rags and polish to spruce up the Ark, like members of the altar guild in an Episcopalian church, its aura of otherworldliness would be dispelled.

Uh . . . *was* there actually an Ark of the Covenant? Sure. There *still is*! Sensationalist writer Graham Hancock[109] attempts to persuade his readers the Ark rests now among the Black Jews of Axum in Ethiopia, brought there in remote antiquity by Menelik, the bastard son of Solomon and the Queen of Sheba (according to medieval legend[110]). The priests in charge of it periodically bring forth what they say is a replica of it for the edification of the crowds. It is a red rectangular chest studded with silver work, easily carried by one man, over his head. Graham's belief that these people do possess the real Ark of the Covenant is groundless TV tabloid stuff.

But in another sense, whatever sacred chest these Ethiopian Jews do have, whether it is a fake relic really hidden away, or whether the "replica" is all they have, the situation is exactly analogous to that of the Bible. There no doubt was some artifact in the Inner Sanctum of Herod's Temple that Jews believed was the Ark in which a historical Moses placed the two tables of the commandments, a souvenir jar of manna, and Aaron's rod that budded. It would have been as genuine as the Stone of Scone on display in Westminster Abbey, which tour guides will tell you is the very rock that rolled along merrily after the Israelites during their wilderness wanderings, spouting water whenever they got thirsty (Exod. 17:1-6; Num. 20:1-11; 1 Cor. 10:1-4).

The story of Menelik taking the Ark to Ethiopia is no more fictive than the biblical myths of Moses having the artisans Bezalel and Oholiab build it according to a heavenly blueprint (Exod. 25:9; 31:1-11). Whatever Ark was housed in the so-called Second Temple[111] was no more an authentic Mosaic artifact than the one shown off in Axum today. The only Ark to ever exist was a "fake." It is a prime example of what Jacques Derrida[112] calls the *simulacrum*: a "copy" without an original which therefore takes the place of an original and *becomes* an original.

The "House" of David

2 Sam. 7

David, having arranged for the construction of an elaborate palace for himself, begins to feel ashamed. Here he is, at ease in Zion, and Yahweh has to camp out in a pup tent! So he proposes to erect a vast temple for his God. But Yahweh pokes fun at his favorite: Does David really think that God Almighty needs a roof over his head? Save yourself the trouble, kid! Tell you what: Let *me* build *you* a house, that is, a *royal* house, a dynasty such as the hapless Saul was unable to establish. Verses 14-16 are very obviously a fictive credential for someone (e.g., Zerubbabel[113]) later vying for authority based on Davidic descent, whether real or imagined. The whole thing is written retrospectively, contemporary with the intended readership.

The sudden change of subject, from the question of building a temple (7:4-7) to the establishment of a dynasty (7:8-29), might imply that, as so often, we are dealing with earlier and later strata in the text. But it seems preferable to take the whole thing as embodying a signature Deuteronomic theme: the superfluity of a temple. God brushes the whole notion of a temple aside in favor of the promise of a perpetual dynasty for David.

Enthroned on an Ejector Seat

2 Sam. 11-20

An extended narrative of two rapid-fire usurpations of David's throne forms a fascinating and beautifully written sequence. It begins with a tawdry affair right out of one of today's political TV soap operas. And, like today's *The West Wing, House of Cards*, etc., this one is purely fictive, despite earlier scholarly claims that the "Succession Narrative" must have been written by an eye-witness. As Niels Peter Lemche observes, "It should never be forgotten who will be best acquainted with inner thoughts of the participants in a narrative or play: of course, the author himself who invented his figures."[114] We might want to call it the "Succession Novella."

One day, King David takes a look out his window and is surprised to see Bathsheba taking a bath of ritual purification on the adjacent rooftop: *hubba hubba!* He wants her. He gets her. Of course, he's already married—to several women in fact, and that's not counting concubines. The problem is that *she's* married, to Uriah[115] the Hittite, one of David's army officers. David has her husband assigned to the thick of the battle, optimistic that he will die in combat, and so he does. Nice going, Dave! With no more competition, the way is clear for David to marry Bathsheba.

But Nathan the court prophet is having none of it. He tells the king a parable, much in the vein of Mark 12:1-12. Picture this: A wealthy man owns great flocks and herds of sheep, while a poor man has but a single lamb which has become a beloved family pet.[116] The rich man needs to provide dinner for a visitor. Instead of roasting one of his own animals, which he would scarcely miss, the rich man appropriates the poor man's pet and serves her up. What do you think should happen to a rat like this?

David is incensed and swears by Yahweh that the rich man deserves death. David has fallen into Nathan's trap. Who is this bastard? The prophet replies, *"You are the man!"* David gets the point and undertakes penance. Nonetheless, God punishes him two-fold. He has the first child of David and Bathsheba, conceived in sin, die after only a week of life.[117] And he will see to it that big trouble will result from David's murder of Uriah: David's enemy will emerge from his own household, and violence will follow him. This foreshadows the overthrow of David by his son Absalom.

The couple has a second child, whom Nathan blesses as loved by Yahweh. So they name him Jedediah ("Beloved of Yahweh"), i.e., he won't kill this one. Later he will take the throne name Solomon (another spelling of the name of the old Jerusalemite sunset god Shalman).

What, if any, might be the pre-history of this episode? Perhaps David's sin was originally not so great given that Uriah was a Hittite, a member of a heathen nation the Israelites were told to exterminate (Josh. 3:10, 11:23; 12:8; 24:11). But, given the repetition of the theme operative in the two versions of Saul setting up David to get killed on the battlefield (1 Sam. 18:17 and 25) in order to prevent David from marrying Saul's daughter, we might wonder if the tale of David, Uriah, and Bathsheba is a third version of the same tale.

Perhaps the characters have simply been reshuffled, as often happens in oral transmission. Remember, the defeat of Goliath was originally credited to Elhanan but was transferred to David. Same thing here? Thus it would not have formed an additional episode in the biography of David at all.

Scions of Zion

2 Sam. 14-18, 1 Kings 1

David names another son for the sunset god Shalman, calling this one Absalom ("Shalman is my Father").[118] This man is full of passion and ambition. When he learns that another brother, Amnon, has raped their beautiful sister Tamar, he invents a scheme to trap and kill the despicable Amnon. David is initially misinformed that Absalom has murdered *all* his brothers (perhaps implying the elimination of potential rivals to the throne), but he is soon relieved to find that Amnon was the sole target. This softens the blow somewhat. But David does not take the death of a son, even a black sheep, lightly. He enters a deep state of mourning, and Absalom takes this as a signal that he'd better skip town, so he takes refuge with the king of Geshur, where he lies low for three years.

Joab, David's military chief of staff, sees that David misses Absalom and probably wouldn't mind if he returned to the fold. So, echoing Nathan's gambit of confronting the king with a fictive parallel to his own situation, Joab sends a woman to David, spinning this yarn: "Alas, I am a widow; my husband is dead. And your handmaid had two sons, and they quarreled with one another in the field. There was no one to separate them, and one struck the other and killed him. And now the whole family has risen against your handmaid, and they say, 'Give up the man who struck his brother, that we may kill him for the life of his brother whom he slew'" (2 Sam. 14:5b-7a, RSV).[119] But then she would have no heir to keep the family name alive. David's case is not really parallel, since he does have more sons.

David smells Joab's involvement and calls him in. He agrees to recall Absalom as long as he stays away from the palace and remains under house arrest. This arrangement holds for two years until Absalom appeals to David for his full liberty. His dad is a softy and agrees. What a mistake! Absalom is a handsome and charismatic figure and begins to curry favor among the people, undermining their loyalty to his father. After four years of this, Absalom makes his move, declaring himself king, establishing a temporary capital at Hebron. When David is told of this, he quickly rounds up his loyalists to flee Jerusalem, knowing that Absalom will soon arrive to take over. Once he does, the usurper makes a public display of copulating with his father's concubines up on the palace roof (2 Sam. 16:22).

In this dramatic fashion, Absalom demonstrates that he has replaced his father. Sitting on the throne might seem to be enough, but intercourse with the harem demonstrates his virility, that he is up to the task of being "the father of his country," a vestige of the ancient Sacred Kingship ideology whereby the king's mandate of heaven waxed and waned with the fertility of the land.

David arranges for a mole in Absalom's court to pass information to him, a confidant named Hushai. He proposes to Absalom a particular plan of attack, which the new king accepts, and Hushai gets the news to David, who is then ready for Absalom's attack.

Absalom flees the scene of his troops' defeat, but he doesn't get far: His long, luxuriant mane of hair becomes tangled in the low-hanging tree limbs, yanking him bodily out of the careening chariot which continues barreling on its way. Though David had issued strict orders that his rebel son be taken alive and uninjured, General Joab disdains such sentimentality, which has already cost David so much, so, when he finds Absalom still alive, twisting in the wind, he dispatches him without a second thought (2 Sam. 18:9-15).

When David gets this news, he collapses in mourning. Joab has to rebuke him bluntly. His soldiers have risked or even sacrificed their very lives to restore David to his throne– and he is most upset about his no-good son? Snap out of it, Dave! Don't make your subjects think you care more for the usurper than for them! You *don't*, do you? So David gets ahold of himself. And his people, ashamed of their fickleness, welcome David back.

But even *this* occasions yet more trouble! Israel's tribes think Judah has positioned itself for greater favor in David's eyes. Affronted, the northern tribes heed the summons of a rebel named Sheba[120] to repudiate the Davidic monarchy and to form an independent Israel. David's forces eventually manage to suppress the secession, besieging the city of Abel where Sheba has taken refuge. The populace decides that Sheba is not worth starving for, and his severed head comes sailing over the city wall like a volleyball, signaling the demise of the revolution–until next time when, after Solomon's death, the whole scenario will replay itself.

With David on his deathbed and using the virgin Abishag as a heating pad (1 Kings 1:1-4), his son Adonijah decides *he* ought to be the next occupant of the throne and proclaims his kingship with the support of several of his father's lieutenants including Joab and Abiathar the high priest (1 Kings 1:5-7). One little problem: David had already named Solomon as his successor. Adonijah and his buddies are celebrating (a bit prematurely, as it turns out), when Solomon and his supporters arrive in force.

Uh-oh! Adonijah backs down at once, begging mercy from his younger brother, who is willing to grant it. But soon after, Adonijah sends their mother Bathsheba to the new king to request that Solomon grant him Abishag as his wife, now that David, being dead, no longer needs her.

For some reason, this request causes Solomon to go ballistic, and he has his brother executed! Why? My guess is that we are to understand Solomon to be suspecting a more subtle version of Absalom's stunt of having public sex with David's concubines in order to reinforce his claim to his father's throne. Adonijah, then, would not be interested in Abishag so much as being seen as the heir to David's voluptuous bed-warmer and thus to his kingship.

Abiathar the priest, an old compatriot of King David, backed the wrong horse when he threw in with Adonijah. This cost him, not his life (Solomon appreciated the support Abiathar had given David during the Absalom mess), but his position. Solomon promoted Zadok to the high priesthood instead. Actually, the whole office of high priest was a much later invention, after the Exile,[121] to replace the monarchy in the absence of Jewish sovereignty under colonial rule. But once it got started, there was the typical vying for power, and this bit of the Succession Novella incorporates a fictive precedent for the Zadokite priesthood supplanting the Aaronide line.

Marginally, we must not ignore a few interesting bits mentioned in passing in the course of the larger story. For one, there are three vestiges of the cult of Nehushtan. We read in 1 Kings 1:9 that the over-ambitious Adonijah was offering inaugural sacrifices at a sacred site called the Serpent's Stone. That has to have been a shrine of Nehushtan, also called Leviathan, the divine dragon. In 2 Samuel 17:25 and 27 we find a woman called Abigail the daughter of Nahash, as well as a man named Shobi the son of Nahash. Remember Nahash, king of Ammon in 1 Samuel 11:1. And then there's Hanun the son of Nahash over in 2 Samuel 10:2. Second Kings 24:8 mentions King Jehoiachin's mother, named Nehushta. All these people have theophoric names, and the deity for whom they are named is none other than the snake god Nehushtan (2 Kings 18:4), worshipped in the

Jerusalem Temple. These names indicate the widespread and deeply rooted devotion to this god.

Wicker Men

2 Sam. 21:1-14

There is a famine in the land, and that can't be a coincidence, not when there are gods in charge of such things. And so David "sought the face of Yahweh," which means he asked an oracle priest to consult Yahweh by means of the Urim and Thummim, the ephod, or some such. The priest "receives" an answer for David: "There is blood guilt on Saul and on his house, because he put the Gibeonites to death" (verse 2). You see, back when Joshua was steamrolling the Canaanites, the Gibeonites escaped eradication by means of a clever stratagem (Joshua chapter 9): They disguised themselves in threadbare rags and claimed to be foreigners from outside Canaan, who had heard of Joshua's victories and wanted to hitch their wagon to the winner.

So they asked to make a treaty with Israel whereby they would live among them as a servant class, like the Shudra caste of India. Okay, why not? Only too late did the Israelites discover the ruse, and by then it was too late to do anything about it. So Israel decided they had no choice but to tolerate the continued breathing of the Gibeonites. But centuries later, King Saul decided he was sick of them and wiped most of them out. Apparently no one in Israel made a peep. And so the Almighty phoned in a wake-up call.

David invites some Gibeonites to his court and explains the situation. What will it take to satisfy them? (Are we to imagine that perhaps the Gibeonites had previously gained the ear of David's oracle and suggested their complaint as the cause of the famine? They certainly seem to have given the matter some thought already!) The Gibeonites request that David hand over seven of Saul's descendants, execute them, and display their corpses on a row of trees at Saul's old city of Gibeah. David readily agrees. So "in the first days of harvest, at the beginning of barley harvest" (2 Sam. 21:9), they kill them and string them up.

According to 21:8, one of the seven tree ornaments turns out to be poor, lame[122] Mephibosheth, whom David had previously promised protection, even assigning him a permanent seat at the royal banqueting table (2 Sam., chapter 9). Ouch! Some scribe found this pretty scandalous and added the contradictory verse 7, "But the king spared Mephibosheth, the son of Saul's son Jonathan." This verse immediately precedes the one that tells us that David handed him over! Apparently, the copyist did not feel at liberty to omit Mephibosheth's name from verse 8 but sought to confuse the issue by inserting verse 7, trying to get David off the hook.

It almost looks like the whole Gibeonite business is a secondary overlay onto an earlier version in which David simply offered up seven human sacrifices aiming to fertilize the ground with their blood. Otherwise, what is the point of coordinating the sacrifice with the start of the harvest? The compensation of the Gibeonites, if that had been the real issue, would not seem to have required this. Additionally, we learn that Mephibosheth's mother keeps vigil over her sons' bodies (see below) *until the rain starts to fall.*

But once we have the Gibeonite material added, striking parallels with Sophocles' *Oedipus* Cycle become evident. In the latter, a plague breaks out in Thebes. No one knows why, so the king consults an oracle, who says Apollo has told him the trouble is an unresolved problem with a former king, Laius, Oedipus' predecessor (and, unbeknownst to him, his father). Laius had vanished while away on a journey.

In the meantime, Oedipus appeared and, having slain the menacing Sphinx, was acclaimed the city's new king. In the wake of all this, everybody just kind of forgot about the old king. Apollo doesn't like this; they ought to resolve the mystery of Laius' disappearance. Oedipus is all for it and launches an investigation, utterly ignorant of the fact that it was none other than Laius that *he* killed in a fight on the road when Oedipus was heading toward the city and Laius was departing it! *Hoo boy*. When this news finally comes out, Oedipus knows he is the cause of the plague and that he must bear the brunt of divine justice. He blinds himself and goes into exile.

Like Oedipus, King David consults an oracle to disclose the cause, this time, of a famine. Again, the cause turns out to be an unresolved issue of justice involving the present king's predecessor, though in 2 Samuel the former king was the offender, while in *Oedipus the King*, the former king was the victim, the present king the offender.

We have to suspect a more comprehensive implicit scenario in which David, fearing that the blame for the famine should fall on him (since the vitality of the land was believed to vary with the power and virtue of its king), arranged for the oracle to finger the house of Saul as the scapegoat. In 2 Samuel 24:13-17 David *was* blamed for a plague. His staff prophet Nathan was apparently peeved that David had taken a census to assess the number of fighting men available instead of heedlessly leaving the outcome of the battle in Yahweh's hands as per the ancient conventions of holy war. So when a plague broke out, he editorialized that it must be God's punishment of David. But in the case of the famine, he managed to shift the blame to others. In cases like these, we can infer, it was up to the oracles to decide, under "divine inspiration," who was guilty. And a shrewd king might bribe the oracle to sidestep the blame.[123]

After the sacrifice of the seven surviving sons of Saul,[124] David is told that Rizpah, the mother of two of them, Mephibosheth and Aiah (the other five actually being Saul's grandsons), has camped out at the execution site to protect the bodies from depredation by jackals and vultures (2 Sam. 21:10-14). The touching spectacle inspires David to exhume the remains of Saul and Jonathan which the men of Jabesh-Gilead had recovered from the Philistines (who had displayed the corpses on the city wall of Beth-Shan, then buried them in Jabesh, 1 Sam. 31:8-13).

David reinterred the remains of Saul and Jonathan (with those of the seven?) in the tomb of Saul's father Kish (2 Sam. 21:11-14). Here we have to think of Sophocles' *Antigone* in which Oedipus' daughter risks her life to prevent the body of her slain brother Polyneices from defilement by carrion animals. She knows her brother had been dumped outside the city wall by King Creon who thought him a traitor and forbade his burial. Has there been influence from one story on the other? Or are they independent variants of the same tradition?

War of the Demigods

2 Sam. 21:15-22

During a new round of fighting with the Philistines, David and his battle companions take on four of the Nephilim, superhuman heroes descended from the Watchers (Gen. 6:1-4): Ishbibenob, who wielded a huge spear weighing 300 bronze shekels; Saph; Goliath; and an unnamed titan who possessed six digits on each hand and foot! It is striking that it is not David but a warrior named Elhanan who dispatches Goliath. Of course more than one person might share the name Goliath, but this has to be the same one David is said to have slain with his slingshot back in 1 Samuel 17. He hails from Gath (thus a "Gittite" as in 2 Sam. 21:19) and hefts a spear as big and heavy as a weaver's beam (as in 1 Sam. 17:7). It seems pretty clear that someone thought the heroic deed of slaying this "giant" should be credited to the great King David, not to some otherwise-unknown also-ran. But this original version survived as well, relegated to the end of David's epic.

Who were David's "mighty men" who fought with him or for him? Chapter 21 lists several. Remember that Genesis 6:4 uses the same term for the ancient half-divine heroes, descended from the Nephilim, "the mighty men that were of old, the men of renown." Were David's retainers originally imagined as remnants of the Nephilim, like the four they battled in 2 Samuel 21? One of them, Josheb-basshebeth, is credited with having killed a grand total of 900 men in a single battle (2 Sam. 23:8), a feat worthy of Samson, implying that the former, too, was a demigod.

The description of the unnamed Philistine giant hints at an interesting possibility. In our chapter on Genesis, we saw that Genesis 6:1-4 was an ethnological myth seeking to account for the towering six-foot height of the Rephaim/Anakim of Canaan by positing that they were the offspring of the sons of God. If any of these huge men are said to have had six fingers per hand and six toes per foot, we have to suspect that these legendary characters reflect the ancients' marveling at what we would call pituitary cases.

The Book of Kings

Solomon

Solomon, ruler of a great Near Eastern empire and builder of the Jerusalem Temple, stands in mid-air unsupported by the slightest archaeological evidence.[125] And this is another one of those cases where the absence of evidence *does* amount to evidence of absence.[126] That's because there is no way to explain what could have happened to the evidence one would expect to find if Solomon's grand buildings, humanistic enlightenment,[127] and vast domains really had existed. Where'd they go? Vaporized by a nuke?

Granted, "biblical archaeologists" claim to have identified occasional relics like Solomon's stables, but these have been instances of "pin the tail on the Bible." Somebody digs up something that more or less corresponds with a biblical item, albeit with nothing to explicitly identify it as that item, and, *bingo*, the historical accuracy of scripture is vindicated! Someone finds an ancient boat in Galilee and *voila*, it's the one Jesus crossed the Sea of Galilee in! Did he carve his name into the hull? The foundation of some house in Capernaum? Must have been Simon Peter's!

Someone came up with a single knob carved into a pomegranate shape. Aha! Must be a vestige of Solomon's Temple! Really? Then where's the *rest* of it? It's the exception that proves the rule: The very notion of it being part of the Temple rules itself out because, if it really were, it wouldn't be the only one found!

If there was a real "historical Solomon," the best candidate must be Alexander the Great.[128] Like the biblical character, Alexander was an enthusiastic champion of culture. He caused whole cities to be built, just as Solomon was a great builder. And his vast empire fragmented after his death, just as Alexander's did. Rehoboam and Jeroboam divided Solomon's kingdom, just as Ptolemy, Antiochus, and Seleucus carved up Alexander's.

Solomon's Choice

1 Kings 3:5-15

In a dream, the new king faces God, who offers him a fateful choice. He will grant one boon to Solomon. He has two options. He can have fantastic wealth *or* surpassing wisdom. Which will it be? Solomon asks for wisdom, which he knows he will need to reign as king, especially since he will spend much of his time hearing and judging legal cases, as ancient kings did. God is pleased to hear this and rewards him by giving him the wisdom he requested *and* the wealth he did not request. Perhaps the lesson the reader is to learn is that if one has wisdom he will sooner or later grow rich as well. But note that Solomon is *already* wise or he would scarcely make the choice he made. And as king of Israel, he was obviously already very wealthy. I have to think of two popular culture parallels.

At the conclusion of *The Wizard of Oz*, Professor Marvel confers a diploma upon the Scarecrow in answer to his request for wisdom—a wisdom he has many times shown that he already has. And in the comic book origin story of Captain Marvel, the wizard Shazam imparts several divine abilities to boy reporter Billy Batson, including the wisdom of Solomon. Billy need only say the old wizard's name to transform into the World's Mightiest (and wisest!) Mortal, Captain Marvel. I think both the Scarecrow and Captain Marvel are powerful illustrations of young Solomon gaining the wisdom of God for the benefit of his subjects.

It is interesting to consider what "wisdom" was thought to include. Three of the collections of aphorisms in the Book of Proverbs are credited to Solomon. But the whole idea of a proverb is that, once you hear it, it rings true. "Of *course!* I should have realized that!" It's not the kind of thing you have to take on faith, which is why proverbs circulate anonymously. It doesn't matter who first said them. Because of its self-evident wisdom, the saying has "gone viral."

Thus it seems unlikely that anyone actually knew who had coined any of these proverbs. It must have been the compilers of the collections who ascribed them all to Solomon as the paragon of wisdom. Using his name was more of a title than an authorship claim. But invoking his name does tell us what kind of thing people had in mind when they spoke of Solomon's wisdom. The same goes for another, similar book, The Wisdom of Solomon.[129]

But we can see from the stories of those other paradigmatic wise men Joseph and Daniel, that "wisdom" also included foretelling the future and interpreting dreams and visions (Gen. 37:5-10; 40:6-19; chapter 41; 44:2, 5, 15; Dan. 2:19-49; 4:4-27; chapters 5, 7-11). Outside the biblical canon, Solomon, too, is credited with esoteric wisdom, in his case magic and exorcism. We read of these aspects of his wisdom in several later works including The Testament of Solomon, The Sword of Solomon, The Greater Key of Solomon, and The Lesser Key of Solomon.[130]

The first of these works contains a kind of field guide to demons, providing the infernal names of the major ones together with the chimera-like[131] details of the hideous appearance of several. This provision of the names is to aid exorcists in their work; standard exorcistic practice[132] entailed ordering the demon to "name thyself!" (Mark 5:9). This is ostensibly how they got the names listed by "Solomon." The Testament of Solomon also informs us how Solomon managed to bind the demons to his service transporting the massive stones to build his Temple.[133] This legend exactly parallels modern speculations that, since the ancient Egyptians supposedly could not have lugged the huge stone blocks to the construction sites of the Pyramids, space aliens must have done it with tractor beams!

Splitting the Difference

1 Kings 3:16-28

This is probably the best known Solomon story, provided as a representative example of his wisdom in action. It reads almost like a "hypothetical" in a law book. A pair of prostitutes who are room-mates appear before the king, baby in tow. They have taken a day off from flat-backing to settle a dispute. Each claims to be the mother of the infant and that the other also had a baby but accidentally rolled over on it in the night, smothering the little one. Then the bereaved mother (whichever of the two she was) snatched the living baby from her colleague. Unlike most of today's baby-nappers, this one did not flee, stolen infant in her arms. Apparently she figured she had an even chance of securing her claim on the baby by bringing the case to the king.

There are no witnesses, so maybe Solomon will just flip a coin (which wouldn't be much different from using the Urim and Thummim, come to think of it!). But Solomon is shrewder than that. He suggests chopping the baby in two and letting each harlot keep one half! Glass half full, you know. Of course it's a ploy to smoke out the real mother. The kidnapper may go along with it: It's not her kid anyway, so what has she got to lose that she hasn't already lost? But the mother's love will cause her to give up her claim: Better that her child live, even with the wrong mother, than die with the right one.[134]

The Temple
1 Kings 5-8

Here is a very long description of the construction and design of a vast building that can never have existed. As we have seen, there are no archaeological remains of it, and there would have to be. Did Satan hide all the debris after he got done planting fake dinosaur bones? But really it is not much of a puzzle. Apparently the desert Tabernacle was a fanciful attempt to read the Temple back into the era of Moses, the goal being to strengthen the pedigree of the Temple since some Israelites/Jews did not think it was a good idea.[135] God could not have needed it (2 Sam. 7:5-7), and it constituted a constant temptation to idolatry. Maybe it even *was* an idol (Acts 7:45-50). Moses' Tabernacle provided a (fictive) precedent legitimating the Jerusalem Temple.

Well, in just the same way, I suggest, the Temple of Solomon was a fictive retrojection of the Temple "re"built by the Persian-appointed Jewish governor Zerubbabel. In short, the account of the erection of Solomon's Temple was of a piece with the larger attempt of the Persian state to provide a fictive national identity for the subjects they had caused to immigrate to Palestine, to give them a reason to feel at home in what they told them was their ancestral homeland.

Look at the literary trajectory here. Based on this long passage, the Freemasons of the eighteenth century fabricated a founder, Hiram Abiff, loosely based on King Hiram of Tyre who designed the Temple for Solomon and administered its construction. In their modern foundation myth, the Masons retrojected their own belief in the esoteric symbolism of the Temple's architecture into Solomon's time, to connect it with his much-vaunted wisdom.

Similarly, as already noted, the Black Jews of Ethiopia extended the biblical episode of Solomon and the Queen of Sheba to create a ceremonial etiology for their own poor man's Ark of the Covenant, thus claiming the mystique of antiquity for it (and for them). What I am saying is that the 1 Kings account of the Temple was already the same sort of mythopoeic fabrication.

All ancient temples were designed as microcosmic counterparts to the great macrocosm, the universe as the ancients imagined it.[136] That is certainly true in this case. Once there *was* an actual Jewish Temple in Jerusalem (Zerubabbel's, Herod's), the priests believed their liturgy mirrored that of the unseen angels worshipping in heaven. This was even true of the schismatic priesthood who wrote the Dead Sea Scrolls, the bitter, sulking Zadokites whom the Hasmoneans had replaced in the mid-second century B.C.E.

In a case of sour-grapes theology, these Zadokites maintained that the Jerusalem Temple was irreparably defiled by the revisionist practices of the entrenched Hasmonean priesthood, so that the Zadokites wouldn't have set sandaled foot in the no-longer-holy precincts anyway. So what did they do? They followed the old script in a new theatre: in their complex at Qumran. As Barbara Thiering[137] suggests, they reproduced the Temple set-up in make-believe form, part of their microcosm version of Jerusalem, Bethany, Galilee, etc., as they dubbed their various outbuildings.

And this raises the question whether "Temple" worship was pantomimed in Judea *before* an actual Temple ever existed in Jerusalem. The long and detailed description of the Temple we read in 1 Kings may simply have been a theoretical blueprint. After all, that's exactly what the Temple blueprint laid out in Ezekiel 40-46 was: An angel measured it out for the prophet in a heavenly vision, just as Moses was said to have seen the celestial prototype for the Tabernacle atop the holy mountain, and as the plan for Solomon's Temple was revealed to David (1 Chron. 28:19). Revelation 6:9; 11:19 also refers to a heavenly Temple including the Ark of the Covenant. To represent the Temple as actually having been built in Solomon's time does not tie it down to real history; it is merely to place it in a halcyon Golden Age instead of an equally mythical heavenly realm.

But what about the destruction of the Temple by the Babylonians in 586 B.C.E.? This supposed event was but another retrojection into an earlier, more venerable, era. In 4 Ezra (and the related 2 Baruch), we seem at first to witness Ezra's soul-searching in the wake of the Babylonian destruction of Solomon's Temple, but all scholars[138] agree that the real occasion for these profound musings was the Roman destruction of the Temple in 70 C.E. The explicit references to the Babylonian destruction are a literary pose. I suggest that the very same thing is true of the Deuteronomic story of Nebuchadnezzar's laying waste to Solomon's Temple. Why not?

In the ancient Near East it was commonly believed that the gods dwelt in temple palaces atop a (or the) sacred mountain, the cosmic mountain or *axis mundi* connecting heaven and earth.[139] We are familiar with this notion from Greek mythology where Zeus, Hera, Apollo and the rest make their home atop Mount Olympus, an actual mountain (for which there are several candidates even today, like the rival sites for Golgotha in Jerusalem). Heaven was not imagined in science-fiction terms as many vaguely picture it today, as "another dimension," whatever that means.

In the Bible, both testaments, the word used for "heaven" is simply the word for "the sky." The Bible sometimes speaks of the cosmic mountain as Mount Zaphon (shared with Canaanite myth), e.g., Isaiah 14:13-14 (in newer, more accurate translations), sometimes as Mount Zion, the supposed location of Solomon's Temple. It seems likely that they eventually identified the two. Thus we might infer that, once a brick-and-mortar Temple did occupy the top of Mount Zion in Jerusalem, it was considered to *be* the very Temple of heaven. This inference seems inevitable once we remember that the Valley of the Sons of Hinnom (Gehenna, Tophet), down at the base of Mount Zion, was believed to be the very gateway to the fiery underground realm of the demon-god Molech (the same as the Babylonian Nergal),[140] which is why infants were sacrificed to feed him there (Jer. 7:31-32; 19:6).

Eden Indoors

As Margaret Barker[141] demonstrates, there was one version of the Garden of Eden myth that situated it atop the Mountain of God (Ezek. 28:13-14). It was from this height that Adam, ruined by pride, was cast out, losing his original jewel-like splendor. Once the familiar Yahwist version of the Eden myth (Gen. 2:3b-chapter 3) prevailed, the alternative version preserved in Ezekiel 28 was transferred to the character of Lucifer, an angel who fell through pride.[142] The original also trickled down to appear in the Jewish Kabbalah, where we read that Adam was at first a celestial giant of divine splendor who, after his failure, was reduced to today's human proportions.[143] The "coats of skin" in which Yahweh clothed him (Gen. 3:21) would refer to the now-standard body of flesh.

All this implies that the Garden of Eden, the Garden of God, *was* heaven. "Heaven" and "Paradise" are used interchangeably in the Bible (Luke 23:43; 2 Cor. 12:2-3). Now we can understand why the design of the Jerusalem Temple included important features shared with the description of Eden in both Genesis 2-3 and Ezekiel 28: flowers and pomegranates, cherubs, and the twin pillars Boaz and Jachin, which must have been the Tree of Life and the Tree of the Knowledge of Good and Evil. And, as Margaret Morris[144] shows, the geographical description of Eden in Genesis 2 is nonsensical if it is supposed to refer to the lay-out of the Fertile Crescent and the four rivers.

It's not as if the ancients were unfamiliar with local geography; the environs of Babylon and Assyria were not exactly Terra Incognita. The four rivers of Eden stemming from one common source are the mythical rivers gushing forth from the *tehom*, the subterranean ocean depth upon which the flat earth was believed to float. This cosmic ocean was represented in the Temple as the Molten Sea,[145] resting on the backs of a dozen bronze oxen (recalling various ancient cosmologies in which the earth rests upon the backs of a series of animals, e.g., elephants and tortoises).

The Temple was understood to have been built over the great navel stone of the world which served as a bulwark against the *tehom* lest its waters burst forth and submerge the world as they did in the days of Noah.[146] Yahweh sits enthroned above the flood (Psalm 29:10), and this was represented in the Temple's design, too. The Ark of the Covenant was his throne. Ezekiel beheld Yahweh sitting in state upon his throne chariot borne by cherubs (Ezek. 1:4-11). Psalm 63:2, written by one of the Levites on duty in the Temple, contains the confession, "So I have looked upon thee in the sanctuary, beholding thy power and glory." The reference seems to be to a repeated sight, not a single, rapturous vision like Ezekiel's and Isaiah's. How had the priests and Levites "routinely" *seen God*?

It appears that when the high priest (or the Jewish priest-king) penetrated the veil, entering the Holy of Holies, the Inner Sanctum, he was doing what the ancient Mesopotamian, Babylonian, and Canaanite kings did every New Year's Day. To renew his heavenly mandate for the coming year, the king, God's (Marduk's, etc.) son or vicar on earth, would enter the temple doors, which were then closed behind him. He was believed to have ascended to heaven where he would be vouchsafed a glimpse of the Heavenly Tablets of Destiny.[147] He would be reaffirmed as God's Son (Psalm 2:7).[148]

We have until recently imagined the king of Judah performing the same ritual process and that, when the Judean monarchy was ended by the Babylonian Conquest, the symbolism and ritual formerly connected with the king passed to the high priests after the Exile. But in light of the revelations of archaeology which render all our assumptions about a pre-Exilic monarchy dubious, we have to ask if it makes most sense to place the adoption of this "royal ideology" of Sacred Kingship very late, in the time of the Hasmoneans of the second century B.C.E., when John Hyrcanus became both priest and king (a move opposed by many). In this case we do not need to envision the purely sacerdotal priesthood inheriting the prerogatives and accoutrements of the "secular" kingship. It may always have been the role of a priest-king like those of the surrounding nations.

Barker makes it pretty clear that, as the high priest emerged again from the Inner Sanctum to the waiting congregation, he had been divinized. In plain terms, he had *become God*. As Philo and the Letter of Aristeas tell us, the golden tiara on the High Priest's turban bore the Tetragrammaton: the four-letter name of God, YHWH.[149]

We see the same thing in the apocalyptic myths of Enoch ascending to heaven, transfigured into fiery form, to sit at God's right hand, henceforth to bear the designation "the Lesser Yahweh." He is the high priest. Emerging from the Holy of Holies, the high priest was himself a divine epiphany.[150] This is how the priests and Levites would, in the normal course of things, see God, clothed in splendor, in the sanctuary.

Many of these features of the Temple décor and ritual seem to have been suppressed by the Deuteronomic editors and must be restored from parallel accounts in Chronicles, Philo, and apocalyptic literature.[151] The "Protestant" agenda of the Deuteronomists included the streamlining of the traditional Israelite polytheism into a strict monotheism. Yahweh was fused with his Father Elyon. The resultant deity was believed to be invisible to the mortal eye, hence the "aniconic"[152] character of Jewish worship.[153]

God could not be visually represented in graven or molten images, in anthropomorphic description. He could not be localized in an earthly building, no matter how grand. At most, he had caused his "Name" to dwell there, to be remembered.[154] The production of further scripture was banned,[155] and new prophets were taking their lives into their hands. Though the Deuteronomic History places this reform in the reign of Josiah (seventh century B.C.E.), I have suggested that it fits more naturally in the second-century B.C.E. Hasmonean period. It would have coincided with the displacement of the old Zadokite priesthood by the Hasmonean.

As Rachel Elior[156] makes clear, the old ways lived on in the Zadokite community of the Dead Sea Scrolls (and elsewhere). In this type of Judaism, apocalyptic visions, a visible deity, new prophecy, and even new scriptures continued unabated. For instance, the Temple Scroll seems to have been composed as a sequel to Deuteronomy.[157] It is here also that we must place the preservation of the Sacred King theology while Hasmonean Judaism scaled down the Anointed One to the shrunken proportions of the Davidic Messiah as no more than a righteous human king who would resume the Davidic succession. Christianity, with its Christology of divine Incarnation and atonement, had, as in so many areas, simply retained the more spectacular belief system of "Enochian" Judaism.

We must conclude that the various statements to the effect that both Tabernacle and Temple were reproductions of heavenly patterns were quite accurate. But they were *literary* incarnations, not *historical* incarnations.

To sum up, then: If there was no Temple of Solomon, what was the point of the 1 Kings description? I think it is a blueprint for a temple, a *pre*scription, not a *de*scription. Just like Ezekiel's and the Qumran Temple Scroll. It is placed as a fact of past history for the same reason the Tabernacle was: to root it in the sacred past for credentials' sake. The "First Temple" must have been Zerubbabel's. The "Second Temple" must have been, of course, Herod's Temple which replaced it. Fourth Ezra similarly retrojects (the destruction of) Herod's Temple into the past, making it fictively into Solomon's Temple. There is a hint of this in the story of God telling Moses to have the Tabernacle constructed according to the heavenly pattern. That's what the 1 Kings "description" is.

The Deuteronomic Reform must be identified with the Hasmonean usurpation, supported by the Pharisees. Their scribes and successors, the rabbis, rejected the earlier, more elaborate Temple mythology (which had provided the pattern for the Temple's décor in the first place) and edited it out of the Bible, as well as excluding the Zadokites' new revelations (the Enochian traditions/literature).

The priestly mythology incorporated much of the old royal ideology borrowed from the surrounding monarchies. It was transferred to the high priest. The ascension of the king/priest/prophet in the Temple to view the Heavenly Tablets comes right out of the New Years ritual with its renewal of nature and of the royal (priestly) mandate of heaven. In the Enochian framework it was the renewal of the cosmic covenant on Pentecost. The rabbinic concept of the Messiah as a human king is part of the repudiation of the royal ideology.

Chock Full o' Gods

1 Kings 11:1-8

Solomon, if the text is to be believed, was quite the marrying man. Let's see now: seven hundred wives and three hundred concubines. Where did he get the time? He couldn't have been doing much but having sex. It's got to be hyperbole, magnifying Solomon by ascribing infinite libido to him. Why? Because, again, the ancient kings were the lynch pin of their countries' fertility. "You and the land are one!"[158]

On the other hand, we might imagine that Solomon did actually amass such a harem for purposes of public relations, but that these women were his lovers (or sex objects) in name only. Who knows what arrangements might have been made for these women? Did they have boy-toys on the side? The kings and queens of Egypt were brother and sister unions, but this was apparently purely formal, to keep the throne (ostensibly) in the family. The queen would be impregnated by a priest acting as a temporary incarnation of one of the gods, which is how they could claim that each new king was himself a demigod: "Thutmose" = "Thoth has begotten him," Ramases" = "Ra has begotten him," etc.

But there is another reason for Solomon's mega-marriages, worthy, one might suggest, of one of Reverend Sun Myung Moon's mass weddings.[159] We are told these were diplomatic in nature. Solomon sought to forge bonds of peace via marriage alliances. Your father-in-law would presumably be less inclined to attack you as long as you treated his little girl well, a lesson Herod Antipas learned the hard way when he famously traded in the daughter of Aretas IV of Nabatea for his own brother's wife Herodias–and got soundly clobbered in a subsequent war with Aretas (Josephus, *Antiquities of the Jews* 18:4:6; 5:1-2, 4). In a sense, the foreign wives would have functioned as hostages.

So the biblical story makes some kind of sense politically. But *seven hundred wives*? There aren't that many countries in the United Nations! Did Solomon marry the daughters of all the Chinese, Indian, and sub-Saharan African kings? Plus American Indian chiefs' daughters?[160] Or did he seek the hands of the princesses of petty micro-states? Why would he bother? Could some crummy city-state pose serious danger to his empire (incredibly vast according to the text: all the real estate between the River Euphrates and the Wadi-el-Arish in Egypt!)? This is more fiction.

The story was that, in order to make his brides feel at home away from home, Solomon directed that temples be built where his spouses could worship their ancestral gods. The intent would have been pretty much the same as Elisha giving the Syrian general Naaman leave to carry two mule-loads of Israelite soil back home so he could arrange a small shrine where he could worship the God of Israel (2 Kings 5:17). The assumption was, as we have seen, that gods were to be worshipped only in the specific domains assigned them by El Elyon at the dawn of human history (Deut. 32:8-9). If a Syrian wanted to worship the Hebrew God, he had either to travel to Israel on pilgrimage (like the Islamic *hajj* to Mecca) or do what Naaman did: build an "embassy" of Yahweh in foreign territory. Solomon is pictured as extending this courtesy to his foreign wives and their accustomed gods.

The Deuteronomist, from a very different, later perspective, considers this to have been a terrible idea, apparently blurring the line between Solomon's diplomatic respect for the religious needs of his foreign princesses and the wholesale Baal-evangelism of the Sidonian Jezebel, Ahab's queen. This confusion served the interests of our compiler, since it seemed to provide an explanation for the presence of very many "pagan" gods and their shrines sprinkled throughout Israel and Judah in his day.[161] In reality, these gods and temples were part and parcel of traditional Hebrew religion, which was itself polytheistic.

But according to the revisionist history constructed by the Deuteronomistic/Hasmonean reformation, these old temples *cannot* have been home-grown; thus they *weren't*.

The Kingdom Divided

The Deuteronomist blames the vivisection of Solomonic Israel on Solomon's courting of foreign hussies and their idols. Turns out Sol was not so wise after all! At least according to the agenda of later story-tellers. Already during Solomon's reign, he sowed seeds of rebellion with his high-handed exploitation of the peasants as a conscripted labor force (think of the ant-like *fellaheen* building the Pyramids for the Pharaohs).

There were at least three opposition leaders: Hadad, an Edomite prince sojourning in Egypt; Rezon, a bandit chief who became king of Syria; and Jeroboam, a foreman over Solomon's work crews. Ahijah the prophet popped up one day and surprised Jeroboam with the news that Yahweh had decided to cut off the northern tribes from the Davidic monarchy and give them to Jeroboam, if he would only keep God's laws better than that strike-out Solomon.

Wait a second: Hadn't God made a much-vaunted pledge to stick with the house of David in perpetuity, even if some of its kings wound up misbehaving? He promised he wouldn't just ditch David's line, as he had poor Saul's, only to start over again. Yet here he is, transferring the kingdom to Jeroboam? Oh, but Yahweh *does* keep his promise–by the skin of a technicality: He leaves David's heirs one single tribe, Judah, to be their modest domain.

But Jeroboam does not take the throne immediately: Solomon hears the "God likes me better" rumors put about by Jeroboam and, playing Saul to Jeroboam's David, Solomon attempts to have him killed. And as David took refuge among the Philistines, Jeroboam takes it on the lam into Egypt. The striking parallels between Saul/David and Solomon/Jeroboam suggest two fascinating possibilities.

First, the story reflects pro-Jeroboam propaganda, just as the Saul/David material served as legitimation for the supplanting of Saul's royal house by David's. Remember, in this story Jeroboam himself had no thought of usurpation. He is not another Absalom. No, it is a prophet who ordains him as Solomon's replacement, just as Samuel told David of God's choice of him to replace the miserable Saul. (By contrast, we will soon read a very different depiction of Jeroboam as an idolatrous louse, a story told by an opponent of his dynasty.)

Second, we have to wonder if perhaps the Saul/David sequence is a doublette (a variant version) of the Solomon/Jeroboam sequence. Neither can be historical anyway, since all these stories are part of a larger narrative of Hebrew kingdoms planted not in terra firma, but in the airy fields of legend.

Solomon dies in peace, just missing the crashing echoes of his empire dying with him. His son Rehoboam[162] takes the throne and is faced at once with an impossible choice. Who but Jeroboam should arrive at the head of a delegation from the northern tribes? They will, they say, be happy to serve the new king as they served his famous father if only he will lighten up on them. They do not appreciate being treated like slaves breaking rocks in a prison yard. If Rehoboam refuses, he can say goodbye to the northern tribes. Rehoboam agrees to think it over and tells them to come back in three days. He then summons the graybeards who advised Solomon and asks their advice. They say they consider the demands to be fair. Acceding to them will create much-needed good will between the new king and his subjects.

Desirous of a second opinion, Rehoboam calls in a group of his contemporaries, and they give him very different counsel. With some justification, these Young Turks advise

Rehoboam not to give in, presumably because he would be starting his reign with a fatal display of weakness. His opponents will smell blood in the water, or else they will realize the new monarch is a pushover, a captive to lobbyists and labor unions (so to speak). So Rehoboam decides to double down. When the delegation returns, he rubs their noses in it! "You think your burden was heavy *before*? You're going to *wish* you had it so good! My pinky finger is thicker than my father's penis! If he lashed you with whips, watch me whip you with scorpions' tails!" (1 Kings 12:10-11, 14).[163] He does a mean impression of Pharaoh (Exod. chapter 5), no?

Repeating the rallying cry of the rebel Sheba in 2 Samuel 20:1, the men of the northern tribes call it quits with the Davidic monarchy (1 Kings 12:16, ASV):

> What portion have we in David?
>   neither have we inheritance in the son of Jesse:
> to your tents, O Israel:
>   now see to thine own house, David.

Uh, just how often did this *happen*? You have to wonder if, again, we are reading a rerun. Is this just a retelling of the tale of Sheba leading Israel to secede from Judah? The possibility is important because it suggests that the basis for believing in a united monarchy splitting up is as insecure in terms of literary sources as it is in terms of hard archaeological evidence.

One might expect that King Rehoboam would get busy preparing for war with Jeroboam to regain the larger Israel that he ruled, apparently, only for a few days. And so he does, but no sooner does a prophet named Shemaiah[164] warn him not to do it than Rehoboam backs down. Would a king so concerned not to appear weak have been scared off that easily? Imagine the reaction of his remaining subjects! Wouldn't they have become as angry with Rehoboam as the Israelite tribes had in response to his earlier show of macho stubbornness?

We have to suspect that this is really just a cloak for editorial and narrative fiat. It's not as if the oracular pronouncement of a prophet would have automatically been taken seriously enough that Rehoboam would immediately hit the "emergency stop" button. Think of the duel of the prophets in Jeremiah 28; the king, listening to a self-styled prophet, would certainly not obey him without question. It would still be up to the monarch to make his own decision. A prophet need not have been more than one of several advisors (cf., 2 Sam. 17:1-14). We will see this again in 2 Kings 22.

Another zigzag carries us from "pious Jeroboam" to "idolatrous apostate Jeroboam." He has rapidly turned from Dr. Jeckyll to Mr. Hyde, lapsing from the purity of the freshly-chosen David to the abominations of the no-longer-wise Solomon, founding false temples. The whole section presupposes the centralization of worship in Jerusalem, which often serves as a source of distortion from a subsequent and artificial standpoint.

Jeroboam suddenly realizes that an Israel without the Jerusalem Temple is a risky proposition. What if his new subjects get nostalgic for the Temple service and periodically hit the road in pilgrimage? They might get homesick, like the Israelites in the wilderness who thought that maybe life as slaves in Egypt hadn't been so bad after all. Then you're talking about a reunified Israel and Judah under Rehoboam!

What is Jeroboam's solution? Well, if Disneyland is off limits, why not build Disney World? Or at least Dollywood? And so, apparently with considerably less trouble than Solomon had, Jeroboam has not one but *two* new temples constructed at Dan and Bethel. We read of nothing like the extravagant measures taken by Solomon in the construction of the Jerusalem Temple, nor of a recruitment of Israelite press gangs to build the two new structures. Remember, that use of forced labor was the very thing that led to Israel's secession under Jeroboam! How did he avoid history repeating itself? The answer is that fiction repeats itself more easily.

The Deuteronomist narrator heartily disapproves of Jeroboam's temples. Why? Of course, for him there can be but one legitimate Temple: Solomon's. These other two are counterfeits, like the outlying altar east of the Jordan in Joshua 22:10-34. But that's not all. The Deuteronomic theology held that God could be neither seen nor visually represented, but the tradition was that Jeroboam's temples each displayed a Golden Calf, a young bull, representing Yahweh. (Bull imagery for gods was very common in the ancient Near East; many examples have been unearthed over the decades.)

I discussed these divine effigies in connection with the Golden Calf episode in Exodus, suggesting that Jeroboam/Aaron should be understood as referring to Yahweh, not other gods, when he tells the worshippers, "Behold your Elohim, O Israel, who brought you up out of the land of Egypt!" (Exod. 32:8 and 1 Kings 12:28). It has to be a reference to (statues of) Yahweh: It makes no sense to suppose Jeroboam was trying to entice his people to worship new and alien deities. Who did not know it was Yahweh who had liberated the Hebrew slaves with a mighty hand? "Oops! Guess we had a case of mistaken identity! Must have been Dagon or Baal who arranged the Exodus!" Jeroboam's whole rationale was to make it easier for his subjects to undertake their accustomed Yahweh worship closer to home. Would he, in order to satisfy their nostalgia for their old-time religion, have introduced a *new* one? Hardly.

And yet there remains an element of ambiguity because of the plural verb "brought." Keep in mind that "Elohim" has what would normally be construed as a plural ending ("gods") even if the reference was to the one God Yahweh. It looks to me like the redactor has changed a singular "brought" to a plural (not evident in English) in order to blur the text, opening the possibility of the reader seeing Jeroboam as "a preacher of foreign divinities" (Acts 17:18).

Again, I'm guessing the adjustment was made in order to make Jeroboam like the fallen Solomon. But that almost doesn't matter, because in chapter 15 Jeroboam fully embraces idolatry and polytheism, making sure the local high places (hilltop shrines) have adequate staffing. Of course, in those days no one saw anything wrong with this, right? We are reading it through the disapproving lens of the much later Deuteronomic theology which forbade all these things.

But that's not the only thing wrong with this picture. If Jeroboam was an advocate and enabler of local idol-worship, why had he gone to the trouble of erecting the huge temples at Dan and Bethel? Remember, these two structures were piggy-backing on the (fictive) Deuteronomic centralization of worship, just slightly "de-centering" it. But who needed even *this* compromise if you could offer sacrifice at your local consecrated barbecue pit? At any rate, Yahweh sends a prophet with the same old tidings: God is taking the kingdom away from you and giving it to someone who won't wallow in apostasy. Yahweh would seem to be a pretty poor judge of character.

Naturally, the Deuteronomist didn't mean to leave this impression; it was just the by-product of his tendency to vilify the Israelite and Jewish kings in order to justify the destruction of both kingdoms at the rude hands of heathen empires (the Assyrians and the Babylonians, respectively) to which God had abandoned them. The Deuteronomist's procedure here is fully as arbitrary as his earlier shoe-horning of the individual Judges episodes into the Procrustean bed of the same theology.

If none of this makes much sense, if there is no plausibility to it, can we suggest some actually historical germ to the division of the kingdom into North and South? We have already noted the difficulties besetting the Bible's portrayal of even a temporary union between Israel and Judah, and the likelihood that the whole business reflects the temporary unification of the Mediterranean world and Central Asia under Alexander the Great, the historical prototype for Solomon "in all his glory" (Matt. 6:29). And, continuing the parallel, just as Alexander's empire fragmented after his death, divided into Ptolemaic Egypt in the south and Seleucid Syria to the north, so Solomon's imaginary empire split into Judah and Israel once he died.

Another attractive possibility is that the whole business reflects the post-Exilic schism between the Jerusalem Temple cultus and that of the Samaritans centered upon Mount Gerizim. Noth understands the Chronicler's antipathy for Northern Israel, all the way back to the Jeroboam secession, as a reflection of this post-Exilic, purely cultic schism (neither group of tribes any longer having political independence).

I suggest that one can understand the original Deuteronomic version of Jeroboam's secession in exactly the same way. It would be just one more instance, as we will see in the next chapter, of the Chronicler further extending the themes he found (and that we find) already present in Deuteronomy. It is a matter of dueling foundational and credentialing myths.[165]

Dare one even suggest that the hard-to-keep-straight names "Rehoboam" and "Jeroboam," being pretty much synonymous in meaning (both mean "he who enlarges the people") denote the fictive character of both? I would interpret this as one more case of a common mythic-symbolic theme discussed by Girard,[166] that of the "monstrous double." In such cases, the myths reflect (albeit in a glass darkly) historical struggles between closely associated groups (clans, tribes, classes, castes, factions) which have become mirror images of one another.

The original ground for the enmity has been lost sight of, and thus where the guilt lies can no longer be determined, especially since both sides, "fighting fire with fire," have sunk to the same moral level. They are "mimetic twins" and thus naturally symbolized as physical doubles, fraternal twins, or at least close counterparts. I understand the rhyming Rehoboam and Jeroboam in this way. They are figureheads of post-Exilic factions in Hellenistic Palestine. And the Deuternomic stories of their carving up of Israel sprouted from there. It goes to show that it is not just dawn-age myths of patriarchs and eponymous ancestors but also quasi-historical narratives that function as what Gunkel calls *ethnological* legends.[167]

Elijah & Elisha

Elijah and Elisha belong in the early period of the Hebrew Prophets, or at least they are placed there. But they do not look much like the preaching ("writing") prophets like Isaiah, Ezekiel, and Jeremiah. This may be because these last are actually literary fictions, names attached to collections of prose and poetry composed by later, unknown writers and initially circulated in written form, never delivered as oral preaching.[168] The situation would exactly parallel the case of still later apocalyptic texts like Daniel, 4 Ezra, 1, 2, and 3 Enoch, 2 Baruch, and Revelation, which were literary creations whose ostensible authors were really pseudonyms employed by much later, anonymous writers.

Elijah and Elisha are on record with virtually no memorable sayings or important revelations. They are instead wonder-workers, thaumaturges whose closest analogues are Jesus and the Jewish miracle-workers and rain-makers Honi the Circle-maker and Hanina ben Dosa. And just as rabbinic tradition later co-opted these miracle-workers, "rabbinizing" them,[169] and as Christian theology remade and domesticated Jesus the magician,[170] so has the Deuteronomic Historian adapted Elijah and Elisha into his polemical narrative, exalting the power of prophets over against that of kings, both good and bad.[171]

But this represents a late stage of the Elijah and Elisha traditions. It is fairly easy to demonstrate that Elijah (like Samson) was at first simply a sun god, matched by his successor and rival, Elisha, as a moon god. Once these mythic figures were demoted to legendary (i.e., quasi-historical) heroes with the powers of demigods (again, like Samson), stories about them seem to have been circulated in connection with a kind of "cult of the saints,"[172] a devotion rendered to the "memories" (i.e., legends) of these supermen, and/ or of self-proclaimed contemporary avatars/epiphanies of them (Mark 6:14-15; 8:27-28; Matt. 17:10-13; John 1:21).[173] Finally, Elijah and Elijah are manipulated for propaganda/ legitimization purposes in the Deuteronomic framework, where they are portrayed as "prophets like Moses."[174]

Acts of Elijah

Elijah Decrees Three Years of Famine
1 Kings 17:1-7

This feat befits Elijah's origin as a sun god, who parches the crops.[175] It becomes a Deuteronomic showpiece for the power of Yahweh's prophets as superior to the dubious kings (dubious not only because of personal character flaws, but because the whole institution permits, or even invites, corruption). Note that famine and drought were prominent among the curses threatened by the Deuteronomic Moses (Deut. 28:22-24).

The Ever-Renewing Meal and Oil
1 Kings 17:8-16

This story makes Elijah a champion of the poor and oppressed, especially the pious widows, who must have been the ones to circulate such stories.[176] But why? Would even the most avid fans of Elijah, hearing these tales, expect such a miracle for themselves? Whether at the hands of some successor of Elijah or in answer to a prayer to the "original" Elijah? It is hard to imagine. What, then, might be the larger point of the story? On the one hand, the story looks like it is intended to magnify the greatness of a popular saint and so to spread his cult. On the other, the whole thing may be a Deuteronomic creation, paralleling Moses' miraculous provision of food for his followers: manna and quails in Exodus 16; Numbers 11; Deuteronomy 8:16. In the same way, of course, John explicitly compares and contrasts Jesus with Moses in John 6:30-51.

Elijah Raises the Widow's Son
1 Kings 17:17-24

As the sun god, Elijah is able to reverse the effects of fatal sunstroke. Also note the action on behalf of the defenseless widow, whose son is her only chance for any kind of a financially secure future (precisely as in Luke 7:12).[177] It seems likely that stories like this were circulated not only to cultivate devotion to the Elijah cult,[178] but also to encourage women like the one depicted here to provide material support for wandering prophets in their own day, for whom the figure of Elijah stands.[179] Support the prophet and you won't go away empty-handed.

Many of these individual, self-contained miracle stories may have originally depicted the prophet answering his devotees from heaven, sometimes "beaming down" in person, as in later Jewish legend.[180] After all, Elijah did not die but ascended directly into heaven.

We have an ancient parallel in the testimonial tablets lining the walls of the healing shrines of Asclepius, the healing god, son of Apollo, who had ascended to heaven but regularly appeared to his customers in dreams as they spent the night in the shrine.

Elijah Calls Down Fire from Heaven

1 Kings 18:17-40

The derisive disdain for Baalism, as well as the spectacularly easy victory over Baal, mark the story as a piece of anti-pagan satire long after the fact.[181] Von Rad's comments on the satire on idolatry in Isaiah 44:9ff seem to me to apply here, too. "The speaker here is no longer speaking from the depths of a real temptation [to idolatry] . . . . It is rather the voice of a certain enlightenment which finds expression . . . the images of foreign deities have become ludicrous." In this case, it's the deities themselves.

Is faith ever really vindicated in this comic book fashion? People in historical times knew it was not, hence the mockery at the cross: "Wait! Let us see if Elijah will come and rescue him!" (Mark 15:36).

Notice, too, that Elijah calls down *fire from heaven*, appropriate for the sun god.

The Baal prophets lash themselves in penance, hoping to move the god to act, just like medieval Christian flagellants and modern Shi'ite Muslims. They also "limp" about the altar, performing a sacred dance also performed by Israelites at Penuel (Gen. 32:31).[182]

The Elijah Whisperer

1 Kings 19:1-18

This episode is artificially juxtaposed with that of Elijah's victory over the Baal prophets. After the decisive humiliation of his (and Yahweh's) rivals, does it make sense for Elijah to flee and hide, complaining that he is the endangered last vestige of Yahweh-worship? The very ingenuity of the suggested harmonizations is proof enough that the task is hopeless. When we take the story by itself it makes plenty of sense as a Deuteronomic creation out of whole cloth. The point of it is to drive home Elijah's identity as one of the Moses-like prophets predicted in Deuteronomy 18:15: "[Yahweh] your God will raise up for you a prophet like me from among you, from your brethren–him you shall heed."

The Moses-Elijah parallels come fast and thick, signaling direct literary dependence. Fearing for his life, Elijah journeys to Mount Horeb, where Moses met Yahweh after taking it on the lam from Pharaoh's threats. God tells Elijah to stand in the cave mouth there because Yahweh is about to pass by, just as Moses was told to hide in a cleft in a rock while Yahweh passed by. Moses saw only God's back as he passed (Exod. 33:21ff), while Elijah only hears God's voice; both are oblique epiphanies. Elijah's epiphany is presaged by special effects including storm, earthquakes, and fire such as preceded Moses' meeting with God to receive the commandments in Exodus 19:18-19.[183]

Elijah Calls Elisha

1 Kings 19:19-21

This is a credential story on behalf of Elisha, claiming "apostolic succession" from Elijah. The basic notion of Elisha succeeding Elijah comes from the cyclical replacement of the setting sun with the rising moon. It is much like the myth (in Isaiah 14) of Helal, the planet Venus which dominates the heavens before the sun rises and after it sets. The personified Morning Star schemes to supplant the sun ("the Most High") but is cast down as soon as the greater light appears.

This passage provided the inspiration for the gospel episodes of Jesus calling Peter and Andrew, James and John, and Levi (Mark 1:16-20; 2:14). Luke's anecdote (9:61-62) of

Jesus warning a would-be disciple to think again is even more closely based on 1 Kings 19:19-21: "Another said, 'I will follow you, Lord; but let me first say farewell to those at my home.' Jesus said to him, 'No one who puts his hand to the plow and looks back is fit for the kingdom of God'" (RSV). Jesus takes the role of Elijah; the unnamed recruit plays Elisha. He asks permission to stop home to say goodbye to his parents, just like Elisha did, but Jesus is not so lenient as Elijah and calls the man's sincerity into question. The plowing reference obviously harks back to Elisha's farm labors.

Naboth's Vineyard

1 Kings 21

This is not an oral-traditional, self-contained Elijah story, but a piece of Deuteronomic fiction, using Elijah as the voice of Deuteronomic criticism against godless kings. The characters of the spineless, petulant, hen-pecked Ahab and the contemptuous witch-queen Jezebel are beautifully drawn.

As Thomas L. Brodie demonstrates, the story of Stephen's martyrdom (Acts 6:8-15; 7:58-8:1a)[184] is derived from this tale, combined with elements of the Achan story (Josh.7). It is also masterfully retold in Goethe's *Faust*, Part 2, Act 5.

Micaiah's Mockery

1 Kings 22

This fascinating tale tells us much about the institution of the court prophets in Israel and how they functioned, as well as about the mythology underlying it. "Jumping" Jehoshaphat, king of Judah, meets with Ahab, his counterpart in Israel, to consider joint military action to take Ramoth-gilead away from Syria. Jehoshaphat likes the idea but, just to be sure, requests that the king of Israel consult his staff prophets of whom there are around four hundred.[185] Jehoshaphat would feel more secure if they could obtain divine approval. And the king's yes-men are happy enough to oblige, unanimously pronouncing Yahweh's blessing on the endeavor.

But this seems a bit too easy to Jehoshaphat who can see that these "kept" prophets know where their *matzoh* is buttered. They are chaplains, not real prophets at all. Their job is to parrot the king's wishes back to him. So Jehoshaphat asks for a second opinion. Grudgingly, the Israelite king comes up with a name: "Micaiah the son of Imlah, but I hate him, for he never prophesies good concerning me, but evil" (1 Kings 22:8).

It is tempting to imagine Micaiah as a free-lancer, not on the royal payroll, a man like Amos, who prophesied judgment and doom on King Jeroboam of Israel. Amos made no pretense of possessing prophetic status or credentials but earned his living as a sheep-shearer and sycamore dresser (Amos 7:10-15). As he stood fulminating on the steps of the temple at Bethel, the chief prophet attached to the place stormed out and told him to beat it! Amos answered that he had no choice. Yahweh could not find a listening ear among Amaziah and his prestigious colleagues and was forced to go outside Israel to bring a layman up from Judah to get his words broadcast.

But I think we are supposed to understand Micaiah as another of the king's staff oracles, just one who has not sold out. He says what he hears from God whether or not the king wants to hear it. Up to now, the king must have feared to lay hands upon him lest God blast him for mistreating one of his own. Think of 2 Kings 2:23-25, where forty-two brats mock Elisha and do not live to tell the tale. Or Herod Antipas' fear of touching John the Baptist despite the latter's public denunciations of him (Mark 6:19-20). But Herod did feel the need to shut the Baptist up, so he figured it was worth the risk to throw him in prison; likewise, the king of Israel just told Micaiah to keep quiet if he had nothing nice to say.

I see the story as paralleling two other Old Testament stories as well. Both Genesis 41 and Daniel 2 set up a similar scenario: A king needs the expertise of his staff of sages and diviners, who, however, find themselves stymied. Then someone suggests he summon an outsider who has the necessary skills, Joseph and Daniel respectively, and, sure enough, they provide the prophetic truth the king had fruitlessly demanded of his paid charlatans. The same thing is going on here, the only real difference being that Micaiah's dissident voice is not heeded.[186]

Micaiah first mocks the king, pretending to agree with his more optimistic colleagues, but the king knows Micaiah well enough to know he can't be serious and commands him to level with him. "You want straight talk, Your Majesty? All right, here it is . . . ." The whole enterprise is doomed from the start. Not surprisingly, the king waves away the truth and pursues his ill-starred scheme.

But what is of more interest to us is Micaiah's astonishing account of a vision he had before being ordered to appear before the king: Micaiah was present as a fly on the wall in the heavenly court, witnessing a convocation of all the heavenly beings. Yahweh sought their advice, asking for suggestions on how best to make a fool of the king and trick him into disaster at Ramoth-gilead.

Like junior executives at a corporate board meeting, one godling proposes one idea, another something else.[187] "Clarence, you've been doing some work on this. What have you got?" Just this: "I will go forth and will be a lying spirit in the mouths of all the king's prophets!"[188] "Okay! You're on! And there'll be a nice fat bonus waiting for you when it's over!" (cf., vv. 19-23).

We have a similar depiction of the heavenly council at Job 2:1-7, where we even see God again conferring with one particular spirit and endorsing his proposed scheme, then sending him on his way to get busy. Psalm 82 begins the same way: "God takes His stand in His own congregation; He judges in the midst of the rulers" (Psalm 82:1, NASB). Where did this august assemblage meet? Mount Zaphon.[189] The young god Helal (the morning star), son of the winged goddess of the dawn, Shahar, had coveted the chief seat there. Here's Isaiah 14:12-14 (ASV):

> How art thou fallen from heaven,
>   O day-star, son of the morning!
> how art thou cut down to the ground,
>   that didst lay low the nations!
> And thou saidst in thy heart,
>   I will ascend into heaven,
>   I will exalt my throne above the stars of God;
>   and I will sit upon *the mount of congregation*,
>   in the uttermost parts of the north [literally, "on Zaphon"];
> I will ascend above the heights of the clouds;
>   I will make myself like the Most High.

Talk about the Siege Perilous! Helal should have taken the advice of Jesus in Luke 14:7-11! But instead, he got the boot and wound up in Sheol, the Netherworld.[190]

Isaiah 6 depicts God enthroned amid the divine Seraphim, asking, "Whom shall I send? And who will go for *us*?" The prophet, seemingly an interloper on the scene, at once realizes he has been invited there so he may hear and accept this summons. Then he, too, is to get to work on his mission.

Elijah Preempts the Oracle of Baal-Zebub
2 Kings 1:2-8

The story is strikingly parallel to that in 1 Samuel 28:3-25. In both, an Israelite king (Saul, Ahaziah) goes to consult a forbidden oracle (the witch of Endor, the priest of Baal-Zebub at Philistine Ekron) to learn of his impending fate (the outcome of a battle, recovery from an injury). In both, the king is caught up short by the appearance of a prophet (Samuel's ghost, Elijah), who is recognized by his distinctive dress (Samuel's long robe, Elijah's hair shirt). And the news is not good. Why are the two stories so similar? It is entirely possible they are versions, "separated at birth," of one original story. But in any case, they are both cautionary tales, emphasizing the Deuteronomic prohibition of "Brand X" methods of divination (Deut. 18:9-14). Thus it may simply be that both stories are the creations of the Deuteronomist, who, like many authors, reused the same plot for different stories.

Baal-Zebub[191] means "Lord of the Flies," denoting the buzzing sound of the roaming spirits that would whisper the desired information into the ear of the oracle-priest.[192]

The description of Elijah as "a hairy man" (translators paraphrase it as "wearing a garment of hair") originally denoted the rays of the sun, as with Samson's long hair.[193]

Elijah Calls Down Fire from Heaven
2 Kings 1:9ff.

Again, Elijah wields the power of the sun god because he *is* the sun god. Of course, the Deuteronomist no longer knows that (or doesn't want anyone *else* to know it). For him, Elijah is a human being with super powers, much like the Human Torch. He doesn't even need to petition God to roast these unfortunate flunkies. He orders up the solar flares all by himself.

Note the wonderful cartoonish character of this tale: the classic threefold structure of folktales and jokes, the increasing anxiety of each party of troops dispatched to apprehend Elijah, the ultimate reversal whereby the once-imperious troops finally become sniveling chickens, begging Elijah for mercy. It is beautifully done.

What we see here is the *other* way things could have gone in two gospel versions of Jesus' arrest in the Garden of Gethsemane. Matthew's Jesus counters his disciples' eagerness to resist by force of arms: "Do you think that I cannot appeal to my Father, and he will at once put at my disposal more than twelve legions of angels?[194] How then should the scriptures be fulfilled, which says that it must happen this way?" (Matt. 26:53-54, NASB). John has "When he said to them, 'I am he,' they drew back and fell to the ground. Therefore he asked them, 'Whom do you seek?' And they said, 'Jesus the Nazarene.' Jesus answered, 'I told you that I am he; so, if you seek me, let these men go their way'" (John 18:6-8, NASB).

And yet, in a sense, the logic of the Elijah version turns out to be the same, since Elijah does in the end come along quietly to stand before the king. Was it really necessary to barbecue the first two groups of fifty arresting officers? Here it is important to realize that all three groups, though technically different characters (150 soldiers in all), function as a single *actant*,[195] or narrative role, just as, in the larger framework, Elijah and Elisha do. "Elisha is represented not just as a disciple but almost as a continuation of Elijah."[196] We are to feel that there is a single narrative entity, "the soldiers," upon whom Elijah finally shows mercy.

Elijah's Ascension

2 Kings 2:1-18

Elijah is depicted as a circuit-rider, like Samuel, as well as the leader of schools of disciples. In this episode we see him making his rounds, as we will subsequently see Elisha doing.

Elijah parts the Jordan (2:19-22) on his way to the launch site, and, after Elijah makes his ascension, Elisha repeats the feat using Elijah's mantle to strike the river, symbolizing his status as Elijah's successor. Note that Elijah's parting of the river paints him as repeating Joshua's miracle, which confirmed him as a prophet like Moses. Likewise, for Elisha to repeat Elijah's feat secures his status as Elijah's successor.

This pattern is so pronounced in the Deuteronomist's narrative that we have to suspect it is the creation of that author.[197] But the ascension story itself was much older, a vestige of Elijah's original identity as a solar deity. Elijah ascends to the zenith of the heaven in a fiery chariot, just like Apollo.[198]

The inability of searchers to find any remains is a common feature of apotheosis legends.[199] But, as Scott D. Hill[200] notes, there might be more to this particular story. Namely, why do Elijah's disciples insist on searching for the departed prophet's corpse? Do they suspect foul play on Elisha's part? Do they imagine Elisha was impatient to succeed him, murdered him,[201] and stashed the body in some remote place? That might be. But it is more likely that the tale presupposes a frequent motif in the stories of local heroes and prophets when they die: Sometimes their bodies are about to be buried in some location other than the one God or the prophet had in mind, and the body flies away to the desired place of interment.

Possibly the sons of the prophets think Elijah's dead body has found its own way to its divinely appointed burial place, and they want to find it. No doubt such tales served as propaganda on behalf of rival shrines, both (or all) of which claimed to be the *real* burial place and thus deserving of the pilgrimage trade, just like the rival Golgothas and empty tombs of Jesus in Jerusalem today.[202]

Elisha wins the privilege of a double share of Elijah's thaumaturgical spirit, as demonstrated in his saga. Accordingly, he performs *twice* as many wonders (count 'em!) as his predecessor. One might speculate that the redactor is already doing with these two mighty prophets what F.C. Baur[203] showed that the Book of Acts does with the apostles Peter and Paul, paralleling them so closely that the partisans of the one can no longer disparage or vilify the other. The intent was to heal a rift between Petrine and Pauline factions (cf., 1 Cor. 1:11-12).

Still, however, Acts finally prefers Peter, portraying him as the venerable figurehead of the Twelve, while Paul (otherwise his equal) is subordinated to the Twelve. Might we imagine a sectarian rivalry between two groups of "the sons of the prophets," one devoted to Elijah, the other to Elisha? The Deuteronomist depicts them as performing many of the same feats, implying that both are genuine prophets of Yahweh, though he does prefer Elisha, to whom he ascribes twice as many miracles.

Acts of Elisha

Elisha Purifies the Water

2 Kings 2:19-22

This one started out as a *geological* story parallel to Exodus 15:25. But it might well be a Deuteronomic rewrite of that Moses story in order to underline the Moses-like character of Elisha. Or the story might have been traditional anyway, and the Deuteronomist found it useful.

Elisha and the Bears

2 Kings 2:23-25

Here is a *cautionary* tale: Don't mock the man of God! It is reminiscent of the warning issued by early Jesus prophets to those who heckled their preaching: "Whoever is ashamed of me and of my words in this sinful and adulterous generation, of him will the Son of Man likewise be ashamed when he comes in the glory of his Father with the holy angels" (Mark 8:38).[204]

But underlying this Elisha the story is another astronomical allegory. It offers one of the major clues that Elisha is the moon (god): He is bald, lacking the hair which, as in the cases of both Samson and Elijah, would mark him as a sun god. The hairlessness of Elisha has survived in oral transmission for this reason only. How often does biblical narrative offer *any* description of a character's appearance?[205] It has to be there for some pretty good reason. In just the same way, Genesis 27:11 tells us that Jacob was a "smooth man," unlike his brother and rival Esau, a "hairy man." Their rivalry is yet another "moon versus sun" allegory.

When the gang of smart-mouth brats harass Elisha, shouting, "Go up, you bald-head!" we understand it in the Deuteronomic context as equivalent to the "bald" jokes Buddy used to torment Mel with on *The Dick van Dyke Show*: "Hey, baldy!"[206] But this is a historicizing reinterpretation of an original moon-rise chant. The ancients thought that such rituals facilitated the motions of nature.

Whence the ravenous bears? Even in the ancient Near East, the Big and Little Dipper were known as the Great Bear and the Small Bear. There must have been some mythic-ritual connection here, too.

Elisha's Role in the Moabite War

2 Kings 3

This is another bit of Deuteronomic composition, using Elisha as a mouthpiece for Deuteronomic theology. It is interesting that Elisha is a counselor of the king of Israel, the very opposite of Elijah's adversarial relationship with Ahab. The story preserves the coloring of ancient prophethood: the use of music to induce prophetic consciousness (3:15), as in 1 Samuel 10:5-6.

Elisha Multiplies the Oil

2 Kings 4:1-7

Again, he is the champion of the widows. This story also serves the Deuteronomic tendency to parallel the various prophets with Moses, as fulfillments of "his" prediction that God would send Moses-like successors, because Moses, too, miraculously provided food to the starving. The underlying tradition portrayed Elisha as another glorified saint whose help one might seek.

It has the basic outline of all miracle stories: the setting of the stage, the location, characters, etc. We find ourselves among the disciples of Elisha when a widow, whose husband had been one of this group, appears and asks for help. Then the story adds the "case history": What is the plight, and how bad is it? It's pretty bad, all right! She is destitute, and her creditors are threatening to confiscate her children as collateral for her debts. The miracle-worker in these tales usually says something that signals he will save the day. Elisha tells her to pour the oil from her single jar into as many vessels as she can scrounge, and there will be more than enough to pay her debts.

Elisha and the Shunammite

2 Kings 4:8-17

This is another biblical "type scene,"[207] the miraculous impregnation of a barren woman, as in the cases of Hannah, Samson's mother, Sarah, and Elizabeth. Underlying all such stories seems to be another aspect of the ancient prophetic role. The "angel" (messenger) or man of God would himself impregnate the woman, who had falsely been blamed for her childlessness. In reality, the husband was sterile, but the prophet was not. His intervention saved face for the husband.[208] If an angel or a spirit impregnated his wife, where's the shame?

The story, with the next one, provides the model for that of the raising of the Widow of Nain's son (Luke 7:11-17), as well as those of the Syro-Phoenician's daughter (Mark 7:24-30), Jairus' daughter plus the woman with the issue of blood (Mark 5:21-43), and the healing of Peter's mother-in-law (Mark 1:30-31).

Elisha Raises the Shunammite's Son

2 Kings 4:18-37

This is a special type of miracle story meant to highlight the unique power of the hero. Not even his own disciple, using Elisha's own staff or techniques, can bring it off. See Mark 9:14-29, where the disciples of Jesus, despite previous success in exorcism, just cannot cast out a particularly ornery demon. Jesus, once he shows up, does the deed without breaking a sweat. Another miracle story of the same kind occurs in this testimonial inscription at the ancient Epidaurus healing shrine:

ARISTAGORA OF TROIZEN

She had tape-worm, and while she slept in the Temple of Asklepios at Troizen, she saw a vision. She thought that, as the god was not present, but away in Epidauros, his sons cut off her head, but were unable to put it back again. Then they sent a messenger to Asklepios asking him to come to Troizen. Meanwhile day came, and the priest actually saw her head cut off from the body. The next night Aristagora had a dream. She thought the god came from Epidauros and fastened her head on to her neck. Then he cut open her belly, and stitched it up again. So she was cured.[209]

The story also functions as "fundraising theology," implying that those who patronize the wandering prophets will by no means lose their reward.

Elisha Purifies Poisoned Food

2 Kings 4:38-41

It seems possible that this story was repeated as a charm to (try to) counteract food poisoning, just as a medieval Elijah story involving Lilith formed part of an exorcism ritual. In that story, Elijah "was walking on the road and met the Evil Lilith and her band. He said to her: 'Where are you headed for, O you Unclean One, and you Spirit of Defilement, and all your band, where are they going?'"

Her reply: "My lord Elijah, I am on my way to the house of a woman in childbirth, Mercada, daughter of Donna, to give her the sleep of death and to take her child which is being born to her, to suck its blood, and to suck the marrow of its bones, and to seal its flesh."

Elijah called for her to be restrained in the name of God, to be "like a stone." And she said: "For the sake of Yahweh, release me from the ban and I shall flee and swear to you in the name of Yahweh, the God of Israel, that I shall desist from this woman in childbirth and her child which is being born to her, and shall surely not harm her. And every time that they mention my names, or I see my names written, I and my band shall have no power to do evil or to harm." Then she listed off a whole series of her names, in addition to Lilith.

Elijah responded with some impressive name recitation of his own:

> Behold, I adjure you and all your band in the Name of Yahweh, the God of Israel, with the number value 613, [the God of] Abraham, Isaac, and Jacob, and in the name of His Holy Shekhina, and in the name of the ten Seraphim, Ophanim, and Holy Beasts, and the ten books of the Law, and by the might of the God of the Hosts, blessed be He, that you and your band not go to injure this woman, or the child she is bearing, neither to drink its blood, nor to suck the marrow of its bones, nor to seal its flesh, nor to touch them, either their 256 limbs, nor their 365 ligaments and veins. Just as she cannot count the stars of heaven, and cannot dry up the waters of the sea. In the name of Him who rent Satan, Hasdiel, Shamriel.[210]

Elisha Multiplies the Loaves

2 Kings 4:42-44

The sons of the prophets, devoted to Elisha, were like Buddhist monks, dependent upon the food donated by local sympathizers. Here they receive such largesse, but it falls woefully short for the many hungry stomachs. Of course, Elisha takes the situation in hand, miraculously multiplying the food. He is thus the *Bhagavat*, the Lord of Bounty. I think that Elisha's personal presence is, as often, a concretization of the nebulous "presence" (precisely as in Matt. 18:19-20; 1 Cor. 5:3-4) and trustworthy providence of the glorified saint. His disciples' request for help is tantamount to praying, "Give us this day our daily bread."

This story would seem to be the prototype for the gospel stories of Jesus' miraculous multiplying loaves and fish (Mark 6:35-44; 8:1-10). One doubts that early Christians expected such wonders to occur among them. For them, the food miracles of Jesus probably served as symbols for the Eucharist, the multiplication of physical food signifying the supernatural (i.e., spiritual) abundance of the communion elements.[211]

Elisha Heals Naaman the Syrian

2 Kings 5:1-19a

This is probably more Deuteronomic material, demonstrating the power of the Hebrew God over the nations, though it must be based on an earlier underlying story. We can tell this because the redactor has overlaid his own theology ("Now I know that there is no god in all the earth except in Israel!" verse 15) on top of an original monolatrous understanding integral to the story, verses 17-18, according to which Yahweh can be worshipped only on Israelite soil (literally!) while Rimmon has legitimate claim to Syria.

One note: I feel sure that we are to identify the servant who urges the outraged Naaman to heed Elisha's silly-seeming instructions (2 Kings 5:13) with the servant girl who urged Naaman to seek Elisha's help in the first place (5:2-3). It makes most sense dramatically that way. I realize verse 13 has "his servants" speak collectively,[212] but "their" words are those of a single voice, unless we are to imagine all of them speaking in unison.

Gehazi's Greed

2 Kings 5:19b-27

A cautionary tale: Don't use religion to seek personal gain! A similar tale is found among the Epidaurus inscriptions.

PANDARUS, A THESSALIAN, WHO HAD MARKS ON HIS FOREHEAD:

He saw a vision as he slept. It seemed to him that the god bound the marks round with a headband and enjoined him to remove the band when he left the Abaton and dedicate it as an offering to the Temple. When day came, he got up and took off the band and saw his face free of the marks; and he dedicated to the Temple the band with the signs which had been on his forehead. Echedorus received the marks of Pandarus in addition to those which he already had. He had received money from Pandarus to offer to the god at Epidaurus in his name, but he failed to deliver it. In his sleep he saw a vision. It seemed to him that the god stood by him and asked if he had received any money from Pandarus to set up as an offering to Athena in the Temple. He answered that he had received no such thing from him, but if he [Asclepius] would make him well, he would he would have an image painted and offer it to him. Thereupon the god seemed to fasten the headband of Pandarus round his marks and ordered him upon leaving the Abaton to take off the band and to wash his face at the fountain and to look at himself in the water. When day came he left the Abaton, took off the headband, on which the signs were no longer visible. But when he looked into the water he saw his face with his own marks and the signs of Pandarus in addition.[213]

Note how the god asks him an incriminating question, just as Peter asks Sapphira (Acts 5:8). And just as Gehazi acquires Naaman's leprosy for himself, so does Echedorus inherit the disfigurement of the healed Pandarus.

Elisha Makes the Axe-Head Float

2 Kings 6:1-7

Again, the petty nature of the miracle indicates its origin among the poor for whom the borrowed axe-head would have been a significant loss. One has to infer that a story like this advertised Elisha as a saint to whom one might pray in order to find lost objects, like Samuel in 1 Samuel 9:3-20a, not one's contemporary, but a saint of the remote past now residing in heaven. His devotees would have petitioned Elisha for help finding lost possessions just as Catholics seek St. Anthony's help today.

One wonders if we detect a Deuteronomic fingerprint in this story, as the situation ("I lost my neighbor's axe-head! What do I do?") is reminiscent of the tort laws in Deuteronomy 22:1-4; 23:24-25; 25:1-3 (not to mention those of the Covenant Code in Exodus 21-22, especially 22:14-15).

Elisha Reveals the Army of God

2 Kings 6:15-17

Classic Deuteronomic theology: The eye of faith beholds the power of God where the eye of flesh sees only human weakness. The usually invisible armies of heaven were expected to appear in plain sight at the climax of salvation history when God or Christ should lead them to victory against sinners and heathen oppressors, the minions of Gog and Magog (Rev. 19:14; War of the Sons of Light and the Sons of Darkness). Joshua had encountered their commander (Josh. 5:13-15). When God is called "Lord of Hosts" (Yahweh Sabaoth), the reference is to this army of angels. "[Yahweh] is a man of war!" (Exod. 15:3). Apparently, the starry hosts of the night sky were identified with the angelic army (Luke 2:13).

Elisha, Gehazi, and the Shunammite

2 Kings 8:1-6

This and the aftermath appear to be Deuteronomic elaboration of the originally self-contained episode of the Shunammite. The after-the-fact embellishment reminds one of the Gospel of Nicodemus/Acts of Pilate, where those healed by Jesus testify to Pontius Pilate long afterward.

Elisha Ordains Hazael King of Syria

2 Kings 8:7-15

Here is a prime case of the Deuteronomic theology of history: God brings the evil Hazael to power precisely to bring sorrowful judgment upon his people Israel. Too bad it was necessary. Again, as awful as this may seem, the alternative was to conclude either that God had washed his hands of them or, worse yet, that he had been routed by the mightier gods of Syria.

Elisha Ordains Jehu King of Israel

2 Kings 9:1-13

Again, this passage is Deuteronomic fiction, allowing Elisha to initiate the slaughter of the Baal prophets just as Elijah did in 1 Kings 18. The Rechabites were like Saudi Arabia's Wahabi sect of Islam—a desert Puritanism, looking back to the imagined halcyon days of nomadic austerity in the wilderness before settlement of the land caused the people to embrace the corrupt ways of paganism with its nature-worship and worldly affluence. As a sect, the Rechabites endured on into New Testament times and perhaps beyond, even feeding into Carmelite monasticism.[214] Probably the Rechabite order arose long after the era of Jehu and has been retrojected into that past by way of self-aggrandizing legend-mongering.

Elisha's Deathbed Prediction

2 Kings 13:14-19

It seems the original story stopped at 13:17 with Elisha's promise of victory over Aram (Syria). But there was no lasting victory after all, so someone added verses 18-19, which blame the Israelite king for flubbing Elisha's blessing.

Elisha's Postmortem Miracle

2 Kings 13:20-21

Elisha has apparently been interred in a mausoleum where his bones are on display for the sake of visiting pilgrims. This story sees his bones as potent relics, still able to work the old magic. It seems likely that this is a *ceremonial* etiology for a sacred grave, told at a healing shrine that purported to be the tomb of Elisha. Similarly, early Christians believed that the saints and martyrs lingered invisibly near their relics, available to perform healings and miracles on behalf of faithful pilgrims gathered there to celebrate the anniversaries of their martyrdoms.[215]

The Savage Sword of Jehu

2 Kings 10

Having been anointed king by Yahweh's prophet Elisha (fulfilling God's command to Elijah), Jehu decides to strike a decisive blow against Yahweh's rival Baal, whose worship Queen Jezebel had promoted. So he pretends to be a great fan of Baal in order to win the trust of the state-supported priesthood of the god. He summons them all to a revival meeting.

On his way there, Jehu runs into Jehonadab the Rechabite, whose hereditary sect detested Baalism and believed Israel had no business worshipping him. Jehu invites Jehonadab to climb aboard his chariot to witness first-hand the carnage he plans to unleash. "Come and see my zeal for Yahweh!"[216]

Once they pull up to the Baalist moose lodge, Jehu gives final orders to the eighty men he had earlier stationed about the perimeter, telling them to be sure that no Baal cultist gets out alive. And none does. Here Jehu shows himself to be following in the bloody footsteps of Elijah, who happily had four hundred Baal prophets slaughtered on Mount Carmel.

Traditionally, Bible readers have perused this story without a qualm. The butchering of the Baal worshippers seems to them no more a tragedy or a moral outrage than the herd of pigs perishing in the sea (Mark 5:13). Their reaction does not show moral insensitivity, but rather literary sensitivity. They have tuned into the proper wavelength presupposed by the story which is not an actual account of a pogrom against members of another religion, as are today's disgusting reports of Islamo-fascists mass-murdering whole groups of Christians, Jews, and Yezidis. Remember, it is all fiction, the point of which is to redouble the zeal of post-Deuternomic Jews to eliminate from their own practice all traces of previous Israelite-Canaanite religion, now deemed heretical and heathen.

The Messiah Hezekiah and Josiah's Reformation

2 Kings 18:1-8, 22-23

The Talmud tractate *Sanhedrin* (99a) contains a startling piece of what we would now call Preterism,[217] the belief that we should no longer await events once prophesied for the future because they have already been accomplished without anyone noticing. Today's Evangelical Preterists believe that the Second Coming of Christ, a future event when Jesus predicted it ca. 30 C.E., is now long past, having occurred coincident with the fall of Jerusalem in 70 C.E. According to *Sanhedrin* 99a, "R. Hillel said 'There shall be no Messiah for Israel, because they have already enjoyed him in the days of Hezekiah.'" No Messiah could be better than him![218]

I have already suggested that the reforms of Hezekiah and Josiah are two versions of the same original story. Both reflected the Hasmonean-era Deuteronomic Reform and tried to provide for it a more ancient pedigree by retrojecting it into earlier centuries, just as the "rebuilt" Temple of Zerubbabel was retrojected into the fictive Golden Age of Solomon, then back further (as the mini-Temple called the Tabernacle) into the fabled time of Moses.

Yet another one of these retrojections occurs in 4 Ezra 14:38-48 (RSV). A voice called to Ezra, saying, "open your mouth and drink what I give you to drink." He did so, "and behold, a full cup was offered to me; it was full of something like water, but its color was like fire. And I took it and drank; and when I had drunk it, my heart poured forth understanding, and wisdom increased in my breast, for my spirit retained its memory; and my mouth was opened, and was no longer closed."

The "Most High gave understanding to the five men," he went on, "and by turns they wrote what was dictated, in characters which they did not know. They sat forty days, and wrote during the daytime, and ate their bread at night." As for Ezra, he "spoke in the daytime and was not silent at night," and during the forty day session, 94 books got written. When it was over, the Most High spoke to him:

> Make public the twenty-four books that you wrote first and let the worthy and the unworthy read them; but keep the seventy that were written last, in order to give them to the wise among your people. For in them is the spring of understanding, the fountain of wisdom, and the river of knowledge.

The first 24 books are the books of the Hebrew biblical canon.[219] The other 70 most likely denote the Septuagint, the Greek version of the Jewish scriptures. By now, I think the implication is clear: The notion that Ezra miraculously restored the whole Jewish Bible, all copies having been destroyed during the Babylonian Exile, is a wink to the reader, admitting that none of the scriptures predated the post-Exilic period of Ezra. They were not *restored* in Ezra's time but rather *composed* then–if not later!

It is like the fictive claim that the Book of the Covenant (the core of Deuteronomy) was, ahem, *rediscovered* in Josiah's day–a pious fraud. To say that Ezra mystically restored the scripture texts is like John having Jesus assure his readers that everything would come back to the disciples by the inspiration of the Paraclete (John 14:25-26; 16:12-14). Of course, this is a clever, if clumsy, attempt to retroject the decades-later teaching of the Gospel of John, placing it in the mouth of the Jesus of seventy years before (and which no one remembered him saying).

But there is no reason whatever to believe 4 Ezra actually goes back to the fifth century B.C.E., and no one thinks it does. The book is generally dated to the late first century C.E. This implies that the idea of an Ezra-era origin of the scriptures reflects an even later attempt to push the date of scripture's writing back *to* the remote-seeming time of Ezra the scribe, implying a *very* late date for scriptural composition. Plus, the fact that 4 Ezra has the *simultaneous* origin of both the Hebrew and Greek Old Testaments brings us very close to the theories of Lemche, who says

> there is really no reason to believe that the Hebrew versions must perforce have been much older than their translations into Greek. To discuss an interval of, say, a hundred years, or a decade, or just one year, is simply a hopeless affair, as no hard evidence of the correct interval between the appearance of the Hebrew original and the Greek translation can be found in favour of any of these positions. [220]

The earliest known manuscript fragments of the Greek Septuagint date from the second century B.C.E., which is pretty close to the time I posit for a Hasmonean Deuteronomic "reform."

The Mouse that Roared at Sennacherib

2 Kings 19:32-37

Isaiah, in 2 Kings 19:32-34, declared that God would never allow Jerusalem to fall to Assyria. The Assyrians were encamped right outside the gates. When morning dawned, there was no longer any threat. The Angel of Yahweh had, during the night, descended upon the sleeping Assyrian army and wiped them out. Even for one of these biblical miracle stories, this seems surprisingly abrupt. How did he do it? One feels there must have been more to the story, and many think that Herodotus preserves the rest of it.

So when presently king Sanacharib came against Egypt, with a great force of Arabians and Assyrians, the warrior Egyptians would not march against him. The priest, in this quandary, went into the temple shrine and there before the god's image bitterly lamented over what he expected to suffer. Sleep came on him while he was lamenting, and it seemed to him the god stood over him and told him to take heart, that he would come to no harm encountering the power of Arabia: "I shall send you champions," said the god. So he trusted the vision, and together with those Egyptians who would follow him camped at Pelusium, where the road comes into Egypt; and none of the warriors would go with him, but only merchants and craftsmen and traders. Their enemies came there, too, and during the night were overrun by a horde of field mice that gnawed quivers and bows and the handles of shields, with the result that many were killed fleeing unarmed the next day. And to this day a stone statue of the Egyptian king stands in Hephaestus' temple, with a mouse in his hand, and an inscription to this effect: "Look at me, and believe."[221]

What hath one to do with the other, you ask? Apologists attempt to rationalize this report, jettisoning the business about Mickey, Minnie, and Mighty nibbling away at the leather fittings of the Assyrians' weapons, and suggesting that instead the little buggers unleashed a flash flood of Bubonic Plague in the camp. This sounds more than a little like the eighteenth-century Protestant Rationalists suggesting that Jesus walked not on the sea but on the stepping stones, or that Exodus 19 records a volcanic eruption on Sinai.

And yet it does make you wonder. Maybe Herodotus' story is a variant of 2 Kings 19:32-37 (or vice versa, as you prefer). Despite significant differences, both stories concern Sennacherib's troops being turned back by divine intervention. And the notion of the Angel of Yahweh acting through deadly pestilence is explicit in 2 Samuel 24:15-17 and implicit in Exodus 12:29-30; Wisdom of Solomon 18:14-16. I do not mean to suggest that this is what actually happened, but it possibly fills in the intent of the Deuteronomist.

Isaiah Turns Back the Clock

2 Kings 20:1-11

Isaiah drops in to share the bad news with King Hezekiah: He is doomed. Somehow a boil from which he is suffering is quickly going to poison his system so thoroughly that he will succumb to it. As can well be imagined, the king does not take it well and tearfully prevails on Isaiah to ask Yahweh for mercy. Lucky for him, Yahweh is willing to grant him another fifteen years.

Not bad. But Hezekiah knows that talk is cheap, and he dares to ask Isaiah if God would be willing to put it in writing via some miraculous stunt. Sure, why not? What'll it be? How about having the shadow retreat by ten degrees on the sun dial? And so it happens. We can't help thinking of another meteorological prodigy in the Deuteronomic History: Joshua making the sun and moon to stop orbiting for about a day (Josh. 10:12-14). Is it the same author reusing a good idea? Or two independent legends utilizing the same mytheme?

But the myth-making did not stop here. A modern urban legend holds that NASA scientists noticed a gap in cosmic history: There seemed to be a missing day, and, lo and behold, its duration matched perfectly the hours affected by the miracles of Joshua plus Hezekiah! Hallelujah, the inerrancy of scripture is vindicated!

This whole notion is absurd. How would the astronomers become aware of a "missing day" in the first place? It's not as if they can consult outer space surveillance tapes or something. They only "know" what happened (i.e., what *should* have happened or *must* have happened) by extrapolating backwards based on the present positions and regular motions of heavenly bodies. If Joshua or Hezekiah (or McNulty with his stopwatch)[222] temporarily halted time or planetary motion, there would be no way to detect it. One website traces this hokum back to Harold Hill, a Pentecostal industrialist who wrote it up for the Spencer, Indiana, paper, *Evening World* (October 1969).[223] But Harry Rimmer had already promoted it back in 1936.[224]

Notes

1. Some restrict the term "Deuteronomic" to refer to the Book of Deuteronomy and employ the longer "Deuteronomistic" for the narrative I am discussing in this chapter. Personally, I don't think the nuance is worth the extra syllable.

2. Martin Noth, *The Deuteronomistic History*. Trans. E.W. Nicholson. Journal for the Study of the Old Testament Supplement Series 15 (Sheffield: University of Sheffield Press; 2nd ed., 1991).

3. Again, these laws seem never to have governed anyone in public life but constituted an ideal blueprint intended to regulate personal conduct, much like the "laws" of the Talmud. See Thomas L. Thompson, *The Mythic Past: Biblical Archaeology and the Myth of Israel* (New York: Basic Books, 1999), p. 312; Philip R. Davies, *In Search of 'Ancient Israel.'* Journal for the Study of the Old Testament Supplement Series 148 (Sheffield: Sheffield Academic Press, 1992), p. 39.

4. Woody Allen, "Hassidic Tales." In Allen, *Getting Even* (New York: Vintage Books, 1978), p. 50: Woody imagines a "sacred Jewish holiday commemorating God's reneging on every promise."

5. Richard L. Rubenstein: "the question of God's responsibility for the death camps ... must plague every Deuteronomist." *After Auschwitz: Essays in Contemporary Judaism* (New York: Bobbs-Merrill, 1966), p. 182.

6. Noth, *Deuteronomistic History*, p. 18.

7. Friedrich Schleiermacher, *The Christian Faith*. Trans. D.M. Baillie. Cloister Library (New York: Harper & Row, 1963), vol. I, e.g., p. 17.

8. Peter Worsley, *The Trumpet Shall Sound: A Study of "Cargo" Cults in Melanesia* (New York: Schocken Books, 2nd ed., 1968), pp. 141-42; Stephen Fuchs, *Rebellious Prophets: A Study of Messianic Movements in Indian Religions* (New York: Asia Publishing House, 1965), pp. 29-30, 32, 41, 96, 98, 107, 123, 149-50, 220.

9. Gerhard von Rad, *Holy War in Ancient Israel*. Trans. Marva J. Dawn (Grand Rapids: Eerdmans, 1991).

10. Von Rad, *Holy War*, p. 126.

11. Von Rad at pp. 132-33.

12. Ben C. Ollenburger, "Introduction," Gerhard von Rad, *Holy War in Ancient Israel*. Trans. Marva J. Dawn (Grand Rapids: Eerdmans, 1991), pp. 7, 31, notes that Von Rad was following in the footsteps of Max Weber in connecting holy war with the old-time charismatic prophets.

13. Aubrey R. Johnson, *The Cultic Prophet and Israel's Psalmody* (Cardiff: University of Wales Press, 1979); Sigmund Mowinckel, *The Psalms in Israel's Worship*. Trans. D.R. Ap-Thomas (New York: Abingdon Press, 1962), Chapter XII, "The Prophetic Word in the Psalms and the Prophetic Psalms," vol. 2, pp. 53-73.

14. "Woe to those who go down to Egypt for help and rely on horses, who trust in chariots because they are many and in horsemen because they are very strong, but do not look to the Holy One of Israel or consult Yahweh!" (Isa. 31:1). Cf. Hosea 10:13.

15. It is the custom nowadays to deny Dagon's merman character and to contend that he was instead a grain deity, but Goldziher already demonstrated the unity of these motifs (Ignaz Goldziher, *Mythology Among the Hebrews and its Historical Development*. Trans. Russell Martineau [1877; rpt: New York: Cooper Square Publishers, 1967], pp. 214-15). The fish was also a symbol for fertility, as in the gospel stories of Jesus miraculously multiplying the loaves and fish (Mark 6:32-44; 8:1-10). Julius Wellhausen found a reference to Dagon's "fishiness" in 1 Samuel 5:4 ("only the trunk of [the statue of] Dagon was left to him") by emending the Hebrew so that it read "only his fishy part was left on him." It appears that an ancient mistranscription of a single Hebrew letter changed "fishy part" to "trunk."

16. Another possibility is that "son of Nun" is a very early scribal alteration of an original "son of Yahweh" as per Saul Levin, *The Father of Joshua/Jesus* (Binghamton: State University of New York, 1978). This, too, would imply Joshua's divine status.

17. Jaan Puhvel, *Comparative Mythology* (Baltimore: Johns Hopkins University Press, 1987), p. 39.

18. R.D. Nelson, "Josiah in the Book of Joshua." *Journal of Biblical Literature* 100, 1981, pp. 531-40; Nelson, *The Double Redaction of the Deuteronomistic History.* Journal for the Study of the Old Testament Studies Supplement Series 18 (Sheffield: JSOT Press, 1981), pp. 125-26.

19. Giovanni Garbini, *History and Ideology in Ancient Israel.* Trans. John Bowden (New York: Crossroad, 1988), Chapter 11, "Joshua's Exploits," p. 130. If we accept this, we must posit subsequent interpolations at this point. We know, on the one hand, that the Chronicler rewrote the Deuteronomic History, embellishing it in a priestly direction and, on the other, that the Deuteronomic History itself received numerous redactional additions before it reached its canonical form. Maybe the Chronicler wasn't satisfied with making a whole new version and could not resist "correcting" the text of his Deuteronomic predecessor's work as well. On additions to the text see Noth, *Deuteronomistic History,* passim.

20. Thompson, *Mythic Past,* pp. 149, 207, 259; cf., Niels Peter Lemche, "The Old Testament–a Hellenistic Book?" *Scandinavian Journal of the Old Testament* 7/2 (1993), p. 179: "It can also be argued that the deuteronomists very much needed a Josiah to make their own religious program legitimate, and here it is of no consequence whether the Deuteronomistic History was a work of the exilic or the post-exilic periods."

21. E.g., Arthur W. Pink, *Gleanings in Joshua* (Prisbrary Publishing, 2012).

22. "He who is slow to anger is better than the mighty, and he who rules his spirit than he who takes a city."

23. Davies, *In Search,* p. 53.

24. Or, as I like to call them, "priestitutes."

25. Thanks to the erudite Geoffrey Tolle for this suggestion.

26. Similarly, Exodus 14:21 says the Sea of Reeds was divided by a strong east wind, not by a snap of the divine fingers. According to Exodus 10:13 and 19, the locusts wound up in Egypt because a strong east wind blew the insects off their usual migratory path. They exited the country once a stiff west wind carried them into the sea. More Hellenistic rationalism?

27. Good thing, too, or else we'd be calling it "Reme"!

28. Thomas L. Brodie, "Luke the Literary Interpreter: Luke-Acts as a Systematic Rewriting and Updating of the Elijah-Elisha Narrative in 1 and 2 Kings." Doctoral Dissertation (Vatican City: Pontificia Universita S. Tommaso d'Aquino, 1981), p. 275.

29. Von Rad, *Holy War,* p. 49.

30. René Girard, *Violence and the Sacred.* Trans. Patrick Gregory (Baltimore: Johns Hopkins University Press, 1977), p. 219: "Henceforth everything touched by the sacred violence belongs to the gods; as such, it becomes the object of a most solemn prohibition."

31. Girard, *Violence and the Sacred,* pp. 27-28.

32. Girard at p. 28.

33. The view of D. Maunder and A.L. Shute, sympathetically discussed in Bernard Ramm, *The Christian View of Science and Scripture* (Grand Rapids: Eerdmans, 1954), p. 109.

34. Ramm, p. 108, was also friendly to the view of A.F. Fleming (1914), A. Rendel Short (1942), and J. Lowell Butler (1951) that what God did was to adjust the refractive index so that the sun would *seem* to have stood still in the sky. That an apologist can say such a thing with a straight face is an index of how severely theological desperation can distort one's sense of proportion. Ignaz Goldziher puts it well: "But what will the theological exegete not attempt in his desperate ingenuity?" *Introduction to Islamic Theology and Law.* Trans. Andras and Ruth Hamori. Modern Classics in Near Eastern Studies (Princeton: Princeton University Press, 1981), p. 109.

35. I am reminded of a *Saturday Night Live* skit in which guest host Charlton Heston reprised his iconic *Ten Commandments* role as Moses, flowing robes, skyscraper wig and all. Rob Schneider portrays Edward G. Robinson playing Dathan, who is urging the people, sick of waiting for Moses to return from Mount Sinai, to worship the Golden Calf. Suddenly Moses himself appears and asks what the heck is going on. Dathan thinks fast and replies, "It's just a par*ade* float, Moses! Yeah, *that's* right: a par*ade* float!"

36. In fact, depending on how late you feel comfortable dating the Deuteronomic History, it might be that this story actually refers to one of these outlying temples. "Joshua 22 is apparently an apology for an altar in Israelite Transjordan." (Morton Smith, *Palestinian Parties and Politics that Shaped the Old Testament* [1971; rpt: London: SCM Press, 1987], p. 70).

37. Vittorio Lanternari, *The Religions of the Oppressed: A Study of Modern Messianic Cults.* Trans. Lisa Sergio (New York: Mentor Books/ New American Library, 1965), p. 113. Deborah also bears comparison to numerous millenarian prophets worldwide. See Worsley, *The Trumpet Shall Sound;* Sylvia L. Thrupp, ed., *Millennial Dreams in Action: Studies in Revolutionary Religious Movements* (New York: Schocken Books, 1970); Fuchs, *Rebellious Prophets.*

38. Moses' father-in-law is named Jethro in Exodus 3:1; 4:18; 18:1. He is called Hobab here and Reuel in Exodus 2:18. The three names must reflect disparate versions of the Moses story. Numbers 10:29, which refers to

"Hobab the son of Reuel the Midianite, Moses' father-in-law," looks like an attempt at harmonization, but which one is supposed to be Moses' father-in-law in this verse, Reuel or Hobab? Is Hobab Moses' *brother*-in-law or his *father*-in-law? It depends on whether we punctuate the phrase as "Hobab (the son of Reuel), Moses' father-in-law" or "Hobab (the son of Reuel, Moses' father-in-law)."

39. Archaeological evidence makes this clear anyway. "Yahweh existed before the Hebrew people existed and was worshipped in the land of Canaan when the Hebrew tribes were still practicing the cults of their 'fathers.'" Garbini, Chapter 4, "The Origin and Development of Yahwism," p. 57. Garbini even shows that "Yahweh," like "El," was both a proper name and a generic term for deities in general. See also Thompson, *Mythic Past*, pp. 171, 175-76, 256; Davies, *In Search*, p. 85. Morton Smith, *Palestinian Parties*, pp. 69-71, discusses evidence that non-Israelite Yahweh worship, not necessarily monotheistic, survived for centuries in the area.

40. Garbini, *History and Ideology*, Chapter 10, "The Twelve Tribes," p. 124, suggests, however, that "Machir" was just an earlier name for the tribe of Manasseh.

41. No, this is not the origin of Oprah Winfrey's first name. Rather, her mother meant to name her for Ruth's mother-in-law, Orpah, but misspelled it.

42. For my money, the definitive commentary on the story of Gideon is Paddy Chayefsky's 1961 play, *Gideon* (New York: Random House, 1962).

43. Goldziher, *Mythology Among the Hebrews*, pp. 96-97: "This story is especially worthy of consideration in connexion with the science of Mythology, because a Hebrew custom similar to the mourning for Osiris or Adonis and Tammuz was fastened onto it, as appears in v. 40."

44. Goldziher, *Mythology Among the Hebrews*, p. 409: "The character of the Herakles-Melkart of the Ph[o]enicians appears in Samson in greatly shrunken proportions."

45. Goldziher, *Mythology Among the Hebrews*, p. 408.

46. Goldziher at pp. 408-409.

47. Puhvel, *Comparative Mythology*, p. 39. See also Goldziher, *Mythology Among the Hebrews*, p. 249: "The Myth is converted either into Religion or into History; the figures of the myth become either Gods and god-born Heroes, or Ancestors of the nation to which the myth belonged."

48. Goldziher, *Mythology Among the Hebrews*, p. 138.

49. Keep in mind that the original Hebrew text lacks punctuation, vowels, even spaces between words! Thus it is frequently possible to construe words and phrases rather differently.

50. Goldziher, *Mythology Among the Hebrews*, p. 406.

51. Goldziher at pp. 403-404.

52. Thus exactly equivalent to "Iscariot" ("the False One," "the Betrayer") in the gospels. See Bertil Gärtner, *Iscariot*. Trans. Victor I. Gruhn. Facet Books, Biblical Series–29 (Philadelphia: Fortress Press, 1971), pp. 5-7; Tzvetan Todorov, *The Poetics of Prose*. Trans. Richard Howard (Ithaca: Cornell University Press, 1977), Chapter 5, "Narrative-Men," pp. 66-79.

53. Goldziher, *Mythology Among the Hebrews*, pp. 408-409.

54. Professor Kogan said this during a dialogue with an atheist on a local TV show in Nutley, NJ, in, let's see, the late 70s or early 80s.

55. G.B. Caird, *Principalities and Powers: A Study in Pauline Theology*. The Chancellor's Lectures for 1954 at Queen's University, Kingston Ontario (Oxford at the Clarendon Press, 1956); Clinton D. Morrison, *The Powers That Be: Earthly Rulers and Demonic Powers in Romans 13.1-7*. Studies in Biblical Theology No. 29 (Naperville: Alec R. Allenson, 1960); Heinrich Schlier, *Principalities and Powers in the New Testament*. Quaestiones Disputatae 3 (New York: Herder and Herder, 1961); Hendrikus Berkhof, *Christ and the Powers*. Trans. John Howard Yoder (Scottdale: Herald Press, 1962).

56. I'm guessing he is not supposed to be a member of the *tribe* of Levi but rather, like the Judean Levite in Judges 17:7-13, a professional oracle-monger.

57. A concubine was a kind of unofficial wife, perhaps a slave, sometimes a man's wife's handmaid to whom she allowed her husband sexual access, as Sarah gave Hagar to Abraham.

58. See the discussion of the Sodom story in Derrick Sherwin Bailey, *Homosexuality and the Western Christian Tradition* (London: Longmans, Green, 1955), pp. 4-5. He thinks the Judges story has been rewritten on the basis of the Sodom story. If he is right, that only makes my case stronger, since it would mean the Deuteronomist interpreted the Genesis original as saying the mob who wanted to "know" Lot's guests meant to kill them, not to rape them.

59. To say nothing of the movie *Seven Brides for Seven Brothers*!

60. Much like John the Baptist, the pivot point between the Torah and the kingdom of God (Luke 16:16; Matt. 11:12-13). See Hans Conzelmann, *The Theology of St. Luke*. Trans. Geoffrey Buswell (New York: Harper & Row, 1961), pp. 26, 101, 185.

61. Noth, *Deuteronomistic History*, p. 85.

62. Smith, *Palestinian Parties*, p. 9.

63. I can't help picturing a little kid back in the 1940s, fallen asleep on the floor in front of the big cathedral radio console.

64. Compare how Jesus rides a donkey that had never carried anyone else (Mark 11:2; Luke 19:30) and how he is buried in a tomb no one had previously been interred in (Matt. 27:60; Luke 23:53; John 19:41).

65. Precisely as the eleven disciples cast lots to decide who will replace Judas (Acts 1:26). On the role of chance in revealing the divine will, see Girard, *Violence and the Sacred*, pp. 311-314.

66. Need I point out that the name marks the town as host to a temple to the sun god who eventually got reduced to the legendary hero Samson?

67. I imagine this is the inspiration for the scene in *Raiders of the Lost Ark* in which nefarious archaeologist René Belloc (hopefully not an Albright disciple!) opens the Ark and melts like a wax figure on a hot day.

68. Noth, *Deuteronomistic History*, pp. 81-82.

69. Josephus, in his *Antiquities of the Jews*, summarizing biblical history, had the section, too, but until now there was no concrete evidence he had gotten it from the Bible.

70. Remember that the tribes wiped out this town because it sat on the sidelines while they combined against Benjamin, avenging the outrages performed upon the Levite's concubine in chapter 19. Are we to understand that the Gadite and Reubenite refugees now fled to an empty ghost town with plenty of room for them? Maybe so.

71. One sometimes reads that Saul was threatening the recipients of his beef-o-grams with dismemberment if they refused his call to arms: "Men, don't let *this* happen to *you*!" But certainly the point is that, just as the sundered bits of the ox belong together, so should the disparate tribes of Israel come together to act.

72. This king bears the theophoric name "Nahash," marking him as a worshipper of Nehushtan/Leviathan, implying that this god's cult extended beyond Israel.

73. Nelson, *Double Redaction*, p. 108.

74. Thompson, *Mythic Past*, p. 206.

75. Nelson, *Double Redaction*, p. 108.

76. Davies, *In Search*, p. 112: "The persistent argument of the Former Prophets, that Israel was inherently disobedient and that monarchs precipitated its downfall is a theme perfectly manufactured to justify hierocracy."

77. "His arrogance has no bounds by day or night. No son is left to his father, for Gilgamesh takes them all ... His lust leaves no virgin to her lover, neither the warrior's daughter nor the wife of the noble; yet this is the shepherd of the city, wise, comely, and resolute." *The Epic of Gilgamesh: An English Version with an Introduction*. Trans. N.K. Sandars. Penguin Classics (Baltimore: Penguin Books, 1960), p. 60.

78. I feel sure that one day an archaeologist's spade will turn up a Philistine *Goliath Epic* featuring him as a great hero. The Deir Alla inscription (from the late eighth century B.C.E.) provides a set of prophecies ascribed to the Moabite seer Balaam, featured in Numbers 22-24. If Balaam, why not Goliath?

79. This episode looks like another version of the immediately preceding story of Merab, just a bit more colorful.

80. Of course, he requires only the foreskins as tokens of the number of Philistines killed, the same rationale for American Indian scalping, introduced by Dutch settlers who set one tribe against another. You don't need the whole corpse brought back. Likewise, newsstand proprietors do not send unsold paperbacks and comic books back to the distributors, only the torn-off covers.

81. Now what do you suppose Saul did with these trophies? Once, back in 1986, I noticed a sign in front of some fast food joint in Raleigh: "Furskins are here!" Instantly I thought, "So *that's* what they do with 'em!"

82. This has to denote Israelite ancestor worship. Doubtless food offerings would be set before the effigy of Uncle Mel to placate him (like leaving cookies for Santa, hoping to butter him up), letting him know that he had not been forgotten as he cooled his heels in the Netherworld (Isa. 14:9; Job 26:5). If he were ignored, he would exercise his baleful influence to cause misfortune and disaster. And somehow the image could be manipulated to elicit oracles from the Other Side.

83. I'm guessing both versions were attempts to situate in past history what actually began as a factional slogan among Jewish scribes over which representation should govern the Deuteronomic narrative, "Saul the hero" or "Saul the bum." Obviously, the latter won out. It almost sounds as if the issue was whether to include some (now lost) "Book of Saul" in the canon of the Former Prophets.

84. But the story may originally have meant to describe David's *castration* of Saul, as the word used for "skirt" (*kanaf*) may mean, as in Deuteronomy 23:1, "penis." David manages to cut off the "skirt" while Saul is in a cave relieving himself. If David took him by surprise and emasculated him as he was urinating, he didn't exactly refrain from laying violent hands on him after all. See Thompson, *Mythic Past*, p. 46.

85. Is it possible that the character of Saul, the persecutor of David, is the literary basis for Acts' character Saul of Tarsus, persecutor of Christians?

86. If one insists that these chapters preserve a single, continuous account of what really happened, then one invites the conclusion that the biblical author was a stupid incompetent. If, however, one recognizes that the Deuteronomist compiler has instead taped together numerous snippets and fragments in order to preserve them all instead of choosing some and dropping others, we emerge with a much higher regard for the narrator. He was stuck: He couldn't very well keep doubling back, saying, "Here's another way that some say it happened."

87. Not that it matters much, but might this be the origin of Samantha's mother's name, *Endora*, on the TV sitcom *Bewitched*? I bet it is!

88. This episode is one of the readings for the Service for All Hallows' Eve in the Episcopalian *Book of Occasional Services* (New York: Church Hymnal Corporation, 1979), p. 106, along with the similarly scary Vision of Eliphaz the Temanite (Job 4:12-21), the Valley of Dry Bones (Ezek. 37:1-4), and the War in Heaven (Rev. 12:1-12).

89. Just like the old joke about the Atheist Dial-a-Prayer.

90. "And when they say to you, 'Consult the mediums and the wizards who chirp and mutter' should not a people consult their God? Should they consult the dead on behalf of the living?"

91. Which also tends to confirm that the teraphim statue in David's house was a necromantic device.

92. Henry H. Halley, *Halley's Bible Handbook: An Abbreviated Bible Commentary* (Grand Rapids: Zondervan Publishing House, 1965), p. 183, implies this. Not all evangelicals share this opinion. Dennis F. Kinlaw thinks the witch did manage to conjure up Samuel's shade. See Kinlaw, "The Demythologization of the Demonic in the Old Testament." In John Warwick Montgomery, ed., *Demon Possession: A Medical, Historical, Anthropological and Theological Symposium*. Papers Presented at the University of Notre Dame January 8-11, 1975 (Minneapolis: Bethany House Publishers, 1976), p. 31.

93. Harry Emerson Fosdick, *A Guide to Understanding the Bible: The Development of Ideas within the Old and New Testaments* (New York: Harper & Brothers Torchbooks, 1938, 1956), p. 12.

94. When [Elyon] gave to the nations their inheritance,
    when he separated the sons of men,
    he fixed the bounds of the peoples
    according to the number of the sons of God (Deut. 32:8, NASB).

95. R.G. Collingwood, *The Idea of History* (New York: Oxford University Press, 1946), pp. 257-59, explains the practice of ancient, pre-critical "scissors-and-paste" historians who accorded their source materials the status of "authorities" and did not feel entitled to weigh them, accepting some and rejecting others. The biblical redactors went even farther in the same direction, often leaving contradictions unresolved in order to preserve as much revered tradition as possible.

96. There have been several attempts to fill this gap over the centuries by creative writers offering their own takes on what might have been in the book. Edgar J. Goodspeed (*Famous Biblical Hoaxes, or Modern Apocrypha*. Twin Brooks Series [Grand Rapids: Baker Book House, 1956], pp. 81-82) tells of three different medieval texts with this title. "One is a moral treatise, composed by Rabbi Shabbatai Carmuz Levita in 1391, and preserved in a Vatican manuscript. An earlier one, in the form of an Introduction to the Hexateuch, written probably by a Spanish Jew in the thirteenth century, was published in Venice in 1625 . . . A third medieval version, written by Rabbi Tham, who died in 1171, was a treatise on Jewish ritual; it was first printed in Italy in 1544." The 1391 version appeared in English in 1840. There have been a few others as well, but the most widely known appears to be a hoax volume that appeared in 1879 and was reprinted by the Rosicrucians and by numerous others since (*The Book of Jasher: One of the Sacred Books of the Bible Long Lost or Undiscovered* [San Jose: The Rosicrucian Order, 1934]).

97. Thompson, *Mythic Past*, p. 190. Davies contends that "The idea of Israel breaking away from Judah is highly implausible. It is quite likely that Judah was formed as a secondary state, perhaps in the 9th century . . . Judah became a state, and Jerusalem a major administrative centre, only in the 8th century BCE *at the earliest*" (Davies, *In Search*, p. 66).

98. Davies, *In Search*, pp. 65-66.

99. Bernard Lewis, *History: Remembered, Recovered, Invented*. Gottesman Lectures for 1974 at Yeshiva University (Princeton: Princeton University Press, 1975), pp. 62-63.

100. Thompson, *Mythic Past*, pp. 149, 207-208.

101. Thompson at p. 206; Davies, *In Search*, p. 64.

102. Cf., Smith, *Palestinian Parties*, p. 87.

103. Lewis, *History*, pp. 44-45, 59.

104. Thompson at p. 95.

105. Id.

106. Thompson at p. 204.

107. Id.

108. To let the Ark splash into the mud might have been construed as a wholesome reminder that it was not divine in its own right, i.e., an idol like the Golden Calf. But then why have it crackling with divine power, like Jesus in Mark 5:30?

109. Graham Hancock, *The Sign and the Seal: The Quest for the Lost Ark of the Covenant* (New York: Random House, 2012).

110. E.A. Wallis Budge, ed. and trans., *Kebra Nagast: The Queen of Sheba and Her Only Son Menyelek* (Forgotten Books, 2007).

111. For evidence that the Temple of Herod did contain an Ark, see Raphael Patai, *The Hebrew Goddess* (New York: Avon/Discus Books 1978), pp. 70-75.

112. Jacques Derrida, *Dissemination*. Trans. Barbara Johnson (Chicago: University of Chicago Press, 1981), e.g., p. 206: "But it is a difference without reference, or rather a reference without a referent, without any first or last unit, a ghost that is the phantom of no flesh, wandering about without a past, without any death, birth, or presence. Mallarmé thus preserves the differential structure of mimicry or *mimesis*, but without its Platonic or metaphysical interpretation, which implies that somewhere the being of something that *is* is being imitated."

113. No, contrary to general opinion, not a character from *The Flintstones*.

114. Lemche, "The Old Testament–a Hellenistic Book?" p. 169.

115. "Uriah" is another version of the name "Uriel," one of the archangels. The only difference is that the first uses the theophoric suffix "Yah" and the second uses "El" ("God"). Uriel is the revealer and appears as such in 2 Esdras (4 Ezra). Presumably, the name is cognate with the mysterious Urim, an oracular device. The name means "Light of God/Yahweh" or "Fire of God/Yahweh." (He's looking down at me right now from atop a bookcase–unless that's just a cheap statuette of him. Oh, never mind.)

116. Think of Lambchop and Shari Lewis.

117. So God punishes, *kills*, an innocent for something his parents did. Nice.

118. When today's Bible dictionaries (re)define this name (and Solomon's) as if it meant "Man of Peace," they are doing exactly as the scribes did when they ventured to redefine "Jerub-Baal" and to alter "Ish-Baal" to "Ish-Bosheth." They do not like the idea of David, imagined anachronistically as a strict monotheist, as having been a polytheist, naming his children for various Jerusalemite deities.

119. Robert Graves and Raphael Patai, *Hebrew Myths: The Book of Genesis* (New York: Greenwich House, 1983), pp. 95-96, regard this as a popular tale that also became the basis of the story of Cain and Abel (Gen. 4:8).

120. David's wife Bathsheba might conceivably have been understood as this man's daughter. Her name means "Daughter of Sheba." Perhaps there was a different version of the story in which Sheba's motive for leading the revolt was a never-assuaged anger over David's having had his son-in-law Uriah killed.

121. Julius Wellhausen, *Prolegomena to the History of Ancient Israel*. Trans. Allan Menzies (1878; rpt: New York: Meridian Books/World Publishing Company, 1957), pp. 148-151.

122. Girard (*Violence and the Sacred*, p. 12) calls attention to the frequent choice of cripples and other "defectives" as scapegoats when ancient societies sought to settle violence or to resolve crises by blaming them on the supposed nefarious magic of some marginal figure. See also René Girard, *The Scapegoat*. Trans. Yvonne Freccero (Baltimore: Johns Hopkins University Press, 1986), p. 25.

123. Girard, *Violence and the Sacred*, p. 78: "Having oscillated freely among the three protagonists [Oedipus, Creon, and Tiresias], the full burden of guilt finally settles on one. It might very well have settled on another, or on none. What is the mysterious mechanism that determines how the guilt shall fall? The attribution of guilt that henceforth passes for 'true' differs in no way from those attributions that will henceforth be regarded as 'false,' except that in the case of the 'true' guilt no voice is raised to protest any aspect of the charge. A particular version of the events succeeds in imposing itself; it loses its polemical nature in becoming the acknowledged basis of the myth, in becoming the myth itself."

124. Cf., "Samson the Sadducee strangler, sir. Silus the Syrian assassin, several seditious scribes from Caesarea . . ." Graham Chapman, John Cleese, Terry Gilliam, Eric Idle, Terry Jones, Michael Palin, *Monty Python's The Life of Brian (of Nazareth)* (New York: Ace Books, 1979), p. 145.

125. Thompson, *Mythic Past*, p. 164.

126. Id.

127. Von Rad, *Holy War*, pp. 81-84.

128. Thompson, *Mythic Past*, p. 207.

129. One might point to Sirach (AKA Ecclesiasticus) as a counter-example, since the sage's grandson introduces the collection as the work of his grandfather, Jesus ben Sira. But does that necessarily mean the old man coined all those sayings himself? Ben Sira himself may have been the compiler of his favorite wise sayings.

130. See the discussions of these texts in Owen Davies, *Grimoires: A History of Magic Books* (New York: Oxford University Press, 2009), pp. 12-18; Sayed Idries Shah, *The Secret Lore of Magic: Books of the Sorcerers* (New York: Citadel Press, 1957), pp. 9-60.

131. Victor Turner, *The Ritual Process: Structure and Anti-Structure*. The Lewis Henry Morgan Lectures, 1966, Rochester University (Ithaca: Cornell University Press, 1977), Chapter 3, "Liminality and Communitas," pp. 94-130. Exorcism functions as a kind of transitional ritual, from sickness to health, from the realm of evil spirits to the earthly plane. The visual appearance of the demons symbolizes the "neither here nor there . . . betwixt and between" (Turner, p. 95) character of the one undergoing the rite. Liminal rituals are typically set in a larger context of society.

Accordingly, as Gerd Theissen (*Sociology of Early Palestinian Christianity*. Trans. John Bowden [Philadelphia: Fortress Press, 1978], p.36) suggests, "Anyone who was dissatisfied with things as they were could become a criminal or a healer, a beggar or a prophet, a man possessed or an exorcist. He could . . . lose his identity completely and become a helpless victim of 'demons.'" Thus an exorcism served to reintegrate the demoniac into society.

132. John M. Hull, *Hellenistic Magic and the Synoptic Tradition*. Studies in Biblical Theology, Second Series 28 (Naperville: Alec R. Allenson, 1974), pp. 17, 68-69; Graham H. Twelftree, *Jesus the Exorcist: A Contribution to the Study of the Historical Jesus*. Wissenschaftliche Untersuchungen zum Neuen Testament. 2. Reihe 54 (Tübngen: J.C.B. Mohr [Paul Siebeck], 1993), pp. 36, 84.

133. M.R. James, *Old Testament Legends: Being Stories out of Some of the Less-Known Apocryphal Books of the Old Testament* (London: Longmans, Green and Co,, 1913), "Solomon and the Demons," pp. 105-19.

134. We have to wonder, however, what Solomon would have done had *both* women, as seems pretty likely, renounced their claims and exclaimed in unison: "*No!* Give it to *her*, for Baal's sake!" I'm guessing he would have resorted to that coin after all.

135. Margaret Barker, *The Gate of Heaven: The History and Symbolism of the Temple in Jerusalem* (London: SPCK, 1991), p. 11.

136. Mircea Eliade, *The Sacred and the Profane: The Nature of Religion*. Trans. Willard Trask (New York: Harcourt, Brace & World, 1959), pp. 58-59.

137. Barbara Thiering, *Jesus the Man: A New Interpretation from the Dead Sea Scrolls* (London: Corgi Books, 1993), pp. 51-53, 140-41.

138. Barker, *Gate of Heaven*, p. 52.

139. Eliade, *Sacred and the Profane*, p. 38; Richard J. Clifford, *The Cosmic Mountain in Canaan and the Old Testament* (Cambridge: Harvard University Press, 1972), "Cosmic-Mountain Symbolism in the Solomonic Temple," pp. 177-181; Barker, *Gate of Heaven*, pp. 63-64.

140. John Day, *Molech: A God of Human Sacrifice in the Old Testament*. University of Cambridge Oriental Publications No. 41 (New York: Cambridge University Press, 1989), pp. 48-55.

141. Margaret Barker, *The Older Testament: The Survival of Themes from the Ancient Royal Cult in Sectarian Judaism and Early Christianity* (London: SPCK, 1987), Chapter 10, "Transformations in the Post-Exilic Period: (2) The Eden Stories," pp. 233-45.

142. This was not much of a stretch, since the Primal Man Adam would have been a "light-bearer" (the meaning of "Lucifer") and a disgraced lieutenant of God anyway. See Henry Corbin, *The Man of Light in Iranian Sufism*. Trans. Nancy Pearson (New Lebanon, New York: Omega Publications, 1994), pp. 14-16.

143. Gershom G. Scholem, *Major Trends in Jewish Mysticism*. Trans. George Lichtheim. The Hilda Strook Lectures, Jewish Institute of Religion, New York, 1941 (New York: Schocken Books, 1954), pp. 265, 269, 275, 279-80.

144. Margaret Morris, *Eden Unveiled: Book of the Tetrad Mysteries*, forthcoming.

145. Clifford, *Cosmic Mountain*, p. 179; Barker, *Gate of Heaven*, p. 30.

146. Barker at pp. 18-19.

147. Geo Widengren, *The Ascension of the Apostle and the Heavenly Book*. King and Saviour III. Uppsala Universitets Årsskrift 1950: 7 (Uppsala: A.B. Lundequistska Bokhandeln, 1950).

148. Moses entering the Tent of Meeting to emerge, face radiant with divine splendor, bearing new commands from God, is based on the same ritual and myth.

149. Barker, *Gate of Heaven*, p. 117; John L. Brooke, *The Refiner's Fire: The Making of Mormon Cosmology, 1644-1844* (New York: Cambridge University Press, 1994), provides a startling modern parallel in this 1793 quote from Ezra Stiles, reporting on a recent "Immortalist" sect: "Nat Smith proceeded to presume & declare himself to be the Most High God & wore a cap with the word GOD inscribed on its front." At least it's better than wearing a "My Name Is" sticker with the Tetragrammaton scrawled on it in magic marker. (I guess.)

150. Barker at p. 120.

151. Barker at pp. 22.

152. Gerhard von Rad, *Old Testament Theology Volume I, The Theology of Israel's Historical Traditions.* Trans. D.G.M. Stalker (New York: Harper & Row, 1962), Part Two, B., IV, 4, "The Veto on Images in the Old Testament," pp. 212-18; G. Ernest Wright, *The Old Testament Against its Environment.* Studies in Biblical Theology No. 2 (London: SCM Press, 1960), pp. 23-25. Wright's book is a blatant exercise in what I call "dissimilarity apologetics," grossly exaggerating the supposed contrasts between Israelite and Canaanite religions (when it is really a contrast between Israelite-Canaanite religion on the one hand and radically reformist Deuteronomic religion on the other). Wright is arguing that biblical religion cannot be merely a product of historical-cultural evolution but must be the result of a direct revelation from God, an endeavor pretty much on the same level as the claim that it must have been space aliens who built the Pyramids.

153. Barker, *Gate of Heaven*, pp. 134-35.

154. Barker at pp. 135-36.

155. Rachel Elior, *The Three Temples: On the Emergence of Jewish Mysticism.* Trans. David Louvish (Portland, OR: Littman Library of Jewish Civilization, 2004). pp. 205-207.

156. Ellior, *Three Temples*, passim.

157. Barker, *Gate of Heaven*, p. 11. "We shall hex the Pentateuch, and slip you in neatly between Numbers and Deuteronomy!" Henry Drummond to Matthew Harrison Brady in Jerome Lawrence and Robert E. Lee, *Inherit the Wind* (New York: Bantam Books, 1963), p. 90.

158. Perceval to Arthur (reinterpreted as the Fisher King or Grail King) in John Boorman's classic 1981 film *Excalibur*.

159. Pretty impressive. I attended two of them (not as a groom, though!).

160. I prefer the term "American Indians," since the only actual "Native Americans" we know of are Bison. The people called "Native Americans" today are descended from hardy Siberian immigrants, thus no more indigenous to America than European settlers.

161. Thompson, *Mythic Past*, p. 208: "It is the story in I Kings 11–the story of Solomon's acceptance of the foreign gods of his 700 wives and 300 concubines–that offers an explanation as to why gods such as Astarte, Chemosh and Moloch were still worshiped in Palestine."

162. Yes, it's a bit difficult to keep these names straight. But if you have trouble with Jeroboam and Rehoboam, wait till we get to Elijah and Elisha!

163. Obviously, this is my colloquial paraphrase, but the Hebrew text actually does have "penis." English translators quail at this and substitute the euphemism "loins." You don't want to hear the word "penis" during the Sunday morning scripture reading.

164. This is the "Yahweh" version of the prophet Samuel's name ("Shemuel").

165. Martin Noth, *The Chronicler's History.* Trans. H.G.M. Williamson. Journal for the Study of the Old Testament Supplement Series 50 (Sheffield: JSOT Press, 1987), pp. 100-106.

166. Girard, *Violence and the Sacred*, pp. 62-67, 161-62.

167. Gunkel, *Legends*, pp. 19-23.

168. Terence Collins, *The Mantle of Elijah: The Redaction Criticism of the Prophetical Books.* The Biblical Seminar (Sheffield: Sheffield Academic Press, 1993), pp. 26, 41, 92, 102, 110, 120; Davies, *In Search*, p. 118.

169. William Scott Green, "Palestinian Holy Men: Charismatic Leadership and Rabbinic Tradition." In *Aufstieg und Niedergang der Romischen Welt* II. 19. 2, pp. 619-647; Scott D. Hill, "The Local Hero in Palestine in Comparative Perspective." In Robert B. Coote, ed., *Elijah and Elisha in Socioliterary Perspective* (Atlanta: Scholars Press, 1992), p. 66.

170. Morton Smith, *Jesus the Magician* (New York: Harper & Row, 1978).

171. Collins, *Mantle of Elijah*, p. 130.

172. Peter Brown, *The Cult of the Saints: Its Rise and Function in Latin Christianity.* Haskell Lectures, School of Divinity at the University of Chicago, April 1978 (Chicago: University of Chicago Press, 1981).

173. Hill, "Local Hero," p. 43.

174. Collins, *Mantle of Elijah*, pp. 133-38.

175. Goldziher, *Mythology Among the Hebrews*, p. 168.

176. Tamis Hoover Renteria, "The Elijah/Elisha Stories: A Socio-cultural Analysis of Prophets and People in Ninth-Century B.C.E. Israel." In Robert B. Coote, ed., *Elijah and Elisha in Socioliterary Perspective* (Atlanta: Scholars Press, 1992), pp. 75-126.

177. Renteria, "Elijah/Elisha Stories," pp. 103, 108.

178. Renteria, "Elijah/Elisha Stories," p. 101.

179. Steven L. Davies, *The Revolt of the Widows: The Social World of the Apocryphal Acts* (Carbondale: Southern Indiana University Press, 1980), Chapter III, "The Apostles," pp. 29-49, argues that the itinerant "brethren," apostles, and prophets glimpsed in the *Didache*, Matthew 25, and 3 John hide behind the "big names" of the superstar apostles in the Acts of John, Acts of Paul, Acts of Peter, Acts of Thomas, etc. Likewise, "Elijah" would be the symbolic figurehead for wandering prophets for whom these stories seek support.

180. There are a great many legends of post-ascension mercy missions undertaken by Elijah. Louis Ginzberg collects very many of them in his monumental *The Legends of the Jews. Volume IV: Bible Times and Characters From Joshua to Esther.* Trans. Henrietta Szold and Paul Radin (Portland, OR: Dragon Key Press, nd), pp. 100-113; Hill, "Local Heroes," p. 54: "Often the figure is said to appear to someone in a later age." Also: "Elijah could appear anywhere now ... It tempts me to wonder whether he was indeed 'alive' even in the time of Ahab, or whether it was his presence that was given credit for miraculous events in those days" (p. 71).

181. Von Rad, *Old Testament Theology*, p. 217.

182. Gunkel, *Legends*, p. 31.

183. Collins, *Mantle of Elijah*, pp. 133-35.

184. Brodie, "Luke the Literary Interpreter," pp. 281-87.

185. About the same number of Baal prophets, four hundred and fifty, serving Ahab and Jezebel in 1 Kings 18:22.

186. We might even include in this category the story of the sorcerer-priests of Pharaoh trying and finally failing to duplicate the wonders of Moses in Exodus 7:8-25; 8:1-19.

187. In fact, Yahweh is pictured here as analogous to the king of Israel, asking guidance from *his* "prophets"! There is a similar scene in L. Sprague de Camp's novel, *The Tritonian Ring* (1953; rpt. New York: Paperback Library, 1968), pp. 9-10: "When the gods of the West were gathered in their place of assembly, Drax, the Tritonian god of war, said in his ophidian hiss: 'Events will take a deadly turn for us in the next century unless we change this pattern.' [...] 'We might pray to *our* gods for guidance,' said the small bat-eared god of the Coranians, whereupon all the gods laughed, being hardened skeptics."

188. Strangely, this passage never gets brought up in discussions of how biblical inspiration guarantees the absolute inerrancy of scripture.

189. E. Theodore Mullen, Jr., *The Divine Council in Canaanite and Early Hebrew Literature.* Harvard Semitic Monographs Number 24 (Chico: Scholars Press, 1980), pp. 205-10.

190. This was originally an astronomical myth, "explaining" what happened daily to the Morning Star (the planet Venus) as soon as the sun rose and blotted out its light, which had just previously seemed so brilliant. It sank into the abyss under the earth till it should emerge again at dusk to begin the whole cycle again. See Goldziher, *Mythology Among the Hebrews*, pp. 116-17.

191. By the way, according to the earliest manuscripts of Mark 3:22, Jesus is said to have cast out demons by invoking Beel-Zebul ("Lord of the House"), though later copies change this to Beel-*Zebub*. The former was an old composite exorcism god (Bel-Ea, "Lord of the World," plus Baal-Mul-lil, "Lord of Evil Spirits"), not the oracle god of Ekron. See William Menzies Alexander, *Demonic Possession in the New Testament: Its Historical, Medical, and Theological Aspects* (Edinburgh: T. & T. Clark, 1902), pp. 181-83.

192. H.P. Lovecraft, having picked up this information from William Beckford's novel *Vathek*, used it in connection with his invented tome the *Necronomicon* ("Concerning the Dead"), supplying a title for the Arabic original, *Al Azif*, "the Buzzing," denoting the horrid revelations of the *jinn* to the soothsayer Abdul Alhazred. Brian McNaughton (*Satan's Seductress* [London: Star Books, 1981]) derived from 2 Kings 1:1-8 his references to the dimension-hopping swarm of demons, "the Host of Ekron."

193. Goldziher, *Mythology Among the Hebrews*, pp. 127-28., 162-63.

194. Wow! That's *thousands and thousands* of angels! Jesus sounds like he is saying he could unleash the Battle of Armageddon right there and then if he wanted to.

195. Algirdas Julien Greimas, *On Meaning: Selected Writings in Semiotic Theory.* Trans. Paul J. Perron and Frank H. Collins. Theory and History of Literature, Volume 38 (Minneapolis: University of Minnesota Press, 1987), Chapter 6, "Actants, Actors, and Figures," pp. 106-20; Jonathan Culler, *Structuralist Poetics: Structuralism, Linguistics, and the Study of Literature* (New York: Cornell University Press, 1975), pp. 82-83, 233-34.

196. Collins, *Mantle of Elijah*, p. 136. See also Gunkel, pp. 49-50.

197. Collins at pp. 136-38.

198. Goldziher, *Mythology Among the Hebrews*, Ibid.

199. Charles H. Talbert, *What Is a Gospel? The Genre of the Canonical Gospels* (Philadelphia: Fortress Press, 1977), pp. 28-33.

200. Hill, "Local Heroes," pp. 58-59.

201. "Might fervent candidates for this gruesome communion not sometimes grow too impatient and refuse to wait for the natural death of the holy one? Might they not hurry it forward?" Alexandra David-Neel, *Magic and Mystery in Tibet* (1929; rpt: Baltimore: Penguin Books, 1971), p. 134.

202. Conceivably, such stories might also have been told to justify the removal of relics to a new resting place. Religious authorities coveted the sacred clout the local shrines possessed, as in Brown, *Cult of the Saints*, p. 37.

203. Ferdinand Christian Baur, *Paul the Apostle of Jesus Christ: His Life and Work, His Epistles and Teaching*. Trans. Edward Zeller (1876; rpt: Peabody: Hendrickson Publishers, 2003), Volume 1, pp. 6-10.

204. Theissen, *Sociology*, pp. 27-28. The saying, by placement into the Markan narrative context, is misattributed to Jesus. Originally, the "me" would have denoted the itinerant charismatic himself, the "Son of Man" referring to the apocalyptic Jesus.

205. Gunkel, *Legends*, pp. 53-54.

206. Collins, *Mantle of Elijah*, p. 139.

207. Robert Alter, *The Art of Biblical Narrative* (New York: Basic Books, 1981), p. 110, etc.

208. M.J. Field, *Angels and Ministers of Grace: An Ethno-psychiatrist's Contribution to Biblical Criticism* (New York: Hill & Wang, 1972), Chapter 5, "The Angel as Man of God," pp. 20-39.

209. Mary Hamilton, *Incubation; or The Cure of Disease in Pagan Temples and Christian Churches* (London: W.C. Henderson & Son, 1906), p. 23.

210. Text from James Alan Montgomery, ed., *Aramaic Incantation Texts from Nippur* (Philadelphia: University Museum, 1913), translated by Raphael Patai, in *The Hebrew Goddess*, pp. 188-89.

211. Cf. Arthur C. Headlam, *The Miracles of the New Testament*. Moorhouse Lectures for 1914 Delivered in S. Paul's Cathedral, Melbourne (London: John Murray, 1914), pp. 324-325; Alan Richardson, *The Miracle-Stories of the Gospels* (London: SCM Press, 1941), p. 96; Raymond E. Brown, *New Testament Essays* (Garden City: Doubleday Image Books, 1968), Chapter X, "The Gospel Miracles," p. 240.

212. Gunkel, *Legends*, pp. 49-50.

213. Emma and Ludwig Edelstein, eds. and trans., *Asclepius: Collection and Interpretation of the Testimonies* (Baltimore: Johns Hopkins University Press, 1998), p. 231.

214. Rod Blackhirst, "Herbs and Wild Fruit: Judas Maccabee and Reflections of Rechabitism in the Medieval Gospel of Barnabas." *Journal of Higher Criticism* (9/2) Fall 2002, pp. 291-92.

215. Brown, *Cult of the Saints*, pp. 3-4.

216. If I were Jehonadab, I'd have wondered where Jehu's loyalties really lay: Was he pretending to be a Baalist in order to catch them unaware? Or was he actually a Baal-worshipper pretending to worship Yahweh in order to trap Jehonadab?

217. J. Stuart Russell, *The Parousia: A Study of the New Testament Doctrine of Our Lord's Second Coming* (T. Fisher Unwin, 1887; rpt: Grand Rapids: Baker Book House, 1983). And see the *Gospel of Thomas*, saying 51: "His disciples say to him, 'When will the repose of the dead begin? And when will the new world come?' He said to them, 'What you look for has already come, but you fail to recognize it.'"

218. I remember seeing on TV the stunning spectacle of Secretariat winning the 1973 Belmont Stakes by an incredible *thirty-one lengths*. Ever since then, I have wondered why anyone would still bother watching horse racing: It had been done to perfection, and it had to be all downhill from there. I suppose that's what Rabbi Hillel felt about Hezekiah.

219. The same as the 39 books of the Protestant Old Testament, just divided differently.

220. Lemche, "Old Testament," p. 189.

221. *Herodotus, with an English translation* by A.D. Godley (Cambridge: Harvard University Press. 1920), Book II, pp. 141, 2-6.

222. Rod Serling and Michael D. Rosenthal, "A Kind of a Stopwatch." *The Twilight Zone* October 18, 1963.

223. biblearchaeology.org/post/2005/08/29/Joshuas-Long-Day-and-Mesopotamian-Celestial-Omen-Texts.aspx#Article

224. Ramm, p. 109. Rimmer, of course, didn't implicate NASA. He claimed that the astronomers at the Harvard Observatory made the "discovery."

IV

Chronicles, Ezra, Nehemiah

PRIESTCRAFT TESTAMENT

This book, originally one continuous work, has been split into four books in our Bibles: 1 and 2 Chronicles, Ezra, and Nehemiah.[1] It is an attempt to (re)write the history of the kingdom of Judah from Adam to the return from the Exile. After the secession of the northern tribes under Jeroboam, the Chronicler has no use for them and says nothing about them. (Hence no tales, e.g., of Elijah and Elisha.).

The Chronicler used Genesis through Kings, plus a single extra-biblical source enumerating military installations.[2] He summarizes the earlier period up through King Saul in a series of genealogies. The main portion is based on 2 Samuel and Kings. He refers us to a *Book of the Kings of Israel and Judah*, but this source may be fictive. And he does not hesitate to make ample use of his imagination.

Just as previous historians had done, the Chronicler rewrote the history according to his religious views. The Deuteronomic Historian had (re)written history on the assumption that the laws of Deuteronomy had been in force since Moses' day. Likewise, the Priestly writer had written on the assumption that the Priestly Code had been in effect since Moses.

The Chronicler, himself a priest, continued the work of the Priestly writer, rewriting the later history of Judah as if the Priestly Code had governed religious life since the time of Moses, all through the Monarchy before the Exile. More recent liturgical innovations he ascribes to King David, not to Moses, for the simple reason that they do not appear in the "Mosaic" Priestly Code.

The Chronicler had a definite agenda in mind as he wrote. First, he harmonizes contradictions and difficulties he found in his sources. Second, he omits shameful behavior on the part of his characters.[3] Third, the Chronicler forces the events into a pattern of reward for piety and punishment for sin. The Deuteronomic Historian, of course, had already done this, but the Chronicler pulls out all the stops!

Fourth, the Chronicler adds new episodes where God intervenes to deliver Judah by miraculous means. Fifth, he magnifies the role of the Levitical priests (he is one of them) and introduces them into the narrative where they did not occur in the original. This also explains why the Chronicler recounts only the history of Judah, not Israel: Only Judah had the true Temple. This is also why he has no real interest in anyone before David and Solomon, architects of the Temple.

The anachronistic reading back of the Priestly Code into the pre-Exilic Monarchy period explains a lot of otherwise odd omissions and apparently small alterations made to Kings by the Chronicler. Why did the Chronicler omit the note that the Brazen Serpent of Moses had been kept in the Temple? Because if P had been in force, it could never have been brought into the Temple in the first place. Likewise, whereas Kings had Josiah "read" the "rediscovered" law book, Chronicles has him read "out of" it, implying it was a much larger tome that one could not read on a single occasion. Kings meant Deuteronomy; Chronicles means the whole Pentateuch.

As Marc Zvi Brettler[4] has noted, one of the most important aspects of Chronicles is that, because its major source, Samuel-Kings, has survived intact instead of simply being replaced by what is essentially a new version, Chronicles itself, it provides clear proof that biblical authors felt quite free to rewrite, edit, and embellish previous sacred books. This means both that it is a fundamental error to regard the Chronicler as trying to compose accurate history (instead of edifying fiction) and that we have to reckon with the likelihood that the previous Deuteronomic History was just as fictive, the product not of historical research but of theological imagination.

A Lot of Begats

No less than the first nine chapters of 1 Chronicles are taken up with soporific genealogies, wholly irrelevant to modern readers, but the veritable stock in trade of the priestly bookkeepers, one of whom wrote the book.[5] The purpose of all biblical genealogies is to secure the pedigrees of priests and rulers. Thus they function as credentials. Matthew's and Luke's genealogies serve the same purpose, seeking to demonstrate Jesus' right as heir to the messianic dynasty of David. Thus the lists of ancestors in the Bible are *tendentious*, axe-grinding. And this naturally raises the question of authenticity.

Was Jesus descended from King David? Who can say? The two gospel genealogies are very different and cannot be reconciled despite the valiant but frustrated efforts of apologists over many centuries. And we must suspect that any given "Davidic" king of Judah might well have fabricated his own ostensible Davidic pedigree.

I suggest that the biblical genealogical lists, especially including those in Chronicles, are precisely analogous to the *isnad*, the chain of attesters accompanying every single Islamic *hadith*. These are the names of those individuals who (supposedly) passed down this or that tradition of what the Prophet Muhammad did or said. ("I received it from Iqbal, who heard it from Abbas, who learned it from Hamsa," etc.) They all end up with some eye-witness (an early disciple or a relative) of Muhammad. But the *hadith*, as criticism has demonstrated,[6] are one and all spurious attempts to father someone's own opinions on Muhammad in order to claim his authority for them. What is true for the Islamic *hadith* is equally true of the genealogies in Chronicles.

This is obvious enough in the case of the genealogical links going back to Adam, all borrowed from Genesis. But there are tell-tale marks of sheer fictionalizing later on as well. For instance, 1 Chronicles 25:4 presents itself as a list of names, but it is actually a list of the titles (opening lines) of various hymns: "Have mercy on me, O Yahweh," "Have mercy on me," "You are my God," "I extol the help of . . .," "Sitting in adversity," "I have fulfilled . . .," "He made abundant," and "Visions."[7]

The Fall of Saul
1 Chron. 10:1-14 vs. 1 Sam. 31:1-13

The Chronicler has followed almost verbatim 1 Samuel's story of King Saul's demise, but he adds a brief paragraph onto the end of it to remind readers why God would have allowed his anointed king to suffer such an ignominious end, killing himself minutes before the victorious Philistines could arrive to torture and humiliate him. For the Chronicler, it seems that Saul had it coming! He shouldn't have disobeyed God's commandment, presumably the one where a vengeful Yahweh had ordered the complete eradication of the Amalekite army and livestock. Saul spared their king for some reason and took the sheep to feed his men (1 Sam. 15:19).

Saul's second blooper was to disdain Yahweh's guidance, preferring the ministrations of an outlawed necromancer, the Witch of Endor, instead–only 1 Samuel had said Saul *did* seek Yahweh's counsel via the approved methods, including the (apparently over-rated) Urim and Thummim. He turned to the Wicked Witch of the East only because God had turned a deaf ear to him (1 Sam. 28:6-7). Besides, the Chronicler has forgotten that Yahweh had *already* repudiated Saul by the time he entreated the Witch; that was *why* God refused to reply to Saul's requests for a battlefield forecast. Why does the Chronicler cap the story of Saul this way, with a rap sheet reminder? Because he is here launching his program of correlating a king's misfortunes with his misdeeds. It comes as no surprise, then, for the Chronicler to omit David's lament for the heroic Saul. The Chronicler comes only to bury Saul, not to praise him.

Battle of the Blind

2 Sam. 5:6-8

Our author also sees fit to drop 2 Samuel's material treating the bloody violence subsequent to David assuming the throne. He is happy to recount the early military victories of his hero David, though he makes an odd omission, chopping 2 Samuel 5:6-8 (NASB): "Now the king and his men went to Jerusalem against the Jebusites, the inhabitants of the land, and they said to David, 'You shall not come in here, but the blind and lame will turn you away'; thinking, 'David cannot enter here.' Nevertheless, David captured the stronghold of Zion, that is the city of David. David said on that day, 'Whoever would strike the Jebusites, let him reach the lame and the blind, who are hated by David's soul, through the water tunnel.' Therefore they say, 'The blind or the lame shall not come into the house.'"

Originally, and obviously, the point was the defiant boasting of the over-confident Jebusites: David was so little a threat that they could post the blind and the lame to detect his approach and to fight him off. Hearing it, David turned the taunt around: His invasion force will be so mighty that it will be as if the doomed Jebusites *had* actually posted the blind and the lame to fight him! This text had been popularly ("Therefore it is said . . .") misunderstood as the ceremonial etiology for the Levitical ban on the blind and lame attending Temple services (Lev. 21:16-20).[8]

Rallying the Ranks

1 Chron. 13:1-4

To 1 Samuel 6:1-11's account of David's retrieval of the Ark of the Covenant, the Chronicler has added an opening episode in which David summons people from all over Israel to attend the event. It does not add much of anything to the story—except for a brief mention of his favorites, the priests and the Levites, perhaps implying a contrast between them and those who carried the Ark, as if to suggest that, had Levites carried it instead of Uzzah and the others, who are conspicuously *not* said to be priests or Levites, tragedy might have been averted.

Had a Levite been on hand to grab the Ark and prevent it from falling into the ditch, God would not have blasted him for touching it. This is made explicit in 1 Chron. 15:13. The purpose of this note is to mitigate the seemingly arbitrary ruthlessness of God in the 2 Samuel version, which still disturbs readers today.

After Uzzah's death, David was so freaked out that he left the Ark for a "cooling off period" upon the threshing floor of the Philistine farmer Obed-Edom. Three months later, David decided to make another attempt at transporting the Ark to Jerusalem (recently conquered from the Jebusites), and this time, having realized his mistake, he commanded that no one but Levites be recruited to carry the Ark (1 Chron. 15:2).

The Chronicler has added all this Levite involvement and takes the opportunity to append a long list of Levites appointed by David to various tasks in conjunction with it, including a marching band and singers. (More reminders of the Levites and their ornamental role in the events of that day of celebration occur in 1 Chronicles 15:26-27 and 16:4-7, 37-42.) And what did they sing? The Chronicler plugs in Psalms 105:1-15, 96:1-13, and 106:1, 47-48.

Among the names of Levitical singers and musicians we find that of Obed-Edom (15:18; 16:5), who would later serve as a Temple gate-keeper. This is odd, especially since this was the name of the owner of the threshing floor where the Ark had been parked for three months. He is a Philistine of Gath, Goliath's home town, and his name marks him (or at least his parents who named him) as a worshipper of the mythical divine ancestor of the Edomites, their tradition's First Man, borrowed somewhere along the line to play the same role in Israelite myth: Adam. Here, then, is another vestige of the fact that, originally, being a "Levite" did not denote membership in an Israelite tribe of that name (cf. Judg. 17:7). Apparently, at some point, a "Levite" need not even have been a Jew.

The Editorial Axe

In 2 Samuel 6:19b-23 we read that David's wife Michal (known to her girlfriends as "Mike"?), Saul's daughter, chewed out her husband for dancing, *ahem*, naked before the Ark as it proceeded through the streets, but Chronicles omits the unedifying scene. Likewise, in his account of David's defeat of the Moabites (1 Chron. 18:1-2), the Chronicler cuts from his source, 2 Samuel 8:2, a seemingly gratuitous slaughter of Moabite prisoners of war at David's command. More dirty linen.

David's mercy to Saul's crippled son Mephibosheth (Meribaal) (2 Sam. 9:1-13) was of no interest to the Chronicler, so there is no sign of it in his work. This seems strange, as the incident showed David in a noble and magnanimous light. But perhaps the Chronicler's loathing for Saul and his legacy was so intense that he disapproved of the honor shown Saul's son.

One of the most notorious biblical tales concerns David's sordid affair with Bathsheba, entailing the murder of Bathsheba's husband, Uriah (2 Sam. 11:2-27; 12:1-25). Guess what? The pious PR man known as the Chronicler has omitted it. This tendency to whitewash the characters as portrayed in earlier sources is exactly the same as we saw when comparing the Yahwist's versions of Abraham lying about Sarah (Gen. 12:10-20) and of Abraham, Sarah, and Hagar (Gen. 16), with the Elohist's later, sanitized versions (Gen. 20; 21:8-21). Likewise, the disgusting tale of Prince Amnon raping his sister, Princess Tamar, (2 Sam. 13:1-22) ends up on the cutting room floor.

We hear nothing in Chronicles of the violent succession disputes for the throne of David, written in blood in 2 Samuel 13 23-39; 14:1-33, including the usurpation of Absalom (chapters 15-18). Nothing about David's return to the throne (2 Sam. 19), the rebellion led by Sheba (20), or that of Adonijah (1 Kings. 1:1-53). The Chronicler also cuts the unedifying business about David mollifying the Gibeonites by executing seven sons and grandsons of Saul (2 Sam. 21:1-14).

Goliath and Satan

Another problem bequeathed by 2 Samuel is that of just who killed the six-footer Goliath: David (1 Sam. 17:41-54) or Elhanan (2 Sam. 21:19)? The Chronicler irons this out in 1 Chronicles 21:19 by having Elhanan kill Goliath's *brother!* Later scribes went back and inserted this harmonization into 2 Samuel 21:19, making it agree with 1 Chronicles 20:5, and this is the way it reads in the King James Bible.

Interestingly, the Chronicler enhances the stature and strength of an unnamed Egyptian slain by one of David's warriors, virtually making him into a second Goliath (1 Chron.11:23 vs. 2 Sam. 23:21). Speaking of David's elite warriors, 2 Samuel already lists several (2 Sam. 23:8-39), and not only does the Chronicler retain it; he also appends another very long list of David's champions (1 Chron. 12).

Second Samuel 24:1 says it was God who tempted David to take a census, then turned right around and punished him for it. But the Chronicler changes the identity of the tempter to *Satan* (1 Chron. 21:1)! Though this alteration at first looks like the most outrageous bit of redactional tinkering on record, it does actually make sense given the biblical understanding of Satan ("the Adversary" or "the Prosecutor") as God's henchman in charge of "sting operations" to test the mettle of God's favorites (Job 1:8-12; Zech. 3:1; Matt. 4:1-11; Luke 22:31) in order to make sure that "God is not mocked" (Gal. 6:7). "Tempting" in these contexts really denotes "testing." Thus it seemed entirely natural for the Chronicler to assume that, if God wanted to test David, he must have given the job to Satan: Would David rely upon worldly resources, or upon the name of Yahweh his God (Psalm 20:7)?

To the ensuing story of God's terrible vengeance upon David, the Chronicler adds an eerie and powerful scene: As the plague rages, David beholds the gigantic form of Yahweh's angel of judgment, spanning earth and sky, about to launch his sword of pestilence against Jerusalem (1 Chron. 21:16, with a brief aftermath in 21:27-22:1).

The Testament of David

1 Kings 2:1-9 vs. 1 Chron. 22:2-19; 28:1-29:9

The Chronicler did not much like what he found in his source about David's charge to his son and successor Solomon. Sure, the old king urges the new one to continue faithful to the laws of Moses, but more time is spent telling Solomon to even the score with David's old enemies. In the case of the traitor Shimei, David had promised him clemency, that he should not kill him. But of course the fine print didn't rule out the possibility of David having his *successor* kill him! And he now orders that hit as well as others.[9]

The Chronicler, no surprise, cut this unsavory business and substituted for it an incredibly long (1 Chron. chapters 22-27!) set of instructions on how to build and staff the planned Temple. This sort of thing makes it absolutely clear that the Chronicler was himself a priest. Martin Noth thought that such an identification went too far. He reasoned that, given the importance of priestly and sacrificial piety in the Chronicler's day, all the attention given priestly, Temple, and Levitical matters was simply an expression of general religiosity at the time, and that any pious Jew would have described the piety of David and Solomon in these taken-for-granted terms. But that is simply unbelievable. No layman could possibly have pursued these subjects with such interest and in such detail.[10]

This is the sort of stuff that kills the attempt of modern readers who set the goal of reading straight through the entire Bible. It's about as interesting as reading through the phone book. If you somehow managed to avoid falling into the quicksand pit of Leviticus, Numbers, and Deuteronomy, these chapters ought to do the job. But of course the Chronicler, together with most other biblical writers, never had a thought that his book would be read by anybody but his fellow professionals.[11]

Two needles do manage to stand out from the haystack, however. The first is the reason supplied for God refusing to allow David himself to build the Temple, handing the job off to Solomon instead. David is disqualified because of his career of bloody, if righteous, warfare (1 Chron. 22:8). I see here something like Martin Luther's attitude toward soldiers and executioners in a Christian state. Slaughter is not the proper work for the children of God, true, but it must be done to defend the society from those who would destroy it, and that makes it righteous.

But still, the army and the executioners are "the left hand of God." The right hand would include the ministry, maybe medicine. For David to build the Temple for Yahweh would amount to the left hand of God trying to do the work of the right, and that job is reserved unto Solomon, a man of peace, albeit a peace secured by his father's wars.

Brettler is surely right: Any "historian" who can play with his sources in such a cavalier manner is certainly not writing anything we would recognize as history, and those who maintain the historical accuracy of scripture are simply determined *not* to understand the book they say they believe in. And this leads us to pick out the second needle: Solomon's name. It is here explained as meaning "Man of Shalom, or Peace" (1 Chron. 22:9).

This is a classic etymological legend meant to provide a new, more acceptable, "origin" for a name which had first denoted something no longer deemed, in a later time, sufficiently orthodox. "Solomon" is actually a theophoric name meaning "Man of Shalman," the Jerusalemite god of the setting sun, brother to winged Shahar, the dawn goddess. Likewise, the name of another son of David, Absalom, means "Shalman is my Father." But later sensitivities found it unseemly for David to have named his sons after gods that, from a later theological standpoint, he shouldn't have been worshipping.

Laundering the Emperor's New Clothes

Solomon's lapse into idolatry, for which the Deuteronomist (1 Kings 11:1-40) scolded him, is here passed over in silence. Nothing about his marriage alliance with Egypt by wedding Pharaoh's daughter (1 Kings 3:1), which would lead to his building shrines for the customary gods worshipped by his foreign wives. Nothing about his allowing, even participating in, sacrifices to Yahweh at the local hilltop shrines before the central Temple was finished (1 Kings 3:2-3).

The Chronicler does, surprisingly, follow the Deuteronomist in allowing Solomon to offer up thousands of sacrifices before the Tabernacle at the high place in Gibeon (1 Kings 3:4; 2 Chron. 1:3-6), though he cuts the subsequent sacrifice by Solomon before the Ark of the Covenant in Jerusalem (1 Kings 3:1). Presumably he kept the Gibeon sacrifice because it was the occasion of the dream in which Solomon petitioned God for wisdom, and the Chronicler didn't want to leave out this pivotal scene.

One of the most famous tales of Solomon is that in which he must decide between rival prostitutes, each of whom maintains that the other accidentally smothered her infant, and that the surviving baby is her own (1 Kings 3:16-28). No sign of it in Chronicles, perhaps because it seemed too ribald to the blue-nosed Chronicler.

The Chronicler omits a list of Solomon's administrators (1 Kings 4:1-19), despite his love for catalogues and lists, presumably because the names are those of secular functionaries, not of priests and the various species of Levites.

Blueprints for the Temple

2 Chron. 2:1-18

Solomon enlists the expertise of his neighbor, Hiram, the king of Tyre, or so 1 Kings names him. For some reason, the Chronicler calls him Huram and Huramabi, a name recalling that of the Babylonian lawgiver Hammurabi. The first major inconsistency we notice, though, concerns the terms of the deal made between Solomon and Hiram/Huram/Huramabi: Instead of Solomon trading twenty cities to Hiram in payment for Hiram building the Jerusalem Temple for him (1 Kings 9:11-13), now Solomon exacts twenty cities *from* the king of Tyre (2 Chron. 8:2). Instead of Israelite conscripts (1 Kings 5:13; 9:15), 2 Chronicles 2:17 has Solomon use only Gentiles as his workforce. He no longer appears as the Pharaoh-like oppressor depicted in 1 Kings.

First Kings already offered an exhaustive (and exhausting) catalogue of details describing the Temple (6:1-38; 7:13-51), most of which 2 Chronicles repeats. The major omission is from 1 Kings 7:27-37, notably the Deuteronomistic description of various decorations such as lilies, pomegranates, and cherubim, the very elements that underline the Garden of Eden symbolism. Margaret Barker[12] suggests that the Eden motif had already been suppressed in 1 Kings, and the tendency continues here. My guess is that the Deuteronomist "reform" began in Hasmonean times in the wake of the schism between the more rationalistic Pharisees and the Zadokite priests (who then formed the Dead Sea Scrolls sect) with their more mythic-charismatic theology.[13]

The Zadokites would have identified the Temple with the heavenly Paradise, or its earthly antechamber. Their rivals toned this down. Second Chronicles does retain the cherubs atop (actually looming over) the Ark of the Covenant because that was too integral to the Ark traditions to lose.

Later Than You Think

Yes, this guess regarding the date has me going way out on a limb. Russell E. Gmirkin,[14] makes a pretty convincing case that Genesis 1-11 were based not on millennia-old oral traditions shared with Mesopotamian religion but rather on the *Babyloniaca*, a compendium of cuneiform texts translated into Greek, by Berossus, a Babylonian archivist, in 278 B.C.E.; and that Exodus is not reflected in the *Aegyptiaca* of the Hellenistic historian Manetho (ca. 285-280 B.C.E.) but rather that the latter was the major source for the former. From this Gmirkin infers that the initial composition of the Pentateuch was coincident with its Greek translation by a group of Alexandrian scholars in 273-272 B.C.E., much, much earlier than Old Testament critics have long thought.

This is shocking enough, but I think the Pentateuch is even later (younger). Gmirkin dates the Septuagint as he does based on the statements of Aristobulus and the Letter of Aristeas (also written by Aristobulus, as Gmirkin shows) that the Septuagint translation was produced during the reign of Ptolemy II Philadelphus. Gmirkin admits that Aristobulus is generally unreliable but accepts his date for a pair of reasons. First, the Genesis chronography of Demetrius the Chronographer, writing between 221-204, matches the figures of the Septuagint rather than those found in the Masoretic Text. This seems to me inconclusive, as Gmirkin still thinks that the Pentateuchal editors employed the traditional sources, J, E, D, and P, and it seems possible that Demetrius derived his statistics from a version of one of these, not necessarily from a completed Pentateuch.

Second, Gmirkin[15] appeals to a comment in the Babylonian Talmud that the Alexandrian translators avoided the Greek word for "rabbit" (*lagos*), substituting *dasupous* ("shaggy-foot"), so as not to offend their patron, Ptolemy II Philadelphus, whose wife, Arsinoe II, was, in Hebrew, punningly called Arnebeth, the Hebrew word for rabbit. In addition, the family line of the Ptolemys was called the Lagids for an ancestor named Lagus.

Plus, rabbits were symbolic of sexual profligacy (as when Ralphie, in the movie *A Christmas Story*, recalls that his father could change fuses "faster than a jackrabbit on a date"). Arsinoe was publicly lampooned for having divorced two previous husbands, then marrying her brother, Ptolemy II Philadelphus, in accord with the ancient custom of the Pharaohs. She was pretty touchy about being made the butt of dirty jokes.

But I think Gmirkin has been seduced into accepting an old-fashioned etymological tale as genuine history. It seemed odd to some rabbi, centuries after the fact, that the Septuagint did not use the expected word for bunny rabbits, and he came up with an elaborate and clever shaggy-dog pseudo-explanation like those with which the Pentateuch is filled. It is hardly believable that people of that age would have boycotted a common word on the chance that some paranoid king would find in it a snide innuendo about his wife.

Picture this, if you will: Ptolemy II Philadelphus slogging through Leviticus with a magnifying glass, coming to the word "rabbit" and exploding in rage: "*Hey!* What the hell is *this*? Kill those Jews!" Can the translators of the Septuagint really have considered this a danger? Somehow I doubt it. Who cares *why* they used an odd term for rabbit?

So, if we dismiss the linking of the Septuagint (and with it the Pentateuch) with Ptolemy II Philadelpus, as I think we can, then the Pentateuch may be dated even closer to the C.E./B.C.E. divide. And this means that the "Deuteronomic Reform" may have occurred as late as the Hasmonean split between the Pharisees and the Zadokites, which looks to me like an ideal *Sitz-im-Leben*. The early chapters of Genesis seem already to have been affected by Deuteronomic censorship, as per Margaret Barker.[16]

Launching the Temple

2 Chron. 5:2-7:10

Though the Chronicler does not fundamentally alter the Deuteronomist's story of Solomon dedicating the newly built Temple, his additions are very pronounced and clearly attest his agenda of advancing priestly/Levitical status and importance. The priests and the Levite singers and musicians are on display in 2 Chronicles 5:11-13, and the Chronicler has supplied a bit of what they must have sung, appropriating some lyrics from Psalm 136. This performance, not even mentioned in the Dedication narrative of 1 Kings, is made the cause of the descent of the Shekinah glory cloud into the midst of the Temple, which 1 Chronicles 5:13-14 shares with 1 Kings 8:10-11.

Why has the Chronicler added to the Kings narrative the short passage 2 Chronicles 6:13? Out of the blue he tells us that Solomon had arranged for the construction of a bronze platform in front of the altar. Since before the Priestly Code kings functioned also as priests, 1 Kings had no problem depicting Solomon comporting himself as a priest, standing before the altar, but Chronicles instead pictures him mounting a pulpit on the occasion of the dedication of the Temple.

Our redactor has again cribbed some text from the Psalter (in this case Psalm 132:8-10, then back up to verse 1). It forms the closing of Solomon's dedicatory prayer in 2 Chronicles 6:41-42. He chops the benediction that he found in 1 Kings 8:54-66 to make room for a miracle (2 Chron. 7:1) that must somehow have escaped the notice of the Deuteronomic Historian.

It looks like the Chronicler has salvaged the feat of Elijah calling down fire from the sky (1 Kings 18:36-38), having the flames descend to consume the burnt offering laid out on the altar for the occasion. (He had omitted the Elijah version along with the rest of the northern stories, but why waste a good miracle?) To this he has added a repetition of the filling of the sanctuary by the divine glory cloud he already had happen in 5:13-14 (following his source, 1 Kings 8:10-11).

He adds a reminder of the presence of the priests and the Levitical brass section.

Perhaps the most important (if not the only) contribution the Chronicler made to the abiding spirituality of Jews and Christians is the well-known promise of God in 2 Chronicles 7:14 (NASB) to heed the prayers of a repentant people: "and if My people who are called by My name humble themselves and pray and seek My face and turn from their wicked ways, then I will hear from heaven, will forgive their sin and will heal their land." First Kings 9:1-9, the parallel account of a second vision of God at Gibeon, did not contain this. I suspect that this single verse is all most Bible readers know or *want* to know about Chronicles, nor can one blame them.

When our redactor repeats his predecessor's note (1 Kings 9:24) about Solomon building a new dwelling for his new Egyptian bride, he explains the need for a separate home: She was a Gentile and thus unfit to live in a city which housed the holy Ark of the Covenant (2 Chron. 8:11). At least it seemed so to the Chronicler, given his professional priestly standards.

Second Chronicles 8:13-15 adds more priestly padding and Levitical larding.

First Kings told the sorry tale of Solomon lapsing into idolatry because of his foreign wives (which may have amounted to no more than occasionally "going to church" with them, as Naaman the Syrian, himself a Yahwist convert, attended Rimmon-worship with his king, without guilt, in 2 Kings 5:18). But the Chronicler has omitted all this. He is not shy about reporting the shortcomings of the kings, but presumably this just reflected too poorly on the builder of the Temple. Perhaps, in the Chronicler's mind, such a reproach might be seen as tarnishing the glory of the Temple itself. "Or what agreement has the temple of God with idols" (2 Cor. 6:16a, NASB).

The "historical" books of the Old Testament occasionally make references to non-canonical books, as if the intended readers were in a position to explore such "further reading" recommendations. While The Book of Jasher ("Book of the Just") cited in Joshua 10:13 and 2 Samuel 1:18 and The Book of the Wars of Yahweh (in Numbers 21:14) seem to have been real texts, now lost, the various titles[17] in Samuel, Kings, and Chronicles appear to be spurious garnishing meant to create the impression of antiquity and authenticity for the tales the Deuteronomist and the Chronicler told.

All such citations employ a literary device also found in John 20:30 ("Now Jesus did many other signs in the presence of the disciples, which are not written in this book") and 21:25 ("But there are also many other things which Jesus did; were every one of them to be written, I suppose that the world itself could not contain the books that would be written"): "This is just the tip of the iceberg." The point is not that there is plenty more left to tell, but rather that the author *wishes* he had more to tell but *doesn't!*

The artificiality of the Chronicler's citations is especially clear, as he carelessly alters those already in his sources. What 1 Kings 14:26 ascribes to The Book of the Chronicles of the Kings of Israel, the Chronicler ascribes to The Book of the Kings of Israel and Judah (2 Chron. 27:7).

First Kings refers to The Book of the Chronicles of the Kings of Judah, but the Chronicler changes this to The Book of the Kings of Judah and Israel (2 Chron. 25:26; 28:26; 32:32) and, in 2 Chronicles 35:37 and 36:8, to The Book of the Kings of Israel and Judah. He cannot keep the titles straight because to him that's all they are: titles. Plus, he adds five more: The Chronicles of Samuel the Seer, Chronicles of Nathan the Prophet, Chronicles of Gad the Seer (1 Chron. 29:29), Chronicles of Shemaiah the Prophet, and Chronicles of Iddo the Seer (2 Chron.12:15; 13:22). But Samuel is barely referred to in 1 and 2 Chronicles, while the Gad material in Chronicles (1 Chron. 21:9-19) is simply borrowed from 2 Samuel 24:11-19. The Chronicler's Nathan material (1 Chron. 17:1-15) is likewise merely lifted from 2 Samuel 7:2-17.[18]

Both Boams

The Chronicler omits the 1 Kings 11 introduction to Jeroboam. The less said of that idolater the better. He has also left out Ahijah's prophetic proclamation of Jeroboam's future kingship (1 Kings 11:29-38), apparently because he is embarrassed at Jeroboam's divine ordination. What kind of improvement on the idol-worshiping Solomon was this guy? He bee-lined to false gods even quicker than Solomon! So, if all we had was Chronicles, we would not suspect that God had a hand in bringing Jeroboam to the throne of the northern tribes. And that's the way the Chronicler wanted it.

Little has been done to 1 King's 12's story of Jeroboam's leading the northern tribes of Israel in secession from Judah in the south. Strangely, the Chronicler has elected to pass over Jeroboam's establishing the cult centers of Dan and Bethel as rivals to the Jerusalem Temple (1 Kings 12:25-33). Instead, he substitutes some deeds of Rehoboam, Solomon's son and heir, pausing to note (really, to posit) that all the priests and Levites of the north dropped everything and fled to Judea (like Peter, Andrew, James, and John abandoning their homes and livelihoods, or like Lot fleeing Sodom).

He says Jeroboam would not allow them to continue in service to Yahweh because the new king preferred heathen gods. This reflects 1 Kings 12's invidious interpretation of Jeroboam's temples as dedicated to a polytheistic pantheon to replace Yahweh, whereas originally Jeroboam was understood to have established Dan and Bethel as redundant centers for Yahweh worship, stultifying the need for his Yahwist subjects to cross the border to Judah on pilgrimage to Jerusalem.

Another inherited misconception was the notion that Jeroboam had consecrated a *pair* of new temples. It appears that someone forgot that Bethel replaced Dan as the sole Yahweh temple of the north when Dan was destroyed by the Syrians twenty years after its temple's construction.[19] But Bethel was destroyed in 880 or so, while Dan was rebuilt. Dan was again leveled in the 730s and again replaced by Bethel. So both were Israelite temples, right enough, but alternately, not at the same time.

The Chronicler figures he has devoted just about enough air time to the stinker Jeroboam, so he skips 1 Kings 13-14:1-20 altogether. He takes an interest in 1 Kings again as of 1Kings 14:21-31, which lists the idolatrous practices that flourished under Rehoboam, who seems to have been as much of a disgrace as his similarly named counterpart up in Yankeeland. Why this gross lapse from Yahwistic purity? Remember, the whole notion of a streamlined monotheism restricted to a central, Solomonic shrine in Jerusalem is a gross and tendentious anachronism in the first place.

These "Canaanite" practices were just the traditional ways of Israel, as was only natural since the Israelites simply *were* Canaanites and always had been. When the Deuteronomist and the Chronicler reproach them for assimilating to the abominations of the "people of the land," they are really warning readers and hearers not to return to the old time religion they and their parents once practiced.

But the Chronicler does not care to elaborate in this particular case, merely saying, tersely, that Rehoboam "forsook the law of Yahweh, and all Israel [uh, actually *Judah*, right?] with him" (2 Chron. 12:1). Presumably, as he did with Solomon, he wants to downplay the sins of the Davidic king because he cannot have either sinful kings go unpunished or righteous kings get punished too severely. As in 1 Kings, Rehoboam's (imagined) sins invited divine chastisement in the form of an invasion by the Egyptian Pharaoh Shishak.

But the Chronicler, with no basis in 1 Kings, has a prophet named Shemaiah ("Name of Yahweh") confront Rehoboam, explaining how it was his and his people's sins that got them into this trouble and that, if he repents, the Almighty may see fit to relent. He does, and God mitigates the depredations of Shishak, though the pharaoh does plunder the Temple treasures and makes Judah a vassal state. I suspect that the Chronicler created "The Chronicles of Shemaiah the Prophet" (2 Chron. 12:15) in order to suggest that he had a documentary source for his episode about Shemaiah playing the role of Nathan to

Rehoboam's David. But the fact that the material is clearly tendentious and redactional rules this out. Perhaps there is a hint in the "Seer" epithet in the title that the Shemaiah/ Rehoboam material was a product of visionary revelation, i.e., imagination.[20]

Alias Abijah

First Chronicles 15:1-6 recounts the rise of Rehoboam's son Abijam, who followed in the straying footsteps of his father, wallowing in idolatry (as it came retrospectively and redactionally to be viewed). As far as the Deuteronomic Historian knew, nothing very bad happened to him as a result, so he says God, though displeased, gave him a pass for the sake of David, who had a much better scorecard. In later centuries, this sort of thing would be elaborated as the rabbinical doctrine of the "Merits of the Fathers."[21]

But the Chronicler was even easier on him. You see, he plans to follow the introduction of Abijam (or, as he calls him, "Abijah") with a long account of a miraculous victory for Abijah over the worthless Jeroboam (2 Chron. 13:3-21). Surrounded front and back by Jeroboam's army, twice as big as Abijah's, Abijah's troops cry out to Yahweh, accompanied by the priestly trumpets, and they manage to dispatch the superior host of Jeroboam. We do not see how they did so: there is no description (just as in 2 Chronicles 20:1-30, another product of the Chronicler's pious imagination). It is his own editorial fiat that wins the day. But the Chronicler could not assign such a happy victory to such a sinner as 1 Kings made of Abijam, so he simply cut that earlier account (1 Kings 15:3), wiping Abijah's rap sheet. In this manner is the justice of God vindicated!

Asa Diamonds

The Deuteronomist already liked Asa, son and successor to Abijam, because he put all the priestitutes attached to local shrines out of business (1 Kings 11-12), but the Chronicler pads his righteous resume further: Now he sends in the G-men to smash up the local altars and the Asherah poles, too (2 Chron. 14:2-5). At first God rewards him with a few years of peace. But then an Ethiopian army of a million men moves into place to attack, and Asa cashes in his brownie points: He prays for victory and gets it. His men manage by the end of the day to kill every one of those enemy soldiers, a feat indeed. We hear of no miracle, no stratagem. The secret weapon was, once again, redactional fiat.

Needless to say, the Deuteronomic Historian knew nothing of this. Let us remind ourselves: There is no particular reason to assume *any* biblical narrative is more historically based than this one. Apologists know this right well; it is they who warn in no uncertain terms that, if the Bible errs (i.e., proves unhistorical) at *any* point, it may as well be inaccurate at *every* point.

One more oddity: At the urging of the prophet Azariah, Asa leads his people in repentance (2 Chron. 15:1-15), destroying all the idolatrous altars throughout the kingdom—even though in the previous chapter he had already done this. Now it appears also that Asa had allowed the true altar in Jerusalem to fall into disrepair though neglect (15:8). And God let this slacker beat an army of a million men? Something is mixed up here. But as long as he can find a spot to lard the narrative with some preaching aimed, really, at his readers, narrative coherence takes a back seat.

In any case, Asa's fidelity to the laws of the Chronicler, er, rather, of God, was short-lived. He made what our author, speaking through a conveniently concocted character called Hanani the Seer, considered a bad foreign policy decision. As 1 Kings 15:16-24, his source, had said, the Israelite King Baasha was building fortifications at Ramah, planning to block access by Asa and Judah. To fend off this danger before it was too late, Asa turns to King Ben-Hadad of Syria, offering to trade some of the Temple treasures in return for an alliance against Israel. He agrees, and Baasha drops his project.

First Kings was okay with that, but the Chronicler took a dim view. One might have thought it was the crass use of sacred Temple silver and gold for mundane purposes that rankled him, but instead it was the faithlessness of Asa in not relying upon God alone to deal with Baasha.

After all, God had enabled Judah to obliterate the Million Man March of the Ethiopians ranged against them, so why be afraid of Baasha? A good question! And now we know why the Chronicler inserted the tall tale of the victory over Ethiopia: If Asa had seen this, how could he *not* rely on God to get rid of Baasha's threat? Tsk, tsk.

As a result of this "sin," Asa is told, he will have incessant military conflicts for the rest of his reign. But that's not all. A king might even *enjoy* that. So God gives Asa some debilitating foot disease (gout?). First Kings 15:23b mentioned the foot affliction without further comment, but 2 Chronicles 16:12 takes the opportunity for one last slap at the aged Asa, calling him faithless for having called in physicians instead of relying on God alone to heal him. The Chronicler would have fit in well with today's Christian Science practitioners and fringe Pentecostals who toss their children's insulin into the trash can.

Forgetting the Lessons of History

As far as our redactor was concerned, the day the northern tribes severed themselves from the House of David, they might as well have floated away into outer space. He gives as little coverage as possible to Israel, skipping over all the 1-2 Kings narratives of Kings Baasha, Elah, Zimri, Omri, and Ahab, in other words, all of 1 Kings 15:31 through chapter 21! I have to think that these sections would be lost to history if the Chronicler had gotten his way.

He very likely intended his work not only to supersede the Deuteronomic History but to replace it entirely, but he wrote too late for that to happen.[22] The Deuteronomic History was too well established, too widely received, by the time the Chronicler did his work. You can tell this from the fact that the Hebrew canon places Chronicles in the late "Miscellaneous" section, the Writings, along with other late books like Daniel and Ruth. The Former Prophets section wasn't accepting new members.

Jumpin' Jehoshaphat

2 Chron. 17-20

The Chronicler might have said of King Jehoshaphat what Kasper Gutman (Sidney Greenstreet) in *The Maltese Falcon* said to Sam Spade, "You're the man for *me*, sir!" He gives him a glowing report in 2 Chronicles 19:1-19, all material he did not get from 1 Kings. Then, in chapter 18, the Chronicler just copies the 1 Kings account of the fascinating and humorous episode of Jehoshaphat allying himself with King Ahab of Israel and of the prophet Micaiah ben Imlah exposing the charlatanry of Ahab's staff of yes-men prophets.

As of 2 Chronicles 19 we are back to the free creations of our redactor. He cannot let Jehoshaphat's alliance with the Israelite king go without complaint, so, through his puppet character Jehu the prophet, he rebukes Jehoshaphat for cooperating with the no-good Israelite monarch. God is mad at him, but given Jehoshaphat's previous righteousness, he is willing to give him a pass this time.

So "Jehu" told Jehoshaphat that the wrath of God was brewing against him, and one might regard the subsequent massing of Moabites, Ammonites, and Edomites ("the men of Mount Seir") against Judah as the result. But it turns out instead to be the occasion for a particularly spectacular military miracle on Jehoshaphat's behalf. In chapter 20, Jehoshaphat calls in a favor from Yahweh, who pulls a Tower of Babel on the heathen, causing their armies to turn upon one another, wiping each other out while the men of Judah munch popcorn on the sidelines. Jahaziel, a Levite (what else?) plays the role of Moses at the Reed Sea:

> and he said, "Listen, all Judah and the inhabitants of Jerusalem and King Jehoshaphat: thus says [Yahweh] to you, 'Do not fear or be dismayed because of this great multitude, for the battle is not yours but God's. Tomorrow go down against them. Behold, they will come up by the ascent of Ziz, and you will find them at the end of the valley in front of the wilderness of Jeruel. You need not fight in this battle; station yourselves, stand and see the salvation of [Yahweh] on your behalf, O Judah and Jerusalem.' Do not fear or be dismayed; tomorrow go out to face them, for the Lord is with you." (2 Chron. 20:15-17, NASB; cf., Exod. 14:13-14).

The Levitical singers turn out to be the real heroes of the day, since the miracle occurs as the response to their hymn-singing (20:19-23). Are you surprised? I didn't think so.

Jehoshaphat should have taken Jehu's prophetic rebuke more seriously, because next we see him teaming up with the new king of Israel, Ahaziah, building a fleet of ships to send to Tarshish. Another fictive prophet appears out of the woodwork, Eliezer, to tell Jehoshaphat he hasn't learned his lesson and that, as a result, God will cause the ships to be wrecked. And they are (2 Chron. 20:37). It is interesting to observe what the Chronicler has done here, for 1 Kings 22:48-49 had credited the ship-building to Jehoshaphat alone and had the ships wrecked fortuitously.

Not only that, they were apparently built *in* Tarshish (or possibly on the model of the ships of Tarshish) and were intended for a trip to Ophir. In 1 Kings, once the ships are wrecked, the Israelite king Ahaziah approaches Jehoshaphat, offering to share the venture, apparently in his own ships. Jehoshaphat declines the offer.

This is just the opposite of the Chronicles version, rewritten to make the shipwreck a punishment for an unholy alliance with Ahaziah. Karma, it seems, is a bitch even when it's just a redactional frame-up!

Chronicles leapfrogs another huge swath of its source, 2 Kings 1-8:15, the exciting adventures of the prophets Elijah and Elisha. He rejoins 2 Kings as of the reign of Joram, whom he calls Jehoram. Apparently they broke the mold after Jehoshaphat, because his son is no damn good. In fact the Chronicler (2 Chron. 21:2-10) makes him worse than he appeared in 2 Kings, adding the atrocity of Jehoram eliminating his brothers for fear that one of them might one day try to usurp his throne. Too bad one of them *didn't*.

Jehoram looks like the model for Herod the Great's bloody paranoia. Out of nostalgia for Jehoram's forebear David, God is lenient, though he does nothing to stop a successful revolt by the Edomites who regain their independence from Judah. But then the Chronicler starts composing freely again. He makes Jehoram really pour on the apostasy, reestablishing idolatry and polytheism and reopening the local hilltop shrines. This crosses the line, and Yahweh slaps him down, sending against him an alliance of Philistines and Arabs who sack Jerusalem and exterminate the royal house, all except Jehoram's youngest son, Jehoahaz.

Jehoram himself falls prey to a plague which causes his bowels to erupt from his body. Of all this the Deuteronomic Historian knew nothing. The Chronicler "knew" it because he invented the whole business. It seemed the appropriate ending for an idolatrous bastard like Jehoram. It *should* have happened, so, for the Chronicler, it *did* happen. Well, that's the Bible for you.

The Chronicler skips the colorful exploits of the usurper Jehu, even though he is a staunch and zealous Yahweh partisan, because they occur up north in Israel (and in 2 Kings 9:1-13, 30-37; 10:1-11, 15-36), merely summarizing (2 Chron. 22:7-9) the next passage in 2 Kings (9:14-29) where Jehu assassinates both Joram, king of Israel, and Ahaziah, king of Judah, as well as summarizing 2 Kings 10:12-14 (where Jehu wipes out some of Ahaziah's relatives) in 2 Chronicles 22:8. The Queen Mother, Athaliah, decides to finish the job, exterminating the sons of her slain son, Ahaziah, and seizing the throne of Judah for herself. Only young prince Joash escapes the slaughter.

In terms of redaction criticism, here's where things get interesting: Where 2 Kings 11:1-20 had the royal guard protect the royal heir following the coup, then overthrow his grandmother after she has reigned six years, the Chronicler substitutes the *priests* as the guardians of the boy king who restore his rightful throne (2 Chron. 22:10-23:21). Again, it's all about the priests and Levites, conspicuous by their absence in the 2 Kings version of the story.

The Chronicler passes over the material in 2 Kings 13 (the reigns of the Israelite monarchs Jehoahaz and Jehoash and the death of the prophet Elisha) and 14:23-29 (the reign of Jeroboam II in Israel up north). He rejoins 2 Kings with the reign of Amaziah in Judah (2 Chron. 25:1-28), but he greatly expands the (unflattering) coverage of this king (25:5-11a, 12-16). Kings and Chronicles continue to run parallel for the reign of Azariah, also called Uzziah (2 Kings 14:21-22; 15:1-3; 2 Chron. 26:1-5).

Despite a pretty good track record, Uzziah contracts leprosy as a punishment from God for leaving the hilltop shrines in operation (as if he could have known there was anything wrong in this. Remember, we are reading stories told by redactors who judged the various kings by the anachronistic standards of the redactors' own day). But to the terse account in 2 Kings 15:4-5 the Chronicler has added what he considers an even more grievous offense: Uzziah dared to stride into the Temple and to offer incense on the altar, rightly the prerogative of the priests (2 Chron. 26:17-20). This, of course, is absent from the 2 Kings original. It is pure priestly ax-grinding.

Chronicles skips 2 Kings 15:8-31, and we will follow his example here. Despite amplifications by the Chronicler (notably an episode concerning the otherwise-unknown prophet Oded, 28:8-15), he tells the same stories of Jotham and Ahaz (2 Chron. 27-28) that we find in 2 Kings 15:32-38-chapter 16.

The Chronicler skips the Assyrian conquest of Israel in 2 Kings 17. What does he care? The northern kingdom has been dead to him for many chapters. His ears perk up again when he gets to good King Hezekiah. Most of 2 Chronicles 29-32:8 is fatty meat piled on the relatively bare bones of 2 Kings 18:13.

As we know to expect by now, the Chronicler amplifies the reforms and restoration of Judean worship and the refurbishing and repairs to the Temple in excruciating detail, complete with plenty of involvement by the priests and Levites. Strikingly, in the course of all this, our redactor cuts 2 Kings 18:4, the notice that Hezekiah put the Nehushtan idol out to the curb. As we saw, the ascription of the bronze serpent to Moses in Numbers 21:5-9, upon which the 2 Kings account depends, was already a ceremonial legend to cover up the polytheistic character of the image of the god Nehushtan/Leviathan.

It looks like the Chronicler regarded even this sanitized version as untoward, implicitly blaming the law-giver Moses for creating a relic that would one day come to be worshipped as an idol, as 2 Kings 18 admitted it was. The Chronicler must have understood the matter along the lines of Judges 8:22-27, where Gideon declines to become king, suggesting instead that a golden ephod be made.

This was, among other things, an oracular device (Judg. 17:5), implying that Gideon was proposing that all questions and legal cases should be brought, not to him as a king, but to the Levites who would consult the device for an answer. Perhaps inevitably, the ephod came to be worshiped as an idol, on the belief that, as an ephod is also described as a sacerdotal breastplate (Exod. 28:4-6), Yahweh himself was invisibly present, actually *wearing* the ephod[23] just as the High Priest, representing (or even *incarnating*) Yahweh,[24] wore it during the Temple service.

Sennacherib's Bullying

2 Kings 18:13-37; 2 Chron. 32:1-19

The story basic to both versions, Kings and Chronicles, is that the armies of the Assyrian despot Sennacherib move into place at the gate of Jerusalem and seek to demoralize Judah by mocking their reliance on Yahweh to protect them. Has any other nation's god been able turn the Assyrian host back? By the end of the episode, the desperate prayer of Hezekiah and his friend the prophet Isaiah prompts Yahweh to act in Judah's behalf. He sends a fierce angel who annihilates the whole Assyrian army (2 Kings 19:35-37; 2 Chron. 32:21-23).

The principal embellishment made by the Chronicler is the addition of 2 Chronicles 32:2-8, which describes Hezekiah's bold trust in Yahweh and his industrious preparation for the impending battle. This is quite different from the impression we receive from 2 Kings 18:14-22, which the Chronicler omits: There Hezekiah is shaking in his boots at the threats of Sennacherib and pre-emptively surrenders, offering a ransom if Sennacherib will just call his troops home and let him alone. He strips what's left of the silver and gold plating from the Temple and empties the royal treasury. And even at that, the Assyrians stick with their invasion plans. It is obvious that the Chronicler reveres Hezekiah and is determined to clean up his image for posterity. Talk about political spin!

The Man(asseh) of Sin

2 Kings 21:1-18; 2 Chron. 33:1-20

Suffice it to say that, of all the apostate kings of Israel and Judah whose outrages are enumerated in Kings and Chronicles, Manasseh is by far the worst. Our authors cannot say enough to his discredit. Child sacrifice, polytheism, idolatry, cheating at cards: You name it, Manasseh did it! In Kings, the apostate Manasseh enjoyed a reign of forty-five years.

How could God have put up with him for that long? Why not lower the boom on him? According to the Chronicler, he *did*: He has Manasseh taken hostage by the Assyrian king and held in Babylon (!). While cooling his heels, Manasseh has ample opportunity for self-reflection and repents, whereupon God restores him to the throne to finish that long reign in proper piety! (How did the Chronicler know this happened? He figured it *must* have, so it did.)

Likewise, he makes some good kings bad in order to justify their surprisingly short reigns: If they were as righteous as they appeared in Kings, why didn't God reward them with long reigns? The Chronicler couldn't just add years to their tenure; that would have messed up the official chronology. He says some kings tried to purify worship by shutting down local polytheistic shrines, even though he says the altars still remained at the end of the reforming king's reign.

The efforts of such kings proved ineffective, but God gave them an "A" for effort, a long reign. The leniency accorded these kings by our redactors betrays the awareness that there were in the time of these kings no "Mosaic" laws against the practices that the much later redactors had since come to loathe as pagan and idolatrous. The altars were still there for the simple reason that the kings had never lifted a finger to close them, being pre-Deuteronomy "idolaters" themselves.

Josiah the Second Hezekiah

2 Chron. 34

Hezekiah's successor Amon continues his father's abominations, at least if you read 2 Kings, but, if you prefer 2 Chronicles, Amon undoes Manasseh's latter-day reforms and repeats every rotten thing Manasseh did before his repentance. This particular case highlights what is going on throughout the Deuteronomist History (Judges, Samuel, Kings) and Chronicles, with their pendulum swings between pagan syncretism and repentance/reform. The whole thing is obviously artificial.

Both the Deuteronomist and the Chronicler wish to create the illusion that the laws they ascribe to Moses, having retrojected them into antiquity, were "on the books" ever since the time of Moses until the redactors' own day. But the surviving traditions of Israel and Judah and their kings all take for granted that no such regulations (e.g., against hill-top shrines, polytheism, idols) existed to be disobeyed.

The only way the redactors could depict the existence of the Mosaic Torah through the whole period was to say it was known but continually flouted despite the periodic efforts of judges, prophets, and kings to "restore" the people to obedience. But these reforms had to be shown as frustrated and ephemeral in order to accommodate the original conditions of the old tales.

The strategy is identical to that of the evangelist Mark, who had to juggle rival beliefs about the Messiahship of Jesus. Some believed Jesus had become the Christ only as of the resurrection (Acts 2:36; 13:33-35; Rom. 1:3-4). Others believed he had received Messianic Sonship already at the Jordan baptism (Mark 1:9-11). Mark regarded neither as heresy; he sought to reconcile the two opinions by positing that Jesus did become Messiah at his baptism but carefully kept it a secret (or tried to!) till his resurrection (Mark 9:9). Since most therefore *heard* of his Messiahship only after Easter, they would naturally have assumed the Messiahship stemmed from that time, not before.

Precisely in the manner of the Deuteronomist and the Chronicler, Mark had to produce a narrative of frequent contradictions resulting from sprinkling implausible warnings by Jesus for people not to tell of his miraculous super-powers which, if known, must instantly reveal his Messiahship.[25] For instance, Mark's story of the raising of Jairus' daughter (Mark 5:22-24, 35-43) says that, after the girl awakens, Jesus warns the parents not to tell anyone what happened. How are they supposed to do *that*, since the house is surrounded by friends and neighbors already mourning her death?

Second Chronicles continues its story through to the conquest of Judah by Nebuchadnezzar, but we will not follow the Chronicler to the bitter end, as he makes no significant alteration to the 2 Kings original.

Ezra and Nehemiah

The Chronicler did not drop his pen with the fall of Jerusalem. He pretty much leapfrogged the Babylonian Exile and picked up the thread with the returning (?) exiles, or their descendants. Actually, the whole notion of a substantial return of Jews from the Babylonian, then Persian, Empire seems pretty dubious.

For one thing, given that the Exile was supposed to have lasted fifty years (or, according to Jeremiah 24:11-15, seventy), there could have been hardly any of the original deportees left to return. The narrative loses the distinction, as we would say, between the *characters* of the deportees as a group of individual persons and the *actant* of "the exiles," a collective role in the narrative, a cipher. As an actant, "the exiles" are a stage prop, like the mob at Lot's door who all speak with one voice, as one (artificial) character, or the mob howling for the crucifixion of Jesus. Nehemiah 8:1 nicely sums up the point: "And all the people of Israel gathered as one man."

For another, there is no reference in the Prophets to a mass return of Jewish exiles, but only to a return, someday, of scattered Jews from the Mediterranean Diaspora.[26] "Behold, I will gather them out of all the lands to which I have driven them in My anger, in My wrath and in great indignation; and I will bring them back to this place and make them dwell in safety" (Jer. 32:37, NASB). "For I will take you from the nations, gather you from all the lands and bring you into your own land" (Ezek. 36:24, NASB).

You begin to wonder if the whole idea of the "returning exiles" from Babylon began as one more spurious credential claim for the group sent from Persia to Palestine to take charge of the indigenous population, which is exactly how Ezra, Nehemiah, and the gang are portrayed in the books named for them: high-handed, imperious, and contemptuous toward "the people of the land." In fact, it is very likely that "Ezra" and "Nehemiah" are really the actantial role of the "returning exiles" made into two characters, given two personal names.

There is no reason to dismiss the notion that Nebuchadnezzar of Babylon did deport the Judean leadership. It's just that the people sent back by the Persian successors to the Babylonians need by no means have been related in any way to those original deportees.[27]

Remember, it was the long-standing policy of the Assyrian, Babylonian, and Persian Empires to play musical chairs with groups of deportees, sending them to some territory different from their (or their ancestors') homeland with the lie that they were graciously restoring them to their forgotten patrimony. The point was to stifle their resentment at being removed from their homeland. "*Au contraire!* We're actually *restoring* you *to* your homeland!" And after a while, it stops making any difference anyway, once you put down roots.

We are told that Ezra, though ostensibly Jewish, was a Persian official. His title, "scribe of the law of the God of Heaven," reflects an official Persian office/title, "secretary, advisor for questions of the Jewish religion."[28] According to the story, the Persian government deploys Ezra at the head of a small contingent to travel to Judah ("Yehud" as the Persians called it) to take charge of the natives and to establish ("restore") Jewish worship. This has two important implications.

First, the business about this mission constituting the "return" of the Jews exiled when Nebuchadnezzar laid waste to Jerusalem is very likely simply another fiction to buttress the imperious claims of what were essentially Persian officials to shove indigenous leadership aside (which is what they did) and take over. The story appears to be fiction anyway, and this may explain why it was concocted, just like the long priestly pedigree genealogies.

Second, we begin to suspect (realize?) that the striking similarity of post-Exilic Judaism to Persian Zoroastrianism did not result, as scholars have long assumed, from Jewish thinkers cooling their heels by the waters of Babylon and picking up some intriguing Zoroastrian ideas that seemed worth adding to traditional Jewish belief.

Zoroastrian influence there certainly was: It is only after the Exile that we start hearing, for instance, of Jewish belief in a future resurrection of the dead to face judgment, in a postmortem hell of torment for the wicked, in a division of history into set periods leading to the End, and, especially, in the transformation of Satan (originally a servant of Yahweh to keep everybody honest) into an evil anti-God reminiscent of the Zoroastrian Ahriman.

The resulting Judaism (to be distinguished from "Israelite religion") was so obviously Zoroastrian in color and form that its enemies (e.g., the Sadducees) dubbed its adherents "Pharisees," i.e., "Parsees" (as Zoroastrians are still called in India, where they moved after Islamic persecutions).[29] Such a wholesale "Persianizing" of Jewish religion makes all the more sense if Ezra (i.e., the "returnees") arrived with an agenda commanded by Zoroastrian Persia to transform Judaism into its own image. Now we can surmise what was in that "law of God" which Ezra is said to have brought in his hand (Ezra 7:14).

Indeed, this possibility suggests that there may well have been more going on in the Jewish-Samaritan schism than we thought. It is not difficult to imagine native Israelites recoiling in shock when informed of the tenets of the new creed the party of Ezra demanded they adopt. "There will be weeping and gnashing of teeth, when you see Abraham and Isaac and Jacob and all the prophets in the kingdom of God, and yourselves thrust out. They will come from the east and the west, from the north and the south, and sit down in the kingdom of God" (Luke 13:28-29, RSV).

One of the most important (as well as cringe-inducing) episodes in Ezra-Nehemiah recounts the alienation between the indigenous inhabitants and the "returnees" led by Ezra and Nehemiah. Ezra 4:1-3 (RSV) records an ugly circumstance whereby, hearing of the newly arrived Jews' intention to build a temple to Yahweh in Jerusalem, the locals offer their help ("Let us build with you; for we worship your God as you do, and we have been sacrificing to him ever since the days of Esarhaddon king of Assyria who brought us here."), only to be rudely rebuffed: "You have nothing to do with us in building a house to our God; but we alone will build to the Lord [Yahweh], the God of Israel."

Granted, the narrator introduces these volunteers as "the adversaries of Judah and Benjamin," but this seems to jump the gun, anticipating their status as Judah's enemies *after* this rebuff, which must have been the cause of the enmity in the first place.

The Chronicler seems to be rewriting these "adversaries of Judah" in the image of Sanballat and his buddies who later make several attempts to ambush Nehemiah under the pretext of peace talks (Neh. 6:1-7). I see, scarcely concealed in Ezra 4:1-3, an echo of the pivotal event that prompted the Samaritan schism. We have to suspect that Ezra's rebuff was (or reflects) something more like an excommunication of those who refused to "get with the program" of newly Persianized Judaism.

Traditional scholarly discussion of the origin of the Samaritan schism has taken for granted the substantial historicity of the Deuteronomic History, with the result that scholars tried to discern how far the roots of this schism could be traced back into the longstanding strife between the twin Hebrew kingdoms of Israel in the north and Judah in the south who parted ways after the death of Solomon. As we have seen, this split must have been fictive, as there *was* no mighty empire of David and Solomon in the first place.

There was indeed a northern kingdom which we call Israel and which ancient extra-biblical sources usually refer to as "the House of Omri" after the famous king. But Judah appears as an organized state a bit later, only in the wake of the Assyrian conquest of its neighbor to the north.[30] There was never a splitting of a previously united kingdom.

In light of that, you have to start looking in the opposite direction. Perhaps pre-Minimalist scholars had been looking through the wrong end of the telescope. Maybe we should start with the Samaritan schism and ask if it was the origin of the "original" split! This would mean that the distinction Coggins[31] wanted to draw between "Samarians" (inhabitants of the northern kingdom) and "Samaritans" (members of a rival Jewish sect) is rendered moot: The "Samarians" whose story is recounted in 1 and 2 Kings stand for the "Samaritans" of Ezra and of subsequent Jewish sectarianism.[32]

Noth, I think, was pointing in this direction when he wrote that the Chronicler "projected into the past which he was describing the relationships which prevailed at the time he was writing."

> The opposition whom [the Chronicler] had in view can only have been the Samaritan community with a cult of their own on Mt Gerizim ... The 'apostate' tribes (and here again [the Chronicler] will certainly have been thinking of their successors, the Samaritans of his own day) had renounced the sole legitimate cult ... [The Chronicler] transferred this circumstance of his own day back into the past which he was describing, and so presented the phenomenon as something which was known to have existed from a long time back.[33]

I think, as I've said earlier in this book, that the Temple described as being "rebuilt" by the "returnees" in Ezra, Nehemiah, and Zechariah was the first centralized in Jerusalem. The glorious Temple planned by David and built by Solomon never existed except in someone's head. It was a blueprint for an ideal Temple, much like that outlined in Ezekiel's vision (Ezek. 40-43).

It was part and parcel of the Persian post-Exile propaganda, a pretense to be restoring the ancestral homeland of a displaced population from who knows where. "Uncle Cyrus wants to help you, ahem, 'rebuild' the wonderful Temple of your forbears!" And, just as the Solomonic Temple was retrojected into the time of Moses, in the form of the equally fictive Tabernacle, in order to more deeply root the Temple worship of post-Exilic times in sacred (and imaginary) antiquity, so was the Temple of Solomon a fictive retrojection of the Persian-era Temple of Ezra, Nehemiah, and Zerubbabel. The subsequent Temple of Herod the Great was, as historians rightly call it, "the Second Temple." It's the *first* one they're confused about.

Putting it all Together

The chapters of Ezra and Nehemiah have been clumsily reshuffled by some inept scribe. It looks as if the originally intended sequence of the mixed-up materials would have been: Ezra 7:8; Nehemiah 7:70-8:18; Ezra 9-10; Nehemiah 9-10.[34] The situation is analogous to that regarding the Gospel of John[35] and 2 Corinthians,[36] where scholars have found it necessary to rearrange displaced chapters in order to make better sense of the texts.

So how much of Ezra-Nehemiah did the Chronicler compose out of his own head? Did he use any previous source documents? He seems to have inherited two sources, the Memoir of Nehemiah (or at least attributed to Nehemiah), found in Nehemiah 1-6, and an Aramaic document preserved in Ezra 4:8-6:14, containing spurious letters to and from the Persian emperors Artaxerxes and Darius.

Analysis of vocabulary and redactional tendencies makes it clear that the Chronicler freely created the rest. He tried to imitate the first-person narrative of Nehemiah's Memoirs in order to fabricate a corresponding testament for Ezra. But the Chronicler kept forgetting himself: He randomly switched back and forth between first- and third-person, thus creating an Old Testament version of the problem of the "We-passages" in the Book of Acts.[37] But the solution is simpler in this case: bad writing.[38] The Chronicler also added various bits to the Nehemiah Memoir, including 2:7-9a; 3:1-32, 34.

In conclusion, as for the Chronicler, who can do better than to second Torrey's judgment?

> No fact of OT criticism is more firmly established than this, that the Chronicler, as a historian, is thoroughly untrustworthy. He distorts facts deliberately and habitually; invents chapter after chapter with the greatest freedom, and, what is most dangerous of all, his history is not written for its own sake, but in the interest of an extremely one-sided theory.[39]

Notes

1. Sorry, but I cannot agree with Marc Zvi Brettler, *The Creation of History in Ancient Israel* (New York: Routledge, 1998), p. 22, who returns to the old opinion that Ezra-Nehemiah was not written by the same author as Chronicles.

2. Second Chron. 8:3-5; 11:5-12; 12:4; 14:6-7; 17:2, 12, 19; 26:9-10; 27:4; 32:5; 33:14; Martin Noth, *The Chronicler's History*, Trans. H.G.M. Williamson. Journal for the Study of the Old Testament Supplement Series 50 (Sheffield: JSOT Press/Sheffield Academic Press, 1987), pp. 58-59. Brettler insists on seeing other, non-canonical, sources underlying Chronicles (*Creation of History*, p. 21), but close scrutiny makes it impossible for me to disagree with Torrey: Just about all the unique material (i.e., not directly paralleled in Samuel and Kings) is impossible not to chalk up to redactional (i.e., priestly/Levitical) self-interest. Granted, as Brettler capably demonstrates, the Chronicler has peppered his additions with phrases drawn from elsewhere in the Bible, but that says nothing about extra-canonical sources.

3. Brettler seems to me to follow the example of the Chronicler in this regard when he attempts to mitigate the impression we might naturally get of the redactions of the Chronicler as a mass of pious frauds. His kid- gloves treatment sounds subtly (?) apologetical in nature as he bends over backwards to ascribe the best possible motives to the Chronicler and his strategy.

4. Brettler, *Creation of History*, p. 19.

5. The subtitle "A Lot of Begats" is borrowed from Jerome Lawrence and Robert E. Lee, *Inherit the Wind* (New York: Bantam Books, 1976), p. 81.

6. Henri Lammens, "The Qu'ran and Tradition." Trans. Ibn Warraq. In Ibn Warraq, ed., *The Quest for the Historical Muhammad* (Amherst: Prometheus Books, 2000), pp. 169-87; Ibn al-Rawandi, "Origins of Islam: A Critical Look at the Sources." Trans. Ibn Warraq. In Ibn Warraq, ed., *Quest for the Historical Muhammad*, pp. 89-124; Joseph Schacht, "A Reevaluation of Islamic Traditions." In Ibn Warraq, ed., *Quest for the Historical Muhammad*, pp. 358-67.

7. *The New American Bible: The New Catholic Translation* (Camden: Thomas Nelson, 1971), p. 392, note 25. See also Harold Lindsell, ed., *The Harper Study Bible* (New York: Harper & Row, 1964), p. 606: "While the first two of the nine names appear as valid proper names elsewhere, the other forms are impossible as individual names. With slight change of vowels and division of consonants the list becomes a fragment of an old poem or prayer. No one knows how it was interpreted as a list of names and incorporated here."

   I once asked Dr. Lindsell how this observation in his study edition of the Bible could possibly be compatible with his well-known stance as a strict biblical inerrantist. He replied that some of the notes had been written by someone else. Pseudepigraphy then?

8. Sigmund Mowinckel, *The Psalms in Israel's Worship*. Trans. D.R. Ap-Thomas (Nashville: Abingdon, 1961), Vol. 1, p. 177.

9. In 1 Kings 2:13-46a, Solomon does indeed settle his father's old scores in a tale reminiscent of *The Godfather*, nor is it surprising to see that the Chronicler chops that, too.

10. Noth, *Chronicler's History*, pp. 85, 169.

11. Philip R. Davies, *In Search of 'Ancient Israel.'* Journal for the Study of the Old Testament Supplement Series 148 (Sheffield: Sheffield Academic Press, 1995), p. 104.

12. Margaret Barker, *The Gate of Heaven: The History and Symbolism of the Temple in Jerusalem* (London: SPCK, 1991), pp. 11, 21-22, 134-36.

13. Rachel Elior, *The Three Temples: On the Emergence of Jewish Mysticism*. Trans. David Louvish. (Oxford/ Portland: Litman Library of Jewish Civilization, 2005).

14. Russell E. Gmirkin, in *Berossus and Genesis, Manetho and Exodus: Hellenistic Histories and the Date of the Pentateuch*. T & T Clark Library of Biblical Studies 433. Copenhagen International Series 15. (New York/ London: T & T Clark, 2006).

15. Gmirkin, *Berossus and Genesis*, p. 85.

16. Margaret Barker, *The Older Testament: The Survival of Themes from the Ancient Royal Cult in Sectarian Judaism and Early Christianity* (London: SPCK Press, 1987), Chapter 10, "Transformations in the Post-Exilic Period (2): The Eden Stories," pp. 233-45.

17. Book of the Chronicles of the Kings of Israel. (1 Kings 14:19; 15:31, 36; 16:5, 14, 20, 27; 22:39; 2 Kings 1:18; 10:34; 13:8, 12; 14:15, ,28; 15:11, 21, 26, 31), Book of the Chronicles of the Kings of Judah (1 Kings 14:29; 15:7, 23; 22:45; 2 Kings 8:23; 12:19; 14:18, 15:6, 36; 16:19; 20:20; 21:17, 25; 23:28; 24:5), Book of the Kings of Israel and Judah (2 Chron. 27:7; 35:27; 36:8); Book of the Kings of Judah and Israel (2 Chron. 25:26; 28:26; 32:32); Chronicles of Samuel the Seer, Chronicles of Nathan the Prophet, and Chronicles of Gad the Seer (1 Chron. 29:29).

18. Brettler writes, "Although some modern scholars have doubted the existence of these sources, in antiquity these citations likely bolstered the readers' belief in the work's reliability" (*Creation of History*, p. 22). Of *course* they did–that's why they were fabricated!

19. Michael D. Goulder, *The Psalms of the Sons of Korah*. Journal for the Study of the Old Testament Supplement Series 20 (Sheffield: JSOT Press, 1982), pp. 61-62.

20. In the Qu'ran, Allah vouchsafes hitherto-secret information about biblical characters Mary (3:44), Noah (11:49), Joseph (12:102), Alexander the Great (18:83); and Moses (28:1). Alexander? Yes, he occurs, thinly veiled, in Daniel 8:5-8.

21. Solomon Schechter, *Some Aspects of Rabbinic Theology* (New York: Macmillan, 1910), pp. 170-98.

22. Brettler thinks otherwise (*Creation of History*, pp. 21-22), but his alternative hypothesis of Chronicles as "an 'authoritative commentary,' [Stephen Geller] to be read in conjunction with its sources" (p. 22) strikes me as rank harmonization in the interest of canonical apologetics.

23. Goulder, *Sons of Korah*, p. 56.

24. Barker, *Gate of Heaven*, pp. 117, 120.

25. William Wrede, *The Messianic Secret in Mark*. Trans. J.C.G. Greig. Library of Theological Translations (Altrincham: James Clarke, 1971).

26. Charles Cutler Torrey, *The Composition and Historical Value of Ezra- Nehemiah*. Beihefte zür Zeitschrift für die alttestamentliche Wissenschaft II (Giessen: J. Ricker'sche Buchhandlung, 1896), pp. 53-54.

27. Davies, *In Search*, p. 78.

28. R.J. Coggins, *Samaritans and Jews: The Origins of Samaritanism Reconsidered*. Growing Points in Theology (Atlanta: John Knox Press, 1975), p. 61.

29. T.W. Manson, *The Servant-Messiah: A Study of the Public Ministry of Jesus* (Cambridge at the University Press, 1961), pp. 18-20.

30. Davies, *In Search*, p. 66.

31. Coggins, *Samaritans and Jews*, pp. 8-9.

32. We see the same kind of attempt to hide a religious identity behind a geographical one in recent Politically Correct efforts to pretend that when the Gospel of John speaks of Jesus' detractors as "the Jews" it only means geographical "Judeans."

33. Noth, *Chronicler's History*, pp. 100-104.

34. Torrey, *Composition*, p. 34.

35. F.R. Hoare, *The Original Order and Chapters of St. John's Gospel* (London: Burns, Oates & Washbourne, 1944); Thomas Cottam, *The Fourth Gospel Rearranged* (London: Epworth Press, 1952); Rudolf Bultmann, *The Gospel of John: A Commentary*. Trans. G.R. Beasley-Murray, R.W.N. Hoare, and J.K. Riches (Philadelphia: Westminster Press, 1971), pp. 10-11.

36. Walter Schmithals, *Gnosticism in Corinth: An Investigation of the Letters to the Corinthians*. Trans. John Steely (New York: Abingdon Press, 1971), pp. 96-100.

37. Vernon K. Robbins, "By Land and by Sea: The We-Passages and Ancient Sea Voyages." In Charles H. Talbert, ed., *Perspectives on Luke-Acts*. Perspectives on Religious Studies, Special Studies Series No 5 (Edinburgh: T&T Clark, 1978), pp. 215-42.

38. Torrey, *Composition*, p. 28. I suspect the same explanation works pretty well for 2 Corinthians 12:1-10.

39. Torrey at p. 52.

V
1 Maccabees, 2 Maccabees

THE HEBREW HAMMER

1 Maccabees

Written at the beginning of the first century B.C.E. (i.e., about 100 B.C.E.), this book recounts in classic biblical style (see the Deuteronomic theology of 3:16-22; 4:6-11, etc.) the victory of the Hasmonean insurgents against the Syrian oppressors of the Seleucid Empire, headquartered in Antioch. In particular, they revolted against the attempts of Seleucid tyrant Antiochus IV Epiphanes, who regarded himself as Zeus on earth and sought to wipe out Judaism. Their hard-fought guerilla struggle resulted in the establishment of about a century of Jewish independence, however, under Levitical priest-kings, not Davidic heirs.

These events are the historical referents to which the cryptic prophecies of Daniel point. That is, Daniel, actually a second-century contemporary of the Hasmoneans, himself one of the Hasideans, was creating retroactive "predictions" of the events as if God had predicted them centuries earlier.

It is striking that 1 Maccabees admits that the mass Hellenization of Jews (adoption of Greek education, language, customs, religion, etc.) was not simply an attempted imposition on unwilling Jews, as if those who did Hellenize must have been knuckling under to avoid persecution (which is the impression we do get in 2 Maccabees by a different author). No, the book tells us quite plainly that Jews by and large rejoiced to embrace the new ways (1:43b).

This is enormously significant. It shows us that the Mystery religion of Dionysus had taken root widely among Palestinian Jews in the second century B.C.E. This is important in view of the debate over what sound like pagan myth-motifs in the gospels, e.g., the Last Supper, where, Jesus' blood, like Dionysus', is wine, and his body, like that of Osiris (the Egyptian counterpart to Dionysus), is grain or bread.

We can recognize in the struggle of the priest Mattathias and his sons (the Hasmonean clan) to stem the tide of Hellenization a prime example of what anthropologists[1] call a Revitalization Movement. This is when a traditional culture is assaulted by the influx of a foreign culture, whether it happens by military invasion, missionary incursions, etc. The old ways (culture, mores, religion) are endangered; the outsiders want to change everything. The native people are demoralized and yet seduced. The new gods must be superior, since the old ones could not turn them (and their earthly representatives) back.

So if you can't beat 'em, why not join 'em? (These would be the many Hellenizing Jews in 1 Maccabees, going so far as to have circumcision surgically reversed!) There will also be a smaller group of fatalistic die-hards, who can see which way the wind is blowing but are willing to go down with the ship. The seven brothers and Eliezar the sage in 2 Maccabees, all gladly martyred for their faith, are examples of this tendency.

But a third group, in order to save the substance of the old ways, will learn some new tricks from the conquerors and try to beat them at their own game. In this way American Indians adopted horsemanship and guns to fight the White man. The Melanesian Cargo Cults, in reaction to the Dutch colonizers,[2] claimed the Dutch god Jesus as their own ancestor god and did their best to ape the European technology that had given their colonial masters the advantage over them. They conducted drills with toy wooden rifles and spoke on "radios" made of orange crates, emulating the Dutch. The hope was to induce Jesus to return to cast out the Dutch and give them the modern goods instead. The Ayatollah Khomeini, who despised the Shah's modernization, was happy enough to use modern communications and weapons to gain and cement his hold upon Iran so he could return it to the Middle Ages.

In just this way, Judah Maccabee and his forces, though the most zealous of Jews, were willing to compromise the Sabbath in order to fight effectively. Eventually, the Hasideans ("Pious"), at first the partisans of Judah Maccabee, later became the Essene sect, splitting off to form Pythagorean-style monasteries. Rabbis formed circles of students on the model of the Greek philosophers and applied to the Torah the allegorizing exegesis invented by the Stoics. In this way, what seems to us quintessentially Jewish turns out to be Greek in origin. Thus the Hasmoneans were a creatively hybridizing Revitalization Movement.

The First Book of Maccabees also tells us the origin of Hanukah, the Feast of Dedication (4:59). Antiochus had defiled the Jerusalem temple by sacrificing a pig on the altar in honor of Zeus (1:54). This was the original "abomination of desolation" or "desolating sacrilege" mentioned by Daniel 11:31; 12:11, and again in Mark 13:14. The Hasmoneans regained control of the Temple, tore down the profaned altar and built a new one, rededicating the place to the worship of Yahweh.

As just anticipated, 1 Maccabees also shows us the origin of a major feature of the Antichrist myth: the abomination of desolation, the act of a megalomaniacal tyrant who proclaims his own divinity in the Jerusalem Temple itself. The same thing happens again in 3 Maccabees 1-2, where Ptolemy IV Philopater seeks to enter the Holy of Holies, not to mention the order of Caligula in 44 C.E. to have his own image set up there (2 Thess. 2:3-4), the execution of which was prevented by his own timely death.

Another thing: 1 Maccabees 9:27 attests the belief of the scribal establishment, Josephus, and the later rabbis that the period of God sending prophets had long ago come to an end (see also, ironically, Zechariah 13:2-5). How, then, are we to understand 1 Maccabees 4:46 and 14:41, which seem to look forward to the reappearance of prophets? On the face of it, these passages make it sound like people expected a prophet might come along any moment, as if it were common. But in view of 9:27, maybe they believed the prophetic voice would return as part of some end-time scenario.

2 Maccabees

This book is an epitome, or condensed version, of a longer, five-volume work by one Jason of Cyrene, 2:23. We don't know who prepared this edition. While not quite as historically dependable as 1 Maccabees, 2 Maccabees is enormously fertile in terms of what it tells us about contemporary Jewish belief in the afterlife, the canon of scripture, monotheism, martyrology, and (indirectly) messianism. In the last case, 2 Maccabees delineates important ideas that later figure into New Testament Christology. Let's take these themes one by one.

Afterlife

It is quite clear from the confessions ("testaments") of the seven brothers and of Eliezar that pious Jews expected that the righteous would rise from the dead in physical bodies, with restored limbs and organs intact (7:11; 14:46). The wicked, by contrast, will remain dead, with no hope of resurrection (7:14). Even the righteous will bide the time till the resurrection in Hades (6:23), though presumably not in torment, the implication being either that Hades has two sections, or that the word was sometimes used as just another term for the more neutral *Sheol*.

It is possible they believed the wicked would remain in a part of Hell devoted to torment, but this does not come in for mention, as in 4 Maccabees 10:11, where we hear that Antiochus Epiphanes is doomed to "unceasing torments." "On you he will take vengeance both in this present life and when you are dead" (4 Macc. 12:18, RSV). "You, because of your bloodthirstiness towards us, will deservedly undergo from the divine justice eternal torment by fire" (4 Macc. 9:9, RSV).

Scripture

There seems to be a reference in 2:13-15 to the gathering of whatever old scriptures could be found, whether all of them or not, who knows? "The books about the kings and prophets" would seem to be the Deuteronomic Histories and probably Chronicles, since Nehemiah is also mentioned. "The writings of David" would have to be the Psalms, which would already have been (mis)attributed to him by this time.

What are the "letters of kings about votive offerings"? Beats me. Judah Maccabee collected more scripture, unspecified, mentioned in 2:14 as "all the books that had been lost on account of the war." This seems to intend that he made sure there was a comprehensive collection from which copies could be supplied to any whose copies had been destroyed. Need I point out that such stories must be suspected of being attempts to claim an older origin for writings actually produced when they are said to be "discovered" or "collected"? Remember, I place the Deuteronomic "reform," as well as many psalms, in the Hasmonean period.

Monotheism

Though the belief that Israel's God is the only God appeared with Jeremiah and the Second Isaiah, there is no telling how long it took for monotheism to catch on among the people. There are three interesting notes here. First, the author tells us that Jews participated in the rites of Dionysus only grudgingly, at sword point (6:7)—which seems a bit odd given that they were Bacchantic revels, hard, one would think, to fake!

The author just doesn't want to admit that many Jews were enthusiastic about "false" religion, while 1 Maccabees admits that a great many Jews participated in Hellenistic paganism by free choice. They may, like many Gentiles of the time, have thought that Yahweh was simply another name for Dionysus anyway.

Similarly, we are told that the Jewish high priest Jason ordered an offering to be made to Hercules for the quadrennial games (7:18-20). (Archaeologists have discovered a mosaic picture of Hercules in a synagogue from the second century C.E.) Finally, in 12:40, when the bodies of slain Jewish freedom fighters are examined, some of them are found to be wearing protective amulets of the gods of Jaffa (Joppa), which would have been Semitic gods.

Get that? They're fighting to the death on behalf of Judaism, against Greek polytheism—and they are counting on help from polytheistic gods of their own! It's the mid-second century B.C.E., and they're *still* not monotheistic! Margaret Barker[3] argues forcefully that early Christianity was simply carrying on the popular unofficial Jewish polytheism characteristic of Old Testament Israel, and that they understood Jesus to be Yahweh, with his Father as El Elyon, God Most High.

Martyrology

Here we find a doctrine that would come to flower in later centuries in the Christian cult of the saints.[4] But it may also help explain the origin of the Christian doctrine of the saving death of Jesus. Second Maccabees 7:37-38 has one of the martyrs, as he is about to die, express the hope that God may count his undeserved death toward alleviating the distress which the people's sins have brought upon them.

Fourth Maccabees makes this even more explicit: "You know, O God, that though I might have saved myself, I am dying in burning torments for the sake of the law. Be merciful to your people, and let our punishment suffice for them. Make my blood their purification, and take my life in exchange for theirs" (6:27-29, RSV). Sam K. Williams[5] argues that it was this understanding of martyrdom that was applied to Jesus' death, so that early Christians would have understood his death as hastening the vanquishing of the Romans, or, later, as making it possible for God to accept Gentiles into his household.

The idea would have been that Jews were always ritually clean before God because of the Temple sacrifices, whereas Gentiles had not the benefit of these. But now God would count the sacrificial death of Jesus Christ as washing away their ritual pollution. This doctrine would then eventually evolve into the belief that Jesus died as a substitute to pay for the moral sins of sinners who had committed them, a very different idea, as different as ritual pollution is from immoral activity. (Theft did not render you unclean, but it sure was wrong; nor was leprosy immoral, though it sure did make you unclean.)

Messiahship

Neither 2 nor 4 Maccabees says anything about the Messiah, though the Testament of Levi intimates that some Jews developed a two-messiah framework to accommodate a Hasmonean, priestly messiah alongside a Davidic, royal messiah. The Levite clan of the Hasmoneans had, after all, accomplished what the Davidic heir was traditionally expected to accomplish: freedom for his people. Perhaps some Jews made room for both. And in the Dead Sea Scroll, *The Messianic Rule*, we seem to have not so much a prophecy of a future messianic banquet as a rubric, a breviary, a script for an ongoing sacramental meal, implying that the community venerated living representatives of both messianic lines.

But in 2 Maccabees 15:12 we read of Judah Maccabee's final dream vision which transports him to heaven where, among other things, he beholds the martyred high priest Onias III standing before God's throne, interceding with God on behalf of the Jewish people. This is a role assigned to the ascended Jesus in Romans 8:34; Hebrews 4:14-5:2; and 1 John 2:1.

One must consider the theory of Benjamin W. Bacon[6] that at first Jesus was believed to have ascended to heaven, with no resurrection, and that his original role there was to plead for his people before God, like the similarly martyred Onias. Only later would they have added the notion that he is the temporarily absent Messiah who would shortly arrive to vanquish the pagans. If people of that day could believe it about Onias, they could believe it about Jesus. This way, we can see that there might have been an early period in which Christians believed in the exaltation of Jesus to heaven without believing in a physical resurrection.

Finally, it is striking to note that 2 Maccabees entertains the feats of walking on water (5:21) and commanding the storm to stand still (9:8) as among the delusions of Antiochus about his own divine grandeur. Sound familiar? Are these feats more believable when attributed to Jesus?

Two New Testament Borrowings

First, Luke has borrowed the disgusting death of Herod Agrippa (Acts 12:23, "he was eaten by worms and died") from that of Antiochus in 2 Maccabees 9:9 (RSV), "And so the ungodly man's body swarmed with worms, and while he was still living in anguish and pain, his flesh rotted away."

Second, Hebrews 11:38 ("of whom the world was not worthy, wandering in deserts and mountains and caves and holes in the ground," NASB) is a reference back to 2 Maccabees 10:6 (RSV), "they had been wandering in the mountains and caves like wild animals".

Notes

1. Anthony F.C. Wallace, *Revitalizations and Mazeways: Essays on Culture Change Volume 1* (Lincoln: University of Nebraska Press, 2003).

2. Peter Worsley, *The Trumpet Shall Sound: A Study of "Cargo" Cults in Melanesia* (New York: Schocken Books, 2nd ed., 1968).

3. Margaret Barker (*The Great Angel: A Study of Israel's Second God* (London: SPCK, 1992).

4. Peter Brown, *The Cult of the Saints: Its Rise and Function in Latin Christianity.* Haskell Lectures, School of Divinity at the University of Chicago, April 1978 (Chicago: University of Chicago Press, 1981).

5. Sam K. Williams, *Jesus' Death as Saving Event: The Background and Origin of a Concept.* Harvard Dissertations in Religion 2 (Missoula: Scholars Press, 1975). pp. 32-33, 230-33.

6. Benjamin W. Bacon, *The Story of Jesus and the Beginnings of the Church: A Valuation of the Synoptic Record for History and for Religion* (London: George Allen & Unwin, 1928), pp. 283-84.

VI

Ruth, Esther, Daniel, Jonah, Judith, Tobit

FICTIONS OF FAITH

This odd lot of biblical writings are outright fiction. They are edifying fictions, though in the ancient world there was but a thin line between the edifying and the entertaining,[1] and many texts had both intended functions. It is always possible that some of these little books were intended by their authors to be taken as historical fact, in which case we would have to call them hoaxers, but I do not think there is any reason to suppose so.

Not that it matters anyway. We have access to the text, not to the author, so the questions we ask must be addressed to the text. And these give the answer that they are indeed fictions.

Ruth

The Book of Ruth takes place in the pre-Monarchic period, i.e., the time of the Judges, which is why it is placed between Joshua and Judges in the Christian Bible. It shouldn't be there, though, since it interrupts the Deuteronomic History (Joshua-Kings).

It was probably written during the time of the Chronicler. This is implied by the topic, as we will soon see, but also by the Aramaic coloring of the Hebrew. Also, the author feels the need to explain for the reader's benefit the practice of handing over a shoe to seal a contract (4:7), implying it is long obsolete, or the reader would know about it.

Jews have long read the book publicly during the Feast of Weeks, which celebrates the wheat harvest, because part of the action of the book is set then.

It is a piece of popular narrative, one of the signs of which is the allegorical nature of the characters' names. They are what Tzvetan Todorov[2] calls "narrative-men," people in the story who are barely characters at all, who do not rise above simply and merely filling a necessary narrative role or function, then they are gone. There is no more to them, and often their name assigns that role.

Elimelech is a pious man about whom we need to know nothing else; accordingly, his name means "God is my king." His two dying sons are named Mahlon ("weakness") and Chilion ("consumption"). Orpah[3] seems to mean "the unfaithful," since she breaks with Naomi ("bitter"). Ruth, by contrast, seems to mean "companion."

Later readers (probably correctly, I suspect) understood Ruth's behavior in 3:7-9 as rather risqué, a seduction of Boaz,[4] especially since sometimes in the Bible "feet" is a euphemism for "penis." Also, "to uncover the nakedness of" someone means to have sex with them (Lev. 18).

What is the point of the book? What is Ruth trying to tell its readers? A few things, actually.

First, the book seeks to provide a genealogy for King David by making his grandfather Obed the son of Ruth and Boaz. But on closer inspection, this cannot be the original purpose because 4:17-22, the link to David, appears clearly to be a later interpolation, substituting "Obed" for another name, probably "Ben-Noam" ("son of pleasantness"). You can see this from the fact that it runs contrary to Hebrew idiom to describe the naming of a child as in 4:17. The name must precede the word "saying," followed by the etymological reason for the naming, the pun (see Genesis 4:1 and many others: "They named him _____, saying, 'For God shall _____ him.'").

Also, "Obed" (which means "servant," i.e., worshipper) has nothing to do with the stated rationale, "A son has been born to Naomi." Rather, the link to David suggested itself to some later scribe because the story takes place in Bethlehem, later regarded as the city of David. Also, compare 4:18 with 4:12.

Ruth also emphasizes the law of Levirate marriage (Deut. 25:5-6) and land redemption: A brother-in-law must beget children for his late brother, the children being counted as the late brother's heirs. Also he must buy his brother's property so these children can inherit in the legal father's name. The book might be an object lesson for all this, but more likely that's just an element of the plot.

The main theme of the Book of Ruth must be to oppose the nativist policies of exclusion advocated in Nehemiah 13:23-27 and Ezra 10, where Jewish men are forced to divorce and abandon their Gentile wives. Ruth goes out of its way to make sure you know Ruth is an Edomite, not an Israelite, and this would seem to be a counterblast to this policy.[5] The point of the book would be much like that of the parable of the Good Samaritan (Luke 10:29-37). You have to assume that the most conspicuous element of the story, the one that sticks out like a sore thumb, has something to do with the main point being made.

Esther

This book is one long ceremonial etiology, told to account for the Jewish holiday of Purim, the name of which it explains from the word *pur*, "lot," so that Purim means "casting lots," a game of chance. But in the story, the climactic event occurs on a day chosen by lot. Since the word for "lot" is an Akkadian loan-word, not originally a Hebrew word, it implies that Jews borrowed an already-existing pagan holiday that somehow involved the casting of lots.

The Book of Esther was written to provide, after the fact, a good Jewish pedigree for the custom, just as we celebrate December 25 as the birth of Jesus Christ, when originally it marked the widely-celebrated birthday of Mithras the sun god. Christians could not be dissuaded from going to Mithraist office parties, singing traditional Mithras carols, and watching favorite Mithras TV specials, so the fourth-century bishops decided to co-opt the holiday.

At the root of the story lies the ancient myth of the supercession of the Elamite gods *Human* and *Mashti* by the Babylonian gods *Marduk* and *Ishtar*. Human has become Hamaan, who loses his position to Mordecai, another form of the name Marduk. Mashti becomes Vashti, the modest queen who is rejected and replaced by Esther (=Ishtar). Note that even in the story "Esther" is not a native Jewish name. She is named Hadassah. It is a hint that the story originally had nothing to do with Jews or Judaism.

Other popular folktale motifs include the modesty of the Queen, who refuses to display herself (naked, I assume?) before the king's nobles, a tale also told by Herodotus about Candaules and Gyges (the "Gog" of Ezekiel).

Candaules thought his wife "was the most beautiful woman on earth." He had "a bodyguard whose name was Gyges," to whom the king said one day, "It appears you don't believe me when I tell you how lovely my wife is." Well, buddy, you will "contrive to see her naked." Understandably, Gyges "did his utmost to decline the king's invitation, because he was afraid of what might happen if he accepted it."

> The king, however, told him, "There is nothing to be afraid of . . . I will hide you behind the open door of our bedroom . . . . Near the door there's a chair—she will

put her clothes on it as she takes them off, one by one ... Then, while she's walking away from the chair to the bed with her back to you, slip away through the door–and mind she doesn't catch you."

Then "Candaules brought him to the room," and "Gyges watched her walk in and put her clothes on the chair. Then, just as she had turned her back and was going to bed, he slipped softly out of the room." The queen saw him, though, and "resolved to have her revenge."

The "next morning she sent for Gyges," who "answered the summons without any suspicion that she knew what had occurred on the previous night." You have two options, she said to him:

> Kill Candaules and seize the throne with me as your wife; or die yourself on the spot, so that never again may your blind obedience to the king tempt you to see what you have no right to see.

Gyges "made his choice–to live." That night, "he followed her into the bedroom. She put a knife into his hand, and hid him behind the same door as before. Then, when Candaules was asleep, he crept from behind the door and struck. Thus Gyges usurped the throne and married the queen."[6]

Also, we see again in Esther the popular Diaspora/Exilic theme of a young Jew refusing to sell out his or her principles and rising to a position of prestige and power in the pagan court itself. Other cases of it include Joseph in Genesis, Daniel, Zerubbabel (in 3 Maccabees), and Ahiqar. It is a very important lesson to be imparted to young Jews who fear they are doomed to social marginalization if they remain Jews and do not assimilate to the religions of the Gentiles among whom they live.

It is precisely by following the ancestral ways that you have your best chance at success even in the empire of the Gentiles! And when this did occasionally happen (e.g., Ezra and Nehemiah, who were prized servants of Cyrus), it is no surprise if pagan co-workers became jealous of the Jews who succeeded. This is just what happens in Daniel and Esther.

One of the factors pointing to Esther being a work of fiction is its grossly distorted picture of the succession of Persian kings, imagining Ahasuerus (Xerxes) as the direct successor of the Babylonian king Nebuchadnezzar who destroyed Jerusalem in 586 B.C.E., taking captive Jews including Mordecai. In fact, Esther's King Xerxes is many kings later. Worse yet, Esther cannot have been Xerxes' queen, since during that period his queen was the cruel and superstitious Amestris.[7]

This book's place in Hebrew Scripture has occasionally been questioned for the simple reason that it never once mentions God (despite the obvious "behind-the-scenes" workings of Providence)! It won its place in the Bible by virtue of its Jewish nationalism. (The Feast of Purim, the Jewish Halloween, is not even a particularly religious holiday.) The longer (Greek) version of Esther included in the Apocrypha contains various additions which do mention God by name in order to obviate the difficulty. These are to be plugged in at Esther 11:2-12; 12:1-6; [then come 1:1-3:13]; 13:1-7; [then 3:14-4:17]; 13:8-18; 14:1-19; 15:1-16; [then 5:3-8:12]; 16:1-24; [then 8:13-10:3, the end of the book in Hebrew]; 10:4-13; 11:1.

Daniel

A second-century B.C.E. redactor used a set of Daniel stories, fictively set in the Babylonian Exile, as the launching pad for a set of apocalyptic visions. Even as early as the second century C.E. the Pythagorean critic Porphyry wrote a multi-volume work arguing that Daniel could not have been a genuine predictive prophecy. Modern biblical criticism agrees with him.

For one thing, the stories preceding the visions are filled with anachronisms and mistakes, indicating that someone wrote them much later based on a very vague apprehension of the relevant history. The Hebrew in which the book is written is late, showing linguistic influence and loan-words from Persian Aramaic and Greek. Part of the Protestant canonical version of Daniel is written in Aramaic, and other Aramaic Daniel fragments would be discovered among the Dead Sea Scrolls. A later Greek author added more material, included in the Septuagint.

In chapter 1, Daniel and his chums are deported to Babylon in an early wave of the Exile not attested anywhere else (implying that the author hasn't got his facts straight). Their new masters immediately note the lads' gifts and train them to serve as wise men, advisors to the state, much as Ezra had been to the later Persian Emperor Cyrus, conqueror of Babylon.

Their acclimation includes a diet of rich Babylonian food, actually a privilege and a perk of their position. But this will entail abandoning Jewish kosher laws, not that the Babylonians are trying to get them to flout the Torah, as the Seleucid villains do in 2 Maccabees. It is just routine procedure, as well as a friendly gesture. Nonetheless, Daniel and his buddies beg leave to stick to more modest Hebrew fare: vegetables and water.

They propose an experiment: Let them live for a while on such victuals, and see if their alertness and strength are not actually superior to those of their young Babylonian colleagues. It works. Daniel's second-century readers are to take note: Do not yield to the seduction of Hellenistic culture under Seleucid rule in Palestine!

The Jehovah's Witnesses, Seventh Day Adventists, Black Muslims, and Mormons of our time can certainly sympathize with this: Their peculiar strictures (e.g., against blood transfusions, caffeine, smoking, pork, even all meats), long sneered at as cultic (which of course they are), have gained new respect in recent years when genuine health benefits have become evident. But why do the Hebrew lads eschew meat and wine altogether? The Torah never forbids these things.

My guess is that what we see here represents the sectarian regimen of the Hasideans, the sectarian group to which Judah Maccabee belonged and which later gave rise to the Essenes. Their thinking may have been that they couldn't be sure that even inherently clean foods had been prepared in a proper (kosher) way by pagans (cf., Mark 7:4; 1 Cor. 10:25-29). Better to avoid any chance of ritual contamination.

Remember, in the ancient Near East, wisdom included the ability to decipher dreams and visions. Thus, during his training as a wise man, Daniel's oracular gifts begin to stir. The story is closely parallel to that of Joseph.

In the next chapter, Daniel rises to a position of authority. Just like Joseph in Egypt, he rises to prominence by interpreting a royal dream that none of the native oracles can make sense of. It is the dream of a statue representing four successive Middle Eastern Empires. It is a pre-Danielic text, reinterpreted here. The statue made of the four metals must originally have denoted the succession of historical epochs, especially the Bronze Age and the Iron Age.

Since then, the metaphor had come to be used to stand for a succession of world empires. This sequence intended the Assyrians, followed by the Medes, then the Persians, and finally Alexander the Great and his successors. Daniel, obviously, reapplies it to the Babylonian Empire, then the Medes, then the Persians, then Alexander. But the image first came from the East, composed by someone over in Iran or Armenia, where Babylon never ruled. Babylon and Media were contemporary, adjacent empires. Thus the sequence of empires originally represented the Medes' perspective, not the Babylonian.[8]

One sometimes reads in fundamentalist Protestant commentaries that the statue stands for Babylon, Medes and Persians together, then Alexander, then Rome. But this is in order to "update" the image and to stretch it to fit the coming of Jesus. That is not the point in Daniel.

Chapter 3 features a Sunday School favorite, the story of the Three Young Men in the fiery furnace. Daniel's friends are framed by jealous pagans, then condemned to death. But they are preserved through the flames. The story is a cruel joke if it is meant to inculcate confidence in Jewish readers that the same magical protection will be theirs, as witness the ovens of Auschwitz. But of course that is not the point. The story means to tell Jews that, despite their individual martyrdoms (the like of which is depicted unflinchingly in 2 and 4 Maccabees), Israel itself will survive the furnace of persecution.

Daniel's redactor uses this story to encourage those faithful Jews of his own day not to yield to the threats of the Seleucid persecutors. A valuable theological point occurs in Daniel 3:17-18 (NASB):

> "If it be so, our God whom we serve is able to deliver us from the burning fiery furnace; and he will deliver us out of your hand, O king. But if not, be it known to you, O king, that we will not serve your gods or worship the golden image which you have set up."

Unlike various other biblical texts about prayer, this one is appropriately humble. The Jewish heroes defiantly reject the king's demand for them to worship idols. God, they say, is fully able to deliver them from this persecution, *but even if he doesn't*, they're not bowing the knee! Faith doesn't presume God *will* do what one asks, but rather that he is certainly up to the task if he so chooses, and it is up to him.

In chapter 4 we read the story of the humiliation of the Babylonian king via lycanthropy, told here of Nebuchadnezzar. It was originally told of King Nabonidus, not of Nebuchadnezzer, as witness *The Prayer of Nabonidus* in the Dead Sea Scrolls.

> Words of the prayer, said by Nabonidus, king of Babylonia, the great king, when afflicted with an ulcer on command of the most high God in Temâ:

> "I, Nabonidus, was afflicted with an evil ulcer for seven years, and far from men I was driven, until I prayed to the most high God. And an exorcist pardoned my sins. He was a Jew from among the children of the exile of Judah, and said: 'Recount this in writing to glorify and exalt the name of the most high God.' Then I wrote this: 'When I was afflicted for seven years by the most high God with an evil ulcer during my stay at Temâ, I prayed to the gods of silver and gold, bronze and iron, wood, stone and lime, because I thought and considered them gods ...'"[9]

Daniel 5 tells of Belshazzar's feast and the proverbial "handwriting on the wall." Belshazzar is said here to be the son and heir of Nebuchadnezzer (the king who conquered Jerusalem in 586 B.C.E.), as well as the last king of Babylon. In fact, Belshazzar was never king, though he did rule for three years as a deputy in the stead of Nabonidus, who *was* the last king of Babylon. There were three kings between Nebuchadnezzar and Nabonidus. The story has Babylon conquered by one Darius the Mede, whereas in fact the conqueror was Cyrus the Persian, whose son was Darius the Persian. Of course all these historical difficulties in no way detract from the profundity and skill of this wonderful story about the vain self-sufficiency of the flesh as opposed to God.

Mene, Mene, Tekel, Upharsin–what does it mean? "You have been weighed in the scales and you come up short!" is not a translation. It is more like an interpretation of tongues. Daniel, after all, is not a translator or a linguist. He is an interpreter of supernatural signs.

In chapter 6, Daniel, like his friends, is set up by his frustrated pagan rivals, but thanks to God's protection, he survives incarceration *in a den of hungry lions*. Pretty much the same story circulated in Persia about the infant Zoroaster, prophetic founder of the Zoroastrian faith, only he was tossed, as an infant, into a den of wolves and was divinely kept from harm. This story functions just like its close parallel: that of Shadrach, Meschach, and Abed-Nego in the fiery furnace. It urges Jewish readers in a time of persecution (by the Seleucids in the mid-second century B.C.E.) not to knuckle under.

Susanna

This is an ingenious detective story in which Daniel's skills at deduction and cross-examination are given as the reason for his rise to prominence in the Babylonian court. In many ways the story foreshadows the later stories of Christian virgins (like Thecla in The Acts of Paul and Thecla) whose threatened virtue is rescued by divine intervention.

Bel and the Dragon

This episode is a bit of rationalist debunking of pious fraud. Bel is Baal, the great god of the Canaanites. Here he has been confused with his Babylonian equivalent Marduk. The Dragon, accordingly, must be Kingu or Tiamat. It is significant that we read of the *worship* of the Dragon, reflected in 2 Kings 18, with the worship of Nehushtan in the Jerusalem Temple. But the point of the story is the ingenuity of Daniel, who easily sees through, and exposes, the bunko priestcraft of the scheming prelates.[10]

The Apocalypse of Daniel

Daniel 7 opens what is essentially a separate book, a visionary apocalypse, to which the tales of the pious hero Daniel have been affixed as a preface. Chapter 7 reiterates the succession of the heathen empires who must rule until God puts them down. Here they are symbolized as a sequence of fearsome chimeras erupting from the sea, rather like Godzilla surfacing to wreak havoc in Japan. The writer extends the image of the fourth Beast so as to make it cover "the Little Horn," Antiochus IV Epiphanes, the terrible persecutor from the Seleucid Empire whose evil deeds we read about in 1, 2, and 4 Maccabees.

"Daniel" was writing during these events. Much debate centers upon the question of the identity of the character in this passage, the "one like a son of man," i.e., one in human form, in contrast to the preceding monsters. Most Jewish interpreters have historically taken the "one like a son of man" to be a symbol of the Davidic Messiah who should trample down the oppressive authority of the nations upon his advent. They did not, however, take the phrase "son of man" as a *title* of the Messiah or a different version of the Messiah, as some modern scholars have thought.[11]

Strictly speaking, it is hard to go beyond saying this figure represents "the kingdom of the saints of Elyon" (7:27) rather than some individual, since all the other figures represent regimes, not individuals. But there is an earlier layer of meaning here.

The vision was experienced, the narrator says, "in the first year of Belshazzar king of Babylon." He beheld "four winds of heaven" that "were stirring up the great sea" and "four great beasts [that] came up out of the sea," all of them "different from one another" (7:1-7, RSV). As "Daniel" contemplated these odd creatures, he tells us (7:9-10, ASV) that

> thrones were placed,
> and one that was ancient of days did sit:
> his raiment was white as snow,
> and the hair of his head like pure wool;
> his throne was fiery flames,
> and the wheels thereof burning fire.
> A fiery stream issued and came forth from before him:
> thousands of thousands ministered unto him,
> and ten thousand times ten thousand stood before him:
> the judgment was set,
> and the books were opened.

The "terrible and dreadful" fourth beast proceeds to get dispatched while the other ones have their dominion taken away. Daniel (7:13-14, ASV) then sees "in the night visions" that,

> there came with the clouds of heaven one like unto a son of man,
> and he came even to the ancient of days,
> and they brought him near before him.
> And there was given him dominion, and glory, and a kingdom,
> that all the peoples, nations, and languages should serve him:
> his dominion is an everlasting dominion, which shall not pass away,
> and his kingdom that which shall not be destroyed.

Here the writer of Daniel has used another old piece of sacred lore. It's an account of Yahweh overcoming the dragons of the sea, creating the world, and taking over his Father Elyon's throne as king. This is the classic divine/royal enthronement myth. The imagery gets recycled in the apocalyptic text that comprises the remainder of chapter 7, which concludes with a prophecy of the people of the saints of Elyon being given an everlasting kingdom with all dominions serving and obeying them.

In the same way that the Danielic redactor takes up this piece of creation mythology, so does John of Patmos in the Book of Revelation, where we again witness the rising of seven-headed Leviathan from the sea (13:1-2). In apocalyptic thought, "*Urzeit gleicht Endzeit*." [12] That is, the events of the creation myth are repeated in the myth of the End, issuing in a new and restored paradise on earth. The primordial struggle becomes politicized: In Daniel the Beast becomes Antiochus; in Revelation, it is Domitian.

The Abomination of Desolation (chapter 9) is a "prediction" of Antiochus IV Epiphanes sacrificing a pig on the Jerusalem altar. The "cutting off of the anointed" refers to the assassination of the high priest Onias III. (Priests were anointed for office.) The seventy weeks of years are a scribal reinterpretation of Jeremiah's prophecy of the Exile lasting seventy years. Daniel needs the period of Gentile oppression (not just the literal Exile) to last longer than that, so that the events of his own day may be regarded as the end of it, so he multiplies the 70 years into 490 years. This is not the stuff of genuine prophecy, but of figure-juggling clerical speculation, as is true of the whole apocalyptic genre.

Daniel 10-12 contains detailed "predictions" of the troop movements, etc., of Antiochus Epiphanes and other principals in the Seleucid persecution and the Hasmonean struggle. This is all quite accurate because it is thinly-veiled reporting on contemporary events, attested in Josephus and 1 Maccabees. If the whole thing were really written by Daniel in the sixth century B.C.E., why are the references to Exilic Babylon so confused, while the remote "predictions" are so clear?

Jonah

According to 2 Kings 14:25, the prophet Jonah was active during the glorious reign of Jeroboam II in the northern kingdom, Israel, in the eighth century, and he prophesied during the Syrian wars. In the Book of Jonah he is erroneously placed in the reign of the Assyrian Empire, which had taken over Syria, hence too late for the historical Jonah. The historical Assyrians were bitter tyrants, worse than the Babylonians who replaced them.

Tarshish, where Jonah books passage, was in Tarsus or Spain (or possibly Britain), i.e., as far as possible in the opposite direction to that in which God sent Jonah. The point is to underline Jonah's desire to go as far away as possible. I guess he hadn't yet learned the lesson of Psalm 139:7-12 (KJV): "Whither shall I go from thy Spirit? Or whither shall I flee from thy presence?"

The motif of a Jewish traveler among Gentiles being the only one whose prayers serve to calm the stormy sea also occurs elsewhere, though Jonah may be the first incidence of it.

It is also quite clear that the Markan tale (Mark 4:35-41) of Jesus asleep in the boat in the midst of a storm, being awakened by frantic disciples, and stilling the storm as a concession to their scant faith, is derived from the Jonah story.

The episode of Jonah's gourd growing up and withering instantly marks the story as legendary. It is reminiscent of Jesus cursing the fig tree (Mark 11:12-14, 20-21). It is interesting to speculate whether the gourd episode may have been, all by itself, the original seed of Mark's story.

While being digested by the fish, Jonah passes the time singing a thank-offering psalm (Jonah 2:2-9, ASV):

2I called by reason of mine affliction unto Jehovah,
    And he answered me;
Out of the belly of Sheol cried I,
    And thou heardest my voice.
3For thou didst cast me into the depth, in the heart of the seas,
    And the flood was round about me;
    All thy waves and thy billows passed over me.
4And I said, I am cast out from before thine eyes;
    Yet I will look again toward thy holy temple.
5The waters compassed me about, even to the soul;
    The deep was round about me;
    The weeds were wrapped about my head.

6I went down to the bottoms of the mountains;
    The earth with its bars closed upon me for ever:
    Yet hast thou brought up my life from the pit, O Jehovah my God.
7When my soul fainted within me, I remembered Jehovah;
    And my prayer came in unto thee, into thy holy temple.
8They that regard lying vanities
    Forsake their own mercy.
9But I will sacrifice unto thee with the voice of thanksgiving;
    I will pay that which I have vowed.
    Salvation is of Jehovah.

Of course, the compiler has borrowed such a psalm and inserted it here because of the metaphors of sinking and drowning, plus the reference to the unanswered prayers of idolaters. But I have to suspect that, underlying the whole story, is a Deuteronomic demythologization of the Sacred King mythology, formerly ritualized in the yearly enthronement festival. In it, remember, the king acted the role of Yahweh devoured by Leviathan the sea dragon (just as Marduk was swallowed by Tiamat), then bursting forth resurrected and triumphant.

I think Matthew 12:40 (NASB) reflects this: "for just as Jonah was three days and three nights in the belly of the sea monster, so will the Son of Man be three days and three nights in the heart of the earth." This would be only one of several instances of the Sacred King mythology, censored from formative Judaism, going underground to re-emerge in Christian Christology.

The point of the Book of Jonah is to rebuke the narrow nationalism of the party of Ezra and Nehemiah.[13] What brilliant irony! God sends the prophet on Mission Impossible: converting the worst of the pagans, and it *works*! But the prophet didn't *want* it to! He would have much preferred seeing them all rot!

The chief difficulty in accepting the Book of Jonah as history is not the oddity of a man surviving being swallowed by a whale, which some claim is possible, but rather the fantasy of the Assyrian Empire converting to Judaism! There is no record of such a thing, and you can bet your sweet bippy there would have been if it had happened.

Judith

Her name suggests that our protagonist is supposed to be a symbol for Jewry in general. Judith is more specifically a combination of Rahab from Joshua 2 and Jael from Judges 4:17-22. Like the former, she appears to be a fifth columnist ready to abandon her sinful people and side with the winners, whom she sees God has sent as a scourge of judgment. Only with Judith, this is a pose. Like Jael, she assassinates a powerful enemy of Israel while he sleeps. In both cases, the heroism of a woman is a lesson in Deuteronomic theology: God wins the victory through unconventional and unexpected means, not only by the might of armies.

Judith to some degree shares with the pious Ammonite Achior the role of the heathen prophet (of Yahweh!), Balaam from Numbers 22, who warned Balak, an enemy king, that Israel could not be defeated unless induced to unfaithfulness to God.

It is hard to know what to make of the gross historical inaccuracy of the Book of Judith, even as a piece of historical fiction. *Nebuchadnezzer*, king of the *Assyrians*? He was rather the Babylonian conqueror of Assyria. And all this happens after the return from the Babylonian Exile and the rebuilding of the Temple!

Tobit

Set during the Assyrian Exile, before Nebuchadnezzr, the Book of Tobit sings the virtues of a charity close to the standard advocated in the gospels: Tobit gives all his surplus income away to the poor, even to the point of his own impoverishment. He also goes way out of his way to provide burial for the poor. Burial of the indigent dead was a major act of charity among Jews, presupposed when Joseph of Arimathea petitions Pilate for custody of Jesus' body so he may provide it a decent burial. Tobit even defies the law to bury the dead, just like Antigone in Sophocles' play of the same name.

He counsels the reader that charity brings rewards from God, and most of the book is dedicated to showing how right he is: God sends the healing archangel Raphael to cure his blindness and to expel the demon Asmodeus (his name denotes his Persian origin), who has a romantic obsession for Sarah, a relative of Tobit, who winds up engaged to his son Tobias. She has been married five times previously, but before she could consummate the marriage, jealous Asmodeus has killed each of the grooms in turn (cf., Mark 12:20-22)! But Raphael supplies a smelly demon repellant and saves the day.

As Randel Helms[14] points out, it appears likely that Raphael's farewell speech in chapter 12 forms the basis of the scene in John 20:17, in which Jesus says, in practically the same words, "I am ascending" etc. Here's what Raphael says in Tobit 12:

> Surely I will keep close nothing from you. For I said, it was good to keep close the secret of a King, but that it was honorable to reveal the works of God. Now therefore, when thou didst pray, and Sara thy daughter in Law, I did bring the remembrance of your prayers before the holy one, and when thou didst bury the dead, I was with thee likewise. And when thou didst not delay to rise up, and leave thy dinner to go and cover the dead, thy good deed was not hid from me: but I was with thee. And now God hath sent me to heal thee, & Sara thy daughter in law. I am Raphael one of the seven holy Angels, which present the prayers of the Saints, and which go in and out before the glory of the Holy one. (vv. 11-15, KJV)

His two listeners "were both alarmed; and they fell upon their faces, for they were afraid." Fear not, is Raphael's reponse:

> Then they were both troubled, and fell upon their faces: for they feared. But he said unto them, fear not, for it shall go well with you, praise God therefore. For not of any favour of mine, but by the will of our God I came, wherefore praise him for ever. All these days I did appear unto you, but I did neither eat nor drink, but you did see a vision. Now therefore give [Yahweh] thanks: for I go up to him that sent me, but write all things which are done, in a book.

> And when they rose, they saw him no more. Then they confessed the great and wonderful works of God, and how the Angel of the Lord had appeared unto them. (vv. 16-22, KJV)

And just as Raphael discloses that his seeming physical presence all along has been an illusion, Jesus' command not to touch him may denote the same thing.

Notes

1. Richard I. Pervo, *Profit with Delight: The Literary Genre of the Acts of the Apostles* (Philadelphia: Fortress Press, 1987), pp. xi-xii.

2. Tzvetan Todorov, *The Poetics of Prose.* Trans. Richard Howard (Ithaca: Cornell University Press, 1977), Chapter 5, "Narrative-Men," pp. 66-79.

3. The demigoddess Oprah Winfrey was named for her, but her mom misspelled it—no kidding!

4. Jane Schaberg, *The Illegitimacy of Jesus: A Feminist Theological Interpretation of the Infancy Narratives* (New York: Harper & Row, 1987), pp. 26-29.

5. Harry Emerson Fosdick, *A Guide to Understanding the Bible: The Development of Ideas within the Old and New Testaments* (New York: Harper & Brothers, 1938), pp. 33-34.

6. Herodotus, *The Histories*, Book One. Trans. Aubrey de Selincourt Penguin Classics (Baltimore: Penguin Books, 1954), pp. 44-45.

7. S.R. Driver, *An Introduction to the Literature of the Old Testament*. International Theological Library (Edinburgh: T. & T. Clark, Fourth Edition, 1892), p. 453.

8. Martin Noth, "The Understanding of History in Old Testament Apocalyptic." In Noth, *The Laws in the Pentateuch and other Studies*. Trans. D.R. Ap-Thomas (London: SCM Press, 1984), pp. 201-203.

9. From 4Q242. See Jona Lendering, "Cyrus Takes Babylon: Daniel & Prayer of Nabonidus," livius.org/ct-cz/cyrus_l/babylon04.html.

10. If you like the Bel episode, may I heartily recommend a science fiction novel by Edgar Rice Burroughs, *A Fighting Man of Mars*, in which earthman Ulysses Paxton exposes the sham of the priests of Tur, a great idol worshipped by the backward Phondahlians on Barsoom (Mars). And, of course, take a look at *The Wizard of Oz*: "Er, pay no attention to the man behind the curtain!"

11. Maurice Casey, *Son of Man: The Interpretation and Influence of Daniel 7* (London: SPCK, 1979), Chapter 9, "The Son of Man Problem," pp. 224-40.

12. Hermann Gunkel, *Creation and Chaos in the Primeval Era and the Eschaton: A Religio-Historical Study of Genesis 1 and Revelation 12*. Trans. K. William Whitney, Jr. (Grand Rapids: Eerdmans, 2006).

13. Fosdick, *Guide*, pp. 33-34.

14. Randel Helms, *Gospel Fictions* (Buffalo: Prometheus Books, 1988), pp. 145-48.

VII

Psalms, Song of Solomon, Lamentations, Psalms of Solomon, Prayer of Manassah, The Song of Azariah and the Three Young Men

Music of the Spheres

The Psalms

Words without Music

Have you ever been reading in the Book of Psalms, identifying with the spiritual struggles or joys of the poet–and then you run smack-dab into some strange-sounding verse about the king, or some battle? The spell is broken, and you know you're missing something. Well, this shows that, in Thomas S. Kuhn's terms,[1] you have been reading the text according to a paradigm that doesn't quite fit: the idea that the Psalms were written to be what you read them for, namely devotional poems.[2]

We seek new and better *paradigms*, models for understanding a text (or any body of evidence), when we run up against anomalous data, facts that stick out like a sore thumb in terms of the old paradigm. Can we come up with a new paradigm that will preserve as much as possible of the old understanding while extending the explanation to cover the hitherto puzzling anomalous data? Yes, we can.

Old Testament scholars have long realized the fact, and the implications of the fact, that the Book of Psalms is the hymn book of the Second Temple (i.e., the post-Exilic Temple). The Psalms in it are not poems but rather song lyrics.

With the possible exception of the so-called Wisdom Psalms or Torah Psalms[3] (e.g., Psalms 1, 19, 90, and 119), which are very late additions by the scribes who copied and compiled the book,[4] by far most of the Psalms are song lyrics used on official religious and state occasions. Hence the frequent mentions of the king, the dynasty of David, fortunes of war, etc. Some scholars[5] think virtually every first-person psalm was written to be sung by (or in the name of) the reigning king, perhaps as the representative of the people.

On the other hand, it is possible that some of them, especially lamentation psalms and thank-offering psalms, were at some point made available for an individual worshipper to choose when he wanted to seek divine help or to thank God for it.[6] The lyrics might not be the tightest fit, but that wouldn't make them any more difficult to apply to the common worshipper than it is for modern readers to do so.

Another possibility is that some of those psalms that lack specific references to royalty, battles, and national misfortunes may have been composed by (or for) individual worshippers, using the general pattern of "official" psalms. Sometimes an individual worshipper, probably a wealthier one, would explain his situation, then ask the Levitical musician to compose (or choose) a psalm and perform it, and the worshipper would offer an appropriate sacrifice.[7]

Such commissioned psalms would have been deposited in the Temple archives as a kind of votive offering. These would eventually have been incorporated in the Psalter even though never performed ritually.[8] Or their specific complaints might have been generalized to make the psalm more generally applicable. This is why the predicaments alluded to in the texts are so general and vague: "One size fits all." *Put your name here!*[9]

Some psalms seem to refer, albeit cagily, to specific situations, e.g., military reversals, suggesting the texts were written for the king on particular (now irrecoverable) historical occasions, then "generalized" for subsequent (royal) use when analogous situations should arise. It is this specificity-minus-details that has tempted scholars to connect this or that psalm to some particular occasion recounted in the Deuteronomic History.

Of course, this is exactly the kind of guesswork that led ancient editors of the Psalter (Book of Psalms) to credit various psalms to David at particular points in his career ("A Psalm of David when he lost a game of checkers with Goliath"). But the undermining of our confidence in the historical veracity of the Old Testament narrative has rendered fanciful these scholarly attempts (both ancient and modern)[10] to "pin the tail on the Bible."[11]

We should recognize these attempts to provide possible historical settings for individual psalms as exactly analogous to the process whereby ancient Christians fabricated "pronouncement stories" in order to supply a context for what reached them as isolated aphorisms of Jesus. By positing, after the fact, a "joke" for which the saying would plausibly serve as a "punch line," a Christian thinker sought to interpret the saying. "Maybe *this* is what he was talking about."

Again, the same thing happened when Islamic savants tried to imagine what certain unclear references in the Koran might have presupposed. Such extrapolations eventually accumulated to the point that an entire imaginary biography of the Prophet Muhammad was the result.

Writing Staff

Who wrote the Psalms? No doubt it was the guild of Levitical singers and musicians whose functions are sometimes said to include prophesying. Occasional statements (e.g., Psalm 45:1) imply authorship by a prophesying Levite, or, as they are often called, "cultic prophets."[12] I think the contribution of such individuals has been significantly overestimated. Aubrey Johnson tended to spot a cult prophet around every corner, whenever God is the first-person speaker in a psalm, offering words of rebuke, absolution, or blessing.

Of course, we see a vast amount of this kind of thing in the books of the Prophets. Isaiah, Jeremiah, and the rest constantly speak as the mouthpieces for Yahweh. (Or at least whoever composed the prophetic books employed these names to introduce long speeches "from God" in the manner of Greek tragedians.) Johnson seems to read the Psalms the same way he reads Isaiah and Jeremiah: as transcripts of oral preaching. But just as Isaiah and Jeremiah read like literary compositions, so do the Psalms.

In other words, it seems more natural to picture a Psalmist working like a poet or a playwright, imagining what God would say to the congregation in this or that circumstance. It seems to me that a vitiating confusion runs through Johnson's interpretation paradigm.

Crucial to his theory is the frequent occurrence of sudden turnabouts in the Psalms: The speaker first tells his sob story about sickness, conspiring enemies, impending military disasters, then beams with new courage and confidence that God has heard his plaint and promised the requested deliverance.

Whence the abrupt reversal? With other scholars, Johnson posits that at the pivot point of such psalms we must imagine an auspicious oracle pronounced on the spot by a cult prophet standing by.[13] But since the psalms were pro forma scripts for repeated use, doesn't this imply that the cult prophet merely played a role, giving the oracular thumbs-up as a matter of course? Like the gaggle of yes-men court prophets whose job was to give the rubber stamp to every plan King Ahab ran by them (1 Kings 22:8)?[14] Johnson doesn't seem to envision the possibility of a "no."

Besides, there is an older theory that makes fewer assumptions. The individual singing such a psalm (or paying to have it sung in his name) would ritually (i.e., as part of the script) express confident gratitude that his prayer would be answered (whether he felt it or not!). "Therefore I say to you, all things for which you pray and ask, believe that you have received them, and they will be granted you" (Mark 11:24, NASB). Nowadays we call it an "affirmation."

Only a Northern Song

Relying on form criticism, scholars have inferred the use, as I have said, of many psalms, with their mentions of kings, in the Temple of Solomon and then, after the return from the Babylonian Exile, in the Second Temple. But in light of recent archaeological evidence, it now appears that Judah (Yehud) became any sort of a state only in the wake of the Assyrian conquest of the kingdom of Israel ("the House of Omri" as it is known in ancient records), and that thus there had never been a Davidic monarchy there, much less a Solomonic Temple.

These facts must cause a basic reevaluation of the origin and use of these "royal" psalms. Where did they originate? Who used them, if not the (legendary) Davidic kings of Judah? It is not that scholars have been misreading the "royal psalms" *as* royal; no other interpretation makes nearly as much sense of the texts. But the *Sitz-im-Leben* (life setting) must be reassessed. And there do seem to be some viable possibilities.

First, it has long been theorized[15] that a number of psalms written for the use of the Israelite kings of the north were carried south after the Assyrian conquest. Michael D. Goulder[16] made a powerful case that two important groups of psalms made this journey, the Psalms of the Sons of Korah (originally used in the Temple at Dan) and the Psalms of Asaph (from the Temple at Bethel). Once these psalms were relocated, a number of references were changed, "Dan" and "Bethel" being replaced with "Zion" and "Jerusalem," though leaving enough loose ends to allow Goulder's detective work. There may well have been other northern psalms that moved south at some point.

We would have to adjust our estimate of how late these made their journey south. At the earliest, they would have begun to be sung in the Jerusalem Temple "re"built by Zerubbabel, the so-called "Second Temple," but actually the very first in Jerusalem. Zerubbabel was ordained Davidic king by the prophets Haggai[17] and Zechariah (4:1-10), accounting for the frequent appeals in the psalms to a supposedly ancient covenant struck between the legendary King David (the Jewish King Arthur) and God.

Some suggest that "David" originated as a kingly epithet ("Beloved"), not a proper name of an historical character. It seems to have been used as a title, with no reference to King David, in some semi-nomadic tribes.[18] Could "David" have been the mythical-sacramental identity of the kings as vicars or avatars for Yahweh specifically during the enthronement festival?[19]

But it is also possible that these royal psalms originated among the Hasmonean priest-kings of the second century B.C.E. This date has been defended by a number of scholars[20] even before Minimalism reared its controversial head, but it never gained much support because, until now, even critical scholars have been blithely willing to take the fictive sagas of the Deuteronomic History at face value and to try to locate the origin of various psalms at various points in that "history."[21]

Now, however, archaeological results pretty much force us to take a second look at the possibility of "Maccabean Psalms." Often those who argued against such late dates for specific psalms merely demonstrated that those dates were unnecessary since good enough sense could be made of these texts in a centuries-earlier context. But, again, that earlier period is now rendered off-limits. Besides, the mere "fact" of a viable exegetical fit with an earlier date in no way disproves a snug possible fit with a later one.[22]

Sigmund Mowinckel rejected Hermann Gunkel's opinion that some psalms came from pietistic schismatic sects.[23] But a Hasmonean date might imply that they did, namely that of the schismatic Zadokite priesthood who broke with the Pharisees during Hasmonean times.[24] And doesn't Mowinckel begin to imagine something like this in his discussion of "a religious split in the congregation"?[25] And if many psalms do belong to the Hasmonean era, we have to take a second look at earlier suggestions by scholars that the seemingly royal "I" of many psalms may actually have belonged to the High Priest,[26] who, in the absence of a monarch, played his role in the liturgy.[27] Now we must adjust the theory to suppose that the royal "I" denoted the Hasmonean (Levitical) priest-kings such as John Hyrcanus.

Indeed, this possibility sheds new light on the inaugural Psalm 110, in which the new sovereign is told that Yahweh "has sworn and will not change his mind," still designating him as "a priest for ever after the order of Melchizedek." Scholars[28] have traditionally understood this psalm as reflecting the assimilation of the pre-Davidic royal priesthood of Melchizedek, Adonizedek, etc., in Salem (Jerusalem) to the Davidic monarchy upon David's conquest of the city. The Jebusite priesthood would thus have been co-opted by the Davidic kings, much as Alexander the Great declared himself to be of Pharaonic descent to soften the blow of his conquest of Egypt.

According to this theory, this dual Davidic role of priest-king eventually succumbed to a Deuteronomic "secularization" of the royal office, leaving priestly matters to the Levitical caste. But what if Psalm 110 had its origin among the Hasmoneans, in order to patch their dynasty, all Levites, into the royal line, *creating* the dual office of Jewish priest-king?

The logic would mirror that of Hebrews 7:11-17, where Jesus is made a priest though he hailed from the tribe of Judah, not Levi, by appeal to the higher priesthood of immortal Melchizedek. Only in this case the point would be to legitimate a line of Levites as kings despite their lack of Judean (Davidic) credentials, again, by appeal to Melchizedek, this time as a king.

Or how about this? As all scholars know, the biblical psalms closely conform to the pattern of ancient Canaanite, Assyrian, and Babylonian psalms, used on much the same occasions. What if some or most of the biblical psalms have simply been borrowed lock, stock, and barrel from these cultures? This hypothesis does not even necessitate the suggestion of a systematic substitution of "Yahweh" for the names of heathen deities. Keep in mind, after all, that "Aleyon" (Baal) was only a variant of "Elyon," and that Baal was also known as "Yaw" (the biblical Yahweh, Yah, Yahu).[29]

Hosea 2:16 tells us that Yahweh and Baal were, in Israel, two names for the same God, though eventually some sought to distinguish them: "'And in that day,' says the Lord, 'you will call me, "my husband," and no longer will you call me, "my Baal."'" This should occasion no surprise in view of the extensive parallels between the mythic characterizations of Baal and Yahweh, "both" being cloud-riding storm gods, etc. If, as now seems evident, the Israelites were simply Canaanites themselves, this identity between their religions is just what we should expect. And the royal and ritual psalms of the adjacent monarchies might easily have simply been borrowed later, once Judah had its own monarchy, however late that development occurred.

That Old Time Religion

You know how it creates all sorts of strife and bickering whenever a church denomination announces they are going to revise their hymn books? The revisers want to update hymns, to re-word, censor, or eliminate lyrics that contain old theology that is considered crude or offensive by modern standards ("There is a fountain filled with blood drawn from Emmanuel's veins, and sinners plunged beneath that flood lose all their guilty stains . . ."). But many do not want their beloved old hymns tampered with, even if they themselves no longer hold to the out-dated theology. This explains why many of the psalms preserve bits and pieces of archaic theology and mythology, part and parcel of the "royal ideology" of Sacred Kingship. This involved the belief that the king was Yahweh's caliph or vicar on earth.

> Thy throne, O God, is for ever and ever: A sceptre of equity is the sceptre of thy kingdom. (Psalm 45:6, ASV)[30]

> For unto us a child is born, unto us a son is given; and the government shall be upon his shoulder: and his name shall be called Wonderful Counsellor, Mighty God, Everlasting Father, Prince of Peace. (Isa. 9:6, ASV)

The king was God's son:

> I will tell of the decree: Jehovah said unto me, "Thou art my son; this day have I begotten thee." (Psalm 2:7, ASV)

> He shall cry unto me, "Thou art my Father, My God, and the rock of my salvation." I also will make him my first-born, the highest of the kings of the earth. (Psalm 89:26-27, ASV)[31]

He was also God's anointed:

> The kings of the earth set themselves, and the rulers take counsel together, against Jehovah, and against his anointed. (Psalm 2:2, ASV)

> I have found David my servant; with my holy oil have I anointed him. (Psalm 89:20, ASV)

The king annually renewed his divine mandate to rule, and with it the very vigor of the cosmos and fertility of the land, by re-enacting the myth of how Yahweh became king of the gods. (It was a common myth told all over the ancient world for the same purpose, just with different divine names in different countries.) The story was that the gods were frightened ("Will you be laid low even at the sight of him?", Job 41:9) by the menace of the Chaos Dragons, including seven-headed Leviathan. All from the NASB:

> Let those curse it who curse the day, who are prepared to rouse Leviathan. (Job 3:8)

> You crushed the heads of Leviathan; you gave him as food for the creatures of the wilderness. (Psalm 74:14)

> In that day [Yahweh] will punish Leviathan the fleeing serpent, with his fierce and great and mighty sword, even Leviathan the twisted serpent; and he will kill the dragon who lives in the sea. (Isa. 27:1)

> Behold, a great red dragon having seven heads and ten horns, and on his heads were seven diadems . . . . And there was war in heaven, Michael and his angels waging war with the dragon. (Rev. 12:3, 7)

Nehushtan was apparently another name for Leviathan. "He broke in pieces the bronze serpent that Moses had made, for until those days the people of Israel had burned incense to it; it was called Nehushtan" (2 Kings 18:4, RSV). Rahab was another sea monster, if not still another name for the same one (Job 26:12-13; Psalm 89:10; Isa. 51:9). The monster Behemoth dwelt on land (Job 40:15-24). Yamm was the sea personified, also the enemy of Baal in the Canaanite epics (Psalm 74:13, 89:9).

Tiamat, the dragon slain by Marduk in the Babylonian version, lies behind Genesis 1:2's *"tohu"* ("the deep") and *"tehom"* ("without form"), followed by *"bohu"* ("void"), alluding to Behemoth.[32] Tiamat, in fact, is the plural form of *tehom*, while Behemoth is the plural of *bohu*.[33]

Then the young god Yahweh stepped forth to meet the challenge. He was a war-god, "a man of war" (Exod. 15:3). And he was a storm-god as well: "On the morning of the third day there were thunders and lightnings, and a thick cloud upon the mountain, and a very loud trumpet blast, so that all the people who were in the camp trembled" (Exod. 19:16). Psalm 18:7-15 and Psalm 29:3-9 describe the fearful majesty of this god, who creates a thick darkness of clouds and then breaks through it with hailstones and coals of fire, thundering in the heavens, shaking the wilderness and stripping the forest bare.

Yahweh was one of the sons of El Elyon, the "Most High God":

Ascribe to [Yahweh], O [sons of El], ascribe to [Yahweh] glory and strength. (Psalm 29:1, NASB)

For who in the skies can be compared to [Yahweh]? Who among the [sons of El] is like [Yahweh], a God feared in the council of the holy ones, great and terrible above all that are round about him? (Psalm 89:6-7, RSV)

when men began to multiply on the face of the land, and daughters were born to them, that the sons of God saw that the daughters of men were beautiful; and they took wives for themselves, whomever they chose . . . . The Nephilim were on the earth in those days, and also afterward, when the sons of God came in to the daughters of men, and they bore children to them. Those were the mighty men who were of old, men of renown. (Gen. 6:1-2, 4, NASB)

Now there was a day when the sons of God came to present themselves before [Yahweh], and Satan also came among them (Job 1:6; 2:1, NASB).

God versus Godzilla

Yahweh had been in charge of a single nation, Israel. "When the Most High [Elyon] gave to the nations their inheritance, when he separated the sons of men, he fixed the bounds of the peoples according to the number of the sons of God" (Deut. 32:8, RSV), i.e., he took a head count of the lesser gods and divided the human race into enough nations that each godling would have one to rule and to be worshipped by. But now Yahweh made his bid to take the throne over them all. He volunteered to destroy the dragons if the gods would agree to make him king.

They signed on, and he did destroy the monsters. He crushed "the heads of Leviathan" (Psalm 74:14), punished Leviathan as it fled (Isa. 27:1), and scattered his enemies with his mighty arm (Psalm 89:10). He stilled the sea, smote Rahab, and pierced the fleeing serpent (Job 26:13; Isa. 27:1, 51:9). Per Job 41:1-5, which asks if a mere mortal could play with Leviathan "as with a bird," or "put him on a leash for your maiden," Yahweh subdued and tamed rather than destroyed the dragon.

Then he took the throne (all NASB):

[Yahweh] my King is from of old, Who works deeds of deliverance in the midst of the earth. (Psalm 74:12)

You have a strong arm; Your hand is mighty, Your right hand is exalted. Righteousness and justice are the foundation of Your throne; Lovingkindness and truth go before You. (Psalm 89:13-14)

Your throne is established from of old; You are from everlasting. (Psalm 93:2)

[Yahweh] is a great God, and a great King above all gods. (Psalm 95:3)

[Yahweh] reigns; let the earth rejoice; let the many islands be glad. Clouds and thick darkness surround Him; Righteousness and justice are the foundation of his throne. (Psalm 97:1-2)

He was enthroned alongside El Elyon, perhaps as co-regent. So we read in the already ancient creation myth embodied in Daniel 7:2-7, 9-10, 11b, 13-14. From the carcass of the dragon(s) he created the world, just as Marduk did when he split open the slain Tiamat, using the upper half of her shell for the heavenly firmament, the lower for the flat earth.

You broke open springs and torrents; You dried up ever-flowing streams. Yours is the day, Yours also is the night; You have prepared the light and the sun. You have established all the boundaries of the earth; You have made summer and winter. (Psalm 74:15-17, NASB)

The heavens are Yours, the earth also is Yours; the world and all it contains, You have founded them. The north and the south, You have created them; Tabor and Hermon shout for joy at Your name. (Psalm 89:11-12, NASB)

[Yahweh] reigns, He is clothed with majesty; [Yahweh] has clothed and girded Himself with strength; Indeed, the world is firmly established, it will not be moved. (Psalm 93:1b, NASB).

It is striking that generations of Bible readers have been oblivious of this absolutely fundamental myth system underlying so much of the Bible (even the Book of Revelation in the New Testament). It is equally striking how much the same schema makes new and total sense of certain psalm texts which otherwise seem to be choppy and disjointed to the point of incoherence. There are verses about God slaying dragons, then verses about the foundation of God's kingdom, then verses about how he created the earth. Two prime examples are Psalms 74 and 89.

Where's the train of thought? You scratch your head and chalk it up as yet another of those puzzles to be cleared up one day in the sweet bye-and-bye, in that heavenly seminar on "apparent" Bible contradictions. But you don't have to wait. You just have to read between the lines, supplying the concepts the psalmists left tacit since in their day people understood them.[34]

Yahweh killed Leviathan and Rahab, just as the Babylonian Marduk slew Tiamat and Apsu, just as Baal killed Mot and Yamm. This victory earned him the throne of the immortals, whereupon he used the carcasses of the defeated monsters as the raw materials to make the natural world. We can finally connect the dots. But it remains a mystery to fundamentalist readers who have never had it pointed out to them and wouldn't like it if they did. They espouse the supernatural, but even for them there are limits! Dragons? No thanks!

Mowinckel and others tell us that the enthronement mythology was derived from the Canaanites.[35] This judgment depends on taking at face value the Old Testament portrayal of the Canaanites. But that was before we realized that the Israelites simply *were* Canaanites. It was *their own* religion.

By the time our Old Testament was written, "Canaanite" religion was a kind of fictive scapegoat employed to condemn earlier Israelite beliefs once they had been repudiated. Later biblical writers could not deny the earlier presence of such beliefs and rites among Israelites, so they had to pretend these elements represented syncretism from an alien source.

Unification Theology

Eventually, the two gods Elyon (El, Elohim) and Yahweh were merged into one: "Abram said to the king of Sodom, 'I have sworn to [Yahweh El Elyon], possessor of heaven and earth,'" etc. (Gen. 14:22, NASB).[36] The biblical god El (Elohim, Elyon) was simply the same deity as the Canaanite god El. Baal was El's son and was also called "Yaw,"[37] i.e., Yahweh. He was also known as "Aleyan Baal," which is a combination exactly analogous to "Yahweh El Elyon," since "Aleyan" is the same as "Elyon," "Most High."

Thus Yahweh El Elyon is Aleyan Baal.[38] The sons of El henceforth become a council with whom Yahweh consults. See Psalm 89:5, 1 Kings 22:19-22, and Genesis 3:22 (cf. Gen. 11:6-7) for descriptions of Yahweh being praised "in the assembly of the holy ones," sitting on his throne with "all the host of heaven" on either side, and speaking of the man as becoming "like one of us."

Psalm 82

The Israelite pantheon, like their Canaanite alter egos, would convene up on Mt. Zaphon in Lebanon. "You said in your heart, 'I will ascend to heaven; I will raise my throne above the stars of God; I will sit on the mount of assembly on the heights of Zaphon'" (Isa. 14:13, NRSV). This went on until Yahweh finally condemned them for their misrule of their nations[39] and sent them to the shadowy Netherworld of Sheol, where their blind stumblings provide the ancient explanation for earthquakes. Here's Psalm 82 (ASV):

1God standeth in the congregation of God;
    He judgeth among the gods.
2How long will ye judge unjustly,
    And respect the persons of the wicked? *Selah*

3Judge the poor and fatherless:
    Do justice to the afflicted and destitute.
4Rescue the poor and needy:
    Deliver them out of the hand of the wicked.
5They know not, neither do they understand;
    They walk to and fro in darkness:
    All the foundations of the earth are shaken.
6I said, Ye are gods,
    And all of you sons of [Elyon].
7Nevertheless ye shall die like men,
    And fall like one of the princes.
8Arise, O God, judge the earth;
    For thou shalt inherit all the nations.

Yahweh Resurrected

It seems quite likely that Yahweh was supposed to have been killed and devoured by the dragon, then rose again to defeat him, as did Baal and Marduk.[40] This would have been reflected in the royal humiliation ritual in which, bearing the sins of the nation, the king set aside his crown, was slapped by the priest, donned his crown again, and sat down upon the throne.[41] Isaiah 53 would preserve this liturgy. As Geo Widengren points out, when

Psalm 18:46 proclaims, "[Yahweh] lives!" it sounds an awful lot like the liturgy for Baal's resurrection: "Aleyan Baal lives!"

Many scholars agree that the humiliation ritual was shared with surrounding cultures but slam on the brakes short of positing the death of Yahweh as the mythic basis for the ceremonial humiliation. Mowinckel cannot allow that such pagan notions found a place in Israelite religion,[42] but I cannot help regarding this (essentially theological) distaste as a vestige of the then-popular axiom that Israel's religion was radically different from that of their heathen Canaanite neighbors, however much of their lore Israel might have borrowed at inessential points.[43] Goulder[44] also rejects the notion that Israel thought of Yahweh, like his counterpart Baal, as trapped in the netherworld for half the year.

But he describes an atonement ritual and ordeal in the course of the festival in which the king (later replaced by a priest as surrogate)[45] was confined in a subterranean pit. Through it, the stream at Dan flowed. That certainly seems to imply the king was on such occasions acting the role of the slain God, Yahweh, whose earthly vicar he was (Psalm 42:6-7).[46]

Psalm 88

Other psalms, like Psalm 88:3-7 (ASV), seem to imply the same thing:

3For my soul is full of troubles,
   And my life draweth nigh unto Sheol.
4I am reckoned with them that go down into the pit;
   I am as a man that hath no help,
5Cast off among the dead,
   Like the slain that lie in the grave,
   Whom thou rememberest no more,
   And they are cut off from thy hand.
6Thou hast laid me in the lowest pit,
   In dark places, in the deeps.
7Thy wrath lieth hard upon me,
   And thou hast afflicted me with all thy waves.

As Goulder notes,[47] Widengren[48] understands Psalm 88 as referring to the ritual reenactment by the king of Yahweh's death. Mowinckel admits that Psalms 48 and 68 incorporate the Canaanite myth of Baal's victory over Mot (Death personified, as in Revelation 6:8, 20:13-14), applying it to Yahweh.[49] Goulder[50] admits this was the ritual logic underlying Psalm 88 but gratuitously posits that the death and resurrection element had been removed from the theology when Israel appropriated the ritual from Canaan. Again, he just couldn't imagine biblical Israel entertaining such heresy.

There are no "messianic psalms,"[51] in the usual sense, certainly not Psalm 22.[52] But to think there are represents an understandable near miss. The Jewish hope for a messianic deliverer was a product of chronic oppression by foreign powers. Jews dreamed of a day when some heir to the Davidic dynasty would come forward as God's agent to expel and conquer the Gentile empires and to restore the (legendary) glories of the (equally legendary) King David.

This expectation was much like that according to which King Arthur would one day return from the Isle of Avalon to rescue England in her hour of need. As, in the absence of a Jewish monarchy, the old royal psalms, particularly the psalms of inauguration and enthronement,[53] were no longer understood, the occasion for their use having dropped away, these texts were reinterpreted (misinterpreted) as prophecies of the king who would come.[54]

The more spectacular aspects of the Sacred King mythos dropped out of emerging Judaism (what would become Rabbinic Judaism) as Judaism tightened up its monotheism.[55] The notions of the king as an embodiment of God who had died and been raised, whose battle sufferings, reenacted every year, served to atone for the sins of his people, etc., were officially suppressed in the course of the late Deuteronomic (Hasmonean) Reform.

But this mythic complex lived on in popular belief and came to the surface again in the form of the Christian "messianism" of Christology.[56] Jesus was never really understood as the demythologized, purely human Davidic monarch. Christian belief understood him along the lines of an older prototype, the divine king, Yahweh's embodiment on earth.[57]

The royal mythology evolved via being repurposed in another direction as well. As Paul D. Hanson[58] says, it appears that this myth-and-ritual complex was originally intended as a reinforcement of the political and cosmic status quo, the government being an extension of the divine and cosmic order. The order of the world was renewed every year, and it was ostensibly the order imposed and re-imposed by God, not to be challenged.

Against this static worldview, the prophets argued that Yahweh was freely active in an open-ended history. It could not be taken for granted that he would safeguard Mt. Zion and the Temple. He might even send enemies against Israel if he was not pleased with the behavior of the government or the people.

But after the Exile, the returning priestly hierarchy understood their return to power (with official Persian imperial backing) as a fulfillment of prophecy and a divine vindication. Thus they had co-opted the "historicism" of the prophets. After this, the popular prophets (Deutero-Zechariah, Trito-Isaiah, the Dead Seas Scrolls writers) turned the tables, appropriating the old Divine Warrior myth for their own cause, predicting that God would once again whelm the dragon, now understood as the symbol of institutional evil, including the Temple hierarchy.

Psalms of Praise

Hymns (songs of praise) were often sung to the accompaniment of harps and were performed at the offering of sacrifices (Amos 5:21 ff) or during the threshing of grain at harvest time (Hosea 9:1).

The word *Hallelujah* ("Praise Yahweh!") often occurs at the beginning or end of these psalms. Often the hymn begins with the exhortation to the congregation (or the Levitical choir) to "Give praise," "Give thanks," "Sing unto Yahweh" (Psalm 105). When it opens with "I will sing" (Psalm 34:1), it may be an individual or a group singing, as in our hymns today.

Then follows a recital of various things Yahweh is being praised for. Often-used themes include his creation of the world (Psalm 104), involving myths of his conquest of the Chaos Dragon (Psalms 74:13-14; 89:10), his manifestation in natural phenomena including volcanoes, earthquakes, and thunderstorms (Psalm 29), reflecting Yahweh's origin and character as a storm deity. Also, his great saving deeds of the past, like the exodus from Egypt and the plagues. Of course, the point here is to flatter the deity. "Whatever we heard was done at Capernaum, do here in your hometown as well" (Luke 4:23b, NASB).

We can observe the same tendency in Vedic hymns to Indra, celebrating his primordial victory over the dragon Vrtra, who had hoarded all the waters. Indra killed him, renewing life on earth and winning the divine throne, previously occupied by the elder god Varuna.

Note that, like Yahweh, Indra was a storm god and a warrior. These passages about him are from the *Rig Veda* (1.32):[59]

> I will declare the manly deeds of Indra, the first that he achieved, the Thunder-wielder.
> He slew the Dragon, then disclosed the waters, and cleft the channels of the mountain torrents.
> He slew the Dragon lying on the mountain: his heavenly bolt of thunder Tvastar fashioned.
>
> Impetuous as a bull, he chose the Soma and in three sacred beakers drank the juices.[60]
>
> When, Indra, thou hadst slain the dragon's firstborn, and overcome the charms of the enchanters,
> Then, giving life to Sun and Dawn and Heaven, thou foundest not one foe to stand against thee.
> Indra with his own great and deadly thunder smote into pieces Vrtra, worst of Vrtras.
>
> But he, when he had smitten Vrtra, opened the cave wherein the floods had been imprisoned.

Royal Psalms

Enthronement psalms (e.g., Psalm 2, 21, 72, 110) were sung at the coronation of a new king and at the Feast of Tabernacles when the enthronement of Yahweh, king of gods (Psalm 97:9), and the king of Israel/Judah as his earthly vicar, was renewed. This is, of course, the occasion upon which the whole apparatus of the pan-Near Eastern Sacred King mythos was brought to bear.

The real point of the myth was to provide the mandate of heaven for the king, both upon his inauguration and at the annual renewal of his kingship. "I will ask you one question, and you answer Me, and then I will tell you by what authority I do these things. Was the baptism of John from heaven, or from men?" (Mark 11:29-30, NASB). Was the authority of the king from heaven or from men? If the former, then we mere men had better obey him!

Thus the ritual depiction of Yahweh's (or Marduk's or Indra's or Baal's) primeval victory over Leviathan (or Tiamat or Vrtra or Mot), with the king acting the role of the conqueror deity, reinforced the belief in the king as the son and earthly vicar of God. "[W]hatever you bind on earth shall have been bound in heaven, and whatever you loose on earth shall have been loosed in heaven." (Matt. 16:19b, NASB).

It is not hard to imagine the mock battle[61] staged before spectators: The king appeared in shining armor, perhaps with stylized javelins like jagged lightning bolts, and faced a guy dressed in a Godzilla suit[62] (or, if you prefer, a bunch of guys in one of those dragon get-ups familiar from Chinese New Year parades). They circled each other, music playing, the crowd cheering, the scribes chanting the text of the myth, and finally the king "stabbed" his opponent. Then he mounted the steps to the throne to the acclamation of the people. "[Yahweh] reigns! The earth rejoices!" (Psalm 97:1).

Psalm 2

Psalm 2 is probably the most important of the inauguration and kingship renewal psalms. Verses 1-3 seem to presuppose an extensive Israelite/Jewish empire such as never really existed, though it is so depicted in the David stories. But royal rhetoric is sometimes inflated, as in the United Kingdom, where the monarch is still called the sovereign of

"Great Britain, France, and Ireland." The psalmist sings of restive vassal states such as Edom, Moab, and Ammon, conquered by David but beginning to break away again under Solomon, whose attention was elsewhere. Alas, such efforts are sure to come to naught. Yahweh laughs to scorn the best-laid plans of these little mice (Psalm 2, ASV):

> ⁴He that sitteth in the heavens will laugh:
>   The Lord will have them in derision.
> ⁵Then will he speak unto them in his wrath,
>   And vex them in his sore displeasure:
> ⁶Yet I have set my king
>   Upon my holy hill of Zion.
>
> ⁷I will tell of the decree:
>   Jehovah said unto me, Thou art my son;
>   This day have I begotten thee.
> ⁸Ask of me, and I will give thee the nations for thine inheritance,
>   And the uttermost parts of the earth for thy possession.
> ⁹Thou shalt break them with a rod of iron;
>   Thou shalt dash them in pieces like a potter's vessel.

The king of Judah is no mere humanly-appointed ruler but the very son and anointed of God himself! These would-be rebels are going nowhere. Instead of plotting to rebel, these petty kings are advised to submit to God's king and to kiss his feet:

> ¹⁰Now therefore be wise, O ye kings:
>   Be instructed [RSV: *warned*], ye judges of the earth.
> ¹¹Serve Jehovah with fear,
>   And rejoice with trembling.
> ¹²Kiss the son [RSV: *kiss his feet*],
>   lest he be angry, and ye perish in the way,
>   For his wrath will soon be kindled.
>
>   Blessed are all they that take refuge in him.

"The decree of Yahweh" was probably, as in the corresponding Egyptian ritual, a plaque engraved with the words that come next.[63] "You are my son" (Psalm 2:7) was typical in these rituals across the Near East.[64] Usually commentators hasten to assure us that the royal "sonship" was purely honorific,[65] but I think there is no reason to deny the king was believed to partake of divine nature in some metaphysical sense, like the sacred kings of the adjacent nations.[66] The sonship came only with the inauguration: As of that day divine sonship was imparted.

Noth thinks the adoptionist element renders the sonship merely honorific, but this is to repudiate the very aspect most characteristic of the standard royal ideology which the Israelite version otherwise so closely resembles. But Noth is begging the question of "Christology." The sonship element has implicit in it the whole range of possible options that surfaced in early Christian belief about Jesus: merely honorific adoptionism, adoption as the imparting of divine nature or power, monophysitism, monothelitism, a hypostatic union of natures, etc., etc.[67]

Psalm 110

Nearly as important is Psalm 110, which begins with Yahweh telling "my Lord," the king, to sit at his right hand until the king's enemies are subjugated (v. 1). Yahweh sends out of Zion the king's scepter, and the king will rule in the midst of his enemies (v. 2). Then verses 3-4 (ASV):

³Thy people offer themselves willingly
In the day of thy power, in holy array:
Out of the womb of the morning [*Shahar*]
Thou hast the dew of thy youth.
⁴Jehovah hath sworn, and will not repent:
Thou art a priest for ever
After the order of Melchizedek.

Verse 3b refers to Shahar, the Jerusalemite dawn goddess, as the mother of the king, just as Isaiah 14:12 makes the king of Babylon Shahar's royal son. This has not been readily apparent to Bible readers because translators want the pious to buy their Bibles and do not want to ruffle any feathers by letting readers see the names of Israelite deities other than Yahweh.

In the *battle psalms*, the king petitions God for victory, sometimes in the face of discouraging odds (e.g., Psalms 20, 144). Here is a Vedic hymn cut from the same cloth, *Rig Veda* 1.8.**68**

Indra, bring wealth that gives delight, the victor's ever-
conquering wealth,
Most excellent, to be our aid;
By means of which we may repel our foes in battle hand to hand,
By thee assisted with the [chariot].
Aided by thee, the thunder-armed, Indra, may we lift up the bolt,
And conquer all our foes in fight.
With thee, O Indra, for ally with missile-darting heroes, may
We conquer our embattled foes.
Mighty is Indra, yea supreme; greatness be his, the Thunderer:
Wide as the heaven extends his power
Which aideth those to win them sons, who come as heroes to the fight,
Or singers loving holy thoughts.

Psalm 23

Psalms of confidence or protection (e.g., Psalms 23, 121) seem to be responses to auspicious oracles given by cult prophets to the king. This is what Saul sought unsuccessfully on the eve of battle with the Philistines (1 Sam. 28:6), and what Ahab did get from his yes-men court prophets (1 Kings 22:5-6).

As W. Philip Keller,**69** himself having worked as a shepherd in modern Israel, has shown, the justly cherished 23ʳᵈ Psalm is a brilliant set of double entendres, paralleling the details of a shepherd's care of his sheep with God's tender providence on behalf of those who love him. The King James Version is a classic:

¹[Yahweh] is my shepherd;
I shall not want.
²He maketh me to lie down in green pastures:
he leadeth me beside the still waters.
³He restoreth my soul:
he leadeth me in the paths of righteousness
for his name's sake.

⁴Yea, though I walk through the valley of the shadow of death,
I will fear no evil:

for thou art with me;
   thy rod and thy staff
   they comfort me.

5Thou preparest a table before me
   in the presence of mine enemies:
thou anointest my head with oil;
   my cup runneth over.
6Surely goodness and mercy shall follow me
   all the days of my life:
and I will dwell in the house of [Yahweh]
   for ever.

The metaphors in the first two verses (and the second half of v. 4) are obvious enough. Verse 3 seems to refer to both "paths of righteous conduct" and "the right paths," i.e., not paths leading into dangerous terrain or into the midst of predators.

Verse 4's "valley of the shadow of death" is often said to be a real geographical location, perhaps to be identified with the Valley of the Sons of Hinnom, or Tophet, where Israelite infants were once sacrificed to Molech, the god of the fiery underworld. Some say that shepherds led their flocks through that valley, keeping an eye open for thieves swooping down from concealment to steal their sheep. Of course, the application to the pious reader intends the near danger of death from which God may be trusted to deliver one.

"Preparing a table" (v. 5) refers on one level to God "giving us this day our daily bread," but it also plays off the notion of the shepherd preparing a table land for his sheep to graze without danger of poisonous plants or of predators ("mine enemies").

The anointing of the head was the customary pouring of oil (or water) on the head of a guest (Luke 7:44-46) for refreshment (and the ritual anointing of every new king). But for the sake of the extended metaphor it refers to the unguent applied to the head of each sheep to repel buzzing insects.

Psalm 63

Psalm 63 is another one of confidence. Here it is, also in the King James rendition:

1O God, thou art my God; early will I seek thee:
   my soul thirsteth for thee,
my flesh longeth for thee
   in a dry and thirsty land, where no water is;
2To see thy power and thy glory,
   so as I have seen thee in the sanctuary.
3Because thy lovingkindness is better than life,
   my lips shall praise thee.
4Thus will I bless thee while I live:
   I will lift up my hands in thy name.

5My soul shall be satisfied as with marrow and fatness;
   and my mouth shall praise thee with joyful lips:
6When I remember thee upon my bed,
   and meditate on thee in the night watches.
7Because thou hast been my help,
   therefore in the shadow of thy wings will I rejoice.
8My soul followeth hard after thee:
   thy right hand upholdeth me.

9But those that seek my soul, to destroy it,
   shall go into the lower parts of the earth.
10They shall fall by the sword:

they shall be a portion for foxes.
¹¹But the king shall rejoice in God;
      every one that sweareth by him shall glory:
      but the mouth of them that speak lies shall be stopped.

The notion of the worshipper seeing God in the sanctuary may refer to the sight of the high priest emerging from behind the Temple veil with the sacred name Yahweh emblazoned on his turban, having become the very embodiment of Yahweh.[70] But one has to wonder if it might instead imply that the worshipper, a Levite or a priest, has imbibed some sacred hallucinogen.[71]

That was the practice of the ancient Vedic priests who sacramentally drank Soma, apparently the juice of the mushroom Amanita Muscaria.[72] A Vedic hymn to Soma, the personified mushroom of immortality, offers a vivid account of the visionary ecstasy produced by a hallucinogen. This passage was excerpted from the *Rig Veda* 9.113:[73]

Let Indra the killer of Vritra drink Soma in Saryanavat,[74] gathering his strength within himself, to do a great heroic deed. O drop of Soma, flow for Indra.
[. . .] Pressed with sacred words, with truth and faith and ardour,[75] O drop of Soma, flow for Indra.
[. . .]
You speak of the sacred, as your brightness is sacred; you speak the truth, as your deeds are true. You speak of faith, King Soma, as you are carefully prepared by the sacrificial priest. O drop of Soma, flow for Indra.
The floods of the high one, the truly awesome one, flow together. The juices of him so full of juice mingle together as you, the tawny one, purify yourself with prayer. O drop of Soma, flow for Indra. Where the high priest speaks rhythmic words, O Purifier, holding the pressing-stone,[76] feeling that he has become great with the Soma, giving birth to joy through the Soma, O drop of Soma, flow for Indra.
Where the inextinguishable light shines, the world where the sun was placed, in that immortal, unfading world, O Purifier, place me. O drop of Soma, flow for Indra.
Where Vivasvan's son[77] is king, where heaven is enclosed, where those young waters[78] are—there make me immortal. O drop of Soma, flow for Indra.
Where they move as they will, in the triple dome, in the third heaven of heaven where the worlds are made of light, there make me immortal! O drop of Soma, flow for Indra.
Where there are desires and longings, at the sun's zenith, where the dead are fed and satisfied, there make me immortal. O drop of Soma, flow for Indra.
Where there are joys and pleasures, gladness and delight, where the desire of desires [is] fulfilled, there make me immortal. O drop of Soma, flow for Indra.

Whose experiences are described in Psalm 63? It certainly looks to be a royal psalm, one intended for the king's ceremonial use, but remember who composed the psalms. They were the work of the Levitical singers, and I think the implication is that verse 2 reflects the visionary experience of a Levite poet (just as this Soma hymn depicts that of a Vedic priest) even though the psalm was to be sung by, or on behalf of, the king. So, if the psalm does embody a sacred hallucination, it would be, as we should expect, that of the Levites, not the kings.

Psalms 18, 45

Victory Psalms thanked God for a successful campaign (e.g., Psalm 18). Such gratitude, fulsomely and publicly expressed, must surely incline the deity to grant more of the same in future conflicts. Victory psalms were positive reinforcement for God. You want more praise? What have you done for me lately?

Psalm 45 is a *wedding psalm* for the king and his queen(s). Perhaps surprisingly, this is the only piece of ancient wedding ceremonial we have in the Bible, despite the fact that ministers and priests conducting weddings in movies are always shown reading the service from a Bible. (In reality, they read from a prayer book or clergy manual.) Originally this psalm was part of the royal liturgy of enthronement, which seems to have included the king taking a new bride every year as part of kingship renewal.[79] Kings had harems in order to attest their great virility, since their sexual potency was supposed to be an index of the vitality of nature during his reign. As Percival says to King Arthur in John Boorman's 1981 movie *Excalibur*, "You and the land are one."

Laments of the King

The *lament psalms* seem to have originated as part of state, royal liturgy. These (and other) psalms were first sung by (or in the name of) the king. But some laments show no clear sign of royal use and would make better sense as written by and for common worshippers, borrowing the royal formula. But one must not rule out the royal character of certain psalms too quickly.

Even declarations of innocence (e.g., Psalms 26, 17, 7, 5, 139) against false accusation may fit the king as the speaker and singer because, first, the king was often criticized and condemned by both rebels like Jeroboam and prophets like Jeremiah.[80] "My enemies" in such cases probably refers to invidious reports made against a vassal king by rivals.[81] In particular, references to betrayal by a close associate (e.g., Psalms 55, 62, 71) may reflect scenarios like Absalom's usurpation,[82] or perhaps provided public justification for the political purging of a royal official who has fallen into disfavor, like Lin Pao or Leon Trotsky.

A king might describe himself in such a context as "a poor man" (Psalm 40:17) because this language is held over from the law courts where it began as the pro forma language of the defendant, who *was* frequently a poor farmer defending himself against lawsuits (e.g., for debt collection) brought by rich oppressors (Isa. 5:8; Jas. 2:6).[83]

Community laments were sung by the congregation when a day of mourning or penitence was called. This could be when crops failed, foreign enemies threatened, or some other national peril loomed. People would wear sackcloth, fast, weep and wail (Esther 4:1, 3; Psalm 35:13; Isa. 58:5; Jer. 6:26; Dan. 9:3; Jonah 3:6; Judith 4:11; 9:1; 1 Macc. 3:47; Matt. 11:21).

There are two types of communal laments. First, *penitential prayers* (e.g., Psalm 85). The people recognize that their own sins have brought on the misfortune, so they confess and seek forgiveness. Often these psalms end on an upbeat note. The mood changes from dejected sorrow to hopeful confidence. Probably the turning point would be the priest pronouncing absolution.

Second, there are *confessions of innocence* (e.g., Psalm 44): The people protest that they have done nothing to deserve the calamity, and they try to persuade God to deliver them. They may remind God that his reputation will be ruined if he does not save them:

The heathen will laugh at Yahweh if he doesn't rescue his people, since they'll think he *can't.* "Save us for thy name's sake!"

For comparison, here are some passages from an ancient Sumerian lament psalm, the *Lamentation on the Destruction of Ur*:

Anu may prevent his word.
Enlil may order kindness.
And may my heart be at peace from sorrow.
[_____] the angry word be prevented.
The foundations it has annihilated, and reduced to the misery of
    silence.
Unto Anu I will cry my "how long?"
Unto Enlil I myself will pray.
"My city has been destroyed" will I tell them.
"Ur has been destroyed" will I tell them.
"Its people have been scattered" will I tell them.
May Anu prevent his word.
May Enlil order kindness.
And may my heart be at peace from sorrow.

Her city has been destroyed, her ordinances have been changed.
This is its antiphon.
Enlil utters the spirit of wrath
and the people wail.
The spirit of wrath prosperity from the Land has destroyed
and the people wail.
The spirit of wrath peace from Sumer has taken and the people wail.
He has sent the evil spirit of wrath and the people wail.
The "Messenger of Wrath," the "Assisting Spirit" into its hand he
    entrusted.
He has uttered the spirit of wrath which exterminates the Land and
    the people wail.

Her people without water jars sit without her in desolation
Within her . . . in the ways are placed and the people wail.
The great city gate and the highways with the dead are choked up.
Like a leather vessel all of her the usurper cast asunder(?)
In her . . . streets and roads corpses he heaped up(?)[84]

Psalm 51

In *laments of the individual*, a person faces some crisis or distress. His friends have betrayed him, he is ill, etc. The descriptions of one's dire state may be exaggerated to increase the chances of Yahweh's mercy,[85] paralleling the "case history" in gospel healing stories like Mark's episode of the woman with the flow of blood (Mark 5:25-26).

He comes into the Temple to offer sacrifice and sings (or has sung for him) this appeal for help. These psalms often conclude with a promise to come back and make a thank offering when God does deliver him (e.g., Psalms 22; 60:13-14; 116:17-18). Again, there are two sub-types. *Penitential psalms* (e.g., 51; 71:22-24; 86) are for when you come to the Temple to ask for forgiveness, perhaps reminding God of his merciful and forgiving nature (e.g., Psalms 120:3-4; 103:8-14).

At some point, an act of absolution by the priest, e.g., washing or sprinkling with the brush-like hyssop branch, would assure the repentant sinner that God had forgiven him. Then the singer would express happy confidence that God will remove the affliction. Here's the most famous one, Psalm 51 (ASV):

¹Have mercy upon me, O God, according to thy lovingkindness:
  According to the multitude of thy tender mercies blot out my
    transgressions.
²Wash me thoroughly from mine iniquity,
  And cleanse me from my sin.

³For I know my transgressions;
  And my sin is ever before me.
⁴Against thee, thee only, have I sinned,
  And done that which is evil in thy sight;
That thou mayest be justified when thou speakest,
  And be clear when thou judgest.

⁵Behold, I was brought forth in iniquity;
  And in sin did my mother conceive me.
⁶Behold, thou desirest truth in the inward parts;
  And in the hidden part thou wilt make me to know wisdom.
⁷Purify me with hyssop, and I shall be clean:
  Wash me, and I shall be whiter than snow.
⁸Make me to hear joy and gladness,
  That the bones which thou hast broken may rejoice.
⁹Hide thy face from my sins,
  And blot out all mine iniquities.

¹⁰Create in me a clean heart, O God;
  And renew a right spirit within me.
¹¹Cast me not away from thy presence;
  And take not thy holy Spirit from me.
¹²Restore unto me the joy of thy salvation;
  And uphold me with a willing spirit.

¹³Then will I teach transgressors thy ways;
  And sinners shall be converted unto thee.
¹⁴Deliver me from bloodguiltiness, O God,
    thou God of my salvation;
  And my tongue shall sing aloud of thy righteousness.

¹⁵O [Adonai], open thou my lips;
  And my mouth shall show forth thy praise.
¹⁶For thou delightest not in sacrifice; else would I give it:
  Thou hast no pleasure in burnt-offering.
¹⁷The sacrifices of God are a broken spirit:
  A broken and a contrite heart, O God, thou wilt not despise.

¹⁸Do good in thy good pleasure unto Zion:
  Build thou the walls of Jerusalem.
¹⁹Then wilt thou delight in the sacrifices of righteousness,
  In burnt-offering and whole burnt-offering:
  Then will they offer bullocks upon thine altar.

Psalm 22

Then there are *Psalms of innocence*. The individual sufferer protests that he does not deserve his fate and pleads with God to vindicate him by saving him from his affliction. He may remind God of their long friendship in the past and call on him to be loyal now.

Psalm 22, often interpreted as an explicit prediction of the suffering of Jesus Christ on the cross, turns out to be a classic instance of the psalm of innocence. Here's its American Standard Version rendition:

¹My God, my God, why hast thou forsaken me?
  Why art thou so far from helping me, and from the words of my
    groaning?
²O my God, I cry in the daytime, but thou answerest not;
  And in the night season, and am not silent.

³But thou art holy,
  O thou that inhabitest the praises of Israel.
⁴Our fathers trusted in thee:
  They trusted, and thou didst deliver them.
⁵They cried unto thee, and were delivered:
  They trusted in thee, and were not put to shame.

⁶But I am a worm, and no man;
  A reproach of men, and despised of the people.
⁷All they that see me laugh me to scorn:
  They shoot out the lip, they shake the head, saying,
⁸Commit thyself unto Jehovah; let him deliver him:
  Let him rescue him, seeing he delighteth in him.

⁹But thou art he that took me out of the womb;
  Thou didst make me trust when I was upon my mother's breasts.
¹⁰I was cast upon thee from the womb;
  Thou art my God since my mother bare me.
¹¹Be not far from me; for trouble is near;
  For there is none to help.

¹²Many bulls have compassed me;
  Strong bulls of Bashan have beset me round.
¹³They gape upon me with their mouth,
  As a ravening and a roaring lion.

¹⁴I am poured out like water,
  And all my bones are out of joint:
  My heart is like wax;
  It is melted within me.
¹⁵My strength is dried up like a potsherd;
  And my tongue cleaveth to my jaws;
  And thou hast brought me into the dust of death.

¹⁶For dogs have compassed me:
  A company of evil-doers have inclosed me;
  They pierced my hands and my feet.
¹⁷I may count all my bones.
  They look and stare upon me;
¹⁸They part my garments among them,
  And upon my vesture do they cast lots.

¹⁹But be not thou far off, O Jehovah:
  O thou my succor, haste thee to help me.
²⁰Deliver my soul from the sword,
  My [life] from the power of the dog.
²¹Save me from the lion's mouth;
  Yea, from the horns of the wild-oxen thou hast answered me.

²²I will declare thy name unto my brethren:
  In the midst of the assembly will I praise thee.
²³Ye that fear Jehovah, praise him;
  All ye the seed of Jacob, glorify him;

And stand in awe of him, all ye the seed of Israel.
24For he hath not despised nor abhorred
   the affliction of the afflicted;
Neither hath he hid his face from him;
But when he cried unto him, he heard.

25Of thee cometh my praise in the great assembly:
   I will pay my vows before them that fear him.
26The meek shall eat and be satisfied;
   They shall praise Jehovah that seek after him:
Let your heart live for ever.

27All the ends of the earth shall remember
   and turn unto Jehovah;
And all the kindreds of the nations
   shall worship before thee.
28For the kingdom is Jehovah's;
   And he is the ruler over the nations.

29All the fat ones of the earth shall eat and worship:
   All they that go down to the dust shall bow before him,
   Even he that cannot keep his soul alive.
30A seed [posterity] shall serve him;
   It shall be told of the Lord unto the next generation.
31They shall come and shall declare his righteousness
   Unto a people that shall be born, that he hath done it.

To Christian readers, Psalm 22 looks like a predictive prophecy, but only because they approach it with dogmatic Christian assumptions. And presumably so did Mark, since he structured his crucifixion narrative (Mark 15) around the text of this psalm.

This is a prime example of the *pesher* ("puzzle solution") technique favored by the writers of the Dead Sea Scrolls and the Gospel of Matthew.[86] The key point here is that *pesher* exegesis expressly does *not* expound the literal sense of the text as intended by its human author in his historical circumstances. As far as the *pesher* interpreters were concerned, all that was stale news. They were after an *esoteric* level of meaning accessible only by the leading of the Holy Spirit.

What a passage had originally meant was one thing; what it might reveal about latter-day events was another. Such hitherto-hidden prophecies could be recognized as such only in retrospect, by the eye of faith. This means that, insofar as we are seeking the setting and meaning of the original author and readers, we have to set aside the possible Christian import of the text.

It is, however, no easy task to determine the original character of Psalm 22. Helmer Ringgren[87] understands it as a piece of liturgy for the (re)enthronement festival, specifically during the humiliation segment (something they did up in Babylon, too). The sacred king's power and success were linked directly to the vitality of nature. As vegetation declined, so, it was believed, did the divine empowerment of the king, hence the need for yearly renewal. His re-enthronement coincided with (or signaled) the return of vegetation in the Spring.

At some point, this notion was modified in a moral direction. Now it was the accumulating sins of the people that were believed to attract crop failure, famine, etc., so the ritual suffering and humiliation of the scapegoat king was accordingly penitential in nature. The high priest would knock the crown off the king's head, box his ears and yank on them like he would a naughty schoolboy's. Then the king, having atoned for the sins of his people, would don his crown to the acclaim of his people. (As we will see, Isaiah 53 makes good sense interpreted this way, too.)

I still think the psalm is best read as a classic individual lament, in which one pins desperate hopes on God even at the eleventh hour. The stereotyped enemies and persecutors are represented as savage animals closing in on the supplicant. These ferocious beasts, granted, would make good sense as metaphors for the foreign foes of the king or the conspirators against him. But the business about open public derision seems to me to make better sense applied to an individual.

What about verse 16, "Yea, dogs are round about me; a company of evildoers encircle me; they have pierced my hands and feet"? Does this refer to a man (guess which one?) getting nailed to a Roman cross? I think not. A much more natural interpretation would be to read the piercing of the extremities as wounds suffered as the victim, surrounded by jackals and lions, tries vainly to fend them off, punching with his hands and kicking with his feet.

Verses 22-26 express the supplicant's confidence that, despite all odds, God will yet deliver or vindicate him, whereupon, he hereby promises, he will return to the Temple and choose one of the thank offering psalms. A reception will follow as he shares a sacrificial banquet with the entire congregation invited for the occasion.

Psalm 139

The excellent Psalm 139 is another psalm of innocence, though this becomes clear only at the end. Again, this is from the American Standard Version.

¹O Jehovah, thou hast searched me, and known me.
²Thou knowest my downsitting and mine uprising;
  Thou understandest my thought afar off.
³Thou searchest out my path and my lying down,
  And art acquainted with all my ways.
⁴For there is not a word in my tongue,
  But, lo, O Jehovah, thou knowest it altogether.
⁵Thou hast beset me behind and before,
  And laid thy hand upon me.
⁶Such knowledge is too wonderful for me;
  It is high, I cannot attain unto it.

⁷Whither shall I go from thy Spirit?
  Or whither shall I flee from thy presence?
⁸If I ascend up into heaven, thou art there:
  If I make my bed in Sheol, behold, thou art there.
⁹If I take the wings of [Shahar],
  And dwell in the uttermost parts of the sea;
¹⁰Even there shall thy hand lead me,
  And thy right hand shall hold me.
¹¹If I say, Surely the darkness shall overwhelm me,
  And the light about me shall be night;
¹²Even the darkness hideth not from thee,
  But the night shineth as the day:
  The darkness and the light are both alike to thee.

¹³For thou didst form my inward parts:
  Thou didst cover me in my mother's womb.
¹⁴I will give thanks unto thee;
 for I am fearfully and wonderfully made:
  Wonderful are thy works;
  And that my soul knoweth right well.

¹⁵My frame was not hidden from thee,
  When I was made in secret,
  And curiously wrought in the lowest parts of the earth.
¹⁶Thine eyes did see mine unformed substance;
  And in thy book they were all written,
  Even the days that were ordained for me,
  When as yet there was none of them.
¹⁷How precious also are thy thoughts unto me, O God!
  How great is the sum of them!
¹⁸If I should count them,
  they are more in number than the sand:
  When I awake, I am still with thee.

¹⁹Surely thou wilt slay the wicked, O God:
  Depart from me therefore, ye bloodthirsty men.
²⁰For they speak against thee wickedly,
  And thine enemies take thy name in vain.
²¹Do not I hate them, O Jehovah, that hate thee?
  And am not I grieved with those that rise up against thee?
²²I hate them with perfect hatred:
  They are become mine enemies.
²³Search me, O God, and know my heart:
  Try me, and know my thoughts;
²⁴And see if there be any wicked way in me,
  And lead me in the way everlasting.

Note the mention in v. 9 of Shahar, the winged dawn goddess. (The ASV and KJV translations read "the wings of the morning," while the NASB goes with "wings of the dawn.") In v. 15, the psalm makes a striking equation of the mother's womb with the caverns of the earth. Here is the same juxtaposition of the unshakeable belief of childhood (and of primitive cultures) that humans are, or were, spawned directly from Mother Earth, with the biological fact of human birth from other humans. The clashing of the two beliefs gave rise to myths in which the contradiction is narratized rather than solved conceptually.[88]

Psalm 139 marvelously expresses the absolute and welcome transparency of the soul before the all-seeing eye of God. It is a perfect statement of what Rudolf Bultmann[89] considered the real import of the eschatological preaching of Jesus. His (erroneous) demand for repentance in light of the soon-coming end of the world, Bultmann thought, really amounted to summoning individuals to the recognition that they don't have to wait for the Last Day to face the scrutiny of God: You face it *right now*. The day you stand naked before God is *today*!

Psalm 137

A sub-category of the psalms of innocence is the *imprecatory psalm*: If the sufferer is confident of his innocence, that he does not deserve the suffering, he may be asking God to vindicate him by destroying his enemies. If God is not responsible for his sufferings, it must be wicked mortals. These psalms are little more than magical hexes. Here's the worst of the bunch, Psalm 137 (ASV):

¹By the rivers of Babylon,
  There we sat down, yea, we wept,
  When we remembered Zion.
²Upon the willows in the midst thereof
  We hanged up our harps.
³For there they that led us captive required of us songs,

And they that wasted us required of us mirth, saying,
Sing us one of the songs of Zion.

4How shall we sing Jehovah's song
In a foreign land?
5If I forget thee, O Jerusalem,
Let my right hand forget her skill.
6Let my tongue cleave to the roof of my mouth,
If I remember thee not;
If I prefer not Jerusalem
Above my chief joy.

7Remember, O Jehovah, against the children of Edom
The day of Jerusalem;
Who said, Rase it, rase it,
Even to the foundation thereof.
8O daughter of Babylon, that art to be destroyed,
Happy shall he be, that rewardeth thee
As thou hast served us.
9Happy shall he be, that taketh and dasheth thy little ones
Against the rock.**90**

We are asked to imagine the sadness and rage of a Levite musician and singer deported from Jerusalem and its Temple after Nebuchadnezzar destroyed it. He gathers periodically with his fellow exiles by the River Chebar, as his colleague Ezekiel did (Ezek. 1:1). The Babylonian soldiers who marched them north thought it might brighten up a weary hike if the Jewish musicians would perform a number from their Temple repertoire.

Our psalmist refused. His sacred songs were for God's edification, not man's entertainment. And they were to be performed only in the course of Temple worship, certainly not outside the Holy Land! These things he will never forget. If he were to lose sight of them, getting too comfortable in Babylon, may the tongue that sings be stuck to the roof of his mouth! May the hand that strums be paralyzed!

But wait a minute! If there is no Temple, and psalms are not to be performed anywhere else, then what is this that we are reading? Of course, such psalms accompanied no ritual or sacrifice but only guided the thoughts and prayers of the exiles. (I think the five dirges constituting the Book of Lamentations were composed for the same reason, only for those who gathered in ruined Jerusalem for worship and mutual comfort.)

What is this about Edom in verse 7? Edom exploited Jerusalem's conquest by Babylon (Jer. 49.7-22; Lam. 4.21-22; Ezek. 25.12-14; 35; Joel 3.19; Obad. *passim*; Mal. 1.2-5), and our psalmist was not in a forgiving mood. The Edomite jackals had bashed out the brains of Jewish babies as they victimized the defeated Jews, and the psalmist is eager for somebody to return the favor (v. 9)! This bitter sentiment is tantamount to a curse, calling down the wrath of God on one's enemies.

Psalm 91

Psalm 91 (ASV) is the opposite case. It's a charm to ward off, rather than ask for, sinister supernatural forces:

1He that dwelleth in the secret place of [Elyon]
Shall abide under the shadow of [Shaddai].
2I will say of Jehovah, He is my refuge and my fortress;
[Eloi], in whom I trust.
3For he will deliver thee from the snare of the fowler,
And from the deadly pestilence.

4He will cover thee with his pinions,
  And under his wings shalt thou take refuge:
  His truth is a shield and a buckler.
5Thou shalt not be afraid for the terror by night,
  Nor for the arrow that flieth by day;
6For the pestilence that walketh in darkness,
  Nor for the destruction that wasteth at noonday.

7A thousand shall fall at thy side,
  And ten thousand at thy right hand;
  But it shall not come nigh thee.
8Only with thine eyes shalt thou behold,
  And see the reward of the wicked.

9For thou, O Jehovah, art my refuge!
  Thou hast made [Elyon] thy habitation;
10There shall no evil befall thee,
  Neither shall any plague come nigh thy tent.

11For he will give his angels charge over thee,
  To keep thee in all thy ways.
12They shall bear thee up in their hands,
  Lest thou dash thy foot against a stone.
13Thou shalt tread upon the lion and adder:
  The young lion and the serpent shalt thou trample under foot.

14Because he hath set his love upon me, therefore will I deliver him:
  I will set him on high, because he hath known my name.
15He shall call upon me, and I will answer him;
  I will be with him in trouble:
  I will deliver him, and honor him.
16With long life will I satisfy him,
  And show him my salvation.

The range of divine names (whether intended as several names of a single deity or those of several) indicates we have a magical invocation of mighty Names, analogous to the use of divine names in exorcism, of which Psalm 91 is really just a variation. The reference in verse 3 to "the deadly pestilence" probably intends Namtar, the Akkadian god of death, who unleashes a plague in the Atrahasis Epic. Verses 5-6 refer to a demon of darkness, perhaps Lilith the Night Hag (Isa. 34:14), as well as Qeteb,[91] the sunstroke demon who aims his deadly arrows in the flood of noontide light (cf., 2 Kings 4:18-19).

Psalms 18, 116, 138

Thank offering songs were mostly written in the first-person singular. Originally they were very likely written for (on behalf of) the king, but they were later probably used by and for common worshippers (as they are today).[92]

These songs would be sung when you came to the Temple, grateful to God for seeing you through some very hard time, and wanted to offer a sacrifice of gratitude (Psalm 116:17). One would lie prostrate during or before singing it (Psalm 138:2). The singer would recount his danger or distress and then describe how God saved him from it (Psalm 18:4f). This is like "giving testimonies" about what God has done for you. The psalm ends with a confession that the singer has no one to thank but Yahweh. The individual would choose one of the psalms of this kind from the collection, though some (probably Levites) may have composed their own, which were eventually added to the repertoire.

Psalm 84

Pilgrimage songs were to be sung by those coming from the countryside to Jerusalem for Temple worship at a festival. You would sing them as you walked or rode along the road. For example, Psalm 84 (ASV).

> ¹How amiable are thy tabernacles,
> O Jehovah [Sabaoth]!
> ²My soul longeth, yea, even fainteth
> for the courts of Jehovah;
> My heart and my flesh cry out
> unto the living God.
>
> ³Yea, the sparrow hath found her a house,
> And the swallow a nest for herself,
> where she may lay her young,
> Even thine altars, O Jehovah [Sabaoth],
> My King, and my God.
> ⁴Blessed are they that dwell in thy house:
> They will be still praising thee. *Selah*
>
> ⁵Blessed is the man whose strength is in thee;
> In whose heart are the highways to Zion.
> ⁶Passing through the valley of Weeping
> they make it a place of springs;
> Yea, the early rain covereth it with blessings.
> ⁷They go from strength to strength;
> Every one of them appeareth before God in Zion.
>
> ⁸O Jehovah God of hosts, hear my prayer;
> Give ear, O God of Jacob. *Selah*
> ⁹Behold, O God our shield,
> And look upon the face of thine anointed.
>
> ¹⁰For a day in thy courts is better
> than a thousand.
> I had rather be a doorkeeper in the house of my God,
> Than to dwell in the tents of wickedness.
> ¹¹For Jehovah [Elohim] is a sun[93] and a shield:
> Jehovah will give grace and glory;
> No good thing will he withhold
> from them that walk uprightly.
> ¹²O Jehovah [Sabaoth],
> Blessed is the man that trusteth in thee.

Psalm 122

And consider Psalm 122 (ASV), sung upon arrival at the Holy City:

> ¹I was glad when they said unto me,
> Let us go unto the house of Jehovah.
> ²Our feet are standing
> Within thy gates, O Jerusalem,
>
> ³Jerusalem, that art builded
> As a city that is compact together;
> ⁴Whither the tribes go up,
> even the tribes of Jehovah,
> For an ordinance for Israel,

To give thanks unto the name of Jehovah.
5For there are set thrones for judgment,
The thrones of the house of David.

6Pray for the peace of Jerusalem:
They shall prosper that love thee.
7Peace be within thy walls,
And prosperity within thy palaces.
8For my brethren and companions' sakes,
I will now say, Peace be within thee.
9For the sake of the house of Jehovah our God
I will seek thy good.

The priests and singers posted at the gate would sing or chant to the pilgrims, welcoming them or reminding them that they must be righteous to approach Yahweh in his Temple. "Who shall ascend the hill of Jehovah? And who shall stand in his holy place? He who has clean hands and a pure heart, who does not lift up his soul to what is false, and does not swear deceitfully. He will receive blessing from Jehovah, and vindication from the God of his salvation" (Psalm 24:3-5; 15).

Sometimes it would be sung antiphonally between the priests and the pilgrims (Psalms 118:19, 20, 24-25, 26-27). Decalogues (Exod. 20:2-17; Exod. 34:17-26; Deut. 5:6-21; Josh. 23:6-8 and 24:14) probably originated as parts of entrance liturgies.[94] "Here's a checklist. Are you sure you're ready?" (Cf., Isa. 1:10-17; Matt. 5:24; 1 Cor. 11:28.)

Psalm 100

Entrance songs: Once the pilgrims reached the Temple, they would sing one of these upon arriving at the gate. The most famous is Psalm 100, which children still memorize. Again, the ASV:

1Make a joyful noise unto Jehovah, all ye lands.
2Serve Jehovah with gladness:
Come before his presence with singing.

3Know ye that Jehovah, he is God:
It is he that hath made us, and we are his;
We are his people, and the sheep of his pasture.

4Enter into his gates with thanksgiving,
And into his courts with praise:
Give thanks unto him, and bless his name.

5For Jehovah is good;
his lovingkindness endureth for ever,
And his faithfulness unto all generations.

Psalms of the Levites

There are psalms written not only by the Levites but also *for* the Levites, being taken up with distinctively priestly themes. Some seem to reflect political struggles, actually labor disputes,[95] between the Aaronide priestly hierarchy and the lowly Korah Guild of singers.

Numbers 16 pillories the Korah Levites by depicting their (fictive) eponymous ancestor as demanding full priestly rights–and getting slapped down for it by God. That ought to teach 'em! It looks as if the sentiments expressed in Psalm 51:15-17 were a counterblast from the Levites, a piece of sour grapes theology, as it were.

Psalms 134, 135

Night-watch songs were for Levites on duty in the Temple at night to pass the time piously (e.g., Psalms 134, 135).

I take Psalm 133 to be part of the ordination liturgy for a new Levite or priest. The peaceful unity of "the brethren" denotes the fellowship of these clerics, envisioned as something like a monastic order. The oil mentioned here would be the chrism of ordination dripping down over the beard and onto the collar of the sacerdotal vestments. And the reference is not to just any beard, but the whiskers of Aaron, the original high priest. No coincidence there.

Psalm 24

Songs of the Ark of the Covenant: These would be sung when the Ark was carried forth in the New Year's festival (Tabernacles), then back to the Temple, the king playing the role of David in 1 Samuel 6:13-15. Two examples, the first being Psalm 24 (ASV):

> ⁷Lift up your heads, O ye gates;
>   And be ye lifted up, ye everlasting doors:
>   And the King of glory will come in.
> ⁸Who is the King of glory?
>   Jehovah strong and mighty,
>   Jehovah mighty in battle.
> ⁹Lift up your heads, O ye gates;
>   Yea, lift them up, ye everlasting doors:
>   And the King of glory will come in.
> ¹⁰Who is this King of glory?
>   Jehovah of hosts,
>   He is the King of glory. *Selah*

The second example is found in Psalm 68 (ASV, cf., Num. 10:35):

> ¹Let God arise, let his enemies be scattered;
>   Let them also that hate him flee before him.
> ²As smoke is driven away, so drive them away:
>   As wax melteth before the fire,
>   So let the wicked perish at the presence of God.
> ³But let the righteous be glad;
>   let them exult before God:
>   Yea, let them rejoice with gladness.

Dances accompanied these songs. Second Samuel 6:13-15 explains that, "when those who bore the ark of [Yahweh] had gone six paces, he sacrificed an ox and a fatling. And David danced before [Yahweh] with all his might; and David was girded with a linen ephod. So David and all the house of Israel brought up the ark of [Yahweh] with shouting, and with the sound of the horn." This must have been an etiological story to provide a script for the ritual of transporting the Ark.

Psalm 73

Wisdom psalms meditate on the shortness and futility of life (Psalm 90) and extol wisdom and God's laws, promising rewards to those who are faithful (e.g., Psalms. 1, 119). Some of them, like Psalm 73, reprinted below (ASV), ponder tough questions like why God allows the wicked to prosper.

¹Surely God is good to Israel,
  Even to such as are pure in heart.
²But as for me, my feet were almost gone;
  My steps had well nigh slipped.
³For I was envious at the arrogant,
  When I saw the prosperity of the wicked.

⁴For there are no pangs in their death;
  But their strength is firm.
⁵They are not in trouble as other men;
  Neither are they plagued like other men.
⁶Therefore pride is as a chain about their neck;
  Violence covereth them as a garment.
⁷Their eyes stand out with fatness:
  They have more than heart could wish.
⁸They scoff, and in wickedness utter oppression:
  They speak loftily.
⁹They have set their mouth in the heavens,
  And their tongue walketh through the earth.

¹⁰Therefore his people return hither:
  And waters of a full cup are drained by them.
¹¹And they say, How doth God know?
  And is there knowledge in [Elyon]?
¹²Behold, these are the wicked;
  And, being alway at ease, they increase in riches.
¹³Surely in vain have I cleansed my heart,
  And washed my hands in innocency;
¹⁴For all the day long have I been plagued,
  And chastened every morning.

¹⁵If I had said, I will speak thus;
  Behold, I had dealt treacherously with the generation of thy
    children.
¹⁶When I thought how I might know this,
  It was too painful for me;
¹⁷Until I went into the sanctuary of God,
  And considered their latter end.
¹⁸Surely thou settest them in slippery places:
  Thou castest them down to destruction.
¹⁹How are they become a desolation in a moment!
  They are utterly consumed with terrors.
²⁰As a dream when one awaketh,
  So, O Lord, when thou awakest, thou wilt despise their image.

²¹For my soul was grieved,
  And I was pricked in my heart:
²²So brutish was I, and ignorant;
  I was as a beast before thee.
²³Nevertheless I am continually with thee:
  Thou hast holden my right hand.
²⁴Thou wilt guide me with thy counsel,
  And afterward receive me to glory.
²⁵Whom have I in heaven but thee?
  And there is none upon earth that I desire besides thee.
²⁶My flesh and my heart faileth;
  But God is the strength of my heart and my portion for ever.

²⁷For, lo, they that are far from thee shall perish:

> Thou hast destroyed all them that play the harlot,
>   departing from thee.
> [28]But it is good for me to draw near unto God:
>   I have made the Lord Jehovah my refuge,
>   That I may tell of all thy works.

This is a poignant meditation on the problem of theodicy: How can a righteous God allow the evil rampant in the world? It recounts the personal anxiety of the psalmist and its eventual resolution.

He could not help seeing the prosperity of the boastful wicked and how they take it (as he is tempted to do) as proof either that there is no God or that, if there is, he takes no interest in human affairs. Are they right? What of all the pious promises that the righteous will prosper? Is God asleep at the switch?

The psalmist had very nearly reached the point of saying, "To hell with it!" Why bother to keep taking the trouble, as we might say, to "keep his nose clean" if it brings him no reward? It hasn't so far! So why not switch sides? He came dangerously close to "speaking thus," i.e., as the sinners do: "There is no God." The faithful, especially the young among them, would have had their fragile faith shattered by his example. In retrospect, he realizes his anguish had reduced him to the stupidity of a raging beast.

But he took himself to the Temple to find enough peace and quiet to consider the matter calmly. And there in the holy stillness he had an epiphany: Who *cares* about worldly "fringe benefits" of faith? Is God some kind of genie at our service? No, God himself is the treasure that enriches his worshippers. There is nothing else the psalmist really desires in this world or in the one above, so why bemoan the absence of worldly riches? And pity the poor sinners! Death will rudely interrupt their revels, and they will have nothing to show for it.

Psalm 1

Psalm 1 (obviously) prefaces the whole collection and seeks to set the tone. Again, from the ASV:

> [1]Blessed is the man
>   that walketh not in the counsel of the wicked,
> Nor standeth in the way of sinners,
>   Nor sitteth in the seat of scoffers:
> [2]But his delight is in the law of Jehovah;
>   And on his law doth he meditate day and night.
> [3]And he shall be like a tree
>   planted by the streams of water,
> That bringeth forth its fruit in its season,
>   Whose leaf also doth not wither;
> And whatsoever he doeth shall prosper.
>
> [4]The wicked are not so,
>   But are like the chaff which the wind driveth away.
> [5]Therefore the wicked shall not stand in the judgment,
>   Nor sinners in the congregation of the righteous.
> [6]For Jehovah knoweth the way of the righteous;
>   But the way of the wicked shall perish.

This is a perfect illustration of all three types of the parallelism that constitutes the chief technique of Hebrew poetry, which only very occasionally utilizes rhyme. Verse 2 is a case of *synthetic* parallelism, whereby the statement of the first line is reiterated in the second by paraphrase, two versions of the same idea. Verse 1 features a variation on synthetic parallelism, namely *staircase* parallelism. Here the point is strengthened, carried just a bit further step by step.

Note the progression. The wrong path, shunned by the righteous, is, first, to follow the advice of the wicked, second, to congregate with them (like Peter warming himself at the fire in the crowd of Jesus' persecutors in Mark 14:53-54), and third, to join their company, enjoying fellowship with those who scoff at the righteous (e.g., Wisdom of Solomon 2:12-20). Verse 6 supplies an example of *antithetical* parallelism, in which a positive statement is reinforced by contrast with its opposite. The technique is, of course, quite effective.

It is possible that this one was not for liturgical use, but rather for readers (scribes) to meditate upon. It glorifies the study of scripture much in the fashion of the later *Pirke Aboth* (Sayings of the Fathers), e.g., "The more Torah, the more life; the more schooling, the more wisdom; the more counsel, the more understanding" (II:8). "Whoso honours the Torah will himself be honoured by mankind, but whoso dishonours the Torah will himself be dishonoured by mankind" (IV:8).[96] By "Torah," the *Pirke Aboth* seems to intend the whole canon, and probably so does Psalm 1, since it is hard to see how anyone could hope to become wise by meditating on the Pentateuch's details of kosher laws and sacrifice recipes.

Psalm 90

Psalm 90 has nothing to do with Moses, despite much later scribes tagging it as "The Prayer of Moses the Man of God." But it is the content, not who may have written it, that matters. Here's its ASV rendition:

> 1Lord, thou hast been our dwelling-place
>   In all generations.
> 2Before the mountains were brought forth,
>   Or ever thou hadst formed the earth and the world,
>   Even from everlasting to everlasting, thou art God.
>
> 3Thou turnest man to destruction,
>   And sayest, Return, ye children of men.
> 4For a thousand years in thy sight
>   Are but as yesterday when it is past,
>   And as a watch in the night.
>
> 5Thou carriest them away as with a flood; they are as a sleep:
>   In the morning they are like grass which groweth up.
> 6In the morning it flourisheth, and groweth up;
>   In the evening it is cut down, and withereth.
>
> 7For we are consumed in thine anger,
>   And in thy wrath are we troubled.
> 8Thou hast set our iniquities before thee,
>   Our secret sins in the light of thy countenance.
>
> 9For all our days are passed away in thy wrath:
>   We bring our years to an end as a sigh.
> 10The days of our years are threescore years and ten,
>   Or even by reason of strength fourscore years;[97]
>   Yet is their pride but labor and sorrow;
>   For it is soon gone, and we fly away.
>
> 11Who knoweth the power of thine anger,
>   And thy wrath according to the fear that is due unto thee?

[12]So teach us to number our days,
   That we may get us a heart of wisdom.

[13]Return, O Jehovah; how long?
   And let it repent thee concerning thy servants.
[14]Oh satisfy us in the morning with thy lovingkindness,
   That we may rejoice and be glad all our days.
[15]Make us glad according to the days wherein thou hast afflicted us,
   And the years wherein we have seen evil.
[16]Let thy work appear unto thy servants,
   And thy glory upon their children.
[17]And let the favor of Jehovah our God be upon us;
   And establish thou the work of our hands upon us;
   Yea, the work of our hands establish thou it.

Any way you cut it, this is a potent wisdom psalm. I'd have to call it downright Heideggerian for its sober reckoning of the shocking (when you think about it) brevity of human life and the urgent need to *do something* with what remains of it.

Our existence is barely even *real* compared to the everlasting duration of God. What can we do that will last? Will we merit even a footnote or a mention in someone's diary?

Beyond this, which is quite profound enough, Psalm 90 sounds to me like a commentary on the Eden story of Genesis 2-3. The shortness of the human lifespan is a punishment from God (Psalm 90:7; Gen. 3:22-23) for our sinfulness, which God mercilessly exposed despite our attempts at concealment (Psalm 90:8; Gen. 3:9-13). He sentences us to return to the dust from whence we came (Psalm 90:3; Gen. 3:19). Our lives are overshadowed by the unremitting wrath of God. If only he would relent!

Psalm 8

What Psalm 90 does with time, Psalm 8 does with space (ASV).

[1]O Jehovah, our Lord,
   How excellent is thy name in all the earth,
   Who hast set thy glory upon the heavens!
[2]Out of the mouth of babes and sucklings hast thou established
      strength,
   Because of thine adversaries,
   That thou mightest still the enemy and the avenger.

[3]When I consider thy heavens, the work of thy fingers,
   The moon and the stars, which thou hast ordained;
[4]What is man, that thou art mindful of him?
   And the son of man, that thou visitest him?

[5]For thou hast made him but little lower than God,
   And crownest him with glory and honor.
[6]Thou makest him to have dominion over the works of thy hands;
   Thou hast put all things under his feet:
[7]All sheep and oxen,
   Yea, and the beasts of the field,
[8]The birds of the heavens, and the fish of the sea,
   Whatsoever passeth through the paths of the seas.

[9]O Jehovah, our Lord,
   How excellent is thy name in all the earth!

It is remarkable that, in light of the relatively cozy cosmology of the ancients, with a flat earth enclosed within a solid dome in which sun, moon, and stars had been installed like ceiling lamps, the psalmist could express the same self-abnegating wonder felt by moderns who know the infinite vastness of the universe and our trivial presence within it. Though the ancients imagined the earth was the center of the cosmos, they apparently did not infer from that any smug delusions of self-flattering anthropocentrism. And yet who but a "measly" human being is in the position to *grasp* this fact? And, ironically, that ability to reckon with one's cosmic insignificance is what marks our species as virtually godlike—only less than God![98]

Psalm 8 provides a perfect example of synthetic parallelism, several of them in fact. But the greatest of these is surely verses 3-4. If the psalmist had said only "thy heavens, the work of thy fingers," the point would have been made, but to echo it immediately with the equivalent phrase, "the moon and the stars which thou hast established," makes prose into poetry. Likewise, following up "what is man that thou art mindful of him?" with the twin phrase, "and the son of man that thou dost care for him?" is true poetic diction that conveys, somehow, far more than straight prose.[99] It's great!

Finally, the use of the term "the son of man" here is very instructive. The parallelism with "man" makes it obvious that the two are synonymous, and that "the son of man" is equivalent to "every mother's son." We will see how every biblical use of "the son of man" (e.g., Ezekiel 32:2, Daniel 7:13, and throughout the gospels) depends, not on this particular verse, but upon this phrase and its meaning as attested here.

Psalm 19

Psalm 19 seems to change course rather drastically, but perhaps there is more to it (ASV).

> ¹The heavens declare the glory of God;
>> And the firmament showeth his handiwork.
> ²Day unto day uttereth speech,
>> And night unto night showeth knowledge.
> ³There is no speech nor language;
>> Their voice is not heard.
> ⁴Their line is gone out through all the earth,
>> And their words to the end of the world.
>
> In them hath he set a tabernacle for the sun,
> ⁵Which is as a bridegroom coming out of his chamber,
>> And rejoiceth as a strong man to run his course.
> ⁶His going forth is from the end of the heavens,
>> And his circuit unto the ends of it;
>> And there is nothing hid from the heat thereof.
>
> ⁷The law of Jehovah is perfect, restoring the soul:
>> The testimony of Jehovah is sure, making wise the simple.
> ⁸The precepts of Jehovah are right, rejoicing the heart:
>> The commandment of Jehovah is pure, enlightening the eyes.
> ⁹The fear of Jehovah is clean, enduring for ever:
>> The ordinances of Jehovah are true, and righteous altogether.
> ¹⁰More to be desired are they than gold, yea, than much fine gold;
>> Sweeter also than honey and the droppings of the honeycomb.
>
> ¹¹Moreover by them is thy servant warned:
>> In keeping them there is great reward.
> ¹²Who can discern his errors?
>> Clear thou me from hidden faults.
> ¹³Keep back thy servant also from presumptuous sins;

Let them not have dominion over me:
Then shall I be upright,
And I shall be clear from great transgression.

[14]Let the words of my mouth and the meditation of my heart
Be acceptable in thy sight,
O Jehovah, my rock, and my redeemer.

As Gunkel suggested, Psalm 19 might have originally been a hymn to the sun,[100] but keep in mind that Yahweh (as with El Elyon) was sometimes understood as a solar deity, as in Isaiah 14:12-14 and Psalm 84:11, and Psalm 19 may view him in that capacity. "He who sits in the heavens laughs," in Psalm 2:4, also depicts God as the sun, his laughter denoting the "beaming" (as we still say of a smiling face) of the solar orb. This helps us explain what the two halves of the psalm have to do with one another, for according to ancient myth the giving of a law code was the work of a sun god.

The Babylonian sun god Shamash presented the tablet of the law, the Code of Hammurabi, to that emperor. Apollo promulgated laws for the Greeks. Even the lawgiver Moses is depicted as a solar god when, as he emerges from conference with Yahweh with new laws for Israel, his face is shining like the sun (Exod. 34:29-31). Thus the progression in Psalm 19 from the sun to the laws of Yahweh.

Psalm 104

Nor is this the only solar hymn in the Psalter. Some see close enough parallels between Psalm 104:19-25, 27-30 and Akhenaten's "Hymn to the Sun" to suggest that Psalm 104 borrows from it. Here is Psalm 104 (ASV), with interestingly similar portions of the *Hymn to the Sun* interspersed between them.[101]

[1]Bless Jehovah, O my soul.
O Jehovah my God, thou art very great;
Thou art clothed with honor and majesty:
[2]Who coverest thyself with light as with a garment;
Who stretchest out the heavens like a curtain;
[3]Who layeth the beams of his chambers in the waters;
Who maketh the clouds his chariot;
Who walketh upon the wings of the wind;
[4]Who maketh winds his messengers;
Flames of fire his ministers;

Thy rising [is] beautiful in the horizon of heaven, O Aten, ordainer of life. Thou dost shoot up in the horizon of the East, thou fillest every land with thy beneficence. Thou art beautiful and great and sparkling, and exalted above every land. Thy arrows [rays] envelop [penetrate] everywhere all the lands which thou hast made.

[5]Who laid the foundations of the earth,
That it should not be moved for ever.
[6]Thou coveredst it with the deep as with a vesture;
The waters stood above the mountains.
[7]At thy rebuke they fled;
At the voice of thy thunder they hasted away
[8](The mountains rose, the valleys sank down)
Unto the place which thou hadst founded for them.
[9]Thou hast set a bound that they may not pass over;
That they turn not again to cover the earth.

[10]He sendeth forth springs into the valleys;
They run among the mountains;

¹¹They give drink to every beast of the field;
　　The wild asses quench their thirst.
¹²By them the birds of the heavens have their habitation;
　　They sing among the branches.
¹³He watereth the mountains from his chambers:
　　The earth is filled with the fruit of thy works.

Thou art as Ra. Thou bringest [them] according to their number, thou subduest them for thy beloved son. Thou thyself art afar off, but thy beams are upon the earth; thou art in their faces, they [admire] thy goings. Thou settest in the horizon of the west, the earth is in darkness, in the form of death. Men lie down in a booth wrapped up in cloths, one eye cannot see its fellow. If all their possessions, which are under their heads, be carried away they perceive it not.

¹⁴He causeth the grass to grow for the cattle,
　　And herb for the service of man;
　　That he may bring forth food out of the earth,
¹⁵And wine that maketh glad the heart of man,
　　And oil to make his face to shine,
　　And bread that strengtheneth man's heart.
¹⁶The trees of Jehovah are filled with moisture,
　　The cedars of Lebanon, which he hath planted;
¹⁷Where the birds make their nests:
　　As for the stork, the fir-trees are her house.
¹⁸The high mountains are for the wild goats;
　　The rocks are a refuge for the conies.
¹⁹He appointed the moon for seasons:
　　The sun knoweth his going down.
²⁰Thou makest darkness, and it is night,
　　Wherein all the beasts of the forest creep forth.
²¹The young lions roar after their prey,
　　And seek their food from God.
²²The sun ariseth, they get them away,
　　And lay them down in their dens.
²³Man goeth forth unto his work
　　And to his labor until the evening.

Every lion emergeth from his lair, all the creeping things bite, darkness [is] a warm retreat. The land is in silence. He who made them hath set them in his horizon. The earth becometh light, thou shootest up in the horizon, shining in the Aten in the day, thou scatterest the darkness. Thou sendest out thine arrows (i.e., rays), the Two Lands make festival, [men] wake up, stand upon their feet, it is thou who raisest them up. [They] wash their members, they take [their apparel] and array themselves therein, their hands are [stretched out] in praise at thy rising, throughout the land they do their works. Beasts and cattle of all kinds settle down upon the pastures, shrubs and vegetables flourish, the feathered fowl fly about over their marshes, their feathers praising thy Ka [person].

²⁴O Jehovah, how manifold are thy works!
　　In wisdom hast thou made them all:
　　The earth is full of thy riches.
²⁵Yonder is the sea, great and wide,
　　Wherein are things creeping innumerable,
　　Both small and great beasts.
²⁶There go the ships;
　　There is leviathan, whom thou hast formed to play therein.

O how many are the things which thou hast made! They are hidden from thy face, O thou One God, like whom there is no other. Thou didst create the earth by thy heart [or will], thou alone existing, men and women, cattle, beasts of every kind that are upon the earth, and that move upon feet [or legs], all the creatures that are in the sky and that fly with their wings, [and] the deserts of Syria and Kesh, and the Land of Egypt.

²⁷These wait all for thee,
     That thou mayest give them their food in due season.
²⁸Thou givest unto them, they gather;
     Thou openest thy hand, they are satisfied with good.
²⁹Thou hidest thy face, they are troubled;
     Thou takest away their breath, they die,
     And return to their dust.
³⁰Thou sendest forth thy Spirit, they are created;
     And thou renewest the face of the ground.

Thou settest every person in his place. Thou providest their daily food, every man having the portion allotted to him, [thou] dost compute the duration of his life. Their tongues are different in speech, their characteristics [or forms], and likewise their skins [in colour], giving distinguishing marks to the dwellers in foreign lands. Thou makest Hapi [the Nile] in the Tuat [Underworld], thou bringest it when thou wishest to make mortals to live, inasmuch as thou hast made them for thyself, their Lord who dost support them to the uttermost, O thou Lord of every land, thou shinest upon them, O ATEN of the day, thou great one of majesty. Thou makest the life of all remote lands. Thou settest a Nile in heaven, which cometh down to them.

³¹Let the glory of Jehovah endure for ever;
     Let Jehovah rejoice in his works:
³²Who looketh on the earth, and it trembleth;
     He toucheth the mountains, and they smoke.
³³I will sing unto Jehovah as long as I live:
     I will sing praise to my God while I have any being.
³⁴Let my meditation be sweet unto him:
     I will rejoice in Jehovah.
³⁵Let sinners be consumed out of the earth.
     And let the wicked be no more.
     Bless Jehovah, O my soul.
     Praise ye Jehovah.

Finally, *Acrostic poems* (Psalms 9-10, 25, 34, 37, 111, 112, 119, 145) are mixtures of various kinds of psalms written just for the sake of the acrostic gimmick: Each line begins with the next letter of the Hebrew alphabet in proper order.

The Song of Solomon

Also known as *Canticles*, the Canticle of Canticles, and the Song of Songs (meaning "Best of Songs"), the work may have nothing to do with Solomon at all. The notion that King Solomon actually wrote the work is just a (false) inference from the fact that he is mentioned in it (and, depending on how you interpret it, he may also be a character in it). Also, 1 Kings 4:32 says Solomon wrote 1005 songs. This, someone guessed, must be one of them.

Actually, it was more likely written during the third century B.C.E., the 200s. The idea that the king composed some thousand songs, and that none (or one!) survived, implies the unintentionally humorous scenario of an untalented king writing songs all of his subjects had to pretend to like, all the while gritting their teeth. As soon as Solomon died, into the shredder they went!

Let's survey some of the major ways of interpreting this text. Some understand the text as a love poem tracing the progress of love through courtship on into marriage and married life. Scholars have proposed this, but it is hard to trace any particular plot continuity at all, much less this.[102] Others see it as a drama about Solomon's courtship of the Shulammite maiden, whoever she is. Again, no real plot is in evidence, though one can be reconstructed with a considerable amount of reading between the lines. The idea of it being a drama does make sense of the role of the "Daughters of Jerusalem," who seem to function like the chorus in a Greek play, interpreting the action for the characters and the audience alike.[103]

Or is it a drama about Solomon's unsuccessful attempt to woo Abishag the Shunnamite, his father David's maid and favorite bed-warmer (1 Kings 1:1-4)? But Abishag resists his advances, already being in love with a young shepherd from back home, who visits her in the course of the drama. It is he, then, who stands outside her lattice window, etc.[104]

Or it might be a collection of thematically similar but unrelated love songs, sung sometimes at weddings or just for fun. Compare the text with popular Syrian and Palestinian wedding customs. On the day before the wedding, the bride performs a sword dance to the rhythm of a song sung by the bystanders who praise her beauty and her adornment (cf. 4:1-7; 5:10-16; 7:1-6). During the week-long wedding feast (reception) (cf. Judg. 14:12, 17; Gen. 29:27), the bride and groom are treated as queen and king. A threshing board is set up as a throne. We know from references as late as the first century C.E. that bride and groom were crowned symbolically as queen and king. This sort of thing would fit 3:6, with the groom cast as the greatest (and most married!) king, Solomon.

As for non-wedding use of the text, note that in the second-century C.E., Rabbi Akiba pronounced a curse on those rascals who used to sing it in the taverns as a bawdy song. This probably was nothing new. Michael D. Goulder makes it blushingly clear just how erotic the Song is, dripping with sexual double entendres.[105]

I cannot resist the suggestion of Marvin H. Pope[106] that the Song represents the liturgy of the cult of Ishtar Shalmith and her husband and brother Tammuz. We know there was such worship in Judah.

Ezekiel 8:14 (NASB) says, "Then He brought me to the entrance of the gate of [Yahweh's] house which was toward the north; and behold, women were sitting there weeping for Tammuz."[107] Perhaps identical with the "daughters of Jerusalem" who appear in the Song of Solomon, these women were engaged in ritual mourning for the dying-and-rising god, taking the role of Ishtar, who mourned him, then entered the Netherworld to find him and restore him to life. We see this myth reflected in Song 3:1-3; 6:1-2; 8:6-7. Little of the text as we have it makes reference to Ishtar's rescue of Tammuz from Sheol, but it does celebrate their divine love. This may well have been the liturgy for the imitative sex-magic rituals of the Baal cult condemned by the prophets. "Shalmith" becomes the nameless "Shulammite." "Shalmith" also seems to be related to the name "Shahar," the Jerusalemite dawn goddess. As such, the Song of Songs is a precious fossil of the worship of the Goddess which was celebrated in the Jerusalem Temple itself for two-thirds of the centuries it stood (at least by the traditional chronology).[108]

My guess is that the text survived, at least in fragmentary form (bowdlerized), only once explicit references to the names Tammuz and Ishtar were chopped. Still, it is only the widespread use of the text as a sacred liturgy that can explain why such an anomalous book found a place in the Jewish canon at all. That is pretty hard to account for otherwise. This element of divine love as the subject of the text has survived in a sanitized, monotheistic form: The Rabbis taught that the poem was a series of vivid metaphors for the love between God and Israel.

Lamentations of Jeremiah

A lament, as we saw in our introduction to the Psalms, is a song of distress and mourning. The form "Oh how . . ." denotes a funeral dirge, as in 2 Samuel 1:19, 25, 27; Isaiah 14:4, 12. Such laments were sung by professional mourners (whether in the Temple, by Levitical singers, or publicly, as possibly in Mark 5:38). The dirges collected here commemorate the Babylonian destruction of Jerusalem in 586 B.C.E. They speak bitterly of the desolation of the city, her lost glory, her sin which brought her doom, and of course Yahweh's righteous anger.

Who wrote these five laments? The ascription to Jeremiah, a witness of the destruction, is sheer guesswork. While the literary style has something in common with that of the Book of Jeremiah, there are also some significant differences it would hard to explain if the same author wrote both. The facts that the first four are acrostics (i.e., each verse begins with each successive letter of the Hebrew alphabet), and the fifth at least has the right number of verses, though not the right letters, imply that our author is a scribe, not a prophet. I suppose someone might want to suggest, then, that Baruch, Jeremiah's scribe wrote them. He might have.

Another reason to think Jeremiah did not write the Lamentations is that he was more optimistic than their author. Jeremiah predicted that the Babylonian Exile would last for 70 years. In fact it lasted only 50. But the author of the Lamentations holds out no hope for the future.

We know from the first chapter of Ezekiel that he and his fellow priests led worship among the exiled priests and aristocrats at the bank of the Chebar River in Babylon every Sabbath. The so-called Third Isaiah and Deutero-Zechariah imply that worship had continued among the common people who of course had never left Judah. They probably worshiped amid sacred ruins (not necessarily at Jerusalem),[109] just as Jews do today (at the Wailing Wall), and my guess is that these Laments were sung on that occasion. They were likely written for that purpose.

Psalms of Solomon

These psalms,[110] written in the classic style, are too late for Solomon, and, taking for granted the attribution of the canonical Psalms to David, it may be that using Solomon's name was just a way of acknowledging, with a wink to the reader, that these are *later*, by ascribing them to David's famous successor. And all the more so since Solomon was said to be the Burt Bacharach of his day. Actually, the Psalms of Solomon appear to stem from the middle of the first century C.E., from pietistic circles, perhaps Pharisees or Essenes.

There are abundant clues to this. All the data are consistent with it, but Psalms of Solomon 17 seems to point to this date very specifically.

> Thou, O Lord, didst choose David (to be) king over Israel, And swaredst to him touching his seed that never should his kingdom fail before Thee. But, for our sins, sinners rose up against us . . . They set a (worldly) monarchy in place of (that which was) their excellency . . . They laid waste the throne of David in tumultuous arrogance. But Thou, O God, didst cast them down and remove their seed from the earth, In that there rose up against them a man that was alien to our race.[111]

The "the lawless one" laid waste the land, destroyed young and old and their children, and drove the righteous into hiding in the desert.

The circumstances envisioned here match what happened at the Roman conquest of Judah in 63 B.C.E. To step back a bit further, we need to remind ourselves of the events of the Maccabean/Hasmonean struggle for independence about a century earlier, when Mattathias the priest and his sons, foremost among them Judah Maccabee (Judah the Hammer), rose up against their persecuting Seleucid Syrian overlords (a story that would have fit right into Judges!) and mounted a campaign of guerilla warfare that, for nearly a century, restored independence to Judah.

The Hasmonean line became a dynasty of priest-kings. They were messiahs according to their supporters, but many refused to recognize their right to rule, since their royal claims conflicted with God's promise of a perpetual throne for David and his line. Their suspicions seemed amply borne out as the years went on and the Hasmonean kings became arrogant, worldly persecutors of the pious (Alexander Jannaeus had thousands of Pharisees crucified).

Finally, factional infighting among rival claimants to the throne became so bad that one faction opened the gates of Jerusalem to the Roman general Pompey (Julius Caesar's ally), who, however, proved no friend to Jews. Pompey is the foreigner, the Gentile ("lawless man") mentioned here. The Hasmoneans are the arrogant usurpers of the Davidic throne, etc.

The wicked, the hypocrites, etc., against whom the psalmist rails (in the classic style of the imprecatory psalms, especially sections of Psalm 119) are fellow Jews who held power under the Romans or Herodians, probably the Sadducees (*Syndikoi*, Syndics or Councilmen). The strange references to unnatural sex acts, etc., allegations common in the Dead Sea Scrolls, too, merely refer to different interpretations of how long the ritual uncleanness of a woman after her period ought to be reckoned. These strict pietists judged their "wicked" rivals as making the quarantine too short and thus as defiling the altar when the women (post-menstrual or still menstrual depending on your rule!) visited it.

Our psalmist is happy enough for God to have unseated the corrupt Hasmoneans, even though it required using the cruel Romans to do it. And now he wants God to expel them as well. No fan of the Romans or the Herodians who governed in their name, the psalmist prays for God to bring to the throne a proper Davidic heir.

Here is perhaps our simplest and purest picture of "demythologized" Jewish messianic expectation: a righteous king from David's dynasty. Nothing is said of an immortal or divine superman, no incarnate God, no dying and rising savior. There is nothing reminiscent either of the earlier Sacred King mythos or of later Christian Christology. But in light of this psalm, it is easy to see where the early Jewish-Christian debate over Jesus' Davidic pedigree came from. It mattered to a lot of people that the King of the Jews be descended from David.

It is possible that these psalms might have been sung at the Temple of Herod, though not by the official priests. More likely they were sung by small fellowships of the pious as they met over kosher meals, groups like the later *haberim*, in private homes (cf. Mark 14:17-18, 26).

The Prayer of Manasseh

2 Kings 21, 2 Chronicles 33

We read of the disgusting and blasphemous reign of King Manasseh of Judah in 2 Kings 21:1-28. Pictured by the Deuteronomic Historian as a sort of Gilles de Rais, a perverted decadent, Manasseh's major crime was heresy, at least in the eyes of the Deuteronomic writer. The king no doubt viewed himself as a reformer, restoring "that old time religion," including the ancient hilltop shrines of the Patriarchs, the chapel of Yahweh's queen Asherah in the Temple, and even infant sacrifice, anciently mandated in the Book of the Covenant (Exod. 22:29). Yahweh announces eventual doom upon Judah for Manasseh's apostasy (1 Kings 21:10-15). And yet the king himself had a long reign!

The Chronicler saw a problem here: Shouldn't God have cut off a sinner like this, according to the Deuteronomic theology? So the Chronicler assumes there must have been more to the story: What if Manasseh was defeated, captured and imprisoned? There he might have been brought to his senses at last, like the Prodigal Son awakening from his shameful squalor, and repented, whereupon, a la the Book of Judges, God mercifully delivered him! Sure, *that* would explain how God could assign him a lengthy reign! Why not?

So that's the way it "happens" in 2 Chronicles 33:10-13. That must have been one heck of a prayer of repentance!

What do you suppose such a villain, now with his tail between his legs, might have said to God? Someone kindly obliged us by composing The Prayer of Manasseh. And it made its way into the canon of the Greek Septuagint Bible. It should be obvious that King Manasseh never prayed such a prayer, but that hardly means no one else ever did. No doubt it has been often used as a poignant prayer of repentance.

The Song of Azariah and the Three Young Men
Dan. 3:24-90

This text also occurs only in the Apocrypha as part of the expanded Book of Daniel.

The first-century B.C.E. psalm is put into the mouth of Azariah ("Abed-Nego," "Worshiper of Nergal") and his two friends Hananiah and Mishael, pious Jews like their friend Daniel (the Frodo, Sam, Merry and Pippin of ancient Jewry). Just as Daniel was dropped into a lion's den for his refusal to obey the dictates of the king of Babylon which banned public prayer offered to anyone but the king, so were these three locked into an incinerator for their refusal to bow before idols. They were not so much as singed, but were protected by a Son of God, one of the angel princes, who shared their imprisonment, a powerful symbol of God's promise to his people that he will be with them in the ordeal of persecution, so that Israel may never perish.

Surely that is the story's point, not some vain promise that God will miraculously save the physical lives of all faithful individuals when the pagans try to kill them. The writer simply could not have believed the latter; experience during the Seleucid persecutions had told him different. Azariah and his comrades stand for Jews in general, not any specific individuals. The deliverance of brave individual martyrs was rather a matter of vindication on the Last Day, when the martyrs would shine like stars with their Father's glory (Dan. 12:1-3).

Actually, what we have here is a pair of psalms. The first is a *penitential lament* like, e.g., Psalm 51, consisting of verses 26-45, probably composed by the Levites for the riverside Sabbath worship in Babylon during the Exile. The second, verses 52-90, is a classic *hymn of praise* meant to be sung antiphonally by the (post-Exilic) congregation in the Temple in Jerusalem. It seems to presuppose a greater degree of real, formal worship.

Verse 88 has been added by the Danielic redactor to make it fit the context. He figured these three men were prime examples of the kind of "holy men of humble heart" mentioned in verse 87. What the redactor has done here is just like the insertion of a *thank offering psalm* into the Book of Jonah (2:3-10), for poor Jonah to sing as he is blinking away the digestive juices of the Ichthyosaur.

Notes

1. Thomas S. Kuhn, *The Structure of Scientific Revolutions* (Chicago: University of Chicago Press, 1962).

2. Sigmund Mowinckel, *The Psalms in Israel's Worship*. Trans. D.R. Ap- Thomas (Nashville: Abingdon, 1962), II: p. 43. He admits that some do express the personal feelings of their Levite authors (II: p. 141).

3. Mowinckel, *Psalms* II: pp. 38-39. Levitical singers copied the psalms and thus were scribes, hence the compatibility of (scribal) Wisdom psalms with the rest (Mowinckel, *Psalms* II: p. 94). The Psalter is a combination of four earlier Psalm collections, and they have been simply put together back to back. First comes the Psalms of David (3-41); second, the Elohistic Psalter (42-83) which is further subdivided into the Psalms of the Sons of Korah (42-49, 84-89), another Davidic collection (51-72), plus the Psalms of Asaph (73-78). The fourth collection includes 90-150.

   Much later scribes redivided them into five sections, in imitation of the Pentateuch: Book One includes 1-41; Book Two consists of 42-72; Book Three consists of 73-89; Book Four includes 90-106; Book Five is made up of 107-50. There are J Psalms and E Psalms, preferring the divine names Yahweh (Jehovah) and Elohim respectively..

4. Mowinckel, *Psalms* II: p. 114.

5. J.H. Eaton, *Kingship and the Psalms*. Studies in Biblical Theology, Second Series 32 (London: SCM Press, 1976).

6. Mowinckel, *Psalms* I, p. 80.

7. Mowinckel, *Psalms* II: p. 83.

8. Mowinckel, *Psalms* II, p. 114.

9. Mowinckel, *Psalms* II: p. 8.

10. Michael D. Goulder, *The Prayers of David: Psalms 51-72*. Studies in the Psalter II (London: T&T Clark, 2004).

11. See Rudolf Bultmann, *The History of the Synoptic Tradition*. Trans. John Marsh (New York: Harper & Row, 1968), pp; 39-41, 47 ("the sayings have commonly generated the situation, not vice-versa."); Henri Lammens, "Koran and Tradition–How the Life of Muhammad Was Composed." Trans. Ibn Warraq. In Ibn Warraq, ed., *The Quest for the Historical Muhammad* (Amherst: Prometheus Books, 2000), pp. 169-87.

12. Aubrey Johnson, *The Cultic Prophet in Israel's Psalmody* (Cardiff: University of Wales Press, 1979); Mowinckel, *Psalms* II: pp. 92-93.

13. Johnson, *Cultic Prophet*, pp. 180-81, 222.

14. Mowinckel has a more charitable suggestion, namely, that the auspicious oracles were not supposed to be clairvoyant prognostications but rather powerful words (virtually incantations) that would shape reality and bring about the hoped-for victory (Mowinckel, *Psalms* II: pp. 65-66). See also Eaton, *Kingship*, pp. 41, 131; Steven J.L. Croft, *The Identity of the Individual in the Psalms*. Journal for the Study of the Old Testament Supplement Series 44 (Sheffield: JSOT Press, 1987), p. 136.

15. Mowinckel, *Psalms* II: p. 72.

16. Michael D. Goulder, *The Psalms of the Sons of Korah*. Studies in the Psalter, I. Journal for the Study of the Old Testament Supplement Series 20 (Sheffield: JSOT Press, 1982), *passim*, but especially pp. 220, 228; Goulder, *The Psalms of Asaph and the Pentateuch*. Studies in the Psalter, III. Journal for the Study of the Old Testament Supplement Series 233 (Sheffield: Sheffield Academic Press, 1996), pp. 24-36.

17. "Then the word of [Yahweh] came a second time to Haggai on the twenty-fourth day of the month, saying, 'Speak to Zerubbabel governor of Judah, saying, "I am going to shake the heavens and the earth. I will overthrow the thrones of kingdoms and destroy the power of the kingdoms of the nations; and I will overthrow the chariots and their riders, and the horses and their riders will go down, everyone by the sword of another. On that day," declares [Yahweh Sabaoth], "I will take you, Zerubbabel, son of Shealtiel, my servant," declares [Yahweh], "and I will make you like a signet ring, for I have chosen you," declares [Yahweh Sabaoth].'" (Hag. 2:20-23, NASB)

18. Mowinckel, *Psalms* I, p. 77.

19. Cf., Mowinckel, *Psalms* I, p. 218.

20. Mowinckel rejects this in *Psalms* I, p. 48, II. pp. 260-61, preferring a period of writing from the monarchy down to 400 B.C.E. (*Psalms* II: p. 155), with the Psalter as a whole being compiled no later than 250-200 B.C.E. (*Psalms* II: pp. 199, 201) by the scribes (*Psalms* II: pp. 204-205). Kennet, *Old Testament Essays*, pp. 219ff, places the Psalms at 168-141 B.C.E.

21. The result was parallel to that achieved by pre-critical attempts to plug the Pauline Epistles into various points in the (fictive) narrative of Acts.

22. Charles Lee Feinberg, "Are There Maccabean Psalms in the Psalter?" *Bibliotheca Sacra* 105 (Jan. 1948), pp. 44-55.

23. Mowinckel, *Psalms* I, p. 12-13, 229; II: p. 86.

24. Albert Gelin, *The Poor of Yahweh*. Trans. Kathryn Sullivan (Collegeville: Liturgical Press, 1964), pp. 67-74.

25. Mowinckel, *Psalms* II, pp. 112-13.

26. Cf. Mowinckel, *Psalms* I, pp. 61, 79. Eaton, *Kingship*, pp. 77-78, 177; Goulder, *Korah*, p. 256, n. 29; Johnson, *Cultic Prophet*, p. 312.

27. Ivan Engnell, *A Rigid Scrutiny: Critical Essays on the Old Testament*. Trans. John T. Willis and Helmer Ringgren (Nashville: Vanderbilt University Press, 1969), Chapter 11, "The Messiah in the Old Testament and Judaism," p. 235.

28. Mowinckel, *Psalms* I, pp. 64, 125.

29. Giovanni Garbini, *History and Ideology in Ancient Israel*. Trans. John Bowden (New York: Crossroad Publishing, 1988), p. 56.

30. Most of the time I quote from the Revised Standard Version, and for the few quotes where no version is noted, you can assume that's the source. Since I will need to repeat several verses to make somewhat different points in what follows, I decided to mix it up a bit, using other translations including the American Standard Version, the New American Standard Bible, and the New Revised Standard Version. I replace "the LORD" and "GOD" with the name *Yahweh*, which is what actually stands in the Hebrew text, likewise replacing "God Most High" with *El Elyon*, another proper name. Differences between my quotations and the original translation text are always indicated with brackets.

31. Eaton, *Kingship*, p. 98.

32. Behemoth appears to be intended in the depiction, in Revelation 13:11, of the second Beast, while the first, the seven-headed dragon, is obviously Leviathan.

33. Robert Graves and Raphael Patai, *Hebrew Myths: The Book of Genesis* (New York: Greenwich House, 1983), p. 31.

34. Nor is this particular myth-ritual complex the only aspect of the royal paradigm that allows us to make new and comprehensive sense of many psalms. J.H. Eaton (*Kingship*) says, "In many cases the royal interpretation is especially to be preferred because it allows the psalm as it stands to be seen as a consistent and meaningful whole. Other interpretations spoil this unity as much by assuming the irrelevant use of royal elements (references to enemy nations, world-judgment etc.) as by reckoning with later additions and redactions" (p. 25).

35. Mowinckel, *Psalms* I, pp. 134-35; Goulder, *Korah*, p. 221-22. Engnell, *Rigid Scrutiny*, Chapter 7, "New Year Rituals," p. 184.

36. Margaret Barker, *The Great Angel: A Study of Israel's Second God* (London: SPCK, 1992) , pp. 16-23.

37. Garbini, *History and Ideology*, p. 56.

38. Mowinckel, *Psalms* I, pp. 132-33.

39. Cf., Lord Dunsany's tale, "How the Gods Avenged Meoul Ki Ning," in *Tales of Three Hemispheres* (John W. Luce & Co., 1919):

Meoul Ki Ning was on his way with a lily from the lotus ponds of Esh to offer it to the Goddess of Abundance in her temple Aoul Keroon. And on the road from the pond to the little hill and the temple Aoul Keroon, Ap Ariph, his enemy, shot him with an arrow from a bow that he had made out of bamboo, and took his pretty lily up the hill and offered it to the Goddess of Abundance in her temple Aoul Keroon. And the Goddess was pleased with the gift, as all women are, and sent pleasant dreams to Ap Ariph for seven nights straight from the moon.

And on the seventh night the gods held conclave together, on the cloudy peaks they held it, above Narn, Ktoon, and Pti. So high their peak arises that no man heard their voices. They spake on that cloudy mountain (not the highest hamlet heard them). "What doth the Goddess of Abundance," (but naming her Lling, as they name her), "what doth she sending sweet dreams for seven nights to Ap Ariph?"

And the gods sent for their seer who is all eyes and feet, running to and fro on the Earth, observing the ways of men, seeing even their littlest doings, never deeming a doing too little, but knowing the web of the gods is woven of littlest things. He it is that sees the cat in the garden of parakeets, the thief in the upper chamber, the sin of the child with the honey, the women talking indoors and the small hut's innermost things. Standing before the gods he told them the case of Ap Ariph and the wrongs of Meoul Ki Ning and the rape of the lotus lily; he told of the cutting and making of Ap Ariph's bamboo bow, of the shooting of Meoul Ki Ning, and of how the arrow hit him, and the smile on the face of Lling when she came by the lotus bloom.

And the gods were wroth with Ap Ariph and swore to avenge Meoul Ki Ning.

And the ancient one of the gods, he that is older than Earth, called up the thunder at once, and raised his arms and cried out on the gods' high windy mountain, and prophesied on those rocks with runes that were older than speech, and sang in his wrath old songs that he had learned in storm from the sea, when only that peak of the gods in the whole of the earth was dry; and he swore that Ap Ariph should die that night, and the thunder raged about him, and the tears of Lling were vain.

The lightning stroke of the gods leaping earthward seeking Ap Ariph passed near to his house but missed him. A certain vagabond was down from the hills, singing songs in the street near by the house of Ap Ariph, songs of a former folk that dwelt once, they say, in those valleys, and begging for rice and curds; it was him the lightning hit.

And the gods were satisfied, and their wrath abated, and their thunder rolled away and the great black clouds dissolved, and the ancient one of the gods went back to his age-old sleep, and morning came, and the birds and the light shone on the mountain, and the peak stood clear to see, the serene home of the gods.

40. Geo Widengren, "Early Hebrew Myths and their Interpretation" in S.H. Hooke, ed., *Myth, Ritual and Kingship: Essays on the Theory and Practice of Kingship in the Ancient Near East and in Israel.* (New York: Oxford University Press, 1958), p. 191.

41. Eaton, *Kingship*, pp. 79, 179.

42. Mowinckel, *Psalms* I, pp. 59, 64, 75, 136-38, 243.

43. G. Ernest Wright, *The Old Testament Against Its Environment.* Studies in Biblical Theology No. 22 (London: SCM Press, 1950).

44. Goulder, *Korah*, p. 157.

45. Goulder at p. 196.

46. Cf. Eaton, *Kingship*, p. 79.

47. Goulder at p. 196.

48. Geo Widengren, *Sakrales Königtum in Alten Testament und in Judentum*, pp. 75ff, and in "Konungens vistesle I dödsriket" in *Svensk Exegetisk Aarsbok* 10 (1945), pp. 66-81.

49. Mowinckel, *Psalms* I, p. 152, 174.

50. Goulder, *Korah*, p. 250.

51. Mowinckel, *Psalms* I, pp. 48-49, 111, cf. pp. 190-91; II: p. 64, pp. 224-25; Engnell, *Rigid Scrutiny*, Chapter 11, "The Messiah in the Old Testament and Judaism," p. 227.

52. Croft, *Identity*, p. 122, reads it as a desperate plea in times of famine, sung by and for the king. For more discussion, read on.

53. Plus other royal birth or enthronement oracles like Isaiah 9:6ff and Isaiah 11:9ff. See Thomas L. Thompson, *The Messiah Myth: The Near Eastern Roots of Jesus and David* (New York: Basic Books, 2005).

54. Aage Bentzen, *King and Messiah*. Lutterworth Studies in Church and State. (London: Lutterworth Press, 1955), pp. 38, 73-74.

55. Bentzen, *King and Messiah*, p. 71.

56. Bentzen, *King and Messiah*, pp. 47, 79.

57. Mowinckel, *Psalms* I, pp. 49, 191. But it was Margaret Barker, in *The Great Angel*, who finally put these puzzle pieces together.

58. Paul D. Hanson, *The Dawn of Apocalyptic: The Historical and Sociological Roots of Jewish Apocalyptic Eschatology* (Philadelphia: Fortress Press, 1975).

59. *The Hymns of the Rgveda*. Trans. and ed. Ralph T.H. Griffith (Dehli: Motilal Banarsidass, 1976), pp 20-21.

60. In like manner, the Israelite king (portraying Yahweh) would prepare for the (mock) battle, fortifying himself by quaffing the water from the sacred cup or well or Fountain of Life (Psalm 110:7). Bentzen, *King and Messiah*, pp. 24-25.

61. Engnell, *Rigid Scrutiny*, Chapter 5, "The Book of Psalms," pp. 118-19; Chapter 7, "New Year Festivals," p. 181; Engnell, *Studies in Divine Kingship in the Ancient Near East* (Uppsala: Almqvist & Wiksells Boktryckeri, 1943), pp. 36, 128.

62. What, you don't think that could be impressive? One day in 1976 I was walking down 42nd Street, headed for the Port Authority bus terminal, when I felt a tap on the shoulder. I turned around to face a guy dressed as Godzilla passing out fliers for the premiere of *Godzilla versus Megalon* at one of the grind house theatres that used to line the street. Yikes!

63. Mowinckel, *Psalms* I, p. 62.

64. Mowinckel at p. 54.

65. Martin Noth, *The Laws in the Pentateuch and Other Studies*. Trans. D.R. Ap-Thomas (London: SCM Press, 1984), Chapter V., "God, King, and Nation in the Old Testament," pp. 172-73. Bentzen is, I think, exactly right:

the "interpretation . . . by Noth . . . is a relic of the days when the divinization of the ancient kings was thought blasphemous and it represents the artificiality of the attempts of the old orthodoxy to avoid 'idolatry' and of its sister rationalism to avoid 'enthusiasm'" (*King and Messiah*, p. 96).

66. Engnell, *Rigid Scrutiny*, Chapter 11, "The Messiah in the Old Testament and Judaism," p. 223; Chapter 12, "The Son of Man," p. 238; Engnell, *Studies in Divine Kingship*, pp. 80-84.

67. Bentzen, *King and Messiah*, pp. 19, 23-24.

68. Griffith, trans., *Hymns of the Rgveda*, p. 5.

69. W. Philip Keller, *A Shepherd Looks at Psalm 23* (Grand Rapids: Zondervan, 2007).

70. Margaret Barker, *The Gate of Heaven: The History and Symbolism of the Temple in Jerusalem* (London: SPCK, 1991), p. 117.

71. Cf. John M. Allegro, *The Sacred Mushroom and the Cross: A Study of the Nature and Origins of Christianity within the Fertility Cults of the Ancient Near East* (New York: Bantam Books, 1971).

72. R. Gordon Wasson, *Soma: Divine Mushroom of Immortality*. Ethno-mycological Studies No. 1 (New York: Harcourt Brace Jovanovich, n.d.).

73. *The Rig Veda*. Ed. and trans. Wendy O'Flaherty. Penguin Classics (Baltimore: Penguin Books, 1981), pp. 133-34.

74. The mountain range where the sacred mushrooms grow.

75. The mystical heat emitted by sacrifice and meditation.

76. The Vedic priest would liquefy the mushroom with mortar and pestle.

77. Yama, the god who reigns over the dead.

78. The cosmic springs of heaven.

79. Goulder, *Korah*, p. 122-30.

80. Croft, *Identity*, pp. 92-93.

81. Mowinckel, *Psalms* I, p. 228.

82. Croft at pp. 126-27.

83. Croft at pp. 56-57, 64.

84. Stephen Langdon, ed. and trans., *Sumerian Liturgies and Psalms* (Philadelphia: The University Museum, 1919).

85. Croft at pp. 138-39.

86. Krister Stendahl, *The School of Saint Matthew and its Use of the Old Testament* (Philadelphia: Fortress Press, 1968), "The formula quotations of Matthew and the Habakkuk Commentary from Qumran–The *pesher* manner of quoting Scripture," pp. 183-202; Richard N. Longenecker, *Biblical Exegesis in the Apostolic Period* (Grand Rapids: Eerdmans, 1975), "Pesher Interpretation," pp. 38-45; Barbara Thiering, *Jesus the Man: A New Interpretation from the Dead Sea Scrolls* (Sydney: Random House/Corgi, 1993), Chapter 4, "The Pesher Technique," pp. 28-35.

87. Helmer Ringgren, *The Messiah in the Old Testament*. Studies in Biblical Theology No. 18 (London: SCM Press, 1956), Chapter IV, "The So-Called Servant Psalms," pp. 54-64.

88. Claude Levi-Strauss, "The Structural Study of Myth." In Levi-Strauss, *Structural Anthropology*. Trans. Claire Jacobson and Brooke Grundfest Schoepf (Garden City: Doubleday Anchor Books, 1967), pp. 202-28. See my discussion of the Eden myth back in the chapter on Genesis.

89. Rudolf Bultmann, *Theology of the New Testament*. Vol. I. Scribner Studies in Contemporary Theology (New York: Scribners, 1951), pp. 21, 25.

90. Once, while attending an infant baptism service, I paged over to this passage, then whispered to my daughter Victoria, "You'll never hear *these* verses in church!"

91. William H. Worrell, "The Demon of Noonday and Some Related Ideas" *Journal of the American Oriental Society* Vol. 38, 1918, pp. 163.

92. Engnell, *Rigid Scrutiny*, Chapter 5, "The Book of Psalms," pp. 84-85, 104.

93. Goulder, *Korah*, suggests that "sun" is the wrong translation and that the Hebrew word ought to be rendered "battlement" (as it is in Isaiah 54:12), given the context. That would indeed seem to make more sense (p. 49).

94. Mowinckel, *Psalms* I, p. 158, 178-79; Johann Jakob Stamm and Maurice Edward Andrew, *The Ten Commandments in Recent Research*. Studies in Biblical Theology Second Series 2 (London: SCM Press, 1967), pp. 29-30.

95. Mowinckel, *Psalms* II, p. 82.

96. *Sayings of the Fathers or Pirke Aboth*. Trans. Joseph H. Hertz (New York: Behrman House, 1945), pp. 35, 71.

97. We often hear that in the ancient world people could generally expect to live no longer than thirty or forty years, but here we have it taken for granted that most lived a full seventy years, and that even eighty was not so rare. Surely the low estimate of years is the result of factoring in a high infant mortality rate.

98. Emil Brunner, *The Word of God and Modern Man*. Trans. David Cairns (Richmond: John Knox Press, 1964), p. 33, says, "Just as man as an object, as a piece of the spatial causal world, has diminished to the verge of comparative nothingness, as a subject he has become greater in the same degree. For this incredible extension of the picture of the universe is itself the product of his science, and thus of his mind."

99. Paul Tillich, *Dynamics of Faith* (New York: Cloister Library. Harper & Row, 1958), p. 42, says, "All arts create symbols for a level of reality which cannot be reached in any other way. A picture and a poem reveal elements of reality which cannot be approached scientifically . . . The symbol . . . not only opens up dimensions and elements of reality which otherwise would remain unapproachable but also unlocks dimensions and elements of our soul which correspond to the dimensions and elements of reality."

100. Hermann Gunkel with Joachim Begrich, *An Introduction to the Psalms*. Trans. James D. Nogalski. Mercer Library of Biblical Studies (Macon: Mercer University Press, 1998), p. 62.

101. "Great Hymn to the Aten," trans. E.A.W. Budge (1923). Copied from WikiSource [en.wikisource.org/wiki/Great_Hymn_to_Aten] along with bracketed text.

102. A modern parallel might be H.P. Lovecraft's sonnet cycle *Fungi from Yuggoth*. Scholars have long debated whether there is a continuous thread uniting the thirty-six sonnets, groups of them, or none of them.

103. For a modern romantic comedy with some of the same dramatic trappings, see Woody Allen's 1996 comedy, *Mighty Aphrodite*, that is, if you don't mind some pretty salty language.

104. For a modern drama using the same subplot, see Chow Yun-Fat and Jody Foster in *Anna and the King* (1999).

105. Michael D. Goulder, *The Song of Fourteen Songs*. Journal for the Study of the Old Testament Supplement Series 36 (Sheffield: JSOT Press, 1986).

106. Marvin H. Pope, *Song of Songs: A New Translation with Introduction and Commentary*. Anchor Bible 7C (Garden City: Doubleday, 1977).

107. Excuse my slight paraphrase.

108. Raphael Patai, *The Hebrew Goddess* (New York: Avon/Discus Books, 1978), pp. 38-39.

109. Barker, *Gate of Heaven*, p. 14: "Solomon's was not the first Israelite temple to be built, or even the first temple to be built in Jerusalem. The stories in the books of Judges and Samuel are full of references to older temples. Some are mentioned by name as temples, others are assumed to have existed because events happened there 'before the Lord.'" These include Shiloh, Dan, Bethel, Gilgal, Beersheba, Nob, and Mizpah. Maybe the Lamentations originally mourned the fourth-century B.C.E. destruction of the Jewish Temple at Elephantine, Egypt. Who knows?

110. See "The Psalms of Solomon," trans. S.P. Brock. In H.F.D. Sparks, ed., *The Apocryphal Old Testament* (Oxford: Clarendon Press, 1984), pp. 649-82.

111. G. Buchanan Gray in R.H. Charles, ed., *The Apocrypha and Pseudepigrapha of the Old Testament in English* (Oxford: Clarendon Press, 1913) Vol. 2: 631-52. Reprinted at wesley.nnu.edu/sermons-essays-books/noncanonical-literature/noncanonical-literature-ot-pseudepigrapha/the-psalms-of-solomon.

VIII

Proverbs, Wisdom of Solomon, Sirach, Job, Ecclesiastes, Testament of Solomon

SAGES AND MAGES

Every nation treasures its tradition of wisdom, enshrined in collections of aphorisms. These digests of wise sayings serve as a collective fund of life experience that would provide a considerable head start for any individual willing to make a withdrawal. Unfortunately, it *takes* wisdom to know one *needs* wisdom. Some have theorized that collections of proverbs were not intended for popular consumption (especially since the common population would not have access to them anyway), but rather for the education of scribes in training for service at the royal court. Egypt, for example, employed many such scribes. The Bible contains a few collections of wisdom sayings (and of rejoinders to them!). As with many books of the Bible, I am not prepared to offer specific dates of composition, given the flux state of things in the wake of Old Testament Minimalism.

The Book of Proverbs

Proverbs is a compilation of seven earlier collections which have simply been placed side-by-side. We do not need to apply some source-critical scalpel to dismember a seemingly unitary text; the original titles of the individual collections still introduce each one. If only it were so clear throughout the Bible and its composite writings!

    I.   The Proverbs of Solomon, Son of David, King of Israel (ch. 1-9)

    II.   The Proverbs of Solomon (10:1-22:16)

    III.   The Words of the Wise (22:17-24:22)

    IV.   Also These [Sayings] of the Wise (24:23-34)

    V.   These Too Are the Proverbs of Solomon, Which the Men of Hezekiah, King of Judah, Copied [or Collected]: (ch. 25-29)

    VI.   The Words of Agur, Son of Jakeh of Massa (ch. 30)

    VII.   The Words of Lemuel, King of Massa, Which his Mother Taught Him (31:1-9)

To these someone has appended the acrostic poem about the Good Wife (31:10-31).[1] Three of these collections are credited to the legendary (and probably fictional) King Solomon. I think of Derrida's "iteration paradox": We can only understand the uniqueness of a thing once it is no longer unique, once there come to be multiple iterations of it. Only then can we place it in a category of "those things," which enables us to tell what *kind* of thing it is![2] When we see just how numerous Solomonic pseudepigrapha are (Song of Solomon, Ecclesiastes, Wisdom of Solomon, Psalms of Solomon, Odes of Solomon, Testament of Solomon, Key of Solomon, Sword of Solomon), we have a context in which to understand the authorship of the Book of Proverbs. It is no more likely to be a genuine work of Solomon than the rest.

But, really, the question of authorship makes not the slightest bit of difference, since the whole point of the proverb is that its truth is self-evident. Once you hear it, it rings true: "Of *course*! I should have *known* that!" You don't take it on faith, as if it were some apocalyptic revelation of unguessable secrets (cf., 1 Cor. 2:11-13; 2 Cor. 12:4) vouchsafed by a prophet. In that case, maybe you'd want to know who said it, Jesus or Joe Blow. But that's not how proverbs work. You don't have to take somebody's word for it. No faith involved. (Have I said that enough times?)

The last two collections, the sayings of Agur and Lemuel, are Arabian. Part of the third one, specifically 22:17-23:12, is borrowed from the Egyptian *Wisdom of Amenemophis.* Here are some notable parallels, with all Bible quotes from the NASB:[3]

Proverbs 22:17-18: "Incline your ear and hear the words of the wise, and apply your mind to my knowledge; for it will be pleasant if you keep them within you, that they may be ready on your lips."

Amenemophis, **chapter 1:** "Give thine ear, and hear what I say, and apply thine heart to apprehend. It is good for thee to place them in thine heart; let them rest in the casket of thy belly that they may act as a peg upon thy tongue"

Proverbs 22:22: "Do not rob the poor because he is poor, or crush the afflicted at the gate."[4]

Amenemophis, **chapter 2:** "Beware of robbing the poor, and oppressing the afflicted."

Proverbs 22:24-25: "Do not associate with a man given to anger, or go with a hot-tempered man, or you will learn his ways and find a snare for yourself."

Amenemophis, **chapter 10:** "Associate not with a passionate man, nor approach him for conversation. Leap not to cleave to such an one, that terror carry thee not away."

Proverbs 22:29: "Do you see a man skilled in his work? He will stand before kings; he will not stand before obscure men."

Amenemophis, **chapter 30:** "A scribe who is skillful in his business [is found] worthy to be a courtier."

Proverbs 23:1-3: "When you sit down to dine with a ruler, consider carefully what is before you, and put a knife to your throat if you are a man given to appetite. Do not desire his delicacies, for it is deceptive food."

Amenemophis, **chapter 23:** "Eat not bread in the presence of a ruler, and lunge not forward with thy mouth before a governor. When thou art replenished with that to which thou hast no right, it is only a delight to thy spittle. Look upon the dish that is before thee, and let that alone supply thy need."

Proverbs 23:4-5: "Do not weary yourself to gain wealth, cease from your consideration of it. When you set your eyes on it, it is gone. For wealth certainly makes itself wings like an eagle that flies toward the heavens."

Amenemophis, **chapter 7:** "Toil not after riches. If stolen goods are brought to thee, they remain not over night with thee. They have made themselves wings like geese, and have flown into the heavens."

Proverbs 14:7: "Leave the presence of a fool, or you will not discern words of knowledge."

Amenemophis, **chapter 21:** "Empty not thine inmost soul to everyone, nor spoil thereby thine influence."

Proverbs 23:10: "Do not remove the ancient boundary or go into the fields of the fatherless."

Amenemophis, **chapter 6:** "Remove not the landmark from the bounds of the field . . . and violate not the widow's boundary."

Proverbs 23:12: "Apply your mind to instruction and your ear to words of knowledge."

Amenemophis, **chapter 1:** "Apply your heart to discipline and your ears to words of knowledge."

As if this weren't enough to demonstrate the cosmopolitan character of the Book of Proverbs, we may add the observation that the book seems unconcerned with any contrast between Jews and Gentiles. Instead, we read a constant contrast between the wise and the foolish, those with foresight versus those who impulsively obey their basest instincts or yield to the lure of instant gratification.

The ethical ideal promoted by Proverbs is the wise man who obeys conventional morality and upholds the social order. He is careful to avoid the enemies of the public order and all bad characters (Prov. 1:10-19; 13:20). He fulfills traditional religious duties, not because of some deep interior piety, but because that is what a good citizen does. The several references to "commandments" seem to refer to the admonitions of the author, not those of the Torah, and "the law" is never said to be that ascribed to Moses.

The wise man gives alms to the poor (11:24-25; 14:21, 31; 19:17; 21:13; 28:27) and lives at peace with his neighbors (3:28-29). He is not lazy but works hard for prosperity (6:6-11; 12:27; 13:4; 15:19; 19:15, 24; 20:4, 13; 21:25; 22:13; 24:30-34; 26:13-16). He is always truthful (6:16-19; 12:19; 14:25) and remains humble before the king (25:6-7), trusting that the king knows what he's doing since God guides him (8:15-16; 16:10-15; 20:28; 21:1; 24:21). He maintains a discrete silence because still waters run deep (10:19; 11:12-13; 12:23; 13:3; 15:28; 21:23). Do you want the reputation of being wise, even if you aren't? Simple: Just *keep your mouth shut* (17:28)!

And the wise man very definitely steers clear of adultery and prostitutes, one of the most often-treated issues in the book. Here's Proverbs 5, from the *Living Bible*[5].

> Listen to me, my son! I know what I am saying; *listen!* Watch yourself, lest you be indiscreet and betray some vital information. For the lips of a prostitute are as sweet as honey, and smooth flattery is her stock-in-trade. But afterwards only a bitter conscience is left to you, sharp as a double-edged sword. She leads you down to death and hell. For she does not know the path to life. She staggers down a crooked trail and doesn't even realize where it leads.

> Young men, listen to me, and never forget what I'm about to say: *Run from her! Don't go near her house,* lest you fall to her temptation and lose your honor, and give the remainder of your life to the cruel and merciless; lest strangers obtain your wealth, and you become a slave of foreigners. Lest afterwards you groan in anguish and in shame when syphilis consumes your body, and you say, "Oh, if only I had listened! If only I had not demanded my own way! Oh, why wouldn't I take advice? Why was I so stupid? For now I must face public disgrace."

> Drink from your own well, my son–be faithful and true to your wife. Why should you beget children with women of the street? Why share your children with those outside your home? Be happy, yes, rejoice in the wife of your youth. Let her breasts and tender embrace satisfy you. Let her love alone fill you with delight. Why delight yourself with prostitutes, embracing what isn't yours? *For God is closely watching you,* and he weighs carefully everything you do.

The wicked man is doomed by his own sins; they are ropes that catch and hold him. He shall die because he will not listen to the truth; he has let himself be led away into incredible folly.

And Proverbs 7:6-23, also from, yes, the *Living Bible*:

I was looking out the window of my house one day and saw a simpleminded lad, a young man lacking common sense, walking at twilight down the street to the house of this wayward girl, a prostitute. She approached him, saucy and pert, and dressed seductively. She was the brash, coarse type, seen often in the streets and markets, soliciting at every corner for men to be her lovers.

She put her arms around him and kissed him, and with a saucy look she said, "I was just coming to look for you and here you are! Come home with me, and I'll fix you a wonderful dinner, and after that—well, my bed is spread with lovely, colored sheets of finest linen imported from Egypt, perfumed with myrrh, aloes, and cinnamon. Come on, let's take our fill of love until morning, for my husband is away on a long trip. He has taken a wallet full of money with him and won't return for several days."

So she seduced him with her pretty speech, her coaxing and her wheedling, until he yielded to her. He couldn't resist her flattery. He followed her as an ox going to the butcher or as a stag that is trapped, waiting to be killed with an arrow through its heart. He was as a bird flying into a snare, not knowing the fate awaiting it there.

Listen to me, young men, and not only listen but obey; don't let your desires get out of hand; don't let yourself think about her. Don't go near her; stay away from where she walks, lest she tempt you and seduce you. For she has been the ruin of multitudes—a vast host of men have been her victims. If you want to find the road to hell, look for her house.

This second passage comes across almost as a kind of bedroom farce, nor is it the only piece of comedy in Proverbs. That's no surprise, as there is much wisdom in comedy and satire, and always has been.[6] The text condemns prostitutes who are married women, therefore adulteresses, turning tricks for some extra cookie jar money. It is not at all clear that unmarried prostitutes are condemned here or elsewhere in the Bible.

Also, notice that, despite the warning that no sin escapes the all-seeing eye of God, these passages, like the rest of the book, teach that sinful deeds in and of themselves lead inevitably to bad results. One can avoid such actions if only one tries to see a few steps ahead, if one will just consider the likely results (14:15-16; 22:3). There is no Kantian appeal to do the right thing for its own sake, results be damned. Of course, if it came to martyrdom for the faith, that would be a matter of absolute duty, but even there (e.g., 2 Macc. 7:9, 11, 14, 23, 29, 36) he who faces torture and death for the Torah's sake is still acting from enlightened self interest (as in Prov. 11:17; 19:8) since he thereby assures himself of eternal bliss in heaven, not a bad trade-off. Life is assumed to operate according to a tidy system: Virtue is always rewarded (10:3, 6, 27-30; 11:21; 14:11; 19:23). The wise get the best out of it. Yes, the thinking is sound: Wisdom is the key to avoid much unnecessary trouble. Nonetheless, the book's expectation seems too optimistic. It takes insufficient account of arbitrary disasters and unvindicated depredations at the hands of the wicked. We will see how fatal a flaw this can be when we consider Job, which reads like a rebuttal to Proverbs.

One of my favorite bits of biblical comedy is the merciless mockery of the drunkard in Proverbs 23:29-35 (NASB):

> [29]Who has woe? Who has sorrow?
>   Who has contentions? Who has complaining?
>   Who has wounds without cause?
>   Who has redness of eyes?
> [30]Those who linger long over wine,
>   Those who go to taste mixed wine.
> [31]Do not look on the wine when it is red,
>   When it sparkles in the cup,
>   When it goes down smoothly;
> [32]At the last it bites like a serpent
>   And stings like a viper.
> [33]Your eyes will see strange things
>   And your mind will utter perverse things.
> [34]And you will be like one who lies down in the middle of the sea,
>   Or like one who lies down on the top of a mast.
> [35]"They struck me, but I did not become ill;
>   They beat me, but I did not know it.
> When shall I awake?
> I will seek another drink."

"Hair of the dog that bit me, Lloyd m' man! Hair of the dog that bit me!"

Wisdom of Solomon

This book is very important for understanding the New Testament and is even included *in* the New Testament on one ancient canon list (the Muratorian Canon). It appears to be directly quoted by Matthew, Romans, and the Epistle to the Hebrews. There was a large population of Greek-speaking Jews in Alexandria, Egypt. Jewish thinkers there were much influenced by Stoicism and Platonism. The outstanding example is the great first-century C.E. Jewish philosopher Philo of Alexandria, whose doctrine of the Logos parallels the New Testament Christology at many points. A number of the same parallels may be drawn between the New Testament and the Wisdom of Solomon, written probably in Greek in Alexandria in the first century B.C.E.

Many scholars see some sort of relationship between Wisdom 2:12-20 and the Passion narrative of Jesus underlying the gospels. Wisdom 2 presents the typical fate of the righteous person, persecuted by the worldly, whose consciences are chafed by his presence as a living rebuke. They propose to test his pious claim that he is God's son by plotting his death to see if God will perhaps come to his rescue, and they are profanely sure that he will not. Wisdom 2:12-20 (KJV):

> [12]Therefore let us lie in wait for the righteous;
>   because he is not for our turn,
>   and he is clean contrary to our doings:
> he upbraideth us with our offending the law,
>   and objecteth to our infamy the transgressings of our education.
> [13]He professeth to have the knowledge of God:
>   and he calleth himself the child of the Lord.
> [14]He was made to reprove our thoughts.
> [15]He is grievous unto us even to behold:
>   for his life is not like other men's,
>   his ways are of another fashion.
> [16]We are esteemed of him as counterfeits:
>   he abstaineth from our ways as from filthiness:

he pronounceth the end of the just to be blessed,
and maketh his boast that God is his father.
17Let us see if his words be true:
and let us prove what shall happen in the end of him.
18For if the just man be the son of God, he will help him,
and deliver him from the hand of his enemies.
19Let us examine him with despitefulness [RSV: *insult*] and torture,
that we may know his meekness,
and prove his patience.
20Let us condemn him with a shameful death:
for by his own saying he shall be respected [RSV: *protected*].

The more one reads this passage, the harder it is not to think the Jesus story has in some measure been based on it. Mark's crucifixion account is based on Psalm 22, which Matthew supplements with material from Wisdom 2:13, 18 (in Matt. 27:43). Actually, if you read further in the same Wisdom passage, verses 21-3:8, you see anticipated the final resurrection of the slain righteous and their eventual rulership over all nations a la Revelation 20:4-6. One has to wonder to what extent this passage might have influenced the basic death-and-resurrection outline of the gospels.

Wisdom 7:22-30 depicts Wisdom as a personified aspect of the Godhead, whether metaphysically or metaphorically, who knows? In any case, this character is best understood, as Margaret Barker shows, as a demythologized version of the Israelite goddess Isis/Asherah. It was the only way to preserve her in the wake of the monotheistic house-cleaning ascribed (I think fictively)[7] to Hezekiah and Josiah. From the KJV:

22For in her there is a spirit that is intelligent, holy,
unique, manifold, subtle,
mobile, clear, unpolluted,
distinct, invulnerable, loving the good, keen, irresistible,
23beneficent, humane,
steadfast, sure, free from anxiety,
all-powerful, overseeing all,
and penetrating through all spirits
that are intelligent and pure and most subtle.
24For wisdom is more mobile than any motion;
because of her pureness she pervades and penetrates all things.
25For she is a breath of the power of God,
and a pure emanation of the glory of the Almighty;
therefore nothing defiled gains entrance into her.
26For she is a reflection of eternal light,
a spotless mirror of the working of God,
and an image of his goodness.
27Though she is but one, she can do all things,
and while remaining in herself, she renews all things;
in every generation she passes into holy souls
and makes them friends of God, and prophets;
28for God loves nothing so much as the man who lives with wisdom.
29For she is more beautiful than the sun,
and excels every constellation of the stars.
Compared with the light she is found to be superior,
30for it is succeeded by the night,
but against wisdom evil does not prevail.

New Testament writers appropriated this language and conceptuality for Jesus Christ, making him a form of the same divine entity. Note how Colossians 1:15-20 and Hebrews 1:2-3 seem to be explicitly acquainted with this particular passage. John 1:1-18 reflects the same sort of "sophialogy," or doctrine of Wisdom, but it also seems indebted to Wisdom

18:14-16, which merges the ideas of God's Word (his irresistable command), his personified Wisdom, and the Angel of Death in a retelling of the Exodus story of the tenth plague, the death of the firstborn. Again, the KJV:

> ¹⁴For while all things were in quiet silence,
> and that night was in the midst of her swift course,
> ¹⁵Thine Almighty word leaped down from heaven out of thy royal throne,
> as a fierce man of war
> into the midst of a land of destruction,
> ¹⁶And brought thine unfeigned commandment as a sharp sword,
> and standing up filled all things with death;
> and it touched the heaven,
> but it stood upon the earth.

Here is perhaps the root of John's picture of the Word leaving heaven and journeying to earth.

Wisdom 2:23-24 (KJV) is one of our earliest attestations of the myth of Satan's fall, implying that he engineered the events of Eden out of envy at having lost his place as God's favorite to Adam.

> ²³For God created man to be immortal,
> and made him to be an image of his own eternity.
> ²⁴Nevertheless through envy of the devil came death into the world:
> and they that do hold of his side do find it.

There are such close parallels between Wisdom 12:3-19 and Romans 1:18-32, both of them fierce denunciations of Gentile depravity, tracing their moral blindness to their wrong turn toward idolatry, that scholars either admit Paul is engaging in typical Jewish Hellenistic missionary preaching or that someone has interpolated such a (non-Christian) sermon into the text of Romans.[8]

Sirach

Ecclesiasticus or The Wisdom of Jesus ben Sirach

Jews were made welcome in Hellenistic Egypt, part of the Ptolemaic Empire. It was here and in the same period that the Hebrew Tanakh (Bible) was translated into Greek (the Septuagint). A sage named Jeschu ben Sirach decided to write up a compilation of his favorite wise sayings, perhaps his own creations, in his native Hebrew. Some years later, once his grandson read the book, he decided to invest considerable time and effort translating the large book into Greek.

The Septuagint contains this translated version, and for a long time it was supposed that the Hebrew original had perished. This is more than just historical trivia, since it has everything to do with why the Protestant Bible omits the so-called Apocrypha, of which Sirach/Ecclesiasticus is a part.

You see, Martin Luther was working on a translation of the Bible into German and he insisted that only the original Hebrew and Greek texts were inspired, not the secondary Latin Vulgate, which the Catholic Church had made the official and inspired Bible. Luther was going to translate only from the Hebrew Old Testament and the Greek New Testament.

The problem was that some books of the Apocrypha seemed to have survived only in various translations, the Hebrew originals having perished. Luther was stuck: He couldn't admit into his canon a book translated from a translation, or he would be unable to consistently defend not using the Latin Vulgate. So he relegated the lot of them to the Apocrypha: nothing wrong with them, but not infallible scripture.

What he had done, as far as the Old Testament is concerned, was to accept the judgment of the Yavneh rabbis on the contents of the Tanakh, the Hebrew Bible. The result is that today, Protestants share the Hebrew Bible of Judaism, whereas Catholics and Orthodox Churches have the longer Old Testament of the Greek Septuagint.

But, it turns out, most of Sirach—in the original Hebrew—came to light at the end of the nineteenth century. Had he known of this, Luther might not have cut Sirach from the canon.

My impression of this book is that it is a bigger, better Book of Proverbs. Certainly longer, it deals with more topics and in more detail. It is, like Proverbs, largely aphoristic, but there are more developed discourses about matters such as the wisdom required to balance almsgiving with financial responsibility (29:1-20), the dangers of indiscretion and careless tale-bearing (9:18; 13:12-13; 19:7-17; 20:1-8, 18; 21:26; 22:27; 23:13; 27:16-21; 28:13-18; 32:7-9), the duties and abuses of friendship (6:5-17; 9:13; 22:21-22; 37:1-6), and so on. There is a fascinating disquisition on the social role of professional sages versus the equally necessary, but by no means as noble, callings of craftsmen and merchants (38:24-39:11). Like Proverbs, Sirach assumes that the pious will always come out just fine (2:7-11; 7:1; etc.).

The implicit internationalism evident in Proverbs is made explicit in Sirach, as our author credits travel (34:10-11; 39:4) with enriching one's insight with new perspectives (much the same experience that contributed to the broadmindedness of the Greek Sophists, contemporaries of Socrates). But Sirach also differs from Proverbs in that it equates wisdom with the Jewish Torah (15:1, 15-18; 19:20; 21:11; 39:1).[9] Proverbs was not so parochial, simply setting forth examples of how wise foresight enables the righteous man to avoid the pitfalls of the fool and the wicked.

Sirach takes this approach, too, and it predominates, but this prudence is said to be embodied in the Law (24:23-25; 33:28-33:3), as if one could find such pointers in the sacrifice laws of the Pentateuch, the prophetic tirades against idol worship, or the adventures of the kings and the judges. It looks like Sirach, working with a basic Jewish canon, thought of the whole thing as "Torah" (as in Rabbinic Judaism still today), but highlighted what for him was the real center of gravity: wisdom and prudence.

The genre of apocalyptic visions had its roots in the Wisdom Literature,[10] quite naturally since both predictive divination and astrological/astronomical speculation were considered departments of Jewish wisdom. Joseph and Daniel, remember, were both dream interpreters, and 1 Enoch presents cosmological "secrets" (theories) of the Jewish natural philosophers, mapping out the concentric heavens, the imagined treasuries of stars and snowflakes, etc.

Sirach 43 (KJV) is a beautiful poem about the seasons and the heavenly bodies that might be viewed as the launch pad for these more elaborate speculations:

> ¹The pride of the height, the clear firmament,
>   the beauty of heaven, with his glorious shew;
> ²The sun when it appeareth, declaring at his rising a marvellous instrument,
>   the work of the most High:
> ³At noon it parcheth the country,
>   and who can abide the burning heat thereof?
> ⁴A man blowing a furnace is in works of heat,
>   but the sun burneth the mountains three times more;
>   breathing out fiery vapours,

and sending forth bright beams, it dimmeth the eyes.
⁵Great is the Lord that made it;
and at his commandment runneth hastily.

⁶He made the moon also to serve in her season
for a declaration of times, and a sign of the world.
⁷From the moon is the sign of feasts,
a light that decreaseth in her perfection.
⁸The month is called after her name,
increasing wonderfully in her changing,
being an instrument of the armies above,
shining in the firmament of heaven;

⁹The beauty of heaven, the glory of the stars,
an ornament giving light in the highest places of the Lord.
¹⁰At the commandment of the Holy One they will stand in their order,
and never faint in their watches.
¹¹Look upon the rainbow, and praise him that made it;
very beautiful it is in the brightness thereof.
¹²It compasseth the heaven about with a glorious circle,
and the hands of the most High have bended it.

¹³By his commandment he maketh the snow to fall aplace,
and sendeth swiftly the lightnings of his judgment.
¹⁴Through this the treasures are opened:
and clouds fly forth as fowls.
¹⁵By his great power he maketh the clouds firm,
and the hailstones are broken small.
¹⁶At his sight the mountains are shaken,
and at his will the south wind bloweth.
¹⁷The noise of the thunder maketh the earth to tremble:
so doth the northern storm and the whirlwind:
as birds flying he scattereth the snow,
and the falling down thereof is as the lighting of grasshoppers:
¹⁸The eye marvelleth at the beauty of the whiteness thereof,
and the heart is astonished at the raining of it.
¹⁹The hoarfrost also as salt he poureth on the earth,
and being congealed, it lieth on the top of sharp stakes.
²⁰When the cold north wind bloweth,
and the water is congealed into ice,
it abideth upon every gathering together of water,
and clotheth the water as with a breastplate.
²¹It devoureth the mountains, and burneth the wilderness,
and consumeth the grass as fire.
²²A present remedy of all is a mist coming speedily,
a dew coming after heat refresheth.

²³By his counsel he appeaseth the deep,
and planteth islands therein.
²⁴They that sail on the sea tell of the danger thereof;
and when we hear it with our ears, we marvel thereat.
²⁵For therein be strange and wondrous works,
variety of all kinds of beasts and whales created.
²⁶By him the end of them hath prosperous success,
and by his word all things consist.

²⁷We may speak much, and yet come short:
wherefore in sum, he is all.
²⁸How shall we be able to magnify him?
for he is great above all his works.

29The Lord is terrible and very great,
and marvellous is his power.
30When ye glorify the Lord, exalt him as much as ye can;
for even yet will he far exceed: and when ye exalt him,
put forth all your strength, and be not weary;
for ye can never go far enough.
31Who hath seen him, that he might tell us?
and who can magnify him as he is?
32There are yet hid greater things than these be,
for we have seen but a few of his works.
33For the Lord hath made all things;
and to the godly hath he given wisdom.

Speaking of the apocalyptic genre raises the question of individual eschatology ("the last things" awaiting each of us). I do not see any clear statement of a heavenly afterlife for the righteous in Sirach, except for 49:10, where the sage expresses the hope that the twelve prophets (the so-called "Minor Prophets") may rise up again. Would this be their unique privilege? By contrast, the Wisdom of Solomon makes it clear that the souls of the righteous will cast off the clumsy clay of the flesh, relieved to be done with the tedious sack race of physical life. Sirach several times mentions Hades as the fate of the wicked. Sometimes he seems to equate it with the older Hebrew counterpart, Sheol (14:12, 16; 17:27-28; 41:3-4), but he also associates it, as did the Greeks, with fiery torment (7:17; 28:21-23a). Such inconsistencies may result from the possibility that our author coined some of these sayings but collected others from various sources, preserving a range of views on some matters.

Sirach (1:1-9; 24:1-12) presents a doctrine of personified divine Wisdom. As in Proverbs 8:22-31, Wisdom is made a kind of Demiurge, an intermediary agent in the Creation. We are fast on the way to John 1:1-3 here. The Arian theologians of the fourth century could see that, if New Testament Christology was based on these passages (see especially Proverbs 8:22 and Sirach 1:4), it implied Christ was a created being, albeit the agent of the creation of everything else.

Sirach himself, as Wisdom's spokesman (the job of a sage), welcomes all who may come to him for learning (6:22-30; 51:23-27).[11] Matthew summarizes these verses and makes them into a saying of Jesus in Matthew 11:28-30.

Chapters 44-50 feature a biblical hall of fame ("Let us now praise famous men . . ."), recounting in summary the high points of the careers of chosen heroes spanning the whole of Jewish history up to that point. One cannot help but wonder if these chapters might have been the inspiration for Hebrews chapter 11.

My own favorite saying of Sirach: "What race is worthy of honor? The human race" (10:19a, RSV).

The Book of Job

The Book of Job, a masterpiece of world literature, is a drama in poetry, apparently the work of a Hellenized Jew seeking to write a play in the style of Euripides.[12] The long monologues, however, resemble the Lament psalms (also utilized in the so-called Confessions of Jeremiah). But they function like the poetic speeches of the characters in Greek tragedy, a natural fit. The play is based on an old Near-Eastern folktale which we also find attested in the Babylonian *Poem of the Righteous Sufferer*. As we can see just from a few excerpts of the poem, as translated by B.R. Foster,[13] the ancients could be quite eloquent when complaining about their rotten luck and the capricious whims of their god.

²As I turned around,
  it was more and more terrible;
³My ill luck was on the increase,
  I could find no good fortune.
⁴I called to my god
  But he did not show me his face.
⁵I prayed to my goddess,
  But she did not raise her head.

        . . .

¹⁰What bizarre actions
  there were everywhere!
¹¹I looked behind,
  there was persecution, trouble.

        . . .

³⁶Who can learn the reasoning
  of the gods in heaven?
³⁷Who understands the plans
  of the underworld gods?
³⁸Where might humans
  have learned the way of a god?
³⁹He who was alive yesterday
  is dead today.
⁴⁰For a minute someone is downcast,
  then suddenly full of cheer.
⁴¹One moment
  he sings in exaltation,
⁴²Another
  he groans like a professional mourner.
⁴³The people's condition changes in a twinkling.

        . . .

⁷³My eyes stared, but did not see,
⁷⁴My ears were open, but did not hear.
⁷⁵Numbness had grasped my whole body,
⁷⁶Paralysis had fallen upon my flesh
⁷⁷Stiffness had seized my arms,
⁷⁸Impotence had fallen on my loins,
⁷⁹My feet had forgotten their motion.

        . . .

⁸⁶My way in was barred,
  my drinking place blocked,
⁸⁷My hunger was chronic,
  my gullet constricted.
⁸⁸When grain is served,
  I choke it down like stinkweed.
⁸⁹Beer, the sustenance of mankind,
  is sickening to me.
⁹⁰Truly, the malady drags on.

        . . .

[102]All day long
   the tormentor tormented me,
[103]Even in the middle of the night
   he would not let me breathe freely for an instant.
[104]From writhing,
   my joints were separated
[105]My limbs were splayed
   and knocked about.

What is missing from this version is the philosophical content of Job, though verses 36-38 do kind of leap-frog all the way to Job's final realization. Thus the Babylonian poem is a parallel only to the prose Job tale upon which our present Book of Job is based.

The old tale is preserved in the two prose sections, the prologue and the epilogue. It looks like someone decided to split up a prose version of the traditional tale and to sandwich the long text of the drama in between. In the prose epilogue (Job 42:7), God says Job has spoken rightly of him, while the drama has God rebuke Job for the nonsense he has spouted about him.

In 42:7, God is probably recalling Job's pious words back in 1:21 and 2:10, but the epilogue also has God rebuke Job's three pals for speaking of God falsely. In neither the prologue nor the epilogue do we read anything spoken by Eliphaz, Bildad, or Zophar, so we can infer they did say something in the earlier prose tale, but that our redactor has omitted it in favor of what they say in the drama.

The problem Job deals with is that of individual reward and punishment, an unforeseen result of the shift toward individualism seen in Deuteronomy, Jeremiah, and Ezekiel. After this announced policy shift whereby God should henceforth cease punishing the whole darn nation for the sins of previous generations,[14] a new question arose: It still seemed that innocent individuals were suffering without deserving it. For this Job serves as the poster boy.

We've already had the occasion to observe that Job presents the original conception of "the Satan (Adversary)" as one of the Sons of God, his special assignment being to monitor humankind. He looks for religious pretenders and hypocrites, to expose them to Yahweh, who may be too soft on them—or even naïve about them and their actual loyalties. He deems Job a bit too good to be true and proposes stripping him of the fringe benefits God has showered upon him.

Is Job's heart with God, or with his goodies (Matt. 6:24)? Clearly the Book of Job harbors no notions of God's omniscient knowledge of human hearts and consciences, any more than the Garden of Eden depicts Yahweh as either omnipresent (Gen. 3:8) or all-knowing (Gen. 3:9).

The Book of Job presents a dialogue or debate between the positive, optimistic outlook of traditional wisdom set forth in Proverbs, and a disillusioned skepticism that may have developed later, though it could just as well be a contemporary rebuttal. As Gerhard von Rad demonstrated, this skepticism developed, strange as it first may seem, precisely from the doctrine of Divine Providence that we find well illustrated in the Genesis story of Joseph.

If God works in mysterious ways beyond the capabilities of human beings to fathom, this is not necessarily all that comforting! The implication is that it may be impossible to discern God's will or what he is up to. And such skepticism and resignation are also to be found in Ecclesiastes.[15]

What is the book's solution to the problem of evil? There are two quite different approaches offered by different strata in the text. The prose section tells us plainly that Job is being tested, and that our own sufferings should be viewed the same way. But the drama/poem says that it is hopeless to try to second-guess God. The mysteries and paradoxes of nature should be enough to convince us that the ways of God are inscrutable. So why should we even bother trying to figure them out–much less feel entitled to complain that God is not doing his job right?

Traditional Jewish wisdom blames the victim, who must have deserved the ills that descend upon him. This is a purely deductive approach. We needn't examine the evidence for the sufferer's sinfulness to gauge whether he deserves his troubles. No, we know God doesn't afflict the innocent, only the wicked; hence the sufferer *must* be guilty. This perspective is, of course, that of Job's three "friends." And their position is not a caricature. It is no straw man.

The fourth opponent of Job, Elihu, who suddenly pops up out of nowhere (perhaps a later interpolation into the play), offers yet another possible explanation. He argues that suffering is educative. This is much the same as Stoicism.

Interestingly, a later rewrite of Job, The *Testament of Job*,[16] serves as a kind of commentary of the canonical Job, and it makes Elihu an outright enemy of Job who condemns and defames him. There, the other three "comforters" are mainly just shocked at Job having been brought so low, and their brief speeches just express their astonishment. They are not depicted as pompous, Polonius-like exponents of conventional wisdom as in canonical Job.

It almost sounds as if the author of the *Testament* were expanding on the prose version of Job (was Elihu in that one, too? Was it he whom Yahweh was rebuking?), not the dramatic portion. But the main difference in the *Testament of Job* concerns the theodicy: The reason Job suffers Satan's harassment is that God had commanded Job to destroy a local temple of a heathen god (really Satan), and he did, prompting the devil's vendetta. God had warned him of the consequences, but Job was willing to take whatever Satan had in store for him, glad to face the music if he could strike a blow against heathenism.

The Job of the Bible laments that if only he could take God before an impartial judge he would be vindicated (Job 9, 23). It forms a striking parallel to Abraham's challenge to Yahweh, "Shall not the judge of all the earth do right?" (Gen. 18:25). But there is a significant difference that marks the theological change which Job represents. Abraham hears of God's plan to obliterate the Cities of the Plain if the rumors of their wickedness turn out to be true.

He suddenly thinks of his nephew Lot who has recently relocated there. So he objects that Yahweh cannot very well kill *everyone*, since it seems impossible for the whole population to be corrupt. And this begins a negotiation between God and man. As God acquiesces to each of Abraham's proposals, the patriarch recalls just how vile the population is–and keeps revising the number downward. ("You wouldn't kill them all if, say, fifty, uh . . . forty-five, forty, thirty, twenty, *ten* righteous are found there?").[17] The reason Jehovah is such a pushover is that he already knows he is not going to have to change his plans. There won't even be ten.

But Abraham doesn't know that; he thinks God is about to deal falsely with Lot and those like him. Thus the noble character of his protest: God is obliged to be morally good. The God-concept has already been moralized and rationalized.

Job's accusations against God denote something else entirely: a passage *beyond* divine moralization into *complete inscrutability*.[18] We have returned to something like the original notion of the Holy transcending human standards of good and evil and thus any accountability to obey them. This agnosticism might be the result of disappointment with confident predictions of national deliverance and failed theodicies.

Ecclesiastes

Qoheleth

This controversial book was written in the third century B.C.E. or thereabouts, implicitly under the pseudonym of Solomon, though the actual name is never mentioned ("Son of David, King in Jerusalem"). It was quite common in the ancient world to attribute a book of wisdom to some ancient king, and in fact several such works were eventually ascribed to Solomon, whose name was after all something of a byword for wisdom. If it was a book of wisdom, it was a book of Solomon. Here Solomon is called The Preacher (*Qoheleth* in Hebrew, *Ecclesiastes* in Greek, "the one who speaks to the congregation"). Solomon is pictured here as the great orator, an eloquent speaker.

The standpoint of the book is basically one of cynicism, pessimism, resignation to the meaningless character of life. All human endeavour is meaningless: "Vanity of vanity: all is vanity!" Everything repeats itself pointlessly (1:2-11), and nothing new ever happens. The wiser you get, the more sorrow you are asking for (1:12-18) (which is why psychologists have one of the highest suicide rates!).

Pursuing wealth is pointless, too, because despite its obvious benefits, which only fools deny, you can't take it with you, and you'll have to leave it to some unworthy jerk who didn't lift a finger to earn it (2:18-23, cf. Luke 12:16-21). Women, too, turn out to be a disappointment to the once eager Lothario (7:25-28).

Why even strive for righteousness, since the righteous and the wicked share the same dismal fate in the end (8:14)? Death is the curtain that finally rings down on everyone's life, no matter how well or badly one has played one's role, and this more than anything else makes life pointless (2:12-17). The end of humans is the same as that of animals (3:18-19).

Ecclesiastes repudiates the optimistic assurances of traditional wise men (of whom Job's pious windbag friends are typical) that adversity is always a chastisement for sin, so that the righteous do not suffer (4:1-3; 8:14; 9:11-12). "Vanity of vanities! All is vanity!" (The emptiest charade of all is that the "meaning" of life is: There *is* no meaning!) The Preacher repeats this piece of jaundiced bitterness twenty times!

In that case, what does one do with life? Just this: Rejoice and enjoy life while you can. Make the most of the little time you have left to you. Enjoy your work (11:9-12:8). Almost vestigially, the Preacher advises his audience to be pious (2:24; 3:11, 13, 14), without, however, going over the edge and becoming a fanatic about it (7:16).

No wonder some even in the ancient world had their doubts whether this book belonged in the canon of scripture! Very early on, it seems, some redactor tried to soften the blow of the Preacher's unremitting pessimism by adding a few sunny passages such as 2:26, 3:17; 7:18b, 26b, 13a; 11:9b; 12:7b, 13-14. That's a pretty safe bet, since these passages seem to contradict their context and to interrupt the flow of thought.

Even today fundamentalists have difficulty understanding how a writing like Ecclesiastes can be in the Bible at all. Some resort to the desperate expedient of saying that, even though the sentiments expressed in Ecclesiastes are blatantly false, God has verbally inspired it to serve as an example of the worldly mind without God. "The philosophy it sets forth . . . makes no claim to revelation but . . . inspiration records [it] for our instruction."[19] As contrived as this is, it is not far from the truth at least in that the inclusion in the canon does attest a surprisingly diverse range of beliefs and perspectives.

Testament of Solomon

This book is a demonology, a handbook to the various devils, how to recognize them, what they can do, etc. In its present form, it is a Christian(ized) work, having received heavy Christian interpolation, apparently in order to "officially" subordinate Solomon's supernatural prowess to that of Jesus Christ. This was done because Christian magicians liked the Testament and still wanted to use it, despite the fact that others looked askance at those who did not throw over the exorcistic use of any name but Jesus.

Originally the text may have been written in some Semitic tongue, as Syriac and Arabic manuscripts survive, though most extant copies are in Greek. It must be earlier than the first reference to it, which is about 400 C.E. How much earlier we do not know, but it may be pretty old. The tradition of Solomon as a powerful sorcerer (Moses and Jesus, too, were considered great magicians, even by Jews and Christians) is very old in Judaism. Josephus already tells us he knew of exorcists who employed formulae and charms established by Solomon to rid the sufferers of their demons.

> God also enabled him to learn that skill which expels demons: which is a science useful, and sanative to men. He composed such incantations also by which distempers are alleviated. And he left behind him the manner of using exorcisms; by which they drive away demons; so that they never return: and this method of cure is of great force unto this day. For I have seen a certain man of my own country, whose name was Eleazar, releasing people that were demoniacal in the presence of Vespasian, and his sons, and his captains, and the whole multitude of his soldiers: the manner of the cure was this: he put a ring that had a root of one of those sorts mentioned by Solomon to the nostrils of the demoniac: after which he drew out the demon through his nostrils: and when the man fell down immediately, he abjured him to return into him no more: making still mention of Solomon, and reciting the incantations which he composed. And when Eleazar would persuade and demonstrate to the spectators that he had such a power, he set a little way off a cup or basin full of water, and commanded the demon, as he went out of the man, to overturn it; and thereby to let the spectators know that he had left the man. And when this was done, the skill and wisdom of Solomon was shewed very manifestly. (*Antiquities of the Jews* VIII, 2, 5)[20]

The Testament of Solomon is by no means the only grimoire attributed to him.[21] Why would anyone associate Solomon with demons and exorcism? Because knowledge of demons, causes of sickness, etc., was part and parcel of wisdom[22] as defined in the ancient world. For the same reason, it is taken for granted that the wise men Daniel and Joseph are both dream-interpreters.

This is why I have included the Testament of Solomon in this section. In it, Solomon summons a host of demons, binding them and interrogating them one by one. After learning their names and specialties, he presses them into service to construct the Temple. The appearance of several is described in these passages (not contiguous):[23]

> And I worshipped the Lord God of Israel, and bade another demon come forward. And there came before me a dragon, three-headed, of fearful hue.

And I adored the Lord God of Israel, and bade another demon present himself. And there came before me a spirit in woman's form, that had a head without any limbs.

And I again ordered another demon to come before me. And there came, rolling itself along, one in appearance like to a dragon, but having the face and hands of a man. And all its limbs, except the feet, were those of a dragon; and it had wings on its back.

And there came before my face another spirit, as it were a woman in the form she had. But on her shoulders she had two other heads with hands.

And having praised God, I commanded another spirit to come before me; and there came before my face another demon, having in front the shape of a horse, but behind of a fish.

And I commanded another demon to come before me. And there came before my face thirty-six spirits, their heads shapeless like dogs, but in themselves they were human in form; with faces of asses, faces of oxen, and faces of birds.

Like the beasts from Revelation and Daniel, these creatures combine bits and pieces from various real animals. These monsters are visible representatives of an otherwise hidden realm beyond the mundane world. This accounts for their appearance as hybrid entities which constitute living category-crossings. As anthropologist Victor Turner[24] says, such creatures are symbols of *liminality*, or of the boundary lines (social, moral, life-stages, etc.) about to be crossed in any ritual of transition or transformation, which is what is envisioned here: the calling up of another realm into this one.

In apocalypses, such symbolic chimeras mark the eruption of the future into the present by means of the revelation being recounted in the book. But in the case of the demons, there is another factor: The creatures are living category confusions (the literal meaning of the "abominations" forbidden in Leviticus). This gives them a sense of uncleanness, and of the approach of incarnate defilement, the very opposite of the holiness of God, though with similar numinous feelings of dread and terror. Such category-crossings also explain the horrific nature of movie monsters like the man-monster (the Wolf Man, the Gill-man) and the living dead (Count Dracula, zombies, the Frankenstein Monster), etc.[25]

A final note: You know how today people are baffled by how the ancient Egyptians with their primitive technology (early on, they didn't even have the *wheel!*) could possibly have built the pyramids or the Sphinx and thus sometimes suggest they were erected by space aliens? Ditto the Easter Island statues. Well, I wonder if in the Testament of Solomon we do not have an ancient example of the same tendency: Did they read of the fantastic dimensions and embellishment of Solomon's Temple and think it was too great for mere human builders? Is this perhaps why they resorted to the "possibility" that demons were enlisted to do the heavy lifting?

Notes

1. An old pal of mine from teenage fundamentalism days, Dave Steinhart, used to say that Proverbs, with its thirty-one chapters, was ideal for an even month's worth of daily meditations. He said it was "great devotional filler."

2. Jacques Derrida, "Signature Event Context." In Derrida, *Margins of Philosophy*. Trans, Alan Bass (Chicago: University of Chicago Press, 1982), pp. 328-29; Rodolphe Gasché, *The Tain of the Mirror: Derrida and the Philosophy of Reflection* (Cambridge: Harvard University Press, 1986), pp. 214-15: "The possibility of repetition depends on the recognition of self-identical marks; yet repetition constitutes these very marks in their identity.

[. . .] Although iterability as such is the *becoming* of intelligibility and ideality, the very possibility of repetition as the root of truth also prohibits truth from ever becoming *itself*."

3. en.wikipedia.org/wiki/Instruction_of_Amenemope#Biblical_parallels

4. Trials were conducted at the city gates.

5. Okay, so I like Kenneth Taylor's version of Proverbs. Sue me!

6. In fact, many or most episodes of *Seinfeld* sound like rabbinic debates over the fine points of *halakah*: How many days do you have to keep a birthday card before throwing it into the trash? If you don't tell your fiancé you are having lunch with another woman, is it cheating? Does soup by itself count as a meal? Can you break up with an annoying friend like you would a lover?

7. Margaret Barker, *The Great Angel: A Study of Israel's Second God* (London: SPCK, 1992), Chapter Four, "The Evidence of Wisdom," pp. 48-69.

8. J.C. O'Neill, *Paul's Letter to the Romans* (Baltimore: Pelican Books / Penguin Books, 1975), pp. 40-58.

9. Nor was this identification uncommon in ancient Judaism. See M. Jack Suggs, *Wisdom, Christology, and Law in Matthew's Gospel* (Cambridge: Harvard University Press, 1970), pp. 103-108.

10. Gerhard von Rad, *Old Testament Theology Volume II: The Theology of Israel's Prophetic Traditions*. Trans. D.M.G. Stalker (New York: Harper & Row, 1965), pp. 306-307; Jonathan Z. Smith, "Wisdom and Apocalyptic." In Smith, *Map Is Not Territory: Studies in the History of Religions* (Chicago: University of Chicago Press, 1993), pp. 67-87.

11. These verses are not original with Sirach, either, for they are based on a passage in the Davidic Psalter of the Dead Sea Scrolls (II QPs[a]). See Suggs, p. 80.

12. Horace M. Kallen, *The Book of Job as a Greek Tragedy*. A Dramabook (New York: Hill and Wang, 1959), p. 7.

13. Trans. B.R. Foster. soas.ac.uk/baplar/recordings/the-poem-of-the-righteous-sufferer-ludlul-bl-nmeqi-tablet-ii-entire-tablet-read-by-karl-hecker.html

14. One might think that wisdom would lead one to see that such inherited "punishment" only makes (tragic) sense. Individuals are not *de novo* atoms who are not born into conditions already laid down by one's ancestors and culture. Surely it is wisdom to realize that life is not and cannot be fair. See Melvin J. Lerner, *The Belief in a Just World: A Fundamental Delusion*. Perspectives in Social Psychology: A Series of Texts and Monographs (New York: Plenum Press, 1980).

15. "God's activity has sunk down into an unattainable concealment." Gerhard von Rad, *Old Testament Theology Volume I: The Theology of Israel's Historical Traditions*. Trans. D.M.G. Stalker (New York: Harper & Row, 1962), p. 456.

16. "The Testament of Job." Trans. R. Thornhill. In H.F.D. Sparks, ed., *The Apocryphal Old Testament* (Oxford: Clarendon Press, 1984), pp. 617-48.

17. Whenever I read this passage of Genesis, I can't help thinking of Maxwell Smart, back-pedaling from his initially exaggerated claims on *Get Smart*: "Well, would you believe . . .?"

18. "God only knows. God makes his plans. The information's unavailable to the mortal man" (Paul Simon, "Slip-Sliding Away").

19. C.I. Scofield, Frank Gaebelein, E. Schuyler English, eds., *The New Scofield Reference Bible* (New York: Oxford University Press, 1967), p. 696.

20. William Whiston translation. penelope.uchicago.edu/josephus/ant-8.html

21. Sayed Idries Shah, *The Secret Lore of Magic: Books of the Sorcerers* (New York: Citadel Press, 1970), Chapter 1, "The Complete Ritual of Ceremonial Magic: The Key of Solomon, Son of David," pp. 9-34; Chapter 2, "The Clavicle: Spells and Medallions," pp. 35-60; Owen Davies, *Grimoires: A History of Magic Books* (New York: Oxford University Press, 2009), pp. 12-18.

22. Von Rad, *Old Testament Theology Volume II*, p. 306, notes how dream interpretation was likewise part of the repertoire of what he calls "charismatic wisdom."

23. Trans. F.C. Conybeare. esotericarchives.com/solomon/testamen.htm

24. Victor Turner, "Betwixt and Between: The Liminal Period in *Rites de Passage*." In William A. Lessa and Evon Vogt, eds., *Reader in Comparative Religion: An Anthropological Approach* (New York: Harper & Row, Third Edition, 1965), pp. 344-46.

25. On the latter see Noel Carroll, *The Philosophy of Horror, or Paradoxes of the Heart* (London: Routledge, 1990).

IX

Isaiah, Jeremiah, Ezekiel, Amos

Written on the Subway Walls

The Written Jehovah

Evangelical writers[1] on the doctrine of biblical inspiration tirelessly appeal to various "Thus says the Lord" passages in the Old Testament prophets to buttress their case that "the Bible" (as if it were all one single book, a claim made anywhere applying everywhere) claims "itself" to be inspired by God. A weak (really, a *broken*) link in their chain of reasoning is that, if these passages are supposed to be quotes from the oral preaching of street-corner orators, they must refer to the divine inspiration of the *spoken* words, the *utterances*, not the extant texts which preserves them whether accurately or not.

If Jeremiah was an inspired speaker, does it necessarily follow that his secretary Baruch was an inspired transcriber? Odd as it might seem, it would iron out this difficulty if it could be shown that the contents of the books of the prophets *originated* in written form. In that case, it *would* be the writer who is claiming to be inspired, right? Inspiration aside, that is what I will be suggesting here. The books of the prophets originated on paper.

Author Appendages

First, though extra-biblical sources confirm the existence of prophets of this or that deity and thus the fact that such a role existed, they are always depicted as issuing only terse directives to their kings. Samuel, Nathan, Elijah, and Elisha fit this description well enough (though of course this does not verify the episodes in which they appear as being historically authentic), but there is nothing outside the Bible like the Writing Prophets. Why the disparity? Surely it is because the names of prophets were only later attached to compilations of poetry, sermons, and stories.[2]

Interestingly, the Chronicler imagined there had been similar collections of the oracles of Gad the Seer, Nathan the Prophet, and Iddo the Seer, but he did not compile books in their names. (But medieval writers did, taking the opportunity to fill one of these gaps with The Words of Gad the Seer.) Again, though the Deuteronomists made much of Elijah, Elisha, Samuel, and Nathan in their narratives, they did not choose their names to apply to their books, but the pattern holds good anyway, as when later pseudepigraphists fabricated The Apocalypse of Elijah. In fact, the distance, as we will see, between Old Testament books of the prophets and the Pseudepigrapha seems to be narrowing, in terms of both genre and date.

Get it in Writing

Second, the material credited to Isaiah, Jeremiah, Ezekiel and the rest simply cannot be transcriptions of oral preaching.[3] No one could possibly have remembered either the poetic or the prose material from happening to hear it spoken. Despite the romantic talk about "the marvelously retentive memory of the Oriental," there is just no way it can be done.

Some point to the ability of many modern Middle Eastern Muslims to recite the entire Koran (about three fourths the length of the New Testament), but this ignores the obvious: Children are drilled on their memorization *of a written text*. Traditional Islamic accounts of Koranic origins[4] would have us believe that the Surahs of the Koran were themselves speeches delivered off the cuff by the Prophet Muhammad, then frozen in memory by his hearers. But this is exactly the same implausibility that faces us in the traditional reading of the Old Testament prophets.

In all these cases (including that of the gospels), a pre-literary basis for written texts seems like an *ad hoc* hypothesis to build a bridge between extant written texts and a desired, ostensibly "historical" individual, whether Jeremiah, Muhammad, or Jesus Christ.[5] Without such an imagined "tunnel period," the very existence of a pre-literary prophet or teacher becomes moot, as the only "Jesus," "Isaiah," etc., we know and are talking about is a literary character who arises within a written text.[6] Indeed, the whole scenario of prophetic threats and promises seems to constitute a self-contained narrative world. And of course *it is*: It is an extension of the Deuteronomic History.

Advocates[7] of an oral-traditional basis for the books of the prophets (and the gospels and the Koran) point out that at least the poetic sections of these books lend themselves to faithful transmission, since if it doesn't scan, you know something is amiss: words left out or added. I remember how, years ago, I used to think a line from Clement Moore's "A Visit from Saint Nicholas" ran "And the moon on the breast of the new fallen-snow / gave the lustre of mid-day *to all who were below*." But then I noticed, "This can't be right . . . it doesn't scan!" Sure enough, I looked it up and found the true reading was "*to objects below*." Again, the whole point is that regular meter, etc., makes it easier to remember a *written* original.

Deuteronomic Anachronism

Third, the prophet texts are everywhere vitiated by a major anachronism, namely the now-familiar distinction between good "old" ever-since-Moses monotheism on the one hand and incessant pagan polytheistic syncretism on the other. As we have seen, this artificial distinction was a much later piece of theological revisionism. The Deuteronomists rewrote Israelite/Jewish history much as the evangelist Mark reworked the square peg of the Jesus story to make it fit the round hole of the Messianic Secret theory. They wanted Moses to have commanded monotheism, but Israel's perpetual polytheism could not be denied.

Actually, Israelites simply *were* Canaanites–sometimes kissin', sometimes killin', cousins with the Ammonites, Edomites, and Midianites, and shared the same polytheism and idol-worship. So the Deuteronomists posited that Israel had been radically different from their heathen "Canaanite" neighbors and had always known better in religious matters.

And yet most Israelites, most of the time, had regarded God's covenant with Moses as "just so much chin music."[8] Part and parcel of this revisionist program was the repeated theme, in the Deuteronomic History, of both prophets and (some) kings striving in vain to get the people to ditch their "borrowed" "Canaanite" ways. And, lo and behold, this is just the struggle in which we see Isaiah, Jeremiah, et. al., engaged.[9] This means, of course, that the iconoclastic preachings of the prophets were never spoken, only written to serve the agenda of a later theological program.

The Veil Slips

Fourth, there are several winks to the reader implying a written origin of the contents of the prophetic books. We have already observed how the "discovery" of the Book of Deuteronomy (or the basis of it) amid the cobwebs of the neglected Temple (2 Kings 22:8-13ff) denoted the unveiling of a newly coined scripture, a pseudepigraph grounding its authority in an imaginary Mosaic antiquity. Joseph Smith's claim to have unearthed the Book of Mormon upon Hill Cumorah was likewise fictive fanfare to introduce his own pseudepigraphical scripture.

Isaiah 8:16 ("Bind up the testimony, seal the law among my disciples," NASB), like Daniel 12:4a ("But as for you, Daniel, conceal these words and seal up the book until the end of time," NASB), surely indicates the pseudepigraphical, *written*, character of the work (or some of it at any rate). Someone announced the "discovery" of an Isaianic "time capsule" which no doubt displayed surprisingly "prescient" relevance to the pressing concerns of the day.

Similarly, in 4 Ezra (2 Esdras) 14:23-26, 37-48, Ezra is commanded to replace the Hebrew Scriptures, all of which had perished during the Babylonian Exile. This he is to accomplish by drinking a sacred cup of inspiration which enables him to dictate the entire canon (plus numerous esoteric texts!) to a team of five scribes. While the scene might seem to depict written transcription of orally delivered revelation, a closer look reveals the priority of *written* texts which Ezra, under inspiration, recites. Does this not model the original circumstances of the writing of prophetic texts, written to be read aloud?

I see the same thing going on in the books of the prophets when, e.g., Jeremiah dictates to his scribe Baruch the whole body of his oral preachments (Jer. 36:1-8), which he is depicted as remembering verbatim.[10] First danger sign: Could Jeremiah *himself* have remembered all of them? He sends Baruch to read them publicly; then others read the scroll to the king, who slices the scroll up, page by page, tossing it into the fireplace (Jer. 36:23).[11] Hearing of this, Jeremiah dictates the whole thing to Baruch *again* (Jer. 36:27-28), and this is presumably intended to represent the canonical Book of Jeremiah.

What I see here is a broad hint that Baruch reading aloud a text with Jeremiah's name on it actually depicts what Jeremiah is: a text originally written, and written by someone else. The situation is exactly like that with the Gospel of Thomas, material ostensibly delivered orally by Jesus and taken down by a disciple, Didymus Judas Thomas. Ditto The Book of Thomas the Contender, which opens with, "The hidden sayings that the Savior spoke to Judas Thomas, which I, Mathaias, in turn recorded."[12] Again, The Second Apocalypse of James has, "This is the discourse that James the Just delivered in Jerusalem and Mariem wrote down."[13] I see the role of Baruch in writing down Jeremiah's prophecies as equally fictive.[14]

Ezekiel (2:9-3:3) beholds an unfurled scroll and is told to *eat* it. In this way he receives the oracles he is to announce to his hearers. Note that his prophecy begins in *written* form and only then is preached, essentially read out. Muhammad's revelations, too, were supposedly dictated to him by the angel Gabriel who read them to him from the Mother of the Book, a *written* text kept in heaven. Again, written text is prior to oral prophesying.

The Latter Prophets

Many find it quite puzzling to learn that the Jewish canon denominates the books we are considering here "the Latter Prophets," with the sequence of Joshua-Judges-Samuel-Kings designated "the Former Prophets." In what sense are these narrative books to be considered "prophetic"? Maybe it is because they view Israelite/Jewish history from the perspective of Isaiah, Jeremiah, Amos, Hosea and the rest? These prophets denounce idolatry, polytheism, exploitation, etc., and predict terrible doom if the people do not straighten up and fly right. Thus a history written to demonstrate how correct these spokesmen for God had been would amply deserve the adjective "prophetic."

It makes sense. But there is so much more to it that we can say the reverse is the case! The way I just put it turns out to be putting it exactly backwards. It now seems that the scholars who compiled the Deuteronomic History went on to compile the books of Isaiah,

Jeremiah, Ezekiel, and the Twelve (whom we call "the Minor Prophets").[15] Moreover, they used pretty much the same methods they employed in their earlier work.

Just as the compilers of the Deuteronomic History did not concoct their epic from whole cloth but instead gathered many legendary episodes, bits of hymns and poems, etc., then coated them with their own rather heavy theological varnish, they collected some episodes of renowned prophets of the past and some poetic materials traditionally attributed to them, embedding these items amid stories and prose sermons of their own making.[16]

We might think of the midrashic technique of generating "shaggy dog" stories as a way of interpreting, creating a context for, enigmatic sayings, psalm lyrics, and prophecies. The headings of many psalms try to place the lyrics in this or that plausible circumstance chosen from 1 or 2 Samuel.[17] The gospels' pronouncement stories look to have been created as "ideal scenes" to apply the saying to a circumstance that might have generated it.[18] Many of the Islamic *hadith* began as attempts to supply the *Sitz-im-Leben* of various Surahs of the Koran.[19] Consulting commentaries on the books of Isaiah, Jeremiah, et. al., will quickly reveal just what a mass of guesswork is required to explain what the prophet is talking about, who is being threatened with a divine ultimatum, whose deliverance is being promised.[20]

The endeavor is highly reminiscent of the attempts to plug the various Pauline Epistles into the (artificial) chronology of the Book of Acts,[21] as well as the hypothetical "police artist" reconstructions of "the opponents" attacked in those epistles.

Speaking of this last, one must ask why all the situations, even subjects, of the Psalms, the Prophets, and the Pauline Epistles are so vague? So difficult to pin down? Is it not because *no* historical specifics are in view? And that therefore no probable (though many plausible) ones can be assigned? Why does Paul appear to be aiming his polemics now at Gnostics, now at Judaizers, now at charismatic "super-apostles"?

I think it is a scattershot approach[22] with the motto "If the shoe fits wear it." The Psalmists are sore distressed at . . . *something* or other, because the more general it is, the easier it is to identify the text with your own situation. It is much like the strategically imprecise horoscopes in the newspaper: One size fits all! Different readers in diametrically opposite situations read the same text, amazed at how it seems to be speaking to them personally!

Apocalyptic texts pretend to supply signs heralding the end: "When you see these things taking place, you know that it is near, at the very gates!" (Mark. 13:29). But the signs listed are so commonplace (wars, famines, alienation) that every generation feels it is the last. And of course that's the whole idea: to keep the readers of any generation on their toes.

Who Ya Gonna Call?

What marks so much of the materials in the Prophets as Deuteronomic, at least in their present form? First, numerous prose speeches attributed to the prophets are filled with vocabulary, style, and the theology-of-history familiar from the Book of Deuteronomy and the Deuteronomic History.[23] The Deuteronomic character of the prophetic books may help to explain a striking and otherwise puzzling feature of many of them, namely the frequent juxtaposition of oracles of doom with promises of restoration and blessing. My guess is that the compilers were trying to reproduce the pattern of alternating blessings and cursings found in Deuteronomy 11:8-28; 27:1-28:68.

Second, the characters of the prophets conform to a stereotype occurring all over the Deuteronomic History, as well as in each other. "There are, for example, many connections between the picture of Elijah and the portrayal of prophets such as Ezekiel and Jeremiah."[24]

Deuteronomy is particularly keen on Moses, the standard by which all subsequent prophets must be judged. Prophets like him will appear from time to time, and they must be heeded, but none will be Moses' equal (Deut. 34:10-12; 18:18-19). First Kings 19 goes out of its way to depict Elijah as one of these prophets like Moses, though not quite as great. Elijah seeks God at Mount Horeb, discouraged at being, he thinks, the last of Yahweh's prophets, with Baalism in the ascendancy. His complaint corresponds to that of the burnt-out Moses in Exodus 5:22.

Yahweh's appearing to Elijah in reply is accompanied by thunder, earthquakes, and fire, just like in Exodus 19:18-19 when God descends upon Sinai to deliver the Law. Moses asks to see God but receives only an oblique glimpse of him passing by; likewise, Elijah is told that Yahweh is about to pass by, but all he gets is an anticlimactic whispering voice.[25] Neither Moses nor Elijah is allowed to see the ultimate triumph of their mission. Moses must appoint Joshua as his successor, while Elijah passes the baton to Elisha. And just as Joshua parts the Jordan, imitating Moses parting the Sea, so does the newly ordained Elisha repeat Elijah's parting of the Jordan, both reinforcing the actantial[26] identity between master and successor.

Jeremiah, too, has a lot in common with Moses:

> Just as Moses writes upon the tables of stone the words of the covenant he has received from God (Ex. 34:27), so Jeremiah with the aid of Baruch produces a scroll containing all the words he has received from the Lord. Both Moses and Jeremiah have to go through the whole procedure twice. In carrying out his mission Moses is assisted first of all by Aaron who acts as his mouthpiece and later by Joshua and Caleb. Jeremiah has Baruch as his mouthpiece and the aid of Ebed Melech and the Sons of Shaphan. It is hard to avoid the conclusion that the book *Jeremiah* had as one of its aims the presentation of Jeremiah as a prophet like Moses sent by the Lord in fulfillment of Deut. 18:18-19.[27]

The narratives of the prophets' call to office are suspiciously similar to that of Moses, Samuel, and each other's. Let's take a look at each.

Moses
Exod. 3:1-12; 4:10-13; 6:10-12; 7:1-4

Moses finds himself tending the flock of his father-in-law, Jethro, leading them from one grazing ground to another. Nearing the holy mountain Horeb, he catches sight of a distant thicket which seems to be ablaze but does not fall to ashes no matter how long he watches. So he decides to check it out, discovering the radiance is not in fact any earthly flame but rather the shimmering glory of an unknown deity. When the Entity sees he has attracted Moses' notice he speaks to him from amid the bushes: "Moses, Moses!"

Stunned, the shepherd stammers, "Here am I." Warned to discard his sandals, rendered henceforth holy by contact with the sacred space Moses has blundered upon, he kicks them away.

The voice identifies itself as the ancestral God of the Genesis patriarchs. He should be no stranger to the Hebrew Moses, but much has been forgotten during the Hebrew sojourn in Egypt. Terror-stricken, Moses hides his eyes. Next God informs him he has seen the sufferings of Moses' oppressed people back in Egypt and has chosen Moses to lead them to freedom. "Come, I will send you."

But to this task Moses feels altogether inadequate. Like Bilbo Baggins, he is loath to give up a mundane life of settled routine. "But Moses said to God, 'Who am I, that I should go to Pharaoh, and that I should bring the sons of Israel out of Egypt?'" (Exod. 3:11, NASB)

God assures him of divine support: "But I will be with you."

Feeling cornered, Moses replies, "Please, [Adonai], I have never been eloquent, neither recently nor in time past, nor since You have spoken to Your servant; for I am slow of speech and slow of tongue." (Exod. 4:10). He pleads to be let off the hook, "Please, [Adonai], now send the message by whomever You will." (v. 13). And besides, "the sons of Israel have not listened to me; how then will Pharaoh listen to me, for I am unskilled in speech?" (Exod. 6:12, all NASB)

Well, God admits, in fact Pharaoh *won't* listen, and that's by design. "I will harden Pharaoh's heart that I may multiply My signs and My wonders in the land of Egypt. When Pharaoh does not listen to you" (Exod. 7:3-4, NASB).

Samuel

1 Sam. 3

Young Samuel, an acolyte serving in the temple of Yahweh, sleeps at the foot of the Ark of God. A voice awakens him. "Samuel! Samuel!"

Supposing it to be the voice of his mentor Eli, Samuel answers, "Here I am!" and hastens to the old man's bedside. "Here I am, for you called me."

But Eli says, "I did not call; lie down again." Puzzled, Sammy goes back to bed, but the whole sequence repeats twice more. It does not occur to the lad that it is God summoning him, for it has not happened to him before this night. But old Eli finally realizes what *has* happened, namely that God has passed over him and chosen a more responsive ear to receive his prophetic word.

Thus begins Samuel's prophetic career. As instructed by Eli, he responds directly to the disembodied voice: "Speak, for thy servant hears."

And God answers, "Behold, I am about to do a thing in Israel, at which the two ears of every one that hears it will tingle" (1 Sam. 3:1-11, RSV)

Isaiah

Isa. 6

Isaiah is meditating in the Jerusalem Temple when a vision of God bursts upon his sight. He beholds Adonai upon a great throne surrounded by six-winged seraphim. These proclaim God's glory. "Holy, holy, holy is [Yahweh Sabaoth]; the whole earth is full of his glory." The ground quakes and the glory cloud swells up to hide the awesome spectacle from mortal eyes.

Isaiah feels much like Dorothy and her companions, trembling before the great and powerful Oz. "Woe is me, for I am ruined! Because I am a man of unclean lips, And I live among a people of unclean lips; For my eyes have seen the King," Yahweh Sabaoth (Isa. 6:5, NASB). Thus he deems himself unfit to speak the holy words of God.

But God will take care of that. One of the attendant seraphs carefully removes a red hot coal from the altar and brings it to Isaiah's lips. "Behold, this has touched your lips; and your iniquity is taken away, and your sin is forgiven." Again God speaks, asking for a volunteer from the audience: "Whom shall I send, and who will go for Us?" (vv. 7-8, NASB)

Transformed and purified, Isaiah is now eager! "Here am I! Send me!" God forewarns him that Isaiah's mission is already doomed to failure. No one will heed him, and there will be hell to pay. "Go, and tell this people" the following, God commands: "Keep on listening, but do not perceive; keep on looking, but do not understand." Isaiah is to render their hearts "insensitive, their ears dull, And their eyes dim." Otherwise, Yahweh says, "they might see with their eyes, hear with their ears, understand with their hearts, and return and be healed" (vv. 9-10, NASB).

Jeremiah

Jer. 1

Young Jeremiah has a similar interview with the Almighty, who tells him, "Before I formed you in the womb I knew you, and before you were born I consecrated you; I have appointed you a prophet to the nations." (Jer. 1:5).

He replies, "Alas, Lord [Yahweh]! Behold, I do not know how to speak, because I am a youth" (v. 6).

But Yahweh has come prepared with an answer. "Do not say, 'I am a youth,' because everywhere I send you, you shall go, and all that I command you, you shall speak." Then Yahweh touched Jeremiah's mouth and said to him, "Behold, I have put My words in your mouth. See, I have appointed you this day over the nations and over the kingdoms, to pluck up and to break down, to destroy and to overthrow, to build and to plant." (vv. 7-10, all NASB).

Ezekiel

Ezekiel 1-3

The priest Ezekiel, deported to Babylon, experiences a fantastic vision in which the sky chariot of Yahweh descends to earth, carried by a team of entities (cherubim) with multiple faces and limbs recalling Hindu iconography. At the sight, Zeke fell on his face, and heard a voice speaking (Ezek. 1:28). The voice said to him, "Son of man, stand on your feet that I may speak with you!" (Ezekiel 2:1).

The Spirit entered Zeke and set him on his feet, and the voice continued:

> Son of man, I am sending you to the sons of Israel, to a rebellious people who have rebelled against Me; they and their fathers have transgressed against Me to this very day. I am sending you to them who are stubborn and obstinate children, and you shall say to them, "Thus says the Lord [Yahweh]." As for them, whether they listen or not—for they are a rebellious house—they will know that a prophet has been among them. And you, son of man, neither fear them nor fear their words, though thistles and thorns are with you and you sit on scorpions; neither fear their words nor be dismayed at their presence, for they are a rebellious house. But you shall speak My words to them whether they listen or not, for they are rebellious. (vv. 3-7)

Then Ezekiel saw a hand extended to him, "and lo, a scroll was in it. When He spread it out before me, it was written on the front and back, and written on it were lamentations, mourning and woe" (vv. 9-10). Zeke did as he was told, and ate the scroll, and, he reports, "it was sweet as honey in my mouth" (Ezekiel 3:3, all NASB).

Common Themes

Notice the recurrent motifs: Samuel, Moses, and Jeremiah hear God's summons and reply, "Here I am!" But then Moses, Isaiah, and Jeremiah get cold feet and try to back out of the job on account of unworthiness: Moses says he is inarticulate and unimpressive; who would listen to a nobody like him?

Jeremiah protests he is not the man for the job because, like Samuel, he is a callow youth. Just as Moses confessed to possessing "uncircumcised lips," so Isaiah says he is "a man of unclean lips," both terms denoting the speaker's lack of requisite holiness for speaking God's message. To remedy this lack, God or an angel does a bit of oral surgery, touching Jeremiah's mouth, purging Isaiah's lips with an altar coal, giving Ezekiel a scroll and commanding him to eat it. Thus God equips his reluctant spokesmen with the words he is sending them to convey. But he is not optimistic and warns them that they will be preaching to the deaf. And of course, at some point in the process the prophet sees visions and hears divine voices.

It is obvious there is a recurring pattern here, and it is not hard to explain. The Deuteronomists wanted to portray ideal "prophets like Moses" again and again. They may have derived this pattern from the Moses character as depicted in the sources available to them, namely J and E. But it also seems likely that somewhere along the line scribes tailored the Exodus 3 and 4 accounts of Moses to make *him* look like the prophets of the Deuteronomic History.[28]

> Jeremiah 1 has all the marks of deuteronomistic editing: the identification of the true prophet who is *sent* by Yahweh to speak his words, the divine watching over his word to perform it, the impending doom of an idolatrous nation and the community's opposition to the prophet (the prophet as a person usually sent *against* the community). These elements provide a characteristically deuteronomistic guide to understanding a prophet, and such a concern explains why these specific elements have been singled out in the construction of a call narrative.[29]

The implication of all this is, once again, to vilify Israel and Judah as the price of a convenient theodicy: The ill fortunes of the covenant people must be ascribed to their own sinfulness because who else is there to blame? Yahweh? No, for "he who guards Israel will neither slumber nor sleep" (Psalm 121:4).[30]

The stiff-necked stubbornness of Israel is exactly analogous to the obtuseness of Jesus' disciples when they fail to grasp that Jesus must die, despite his repeated, straightforward announcements of it. The reason is that the evangelists are speaking over the heads of their narrative characters, straight to the reader,[31] but then they must account for the fact that, on the narrative level, the disciples are utterly flummoxed once Jesus is arrested. Didn't they know? Well, er, ah, it must have been *hidden* from them by God (Luke 9:43-45)–an absurdity implying that God did not want them to hear what Jesus *did* want them to hear!

Similarly, there is the parallel between the "anticipated" rejection by Israel of the preaching of Ezekiel and his colleagues on the one hand and the nihilistic cynicism ascribed to Jesus in Mark 4:10-12 where he says he purposely cloaks the truth from his hearers, because if they were to understand it they might repent, apparently the last thing Jesus wants! This looks like an after-the-fact rationalization of the failure of Christian preaching,[32] nicely summed up in the childish defense, "I *meant* to do that!"

Remember, the people of Israel and Judah were *not* persisting in borrowed "Canaanite" worship despite the best efforts of Elijah, Hosea, and Jeremiah to dissuade them. This is all an optical illusion created by the agenda of the Deuteronomists to retroject their much later monotheism back into Israel's history in order to lend it a venerable ancient pedigree. Polytheism and image veneration were the traditional religion of Israel, who were simply one more group of Canaanites. "The tradition about the long history of the communities' refusal to listen to the prophets is part of the deuteronomistic view of history."[33]

Sacred Charades

Jer. 13

Another literary device employed all across the prophetic canon is the *acted parable* in which Isaiah, Jeremiah, Ezekiel, Hosea, et. al., perform bizarre stunts to symbolize their message before the public. These, too, however, appear to be purely literary parables with no basis in historical fact. In other words, the prophets did not actually do these things.

The Book of Jeremiah has a few such stories.[34] Here's one:

> Thus [Yahweh] said to me, "Go and buy yourself a linen waistband and put it around your waist, but do not put it in water." So I bought the waistband in accordance with the word of [Yahweh] and put it around my waist. Then the word of [Yahweh] came to me a second time, saying, "Take the waistband that you have bought, which is around your waist, and arise, go to the Euphrates and hide it there in a crevice of the rock." So I went and hid it by the Euphrates, as [Yahweh] had commanded me. After many days [Yahweh] said to me, "Arise, go to the Euphrates and take from there the waistband which I commanded you to hide there." Then I went to the Euphrates and dug, and I took the waistband from the place where I had hidden it; and lo, the waistband was ruined, it was totally worthless.
>
> Then the word of [Yahweh] came to me, saying, "Thus says [Yahweh], 'Just so will I destroy the pride of Judah and the great pride of Jerusalem. This wicked people, who refuse to listen to My words, who walk in the stubbornness of their hearts and have gone after other gods to serve them and to bow down to them, let them be just like this waistband which is totally worthless. For as the waistband clings to the waist of a man, so I made the whole household of Israel and the whole household of Judah cling to Me,' declares [Yahweh], 'that they might be for Me a people, for renown, for praise and for glory; but they did not listen.'" (Jer. 13:1-11, NASB)

Um ... the Euphrates is about *four hundred miles* from Jerusalem. It took Ezra and company four whole months to cover the ground between Babylon and Jerusalem (Ezra 7:7-9)! And Jeremiah made the round trip *twice*? Just to stuff his dirty underwear between some rocks? And what kind of "sign" (object lesson) could it have been if nobody went along with him to witness this grand gesture? Just try to picture the prophet's luck trying to recruit traveling companions (like Paul's companions on his trip to Jerusalem to present his collection, Acts 20:4): "Hold on, Jerry. You mean you want witnesses to prove you hid a *loin*cloth under a *rock* pile?" No, the only intended witnesses are the intended *readers*.

Wonderful Marriage Counselor

Jer. 16, Ezek. 24, Hosea 1, Isa. 8

A recurrent theme in the Prophets is Yahweh's rather weird marriage counseling. He tells Jeremiah not to take a wife or have sons or daughters while still in Judah, because the sons and daughters born there

> will die of deadly diseases, they will not be lamented or buried; they will be as dung on the surface of the ground and come to an end by sword and famine, and their carcasses will become food for the birds of the sky and for the beasts of the earth. (Jer. 16:4, NASB)

From Ezekiel he promised "to take the delight of your eyes away from you at a stroke." But Yahweh forbade any mourning:

> "you shall not mourn and you shall not weep, and your tears shall not come. Groan silently; make no mourning for the dead. Bind on your turban and put your shoes on your feet, and do not cover your mustache and do not eat the bread of men." So I spoke to the people in the morning, and in the evening my wife died. And in the morning I did as I was commanded. (Ezek. 24:15-18, NASB)

The people asked Ezekiel what all this meant for them. Yahweh's response, per Ezekiel, was that he would profane his sanctuary, "the pride of your power, the delight of your eyes, and the desire of your soul; and your sons and your daughters whom you left behind shall fall by the sword" (v. 21, RSV). And then they, like Ezekiel, would avoid any mourning, contenting themselves to "pine away in your iniquities and groan to one another" (v. 23, RSV).

What Yahweh said to Hosea was even weirder. It begins with the command to "take a wife of whoredom and children of whoredom." The reason, it seems, was that the land was committing a great whoredom by departing from Yahweh. So Hosea "went and took Gomer the daughter of Diblaim; and she conceived, and bare him a son."

Yahweh said to Hosea, "Call his name Jezreel; for yet a little while, and I will avenge the blood of Jezreel upon the house of Jehu, and will cause the kingdom of the house of Israel to cease. And it shall come to pass at that day, that I will break the bow of Israel in the valley of Jezreel."

> And she conceived again, and bare a daughter. And Jehovah said unto him, Call her name Lo-ruhamah; for I will no more have mercy upon the house of Israel, that I should in any wise pardon them. But I will have mercy upon the house of Judah, and will save them by Jehovah their God, and will not save them by bow, nor by sword, nor by battle, by horses, nor by horsemen.

> Now when she had weaned Lo-ruhamah, she conceived, and bare a son. And Jehovah said, Call his name Lo-ammi; for ye are not my people, and I will not be your God.

> Yet the number of the children of Israel shall be as the sand of the sea, which cannot be measured nor numbered; and it shall come to pass that, in the place where it was said unto them, Ye are not my people, it shall be said unto them, Ye are the sons of the living God. And the children of Judah and the children of Israel shall be gathered together, and they shall appoint themselves one head,

and shall go up from the land; for great shall be the day of Jezreel. (Hosea 1:2-11, ASV)

Isaiah's divine marriage advice began with the instruction to take "a large tablet and write on it in ordinary letters" He got some witnesses and "went to the prophetess, and she conceived and gave birth to a son." Then Yahweh said to him, "Name him Maher-shalal-hash-baz; for before the boy knows how to cry out 'My father' or 'My mother,' the wealth of Damascus and the spoil of Samaria will be carried away before the king of Assyria." (Isa. 8:1-5, NASB)

Can you imagine anybody naming his kids "Shear-jashub" (Isa. 7:3) and, even worse, "Maher-shalal-hashbaz"? Picture the snickering every time the teacher took attendance! Such names "would make life at Warren G. Harding School a veritable hell." No, it makes more sense as a prophetic sign *to the reader.*

The Isaiah story is obviously a close parallel to the Hosea passage quoted just above, especially if, as I can't help suspecting, "the prophetess" is a euphemism for a sacred prostitute (a "priestitute," as it were), one of the Vestal "virgins." Hosea's amply experienced wife is very likely supposed to be that kind of prostitute and not some rouged hooker off the street.

God tells Jeremiah not to get married for reasons similar to that set forth in 1 Corinthians 7:26-27, "In view of the impending distress, it is well for a person to remain as he is . . . . Are you free from a wife? Do not seek marriage." Hosea has to marry a prostitute. Isaiah at least sleeps with a "prophetess" to beget some sons to serve as reminders of his prophecies. God tells Ezekiel he is planning to kill his wife so Zeke can tell those who offer their condolences that they will soon not have the luxury of mourning for loved ones slaughtered by the Babylonians. That's pretty cold! But it is all a parable, not one told by Ezekiel but one using him as a character, like the Rich Fool or the Unjust Judge in Luke's gospel.

The Potter's House

Jer. 19

In Jeremiah 19:1-2a and 10-11a, Yahweh instructs,

> Go and buy a potter's earthenware jar, and take some of the elders of the people and some of the senior priests. Then go out to the valley of Ben-hinnom, which is by the entrance of the potsherd gate . . . Then you are to break the jar in the sight of the men who accompany you and say to them, "Thus says the [Yahweh Sabaoth], 'Just so will I break this people and this city, even as one breaks a potter's vessel, which cannot again be repaired.'" (NASB)

As Robert P. Carroll proposes,[35] the mention of the Valley of the Son of Hinnom (the New Testament Gehenna) is probably a subsequent Deuteronomic interpolation, reapplying the story of the ceramic flask to a different purpose, preparing the way for the denunciation (in vv. 3-9) of the baby-sacrificing cult of Molech practiced there. The original lesson would more likely have been a prediction of the irreparable ruination of the Jewish community through the Babylonian conquest. Why was it changed? Someone thought the message was too pessimistic, especially in light of the claims of the Ezra-Nehemiah faction to represent the restored "true Israel."

Drink Ye All of It

Jer. 25

Here there is no attempt at plausibility. Yahweh tells the narrator, "Take this cup of the wine of wrath from My hand and cause all the nations to whom I send you to drink it. They will drink and stagger and go mad because of the sword that I will send among them" (Jer. 25:15-16).

He takes the cup from Yahweh's hand, and guess what? He makes all the nations to whom Yahweh sent him take a drink: "Jerusalem and the cities of Judah and its kings and its princes, to make them a ruin, a horror, a hissing and a curse, as it is this day" (v. 18). There follows a long list of these unfortunates.

Then, the narrator is told he "shall say to them, 'Thus says [Yahweh Sabaoth], the God of Israel, "Drink, be drunk, vomit, fall and rise no more because of the sword which I will send among you."' And it will be, if they refuse to take the cup from your hand to drink, then you will say to them, 'Thus says [Yahweh Sabaoth]: "You shall surely drink!"'" (vv. 27-28, all NASB).

The problem is not the idea that a prophet might presume to send messages and warnings to various heads of state. The nineteenth-century founder of the Baha'i Faith, Bahá'u'lláh, sent various hortatory epistles to rulers including Queen Victoria, the Shah of Iran, the Ottoman Sultan, Napoleon III, Kaiser Wilhelm, Pope Pius IX, and Czar Alexander II,[36] urging them to acknowledge his status as the "Point of Manifestation" of Allah. No, the problem is that Jeremiah is ordered to *go to* all the rulers of the known world and to command them to drink from his grail. Good luck on that one. He'd probably still be at it today!

Battle of the Prophets

Jer. 27-28 // Deut. 18

Jeremiah recounts this word coming from Yahweh in "the beginning of the reign of Zedekiah the son of Josiah, king of Judah":

> Make for yourself bonds and yokes and put them on your neck, and send word to the king of Edom, to the king of Moab, to the king of the sons of Ammon, to the king of Tyre and to the king of Sidon by the messengers who come to Jerusalem to Zedekiah king of Judah. (Jer. 27:1-3, NASB)

He conveyed the message to Zedekiah: "Bring your necks under the yoke of the king of Babylon and serve him and his people, and live!" (v. 12, RSV).

> Then Hananiah the prophet took the yoke from the neck of Jeremiah the prophet and broke it. Hananiah spoke in the presence of all the people, saying, "Thus says [Yahweh], 'Even so will I break within two full years the yoke of Nebuchadnezzar king of Babylon from the neck of all the nations.'" Then the prophet Jeremiah went his way. (Jer. 28:10-11, NASB)

This contest of prophets brings to mind René Girard's discussion of the Oedipus legend as presented by Sophocles. Oedipus has launched an investigation to identify the killer of his predecessor as king of Thebes.

> Accusations fly between Oedipus, Tiresias, and Creon. Oedipus fails to fix the blame on Creon or Tiresias. Creon and Tiresias are successful in their efforts to fix the blame on him . . . . Having oscillated freely among the three protagonists,

the full burden of guilt finally settles on one. It might very well have settled on another, or on none. The attribution of guilt that henceforth passes for "true" differs in no way from the attributions that will henceforth be regarded as "false," except that in the case of the "true" guilt no voice is raised to protest any aspect of the charge. A particular version of the events succeeds in imposing itself.[37] [. . .] And in asserting that there is no difference between the antagonists in a tragedy, we are saying that ultimately there is no difference between the "true" and the "false" prophet.[38]

He might as well have been talking about Jeremiah and Hananiah. How does Deuteronomy tell us to distinguish between true and false prophets? Well, which one's prediction comes true? Simple, no? Uh . . . not really, because, until we know the outcome, we cannot pass judgment, and this means that the white hat of "true prophet" and the black hat of "false prophet" remain floating in the air above the heads of Jeremiah and Hananiah until it is too late for it to make any difference. And thus neither one is "really" a true or false prophet until the coin falls on either heads or tails.

But that is only a problem if one is eagerly awaiting the decision between Jeremiah and Hananiah, before history lowers the boom. And that was not the *Sitz-im-Leben* of Deuteronomy 18:21-22 (NASB):

> You may say in your heart, "How will we know the word which [Yahweh] has not spoken?" When a prophet speaks in the name of [Yahweh], if the thing does not come about or come true, that is the thing which [Yahweh] has not spoken. The prophet has spoken it presumptuously; you shall not be afraid of him.

Robert P. Carroll explains what's really going on. It is, he says, "an axiom of the redactors that Jeremiah is *the true prophet*, so the problem of criteriology does not arise for the tradition."

> The modern concern with a criterion of validation which would allow any community to determine the truth or falsity of the prophets in its midst is not one shared by the deuteronomists. They already knew who the true prophet was, and working from that position constructed the accounts of his relationship with the other prophets, whom they knew to be false by definition.[39]

"Only hindsight could provide an adequate criteriology," in Carrol's estimation. If "the function of prophecy is to forewarn," then "such a validation theory is useless."[40]

At issue was a competition between rival groups of *scriptures* under the names of prophetic figures *of the past*:

> [T]here was a movement in the production and editing of prophetic traditions which aimed at making certain collections authoritative and therefore normative (cf. Isa. 8:16-20). An element of this movement can be seen in the presentation of the conflict between Jeremiah and Hananiah.[41]

We have to view, then, "Jeremiah" and "Hananiah" as we do "Moses/Aaron" and "Korah" or "Simon Peter" and "Simon Magus": as figureheads, eponymous ancestors, for competing sects and factions—and their scriptures. It is no more an accident of history that we have no copies of a "Book of Hananiah" than it is that we lack manuscripts of the Gospel of Basilides. The Nazis did not invent book burning.

Buyer's Market

Jer. 32

Jeremiah 32:1-15 provides us with a speech by the prophet, delivered from the court of the guard in the palace of the king of Judah. Zedekiah had imprisoned Jeremiah there during Nebuchadnezzar's siege of Jersualem, during Zedekiah's tenth year as King. Zedekiah wasn't happy with the bearer of bad news who'd conveyed a judgment from Yahweh that the city would be handed over to the king of Babylon.

Jeremiah gives Zedekiah this long-winded reply:

> The word of Jehovah came unto me, saying, Behold, Hanamel the son of Shallum thine uncle shall come unto thee, saying, Buy thee my field that is in Anathoth; for the right of redemption is thine to buy it. So Hanamel mine uncle's son came to me in the court of the guard according to the word of Jehovah, and said unto me, Buy my field, I pray thee, that is in Anathoth, which is in the land of Benjamin; for the right of inheritance is thine, and the redemption is thine; buy it for thyself. Then I knew that this was the word of Jehovah.
>
> And I bought the field that was in Anathoth of Hanamel mine uncle's son, and weighed him the money, even seventeen shekels of silver. And I subscribed the deed, and sealed it, and called witnesses, and weighed him the money in the balances. So I took the deed of the purchase, both that which was sealed, according to the law and custom, and that which was open: and I delivered the deed of the purchase unto Baruch the son of Neriah, the son of Mahseiah, in the presence of Hanamel mine uncle's son, and in the presence of the witnesses that subscribed the deed of the purchase, before all the Jews that sat in the court of the guard. And I charged Baruch before them, saying, Thus saith Jehovah [Sabaoth], the God of Israel: Take these deeds, this deed of the purchase which is sealed, and this deed which is open, and put them in an earthen vessel; that they may continue many days. For thus saith Jehovah [Sabaoth], the God of Israel: Houses and fields and vineyards shall yet again be bought in this land. (Jer. 32:6-15, ASV).

I suppose this might have happened if God *hypnotized* Hanamel ("This is your lucky day, my boy!") to do something he would never think of doing if he were in his right mind: offering a parcel of land with a hefty price tag to a man whom everyone knew believed that all the land would shortly be seized by the Babylonian conquerors! But it doesn't say that. It would make a bit more sense if the story had God tell *Jeremiah* to take the initiative: to approach his cousin and ask to buy the land at a good price. Furthermore, the punch line doesn't quite fit snugly: wouldn't you think the point was that the Babylonians, despite the looming storm clouds, would *not* wind up conquering Judah?

Crocodile Rocks

Jer. 43

In Jeremiah 43:8-13, we see a close parallel–odd as it may seem to say so–to the story of the Cleansing of the Temple in Mark 11:15-19. In Tahpanhes, Yahweh tells Jeremiah to take large stones in his hands and "hide them in the mortar in the pavement which is at the entrance to Pharaoh's palace in Tahpanhes, in the sight of the men of Judah." Then he is to give them the following speech:

> Thus says Jehovah [Sabaoth], the God of Israel: Behold, I will send and take Nebuchadrezzar the king of Babylon, my servant, and he will set his throne above these stones which I have hid, and he will spread his royal canopy over them. He shall come and smite the land of Egypt, giving to the pestilence those who are doomed to the pestilence, to captivity those who are doomed to captivity, and to the sword those who are doomed to the sword. He shall kindle a fire in the temples of the gods of Egypt; and he shall burn them and carry them away captive; and he shall clean the land of Egypt, as a shepherd cleans his cloak of vermin; and he shall go away from there in peace. He shall break the obelisks of Heliopolis which is in the land of Egypt; and the temples of the gods of Egypt he shall burn with fire. (Jer. 43:8-13, ASV)

Like Jeremiah, Mark's Jesus gets no blowback for his gross disruption of the Temple service. That despite the presence of armed Temple police posted, after all, to deal with events like this one! As the story stands, it just can't have happened. Forget any skepticism about miracles; it just doesn't make sense as a narrative.

Same thing here: Weren't there palace guards on duty? Would they have watched in calm bemusement as old Jeremiah dug up the pavement? "Just what do you think you're doing, sir?" And would he have been capable of it anyway? Did he use a pneumatic drill? Can you picture the old geezer swinging a pick axe?

Book in the Brook

Jer. 51

In Jeremiah 51:59-64 we read what the prophet commanded to "Seraiah the son of Neriah, son of Mahseiah, when he went with Zedekiah king of Judah to Babylon, in the fourth year of his reign." Seraiah, the text tells us, was the quartermaster, and "Jeremiah wrote in a book all the evil that should come upon Babylon, all these words that are written concerning Babylon." Here's what Jeremiah told him:

> When you come to Babylon, see that you read all these words, and say, "You, O [Yahweh], have promised concerning this place to cut it off, so that there will be nothing dwelling in it, whether man or beast, but it will be a perpetual desolation." And as soon as you finish reading this scroll, you will tie a stone to it and throw it into the middle of the Euphrates, and say, "Just so shall Babylon sink down and not rise again because of the calamity that I am going to bring upon her." (Jer. 51:61-64, NASB)

Let me get this straight: Seraiah is a royal official, part of the Jewish king's retinue accompanying him in exile to Babylon—and he's going to give a public reading of Jeremiah's doom threats against Babylon? Isn't Jeremiah ordering the man to commit suicide? The Deuteronomic writer doesn't seem to know what would be at stake here.

Sacred Cow Pies

Ezek. 4

Ezekiel, in the fourth chapter of the book named after him, receives a detailed set of divine instructions about constructing a miniature model of Jerusalem, along with a besieging army of toy soldiers outside it. Here is what he is told to do (quotes are from Ezek. 4, ASV):

> Thou also, son of man, take thee a tile, and lay it before thee, and portray upon it a city, even Jerusalem: and lay siege against it, and build forts against it, and cast up a mound against it; set camps also against it, and plant battering rams against it round about. And take thou unto thee an iron pan, and set it for a wall of iron between thee and the city: and set thy face toward it, and it shall be besieged, and thou shalt lay siege against it. This shall be a sign to the house of Israel.

All that's missing is the model railroad running through it. Choo choo! Then Yahweh commands redemptive bedsores:

> Moreover lie thou upon thy left side, and lay the iniquity of the house of Israel upon it; according to the number of the days that thou shalt lie upon it, thou shalt bear their iniquity. For I have appointed the years of their iniquity to be unto thee a number of days, even three hundred and ninety days: so shalt thou bear the iniquity of the house of Israel. And again, when thou hast accomplished these, thou shalt lie on thy right side, and shalt bear the iniquity of the house of Judah: forty days, each day for a year, have I appointed it unto thee. And thou shalt set thy face toward the siege of Jerusalem, with thine arm uncovered; and thou shalt prophesy against it. And, behold, I lay bands upon thee, and thou shalt not turn thee from one side to the other, till thou hast accomplished the days of thy siege.

The poor guy spends all day for just over a year and two months lying down on the ground beside his toy village. Did he take bathroom breaks? Did he get to go home each night? How many times did he have to rebuild the model, given that mischievous boys cannot have left it undisturbed?

And it gets worse. Ezekiel is told to bake bread with human dung:

> Take thou also unto thee wheat, and barley, and beans, and lentils, and millet, and spelt, and put them in one vessel, and make thee bread thereof; according to the number of the days that thou shalt lie upon thy side, even three hundred and ninety days, shalt thou eat thereof. And thy food which thou shalt eat shall be by weight, twenty shekels a day: from time to time shalt thou eat it. And thou shalt drink water by measure, the sixth part of a hin: from time to time shalt thou drink. And thou shalt eat it as barley cakes, and thou shalt bake it in their sight with dung that cometh out of man. And [Yahweh] said, Even thus shall the children of Israel eat their bread unclean, among the nations whither I will drive them.

But here Ezekiel finally objects: "Then said I, Ah Lord [Yahweh]! behold, my soul hath not been polluted; for from my youth up even till now have I not eaten of that which dieth of itself, or is torn of beasts; neither came there abominable flesh into my mouth."

On this point, Yahweh relents, replying, "See, I have given thee cow's dung for man's dung, and thou shalt prepare thy bread thereon. Moreover he said unto me, Son of man, behold, I will break the staff of bread in Jerusalem: and they shall eat bread by weight, and with fearfulness; and they shall drink water by measure, and in dismay: that they may want bread and water, and be dismayed one with another, and pine away in their iniquity."

There is something perverse and disgusting about a deity who would subject his servant to such hazing. Did the author really think God stooped to such sadism? Is he even *trying* to make a theological statement? Does he realize that he *is*? It's not *quite* so bad if we take the whole thing as a written parable in which Ezekiel figures as a character.

Anyone in the real world who obeyed these "commands of God" would be written off as a pathetic schizophrenic–and rightly so. Here's how it goes: If you *act* crazy, you *are* crazy. That's all it takes to qualify. It doesn't change the diagnosis if you say the voice of God told you to do it–in fact that only makes things *worse*. Sometimes biblical literalists puzzle over whether stories like this (or Abraham nearly sacrificing Isaac) can ever be considered precedents for believers to follow, and their puzzlement highlights the point I am making: These episodes were only ever part of a written text, not "heroic" memorials of things people had actually done.

Baring Witness

Isa. 20

In Isaiah 20 (NASB), another prophet is portrayed as an absolute lunatic:

> In the year that the commander came to Ashdod, when Sargon the king of Assyria sent him and he fought against Ashdod and captured it, at that time [Yahweh] spoke through Isaiah the son of Amoz, saying, "Go and loosen the sackcloth from your hips and take your shoes off your feet." And he did so, going naked and barefoot. And [Yahweh] said, "Even as My servant Isaiah has gone naked and barefoot three years as a sign and token against Egypt and Cush, so the king of Assyria will lead away the captives of Egypt and the exiles of Cush, young and old, naked and barefoot with buttocks uncovered, to the shame of Egypt. Then they will be dismayed and ashamed because of Cush their hope and Egypt their boast. So the inhabitants of this coastland will say in that day, 'Behold, such is our hope, where we fled for help to be delivered from the king of Assyria; and we, how shall we escape?'"

One cannot picture the authorities, much less Isaiah's family, allowing this grotesque spectacle to continue for one minute past the first appearance of the nude prophet on the public street.

"But wait! You don't under*stand*, officer! I'm just trying to show what's going to happen to Egypt and Ethiopia! God *told* me to!"

"Sure, buddy, sure! Now come along."

The story works as part of a written text, but not as something you could picture in your mind as happening in the real world.

Once a New Testament professor of mine was discussing the Nativity story in Matthew. He had seen some movie or cartoon adaptation of the story, including the moving star that guided the Wise Men. He shook his head and said, "There are just some things you shouldn't try to depict." I think he was on the verge of realizing that any attempt to bring some biblical episodes across the barrier into "real life" will only reveal the impossibility of the attempt, impossible because the episode doesn't *belong* in the real world. It only works as a story, hence, e.g., the challenge of translating superhero stories into movies.

This Isaiah episode is not some extravagant miracle; that's not the problem. As an ostensibly real event, it just loses all gravitas and looks ridiculous.

Narratees versus Readers

Literary critics[42] remind us of the need to distinguish between "narratees" and "readers." Narratees are those to whom a narrative or a letter is ostensibly directed, but they may be phantoms, just part of the narrative itself. Likewise, the narrator may be one of the characters in the story, recounting his tale to his family and friends who are thus implicitly fictional characters, too.[43]

A quasi-biblical example of a fictive narrator and his narratees (as opposed to the actual author and his intended readers) is 1 Enoch, or the Ethiopic Book of Enoch. In it the patriarch Enoch tells the story of his ascension into heaven and the many wonders revealed to him there. Who is he telling it to? His family. He is about to return to the celestial realm, this time for good. First Enoch is his swan song. Of course it is all a literary device, a vehicle for some unknown scribe to publish his theological and astronomical speculations for his colleagues to read.[44] The scribe is the actual author; the other scribes are the intended readership. But Enoch is the narrator; his family are the intra-narrative narratees.

In pseudonymous New Testament epistles, e.g., 2 Peter, we must draw the same line: The Apostle Peter is the ostensible writer of the letter, and various congregations in Asia Minor are understood to be his intended audience. But the actual author is some unknown Christian of the second century, and his intended readers are latter-day members of the same churches (or any Christians anywhere). This means "Peter" is in effect the narrator, and the first-century Christians of Asia Minor are the equally fictive narratees.

When it comes to the Old Testament Prophets, the actual authors are unknown, at least by name, but we can identify them with the "Deuteronomists" who compiled the books of the Deuteronomic History. Roughly, we may be pretty sure the books are constructed around earlier written poetry (or hymn lyrics?). Most modern versions of the Bible indent this material to represent the poetic structure.

But who wrote this poetry? It is theoretically possible that individuals named Isaiah, Jeremiah, Ezekiel, etc., wrote those poems. But it really remains up in the air: You can't take it for granted just because there's no decisive evidence against it. On the other hand, it's pretty clear that the greater part of the Book of Isaiah was not the work of the author of chapters 1-39. And even those chapters cannot all be the work of a single poet. So as far as we are concerned "Isaiah" and the rest are narrators, not authors.

So, who were the intended reading public? Generally speaking, they must have been Diaspora Jews[45] of the very latest pre-Christian centuries. It is really to the great number of Jews living among Gentiles throughout the Mediterranean world that the warnings against polytheism and idolatry were aimed, borrowing the authority of an ancient saint (in the fashion of all pseudepigraphists) to drive them home.

These scattered Jews—some flourishing, others discriminated against—were under pressure to assimilate to the cultures, and therefore to the religions, of their Gentile neighbors. It may have been the path of least resistance so as to fit in,[46] but often it was simply because these Jews, no longer secure within the Jewish "plausibility structure" of the Holy Land,[47] felt at liberty to heed the attractiveness of their neighbors' colorful religions, as happened in Palestine itself under Seleucid domination (1 Macc. 1:11-15). They may have identified Yahweh with the Greek Zeus (as in the Epistle of Aristeas) or Dionysus (as many in the Hellenistic world did). They may have added the worship of Hellenistic deities to their own brand of Judaism (I think this is in view in Isa. 42:8, "I will not share my glory with another;" cf., 1 Cor. 10:14-22).

I'm guessing that these prophetic denunciations of polytheism and syncretism originated as accusatory sermons aimed at Diaspora Jews when they made the pilgrimage to Jerusalem, perceived by the Levites to be assimilated, compromising sinners who needed a tongue-lashing. Such a practice might be considered a development or version of the antiphonal Entrance Songs like Psalms 15 and 24:3-6.

The desired reaction is depicted in 2 Kings 22:11-13 when Josiah heard the (Deuteronomic) Book of the Covenant read and found himself stricken with dread: *Oh no! I hope it's not too late to straighten things out!* Hopefully the pilgrims would feel just as a similar group did in similar circumstances: "Now there were Jews living in Jerusalem, devout men from every nation under heaven . . . . Now when they heard this, they were pierced to the heart, and said to Peter and the rest of the apostles, 'Brethren, what shall we do?'" (Acts 2:5, 37, NASB).

One has to wonder whether the many references in the Prophets to a "remnant" returning from "exile" (i.e., the Diaspora) were intended to denote the group of Jews (or supposed Jews) sent by the Persian authorities to reconstruct Judaism in Palestine[48] (fictively depicted in Ezra and Nehemiah) along the lines of Persian Zoroastrianism (which eventuated in Pharisaism, "Parseeism"). Possibly relevant here would be the odd fact that the Persian Empire never comes in for the kind of damning criticism the prophetic writers heap on Assyria, Babylon, Edom, and others.[49] As Philip R. Davies notes, the unremitting denunciations of the rulers of Israel and Judah may have been intended to make another regime look good by contrast.[50] "See, aren't you better off with us?" That is, perhaps, the Persians, under whose regime much of the content of the books of the Prophets was being written.

In the rest of this chapter I want to zero in on particularly interesting passages from the Books of Isaiah, Jeremiah, Ezekiel, and The Twelve. Where there are important thematic overlaps, I will discuss the relevant passages from different books together.

The Book of Isaiah

The first chapter of this book opens with a lament over a devastating defeat of Israel, blaming the victim with the accusation of an all-permeating wickedness that (must have) led to the disaster. The tirade concludes with Isaiah 1:9 (NASB): "Unless [Yahweh Sabaoth] / Had left us a few survivors, / We would be like Sodom, / We would be like Gomorrah," i.e., like Hiroshima and Nagasaki, landmarks of complete destruction.

Isaiah 1

Isaiah 1:10-31 looks like a separate poem urging national repentance, lest such catastrophe ensue, as if it had not yet occurred and might not. This section, comprised of verses 10-17 (ASV), raises an important and controversial question, one also addressed in Micah 6:6-8 and Jeremiah 7:21-23; 8:8-9:

> [10]Hear the word of Jehovah, ye rulers of Sodom;
> give ear unto the law of our God, ye people of Gomorrah.
> [11]What unto me is the multitude of your sacrifices?
> saith Jehovah:
> I have had enough of the burnt-offerings of rams,
> and the fat of fed beasts;
> and I delight not in the blood of bullocks,
> or of lambs, or of he-goats.
>
> [12]When ye come to appear before me,
> who hath required this at your hand,

to trample my courts?
13Bring no more vain oblations;
  incense is an abomination unto me;
  new moon and sabbath, the calling of assemblies,–
  I cannot away with iniquity and the solemn meeting.
14Your new moons and your appointed feasts my soul hateth;
  they are a trouble unto me;
  I am weary of bearing them.
15And when ye spread forth your hands,
  I will hide mine eyes from you;
  yea, when ye make many prayers,
  I will not hear:
  your hands are full of blood.
16Wash you, make you clean;
  put away the evil of your doings from before mine eyes;
  cease to do evil;
17learn to do well;
  seek justice,
  relieve the oppressed,
  judge the fatherless,
  plead for the widow.

It is obvious that the main point here is the sickening farce of religious piety on the part of people who behave wickedly, oppressing and exploiting others outside the walls of the Temple. ("Profane," after all, means "outside the fane, or temple."). The poet warns that God is not impressed with ceremonial mummery if the worshipper's heart is not right.

They're not fooling anybody. "Woe to you, scribes and Pharisees–hypocrites! For you devour widows' houses and for a pretense you make long prayers" (Matt. 23:14). "God is not mocked" (Gal. 6:7). But note that in Isaiah 1:12 the poet has God say, "*Who requires of you* this trampling of my courts?" Nobody requires hypocritical worship. No, our poet seems to be denying that God ever stipulated this traffic in the Temple courts, which he *is* certainly portrayed doing in Exodus 34:22-24 (NASB):

You shall celebrate the Feast of Weeks, that is, the first fruits of the wheat harvest, and the Feast of Ingathering at the turn of the year. Three times a year all your males are to appear before the Lord [Yahweh], the God of Israel. For I will drive out nations before you and enlarge your borders, and no man shall covet your land when you go up three times a year to appear before [Yahweh].

Most commentators assure us that the poet does not object to sacrifice and ritual *per se*, but only as empty gestures when vitiated by moral turpitude and hypocrisy. But this sounds like a harmonization offered by those who don't want one Bible writer contradicting another. We see the same contrast in Micah 6:6-8 (NASB):

6With what shall I come to [Yahweh]
  And bow myself before the God on high?
  Shall I come to Him with burnt offerings,
  With yearling calves?
7Does [Yahweh] take delight in thousands of rams,
  In ten thousand rivers of oil?
  Shall I present my firstborn for my rebellious acts,
  The fruit of my body for the sin of my soul?
8He has told you, O man, what is good;
  And what does [Yahweh] require of you
  But to do justice, to love kindness,

And to walk humbly with your God?

Again, what is it that Yahweh "requires"? It is a simple (though not easy) matter: just, kind, and humble behavior, not the sort of stuff listed, sarcastically, in the preceding verses—and in Leviticus! Walter Kaufmann regarded these sentiments as "one of the central themes of the prophetic books." He calls "the teachings of the Hebrew prophets," even if only implicitly, "consistently and radically anti-theological."[51]

Jeremiah makes that inescapably clear. Here he quotes Yahweh Sabaoth, the God of Israel: "Add your burnt offerings to your sacrifices and eat flesh. For I did not speak to your fathers, or command them in the day that I brought them out of the land of Egypt, concerning burnt offerings and sacrifices. But this is what I commanded them, saying, 'Obey My voice, and I will be your God, and you will be My people; and you will walk in all the way which I command you, that it may be well with you.'" (Jer. 7:21-23, NASB).

And here, a few verses later (Jer. 8:8-9, NASB), he pooh-poohs the wisdom of man vs. that of Yahweh:

> [8]"How can you say, 'We are wise,
>   And the law of [Yahweh] is with us'?
>   But behold, the lying pen of the scribes
>   Has made it into a lie.
> [9]"The wise men are put to shame,
>   They are dismayed and caught;
>   Behold, they have rejected the word of [Yahweh],
>   And what kind of wisdom do they have?

I'd say these are the words of a man who denies that God ever issued the commandments to offer the sacrifices that Temple priests and scribes, whose business was ritual and sacrifice, had penciled into the Torah.

By the way, the early Jewish Christians known as the Ebionites ("the Poor") believed exactly this, that God abhorred blood sacrifices and had never commanded them. The passages in the Torah stipulating such "butcher shop religion" (Harry Emerson Fosdick) were among the "false pericopes" that Jesus came to identify and cancel out.[52] We have already seen how Psalm 51:15-17 seems to scorn animal sacrifices in favor of repentance and the sincerity of the spirit, and that the psalm evidences the same factional dispute displayed in Numbers 16, the contest between Korah (standing for the Levitical singers) and Moses and Aaron (figureheads for the sacrificing priests).

It seems pretty clear that the same opinions, from the same or a similar faction, get some air time in the Prophets. Even on the more harmonistic reading, however, there is yet another profound development observable in these passages. Someone has taken a revolutionary theological step. Hitherto, "sin," offending God, was understood to be uniquely *ritual*, not *moral*, in character, which is why purification sacrifices never had anything to do with assuaging moral guilt but only expiated ceremonial transgressions (like Nadab and Abihu "offering strange fire") and ritual impurity.

This may imply that the kind of worshippers whom Isaiah 1 excoriates were not exactly hypocrites. It may be that they naively showed up to worship without having it occur to them they had better clean up their business practices or their personal lives. They may have been genuinely astonished to hear (or read) that God considers moral infractions to be offenses not only against one's fellows, but against God as well. Those, too, count as sins! Henceforth "sin" carries a moral coloring that in our day threatens to obliterate the original, uniquely religious connotation it first had.

The Temple Epiphany

Isa. 6:1-13

Taking a second look at this fascinating passage, we can follow up our last observation about the moralization of "sin." It can be understood as an aspect of the moralization and rationalization of the God concept itself, of which this very passage is the classic example. Rudolf Otto[53] spoke of a uniquely religious type of experience. He called it the "numinous" experience, the experience of, the encounter with, the Holy. Originally no one sought to confine God within human categories of "good" and "evil." Instead, "holy" meant "wholly other." Our experience with the uncanny Other is two-fold.

First, we experience holy terror before the *Mysterium Tremendum* because it manifests *awe-full-ness*, prompting fullness of awe and religious dread of the uncanny, not fear of some concrete danger, even of going to hell. Second, it carries the feeling of *over-powering-ness*. This is a sense of the fullness of power and therefore of being, producing not moral but rather *ontological* deficiency, humility, not shame or guilt, and prompting the self-negation Otto dubbed "creature-feeling." The beholder of the Holy experiences the urgency-energy of a living Presence, not a static idea.

Consider these accounts from different centuries, religions, and geographical locations.

The **Katha Upanishad** (6:1-4) speaks of an "ancient tree, whose roots grow upward and whose branches grow downward," in such a way as to strike root and form new, stems, eventually creating a whole new forest where there was at first a single tree. That, it says,

> indeed is called the Bright; that is called Brahman; that alone is called the Immortal. All worlds are contained in it, and no one goes beyond. This is that. Whatever there is, the whole world, when gone forth [from the Brahman], trembles in its breath. That Brahman is a great terror, like a drawn sword. Those who know it become immortal. From terror of Brahman fire burns; from terror the sun burns; from terror [the gods] Indra and Vayu, and Death, as the fifth, run away. If a man could not understand it before the falling asunder of his body, then he has to take body again in the worlds of creation.[54]

In **The Sacred Stories**, Aelius Aristides of the second century C.E. (XLVIII 31-33 K., XXIV 298 D.) says a desired remedy

> was revealed in the clearest way possible, just as countless other things also made the presence of the god [Sarapis] manifest. For I seemed as it were to touch him and to perceive that he himself was come, and to be halfway between sleep and waking and to want to get the power of vision and to be anxious lest he depart beforehand, and to have applied my ears and to hear, sometimes as in a dream, sometimes as in a waking vision, and my hair was standing on end and tears of joy came forth, and the consciousness I had of his weighty presence was no burden - what man could even set these things forth in words? But if he is one of the initiates, then he knows and understands.[55]

The **Bhagavad Gita** (XI, 14, 16, 24) describes an encounter of Dhanamjaya (also called Arjuna) with the numinous:

> Then filled with amazement,
> His hair standing upright, Dhanamjaya
> Bowed his head to the God,
> And said with a gesture of reverence:

[. . .]

"With many arms, bellies, mouths, and eyes,
I see Thee, infinite in form on all sides;
No end nor middle nor yet beginning of Thee
Do I see, O All-God, All-formed!

[. . .]

"Touching the sky, aflame, of many colors,
With yawning mouths and flaming enormous eyes,
Verily seeing thee (so), my inmost soul is shaken,
And I find no steadiness nor peace, O Vishnu!"[56]

When we experience the lure of the *Mysterium Fascinans*, we are enthralled and charmed, even while we are frightened, by the Holy. We yearn for it, not just for its possible benefits but for its own sake, for it is both inherently *august*, or worthy of worship and praise, and subjectively *fascinating* to us.

Because the Holy is fullness of Being, we recognize it as our Source. It can fulfill us precisely because it is unlike us, the other half or missing piece. Psalm 63:1-4 (ASV):

¹O God, thou art my God; earnestly will I seek thee:
My soul thirsteth for thee, my flesh longeth for thee,
In a dry and weary land, where no water is.
²So have I looked upon thee in the sanctuary,
To see thy power and thy glory.
³Because thy lovingkindness is better than life,
My lips shall praise thee.
⁴So will I bless thee while I live:
I will lift up my hands in thy name.

Thus we are simultaneously attracted *and* repelled, enthralled *and* afraid. (Think of your ambivalence watching a horror movie: You want to look away but you can't.) While the *Mysterium Tremendum* corresponds to the wrath of God, the *Mysterium Fascinans* corresponds to the love of God, and each is a consuming fire. This is the basic *experiential, pre-rational element of religion* which is subsequently developed and interpreted rationally (and morally) in various ways by various religions.

How did the notion of God and "the Holy" become rationalized and moralized?[57] In the case of biblical religion, it was probably a result of the Persianizing of Judaism. Originally it seems that God was thought to be beyond and above mere human distinctions of good and evil, yet responsible for both. "Does evil befall a city, unless [Yahweh] has done it?" (Amos 3:6). "Is it not from the mouth of [Elyon] that good and evil come?" (Lam. 3:38). Accordingly, there was no need for a theodicy, since there was no incongruity between the Wholly Other and the presence of evil in his world.

But Zoroastrian theology thought differently. It was dualistic, tracing all good back to a good God, Ahura Mazda, and evil to an evil anti-God, Ahriman. Persianized Jews seem to have adopted this schema. Yahweh came to be regarded as good, "holiness" now meaning "moral perfection." Likewise, Satan was originally a loyal servant of Yahweh dedicated to exposing those who only pretended to be righteous, trapping them in sting operations, for God to see what they (Job in Job 1:8-11, David in 1 Chron. 21:1, Joshua the priest in Zech. 3:1-2) were really made of. But now Satan was recast as the enemy of God, not testing his servants to see if they would sin but rather trying to *get* them to sin. Yahweh became Ahura Mazda, with Satan aping Ahriman.

In Isaiah 6 we have a story of Isaiah witnessing an epiphany like those described in our examples above. It is not necessary to take Isaiah 6 as genuine autobiography in order to regard it, like the others, as based on the real experiences of visionaries. This *kind* of thing certainly happened–and still does.

Let's note a few features of the Isaiah version. For one thing, the adoring cry of the seraphim, the so-called Trishagion ("Thrice Holy"), is exactly what we should expect from a numinous experience as Otto described it. It is not God's righteousness that the celestial creatures extol, but his *glory* which fills the earth if men but have eyes to see it. And the visionary is daunted and abashed, just like Moses, who was terrified and as afraid to look at God as Perseus was to glimpse Medusa. As Otto says, Isaiah is filled with the self-reproach of creature-feeling. He does not feel moral guilt but rather *ontological shame*. If the nations of the world are no more than dust before mighty Jehovah, what is Isaiah but an ephemeral speck of cosmic flotsam? Simply *as a poor mortal* he is "a man of unclean lips," anticipating his perceived ill-fittedness to speak the holy words of God, to sing with the tongues of angels.

Yahweh is flanked by a retinue of seraphim, "blazing ones," who are graphically represented in Egyptian iconography as flying serpents[58] who may sprout hands or feet if they happen to need them for whatever errand they are to perform. I have never been quite sure *whose* feet (sometimes a biblical euphemism for genitals) and face the seraphs are supposed to be covering–their own or Yahweh's? It would make sense either way. They might be veiling themselves in the divine Presence, or they might be hiding God from human eyes.

When God asks, "Whom shall I send, and who will go for us?" he is addressing the heavenly council of the Sons of God, his subordinates and advisers. Whether the seraphim are also supposed to be members of this council is unclear, but Yahweh is speaking to the council in any event. As he invited their suggestions for a plan to cross up King Ahab (1 Kings 22:19-23), now he invites nominations for a messenger to Israel.

It is a pose, since he has "beamed up" Isaiah to "overhear" these proceedings, knowing he will pipe up and volunteer. Isaiah has been rapt up to heaven, whether in the body or out of the body, I know not; only God knows. But either way, Isaiah is sharing the same high-flying experience as Micaiah ben-Imlah (1 Kings 22:19-23), Paul (2 Cor. 12:1-10), and John the Revelator (Rev. 4:1-4).

Perhaps the clearest sign that the whole scene is fictive is the retrospective certainty that the people will reject Isaiah's preaching. The skill of the author is such that even supposedly critical readers of Isaiah have blithely been happy to take this narrative at face value: "Oh, sure, Isaiah embarked on his ministry knowing that it was doomed to futility from the get-go. Sure, why not?" Can't they see the whole thing is written in historical retrospect?

Plus, it is hard to take the Temple epiphany story as factual history since there was not yet any Jerusalem Temple!

Birth Announcement

Isa. 7:1-17

This passage tells us of an event that occurred in "the days of Ahaz the son of Jotham, the son of Uzziah, king of Judah." Rezin the king of Syria and Pekah the son of Remaliah went to Jerusalem, in Judah (then divided from its larger neighbor to the north) "to war against it, but could not prevail against it" (Isa. 7:1).

And it was told the house of David, saying, Syria is confederate with Ephraim. And his heart trembled, and the heart of his people, as the trees of the forest tremble with the wind. (v. 2)

Yahweh said to Isaiah,

Go forth now to meet Ahaz, thou, and Shear-jashub thy son, at the end of the conduit of the upper pool, in the highway of the fuller's field; and say unto him, Take heed, and be quiet; fear not, neither let thy heart be faint, because of these two tails of smoking firebrands, for the fierce anger of Rezin and Syria, and of the son of Remaliah. Because Syria, Ephraim, and the son of Remaliah, have purposed evil against thee, saying, Let us go up against Judah, and vex it, and let us make a breach therein for us, and set up a king in the midst of it, even the son of Tabeel . . . (vv. 3-7)

Yahweh went on,

It shall not stand,
   neither shall it come to pass.
[8]For the head of Syria is Damascus,
   and the head of Damascus is Rezin;

and within threescore and five years shall Ephraim be broken in pieces, so that it shall not be a people:

[9]and the head of Ephraim is Samaria,
   and the head of Samaria is Remaliah's son.
If ye will not believe,
   surely ye shall not be established" (vv. 7-9, all ASV).[59]

And Jehovah spake again unto Ahaz, saying, Ask thee a sign of Jehovah thy God; ask it either in the depth, or in the height above. (vv. 10-11)

Ahaz responded thus:

I will not ask, neither will I tempt Jehovah. And he said, Hear ye now, O house of David: Is it a small thing for you to weary men, that ye will weary my God also? Therefore the Lord himself will give you a sign: behold, a virgin shall conceive, and bear a son, and shall call his name Immanuel. Butter and honey shall he eat, when he knoweth to refuse the evil, and choose the good. For before the child shall know to refuse the evil, and choose the good, the land whose two kings thou abhorrest shall be forsaken. Jehovah will bring upon thee, and upon thy people, and upon thy father's house, days that have not come, from the day that Ephraim departed from Judah, even the king of Assyria. (vv. 12-17)

And it shall come to pass in that day, that Jehovah will hiss for the fly that is in the uttermost part of the rivers of Egypt, and for the bee that is in the land of Assyria. (v. 18, all ASV)

It seems pretty clear that someone has added a couple of glosses (explanatory notes) at verses 8b and 18. The first slips in a retrospective "prediction" of the destruction of Ephraim (northern Israel), something King Ahaz would not live to see. It clumsily interrupts the poetic structure. The second specifies the identity of the menace that the rest of the verse predicts.

What is the story about? There is room for a lot of debate on many secondary issues in the passage, but the main theme is pretty clear: Isaiah is shown trying to convince King Ahaz to renounce his plans to seek an alliance with Assyria against a threat from Israel (Samaria) and Syria. Isaiah wants Ahaz instead to stick his neck out and rely on Yahweh alone, a stratagem that has never worked too well, as witness, for example, the ill-fated Boxer Rebellion.

The Deuteronomic Historians who wrote this were armchair generals who had the luxury of rewriting history to support their own ideology. They picture Isaiah challenging the king to name any sign he wants from Yahweh that he will indeed go to bat for Judah without reinforcements from Assyria (kind of like America allying herself with Uncle Joe Stalin against the Nazis). But Ahaz declines this generous offer. He is too pragmatic to gamble everything on an improbable supernatural *deus ex machina.* "Uh, thanks, but no thanks."

But Isaiah (and God, pretty much the same thing) loses patience and saves Ahaz the trouble; Yahweh will grant him a sign (and deliverance) whether he wants it or not, something to remind him once Isaiah's prediction soon comes true: "*Told* you so!" A child is about to be born and given the name "Immanuel" ("God [is] with us"), not in itself any big deal. The sign is the name: "God is on our side!" Plus the fact that this boy will not be more than a few years old before the Samaritan-Syrian axis will have been wiped off the map! (The scribe who inserted the identification of the avenging force as Assyria didn't seem to grasp the fact that Isaiah didn't want Ahaz to rely on Assyria!) This by itself rules out any possibility that Isaiah was predicting the nativity of Jesus Christ more than seven centuries in the future![60] The whole point is that Isaiah places a statute of limitation on the range of his prediction.

I can't believe the evangelist Matthew, who (at Matt. 1:22-23) cites Isaiah 7:14 as a prophecy of Jesus' birth, didn't understand the original reference. He wasn't stupid. Nor do we need to suppose he was cynically prying the text out of context, confident that his gullible readers would have no ready access to a copy of Isaiah to check for themselves.[61]

No, ever since the 1947 discovery of the Dead Sea Scrolls, it has become clear that Matthew was employing an esoteric method of exegesis common in his day, the *pesher* technique,[62] whereby one teased out a hitherto-unsuspected secret meaning in scripture, a meaning predicting the events of one's own day. It was taken for granted that one had to approach the text with the presupposition of faith. They knew that outsiders could never acknowledge the esoteric meaning by a straightforward, literal reading. Matthew was not trying to persuade unbelievers. Instead he was revealing, as he thought, new revelations visible only to the eye of faith (cf., Matt. 13:52; 1 Cor. 2:7, 13). Modern appeals to "fulfilled prophecies" to prove Jesus was the Messiah predicted by the prophets are futile and wrong-headed.

Much has been made of the fact that the word traditionally translated "virgin" in Isaiah 7:14 is *almah,* which might mean "virgin," but could just as easily denote a young woman of marriageable age, whether sexually intact or not. Isaiah does not use the synonym *bethulah,* which, at least originally, referred strictly to women "who know not a man" (Luke 1:34).

But it may all be moot anyway. The Septuagint translators of the Hebrew Bible into Greek rendered Isaiah's *almah* as *parthenos* ("virgin"), and they certainly did not understand Isaiah 7:14 to refer to anyone's miraculous, non-sexual conception. So at some point the word *bethulah,* not to mention the Greek *parthenos,* became ambiguous in meaning, just like *almah.* We have to ask: Did even *Matthew* mean "virgin"?[63]

Isaiah 8

Who was the mother-to-be? Compare this passage to Isaiah 8:1-4 (NASB):

> Then [Yahweh] said to me, "Take for yourself a large tablet and write on it in ordinary letters: Swift is the booty, speedy is the prey. And I will take to Myself faithful witnesses for testimony, Uriah the priest and Zechariah the son of Jeberechiah." So I approached the prophetess, and she conceived and gave birth to a son. Then [Yahweh] said to me, "Name him Maher-shalal-hash-baz; for before the boy knows how to cry out 'My father' or 'My mother,' the wealth of Damascus and the spoil of Samaria will be carried away before the king of Assyria."

As you see, this passage is a virtually exact parallel to the one in Isaiah 7: A woman shall conceive and give birth to a son, and he is to be given a symbolic name denoting the destruction of the Samaritan-Syrian alliance ("The spoil speeds, the prey hastens"), so that, once the boy reaches only a very young age, the enemies of Judah will have been defeated, and the lad's name will remind everyone that Isaiah had been right. The mother is called "the prophetess," and it is explicitly Isaiah who impregnates her. I would have to infer that the parallel is complete, and that Isaiah was the father of Immanuel, too.

But there would seem to be a deeper level here, though not in the *pesher* sense. As Mowinkel points out, the operative phrase "the virgin shall conceive" appears verbatim in one of the Canaanite texts from Ugarit: "Behold, the young woman will bear a son." Here the context makes it plain that the "young woman" (*galmatu*, cognate equivalent of the Hebrew *almah*) is in fact "the Virgin Anath," who is depicted as Yahweh's queen in a bas relief from the Jewish temple in Elephantine, Egypt, where she is called "Anatyahu." She is a warrior and a goddess of love, sort of a combination of Athena and Aphrodite.

The cry, "Behold, the young woman will bear a son" was part of a liturgy celebrating the rebirth of the dying god. Mowinkel, who details all of this,[64] tries to weasel out of the obvious implications with some vague rationalization that Isaiah was merely using familiar Canaanite mythemes in a safely demythologized way as metaphors somehow appropriate to a historical Isaiah addressing Ahaz. Instead, we can see that the Deuteronomic Historian built the Isaiah 7:14 scene on the basis of (or at least utilizing) a mythic-ritual text from the native Hebrew worship of Baal and Anath which he sought to suppress. In fact, repurposing it in this way was part of the Deuteronomic program of suppressing the traditional polytheism.

The maneuver was exactly like the various etymological stories which contrive new "orthodox" meanings for old polytheistic names, as when, in Judges 6:25-33, "Jerubbaal" ("May Baal contend [on his behalf]") gets reinterpreted as "Let Baal fight [his *own* battles]!" It becomes an Elijah-like taunt (cf., 1 Kings 18:27) to the defunct Baal to punish the man (also known as Gideon) for smashing his idol. Does he need a mere mortal to punish the sacrilege? Some god! The text used in Isaiah 7:14 would have hailed the birth of a new royal heir, acclaiming him the son/resurrection of God (Baal? Yahweh? Six of one, half a dozen of the other).

Isaiah 9

The same thing has happened in two other well-known Isaiah passages. The first is Isa. 9:6-7 (NASB):

> [6]For a child will be born to us, a son will be given to us;
> And the government will rest on His shoulders;

And His name will be called Wonderful Counselor, Mighty God,
   Eternal Father, Prince of Peace.
⁷There will be no end to the increase of His government or of peace,
   On the throne of David and over his kingdom,
   To establish it and to uphold it with justice and righteousness
   From then on and forevermore.
   The zeal of [Yahweh Sabaoth] will accomplish this.

This is a perfect specimen of the royal birth (or inauguration) oracle used all across the ancient Middle East.[65] The imagined state of world peace and the eternal reign of righteousness and justice, even peaceful coexistence between predator and prey, were pro forma and obviously hyperbolic. The king is divine as his titles make clear. It would make equal sense if employed at the birth of a new king of the Jews (Matt. 2:2) or at the crowning of the new king when his predecessor has died, as in Psalm 2 ("You are my son; today I have begotten you."), which envisions the new king being adopted as God's son on the day he takes the throne: "His Son, who was descended from David according to the flesh, who was declared the Son of God with power by the resurrection from the dead, according to the Spirit of holiness" (Rom. 1:3-4, RSV).[66]

Isaiah 11

Second we have Isa. 11:1-9 (NASB):

¹Then a shoot will spring from the stem of Jesse,
   And a branch from his roots will bear fruit.
²The Spirit of [Yahweh] will rest on Him,
   The spirit of wisdom and understanding,
   The spirit of counsel and strength,
   The spirit of knowledge and the fear of [Yahweh].
³And He will delight in the fear of [Yahweh],
   And He will not judge by what His eyes see,
   Nor make a decision by what His ears hear;
⁴But with righteousness He will judge the poor,
   And decide with fairness for the afflicted of the earth;
   And He will strike the earth with the rod of His mouth,
   And with the breath of His lips He will slay the wicked.
⁵Also righteousness will be the belt about His loins,
   And faithfulness the belt about His waist.

⁶And the wolf will dwell with the lamb,
   And the leopard will lie down with the young goat,
   And the calf and the young lion and the fatling together;
   And a little boy will lead them.
⁷Also the cow and the bear will graze,
   Their young will lie down together,
   And the lion will eat straw like the ox.
⁸The nursing child will play by the hole of the cobra,
   And the weaned child will put his hand on the viper's den.
⁹They will not hurt or destroy in all My holy mountain,
   For the earth will be full of the knowledge of [Yahweh]
   As the waters cover the sea.

The actual bums who burdened the throne with their posteriors certainly failed to live up to this rhetoric. These formulae are mythic descriptions of the divine blessings that "will surely" attend the new king's reign. They set the bar very high: Maybe this time it will work! Prescription masquerades as description: "Your Highness, this is what we expect from you! You won't let us down, will you, O divine one?" Hope springs eternal. Or maybe it was just groveling flattery. "Forgive us, Lord, for this, our dreadful toadying."[67] It's pretty great poetry any way you cut it, though for my money many of these scripture texts had to wait a long time for Handel to bring them to life again.

The Bigger They Are . . .

Isa. 14:3-20

Does the Bible speak of the fall of Satan from heavenly glory? Yes, but not here. In an earlier chapter, we have seen how the poem is based on the Canaanite astronomical myth of Helal (the planet Venus), son of Shahar (the dawn goddess). Like many of these stories, it depicts the ever-repeating events of the night sky as if a one-time narrative about personified characters. Helal became a bit too full of himself and thought to usurp the throne of El Elyon (conceived here as a sun god) atop Mount Zaphon where the gods dwelt. This referred to the glowing prominence of Venus, "the Morning Star," in the heavens just before the rising of the sun puts his radiance in the shade. Just as the sun was imagined to sink beneath the surface of the earth when it set, so the vanished Helal was depicted as sinking into Sheol.

Isaiah 14:1-22 applies this myth to the fate of some overweening king, recently deposed (or at least dead). It will be when Yahweh "gives you rest from your pain and turmoil and harsh service in which you have been enslaved, that you will take up this taunt against the king of Babylon" (vv. 3-4, NASB) the prose introduction begins, identifying the king in question.

But the poem (vv. 4-21) says nothing about him. Instead Helal may stand for Alexander the Great.[68] The problem with this theory is that Alexander was certainly treated to funereal honors and an opulent tomb, just the things denied to the king in this poem. Another intriguing possibility is that the reference *is* to the last Babylonian ruler (Belshazzar), and that the gloating over his doom reflects the poet's allegiance to the Persian Empire which replaced its Babylonian predecessor. In this case, we would have to look for the poet among the Ezra-Nehemiah faction who owed their position of power and privilege to their imperial sponsors.

Here's the poem itself, quoted from the ASV:

> ⁴How hath the oppressor ceased!
>   the golden city ceased!
> ⁵Jehovah hath broken the staff of the wicked,
>   the sceptre of the rulers;
> ⁶that smote the peoples in wrath with a continual stroke,
>   that ruled the nations in anger,
>   with a persecution that none restrained.
> ⁷The whole earth is at rest, and is quiet:
>   they break forth into singing.
> ⁸Yea, the fir-trees rejoice at thee,
>   and the cedars of Lebanon, saying,
>   Since thou art laid low, no hewer is come up against us.
> ⁹Sheol from beneath is moved for thee to meet thee at thy coming;
>   it stirreth up the dead for thee,
>   even all the chief ones of the earth;
>   it hath raised up from their thrones all the kings of the nations.
> ¹⁰All they shall answer and say unto thee,
>   Art thou also become weak as we?
>   art thou become like unto us?
> ¹¹Thy pomp is brought down to Sheol,
>   and the noise of thy viols [RSV: *harps*]:
>   the worm is spread under thee,

and worms cover thee.

¹²How art thou fallen from heaven, O [Helal], son of [Shahar]!
     how art thou cut down to the ground,
     that didst lay low the nations!
¹³And thou saidst in thy heart,
     I will ascend into heaven,
     I will exalt my throne above the stars of God;
     and I will sit upon the mount of congregation,
     in the uttermost parts of the north;
¹⁴I will ascend above the heights of the clouds;
     I will make myself like [Elyon].
¹⁵Yet thou shalt be brought down to Sheol,
     to the uttermost parts of the pit.
¹⁶They that see thee shall gaze at thee,
     they shall consider thee, saying,
     Is this the man that made the earth to tremble,
     that did shake kingdoms;
¹⁷that made the world as a wilderness,
     and overthrew the cities thereof;
     that let not loose his prisoners to their home?
¹⁸All the kings of the nations,
     all of them, sleep in glory,
     every one in his own house.
¹⁹But thou art cast forth away from thy sepulchre
     like an abominable branch,
     clothed with the slain,
     that are thrust through with the sword,
     that go down to the stones of the pit;
     as a dead body trodden under foot.
²⁰Thou shalt not be joined with them in burial,
     because thou hast destroyed thy land,
     thou hast slain thy people;
     the seed of evil-doers shall not be named for ever.

²¹Prepare ye slaughter for his children
     for the iniquity of their fathers,
     that they rise not up, and possess the earth,
     and fill the face of the world with cities.

Most Bible readers imagine this poem describes the prideful rebellion of Satan, of which we read an abbreviated account in Revelation 12:7-12. Isaiah 14 does not have that scenario in view at all.

But it's quite easy to see how this text was later added to the snow-balling legend of the Prince of Darkness. It does, after all, speak of a heavenly being crashing down to, and under, the earth. But, if this writer even knew of a character called Satan ("the Adversary," not yet even a proper name), he would most likely have understood him to be an angel in God's service, as in the Book of Job.

The poem pictures the arrival of the oppressor king in the gloomy subterranean realm of Sheol, in this case a sort of negative Valhalla where the dead kings of all nations carry on a ghostly half-existence, each "enthroned" upon his slab (cf., Isa. 24:21-22). Their astonished mockery greets the newcomer: He has not been properly interred, a thing necessary for a king to inherit the baleful majesty of the ghost-kings. Thus Belshazzar (or whoever), having been strung up from a lamp post like Mussolini, makes his entrance like a rotting sack of meat thrown into the alley behind the butcher shop. Royal robes?

Mummy wrappings? Not a chance! Instead he must be satisfied with a shroud of squirming maggots (cf., Isa. 66:24).

The Apocalypse of Isaiah

Isa. 24-27

These chapters are very late and look back to the time of Alexander the Great and his successors. It is a patchwork quilt of various oracles and psalms. The first section, 24:1-24, is a fearful oracle of doom, easily as powerful as the New Testament Book of Revelation. It is both world-wide in scope (not restricted to Israel) and absolutely pessimistic. All distinctions between classes and castes, clergy and laity, poor and prosperous, will be swept away by the oncoming tornado of divine wrath, which none shall escape!

The quotations of Isaiah 24-27 are all from the ASV.

Isaiah 24

[1]Behold, Jehovah maketh the earth empty, and maketh it waste,
  and turneth it upside down,
  and scattereth abroad the inhabitants thereof.
[2]And it shall be, as with the people,
  so with the priest;
  as with the servant, so with his master;
  as with the maid, so with her mistress;
  as with the buyer, so with the seller;
  as with the creditor, so with the debtor;
  as with the taker of interest, so with the giver of interest to him.
[3]The earth shall be utterly emptied, and utterly laid waste;
  for Jehovah hath spoken this word.

All mankind has fallen irretrievably into sin and will receive the just punishment. Yahweh will act, not as savior and redeemer, but as merciless executioner.

[4]The earth mourneth and fadeth away,
  the world languisheth and fadeth away,
  the lofty people of the earth do languish.
[5]The earth also is polluted
  under the inhabitants thereof;
because they have transgressed the laws,
  violated the statutes,
  broken the everlasting covenant.

The few who survive will not consider themselves very lucky. What is left to eat or drink? Where is any cause to rejoice? The scenario described is much like that depicted in Cormac McCarthy's novel (and the film adaptation) *The Road*. Survival is a daily struggle and questionably worth it. The covenant sinners have broken must be that which God struck with Noah (Gen. 9:1-17), because the whole human race is indicted—and punished.

[6]Therefore hath the curse devoured the earth,
  and they that dwell therein are found guilty:
  therefore the inhabitants of the earth are burned,
  and few men left.
[7]The new wine mourneth,
  the vine languisheth,
  all the merry-hearted do sigh.
[8]The mirth of tabrets ceaseth,
  the noise of them that rejoice endeth,
  the joy of the harp ceaseth.

9They shall not drink wine with a song;
  strong drink shall be bitter to them that drink it.
10The waste city is broken down;
  every house is shut up, that no man may come in.
11There is a crying in the streets because of the wine;
  all joy is darkened,
  the mirth of the land is gone.
12In the city is left desolation,
  and the gate is smitten with destruction.
13For thus shall it be in the midst of the earth among the peoples,
  as the shaking of an olive-tree,
  as the gleanings when the vintage is done.

Verses 14-16 and 23 seem to be insertions seeking to mitigate the unrelenting doom announced in the rest of chapter 24. The rest of the poem makes it about as clear as you can get that there will be no rescue, no relief, no redemption. Verses 14-16 look like a piece of an Individual Lament psalm, praising God for his wonderful vindications of Israel/Judah, but complaining about "poor me," and petitioning the Almighty to send some of that deliverance the psalmist's way. ("What we have heard you did in Capernaum, do here also in your own country," Luke 4:23.)

14These shall lift up their voice, they shall shout;
  for the majesty of Jehovah they cry aloud from the sea.
15Wherefore glorify ye Jehovah in the east,
  even the name of Jehovah, the God of Israel,
  in the isles of the sea.
16From the uttermost part of the earth have we heard songs:
  Glory to the righteous.
But I said,
  I pine away, I pine away, woe is me!
the treacherous have dealt treacherously;
  yea, the treacherous have dealt very treacherously.

Verses 17-22 continue the theme of complete destruction, describing it in terms similar to the Priestly account in Genesis 7:11b, "on that day all the fountains of the great deep burst forth, and the windows of the heavens were opened." Verses 21-22 imagine Yahweh wreaking his vengeance upon the stars of heaven as well as the mortal kings on earth, coupling these together on the assumption that the stars represent the fallen Sons of God (Gen. 6:1-4) who, despite their disgrace, continued to rule, each one over his own assigned nation (Deut. 32:8; Dan. 10:13), as the power behind the throne. These entities become the wicked Principalities and Powers of the New Testament (Rom. 8:38; Col. 2:15).

This was, of course, an explanation for government corruption and tyranny: What else can you expect with fallen angels whispering into the king's ear like Gríma Wormtongue manipulating King Théoden in *The Lord of the Rings*? And thus oppressed Jews rejoiced at the prospect of a coming day when Yahweh would throw these lame duck devils out of office and take back direct rule of the nations himself, while these gods are confined underground in the pit of darkness, causing earthquakes as they stumble blindly through the caves of Sheol (Psalm 82).

Isaiah 25

Isaiah 25:1-5 is a psalm of victory to be sung following a successful military campaign. Why is the identity of the defeated foe not revealed? Simply because the psalm is a stock piece of liturgy, taken off the shelf whenever the occasion arose. What's it doing here?

Again, I'm guessing, the idea is to lift the mood after the absolute nihilism of the doom-oracle.

> ¹O Jehovah, thou art my God;
> I will exalt thee, I will praise thy name;
> for thou hast done wonderful things,
> even counsels of old, in faithfulness and truth.
> ²For thou hast made of a city a heap,
> of a fortified city a ruin, a palace of strangers to be no city;
> it shall never be built.
> ³Therefore shall a strong people glorify thee;
> a city of terrible nations shall fear thee.
> ⁴For thou hast been a stronghold to the poor,
> a stronghold to the needy in his distress,
> a refuge from the storm,
> a shade from the heat,
> when the blast of the terrible ones is as a storm against the wall.
> ⁵As the heat in a dry place
> wilt thou bring down the noise of strangers;
> as the heat by the shade of a cloud,
> the song of the terrible ones shall be brought low.

Verses 6-12 interrupt the poetic verse with an impressive chunk of prose:[69]

> And in this mountain will Jehovah of hosts make unto all peoples a feast of fat things, a feast of wines on the lees, of fat things full of marrow, of wines on the lees well refined. And he will destroy in this mountain the face of the covering that covereth all peoples, and the veil that is spread over all nations. He hath swallowed up death for ever; and the Lord Jehovah will wipe away tears from off all faces; and the reproach of his people will he take away from off all the earth: for Jehovah hath spoken it.

> And it shall be said in that day, Lo, this is our God; we have waited for him, and he will save us: this is Jehovah; we have waited for him, we will be glad and rejoice in his salvation. For in this mountain will the hand of Jehovah rest; and Moab shall be trodden down in his place, even as straw is trodden down in the water of the dunghill. And he shall spread forth his hands in the midst thereof, as he that swimmeth spreadeth forth his hands to swim; but Jehovah will lay low his pride together with the craft of his hands. And the high fortress of thy walls hath he brought down, laid low, and brought to the ground, even to the dust.

The promise that Yahweh will forever abolish death clearly contradicts the earlier prediction that the earth will be scraped clean, will drop dead, never to get up again. But in a way, contradiction is the point. Ancient scribes, once the texts had reached a certain level of veneration, dared not simply omit material they didn't like, so instead they would just try to negate the offending passage by adding a more congenial one right after it, as if to suggest to the reader or hearer that things must not be as bad as he had thought.

Another contradiction, this time within the block of prose, is the utopian vision of a day when all nations will gather in ecumenical fellowship atop Mount Zion in the glad worship of Yahweh, a scenario quite different from the chop-licking delight over the eradication of the Moabites.

If I may try my hand at the game of speculating about when and why this psalm (for that's what is) was composed, and by whom, I should imagine it commemorates the

Hasmonean victory over the Seleucid Empire in 164 B.C.E. "Open the gates" implies our text is an Entrance Liturgy psalm like Psalms 24 and 100. The designation of the people of Judah as "the righteous nation" would naturally refer to both the devotion of the persecuted, those martyred for their faith by the Seleucid tyrant, and to the valiant heroes, especially the Brothers Maccabee. Our author was likely a Levite scribe, as witness the wisdom emphasis, reflecting the Book of Proverbs and Wisdom psalms like Psalm 1. The suggestions of meditation on the Divine Name reminds us of the Levitical piety of Psalm 63:1-8.

Isaiah 26

In Chapter 26 we have a "song [that] shall be sung in the land of Judah":

¹We have a strong city;
    salvation will he appoint
    for walls and bulwarks.
²Open ye the gates,
    that the righteous nation which keepeth faith
    may enter in.
³Thou wilt keep him in perfect peace,
    whose mind is stayed on thee;
    because he trusteth in thee.
⁴Trust ye in Jehovah for ever;
    for in Jehovah, even Jehovah,
    is an everlasting rock.
⁵For he hath brought down
    them that dwell on high,
    the lofty city:
he layeth it low, he layeth it low even to the ground;
    he bringeth it even to the dust.

⁶The foot shall tread it down;
    even the feet of the poor,
    and the steps of the needy.

⁷The way of the just is uprightness:
    thou that art upright dost direct the path of the just.
⁸Yea, in the way of thy judgments,
    O Jehovah, have we waited for thee;
    to thy name, even to thy memorial name,
    is the desire of our soul.
⁹With my soul have I desired thee in the night;
    yea, with my spirit within me will I seek thee earnestly:
for when thy judgments are in the earth,
    the inhabitants of the world learn righteousness.
¹⁰Let favor be showed to the wicked,
    yet will he not learn righteousness;
in the land of uprightness will he deal wrongfully,
    and will not behold the majesty of Jehovah.
¹¹Jehovah, thy hand is lifted up,
    yet they see not:[70]
but they shall see thy zeal for the people, and be put to shame;
    yea, fire shall devour thine adversaries.
¹²Jehovah, thou wilt ordain peace for us;
    for thou hast also wrought all our works for us.

¹³O Jehovah our God,
    other lords besides thee have had dominion over us;
    but by thee only will we make mention of thy name.

Who are the "other lords" in verse 13? I should think the reference is to the sequence of Gentile empires (Assyrian, Babylonian, Persian, Greek, Ptolemaic, and Seleucid) who dominated Israel and Judah for centuries until the Hasmonean/Maccabean rebellion. Henceforth, Judah owes allegiance to no king but Yahweh.

The heathen foes of Judah, now vanquished, are doomed to spend eternity, forgotten by humanity, in the ghost world of Sheol (precisely as in Isa. 14:15-20). Yahweh's chosen have a very different fate in store: resurrection from the dead. The reference to "the dew" in verse 19 recalls that in Psalm 110:3b, a coronation psalm which speaks of the elevation of the new king to the position of an avatar of the dying-and-rising god (Yahweh, Baal, Tammuz, Hadad-Rimmon): "from the womb of [Shahar] the dew of your youth will come to you." Remember, the king of Babylon, too, was supposed to be the son of Shahar (Isa. 14:4, 12).

> [14]They are dead, they shall not live;
>   they are deceased, they shall not rise:
>   therefore hast thou visited and destroyed them,
>   and made all remembrance of them to perish.
> [15]Thou hast increased the nation, O Jehovah,
>   thou hast increased the nation; thou art glorified;
>   thou hast enlarged all the borders of the land.
>
> [16]Jehovah, in trouble have they visited thee;
>   they poured out a prayer
>   when thy chastening was upon them.
> [17]Like as a woman with child,
>   that draweth near the time of her delivery,
>   is in pain and crieth out in her pangs;
>   so we have been before thee, O Jehovah.
> [18]We have been with child, we have been in pain,
>   we have as it were brought forth wind;
>   we have not wrought any deliverance in the earth;
>   neither have the inhabitants of the world fallen.
> [19]Thy dead shall live; [their] dead bodies shall arise.
>   Awake and sing, ye that dwell in the dust;
>   for thy dew is as the dew of herbs,
>   and the earth shall cast forth the dead.

When the new monarch ascended the throne he became the ever-reborn god. Verses 20-21 promise the faithful that they have nothing to fear. Just relax in your "chambers," i.e., your tombs, till war and persecution shall at last cease and, with the definitive victory of Yahweh, the earth shall no more hide her dead. From her clammy embrace they shall arise.[71] This would seem to be the first biblical reference to the doctrine of the end-time resurrection. We will see it again in another very late book, Daniel.

> [20]Come, my people, enter thou into thy chambers,
>   and shut thy doors about thee:
>   hide thyself for a little moment,
>   until the indignation be overpast.
> [21]For, behold, Jehovah cometh forth out of his place
>   to punish the inhabitants of the earth for their iniquity:
>   the earth also shall disclose her blood,
>   and shall no more cover her slain.

In Isaiah 27:1, a later prose addition to the poem of Isaiah 26, we see another feature of the apocalyptic scenario: a replay of the primordial victory of Yahweh over the seven-headed Chaos Dragon, Leviathan. "In that day Jehovah with his hard and great and strong sword will punish leviathan the swift serpent, and leviathan the crooked serpent; and he will slay the monster that is in the sea" (ASV). Jews believed that the end of all things would recapitulate the beginning of all things.[72] This is why the Book of Revelation locates the war in heaven, the fall of Satan, and the defeat of the seven-headed serpent at the end of history, implicitly a replay of those ancient events.

The Second Isaiah

Whoever may have written the oldest, core material in the Book of Isaiah (perhaps chapters 2-12 and 28-32),[73] the same poet had nothing to do with chapters 40-66. This latter collection of excellent verse seems to be the work of a single gifted author, whom scholars call, for lack of any better alternative, Deutero-Isaiah, i.e., the Second Isaiah. The thematic and stylistic distinctives of this writer would be more than enough to set him apart from "First Isaiah," but the really decisive factor is the different historical setting. No more do we hear about Assyria or the looming threat of Babylon. All that is over; the page has been turned.

Theoretically, even if a clairvoyant could see the events of a future generation, what would be the relevance for his own contemporaries? Furthermore, the material is not even couched in terms of a prediction of "things to come."[74] He seems to be writing for his contemporaries, not for those of some future generation. His oracles are almost not predictions at all.

Torrey argues that Deutero-Isaiah actually begins with chapters 34-35. Chapter 40 originally followed immediately upon 35. Chapters 36-39, narratives lifted from 2 Kings 18-20, were no doubt inserted like a tack to attach the Deutero-Isaianic material to the rag-bag of Isaiah 1-39. In fact, it looks like "First Isaiah" had never circulated (was never published) as a separate book. That material was collected and made to preface the already extant "Second Isaiah."[75] And that raises the question of whether what we call Second Isaiah ought rather to be called *First* Isaiah, a pseudepigraph fathered onto the prophet of 2 Kings, with all the rest as a collection of other bits and pieces.

Most critics would slice off (cf., Jer. 36:23!) chapters 56-66, ascribing them to another writer or group of writers, producing a Trito-Isaiah (Third Isaiah). They admit that it reads much like chapters 40-55, but they are reduced to suggesting that this must be the result of people trying to emulate Deutero-Isaiah. But this looks like an *ad hoc* hypothesis to which these scholars are forced by an extraneous factor. Chapters 56-66 appear to them to presuppose a different *Sitz-im-Leben* from that underlying chapters 40-45. Chapters 40-55 are, they say, squarely placed in Babylon (taken over by Persia), the prophet announcing the imminent decree of Persian emperor Cyrus allowing Jews to return to Palestine (or Canaan or the Holy Land–whatever you want to call it). But there is no hint that this poet lives among fellow exiles.[76] He excoriates his readers for not offering the proper sacrifices (Isa. 43:22-24)–as if sacrifices were even possible for Jews living in Babylon.[77] Rather, chapters 56-66 seem to come from a writer or writers living in Jerusalem. Two different authors, no?

Actually, no, said C.C. Torrey, who demonstrated that the few references to "Babylon" (Isa. 43:14; 48:14, 20) and to "Cyrus" (44:28; 45:1) not only do not properly mesh with their contexts but also pointedly violate the poetic meter of their lines.[78] They scan just fine once one scalpels out "Babylon" and "Cyrus." Then it becomes clear that the whole of chapters 40-66 stem from a poet living in *Jerusalem*. He does not speak of a massive return of Jewish exiles from Persian Babylon, but rather of an envisioned regathering of Diaspora Jews who had relocated all over the Mediterranean world[79] (Isa. 43:5-7; 49:8-13; 60:8-9; 66:20; cf. Psalm 126:1-2). Compare Mark 13:27 (RSV): "And then he will send out the angels, and gather his elect from the four winds, from the ends of the earth to the ends of heaven." In fact, *no* prophet speaks of a wholesale departure or return of Jews *from* Babylon.[80]

Why the addition of Babylon and Cyrus? The interpolations were made in service to the agenda of the priestly party who created the fiction, on display in Ezra and Nehemiah, of a massive "Babylonian Exile" to reinforce their clout as the "returning" guardians of "true" Judaism with every right to enforce an (actually heavily Persianized) "orthodoxy." The tensions between this Persian-sponsored elite and the "people of the land"[81] make new sense if the Ezra-Nehemiah faction were really a clique of Quisling interlopers.

The Deuteronomists and the Chronicler had promoted the fictive notion that Judah had been virtually depopulated by Nebuchadnezzar, just as Joshua and his troops had supposedly exterminated virtually the entire Canaanite population, leaving the land ready for Yahweh's righteous conquerors to move in and take over. "And when he comes he finds it empty, swept, and put in order" (Matt. 12:44b, RSV). But in fact it had been only the royal and priestly aristocracy who had been deported to Babylon.[82]

The idea was to imply that the only "real" Jews were the "returning," Persian-backed elite.[83] (One hates to point this out, but all this is distressingly reminiscent of the attempt by today's "Christian" anti-Semites to dissociate modern Jews from biblical Israel in order to claim the biblical legacy for themselves while demonizing actual, contemporary, flesh-and-blood Jews as Asiatic Khazars or even as sub-human hybrids.)[84]

It is only on this understanding, I think, that it makes any sense at all for Isaiah 45:1 to call Cyrus "my Messiah." It is to make him, to borrow a phrase, "Caesar's Messiah."[85] Torrey measures a wide gap between what we know of the historical Cyrus, worshipper of Nabu and Marduk, and the characterization in (interpolated) Isaiah which has the Persian conqueror calling on the name of Yahweh.[86]

Songs of the Servant

Isa. 42:1-9; 49:1-12; 50:4-11; 52:13-53:12

The 19th-century scholar Bernhard Duhm proposed that four passages of Second Isaiah pre-existed the rest of the work as hymns and were only subsequently incorporated into the larger work. These songs all treated of the so-called "Servant of Yahweh." Many scholars have followed him, and much debate has ensued over the identity of this Servant. As to whether these texts were originally a set of independent poetical compositions, I believe Torrey,[87] anticipating the arguments of Tryggve Mettinger,[88] was correct that themes and vocabulary shared by these passages and their larger contexts make the hypothesis gratuitous.[89]

Who is this servant? Some nominate the Second Isaiah himself, others the people of Israel collectively. Mettinger convinces me that the latter is the case. He has (they have) been punished for stubborn refusal to heed the commands of Yahweh. Israel/Jews find themselves taking refuge, or imprisoned, in various nations, from which Yahweh will recall them. The servant appears now to be the whole people in their disobedience, now the righteous among them who urge repentance.

Isaiah 42

Here's the first Servant Song, Isaiah 42:1-9, in the King James translation that is so familiar to Christian ears:

> [1]Behold my servant, whom I uphold;
>   mine elect, in whom my soul delighteth;

I have put my spirit upon him:
  he shall bring forth judgment to the Gentiles.
2He shall not cry, nor lift up,
  nor cause his voice to be heard in the street.
3A bruised reed shall he not break,
  and the smoking flax shall he not quench:
  he shall bring forth judgment unto truth.
4He shall not fail nor be discouraged,
  till he have set judgment in the earth:
  and the isles shall wait for his law.

5Thus saith [the God Yahweh],
he that created the heavens,
  and stretched them out;
he that spread forth the earth,
  and that which cometh out of it;
he that giveth breath unto the people upon it,
  and spirit to them that walk therein:
6I [Yahweh] have called thee in righteousness,
  and will hold thine hand, and will keep thee,
  and give thee for a covenant of the people,
for a light of the Gentiles;[90]
7To open the blind eyes,
to bring out the prisoners from the prison,
  and them that sit in darkness out of the prison house.
8I am [Yahweh]: that is my name:
  and my glory will I not give to another,
  neither my praise to graven images.
9Behold, the former things are come to pass,
  and new things do I declare:
before they spring forth
  I tell you of them.

Admittedly, verses 1-4 of the first Servant Song would make a good deal of sense if a great future prophet were intended, but verse 6 sounds to me like a reference to the role of Israel to bear witness to the world as to the benefits of keeping Yahweh's covenant.

The last line of verse 4 might fairly be taken to denote the docile submission of the (conquered?) Gentile nations to ascendant Israel, passively awaiting their king's commands. But I take it to denote the happy conversion of the nations, by the quiet persuasion and the example of Diaspora Jews (cf., 1 Pet. 3:1), to Israel's faith and their eagerness for catechism in the Torah (a prospect seen also in Isaiah 2:2-4).

I understand verse 7 to refer to the recovery of Jews mired in oppression among their captors and persecutors. Verse 8 is a forthright declaration of Deuteronomic monotheism. Why here? The point, it seems to me, is to rebuke Diaspora Jews who have assimilated, or are tempted to assimilate, to their Gentile neighbors' religions, or to mix their Judaism with non-Jewish elements. Yahweh does not share worshippers with bogus deities. He is, after all, a jealous God.

Finally, verse 9 seems to appeal to the fulfillment of prophecies made in the past in order to buttress faith in the present prediction of liberation and homecoming. By "present," of course, I mean back when the text was written, not nowadays as evangelical preachers read it today—with Jesus firmly in mind as the servant.

Isaiah 49

In verses 1-5 of the second Song (Isaiah 49, again quoting from the KJV), the servant identifies "himself" plainly as the personification of the people of Israel. Yahweh has called him as his instrument to gather in Gentiles to the household of biblical faith. Israel protests his (nation's) unworthiness, given the sorry record of behavior, but, really, what else can he do but answer Yahweh's call?

¹Listen, O isles, unto me;
    and hearken, ye people, from far;
    The Lord hath called me from the womb;
    from the bowels of my mother hath he made mention of my name.
²And he hath made my mouth like a sharp sword;
    in the shadow of his hand hath he hid me,
    and made me a polished shaft;
    in his quiver hath he hid me;
³And said unto me, Thou art my servant,
    O Israel, in whom I will be glorified.
⁴Then I said, I have laboured in vain,
    I have spent my strength for nought, and in vain:
    yet surely my judgment is with [Yahweh],
    and my work with my God.

Verses 5-6 explain that, though Israel's mission is to win the Jewish people for repentance, that is not enough of a task! Israel, again, will convert her traditional enemies. It will be a spiritual conquest, not a military victory. "To the Jew first, and also to the Greek" (Rom.1:16).

⁵And now, saith [Yahweh]
    that formed me from the womb to be his servant,
    to bring Jacob again to him,
    Though Israel be not gathered,**91**
    yet shall I be glorious in the eyes of [Yahweh],
    and my God shall be my strength.
⁶And he said,
    It is a light thing that thou shouldest be my servant
    to raise up the tribes of Jacob,
    and to restore the preserved of Israel:
    I will also give thee for a light to the Gentiles,
    that thou mayest be my salvation unto the end of the earth.

⁷Thus saith [Yahweh],
    the Redeemer of Israel, and his Holy One,
    to him whom man despiseth, to him whom the nation abhorreth,
    to a servant of rulers,
    Kings shall see and arise,
    princes also shall worship,
    because of [Yahweh] that is faithful,
    and the Holy One of Israel, and he shall choose thee.

⁸Thus saith [Yahweh],
    In an acceptable time have I heard thee,
    and in a day of salvation have I helped thee:
    and I will preserve thee, and give thee
    for a covenant of the people,
    to establish the earth,
    to cause to inherit the desolate heritages;
⁹That thou mayest say to the prisoners, Go forth;
    to them that are in darkness, Shew yourselves.
    They shall feed in the ways,
    and their pastures shall be in all high places.
¹⁰They shall not hunger nor thirst;
    neither shall the heat nor sun smite them:

for he that hath mercy on them shall lead them,
   even by the springs of water shall he guide them.
[11]And I will make all my mountains a way,
   and my highways shall be exalted.
[12]Behold, these shall come from far:
   and, lo, these from the north and from the west;
   and these from the land of Sinim.

The claim of some that Jesus Christ is predicted in Isaiah 49:6 is gratuitous; nothing of the kind is implied. It seems so only if one starts out with the assumption that the servant is supposed to be Jesus, but that is the very opposite of any scientific approach to biblical interpretation, which must always be inductive, starting with the textual data, not deductive, forcing the texts into conformity with prior dogma.

And yet there is a larger point to invoking this verse in connection with Jesus. Many Jews today regard Jesus not as their Messiah but nonetheless as one by whom God spread the knowledge of himself to the heathen nations so that they renounced the worship of idols and false gods, turning to the biblical tradition instead. Not Judaism, but not bad. This would mean that Jesus had in fact expedited the "light to the nations" ministry envisioned for Israel in Isaiah 49:6. He was a Jew doing a good job at the task of Jews in general. This does not mean that Isaiah 49:6 was a prediction of Jesus as an individual. It is significant that this text is never applied to Jesus in the New Testament, but rather to *Paul* (Acts 13:46-47).

Likewise, it is a mistake to take the promises of Isaiah 49:10 as referring to a glorious afterlife in heaven. The context makes it clear that the reference is to a return to security and prosperity for the Jewish people once God delivers them from their national overlords, enemies, and persecutors–on earth. Are you going to get thirsty in heaven? Not likely, so the "springs of water" mentioned in this verse must be located here on earth. Those who read verse 10 as referring to heaven have the wrong verse in mind; they're really thinking of Revelation 21:3-4.

Isaiah 50

In the third sequence, Isaiah 50:4-11 (KJV), the servant is prepared to speak words of comfort to Jewish prisoners in the Mediterranean world, promising them deliverance and pronouncing doom upon their tormentors. Again, this is not about some promise of post-mortem release, but a very real one right here. Yahweh's new sheriff in town will give the bad guys a bitter taste of their own medicine.

Is this sentiment incompatible with the predictions of universal repentance and the conversion of the Gentiles? Of course not; there is no hope for salvation for unrelenting persecutors. The poet by no means commits himself to a belief that *every single* Gentile will turn to Yahweh.

[4][Yahweh] hath given me
   the tongue of the learned,
   that I should know how to speak a word
   in season to him that is weary:
   he wakeneth morning by morning,
   he wakeneth mine ear
   to hear as the learned.
[5]The Lord [Yahweh] hath opened mine ear,
   and I was not rebellious,
   neither turned away back.
[6]I gave my back to the smiters,
   and my cheeks to them that plucked off the hair:[92]

I hid not my face
from shame and spitting.

⁷For the Lord [Yahweh] will help me;
    therefore shall I not be confounded:
    therefore have I set my face like a flint,
    and I know that I shall not be ashamed.
⁸He is near that justifieth me;
    who will contend with me?
    let us stand together:
    who is mine adversary?
    let him come near to me.
⁹Behold, the Lord [Yahweh] will help me;
    who is he that shall condemn me?
    lo, they all shall wax old as a garment;
    the moth shall eat them up.

¹⁰Who is among you that feareth [Yahweh],
    that obeyeth the voice of his servant,
    that walketh in darkness,
    and hath no light?
    let him trust in the name of [Yahweh],
    and stay upon his God.
¹¹Behold, all ye that kindle a fire,
    that compass yourselves about with sparks:
    walk in the light of your fire,
    and in the sparks that ye have kindled.
    This shall ye have of mine hand;
    ye shall lie down in sorrow.

Isaiah 52-53

This next one, the fourth, is the most famous servant poem because of the Christian reading of it as a prediction of Jesus Christ (or at least of a suffering messiah). Again, I do not think the earliest Christians thought this was in the poet's mind at all. Rather, they looked past the original meaning (which they may not even have understood) and thought they recognized an esoteric message about Jesus or Paul (Acts 13:47).

From the KJV again, Isaiah 52:13-15:

¹³Behold, my servant shall deal prudently,
    he shall be exalted and extolled,
    and be very high.
¹⁴As many were astonied at thee;
    his visage was so marred more than any man,
    and his form more than the sons of men:
¹⁵So shall he sprinkle many nations;
    the kings shall shut their mouths at him:
    for that which had not been told them shall they see;
    and that which they had not heard shall they consider.

In Isa. 52:13, the RSV says the servant "shall prosper." It refers to third person observers rather than the reader ("As many were astonished at him") in v. 14. And it uses the word "startle" rather than "sprinkle" in v. 15.

Now (again from the KJV), Isaiah 53:1-12:

¹Who hath believed our report?
    and to whom is the arm of [Yahweh] revealed?
²For he shall grow up before him as a tender plant,

and as a root out of a dry ground:
    he hath no form nor comeliness;
    and when we shall see him,
    there is no beauty that we should desire him.
3He is despised and rejected of men;
    a man of sorrows, and acquainted with grief:
    and we hid as it were our faces from him;
    he was despised, and we esteemed him not.

In 53:2, the RSV uses the past rather than the future tense, avoiding any translation bias of this being a prophecy.

4Surely he hath borne our griefs,
    and carried our sorrows:
    yet we did esteem him stricken,
    smitten of God, and afflicted.
5But he was wounded for our transgressions,
    he was bruised for our iniquities:
    the chastisement of our peace[93] was upon him;
    and with his stripes we are healed.
6All we like sheep have gone astray;
    we have turned every one to his own way;
    and [Yahweh] hath laid on him
    the iniquity of us all.

7He was oppressed, and he was afflicted,
    yet he opened not his mouth:
    he is brought as a lamb to the slaughter,
    and as a sheep before her shearers is dumb,
    so he openeth not his mouth.
8He was taken from prison and from judgment:
    and who shall declare his generation?
    for he was cut off out of the land of the living:
    for the transgression of my people was he stricken.
9And he made his grave with the wicked,
    and with the rich in his death;
    because he had done no violence,
    neither was any deceit in his mouth.[94]

10Yet it pleased [Yahweh] to bruise him;
    he hath put him to grief:
    when thou shalt make his soul an offering for sin,
    he shall see his seed, he shall prolong his days,
    and the pleasure of [Yahweh] shall prosper in his hand.
11He shall see of the travail of his soul, and shall be satisfied:
    by his knowledge shall my righteous servant
    justify many;
    for he shall bear their iniquities.
12Therefore will I divide him a portion with the great,
    and he shall divide the spoil with the strong;
    because he hath poured out his soul unto death:
    and he was numbered with the transgressors;
    and he bare the sin of many,
    and made intercession for the transgressors.

Hugo Gressmann[95] believed that the poet had reworked a cult lamentation originally used in the rites of the dying and rising gods, e.g., Tammuz and Hadad-Rimmon (both well-known in Israel and Jerusalem, Ezekiel 8:14 and Zechariah 12:11). It would have been chanted on "Holy Saturday" between the god's death and resurrection.

Helmer Ringgren[96] suggested that Isaiah 52:13-53:12 formed part of the New Year ritual of royal humiliation. In it, the king of Judah took responsibility for the sins of his people and for the divine punishment seen in the death of nature (vegetation). He would submit to the High Priest slapping his face, yanking his ears, and knocking the crown off his head. Then he would retrieve the crown and receive the mandate of heaven for another year. In this procedure he was symbolically reenacting the death and resurrection of Yahweh. This would provide a perfect *Sitz-im-Leben* for the use of the liturgy Gressmann postulated.

In any case, the poem has repurposed the lamentation, applying it to Yahweh's servant Israel. The astonished witnesses of the servant's sufferings are the nations at whose hands the servant has suffered. They had thought the Diaspora Jews were only getting what they deserved (the usual prejudice of anti-Semites), but now they have come to realize that the servant was innocent and that it was *their* sins for which he suffered.

This is the moment of their conversion from heathenism to the faith of Israel. It amounts to a Jewish version of the Moral Influence theory of Christ's atonement: The display of divine love in the crucifixion of Jesus wins over the sinner who never knew God would go to such lengths to save them (Rom. 5:8; 1 John 4:9-10).

Israel is depicted like Paul in 2 Corinthians 4:7-12: His undaunted faithfulness to God amid trials makes known the power and favor of God within him. Combine this with Paul's timetable for universal redemption in Romans 11:13-15, 25-32: Jews turn away from the gospel so Gentiles may embrace it, which in turn causes Jews to be amazed and to turn to God/the gospel after all. Only here in Isaiah 53 it is the *Gentiles* who observe the sufferings of Israel, of the Jews, and turn to God.

The notion that Jewish sufferings actually *atone* for the Gentiles[97] makes new sense in light of René Girard's work. He maintains that religion is the result of the primitive social mechanism of persecuting and executing a scapegoat as a symbolic and magical means of reconciliation between warring factions in a society. Society is organized into different class or caste divisions, and one of these begins to envy what the other possesses. Social order breaks down, both violence and anomie resulting. People begin to realize this state of disintegration must be reversed or all will be lost. But neither faction is willing to accept responsibility for the chaos. So both sides eventually come together in identifying a minority group or an individual whom they accuse of magically or secretly causing all the problems.

In accusing and persecuting him, all factions unite. Thus the scapegoat, by getting everyone off the hook and giving them something to unite over, becomes a savior. Just as he was first believed powerful enough to send the plague (or whatever), so now is he regarded as powerful enough to solve the social upheaval. He becomes as venerated and worshipped as he once was feared and despised—and by the same people! Historically, Jews have in this way been made scapegoats,[98] with scurrilous and superstitious accusations heaped upon them, yet simultaneously revered as God's chosen people.

Some More about the Servant

Isaiah 41

Mettinger[99] suggests that two more passages naturally belong in the same box with the supposed Servant Songs. Isaiah 41:8-13 flatly states that the servant of Yahweh is the persecuted and redeemed people of Israel. Verse 9 views God's regathering of Diaspora Jews as a *fait accompli*, so sure a prospect is it in the poet's mind. These scattered people need not fear further abuse at pagan hands, for their God will soon free them and call their enemies to account. Here is the passage (ASV), with emphasis added to v. 9.

> 8But thou, Israel, my servant,
>> Jacob whom I have chosen,
>> the seed of Abraham my friend,
> 9thou *whom I have taken hold of*
>> *from the ends of the earth,*
>> *and called from the corners thereof,*
>> and said unto thee,
>> Thou art my servant,
>> I have chosen thee and not cast thee away;
> 10fear thou not, for I am with thee;
>> be not dismayed, for I am thy God;
>> I will strengthen thee;
>> yea, I will help thee;
>> yea, I will uphold thee with the right hand of my righteousness.

> 11Behold, all they that are incensed against thee
>> shall be put to shame and confounded:
>> they that strive with thee
>> shall be as nothing, and shall perish.
> 12Thou shalt seek them,
>> and shalt not find them,
>> even them that contend with thee:
>> they that war against thee shall be as nothing,
>> and as a thing of nought.
> 13For I, Jehovah thy God, will hold thy right hand,
>> saying unto thee,
>> Fear not; I will help thee.

Isaiah 42 (again)

Isaiah 42:18–25 (ASV) looks back on Israel's long blindness and the severity of their punishment, their being scattered to the four winds. But God is willing to regard all that as water under the bridge, and the poem ends with Israel's own confession of former sins.

> 18Hear, ye deaf;
>> and look, ye blind, that ye may see.
> 19Who is blind, but my servant?
>> or deaf, as my messenger that I send?
>> who is blind as he that is at peace with me,
>> and blind as Jehovah's servant?
> 20Thou seest many things, but thou observest not;
>> his ears are open, but he heareth not.
> 21It pleased Jehovah, for his righteousness' sake,
>> to magnify the law, and make it honorable.
> 22But this is a people robbed and plundered;
>> they are all of them snared in holes,
>> and they are hid in prison-houses:
>> they are for a prey, and none delivereth;
>> for a spoil, and none saith, Restore.

> 23Who is there among you
>> that will give ear to this?
>> that will hearken and hear for the time to come?
> 24Who gave Jacob for a spoil,
>> and Israel to the robbers?
>> did not Jehovah?

he against whom we have sinned,
  and in whose ways they would not walk,
neither were they obedient unto his law.
  ²⁵Therefore he poured upon him the fierceness of his anger,
  and the strength of battle;
  and it set him on fire round about,
yet he knew not;
  and it burned him,
  yet he laid it not to heart.

Much more could be said of the very long Book of Isaiah but if all of it were to be covered, the world itself (or at least the library of Harvard Divinity School) could not hold all the books.

The Contrived Christian Isaiah

Let me reiterate an important point, namely just how problematical it is to do what Christian theologians have always done, appropriating these passages from Isaiah (and other prophetic books) for Christian apologetics. I hope I have made it clear that none of the texts so often cited as clairvoyant predictions of Jesus as the Christ were so intended by the ancient writers.

On a popular level, Isaiah 7, 9, 11, and 53 (to take the major examples) are usually quoted out of context with all the mischief entailed when a public figure's words are quoted in isolation today. These believers are not trying to hoodwink anyone. This is the way they have always heard the passages interpreted from the pulpit. They find historical exegesis of the Old Testament tedious and uninteresting. They are interested, really, only in the Christian New Testament, the Old amounting pretty much to a museum relic, like skeletons of our cavemen predecessors.

Did Isaiah 7:14 have relevance to some hoary era when Judah feared the encroachments of Aram and Samaria? Who knows? Who cares? Not them. Why should they? They aren't Bible scholars and aren't pretending to be. For them, the verse is interesting only because it functions as a prophetic proof text for the miraculous conception of Jesus Christ—which it isn't. Even when they defend their out-of-context reading of Isaiah 7:14 by pointing to Matthew 1:23 which quotes Isaiah 7:14 as a prediction of Jesus, they are really appealing to Matthew, not Isaiah.

But what happens when a Bible student learns more and becomes interested in what the Book of Isaiah was actually trying to tell its readers? Once he comes to understand that Isaiah 7:14 was after all about Aram and Samaria? By gaining such knowledge, our Bible devotee has painted himself into a corner. For, as a good Protestant he knows he is obliged to affirm but a single, literal sense of scripture, this being the only way to avoid making scripture into a ventriloquist dummy parroting the opinions of clever manipulators who smuggle their own views into the text by means of arbitrary and self-serving "spiritual," figurative, allegorical exegesis.

That's what Martin Luther saw the Roman Catholic Church doing, and he wanted nothing to do with it. We shouldn't treat scripture that way. But what if that's how the scriptural writers *themselves* treated scripture? For that's just how the New Testament writers treated the Old Testament! This is what *pesher* exegesis was all about: a studied disregard of the no-longer-relevant meaning of a passage in its original context in favor of some imagined esoteric meaning. Matthew, appealing to Isaiah 7:14, then, was not being a good Protestant!

So who is today's Bible reader going to side with? Which way is he to go? Follow Luther with his grammatico-historical method? Or the New Testament writers, blown about by the changing winds of the Holy Ghost's leading?

It's a pickle, to be sure. You abandon either the sane, serious approach of Protestantism or the fanciful approach of the scriptural writers whose meanings you wanted so fervently to discover by a literal, contextual reading. Do you dare to saw off the very limb you are sitting on?

As for me and my house, we will serve the Bible by taking seriously what its writers were trying to say—even if that forces us to disagree with them. And that, it seems to me, is the nub of the issue with biblical criticism: understanding the Bible undistorted by faith. Undistorted by faith in the Bible itself.

The Book of Jeremiah

Given the prominence of this prophet in the events leading to the Babylonian conquest, as we read in the Book of Jeremiah, why does 2 Kings *never even mention him*?[100] The only answer has to be that the Deuteronomic writers had not yet invented him. Terence Collins and Robert P. Carroll agree that Jeremiah is really a literary incarnation of Deuteronomy's ideal of a true prophet of Yahweh.[101]

Carroll supposes that a historical Jeremiah was the author of the core of poetry around which the rest of the book was built, but even he admits this is an *a priori* assumption.[102] This may sound outrageous given the way scholars (as well as ordinary readers) have long opined that Jeremiah is the biblical prophet whose inner life we know best. But as we will see, this is an optical illusion. It arises from too superficial a reading of several passages traditionally called the "Confessions of Jeremiah."

Jeremiah 11-12

The first of these passages (11:18-23; 12:1-6) belongs to a particular subspecies of Individual Lament psalm, namely the Imprecatory psalms, the psalmist protesting his innocence, that he does not deserve the suffering presently inflicted on him by his enemies, and pleading with God to give them a big dose of their own poison medicine. Jeremiah 11:21-23 looks like an insertion made in order to provide a plausible context for the song lyric. The section at Jer. 12:4-6 is one of those pro forma responses from God through the mouth of a cult prophet. It seems likely that there are actually two psalms of innocence here: Jeremiah 11:18-21 and 12:1-6 (the ASV is quoted).

> ¹⁸And Jehovah gave me knowledge of it, and I knew it:
> then thou showedst me their doings.
> ¹⁹But I was like a gentle lamb
> that is led to the slaughter;
> and I knew not that they had devised devices against me,
> saying,
> Let us destroy the tree with the fruit thereof,
> and let us cut him off from the land of the living,
> that his name may be no more remembered.
> ²⁰But, O Jehovah [Sabaoth],
> who judgest righteously,
> who triest the heart and the mind,
> I shall see thy vengeance on them;
> for unto thee have I revealed my cause.

²¹Therefore thus saith Jehovah concerning the men of Anathoth, that seek thy life, saying, Thou shalt not prophesy in the name of Jehovah, that thou die not by our hand; ²²therefore thus saith Jehovah [Sabaoth], Behold, I will punish them: the young men shall die by the sword; their sons and their daughters shall die by famine; ²³and there shall be no remnant unto them: for I will bring evil upon the men of Anathoth, even the year of their visitation.

> ¹Righteous art thou, O Jehovah,
>> when I contend with thee;
>> yet would I reason the cause with thee:
> wherefore doth the way of the wicked prosper?
>> wherefore are all they at ease
>> that deal very treacherously?
> ²Thou hast planted them,
>> yea, they have taken root;
>> they grow, yea, they bring forth fruit:
> thou art near in their mouth,
>> and far from their heart.
> ³But thou, O Jehovah, knowest me;
>> thou seest me, and triest my heart toward thee:
>> pull them out like sheep for the slaughter,
>> and prepare them for the day of slaughter.
> ⁴How long shall the land mourn,
>> and the herbs of the whole country wither?
> for the wickedness of them that dwell therein,
>> the beasts are consumed, and the birds;
> because they said,
>> He shall not see our latter end.

> ⁵If thou hast run with the footmen,
>> and they have wearied thee,
>> then how canst thou contend with horses?
> and though in a land of peace thou art secure,
>> yet how wilt thou do in the pride of the Jordan?
> ⁶For even thy brethren,
>> and the house of thy father,
> even they have dealt treacherously with thee;
>> even they have cried aloud after thee:
> believe them not,
>> though they speak fair words unto thee.

Jeremiah 15

The next passage would make a lot of sense as a Royal Lament psalm, possibly part of the humiliation rite during the New Year Festival. There appears to be a dialogue between the king and a cult prophet speaking for Yahweh. The prophet is heard first in Jeremiah 15:13-14, in which Yahweh, through the prophet, rebukes the king and threatens defeat at the hands of the nation's enemies. The second pro forma "oracle" appears in verses 19-21, a divine promise of forgiveness and restoration, which is the logic of the ritual.

The first verse of the passage (v. 10) is marked by lamentation language that is shared with Job 3:1-10. Here's the NASB version of Jeremiah 15:10-21:

> ¹⁰Woe to me, my mother, that you have borne me
>> As a man of strife and a man of contention to all the land!
>> I have not lent, nor have men lent money to me,
>> Yet everyone curses me.

[11][Yahweh] said, "Surely I will set you free for purposes of good;
   Surely I will cause the enemy to make supplication to you
   In a time of disaster and a time of distress.

[12]"Can anyone smash iron,
   Iron from the north, or bronze?
[13]"Your wealth and your treasures
   I will give for booty without cost,
   Even for all your sins
   And within all your borders.
[14]"Then I will cause your enemies to bring it
   Into a land you do not know;
   For a fire has been kindled in My anger,
   It will burn upon you."

[15]You who know, O [Yahweh],
   Remember me, take notice of me,
   And take vengeance for me on my persecutors.
   Do not, in view of Your patience, take me away;
   Know that for Your sake I endure reproach.
[16]Your words were found and I ate them,
   And Your words became for me a joy and the delight of my heart;
   For I have been called by Your name,
   O [Yahweh] God of hosts.
[17]I did not sit in the circle of merrymakers,
   Nor did I exult.
   Because of Your hand upon me I sat alone,
   For You filled me with indignation.
[18]Why has my pain been perpetual
   And my wound incurable, refusing to be healed?
   Will You indeed be to me like a deceptive stream
   With water that is unreliable?

[19]Therefore, thus says [Yahweh],
   "If you return, then I will restore you
   Before Me you will stand;
   And if you extract the precious from the worthless,
   You will become My spokesman.
   They for their part may turn to you,
   But as for you, you must not turn to them.
[20]"Then I will make you to this people
   A fortified wall of bronze;
   And though they fight against you,
   They will not prevail over you;
   For I am with you to save you
   And deliver you," declares [Yahweh].
[21]"So I will deliver you from the hand of the wicked,
   And I will redeem you from the grasp of the violent."

Jeremiah 17

The third "Confession" is yet another psalm of Innocence and Imprecation. It may have been sung by or for the king in a time of trouble from foreign foes or else from threatening conspirators, calling on Yahweh to vindicate the psalmist and to deliver him from his enemies. Verse fifteen quotes the scoffing of the impious: "Where is (the fulfillment of) Yahweh's promise of deliverance?" We find the same sentiments in Psalm 42:3, 10; Micah 7:10; Malachi 2:17; and 2 Peter 3:3-4. In verse 15 the psalmist says that up to this point he has not invoked God's wrath upon his enemies, but now he will. Jeremiah 17:12-18 (ASV):

[12]A glorious throne, set on high from the beginning,
is the place of our sanctuary.
[13]O Jehovah, the hope of Israel,
all that forsake thee shall be put to shame.
They that depart from me shall be written in the earth,
because they have forsaken Jehovah,
the fountain of living waters.

[14]Heal me, O Jehovah, and I shall be healed;
save me, and I shall be saved:
for thou art my praise.
[15]Behold, they say unto me,
Where is the word of Jehovah?
let it come now.
[16]As for me, I have not hastened
from being a shepherd after thee;
neither have I desired the woeful day;
thou knowest:
that which came out of my lips was before thy face.
[17]Be not a terror unto me:
thou art my refuge in the day of evil.
[18]Let them be put to shame that persecute me,
but let not me be put to shame;
let them be dismayed,
but let not me be dismayed;
bring upon them the day of evil,
and destroy them with double destruction.

Jeremiah 18

Another imprecatory psalm meets us in Jeremiah 18:19-23 (NASB). Its venom is easily equal to that in Psalm 109, though more concise. There is no cheek-turning here!

Do give heed to me, O [Yahweh],
And listen to what my opponents are saying!
Should good be repaid with evil?
For they have dug a pit for me.
Remember how I stood before You
To speak good on their behalf,
So as to turn away Your wrath from them.
Therefore, give their children over to famine
And deliver them up to the power of the sword;
And let their wives become childless and widowed.
Let their men also be smitten to death,
Their young men struck down by the sword in battle.
May an outcry be heard from their houses,
When You suddenly bring raiders upon them;
For they have dug a pit to capture me
And hidden snares for my feet.
Yet You, O [Yahweh], know
All their deadly designs against me;
Do not forgive their iniquity
Or blot out their sin from Your sight.
But may they be overthrown before You;
Deal with them in the time of Your anger!

Jeremiah 20

The same pattern obtains in the last of our Jeremiah passages. The psalmist complains bitterly of the mockery he endures even from his so-called friends. In verses 8b-9 he laments how his reliance upon the promise of God seems to have failed, and his enemies rub it in, reminding him of his former confidence in God, which now seems to have been misplaced. So he resolves to invite no more such ridicule: He will never again profess to trust in God's protection.

But his heart is not in it. Deep down he knows God will not fail him, and he must so testify no matter what scoffing he invites by doing so.

He is backing away from the same brink upon which the writer of Psalm 73:13-15 teetered. When our author resolves no more to speak of Yahweh's protection, in order to avoid further ridicule, but finds he cannot keep silent (20:9), the point is the same as when the psalmist says, "If I had said, 'I will speak thus' [i.e., voice these thoughts aloud], I should have been untrue to the generation of thy children" (73:15).

Here's the passage, Jeremiah 20:7-18, this time from the NASB:

7O [Yahweh], You have deceived me and I was deceived;
   You have overcome me and prevailed.
   I have become a laughingstock all day long;
   Everyone mocks me.
8For each time I speak, I cry aloud;
   I proclaim violence and destruction,
   Because for me the word of [Yahweh] has resulted
   In reproach and derision all day long.
9But if I say, "I will not remember Him
   Or speak anymore in His name,"
   Then in my heart it becomes like a burning fire
   Shut up in my bones;
   And I am weary of holding it in,
   And I cannot endure it.
10For I have heard the whispering of many,
   "Terror on every side!
   Denounce him; yes, let us denounce him!"
   All my trusted friends,
   Watching for my fall, say:
   "Perhaps he will be deceived, so that we may prevail against him
   And take our revenge on him."
11But [Yahweh] is with me like a dread champion;
   Therefore my persecutors will stumble and not prevail.
   They will be utterly ashamed, because they have failed,
   With an everlasting disgrace that will not be forgotten.
12Yet, O [Yahweh Sabaoth], You who test the righteous,
   Who see the mind and the heart;
   Let me see Your vengeance on them;
   For to You I have set forth my cause.
13Sing to [Yahweh], praise [Yahweh]!
   For He has delivered the soul of the needy one
   From the hand of evildoers.

14Cursed be the day when I was born;
   Let the day not be blessed when my mother bore me!
15Cursed be the man who brought the news
   To my father, saying,
   "A baby boy has been born to you!"
   And made him very happy.

¹⁶But let that man be like the cities
    Which [Yahweh] overthrew without relenting,
    And let him hear an outcry in the morning
    And a shout of alarm at noon;
¹⁷Because he did not kill me before birth,
    So that my mother would have been my grave,
    And her womb ever pregnant.
¹⁸Why did I ever come forth from the womb
    To look on trouble and sorrow,
    So that my days have been spent in shame?

Verses 14-18 don't seem to belong here. They look like a fragment from a separate lament psalm, again recalling the suicidal moaning of Job. Whoever tacked it on here in order to preserve it would have done better to place it at the beginning of the psalm, not at the end where the clouds seem to have parted.

By now it is patently obvious that nothing in any of these texts makes specific reference to Jeremiah. All the trials, tribulations, and worries mentioned in them are generic and vague. This, of course, is the style of the psalms, where "one size fits all." And that is hardly the only respect in which these texts resemble lyrics from the Book of Psalms. Job's laments, paralleled here, sound like the laments of the Psalter, too.

Why? Because *these texts are borrowed from Jewish liturgy*. By placing them in the mouth of Jeremiah, the Deuteronomists have created the character of "the Weeping Prophet."[103] (Suffering Job, cursing his luck, is the result of the same process). Jeremiah is, if you'll forgive the metaphor, a Frankenstein monster stitched together from various old psalms.

The Vengeance of Nitocris

Jer. 43-44

In Jeremiah 43, a group of survivors of the Babylonian conquest decide to take refuge in Egypt, against Jeremiah's warnings. They scorn his opinion but wind up taking him along with them, against his will, for his own good. I have to wonder if there is some polemic encoded here.[104]

I think of the Matthean story of young Jesus taken in tow to Egypt to escape the wrath of Herod the Great (Matt. 2:13-15). The second-century critic of Christianity, Celsus, claims that, according to Jewish opinion, Jesus went to Egypt to learn magic there,[105] the power by which he performed his (lying) wonders. Indeed, pagans, Jews, and even some early Christians understood Jesus as a great magician.[106] Is the version attested by Celsus the original (true or not) and Matthew's version a theologically sanitized substitution? Or the other way around? It doesn't matter: The point is that we have two sides of an argument. And I suspect we are reading one side of an argument in Jeremiah 43 as well.

There was an outlying Jewish Temple in Leontopolis and another at Elephantine, both in Egypt. The Deuteronomists certainly despised them, given their restriction of Jewish worship to Jerusalem (Deut. 12:1-7). My guess is that Jeremiah 43's tale of Jeremiah being packed off to Egypt against his will is a Deuteronomistic rewrite of a credential story put forth by Egyptian Jews who would have claimed that Jeremiah had founded their community and their Temple.

Did their colony and Temple pre-date Jeremiah? No matter. They'd have been happy enough to post-date their founding if it would win them an "apostolic" pedigree for their "church." Of course, I mean to parallel the case with those of various prominent Christian churches later claiming to have been established by this or that apostle, the greater the apostolic name, the greater the bishop's clout.

Chapter 44 only adds fuel to this blaze.

> Then all the men who were aware that their wives were burning sacrifices to other gods, along with all the women who were standing by, as a large assembly, including all the people who were living in Pathros in the land of Egypt, responded to Jeremiah, saying, "As for the message that you have spoken to us in the name of [Yahweh], we are not going to listen to you! But rather we will certainly carry out every word that has proceeded from our mouths, by burning sacrifices to the queen of heaven and pouring out drink offerings to her, just as we ourselves, our forefathers, our kings and our princes did in the cities of Judah and in the streets of Jerusalem; for then we had plenty of food and were well off and saw no misfortune. But since we stopped burning sacrifices to the queen of heaven and pouring out drink offerings to her, we have lacked everything and have met our end by the sword and by famine." "And," said the women, "when we were burning sacrifices to the queen of heaven and were pouring out drink offerings to her, was it without our husbands that we made for her sacrificial cakes in her image and poured out drink offerings to her?" (Jer. 44:15-19, NASB)

Listen to this! Here is an alternative to the Deuteronimsts' theodicy: The Babylonian devastation of Judah came about because Asherah, the Queen of Heaven, was displeased at the cessation of *her* offerings! It was *she* who struck down Judah by the hand of Nebuchadnezzer, *not Yahweh*! Her partisans are not described here as rejectors of Yahwist worship. They did not worship Asherah *instead* of Yahweh. No, they believed in a Jewish pantheon in which these two ruled as divine king and queen over the lesser Israelite deities.

A storage jar dating from the eighth century B.C.E., unearthed at Kuntillet Ajrud[107] in the Sinai Desert, features a depiction of seated figures apparently intended to represent King Yahweh and Queen Asherah. It and another jar feature inscriptions. One reads, "Amaryau said to my lord . . . may you be blessed by Yahweh and by his Asherah." Another has, "I may have blessed you by Yahweh of Samaria and his Asherah." It also twice mentions "Yahweh of Teman and his Asherah." An inscription discovered at Khirbet el Qom (the biblical Makkedah), some nine miles to the west of Hebron, says: "Uriah the rich has caused it to be written: Blessed be Uriah by Yahweh and by his Asherah; from his enemies he has saved them."[108] Aramaic papyri from the Jewish colony located at the fortress of Yeb (or Elephantine) in Egypt includes a letter from the priests of the Jewish temple there, and it mentions the worship of Yahweh, Anath (daughter of Asherah), who is called "Anatyahu," meaning "Yahweh's Anath." This last attests the sort of Judaism that must have claimed Jeremiah as its patron and which the Deuteronomic Book of Jeremiah repudiated in his name.

So which deity was "really" responsible for the defeat of Judah? Girard would say that neither one was—until one of the rival ascriptions succeeded in establishing itself, which the Deuteronomic theodicy did by virtue of its inclusion in the canonical scriptures. Now it's settled, retroactively.

O Christmas Tree?

Jer. 10, Isa. 46

Some too-religious Scrooges cite Jeremiah 10:2-4 in order to condemn Christmas trees as survivals of paganism and on this basis to bully more healthy-minded Christians into skipping the holiday. But are they right? The passage quotes Yahweh as follows (RSV):

> Learn not the way of the nations,
>> nor be dismayed at the signs of the heavens
>> because the nations are dismayed at them,
> ³for the customs of the peoples are false.
> A tree from the forest is cut down,
>> and worked with an axe by the hands of a craftsman.
> ⁴Men deck it with silver and gold;
>> they fasten it with hammer and nails
>> so that it cannot move.

So, Christmas tree or what? It's not a stupid reading of the text, but it is wrong nonetheless. One need not treat this passage as a prediction of Christmas trees, their installation, and their ornaments in order to see a possible continuity between modern Christmas decorations and ancient paganism. There were indeed sacred trees, e.g., on Mount Carmel, and worshippers would hang votive offerings on the branches, aiming to please the god whom they believed dwelt in the tree trunk. But this would not have included precious metals. Usually worshippers hung rags or strips of meat.[109]

There is certainly an analogy between this practice and the Christmas tree customs of past generations according to which parents would tie small Christmas presents *for their children* on the tinsel- or popcorn-decked boughs of the Christmas tree. But this ancient practice is not what Jeremiah refers to. First, continue to verse 5 (RSV):

> ⁵Their idols are like scarecrows in a cucumber field,
>> and they cannot speak;
> they have to be carried,
>> for they cannot walk.
> Be not afraid of them,
>> for they cannot do evil,
>> neither is it in them to do good.

Compare this with what the Second Isaiah has to say. Isa. 44:9-20 sniffs at the futile efforts of those "who fashion a graven image," whose "precious things are of no profit." This is something "even their own witnesses fail to see or know." The guy fashioning a god or casting an idol "to no profit" is wasting his time, shameful even.

> Behold, all his companions will be put to shame, for the craftsmen themselves are mere men. Let them all assemble themselves, let them stand up, let them tremble, let them together be put to shame.

> The man shapes iron into a cutting tool and does his work over the coals, fashioning it with hammers and working it with his strong arm. He also gets hungry and his strength fails; he drinks no water and becomes weary. Another shapes wood, he extends a measuring line; he outlines it with red chalk. He works it with planes and outlines it with a compass, and makes it like the form of a man, like the beauty of man, so that it may sit in a house. Surely he cuts cedars for himself, and takes a cypress or an oak and raises it for himself among the trees of the forest. He plants a fir, and the rain makes it grow. Then it becomes something for a man to burn, so he takes one of them and warms himself; he also makes a fire to bake bread. He also makes a god and worships it; he makes it a graven image and falls down before it. Half of it he burns in the fire; over this half he eats meat as he roasts a roast and is satisfied. He also warms himself and says, "Aha! I am warm, I have seen the fire." But the rest of it he makes into a god, his graven image. He falls down before it and worships; he also prays to it and says, "Deliver me, for you are my god."

They do not know, nor do they understand, for [Yahweh] has smeared over their eyes so that they cannot see and their hearts so that they cannot comprehend. No one recalls, nor is there knowledge or understanding to say, "I have burned half of it in the fire and also have baked bread over its coals. I roast meat and eat it. Then I make the rest of it into an abomination, I fall down before a block of wood!" He feeds on ashes; a deceived heart has turned him aside. And he cannot deliver himself, nor say, "Is there not a lie in my right hand?" (Isa. 44:10-20, NASB)

In Isaiah 46:6-7 (back to the RSV), the lady's definitely not buying a stairway to heaven with any of that gold:[110]

>⁶Those who lavish gold from the purse,
>   and weigh out silver in the scales,
>hire a goldsmith, and he makes it into a god;
>   then they fall down and worship!
>⁷They lift it upon their shoulders, they carry it,
>   they set it in its place, and its stands there;
>   it cannot move from its place.
>If one cries to it, it does not answer
>   or save him from his trouble.

Isn't it obvious that this—the futility of making golden idols—is exactly what Jeremiah is pointing out? The tree he mentions is not transferred to somebody's living room; it is chopped down and denuded of bark and branches, carved into the desired shape, then plated with gold and silver, then nailed to a base in a shrine. He is talking not about a Christmas tree but a fancy statue of Baal (or maybe one of his divine colleagues).

The Book of Ezekiel

The very beginning of the Book of Ezekiel contains an important and quite clumsy redactional interpolation.

> In the thirtieth year, in the fourth month, on the fifth day of the month, **as I was among the exiles by the river Chebar,** the heavens were opened, and I saw visions of God. **On the fifth day of the month (it was the fifth year of the exile of King Jehoiachin), the word of** the Lord **[Yahweh] came to Ezekiel the priest, the son of Buzi, in the land of the Chaldeans by the river Chebar; and the hand of** the Lord **[Yahweh] was upon him there.**
> (Ezek. 1:1-3, RSV, emphasis and bracketed text added)

You can't help noticing how there are two openings and that verse 1, like the rest of the book, is in the first person, while verse 2 is written in the third person. That ought to be a big clue. Another oddity is the juxtaposition of two contradictory dates. That in the first verse must refer to the thirtieth year of the reign of the current king, but the date in the second verse places the beginning of Ezekiel's prophesying five years into the Babylonian Exile. The second date occurs in the ill-fitting third-person narration.

C.C. Torrey[111] inferred from all this, surely correctly, that a later hand has interpolated the third-person text, inserting the repeated phrase "by the river Chebar" from this section into the first-person section in a clumsy attempt to harmonize the two. Why is this important? Simply because this is the only grounds for placing Ezekiel's ministry in Babylon, something that does not fit with the rest of the book, all of which seems to be set in Jerusalem.[112]

Who would have made such an alteration? Again, simple: the Chronicler (or an ally) who added the hand-full of references to Babylon, Chaldea, and Cyrus to the text of Deutero-Isaiah. And why? The interpolations aim at promoting the interests of a particular party, the so-called Babylonian Exilarchs, the Persian-backed elite (Ezra, Nehemiah, et. al.), painting them as the authoritative guardians of the "true Judaism" as if they had preserved it while away and were now "returning" to impose their doctrines and policies on that majority of Jews who had remained in the land after Nebuchadnezzer's conquest in 587 B.C.E.

The original text was addressed, not to a Jewish exile community in Babylon, but rather to the Diaspora Jews all over the Middle East and the Mediterranean world, anticipating their regathering in the Jewish homeland. But even the original book was not the work of Ezekiel, son of Buzi, though the actual Deuteronomist writer(s) placed his name upon it. And, as in the case of Jeremiah, no such prophet appears in 2 Kings 24-25, which covers his period, much less in Jeremiah 29:15-21, which discusses Jewish prophets in Babylon. Why? "The omission of any reference to a prophet Ezekiel may be due to the simple fact that such a 'prophet' did not exist until the book *Ezekiel* created him out of the priest and teacher Ezekiel ben Buzi."[113]

This pseudepigraph seems to be set fictively during the reign of the apostate King Manasseh[114] who embraced every pagan abomination his righteous father, King Hezekiah, had extirpated from the land. As we have seen, that whole scenario was a fiction serving the Deuteronomic rewrite of Jewish/Israelite history as if the native polytheism had instead been borrowed from the heathen "Canaanites" and proved impossible to eradicate once and for all.

There are numerous dates provided for when Ezekiel issued his predictions. Why? What's the difference? The point is to make sure the reader "knows" that the prophet made his forecasts *before the event*, even though he didn't.[115] That is the trick of pseudepigraphy, after all. It's pretty easy to make accurate predictions in retrospect. It's called "pious fraud."

Then why, you may ask, the erroneous promise that "Nebuchadrezzar, king of Babylon" would conquer Tyre (Ezek. 26:7-14)? As Torrey[116] shows, the name of the Babylonian emperor is a subsequent scribal/redactional insertion in line with the artificial (re-)focus on Babylon and the supposed Exile. Originally, only the title "king of kings" stood in the text, and it must have referred to Alexander the Great who actually did conquer Tyre, building a bridge to the island kingdom from slabs of masonry salvaged from collapsed city walls.

Interestingly, the Koran (Surah 18:92-99) mentions Alexander ("Dhu'l-Qarneyn," i.e., "the Two-Horned") as he who imprisoned Gog and Magog behind a great barrier wall, warning that they should be loosed from there on the Day of Judgment. Of course, Ezekiel mentions Gog and Magog (chapter 38) as invading nations from the north.

Scholars generally identify Gog and Magog with the fierce Scythians, but Torrey argues they were the Macedonians of Alexander,[117] remembrance of whom likely led to the association of Alexander with Gog and Magog in the Koran. Torrey[118] sees Ezekiel predicting a second invasion of Gog and Magog at the End of Days (38:4; 39:2), corresponding to the Koran's statement that Gog and Magog will break free to menace the world again on the Last Day.

What is the meaning of the names Gog and Magog? "Gog" may be another form of the name of King Gyges of Lydia,[119] with "Magog" ("Land of Gog") referring to Lydia plus his allies the Mushki (Ezekiel's "Meschech"), Tubal (the Black Sea bronze-smiths descended from Tubal-Cain in Genesis 4:22), and the Cimmerians or Scythians (Gomer). "Rosh" has nothing to do with Russia (as Dispensationalists[120] think). The Hebrew word simply means "head" or "chief." Here it stands for Javan (which holds the corresponding place in the equivalent phrase "Javan, Meschech, and Tubal" in Genesis 10:2; 1 Chronicles 1:5; and Ezekiel 27:13. Javan is the Hebrew name for Greece, i.e., Alexander's Macedonians.[121]

Pretty Tired of Tyre

Ezek. 28:1-19

Traditionally cited as recounting the Fall of Lucifer to become the evil Satan, Ezekiel 28:1-19 actually refers to the fall of the king of Tyre, once God's favorite as witnessed by Tyre's maritime prosperity. The king of Tyre was as close to God as the royal signet ring is to the king's finger. But now he is to be destroyed for his pride. He is like Adam, who, though initially under the guardianship of a specially appointed cherub (God's treasure guardians, who also guard the Tree of Life, Gen. 3:24, and the Ark of the Covenant, Exod. 25:18-22), according to this version of the story, was cast out of Eden for his pride.

"The word of [Yahweh] came to me," says the narrator, telling him to convey the following to the prince of Tyre (ASV):

> 2Because thy heart is lifted up [RSV: *proud*],
>   and thou hast said, I am a god,
>   I sit in the seat of God,
>   in the midst of the seas;
>   yet thou art man, and not God,
>   though thou didst set thy heart as the heart of God;–
> 3behold, thou art wiser than Daniel;
>   there is no secret that is hidden from thee;
> 4by thy wisdom and by thine understanding thou hast gotten thee
>   riches,
>   and hast gotten gold and silver into thy treasures;
> 5by thy great wisdom and by thy traffic hast thou increased thy
>   riches,
>   and thy heart is lifted up because of thy riches;–
> 6therefore thus saith the Lord Jehovah:
>   Because thou hast set thy heart as the heart of God,
> 7therefore, behold, I will bring strangers upon thee,
>   the terrible of the nations;
>   and they shall draw their swords against the beauty of thy wisdom,
>   and they shall defile thy brightness.
> 8They shall bring thee down to the pit;
>   and thou shalt die the death of them that are slain,
>   in the heart of the seas.
> 9Wilt thou yet say before him that slayeth thee, I am God? [RSV: *a
>   god*]
>   but thou art man, and not God,
>   in the hand of him that woundeth thee.
> 10Thou shalt die the death of the uncircumcised
>   by the hand of strangers:
>   for I have spoken it, saith the Lord Jehovah.

And, the narrator continues, the word of Yahweh told him to "take up a lamentation over the king of Tyre, and say to him" the following from the Lord Yahweh:

> 12Thou sealest up the sum[122]
>   full of wisdom, and perfect in beauty.
> 13Thou wast in Eden, the garden of God;
>   every precious stone was thy covering,
>   the sardius, the topaz, and the diamond,

the beryl, the onyx, and the jasper,
the sapphire, the emerald, and the carbuncle, and gold:
the workmanship of thy tabrets and of thy pipes was in thee;
in the day that thou wast created they were prepared.
¹⁴Thou wast the anointed cherub that covereth:
and I set thee, so that thou wast upon the holy mountain of God;
thou hast walked up and down in the midst of the stones of fire.
¹⁵Thou wast perfect in thy ways
from the day that thou wast created,
till unrighteousness was found in thee.
¹⁶By the abundance of thy traffic
they filled the midst of thee with violence,
and thou hast sinned:
therefore have I cast thee as profane
out of the mountain of God;
and I have destroyed thee, O covering cherub,
from the midst of the stones of fire.
¹⁷Thy heart was lifted up because of thy beauty;
thou hast corrupted thy wisdom by reason of thy brightness:
I have cast thee to the ground;
I have laid thee before kings,
that they may behold thee.
¹⁸By the multitude of thine iniquities,
in the unrighteousness of thy traffic,
thou hast profaned thy sanctuaries;
therefore have I brought forth a fire from the midst of thee;
it hath devoured thee,
and I have turned thee to ashes upon the earth
in the sight of all them that behold thee.
¹⁹All they that know thee among the peoples
shall be astonished at thee:
thou art become a terror,
and thou shalt nevermore have any being.

None of this has anything to do with Lucifer as popular imagination supposes. So where did that identification come from? It all comes down to verse 14a, which is unclear in the original Hebrew. It might mean "*with* a guardian cherub" or "*as* a guardian cherub." If you go with the first possibility, the text speaks of a glorious cherub who fell due to his pride, and you've got something that looks like the familiar "fall of Lucifer" myth. I'm not sure anyone would have made that connection unless it reminded them of the "fall of the Sons of God" myth in Genesis 6:1-4.

But if you understand the Hebrew to mean "*as* a guardian cherub," you have a variant (probably older) version of the "fall of *Adam*" myth.[123] The latter, I think, must be the original intent because of verse 16, "and the guardian cherub drove you out," which also parallels Genesis 3:24, "He drove out the man; and at the east of the garden of Eden he placed the cherubim, and a flaming sword which turned every way, to guard the way to the tree of life." Verse one makes the sin of Adam to be pride; he was so great that he became too full of himself and decided he was no mere man but a god in his own right. We see this notion also in Genesis 3, where Yahweh expels the man from the garden because, having gained the knowledge proper only to gods, he has become like one of Eden's gods. Ezekiel's Adam, too, has gained ultimate knowledge, and that is what leads to his overweening pride.

The hymn about Christ in Philippians 2:6-11 presupposes this version of the Adam story, since we are to understand that the pre-incarnate Christ was in the same position Adam was, godlike in form and power. Like this heavenly Adam (Adam Kadmon),[124] he faced the temptation to "seize equality with God" but, unlike his predecessor, he declined it and instead undertook humiliation by assuming mortal form down on earth.[125]

Verses 4-5, 16a mix the Adam myth with the actual cause of the king of Tyre's coming punishment: He had become proud and arrogant because of the vast wealth his maritime trade had garnered, and he was due to be taken down a peg, just like Herod Agrippa in Acts 12:20-23. The author of Ezekiel wanted to make sure the reader remembered who this passage was really about. But as far as most of his readers were and still are concerned, his metaphoric efforts turned out to be in vain: People insist on seeing Satan in the poem.

Dem Dry Bones

Ezek. 37

I have to admit I kind of like the Living Bible's translation of this chapter, though I pretty much loathe it otherwise. Go figure. What's quoted is exactly how the translation reads; I'll let you do the replacement of "the Lord" and "God" with the actual Hebrew word "Yahweh" in your head:

> The power of the Lord was upon me and I was carried away by the Spirit of the Lord to a valley full of old, dry bones that were scattered everywhere across the ground. He led me around among them, and then he said to me:
>
> "Son of dust, can these bones become people again?"
>
> I replied, "Lord, you alone know the answer to that."
>
> Then he told me to speak to the bones and say: "O dry bones, listen to the words of God, for the Lord God says, 'See! I am going to make you live and breathe again! I will replace the flesh and muscles on you and cover you with skin. I will put breath into you, and you shall live and know I am the Lord.'"
>
> So I spoke these words from God, just as he told me to; and suddenly there was a rattling noise from all across the valley, and the bones of each body came together and attached to each other as they used to be. Then, as I watched, the muscles and flesh formed over the bones, and skin covered them, but the bodies had no breath. Then he told me to call to the wind and say: "The Lord God says: Come from the four winds, O Spirit, and breathe upon these slain bodies, that they may live again." So I spoke to the winds as he commanded me, and the bodies began breathing; they lived and stood up–a very great army.
>
> Then he told me what the vision meant: "These bones," he said, "represent all the people of Israel. They say: 'We have become a heap of dried-out bones–all hope is gone.' But tell them, 'The Lord God says: My people, I will open your graves of exile and cause you to rise again and return to the land of Israel. And, then at last, O my people, you will know I am the Lord. I will put my Spirit into you, and you shall live and return home again to your own land. Then you will know that I, the Lord, have done just what I promised you.'" (Ezek. 37:1-14, Living Bible)

Fundamentalists, who dislike the notion that biblical/Israelite belief changed rather drastically over the centuries, cite this portion of the vision of the valley of dry bones as evidence for a relatively early Jewish belief in bodily resurrection. But this is to disregard the plain statement that the prophet was experiencing a *vision*. Granted, one might be vouchsafed a vision of future events just as they will one day happen, but usually the visions ascribed to the biblical prophets were symbolic and dreamlike in nature, e.g., Jeremiah 1:11-15. Here's another of the same kind from Ezekiel.

> The word of the Lord came again to me saying, "And you, son of man, take for yourself one stick and write on it, 'For Judah and for the sons of Israel, his companions'; then take another stick and write on it, 'For Joseph, the stick of Ephraim and all the house of Israel, his companions.' Then join them for yourself one to another into one stick, that they may become one in your hand. When the sons of your people speak to you saying, 'Will you not declare to us what you mean by these?' say to them, 'Thus says the Lord [Yahweh], "Behold, I will take the stick of Joseph, which is in the hand of Ephraim, and the tribes of Israel, his companions; and I will put them with it, with the stick of Judah, and make them one stick, and they will be one in My hand."' (Ezek. 37:15-19, NASB)

Mormons claim that this passage predicts the discovery of the Book of Mormon and its addition to the Christian canon. According to this reading, the stick of Judah is the Old and New Testaments, while the Ephraim (Israel) stick is the Book of Mormon. Mormons suggest that wooden staffs were sometimes inscribed with sacred texts (as depicted in the 1966 movie *The Bible: In the Beginning* in which Abraham inherits his gnarled stave from the antediluvian Patriarchs who recorded upon it the biblical lore up through Noah). But wait a second! Isn't the Book of Mormon supposed to be the work of *Judean* expatriates from Jerusalem to ancient America? I think they've got the wrong stick!

> Thus says the Lord [Yahweh], "Behold, I will take the sons of Israel from among the nations where they have gone, and I will gather them from every side and bring them into their own land; and I will make them one nation in the land, on the mountains of Israel; and one king will be king for all of them; and they will no longer be two nations and no longer be divided into two kingdoms. They will no longer defile themselves with their idols, or with their detestable things, or with any of their transgressions; but I will deliver them from all their dwelling places in which they have sinned, and will cleanse them. And they will be My people, and I will be their God." (Ezek. 37:21-23, NASB)

Once again we see that the Jewish "exiles" are simply Diaspora Jewish emigrants and colonists, not just deportees to Babylon.

Ezekiel 37:24-28 (RSV) has Yahweh proclaim that David, his servant[126], "shall be their King, their only Shepherd; and they shall obey my laws and all my wishes. They shall live in the land of Israel where their fathers lived, the land I gave my servant Jacob. They and their children after them shall live there, and their grandchildren, for all generations." Yahweh's servant David[127] will be "their Prince forever." Yahweh promises to "make a covenant of peace with them, an everlasting pact," to "bless them and multiply them and put my Temple among them forever," and to make his home among them. Yes, he says, "I will be their God, and they shall be my people. And when my Temple remains among them forever, then the nations will know that I, [Yahweh], have chosen Israel as my very own."

Does Ezekiel mean to predict some Arthurian return from Avalon for old King David? Such a reading is by no means implausible or even improbable, so common are such beliefs throughout history. The Emperor Constans, the Hidden Imam Muhammad al-Mahdi, Friedrich Barbarosa, Napoleon Bonaparte, and others have been the objects of such hopes. But the passage could just as easily denote Jewish expectations of an eventual resumption of the Davidic dynasty. Both possibilities entail reading a good bit into the text, but any interpretation must do so, since the David references are so terse.

The Stoneheart Group

Ezek. 36, Jer. 31

Ezekiel 36:25-27 (RSV) predicts the giving of a new heart and a new spirit to the people, so they will no longer be stubborn and inclined to apostatize from the Torah:

> I will sprinkle clean water upon you, and you shall be clean from all your uncleannesses, and from all your idols I will cleanse you. A new heart I will give you, and a new spirit I will put within you; and I will take out of your flesh the heart of stone and give you a heart of flesh. And I will put my spirit within you, and cause you to walk in my statutes and be careful to observe my ordinances.

Jeremiah 31:31-34 similarly predicts a new covenant in which people will be faithful to the Torah because it will become second nature: written on their hearts.

> "Behold, days are coming," declares [Yahweh], "when I will make a new covenant with the house of Israel and with the house of Judah, not like the covenant which I made with their fathers in the day I took them by the hand to bring them out of the land of Egypt, My covenant which they broke, although I was a husband to them," declares [Yahweh]. "But this is the covenant which I will make with the house of Israel after those days," declares [Yahweh], "I will put My law within them and on their heart I will write it; and I will be their God, and they shall be My people. They will not teach again, each man his neighbor and each man his brother, saying, "Know [Yahweh]," for they will all know Me, from the least of them to the greatest of them," declares [Yahweh], "for I will forgive their iniquity, and their sin I will remember no more." (NASB).

It is plainly the same idea. Such close similarities have led scholars to suggest either that the Book of Jeremiah copied from the Book of Ezekiel[128] or vice versa.[129] Surely, in view of the pseudepigraphical character of these books, the "predicted" new order was either a religious arrangement in the writer's own day or one whose imminent arrival he hoped to bring about. I would venture to guess that the emergence of the pious Hasidim in Hasmonean Judea is in view. After all, the Qumran community of the Dead Sea Scrolls considered themselves to embody Jeremiah's New Covenant, and in this case I think they did not have to borrow an earlier, then-ancient text to apply to themselves. The relevant prophecies were likely composed by themselves or likeminded contemporaries.

Invidious Individualism

Jer. 31, Ezek. 18

Deuteronomy seems to reject the old idea that God would make subsequent generations suffer for the sins of their ancestors: "The fathers shall not be put to death for the children, nor shall the children be put to death for the fathers; every man shall be put to death for his own sin" (Deut. 24:16, RSV).

Jeremiah, not surprisingly for a Deuteronomist work, reiterates the same notion: "In those days they shall no longer say: 'The fathers have eaten sour grapes, and the children's teeth are set on edge.' But every one shall die for his own sin; each man who eats sour grapes, his teeth shall be set on edge" (Jer. 31:29-30, RSV). Ezekiel echoes it again in 18:2 (RSV): "What do you mean by repeating this proverb concerning the land of Israel, 'The fathers have eaten sour grapes, and the children's teeth are set on edge'?"

This sounds pretty good—a real advance in the concept of justice, recognizing the responsibility of the individual—but of course nothing changed. The innocent still got screwed. Ask Job. At least the idea of inherited guilt and punishment served as a kind of theodicy. However bitter a pill, it at least left some semblance of divine justice intact.

It was the failure of this new change in policy to materialize that eventually led to the borrowing of the Zoroastrian concept of resurrection. The logic was simple: If you did not get the justice due you in this life, there must be another in which the score will be evened.

Ezekiel the Architect

Ezek. 40-46

Our author takes the role of Moses in Exodus 25:40; 26:23-27:21, receiving the blueprints of the Tent of Meeting directly from Jehovah, who revealed the pattern to him atop the mountain. And of David, to whom God revealed the plans for Solomon's Temple (1 Chron. 28:19). An angel using a tape measure leads Ezekiel around the heavenly Temple, stipulating the exact measurements so that an earthly counterpart might be constructed that would perfectly match it.

We have already seen that the Tabernacle was a fictive precedent for the Temple in order to provide a Mosaic pedigree for the Jerusalem Temple, and that, furthermore, the Deuteronomic account of Solomon's Temple was itself a sketch of what Israelite priests hoped one day to see built. It would now appear that Ezekiel was attempting to publish his own plan for such a Temple. It pointedly does not match that described in 1 Kings. This implies either that the author of the Book of Ezekiel did not know of the Deuteronomic blueprint or that he did not consider it authoritative and preferred his own design.

The first real-world Temple in Jerusalem would have been the one built under Zerubbabel. We don't know the plan on which it was constructed. It may not have matched either 1 Kings or Exodus. Apparently some rabbis eventually challenged the inclusion of the Book of Ezekiel in the canon of scripture because, since his design was not used, his vision of it qualified as a false prophecy.

Ezekiel's Close Encounter

Ezek. 1

The calling vision of Ezekiel is much longer and far more elaborate and detailed than that of any other prophet, despite the fact that it shares several points of similarity with Isaiah 6. Many today, though no Old Testament scholars, believe that Ezekiel witnessed the touching down of a spacecraft and recorded the incident in chapter 1.[130] This is a fascinating reading of the text.

It was easy to dismiss until NASA engineer Josef F. Blumrich,[131] initially scoffing at the notion, took a close look at the text. To his utter astonishment, he found that the description of the Merkavah, or Throne Chariot of God, made sense as a description of a landing module descending from a larger mother ship. Piece by piece, Blumrich explains how virtually every detail of the description of the Throne Chariot and the four-faced cherubim supporting it corresponds to the necessary parts of such a mechanism, most of which would not be beyond the capability of twentieth-century technology. In short, it would work!

Blumrich is no wild-haired pseudo-scholar on the *History Channel* grinding an axe. His analysis is quite serious and most impressive. Should we accept it? If we reject it, it should not be because we approach it deductively with the assumption that there cannot have been extraterrestrial visitations. I should think it better to examine the evidence and arguments on their own merits, come what may.

Personally, though impressed, I am not convinced. For one thing, much of Blumrich's case depends on the traditional but now untenable assumption that the writer of Ezekiel was an actual eyewitness. But I suppose one might suggest that the author, whoever he was, had access to an eyewitness account by someone else and decided to insert it into his own book.

The eyewitness theory, it must be admitted, does seem to explain one puzzling feature of the text, namely that the scene goes into *much* more detail than would be necessary if the point were simply to depict a prophetic calling vision. Just compare it with Isaiah 6. But then we must ask whether an eyewitness, especially given the astonishing sight in question, could have possibly recalled everything in such minute detail.

We possess a number of pieces of Near Eastern iconography depicting divine thrones upheld by winged, even four-winged, creatures, even "full of eyes."[132] So such imagery was likely familiar to our author, implying he could simply have adapted several features of it to his own composition, even as the author of the Book of Revelation borrowed and reshuffled bits of the inaugural visions of both Isaiah and Ezekiel in Revelation 4:6-11. In fact, that is what I think he did. But still—why all the details about the design and motion of the wheels, etc.?

Here is my theory: The minutely detailed description of the Throne Chariot of Yahweh is of a piece with the similarly (and tediously) explicit blueprint of the Temple (Ezek. 40-46). The description of the Merkavah is intended as a model for an Ark of the Covenant to go in it. Like the familiar design in Exodus, Ezekiel's would represent the divine throne with attendant angels. And as the one described in Exodus 25:1-22 was portable, to be carried by poles running through metal rings along the sides, Ezekiel's was designed to be *rolled* along and to change direction easily as needed. Thus the intricate details: a set of directions for building it.

Would Ezekiel's Ark have featured a bejeweled effigy of the God Yahweh on his throne? Perhaps so, given the careful phraseology (Ezek. 1:26-27) attempting to distance the sitting figure from the genuine article, which not even a gifted Bezalel or an inspired Oholiab (Exod. 31:1-11) could ever approximate. Wouldn't this make sense if the point were to say, "This figure stands for Yahweh, as inadequate as it must needs be in depicting the real thing"? I suspect that the Exodus Ark, too, originally featured an enthroned Yahweh statue, since the aniconic refusal to depict Yahweh must have begun with the Deuteronomic "reform,"[133] which I place much later than most, in the Hasmonean period.

This passage from Ezekiel became the basis for an esoteric practice of visionary meditation in the centuries to follow, the so-called "Merkavah Mysticism"[134] whereby ambitious adepts would meditate on the vision of the Throne Chariot, hoping to experience the same vision for themselves. But such an out-of-body journey was not to be undertaken lightly, as the famous rabbinic anecdote of the Four Who Entered Paradise makes clear.

> Our Rabbis have taught, four entered into the Pardes. They were Ben Azai, Ben Zoma, Aher, and Rabbi Akiba. Ben Azai gazed and died. Of him it is written, "precious in the eyes of HaShem is the death of his pious ones" (*Tehilim* 116, 15). Ben Zoma gazed, and went insane. Of him, it is written, "have you found honey, eat your share lest you become full, and vomit it up." (*Mishlei* 25, 16). Aher became an apostate. Rabbi Akiba entered, and exited in peace. (*Hagigah* 14B)[135]

This striking tale is a variation on the biblical warning (Exod. 33:20): "You cannot see my face; for man shall not see me and live." (Compare Gen. 16:13 and Judg. 13:22.) How powerful is this cautionary tale! One of the visionaries died of shock at what he saw. Another went insane, his circuits blown by what he had seen. A third could not understand it adequately and began to teach heresies inferred from his vision. Only the great Rabbi Akiba had what it took to return safe, sane, and orthodox. Would-be mystic, do you really think you're in *his* class?

The Book of the Twelve

The Jewish canon lists twenty-four books. Isn't that fewer than its counterpart, the Protestant Old Testament, with thirty-nine? No, it's the same cake, just cut differently. The Tanakh (Jewish Bible) does not divide Samuel, Kings, or Chronicles into two separate books, and it counts all the prophetic books after Ezekiel as a single book, that of "the Twelve." As Terence Collins[136] notes, that is more than a format change, because it reflects the fact that the Book of the Twelve is a redactional unity. The originally separate writings have not only been edited, but *edited together*, fused into a single, more-or-less coherent work.

We ought to view it much as we do the Books of Isaiah[137] and Jeremiah, both of which, unlike Ezekiel, which is the work of single author, are compilations of a brief original core with much subsequent embellishment by various Deuteronomists. The main difference is that no one preserved the names of these later "Isaiahs" and "Jeremiahs," retaining the names "Amos," "Hosea," "Micah," etc., instead. Why this difference? Probably because most of the secondary material in Isaiah and Jeremiah was committee work from the start, consciously intended to ride on the coattails of the eponymous prophets, whereas in the case of the Twelve the role of the Deuteronomists was more like mortar between pre-existent bricks.

We must keep in mind that these short writings are everywhere permeated by the Deuteronomic revisionism which promoted the (false) notion that Israelite religion had been officially monotheistic from its Mosaic beginnings, with the undeniably rampant polytheism resulting from the forbidden borrowing of alien "Canaanite" gods and rites, whereas actually the inherited religion of Israel had always *been* Canaanite polytheism. This means that an awful lot of the material now found in Amos and the rest must be Deuteronomic in origin, not actually the preaching of the credited prophets. Remember, the texts cannot very well have resulted from transcriptions of anyone's oral preaching anyway.

Because of space limitations, this chapter already being quite long, I have chosen to discuss only Amos. In earlier chapters I have already discussed various striking passages from some of the other "Minor Prophets," so I don't feel too bad about it.

Amos

Amos 7

Amos 7:12-17 depicts a showdown between Amos, a self-appointed prophet, as we might call him, and Amaziah,[138] an official prophet of the royal court of Israel. Amaziah had all the prophetic credentials one might ask, not to mention an official post in the government. The trouble is that Amos, a loud-mouthed upstart and an outsider from Judah, a lowly shepherd and sycamore tender, had been appearing in public, on a soap-box, so to speak, railing against the government, its foreign policy, and its official worship. It is all a sham, he says, and for that reason an abomination in the sight of Yahweh. God, it seems, is ever the outsider, ever the lone wolf, like Amos himself. Or at least Amos cannot help seeing him that way. Amaziah tries to shoo his unlettered rival away. What business has Amos, with no prophetic ID card, no official sanction, in declaring the word of Yahweh, especially since it's making the state and the state church look bad?

How, one might ask, could Amaziah be so sure that Amos was wrong? Simply this: He *had* to be wrong. By definition, a true prophecy was one that toed the party line. Prophecy had become an institution. The court prophets (staff prophets) were a group of oracle-mongers whose job it was, ostensibly, to advise the king in light of God's wisdom. But in fact they were a group of well-paid yes-men who were expected to pronounce God's blessing on any plan the king might float. Prophecy *was* the party line. Amaziah followed that line well. Amos called its bluff. No wonder he didn't have credentials: He wouldn't play the game.

The court prophets were simply the embodiment of the divine right of kings. Today we would call them spin doctors. Notice that Amaziah tells Amos he'd better stop bad-mouthing Bethel because, after all, it's the king's own chapel. Significant choice of words. What is the difference between a prophet and a chaplain?[139] A chaplain is a clergyman retained by an institution to perform certain religious functions for them. And there is no problem with that as long as there is no question of speaking the truth. There are plenty of aspects of religion that are purely ceremonial, ornamental, aesthetic. And a chaplain does these things quite properly.

The problem comes when the chaplain is told to prophesy and yet is really expected to speak the comforting words of a chaplain. Can an institution take seriously what a prophet says and survive *as* an institution? Jesus points out the irony of those undertakers of the prophets who venerate their safely silent corpses. "You who erect the tombs of the prophets! You say you would never have killed them? Then tell me why you're building that new one over there?" Maybe that's the point of the business of Joseph of Arimathea burying Jesus in a brand new tomb: It was just waiting for him, since it was only a matter of time.

And note that the fact that the names "Amos" and "Amaziah" are so similar fits in perfectly with Girard's observation[140] that narrative antagonists ("monstrous doubles" of one another) often bear names that reflect each other. This implies the fictive character of the whole episode, as does the fact that Tekoa, the area in Judah from which Amos is said to hail, sat at too high an altitude for sycamore trees to grow there.[141] *Sounded* good, though.

Amos 2-3

This episode reflects a persistent motif in Amos: the suppression of prophecy. There are two passages—first, Amos 2:12 (NASB): "But you made the Nazirites drink wine, And you commanded the prophets saying, 'You shall not prophesy!'"

Then, Amos 3:7-8 (NASB):

> 7Surely [Yahweh] does nothing
>   Unless He reveals His secret counsel
>   To His servants the prophets.
> 8A lion has roared! Who will not fear?
>   [Yahweh] has spoken! Who can but prophesy?

What is going on here? What is Amos so upset about? It looks like he was reacting to a systematic attempt by the religious authorities to silence prophets because of their well-known tendency to rock the boat. Amos 2:12 and 3:7-8 (see just above) seem to parallel Peter's response to the Sanhedrin in Acts 4:17-20, who'd told the apostles not to speak or teach at all in the name of Jesus. Peter and John answered them, "Whether it is right in the sight of God to listen to you rather than to God, you must judge; for we cannot but speak of what we have seen and heard."

Amos 8

Amos warns (8:11-12, NASB) that, if these efforts should succeed, a clueless nation will bemoan the lack of any available oracle from God.

> 11"Behold, days are coming," declares the Lord [Yahweh],
>   "When I will send a famine on the land,
>   Not a famine for bread or a thirst for water,
>   But rather for hearing the words of [Yahweh].
> 12"People will stagger from sea to sea
>   And from the north even to the east;
>   They will go to and fro to seek the word of [Yahweh],
>   But they will not find it.

The whole people will find themselves sharing the desperation of Saul in 1 Samuel 28:3-6 (NASB):

> Now Samuel was dead, and all Israel had lamented him and buried him in Ramah, his own city. And Saul had removed from the land those who were mediums and spiritists. So the Philistines gathered together and came and camped in Shunem; and Saul gathered all Israel together and they camped in Gilboa. When Saul saw the camp of the Philistines, he was afraid and his heart trembled greatly. When Saul inquired of [Yahweh], [Yahweh] did not answer him, either by dreams or by Urim or by prophets.

Perhaps more can be inferred from Zechariah 13:2-5 (NASB), where we read of a climate in which prophecy is no longer welcome because of the possibility that a prophet will preach doctrines the authorities deem heretical. It is significant that, though image-worship was the fear, the ban is on *anyone* who comes forward as a prophet.

> "It will come about in that day," declares [Yahweh Sabaoth], "that I will cut off the names of the idols from the land, and they will no longer be remembered; and I will also remove the prophets and the unclean spirit from the land. And if anyone still prophesies, then his father and mother who gave birth to him will say to him, 'You shall not live, for you have spoken falsely in the name of [Yahweh]'; and his father and mother who gave birth to him will pierce him through when he prophesies. Also it will come about in that day that the prophets will each be ashamed of his vision when he prophesies, and they will not put on a hairy robe in order to deceive; but he will say, 'I am not a prophet; I am a tiller of the ground, for a man sold me as a slave in my youth.'"

The imagined words of the would-be prophet, fearful of reprisals, now trying to deny that he had ever claimed to be one, sound suspiciously similar to Amos 7:14-15. But whereas Amos was freely admitting he was not a "licensed" (paid) prophet like Amaziah, Zechariah's prophet is clucking like a chicken, like Peter denying Jesus.

So why are we reading such defiant defenses of "freedom of prophetic speech" as we find ascribed to Amos in the Book of the Twelve, compiled by the very religious establishment responsible for suppressing prophecy? Because the canon of scripture is the tomb of the prophets. Embalmed in the canon, their stilled voices can safely be reinterpreted, de-fused, by the Deuteronomist ventriloquists.

Amos 2, 4-5

Another of the main emphases in Amos (perhaps the original core?) is his scathing denunciations of those who oppress the poor, as witness Amos 2:6-7a (NASB), which quotes Yahweh as saying

> "For three transgressions of Israel and for four
>   I will not revoke its punishment,
> Because they sell the righteous for money
>   And the needy for a pair of sandals.
> 7"These who pant after the very dust of the earth
>   on the head of the helpless
>   Also turn aside the way of the humble;

Elsewhere, Amos scolds the "cows of Bashan" for oppressing the poor and crushing the needy (4:1), for trampling upon the poor. Like downtrodden rural locals glaring across the waters of their fishing hole at some mostly vacant McMansion built by an out-of-state millionaire, he criticizes those who "impose heavy rent on the poor and exact a tribute of grain from them," and then flaunt their ill-gotten gains (5:11-12, NASB):

> Though you have built houses of well-hewn stone,
>   Yet you will not live in them;
> You have planted pleasant vineyards,
>   yet you will not drink their wine.
> 12For I know your transgressions are many and your sins are great,
>   You who distress the righteous and accept bribes
>   And turn aside the poor in the gate.

"Hear this," Amos (8:3-6, NASB) has Yahweh warn those "who trample the needy, to do away with the humble [poor] of the land," who "cheat with dishonest scales." A lot of people are going to die. Yahweh will darken the earth and turn the feasts into mourning. It will be "like a time of mourning for an only son, And the end of it will be like a bitter day" (v. 10, NASB).

Amos begins with a catalogue of the atrocities and sins committed by all the surrounding nations–and then levels his guns at Israel and Judah! Thus says Yahweh, he warns (2:4-5, NASB):

> "For three transgressions of Judah and for four
>   I will not revoke its punishment,
>   Because they rejected the law of [Yahweh]
>   And have not kept His statutes;
>   Their lies also have led them astray,
>   Those after which their fathers walked.
> 5"So I will send fire upon Judah
>   And it will consume the citadels of Jerusalem."

And, continuing Yahweh's speech (2:6-8, NASB):

> "For three transgressions of Israel and for four
>   I will not revoke its punishment,
>   Because they sell the righteous for money
>   And the needy for a pair of sandals.
> 7"These who pant after the very dust of the earth
>   on the head of the helpless
>   Also turn aside the way of the humble [RSV: *afflicted*];
>   And a man and his father resort to the same girl

In order to profane My holy name.
8"On garments taken as pledges they stretch out beside every altar,
   And in the house of their God
   they drink the wine of those who have been fined.

The scope of his denunciations is so wide, it is obvious he means to announce the impending Day of Yahweh, a universal Day of Judgment which no one will escape. And he is not alone in this expectation. But Amos (5:18-20, NASB) warns the bloodthirsty pious in Israel: Are you sure you *want* this? Careful, now. You may turn out to be on the losing side!

18Alas, you who are longing for the day of [Yahweh],
   For what purpose will the day of [Yahweh] be to you?
   It will be darkness and not light;
19As when a man flees from a lion
   And a bear meets him,
   Or goes home, leans his hand against the wall
   And a snake bites him.
20Will not the day of [Yahweh] be darkness instead of light,
   Even gloom with no brightness in it?

Notes

1. The Universalist theologian Hosea Ballou once referred to the Bible as "the written Jehovah." I think it appropriate here because what millions revere as the God who supposedly stands behind these first-person tirades exists, first and last, as a literary character in these books. The *only* Jehovah is the *written* Jehovah.

   Bernard Ramm, *Special Revelation and the Word of God* (Grand Rapids: Eerdmans, 1961), p. 164: "Whatever the prophet cast into written form was held with the same regard as the oral word of the prophet." Clark H. Pinnock, *Biblical Revelation–The Foundation of Christian Theology* (Chicago: Moody Press, 1971), p. 33: "Scripture grew out of the divine speaking as it was cast into writing for the welfare of God's people." See also John R.W. Stott, *Understanding the Bible.* Special Crusade Edition (Minneapolis: Billy Graham Evangelistic Association / World Wide Publications, 1972), p. 185.

2. Terence Collins, *The Mantle of Elijah: The Redaction Criticism of the Prophetical Books.* The Biblical Seminar (Sheffield: JSOT Press, 1993), p. 13.

3. Collins, *Mantle of Elijah*, pp. 26, 28.

4. H.A.R. Gibb, *Mohammedanism: An Historical Survey* (New York: New American Library / Mentor Books, 1955), pp. 45-46.

5. Robert P. Carroll, *From Chaos to Covenant: Uses of Prophecy in the Book of Jeremiah* (London: SCM Press, 1981), p. 26; Collins, *Mantle of Elijah*, p. 28; Walter Schmithals, "The Parabolic Teachings in the Synoptic Gospels." Trans. Darrell J. Doughty. *Journal of Higher Criticism* 4/2, Fall 1997, pp. 3-32.

6. Collins, *Mantle of Elijah*, p. 148: "Isaiah and his children exist as symbols within the pages of a book rather than as real people." Also p. 26.

7. F.F. Bruce, *The New Testament Documents: Are They Reliable?* (Grand Rapids: Eerdmans, 1960), pp. 39-40; C.F. Burney, *The Poetry of our Lord: An Examination of the Formal Elements of Hebrew Poetry in the Discourses of Jesus Christ* (Oxford at the Clarendon Press, 1925), p. 6.

8. Woody Allen, "Hassidic Tales, with a Guide to Their Interpretation by the Noted Scholar." In Allen, *Getting Even* (New York: Random House / Vintage Books, 1978), p. 51.

9. Carroll, *From Chaos to Covenant*, pp. 62-63, 66, 67, 70, 80, 84, 90, 104, 142; Collins, *Mantle of Elijah*, p. 32, 129.

10. Carroll at pp. 15-16, 103-104.

11. Something about this story strikes me as strange: The seemingly simple scenario has the king razoring off section after section, three columns at a time, as soon as Jehudi finishes reading each portion aloud. Somehow this is difficult to envision: Did the king keep grabbing the scroll whenever the reader reached the end of each third column? This is easier said than done if the king was not himself doing the reading. Just hearing someone else reading it, how would he know when to start slicing? Or did he tell Jehudi to stop after every three columns and hand over what was still left of the scroll, then hand it back after he'd cut more off? It looks like an attempt at a story that someone did not think out adequately. In the same way, how did the Lamb (in Revelation chapter 6)

display more and more of the apocalyptic scroll by breaking one seal after another? The seals must have run vertically along the edge of the scroll. You'd have to break all seven even to read the first page! This is not something somebody *saw*, even in a vision. In the 1988 movie *The Seventh Sign* they solve the problem by assigning each seal to a *separate* prophetic scroll. Unlike the *written* text of Revelation, the movie had to *show* it.

12. "The Book of Thomas." Trans. Marvin Meyer, in Meyer, ed., *The Nag Hammadi Scriptures* (New York: HarperCollins, 2007), p. 239.

13. "The Second Revelation of James." Trans. Wolf-Peter Funk, in Mayer, ed., p. 333.

14. Carroll, *From Chaos to Covenant*, p. 151.

15. Carroll at p. 14; Collins, *Mantle of Elijah*, p. 26.

16. Collins at p. 62

17. Carroll at pp. 11, 109. 123, 140, 165.

18. Rudolf Bultmann, *The History of the Synoptic Tradition*. Trans. John Marsh (New York: Harper & Row, 1972), pp. 47-48.

19. Henri Lammens, "The Koran and Tradition: How the Life of Muhammad Was Composed." Trans. Ibn Warraq. In Ibn Warraq, ed., *The Quest for the Historical Muhammad* (Amherst: Prometheus Books, 2000), pp. 169-187.

20. Carroll, *From Chaos to Covenant*, p. 116.

21. John Knox, *Chapters in a Life of Paul* (New York: Abingdon-Cokesbury Press, 1950); Gerd Lüdemann, *Paul, Apostle to the Gentiles: Studies in Chronology* (Philadelphia: Fortress Press, 1984).

22. Dennis Ronald MacDonald, *The Legend and the Apostle: The Battle for Paul in Story and Canon* (Philadelphia: Westminster Press, 1983), p. 56; Darrell J. Doughty, "Pauline Paradigms and Pauline Authenticity." *Journal of Higher Criticism* Vol. 1, Fall 1994, pp. 109-110, 126.

23. Carroll, *From Chaos to Covenant*, pp. 9-10, 13-14, 27, 53-55, 87, 89, 90-91, 96, 105, 137, 139, 141-142, 149, 171, 229, 236, 253, 255, etc.; Collins, *Mantle of Elijah*, p. 39.

24. Collins, *Mantle of Elijah*, p. 23; cf., p. 55

25. These parallels are set out in Collins at pp. 133-37.

26. "Indeed, Elisha is represented not just as a disciple but almost as a continuation of Elijah." Collins, *Mantle of Elijah*, p. 136.

27. Collins at p. 141.

28. Carroll, *From Chaos to Covenant*, p. 33.

29. Carroll at p. 53.

30. Carroll at pp. 71, 73. 89.

31. Robert M. Fowler, *Let the Reader Understand: Reader-Response Criticism and the Gospel of Mark* (Minneapolis: Fortress Press, 1991), pp. 139, 249, 251.

32. C.H. Dodd, *The Parables of the Kingdom* (New York: Scribners, 1961), p. 4.

33. Carroll at p. 171.

34. Carroll at pp. 130-35.

35. Carroll at p. 131.

36. H.M. Balyuzi, *Bahá'u'lláh: A Brief Life, Followed by an Essay on the Manifestation of God Entitled The Word Made Flesh* (London: George Ronald, 1963), pp. 39-50.

37. René Girard, *Violence and the Sacred*. Trans. Patrick Gregory (Baltimore: Johns Hopkins University Press, 1979), p. 78.

38. Girard, *Violence and the Sacred*, p. 70.

39. Carroll at p. 192.

40. Carroll at p. 178.

41. Carroll at p. 189; cf., also p. 26.

42. Gérard Genette, *Narrative Discourse: An Essay in Method*. Trans. Jane E. Lewin (Ithaca: Cornell University Press, 1980), pp. 213-214; Seymour Chatman, *Story and Discourse: Structure in Fiction and Film* (Ithaca: Cornell University Press, 1980), pp. 147-51.

43. Collins, *Mantle of Elijah*, p. 156.

44. Collins at p. 160.

45. Carroll, *From Chaos to Covenant*, pp. 54-55, 85, 141, 147, 203, 241, 243; Collins, *Mantle of Elijah*, p. 51. Likewise, Jeremiah's letter, ostensibly to the Jewish exile community in Babylon (at least Jer. 29:4-7, perhaps the original, the rest added subsequently) must really have been a pseudonymous encyclical addressed to all Diaspora Jews. These would be the actual intended readers, while the deportees in Babylon would be the fictive narratees. We have another of these in Baruch chapter 6, The Epistle of Jeremiah.

46. As on an episode of *King of the Hill* when Laotian immigrant Ted Wassanasong converts from Buddhism to Episcopalianism because "It's good for business."

47. Peter L. Berger and Thomas Luckmann, *The Social Construction of Reality; A Treatise in the Sociology of Knowledge* (Garden City: Doubleday Anchor Books, 1967), pp. 154-56.

48. Carroll, *From Chaos to Covenant*, 72-73, 84, 258-59.

49. Carroll at p. 252.

50. Philip R. Davies, "The Audiences of Prophetic Scrolls: Some Suggestions." In Stephen Breck Reid, ed., *Prophets and Paradigms: Essays in Honor of Gene M. Tucker*. Journal for the Study of the Old Testament Supplement Series 229 (Sheffield: Sheffield Academic Press, 1996), p. 61.

51. Walter Kaufmann, *The Faith of a Heretic* (Garden City: Doubleday Anchor Books, 1963), p. 127.

52. Hans-Joachim Schoeps, *Jewish Christianity: Factional Disputes in the Early Church*. Trans. Douglas R.A. Hare (Philadelphia: Fortress Press, 1969), Chapter 5, "The Message of the Ebionite Christ I," pp. 74-98.

53. Rudolph Otto, *The Idea of the Holy: An Inquiry into the Non-rational Factor in the Idea of the Divine and its Relation to the Rational*. Trans. John W. Harvey (New York: Oxford University Press, 1924).

54. Max Müller, trans (1879), www.sacred-texts.com/hin/sbe15/sbe15015.htm

55. In André-Jean Festugiére, *Personal Religion Among the Greeks*. (Berkeley: University of California Press, 1960), p. 97.

56. *The Bhagavad Gita,* Trans. Franklin Edgerton. Harper Torchbboks, Cloister Library (New York: Harper & Row, 1964), pp. 56-57.

57. René Girard, *The Scapegoat*. Trans. Yvonne Freccero (Baltimore: Johns Hopkins Press, 1986), p. 79: "There comes a time, however, when men want only models of morality and demand gods purified of all faults."

58. Since the cherubim seem to be personified storm clouds upon which Yahweh, like his alter ego Baal Hadad, rides through the stormy skies, it seems quite likely that the seraphim, fiery serpents as they are, should be understood as personified lightning bolts (Arthur S. Peake, "Isaiah I:I-XXXIX." In Peake, ed., *A Commentary on the Bible* [London: T.C. & E.C. Black, 1929], p. 441). "Of the angels he says, 'who makes his angels winds, and his servants flames of fire'" (Heb. 1:7).

59. Poetic formatting added for vv. 7-9.

60. Sigmund Mowinkel, *He That Cometh: The Messiah Concept in the Old Testament and Later Judaism*. Trans. G.W. Anderson (New York: Abingdon Press, 1959), p. 111; Joseph Wheless, *Is It God's Word? An Exposition of the Fables and Mythology of the Bible and of the Impostures of Theology* (New York: Alfred A. Knopf, 1926), p. 281.

61. As charged by Wheless, *Is It God's Word?*; Morton Smith, *Jesus the Magician* (New York: Harper & Row, 1978), p. 27: "Matthew . . . is notoriously unscrupulous in ripping Old Testament verses out of context to make them prophecies of gospel stories."

62. Krister Stendahl, *The School of St. Matthew and its Use of the Old Testament* (Philadelphia: Fortress Press, 1968); Richard N. Longenecker, *Biblical Exegesis in the Apostolic Period* (Grand Rapids: Eerdmans, 1975), pp. 38-45.

63. Jane Schaberg, *The Illegitimacy of Jesus: A Feminist Theological Interpretation of the Infancy Narratives* (New York: Harper & Row, 1987), pp. 69-70. Despite the subtitle, this fascinating study is not a mere exercise in ideological axe-grinding.

64. Mowinkel, *He That Cometh*, pp. 113-15.

65. Mowinkel at pp. 102-109; cf. Thomas L. Thompson, *The Messiah Myth: The Near Eastern Roots of Jesus and David* (New York: Basic Books, 2005), Chapter 5, "The Myth of the Good King," pp. 139-69; Collins, *Mantle of Elijah*, p. 50.

66. Lin Carter, in his heroic fantasy novel, *Lost World of Time* (New York: Signet Books, 1969), pp. 15, 74-75, showed more clearly (and in fewer words) than any theologian known to me how a king being the "son" of a god would naturally mean the same thing as his being the incarnation or avatar of the god. His "begetting" is a synonym for his incarnating on earth. Carter's idea is somewhat akin to that of Raymond Panikkar in *The Unknown Christ of Hinduism* (London: Darton, Longman & Todd, 1964, 1968), pp. 126-29.

Most scholars take the formula in Romans 1:3-4 as a quotation by Paul from an early Christian hymn, but I suspect it is instead a fossil of the sacred coronation rhetoric, with the Jesus business added, which, for example, would explain the overburdening of the second clause by the apparent addition of "via his resurrection from the dead."

67. *Monty Python's The Meaning of Life*, 1983.

68. Charles Cutler Torrey, *The Second Isaiah: A New Interpretation* (New York: Scribners, 1928), p. 96.

69. The NASB formats Isa. 25:6-12 as poetry along with vv. 1-5.

70. I suspect this verse is the basis of a passage in H.P. Lovecraft's fictional *Necronomicon*: "Their hand is at your throats, yet ye see Them not" ("The Dunwich Horror").

71. Might this have been the seed that grew into Matthew 27:51-53?

72. Hermann Gunkel, *Creation and Chaos in the Primeval Era and the Eschaton: A Religio-Historical Study of Genesis 1 and Revelation 12*. Trans. K. William Whitney. Biblical Resource Series (Grand Rapids: Eerdmans, 2006).

73. Collins, *Mantle of Elijah*, p. 37.

74. Cf., H.G. Wells's science fiction novel (and movie which he scripted) of this title.

75. Torrey, *Second Isaiah*, p. 100; Collins, *Mantle of Elijah*, pp. 42-43, referring to W.A.M. Beuken, "Isaiah Chapters lxv-lxvi: Trito-Isaiah and the Closure of the Book of Isaiah," in J.A. Emerton, ed., *Congress Volume Leuven 1989*. Proceedings of the 13th Congress of the International Organisation for the Study of the Old Testament [Leiden: Brill, 1991], p. 204.

76. Torrey, *Second Isaiah*, p. 31.

77. Torrey at p. 31

78. Torrey at pp. 32, 45.

79. Torrey at pp. 59-60.

80. Torrey at p. 32.

81. A big clue to the real nature of the situation is the fact that Ezra-Nehemiah classifies and vilifies the Jews left in the land as mixed-race mongrel Canaanites, exactly the strategy of the Deuteronomic Historians, who made traditional Hebrew polytheism appear to be non-Jewish Canaanite paganism plus naughty Jewish "borrowing" from paganism.

82. Torrey at pp. 28-29; Carroll, *From Chaos to Covenant*, 231, 247-48.

83. Torrey at pp. 29-30.

84. Michael Barkun, *Religion and the Racist Right: The Origins of the Christian Identity Movement* (Chapel Hill: University of North Carolina Press, 1994), chapter 7, "The Demonization of the Jews, 1: Racial Anti-Semitism," pp. 121-47; chapter 8, "The Demonization of the Jews, 2: Children of Cain," pp. 149-72; chapter 9, "The Demonization of the Jews, 3: 'Satan's Spawn,'" pp. 173-96 ; Nicholas Goodrick-Clarke, *The Occult Roots of Nazism: Secret Aryan Cults and Their Influence on Nazi Ideology; The Ariosophists of Austria and Germany, 1890-1935* (Washington Square: New York University Press, 1992), chapter 8, "Jörg Lanz von Liebenfels and Theozoology," pp. 90-105; Goodrick-Clarke, *Black Sun: Aryan Cults, Esoteric Nazism and the Politics of Identity* (New York: New York University Press, 2002), pp. 237-38; Lanz von Liebenfels, *Theozoologie: Das Urchristentum Neu Erschlossen; Was Lehrt die Bibel Wirklich?* (Deutschherrenverlag, 2001).

85. Joseph Atwill, *Caesar's Messiah: The Roman Conspiracy to Invent Jesus.* (Berkeley: Ulysses Press, 2005).

86. Torrey at pp. 24-25.

87. Torrey at p. 137.

88. Tryggve N.D. Mettinger, *A Farewell to the Servant Songs: A Critical Examination of an Exegetical Axiom.* Trans. Frederick H. Cryer. Scripta Minora. Regiae Societatis Humaniorum Litterarum Lundensis. Studier utgivna av. Kungl. Humanistika Vetenskapssamfundet i Lund 1982-1983: 3 (Lund: CWK Gleerup, 1983).

89. Similarly, Earl Richard, *Acts 6:1-9:4: The Author's Method of Composition.* Society of Biblical Literature Dissertation Series 41 (Missoula: Scholars Press, 1978), and Marion L. Soards, *The Speeches in Acts: Their Content, Context, and Concerns* (Atlanta: Westminster John Knox Press, 1994), demonstrate that the apostolic speeches in the Book of Acts are not records of what Peter, Paul, or Stephen said on some particular occasion but are the free compositions of the Acts author.

90. In the RSV and NASB, "nations" is used instead of "Gentiles."

91. This line in the RSV: "and that Israel might be gathered to him."

92. Believe it or not, this is the sole biblical verse cited to prove that Jesus had a beard! Of course it is based on the ahistorical Christian reading of the passage as a prediction of Jesus.

93. RSV: The "chastisement that made us whole."

94. In v. 8, the RSV provides a significantly different sense of the text, rendering it as asking, "as for his generation, who considered / that he was cut off out of the land of the living, stricken for the transgression of my people?" In v. 9, the RSV says "although he had done no violence," rather than "because."

95. Hugo Gressmann, *Der Ursprung der Israelitisch-jüdischen Eschatologie.* Forshungen zur Religion und Literatur des Alten und Neuen Testaments (Göttingen: Van den Hoeck und Ruprecht, 1905), Chapter 31, "Der sterbende Gott," pp. 328-33.

96. Helmer Ringgren, *The Messiah in the Old Testament.* Studies in Biblical Theology No. 18 (London: SCM Press, 1956), Chapter Four, "The So-called Servant Psalms," pp. 54-64.

97. Torrey, *Second Isaiah,* p. 146.

98. Girard, *The Scapegoat,* Chapter One, "Guillaume de Machaut and the Jews," pp. 1-11; Richard L. Rubenstein, "Religion and the Origins of the Death Camps, A Psychoanalytic Interpretation." In Rubenstein, *After Auschwitz: Radical Theology and Contemporary Judaism* (New York: Bobbs-Merrill, 1966), pp. 1-45.

99. Mettinger, *Farewell to the Servant Songs,* p. 10.

100. Collins, *Mantle of Elijah,* p. 108.

101. Collins at pp. 108-10; Carroll at p. 27, 260.

102. Carroll at p. 9.

103. Collins, *Mantle of Elijah,* p. 174; Carroll at pp. 9, 28, 111, 116, 118, 224.

104. The subtitle above borrows the title of a story by Tennessee Williams (*Weird Tales* August 1928) based on Herodotus' account of Egyptian Queen Nitocris whose brother had been assassinated: She invited the conspirators to a banquet in an underground chamber, then excused herself while she had the chamber flooded (*Histories* II: 100).

105. Smith, *Jesus the Magician,* pp. 48, 58.

106. Smith at pp. 60-64.

107. Nick Wyatt, "Asherah." In Karel van der Toorn, Bob Becking, and Pieter W. van der Horst, eds., *Dictionary of Deities and Demons in the Bible (DDD).* (New York: Brill, 1995), cols. 191-92; Saul M. Olyan, *Ashera and the Cult of Yahweh in Israel.* Society of Biblical Literature Monograph Series Number 34 (Atlanta: Scholars Press, 1988), Chapter 2, "Epigraphic Sources Pertaining to the Cult of Asherah," pp. 23-37; William G. Dever, *Did God Have a Wife? Archaeology and Popular Religion in Ancient Israel* (Grand Rapids: Eerdmans, 2005), pp. 160-67; Darlene Kosnik, *History's Vanquished Goddess: Asherah* (Sanford: Emergent Press, 2014), "Introduction to Kuntillet Arjud Drawings," pp. 161-95.

108. Huh? Didn't he mean "*they* have saved *him*"? I guess that's just one of those puzzles we'll have to wait to hear solved when we get to heaven.

109. Samuel Ives Curtiss, *Primitive Semitic Religion To-day: A Record of Researches, Discoveries and Studies in Syria, Palestine and the Sinaitic Peninsula* (Chicago: Fleming H. Revell, 1902), pp. 91-94.

110. *See* Robert Plant and Jimmy Page, "Stairway to Heaven." *Led Zeppelin IV* (London:Island Studios, 1971).

111. Charles Cutler Torrey, *Pseudo-Ezekiel and the Original Prophecy.* Yale Oriental Series Researches Volume XVIII (New Haven: Yale University Press, 1930), pp. 17-19.

112. Actually, Torrey identifies a whole series of such scribal "Babylonian" redactions throughout the Book of Ezekiel: "to them of the captivity" (in 3:11); "And I came to them of the captivity at Tell Abib, that dwelt by the river Chebar, where they were dwelling, and I sat there appalled among them seven days. And it came to pass at the end of seven days" (in 3:14-16); "like the glory that I saw by the river Chebar" (in 3:23); "in the sixth year" (in 8:1); "And he put forth the form of a hand, and took me by a lock of the hair of my head" and "between the earth and the heaven" and "in the visions of God to Jerusalem" (in 8:3); "this is the living creature that I saw by the river Chebar" (in 10:15); "this is the living creature that I saw under the God of Israel by the river Chebar" (in 10:20); "they were the faces which I saw by the river Chebar, their appearances and themselves" (in 10:22); "to Chaldea, to the Golah [exile community]" and "And I spoke unto them of the captivity all the things that the Lord had shown me" (in 11:24f); "in the seventh year" (in 20:1); "in the ninth year" and "write the name of the day, even of this selfsame day: the king of Babylon drew close unto Jerusalem this selfsame day" (in 24:1f); "whom ye have left behind" (in 24:21); most of 24:24-27; "in the ninth year" (in 26:1); "in the tenth year" (in 29:1); "in the eleventh year" (in 30:20; 31:1; 32:1); most of 33:21f; "these waste places" (in 33:24, 27); and "the twenty-fifth year of our captivity" and "in the fourteenth year after that the city was smitten, in the selfsame day" and "thither; in the visions of God he brought me to the land of Israel" (in 40:1f.). In Torrey, *Pseudo-Ezekiel,* pp. 110-12.

I have retained Torrey's use of the English Revised Version in these quotes. Notice the contrived and clearly harmonistic device explaining how, though trapped in Babylon, the prophet was up on all developments in Jerusalem: out-of-body travel from the former to the latter!

113. Collins, *Mantle of Elijah*, p. 102. The problem is precisely the same as the absence of Jesus from any contemporary writings. Collins is willing to grant a hypothetical "historical Ezekiel" as the seed from which our Book of Ezekiel sprang. Sounds like Euhemerism to me.

114. Torrey, *Pseudo-Ezekiel*, pp. 64-66.

115. Torrey, *Pseudo-Ezekiel*, Chapter IV, "The Dates, Original and Secondary," pp. 58-70.

116. Torrey at pp. 62-63, 94.

117. Torrey at pp. 94-97. Here he follows Theodor Nöldeke and Hugo Winckler.

118. Torrey at p. 96.

119. Or Gog may be intended as another Gyges, one of the monstrous offspring of the Titan Ouranos; "From their shoulders shot a hundred arms / unimaginable, and fifty heads on the shoulders / of each grew over their strong bodies; / great and mighty strength was in their huge shape" (Hesiod, *Theogony*, lines 150-153). I think this likely, given the apparent description of Gog in Ezekiel 38:4 (cf., Job 41:1) as a Leviathan-like sea dragon. Richard S. Caldwell, trans., *Hesiod's Theogony*. Focus Classical Library (Newburyport: Focus Information Group, 1987), p. 37.

120. E.g., Hal Lindsay with C.C. Carlson, *The Late Great Planet Earth* (New York: Bantam Books, 1973), pp. 51-55. Even where some of their attempts to identify peoples mentioned in Ezekiel with modern nations are valid, fundamentalist prophecy mavens are basically reviving ancient *pesher* exegesis, since it is otherwise nonsensical to suggest that Ezekiel meant to predict events (e.g., with modern Russia) thousands of years after the generation he was addressing.

121. Torrey, *Pseudo-Ezekiel*, p. 96.

122. RSV: "You were the signet of perfection."

123. Margaret Barker, *The Gate of Heaven: The History and Symbolism of the Temple in Jerusalem* (London: SPCK, 1991), pp. 71, 74-75.

124. Hugh J. Schonfield, *Those Incredible Christians* (New York: Bantam Books, 1969), pp. 250-51.

125. Ralph P. Martin, *Carmen Christi: Philippians ii.5-11 in Recent Interpretation and in the Setting of Early Christian Worship*. Society for New Testament Studies Monograph Series 4 (Cambridge at the University Press, 1967), pp. 142, 161-64.

126. Living Bible translator (well, paraphraser, actually) Kenneth Taylor gratuitously adds "their Messiah" at this point.

127. Ditto.

128. Collins, *Mantle of Elijah*, p. 114.

129. Torrey, *Pseudo-Ezekiel*, p. 69.

130. Erich von Däniken, *Chariots of the Gods? Unsolved Mysteries of the Past* (New York: Bantam Books, 1971), pp. 37-40; R.L. Dione, *God Drives a Flying Saucer* (New York: Bantam Books, 1973), pp. 79-81; Barry H. Downing, *The Bible & Flying Saucers* (New York: Avon Books, 1970), pp. 105-106.

131. Josef F. Blumrich, *The Spaceships of Ezekiel* (London: Corgi Books, 1974).

132. sitchiniswrong.com/ezekielnotes.htm

133. Barker, *Gate of Heaven*, p. 15.

134. Gershom Scholem, *Major Trends in Jewish Mysticism*. Hilda Strook Lectures (New York Schocken Books, 1973), Second Lecture: "Merkabah Mysticism and Jewish Gnosticism," pp. 40-79; Gershom G. Scholem, *Jewish Gnosticism, Merkabah Mysticism, and Talmudic Tradition*. Israel Goldstein Lectures (New York: Jewish Theological Seminary of America, 1965).

135. See Scholem *Major Trends*, p. 52.

136. Collins, *Mantle of Elijah*, pp. 59-61.

137. Collins at pp. 60-61.

138. Not to be confused with Amazo the android.

139. Jim Wallis, *Agenda for Biblical People: A New Focus for Developing a Life-style of Discipleship* (New York: Harper & Row, 1976), pp. 1, 24.

140. Girard, *The Scapegoat*, p. 129.

141. T.K. Cheyne, "Amos." In T.K. Cheyne and J. Sutherland Black, eds., *Encyclopædia Biblica: A Dictionary of the Bible* (London: Adam and Charles Black, 1914), col. 148.

Printed in Great Britain
by Amazon

44274288R00197